Law,
Politics,
and Society

Law,
Politics,
and Society

Suzanne Samuels
Seton Hall University

WADSWORTH
CENGAGE Learning™

Australia • Brazil • Japan • Korea • Mexico • Singapore • Spain • United Kingdom • United States

WADSWORTH
CENGAGE Learning™

Law, Politics, and Society
Suzanne Samuels

Publisher: Charles Hartford

Sponsoring Editor: Katherine Meisenheimer

Senior Development Editor: Jeffrey Greene

Editorial Assistant: Kristen Craib

Project Editor: Reba Libby

Editorial Assistant: Deborah Berkman

Senior Art and Design Coordinator:
   Jill Haber Atkins

Senior Photo Editor: Jennifer Meyer Dare

Executive Marketing Manager: Nicola Poser

Cover image: Black and white photo/statue
outside courthouse. Cover photograph
© by Gary Gnidovic for Solus
Photography/Veer.com.

For product information and technology assistance, contact us at
Cengage Learning Customer & Sales Support, 1-800-354-9706

For permission to use material from this text or product,
submit all requests online at **www.cengage.com/permissions**
Further permissions questions can be e-mailed to
permissionrequest@cengage.com

Library of Congress Catalog Card Number: 2005927842

ISBN-13: 978-0-618-37651-3

ISBN-10: 0-618-37651-8

Wadsworth Cengage Learning
20 Davis Drive
Belmont, CA 94002-3098
USA

Cengage Learning is a leading provider of customized learning solutions
with office locations around the globe, including Singapore, the United
Kingdom, Australia, Mexico, Brazil, and Japan. Locate your local office at
www.cengage.com/global

Cengage Learning products are represented in Canada by
Nelson Education, Ltd.

To learn more about Wadsworth, visit **www.cengage.com/wadsworth**

Purchase any of our products at your local college store or at our preferred
online store **www.cengagebrain.com**

To Charlotte Rose and Sebastian Raphael

Printed in the United States of America
3 4 5 15 14 13 12

Contents

Chapter 3   **The Foundations of American Law**   57

The Historical Foundations of U.S. Law: The Anglo-American Common Law Tradition   57

PART III

Controversial Issues in American Law   263

Chapter 11 Law, Race, and Ethnicity   265

Preface

The first plane hit the tower, then the second, and the very foundations of American society and political culture were shaken to their core. After the events of 9/11, I had no shortage of examples to illustrate for my students the close relationship between law, politics, and society. In the aftershocks of 9/11, we all asked ourselves how we could prevent another horrific act of terrorism in the future, and many of us looked immediately at the laws in place. After the first wave of laws aimed at protecting against future terrorist acts were passed by Congress and law enforcement agencies, and the shock of the attacks had begun to subside, we looked again at how our new laws affected our deeply rooted commitment to individual rights and liberties. In our fervor to ensure that we were protected, we had been willing to accept many governmental encroachments on our civil liberties that we probably never would have considered before.

In the period following the terror attacks, I began to look much more closely at how I was teaching my introductory course on American law. My undergraduates at Seton Hall University have always challenged me to make my courses relevant to their lives, and the 9/11 attacks added even greater urgency to their challenge.

It was after 9/11 that I began thinking seriously about writing this book. For a long time, I had been dissatisfied with the books that I had been using for my introductory course on American law. I found that these texts fit into two very separate categories—either they were texts that taught this course as a "mini-law school class," covering the subject areas, like torts, contracts, and civil procedure, that are taught in the first year of law school; or they were texts that examined law without looking at any cases, statutes, or regulations at all. I began supplementing these texts with reading packets, but each semester, the packets got longer and my reliance on the texts diminished, until finally, I just stopped using the texts altogether. What I wanted was a text that would offer my students the opportunity to look at actual laws, but also provide the theoretical background for understanding the laws. My training in law and social science helped me to appreciate the value of studying law from an interdisciplinary perspective, and I was committed to helping my students to understand the fascinating and complex interrelationship between law and the larger society.

Approach

Law, Politics, and Society is an interdisciplinary text. It draws on the scholarship in a variety of fields, including sociology, political science, anthropology, history, economics, philosophy, and psychology, using readings and background materials from these fields. It provides a comprehensive, timely and relevant introduction to the study of law and society, drawing in students and instructors with examples that are current and up to date. This text provides an excellent backdrop for more advanced studies of law, politics, and society, offering students the tools to understand and critically assess American law. It is designed as the core text to be used in courses on law and society, American law, and legal studies. It makes excellent use of materials that students and instructors can use to place the U.S. system in a comparative perspective.

Features

There are a number of unique features in *Law, Politics, and Society*, all aimed at making the study of law relevant, interesting, and challenging. Among these are the Law in Action, Debate, and Law and Popular Culture features, extensive active learning exercises, an interactive glossary, and an up-to-date website.

Writing nearly one hundred years ago, Harvard Law School Dean and jurist Roscoe Pound praised the study of "law in action," claiming that one could only really understand what law was by examining how it actually functioned in the society. One of the central features of this book is the Law in Action feature, which uses an actual law to illustrate a course concept or theme. This feature runs through every chapter, providing instructors and students the opportunity to discuss how law operates in the larger society, and offers another opportunity to demonstrate the relevance of this course to students' lives.

Each chapter also provides a Debate feature that allows students to think critically about some issue that is currently in the news. This feature asks a question, and then provides both positive and negative answers illustrating both debate positions. The Debate feature guides students in beginning to evaluate law and assess what impact laws have on social, political, and economic systems. It also challenges the assumptions students often have that legal disputes have obvious solutions.

Another novel feature that *Law, Politics, and Society* offers is the Law in Popular Culture feature. Law and popular culture is an emerging theory of jurisprudence that contends that law both informs and is informed by our popular culture, that is, our literature, film, music, and other media sources. In every chapter, a photograph from a film offers a glimpse of how law and culture are interwoven. Students are fascinated by popular culture and this feature further demonstrates the relevancy of the law to their lives. The text, website, and instructor's manual provide many additional recommendations about how popular culture can be integrated into the course materials.

This text also aims at helping students to think critically and to develop their analytical reasoning skills, and to this end, it provides extensive Active Learning exercises, both at the end of the chapters and on the website. It is the central goal of this text to draw students into the study of law—to make it interesting, engaging, and fun, and these exercises and group learning projects aim at advancing this goal.

Organization

This book is divided into three sections. Part I offers an engaging discussion of the origins and context for American law. Chapter 1 examines the similarities and differences between law and other kinds of norms, focusing on the ways in which law expresses shared values and is enforced by the government. In this chapter, we also talk about what happens when laws are not based on values or when some other, nongovernmental actor assumes the role of the government in law enforcement. Chapter 2 provides an overview of different theories of jurisprudence, distinguishing between normative theories, which tell us how law *should* function, and empirical theories, which inform our understanding about how law *does* in fact function. Chapter 3 focuses on the foundations for American law, talking about the historical background and the development of both code and common law traditions in the United States. This chapter also introduces the case law method and provides several cases for students to work on in writing legal briefs. Chapter 4 widens the lens again, laying out the comparative context for American law, and discussing the legal traditions in place throughout the world. In this chapter, we talk specifically about developments in the European Union and the Islamic legal community. And finally, in Chapter 5, we talk about the relationship between American domestic law and international law, focusing specifically on how the war on terror has further entangled these two sources of law.

Part II focuses on the institutions for lawmaking in the United States, looking specifically at the structure, function, and participants in these institutions. Chapters 6 and 7 focus on the American judicial system. Chapter 6 examines the dual structure of this system, and focuses on how jurisdiction determines which courts hear what issues, and about why this actually matters. This chapter encourages students to think about who actually participates in judicial decision-making, and about how race, class and other factors affect participation by judges, juries, lawyers, and litigants. Chapter 7 examines the function of courts in the American system, focusing on the dispute resolution function. Here, we talk about the limitations of judicial resolution, and focus on the growth in alternative dispute resolution devices, like mediation and negotiation. Moving to legislative lawmaking, Chapter 8 looks at how legislatures create statutes and how this differs from other forms of lawmaking. Specifically, we talk about how the lawmaking process results in laws that, by necessity, are ambiguous and about the interrelationship of legislatures, courts, and administrative agencies in the construction of statutes. Chapter 9 examines the growth in lawmaking by executives, focusing on how laws are made by chief executives, their executive departments, and administrative agencies. We discuss lawmaking by the president and his executive departments in the post-9/11 world in an attempt to appreciate the complexities of this process. And in Chapter 10, we look at lawmaking by law enforcement agencies, examining how police function as agents of social control, and how police discrimination is the flip side of discretion.

And finally, in Part III, *Law, Politics, and Society* aims at engaging students in a discussion about some of most controversial issues in American society. Chapters 11, 12, and 13 examine civil rights and the law governing discrimination in three areas—race, gender, and class. The law approaches each of these areas quite differently and is most aggressive in responding to charges of race discrimination, less stringent in dealing with gender discrimination, and least hostile to charges of class discrimination. Chapter 11 discusses the relationship between law, race, and ethnicity, focusing on the experience of Native Americans and African Americans in the American legal system. This chapter examines institutional racism and affirmative action in an attempt to better understand how law can be used to advance or hinder racial justice in the United States. Chapter 12 looks at the relationship between law and gender, focusing on three areas—gender roles, reproductive rights, and gender identity and orientation—to better understand how our law responds to and shapes societal expectations about gender and sex. Chapter 13 expands this discussion, talking about the relationship between law and social class in the United States. This chapter offers a discussion about how law treats class far differently than race or even sex and how class discrimination is generally permissible in the United States. Chapters 14 and 15 examine specific issues in the law. Chapter 14 discusses law and medicine; Chapter 15 looks at law and corporations, and both attempt to understand how law has responded to radical changes in these areas, especially in the last one hundred years. The Law and Medicine chapter examines the changing role of physicians and the impact of emerging technologies on the kinds of laws that we have. Chapter 15 looks at how law relates to our entrepreneurial system, and specifically, the laws governing stock trading, environmental hazards, and products liability.

Supplements

Law, Politics, and Society comes with a website that contains a rich assortment of resources for the instructor, including a test bank. This website provides group activities; PowerPoint slides; and research, critical thinking, and additional resources to aid in teaching the course. A test bank with multiple-choice and short-answer questions is provided for assessment.

Acknowledgments

First and foremost, I want to thank my students at Seton Hall University. They were the first audience for this book and profoundly shaped its structure and focus. Students in my Introduction to Law, Society, and Politics course constantly challenged me to consider the impact of law on the larger society, and I could count on them to ask the "who cares?" question that is at the heart of the study of law in action. They wanted to know *why* law mattered and how law actually was functioning and prodded me to make it all interesting and engaging! I also thank my wonderful colleagues at Seton Hall, especially my chairman, Joe Marbach, and my friends, Jo Renee Formicola, Mary Boutilier, Jeff Togman, and Roseanne Mirabella, whose enthusiasm for teaching and learning are at the heart of this project. My gratitude to Nancy Hall for all of her help throughout the project. Thanks also to Tom Lindsay, Molly Smith, Deborah Ward, Patrick Fisher, and Michael Taylor for their enthusiastic and continuing support of this book.

I also want especially to thank these colleagues whose thoughtful reviews contributed to making this a better book:

Steven P. Brown, *Auburn University*
C. Augustus Martin, *California State University-Dominguez Hills*
Karen A. Donahue, *Hanover College*
Mike Males, *University of California-Santa Cruz*

Many thanks to Katherine Meisenheimer for her keen interest in this project from the very start, and to Jeff Greene and Terri Wise for their solid guidance throughout the writing and production phases. I am especially thankful to Katherine and Jeff for their enthusiasm and willingness to incorporate those features that distinguish this project. My warm thanks to Rachel Zander for overseeing the book's production and Jane Sherman for her careful editing of the manuscript, and to Susan Holtz, for her help in finding the appropriate photo stills for the pop culture feature.

As always, my love and deepest gratitude to my husband, Steven, for his enthusiastic support. It was he who kept encouraging me to develop this project, and he who has been my loudest and most persistent cheerleader throughout. My warm thanks, too, to my parents, Camille Uttaro Stern and Aaron Stern, for all their help these last two years. Thanks to my brothers, Tom and Jim Uttaro, for all the debates across the kitchen table—they were the first ones to help me find my voice and to speak up for myself and my ideas. And finally, my unending love and gratitude to my children, Charlotte Rose and Sebastian Raphael, who made me stop and smell the roses (and play with groovy girls and knights) along the way.

S.U.S

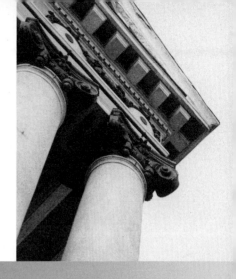

PART ONE

The Origins and Context of American Law

Where does American law come from and what purposes does it serve? These questions are central to understanding the American legal system. American law has deep roots in the U.S. historical experience and in its social and economic institutions. This section explores both the origins and contexts of American law. Specifically, it examines the norms that are the basis for most laws and distinguishes between laws and other kinds of norms. It also explores the predominant theories of jurisprudence and provides a foundation for distinguishing between theories that focus on how law *should* function and those that focus on how law *does* function.

This section of the book also examines the two central strands of the American system—the common law tradition and the code law tradition. It then compares these traditions with the common and code law traditions in other nation-states, as well as with the Islamic and socialist legal traditions. This section also explores the study of legal anthropology, which looks at how legal systems change over time, and uses sociology and anthropology to better understand this change or evolution.

And finally, this segment of the book examines the overlap between international law and domestic law in the United States and focuses on the sources of international law. It looks at two sides of the same coin—first, how American law is increasingly used abroad, especially in the War on Terror; and second, how international law and norms are used in American courts. Part I is intended to place American law in a historical and comparative context. It uses the writings of legal analysts, as well as the work of scholars in many other fields, to illuminate the theoretical and actual basis for law in the United States.

CHAPTER 1

An Introduction to American Law: Defining "Law"

Law is ubiquitous in the United States—it is everywhere! Think about a typical weekday. Maybe you wake to the sound of a clock radio, set perhaps to music from a local radio station. Then you shower, eat breakfast, get dressed, and get into your car, or onto a bus or train, which takes you to your destination. Some law or set of laws guides every step of this process. For example, many federal and state regulations require that alarm clocks, or the electricity that powers them, be manufactured and distributed according to certain codes. The same is true of the water you showered with, the soap and shampoo you used, the food you ate, and the car you drove. Additional regulations apply to licensing radio stations (remember your clock radio?), registering automobiles, and licensing drivers. In any given day, or even hour, a myriad of legal rules and regulations guide your behavior. And we've only touched on the rules that affect you as an individual; there are many more rules that govern your interactions with others.

NORMS AS SOCIAL CONTROLS

social control

device that establishes norms to guide individual and group behavior

Law in the United States functions primarily as a **social control:** it establishes norms, or rules of behavior, that are intended to guide individuals and groups. The law is an enormous source of power for those individuals and groups authorized to engage in lawmaking and law enforcement because it provides a powerful tool for shaping behavior. Because of concerns about how this power might be used and abused, a central feature of American law has always been procedural due process. Due process is at the core of a number of our constitutional provisions; it demands that all persons have sufficient notice of what the law requires of them and that they be aware of the penalties for not obeying these legal rules. For example, both the Fifth and Fourteenth amendments to the U.S. Constitution require that all persons have "due process of the law," the Fourth Amendment requires that governments and their agents be very specific about premises that they want to search and property that they seek to seize, and the Sixth Amendment requires that a person accused of a crime will have the right to "be informed of the nature and cause of the accusation [and] to be confronted with the witnesses against him." At the heart of these constitutional guarantees was a profound concern about the tremendous powers that lawmaking and law enforcement would confer upon the government, and about how officials might use these powers to undermine individual rights.

Informal Norms as the Basis for Laws

informal norms

social controls that are self-imposed by the individual

folkways

informal norms that are part of day-to-day living and guide dress, patterns of speech, and interactions with others

mores

informal norms that are based on common values and establish rules for moral behavior; more intensely held than folkways

While law creates enormous opportunities for governmental actors to shape behavior, it is not the only social control in our society. There are many other norms that establish standards of conduct and tell us how we must act in a given circumstance. In fact, our legal rules are only a relatively small subset of this rather large universe of rules. While you have likely had significant interaction with "the law" today, other **informal norms,** namely **folkways** and **mores,** have probably had an even more pervasive impact on your behavior. These norms operate at the micro level; that is, they are self-imposed by the individual and are created, maintained, and reinforced by interactions with others. Through socialization from childhood into adulthood, individuals learn what is preferred or acceptable within their communities. My toddler son is already well on his way to being socialized in our patterns of speech: this morning, he corrected me when I told him he was beautiful, telling me that only girls are beautiful and that he is handsome!

■ **Folkways** Unlike law, which is imposed on the individual by an outside actor (the government), micro norms operate through the individual's conscious and often subconscious acceptance. Folkways are those activities that are part of our customs for day-to-day living, and they guide such aspects of our lives as our dress, patterns of speech, and interactions with others. The way you wear your hair, the place you live, the manner in which you greet your teachers and peers, and even what you chose to eat for breakfast this morning, all are guided by folkways. These folkways can be incredibly pervasive: every time I talk with my students about this topic, I encourage them to look around their classroom and make note of how much black and blue they are wearing, and to consider how many of us actually dress in uniforms (jeans, tees, sweats) without being required to do so! Similarly, folkways dictate social courtesies, like saying "thank you," holding the door for someone, and "waving on" other drivers who are having a difficult time merging into traffic. While these folkways are pervasive, they can usually be flouted—if you don't say "thank you," the worst that someone will think is that you have poor manners; if you wear a formal gown or tuxedo to class, you will certainly be noticed, but probably the worst thing that can happen to you is that people will snicker and point.

Not all folkways are as mundane as dress and social courtesy. For example, over time, physicians in the United States have developed their own customs for treating Jehovah's Witnesses who refuse blood transfusions. Reviewing cases in which Jehovah's Witnesses refuse this treatment because they view these procedures as conflicting with their religious principles, courts have issued holdings that are inconsistent and provide little guidance to physicians. Given this lack of guidance, doctors have developed their own norms to help them to decide what to do when treating Jehovah's Witnesses. Employing these informal norms, the vast majority of physicians transfuse incompetent adults and those children whose parents refuse to allow them to be treated; and relatively few physicians transfuse competent adults who refuse treatment.

■ Mores The other kind of informal social norm, the more (pronounced MORE-ay), is much more closely and intensely held than is the folkway. While both are self-imposed by the individual, they differ in that mores tend to be much clearer and carry heavier moral weight. Mores, which are based on our common values, establish rules for moral behavior. Nearly every society has mores against murder, cannibalism, and incest: these are universal rules that strictly prohibit certain activities. On the website, you will find "One Man's Meat Is Another's Person," a reading that suggests the universality of human revulsion against the practice of cannibalism. As this reading discusses, nearly every human society rejects the eating of human flesh and there are very few exceptions to this taboo. In those few societies where cannibalism was accepted, namely among tribes in Fiji, Papua (also known as British New Guinea), and the Amazon, it is interesting to note that the practice was part of war making and conquest, and that the vanquished were consumed for largely ritualistic purposes.

While the taboos against cannibalism, murder, and incest appear to be nearly universal, there is variation across cultures with regard to other mores. For example, in the United States, most people accept that marriage should be exclusive and that it can be entered into by only two people. There is some disagreement about whether marriage must be between men and women, or whether same-sex marriages are valid; however, as a society, we embrace the view that only two people can enter into a legal union. The vast majority of Americans reject the practice of **polygamy**, or marriage between more than two people. In 2002, Tom Green, a self-proclaimed "fundamentalist Mormon" who had publicly flaunted his marriage to five

polygamy
marriage between more than two people

women in Utah, was convicted of polygamy and sentenced to five years in prison. While it is estimated that between thirty thousand and fifty thousand people live in polygamous families in Utah, Tom Green's vocal advocacy of polygamy as part of "God's plan" and his very public display of his very young wives (all of his wives were under sixteen when they married Green and one, Linda, was only thirteen years old) and twenty-nine children, likely compelled the state to enforce its polygamy ban. Tom Green was also recently convicted of the 1986 rape of thirteen-year-old Linda, and the state of Utah sentenced him to an additional five years in prison.

In contrast to the U.S. ban on marriage between more than two people, there is an accepted norm of polygamy—specifically, polygyny, or marriage between one man and more than one woman—in many other cultures, among these, many Muslim societies and Senegalese culture. Within such polygynous marriages, there are significant status differences between senior and junior wives, and children of senior wives usually enjoy higher status than those of junior wives. While polyandry, marriage between one woman and more than one man, is rare, polygyny is fairly common in the world today.

Mores are widely observed and have great significance in a society. While there is some discretion permitted with regard to the observance of folkways, there is none with regard to mores. Everyone must observe these rules and failure to abide by them constitutes the violation of a taboo. There is no ambiguity in terms of whether a behavior will be tolerated—an individual either abides by these rules or disobeys them, and disobedience usually triggers a strong and negative reaction from the community. While there are only a few hundred cases of infanticide or filicide each year according to the Bureau of Justice Statistics, these cases engender an intense and often visceral public reaction, likely because they violate the norm that parents, especially mothers, will give their children unconditional love and do whatever they can to safeguard their children's well-being. For example, the press revealed the depth and intensity of the norm against filicide in its coverage of cases involving Andrea Yates, the Texas mother of five who drowned all her children; Susan Smith, who drove her Mazda Protegé into a lake, drowning her two sons; and the "prom mom," who gave birth to her child at the prom, killed him, and then went back to dancing.

Sometimes norms can be unclear or even contradictory. For example, American norms about what makes a good mother or father, and about parents' responsibilities for their offspring's well-being, appear in far less extreme forms, as well. In the United States, we continue to be fairly ambivalent about gender roles, especially with regard to parenting, and many believe that there has been a backlash against working-class and middle-class mothers who work outside the home. This ambivalence is apparent in the lack of strong public support for quality, affordable care for children under five. This lack of support makes it much more difficult for working families to juggle work and home obligations. In contrast, the social policies of Sweden historically have supported working parents, and in France strong support for "the employed mother" is demonstrated in popular attitudes towards childcare outside the home.

Mores are very intensely held feelings of right and wrong, and some mores, like the one governing cannibalism, have changed little throughout recorded history. This doesn't mean, however, that mores can't change. In fact, there has been significant alteration in a number of norms in the United States, and these changes are reflected in our laws. For example, protection of **private property rights** has always been an important value in American society. Private property includes real property, like land or buildings, and personal property, like objects, money, or stocks. The idea of private property is based on the understanding that these items are owned exclusively by the individual, as opposed to the government or some other entity. Historically, Americans have believed in the primacy of private property and in the individual's right to make decisions about how this property will be used and disposed of. While we strongly embrace this more of property rights, our definition of what is property has substantially changed over the last two hundred years. For example, when our nation was founded in 1776, slavery and slaveholding were well accepted, or at least tolerated, by most white Americans, and slaves were considered to be the property of their owners.

private property rights

in the United States, the claim of individuals to make decisions about real property and personal property in which they have an ownership interest

But our views on slavery have changed dramatically in the last two hundred years, as we have come to embrace the view that all people have certain inalienable rights, including the right to self-determination. More recently, our mores about capital punishment, and in particular, the execution of juveniles, have also begun to change. Individuals who are investigated, tried, and punished for committing crimes have certain rights that are guaranteed under the federal and state constitutions. These rights, known collectively as **criminal due process rights**, ensure that those who are subjected to the criminal justice system are protected against arbitrary or unreasonable actions by the government. Among these criminal due process rights is the right to be free from unreasonable search and seizure, the right to a fair trial, and the prohibition against cruel and unusual punishment. Most of these have existed since the colonial era and were present when the first states wrote their constitutions and when the federal Bill of Rights was ratified in 1789. Our understanding of what these rights require, however, has profoundly changed. This shift is perhaps nowhere as clear as in our use of capital punishment.

criminal due process rights

those rights that protect individuals against arbitrary and unreasonable actions taken by the government in enforcing the criminal code

The Eighth Amendment encapsulates the legal norm that governs punishment in the criminal justice system and bars courts from imposing cruel and unusual punishment on those convicted of crimes. For several decades, the U.S. Supreme Court has interpreted this provision by considering what are known as "evolving standards of decency" in the community in which

www ▶ ▶ ▶

the execution is to take place. These standards are mores or norms, and they create the parameters for determining who should be put to death and how the execution should be carried out. In the last several years, some U.S. Supreme Court justices, along with a number of state legislators and governors, have begun to seriously question whether it is fair or just to execute minors. They have suggested that the execution of juveniles is inconsistent with public opinion and popular will. In 2005, the Supreme Court decided that the execution of minors in fact did violate the Eighth Amendment prohibition against cruel and unusual punishment. In this case, *Roper* v. *Simmons,* a majority of the justices contended that their decision reflected evolving standards of decency, both in the United States and in the larger international community, which mandate the banning of juvenile execution. Our understanding of what forms of punishment are acceptable and who may be subjected to the ultimate penalty—death—is clearly changing, and our law in this area is also changing, as did our laws defining property more than one hundred years ago.

www ▶ ▶ ▶

LAWS DISTINGUISHED FROM NORMS

Norms are at the core of all laws, and the first set of laws adopted in virtually all societies is based on religious mores. The Ten Commandments and the Qur'an both articulate basic rules about human behavior. The Ten Commandments, the first "laws" set forth in the Bible, very clearly prohibit murder, adultery, and the worship of more than one god. Similarly, the Qur'an, the most sacred text for Muslims, prohibits murder, adultery, theft, or other "evil deeds." Other norms also lie at the heart of our legal system. For example, our commitment to equality of opportunity is evident in the laws that ban discrimination on the basis of national origin, age, and sex, and our contract law is premised on an assumption about fair play and fair dealings. In some cases, folkways can become laws, as well. For example, the requirement in some towns that property owners clear their sidewalks of snow or that they mow their lawns is probably based on customs or practices dictating how homes and businesses should be maintained.

Norms as the Basis for Law

formal norms

social controls that are imposed on the individual by some outside actor—either a nongovernmental entity, or a governmental control, known as a law

Norms are not only self-imposed—they may also be created and imposed by external actors. These external controls are called **formal norms**, and they may be used by either nongovernmental entities, like churches, schools, or professional organizations, or governmental entities. Formal governmental controls are called laws. When a law is created, this means that the state has the final and often *sole* authority for implementing the norm through the exercise of its enforcement powers. This is a very important distinction. You may want to remember that other nongovernmental organizations, like churches, temples, or mosques, may also have rules, as may schools, businesses, or private clubs. These rules may be very strict, and the organization may impose even heavier penalties for noncompliance than does the law. Consider that the ultimate penalty for noncompliance in the Christian, Muslim, or Hindu religions may be eternal damnation, consignment to purgatory, or rebirth into a lower status!

Nongovernmental rules may be even more effective in shaping behavior than are formal laws. For example, during the early colonial era, the use of shame by the church elders was incredibly effective in controlling behavior. Many have argued that this institution had a greater impact on sexual activity than laws ever could, despite the fact that the government's penalty for noncompliance—whipping, mutilation, and death—would seem much more severe than shaming someone. Again, law is not distinguished from norms or mores by its greater severity or by being more—or less—effective in shaping behavior. Instead, the most important distinction between norms and laws is that once the government adopts a norm as law, it is able to use its often considerable power to enforce that norm. For example, when church elders were no longer able to police sexual and nonsexual misconduct by the early 1700s, the colonial governments stepped in, increasing the number and scope of criminal laws and taking steps to enforce these laws.

The Expansion of American Law

Beginning in this period, the colonies, and later the states, became the primary enforcers of what we now know as criminal law, which is found in the penal codes of the state and federal governments. Criminal law encompasses prohibitions on certain actions that are seen as serious threats to individuals and to the larger society. Usually, these are actions that deprive an individual of his or her property or that cause serious bodily harm or death. The state has had a virtual monopoly in the area of criminal law since the early 1700s and has aimed at excluding other groups from making and enforcing their own codes of conduct in this area. Moreover, while the colonies and states largely accepted the views of nongovernmental institutions about which activities would be deemed criminal, they often adopted much stricter penalties than had these predecessors. For example, the Quakers had a dominant role in the creation and implementation of norms about criminal conduct in the early 1600s in the Pennsylvania colony, and these laws reflected the Quaker focus on redemption and rehabilitation, as opposed to punishment. When the criminal code was rewritten in the early 1700s when the Quakers were no longer as powerful, the code imposed much stricter and more punitive penalties.

Colonial and state governments effectively supplanted all other institutions in the regulation of criminal activities. In the civil arena, however, governmental actors have allowed nongovernmental entities, like religious institutions, businesses, and professional and community groups to predominate. It is only in the last fifty years that there has been an explosion in the number and scope of civil laws. This is true not only of laws passed by the U.S. Congress and state legislatures, but of federal and state regulatory agencies, as well. A number of domains that were until recently viewed as private and off-limits to governmental regulation, like places of business, property that was privately held, educational institutions, and families, are now subject to a sometimes dizzying array of laws.

Entirely new areas of law, like environmental law, occupational safety and health law, and employment discrimination law, have imposed many new obligations on actors that were, until recently, able to perform their functions relatively free of governmental interference. In many other areas, there may have been laws on the books, but the last several decades have seen a steady expansion in the number and the reach of these laws. For example, securities law looks very different today and imposes much greater duties on corporations than it did when it was first created in 1930. The collapse of Enron and other scandals in the late 1990s and early 2000s will likely result in even more regulations, which will probably mandate heightened accounting disclosure requirements. Moreover, the vast expansion in the activities of multinational corporations will very likely lead to a proliferation of new laws in this area. Law is increasingly employed to enforce norms of social behavior, and it is being used in contexts where private arrangements have traditionally structured the rights, responsibilities, and remedies of private actors.

This huge expansion of law creates serious challenges for U.S. lawmakers. For example, one of the fastest growing problems in the U.S. economy is the cost of theft of intellectual property. The U.S. State Department estimates that worldwide losses to the U.S. economy for copyright infringement and piracy range from $200 billion to $250 billion each year. Intellectual property includes all creations of the mind, among these, industrial products and designs, and literary and artistic works. This property is protected under law through the use of various legal devices, principally, trademarks, patents, and copyrights—typically, trademarks and patents are used for industrial products, and copyright protection is given to artistic or literary pieces. Unlike the law governing real property, like land and buildings, which developed over the course of several hundred years, intellectual property law has been developing incredibly quickly. In fact, our laws lag far behind our technological abilities. In 2004, the U.S. Department of State identified two crimes that have imposed huge costs on the U.S. economy. The first is the crime of product counterfeiting, which includes the practice of manufacturing "fake" products, like handbags, watches, cell phones,

www ▶ ▶ ▶

and printer cartridges, with the labels of products that have the trademark or patent protection. The second crime is that of piracy of protected artistic or literary works. Many of us have CD burners on our computers and at least some have been tempted to use these devices to get free music and movies—but this practice is a violation of existing copyright laws. The State Department estimates that worldwide product counterfeiting and piracy cost the U.S. economy between $200 billion and $250 billion a year, and law enforcement agencies claim that they have begun to crack down on these practices. Cases have been initiated by both the music industry and the federal government, and in many of these, the people charged with piracy have been ordered to pay substantial awards. In one case decided in 2003, a man charged with selling pirated music was found guilty of criminal copyright infringement and sentenced to six months imprisonment.

The Nature of Government Sanctions

Those who violate the criminal and civil laws of the United States face certain sanctions, and these punishments have several distinguishing characteristics: first, they may be imposed only by governmental actors; second, they are almost entirely negative; and third, they are governed by the principle or proportionality, which requires that they "fit" the crime.

■ **State Monopoly on the Imposition of Punishments** What distinguishes law from other forms of social control is that the government uses law to establish standards of conduct and then has the sole authority to impose sanctions on individuals who fail to comply with the rules. Where the government steps in to act on some issue or to combat some problem, it usually establishes itself as the exclusive actor in this area. For example, by formulating a regulation that limits the allowable level of arsenic in drinking water, the Environmental Protection Agency is basically "bumping" any other private entity that might want to mandate a higher or a lower level. The federal EPA establishes a floor—other states may mandate more protective standards, or ceilings, but private actors are barred from ignoring the federal and state laws. By enacting laws, these governments are signaling that they are going to monopolize rule making in a given area.

www ▶ ▶ ▶

■ **Negative Sanctions** Unlike other social controls, which may reward you for internalizing the rules—by offering you a promotion, a college degree, or membership in the community pool—law offers no such rewards. There are few intrinsic rewards for compliance, and in fact, the "long arm of the law" is something you usually feel when you are suspected of not complying with it. In fact, when most people, and in particular, most African Americans, are asked about their exposure to law, they talk only about negative encounters that either they or their friends and family have had with police officers. American law is negative; that is, it is characterized by punishment and not reward, and punishment has been administered more harshly for people of color throughout our nation's history.

The sanctions that government may impose on those who don't abide by the rules can range from minor ones, like small fines or notices, to very severe ones, like capital punishment or imprisonment. The key element is that is that the state is the only actor with the authority to impose these sanctions. While other organizations can impose monetary sanctions or fines or can remove your right to engage in certain activities, only the state can remove you from the larger society, either temporarily, through imprisonment, or permanently, through imposition of the death penalty. In other words, a private high school can expel a student for cheating and a credit card company can either impose a late charge on a customer who doesn't pay her bill on time or revoke her card privileges and ruin her credit rating, but these are the limits on the types of penalties that a private institution can impose. Ultimately, if the credit card company wants to collect its money and the customer refuses to pay, the company must turn to a governmental entity, likely the courts, for assistance.

proportionality

the requirement that the punishment fit the crime, that is, that it be neither too lenient nor excessive

www ▶ ▶ ▶

■ **Requirement of Proportionality** Again, for a governmental action to constitute a law, rather than a decree or proclamation, it must stipulate the penalties for noncompliance and must notify the public about the rule and its penalties. Our legal and political culture mandates that there be **proportionality** in the punishments exacted for a violation of law, and in the realm of criminal law, this is expressed in the U.S. Constitution's Eighth Amendment prohibition against excessive punishments. Much of the debate about proportionality in the last several decades has centered on capital punishment. At the time of our nation's founding in the early 1600s, the number of death-eligible crimes was substantial; they included not only murder and treason but also rape, sodomy (which was usually defined as either homosexual contact or sex with animals), witchcraft, and arson. Over the last three centuries, courts and legislatures have sharply reduced this number, and in the 1977 case *Coker* v. *Georgia* (433 U.S. 884), the U.S. Supreme Court established that the only offense that was death eligible was murder. In *Coker,* the Court rejected the imposition of capital punishment for the crime of rape, holding that this penalty was grossly out of proportion to the severity of this crime and that the Georgia law that provided for this penalty violated the Eighth Amendment's prohibition against cruel and unusual punishment. As a result, the only offense for which states and the federal government may impose death is murder. Consider the Federal Law Against

Terrorism and Weapons of Mass Destruction, passed in the wake of the first terror attack on the World Trade Center in 1993. In the wake of the 9/11 attacks, this law was amended in the USA Patriot Act (50 USC 1701 (2001)) to broaden the definition of terrorism to include attacks occurring solely on U.S. soil and aimed at intimidating or coercing the civilian population, influencing policy through intimidation or coercion, or affecting the conduct of government through mass destruction, assassination, or kidnapping.

LAW IN ACTION

1.1 The Principle of Proportionality

THE FEDERAL LAW AGAINST TERRORISM AND WEAPONS OF MASS DESTRUCTION (18 USC 2332A)

TITLE 18—CRIMES AND CRIMINAL PROCEDURE
PART I—CRIMES
CHAPTER 113B—TERRORISM
Sec. 2332a. Use of certain weapons of mass destruction

(a) Offense Against a National of the United States or Within the United States.—A person who, without lawful authority, uses, threatens, or attempts or conspires to use, a weapon of mass destruction (other than a chemical weapon as that term is defined in section 229F), including any biological agent, toxin, or vector (as those terms are defined in section 178)—

(1) against a national of the United States while such national is outside of the United States;

(2) against any person within the United States, and the results of such use affect interstate or foreign commerce or, in the case of a threat, attempt, or conspiracy, would have affected interstate or foreign commerce; or

(3) against any property that is owned, leased or used by the United States or by any department or agency of the United States, whether the property is within or outside of the United States,

shall be imprisoned for any term of years or for life, and if death results, shall be punished by death or imprisoned for any term of years or for life.

QUESTIONS:

1. What is the goal of this law?
2. Which crimes are death eligible?
3. Is this law consistent with the principle of proportionality enshrined in the Eighth Amendment? Why or why not?

TYPES OF LAW IN THE UNITED STATES

criminal law

law whose primary goal is the protection of persons and property and maintenance of public order; government is the central actor

civil law

law whose primary goal is the enforcement of rights and obligations usually between private entities

There are basically two kinds of law in the United States: **criminal law** and **civil law**. These two sets of law differ in their basic goals, the penalties available to punish transgressors, and the role the government plays in bringing suit. The primary goal of criminal law is the protection of persons and property and the maintenance of public order, and the government plays a pivotal role in advancing this goal. In contrast, the goal of civil law is to enforce rights and obligations that are primarily between private entities. While civil law remedies are almost always limited to monetary damages, violations of the criminal code are punishable by fine, imprisonment, or death.

Criminal Law

www ▶ ▶ ▶

rehabilitation

a controversial goal of the criminal justice system—over the last several decades, it has given way to retribution and incapacitation

retribution

the oldest goal of criminal law; encompasses both simple retribution ("an eye for an eye") and pecuniary compensation

incapacitation

a goal of criminal law that aims at protecting society by incarcerating criminals or putting them to death

Criminal law is the most ancient form of law, and the government's commitment to protecting its citizens is so powerful that violations of this criminal code are punished only by the state. That is, the full power of the state is employed to enforce criminal laws both at the state and federal level. The central role that the government plays is apparent in how these laws are implemented. In criminal cases, the government itself challenges the offender. This is why cases are brought by the state or federal government directly against the offender. For example, the United States government, rather than some private parties, is bringing the case against Zacarias Moussaoui, who is alleged to be the "twentieth hijacker" in the 9/11 attack and is charged with conspiracy to commit terrorism. If Moussaoui is found guilty of violating the federal terrorism statute, he will be subject to penalties under this law.

The criminal justice system can be seen as serving a number of possible goals, and people sharply disagree not only about what the central goal should be but also about how well the system is achieving this goal. One of the most controversial goals, the goal of **rehabilitation**, has become less popular, at least among politicians and governmental officials. Throughout the 1960s and early 1970s, many believed that crime was largely the result of failures in our nation's social policies and that the goal of the criminal justice system was to reform criminals through treatment, education, and training. This focus on the individual offender required that the judge be given greater flexibility and discretion in sentencing. When crime rates dramatically increased in the 1970s, 1980s, and 1990s, many blamed what they saw as a lax approach to sentencing, and the goal of the system shifted, very dramatically, from rehabilitation to **retribution** and **incapacitation**, as politicians promised to "get tough on crime." This shift brought with it less discretion in sentencing, more mandatory sentences, and a heavier reliance on sentencing guidelines.

■ **Retribution** This is the oldest goal of criminal law, and all early civilizations used their laws, both religious and governmental, to advance this goal. These cultures, however, had differing views of what was necessary to achieve retribution, and sometimes this conflict is apparent within cultures. For example, the Code of Hammurabi, penned in ancient Sumer at about 2500 BCE, incorporates two very different views of retribution. The first of these, which is very well known, mandated a simple reciprocal arrangement, known as the principle of "an eye for an eye." This phrase appears pretty far into the Code, and is part of a larger, fairly gruesome, retributive framework based on the principle that retribution could be accomplished only by harsh physical harm to the wrongdoer. Embedded in the Code is a second, far less well known principle—that of pecuniary compensation. Few people know that the Code was superimposed on a society that relied heavily on pecuniary compensation, and that the Code itself incorporated this earlier practice by providing a detailed and complex system for providing compensation for those who had been wronged. The nature of this compensation was monetary and did not hinge on physical harm to the transgressor. For example, the Code establishes that "If a Shepherd, without the permission of the owner of a field, and without the knowledge of the owner of the sheep, lets the sheep into a field to graze, then the owner of the field shall harvest his crop, and the shepherd, who had pastured this flock there without permission of the owner of the field, shall pay to the owner twenty gur of corn for every gan."

www ▶ ▶ ▶

This ambiguity about what retribution requires is apparent not only in ancient Sumer, but in both the Judeo-Christian and Islamic traditions, as well. There is significant variation in how retribution is defined and in the role to be played by forgiveness and redemption. For example, both the Hebrew Scriptures, or Old Testament, and the Qur'an call for proportionate punishment. The Old Testament articulates the notion that justice is served where "an eye [is taken] for an eye," and the Qur'an states that "the law of equality is prescribed" in cases of murder; that is, retribution for the murder of a free man is the death of another free man. Both the Judeo-Christian and Islamic legal traditions, however, also envision a role for compensation and forgiveness of those who transgress the law.

For example, in Exodus, one of the first books in the Bible, the "eye for an eye" rule is first established; but even here there is a call for compensation for the person who has been harmed by the death of a fetus, namely the father. Similarly, the Qur'an lays out a system for compensating those harmed from bad deeds: where a believer is killed by accident, a guilty party must free a believing slave and pay compensation to the victim's family, or if he cannot afford this, he must enter into a long period of fasting. While both texts call for retribution, they also seem to rely on compensation, seeing this as the path to forgiveness and redemption. In these ancient texts, retribution has two aspects: first, it requires proportional punishment, that is, that the perpetrator be subjected to the same harm he or she has inflicted on the victim; and second, these texts mandate that there be pecuniary retribution, and that a certain sum of money be paid to redress whatever harms the offender has caused. It bears noting that in other parts of these texts, the "eye for an eye" rule seems to have been tempered by compassion, or at least the possibility of forgiveness.

In the United States, we believe strongly in the retributive function of the criminal justice system. In fact, the policies adopted by the federal and state governments in the last two decades demonstrate that this is the predominant role of this system. For example, the creation of victims' rights hearings and compensation hearings echoes the texts of the Judeo-Christian and Islamic heritages. Similarly, the creation of work programs, intended to reduce the taxpayers' costs for maintaining the prisons and to provide funding for victims' programs, are also based on the concept of retribution. Moreover, we are increasingly relying on what is known as **punitive restitution**. For example, Megan's Laws, in place now in all fifty states, mandate that after serving a prison term for a sex offense, the offender must register with a state agency, which will post the individual's address, the specifics of the crime that he or she was convicted of, his or her physical characteristics, and in some states, a current photograph.

Laws that consider the impact of the crime on victims' lives and require lifelong registration of some offenders even after the term has been served, probably achieve a number of purposes. Not all of these, however, are about reducing crime or even about making the victim whole by punishing the perpetrator. Some have argued that these laws are motivated by social outrage about crime, rather than a concern about the victim's injuries. This use of social retribution harkens back to an earlier era in American history when stigma and moral outrage, not crime control, were at the heart of the criminal justice system.

■ Incapacitation The second goal of the criminal justice system, incapacitation, is also one that we seem to have embraced, especially in the last two decades. Through incapacitation, people convicted of crimes are removed and isolated from the public, either permanently or for a determined number of years. Our commitment to this goal is clearly demonstrated by the recent proliferation of mandatory sentencing and "three strikes, you're out" laws. By imposing predetermined sentences, mandatory sentencing limits the ability of judges to individualize punishment. For example, when the U.S. Congress passed its Anti-Drug Abuse Act in 1988 as part of the federal government's "War on Drugs," it created strict guidelines for people convicted of possession and sale of narcotics. This act continues to generate vigorous debate, especially those provisions that mandate much longer prison terms for crack cocaine than for powder cocaine, because these

---

www ▶ ▶ ▶

punitive restitution
a goal of criminal law that focuses on both punishment and compensating the victim

www ▶ ▶ ▶

www ▶ ▶ ▶

www ▶ ▶ ▶

provisions have resulted in much lighter terms for powder users, who are often white, and heavier terms for minorities, who tend to use crack. Similarly, the creation of "three strikes, you're out" (or *in*) laws, which mandate incarceration for life or for a term of years for those who are convicted of more than two crimes, effectively isolate those convicted of crime from the general public.

These laws, coupled with state and federal laws that now sharply limit probation and parole, have dramatically increased the number of people incarcerated in U.S. prisons. In 2002, this population numbered more than 2 million men and women. The United States imprisons between five and eight times as many citizens per capita as do Western European nations. Moreover, only 10 percent of those now imprisoned were found guilty of committing violent crimes; the remaining 90 percent were found guilty of property and narcotics violations. Even more troubling is the fact that these laws have a disproportionate impact on African American and Latino men. For example, in California, these groups made up more than 70 percent of "three strikers" in 2001, and most of these were too poor to hire their own attorneys.

deterrence

the most controversial goal of criminal law; it focuses on using punishment to dissuade either the individual offender or the larger public from breaking the law in the future

■ **Deterrence** The third goal of the criminal justice system, **deterrence**, is perhaps the most controversial, probably because it has been a central feature of the debate about capital punishment in this country. Advocates of the death penalty claim that it is a strong deterrent to the most egregious criminal acts; opponents argue that it has no deterrent effect. Criminal sanctions or the threat of sanctions effectively deter someone when they cause the person to make a conscious decision to obey the law because of fear of the threatened sanctions. There are two types of deterrence: individual and general. Individual deterrence works when an individual, having been punished in the past, is deterred from committing future criminal acts. In contrast, general deterrence posits that making an example of someone by imposing punishment that is swift, certain, and severe will deter others from committing similar acts. There is substantial disagreement among scholars and government officials about whether violent crime, and especially murder, can be deterred by law. Consider the debate on the following page about capital punishment and deterrence.

Civil Law

In the last forty or fifty years, there has been a virtual explosion in the number and scope of civil laws in the United States. This body of law encompasses traditional subjects that have existed for many years, like family, tort, and contract law, and emerging fields, like environmental, health, intellectual property, and copyright law.

DEBATE

Can capital punishment be an effective deterrent?

Yes: Many people claim that the fact that the United States continues to have one of the highest per capita rates of homicide in the world is proof that the death penalty does not function effectively as a deterrent. Individual and general deterrence can only work if punishment is swift, certain, and severe, and the practice of capital punishment in the United States meets none of these requirements. Many advocates of capital punishment argue that it could serve as an effective deterrent, if only it were altered to ensure that punishment was both swift and certain. At present, it takes nearly one decade to move through all of the appeals in a capital punishment case. These appeals and this long delay are costly to the state and interfere with the closure that the victim's family needs to move forward. What is needed are more laws like the 1996 Effective Death Penalty and Anti-Terrorist Bill, which requires that appeals in federal death penalty cases be initiated within one year of the sentence. Many states have also passed laws limiting appeals in death penalty cases. These changes in the law increase the chances that capital punishment will be both swift and certain, and thus will function as an effective deterrent in the future.

No: One of the most often cited arguments in favor of capital punishment is that it deters criminals from committing homicide. In fact, there is little evidence that the threat of capital punishment serves as an effective general deterrent. The "yes" side argues in favor of amending death penalty law to limit appeals and expedite executions, but these changes will increase the chances that an innocent person will be executed. And it is not entirely clear that the public speaks with one voice on this issue—in reality, debate about capital punishment continues to rage in many states, with many opponents calling for an end to its practice. The governors in two states, Maryland and Illinois, have imposed moratoriums on executions, halting them while the states conduct investigations into the prevalence of wrongful convictions and racial bias in the application of capital punishment. We should be skeptical about policy arguments that justify and in fact seek to expedite the use of capital punishment at a time when many abuses and wrongful convictions are beginning to see the light of day.

■ **Role of the Government** While criminal law aims at ensuring order and protecting individuals and their property, civil law focuses on the rights and obligations that arise among individuals and groups. Government usually has only a peripheral role in safeguarding these rights, and damages are almost always limited to a monetary award. While the burden of proof in a criminal suit is beyond a reasonable doubt, in a civil suit it is usually far less vigorous, most often requiring only that the person bringing the suit prove her or his case by preponderance of the evidence, sometimes thought of as a 51 percent certainty.

■ **Nature of the Remedy** Criminal and civil suits operate largely independently of each other. For example, following the completion of the criminal trial of Zacarias Moussaoui, a subsequent civil suit could be brought against him, by either the government or a private actor. It is possible that a victim of the World Trade Center attack could sue Moussaoui under civil law principles, alleging that Moussaoui's actions helped to bring about the bombing and that monetary damages are owed to him or her. Monetary damages can be sought for one of two purposes. First, these damages can aim at compensating the victim; that is, making him or her "whole" by paying for such things as lost wages, medical expenses, or pain and suffering. Second, an award can be used to punish the wrongdoer in an attempt to deter him or her, as well as other potential transgressors. This second kind of award is called punitive damages, and it is highly controversial because it can result in tremendous liability for the individual or organization that is found guilty.

So, the two main differences between criminal and civil law are in the government's role and the available remedies. The government is at the center of a criminal suit, and the case can only go forward if the federal, state, or local government decides to pursue it. Private actors, even victims, cannot bring these suits. On the other hand, a civil suit may go forward either with or without the government's involvement, since a civil suit, unlike a criminal one, may be brought by private individuals or groups. Although some civil suits are brought by, or against, a governmental actor, this involvement is not mandated as it is in a criminal case. Second, in a criminal suit, the available penalties are, in a sense, broader than they are in a civil suit. A violation of criminal law can bring with it a monetary fine, imprisonment, or death. In contrast, civil suits are only for money damages, either to compensate the victim or to deter the wrongdoer, or others, from violating the law in the future.

CONTROVERSIAL LAWS

In general, social norms both establish and reflect rules of conduct that are accepted in a community. Norms that are not based on popular values or belief systems will not be effective. Similarly, to be effective, laws must be based on norms about acceptable and desirable behavior. Laws that are not based on a shared consensus about whether an act is wrong or not will probably not be obeyed or consistently enforced. Often, there will be a split among the populace about whether a law is just or fair. For example, in the 1830s, many Americans, particularly white Americans, were divided about whether slavery was just, and there were many who believed that slavery could be justified by a belief in what was known as manifest destiny.

Civil Disobedience

civil disobedience

the view that individuals have no obligation to obey laws that they deem unfair or unjust

www ▶ ▶ ▶

Henry David Thoreau, writing in 1849, first articulated the notion of **civil disobedience** in the United States. In his essay, "Civil Disobedience," he argues that individuals have no responsibility to obey "unjust laws," and that they in fact have a duty to disobey them. He contends that individuals should obey their consciences first and should not support governments that create laws that are evil or unjust. This essay called upon individuals to oppose activities and laws that maintained the practice of slavery and expansionism into Mexico. Thoreau argues that all abolitionists, that is, those who opposed slavery, should withdraw their support for their state governments by refusing to pay the poll taxes that enabled them to vote. Nonpayment of taxes subjected individuals to jail, and he argued that if enough protesters were imprisoned for nonpayment, it would "clog the machine," causing it to break down.

As the abolitionist movement failed to achieve its goal of eliminating slavery, he called for more active means. For example, he was often a "conductor" on the Underground Railroad, a system of safe houses that enabled runaway slaves to reach freedom in the North. This "railroad" was operated in clear defiance of the 1854 Fugitive Slave Act, a congressional statute that made it a crime to assist fugitive slaves in reaching the North. The practice of civil disobedience has been embraced many times since Thoreau wrote his influential essay, probably most significantly in the civil rights movement of the 1950s and 1960s.

While Thoreau's notion of civil disobedience was based on individual action, the principle of civil disobedience articulated in the twentieth century was based on mass action. Mahatma Gandhi, who advocated this principle, called on his people to oppose British rule in India by nonviolent means, among these, marches, sitting down or lying in the streets, striking, fasting, or boycotting British goods. He argued that protesters should "fill the jails" and willingly be imprisoned for disobeying the unjust laws of the British. Gandhi's nonviolent protest was ultimately successful, and India achieved independence in 1947. Martin Luther King, Jr., drew upon both Gandhi's actions and Thoreau's principle of civil disobedience and urged people to actively protest unjust laws that segregated African Americans. The first mass act of civil disobedience in the United States was a bus boycott in Montgomery, Alabama, in 1955, which followed the arrest of a black woman, Rosa Parks, who had refused to give up her seat on a public bus to a white man. This boycott was followed by many other acts of civil protest by African Americans and whites both in the South and the North. Ultimately, the segregation laws were struck down and the 1964 Civil Rights Act was passed barring race discrimination in education, employment, and public establishments.

Today, many pro-life groups employ civil disobedience tactics to demonstrate their opposition to abortion. Members of these groups offer "sidewalk counseling" to women who are approaching health care clinics where abortions are performed. These groups also make extensive use of the Internet to provide information about adoption and avenues for lobbying of governmental officials. While many groups disavow violence, some advocate its use, arguing that clinic violence and violence against health care providers is justified by a higher value, that is, the protection of the unborn. In fact, there has been a sharp increase in the last five years in clinic bombings and other forms of violence. Those concerned about the impact of both violent and nonviolent protest on access to abortion services have been actively engaged in countering these activities. For example, the

"Sidewalk counseling" outside abortion clinics by pro-life groups is a form of civil disobedience intended to counter legal precedent that establishes the right to choose abortion.

National Organization for Women used federal extortion law to sue both clinic protestors and the pro-life groups that vigorously support them in an attempt to seize their assets and undermine their effectiveness.

Mala in se v. Mala prohibita

mala in se

acts that are viewed as evil in themselves, like murder and rape

mala prohibita

activities that are prohibited by law but about which there is substantial societal disagreement, including "victimless" crimes

The role of governmental officials in enforcing the laws that those engaged in civil disobedience are breaking matters greatly, because lack of enforcement can further weaken a law with questionable public support. There is an important distinction in criminal law between crimes that are considered to be *mala in se,* that is, inherently wrong, and those that are *mala prohibita.* As a society, we believe that there are some actions that are *mala in se,* that is, wrong in themselves, like murder, rape, theft, arson, kidnapping, and extortion. Nonenforcement of these crimes would almost certainly be sharply criticized in the public arena. For crimes that are simply *mala prohibita,* however, there is no such consensus: although these crimes are prohibited by law, there is usually disagreement about whether the acts are wrong in and of themselves. For example, there exist a category of "victimless crimes," like drug use and addiction, prostitution, and gambling that are engaged in by consenting adults. These crimes are considered to be victimless because most people see them as actions that impose no harm on others. Historically, these crimes have not been uniformly prosecuted in the United States, and at times, there has been strong public resistance to the enforcement of these laws. Effective use of civil disobedience and lack of law enforcement often suggest that the law in question may not be based on popular values or belief systems. To be most effective, law must be based on widely accepted norms that establish desirable behavior, and unpopular laws will likely not be obeyed or enforced.

OTHER ACTORS STANDING IN THE PLACE OF GOVERNMENT

Law is made by government, and there has been an explosion in the number and kind of laws created in the United States in the last forty to fifty years. We have more law now, in terms of statutes created by legislatures, regulatory law created by agencies, and case law written by courts, than we have had at any point in our nation's history. The primary function of law is social control, that is, the maintenance of order and the construction and enforcement of a code of behavior for individuals and groups. It bears noting, however, that there have been times in our nation's history that other actors have effectively replaced the state in enforcing this code and at times have implemented a code that violates the basic rights of certain groups in the polity.

Vigilante Justice

vigilante justice

actions by persons outside of government who step in to ensure order and the protection of life and property

At times, mobs have stepped in to administer justice because no state actor or apparatus was available to counter criminal acts. For example, frontier culture relied heavily upon the use of "posses," or **vigilante justice**, to implement the criminal code. Many of these settlements were hundreds, if not thousands, of miles from law enforcement personnel or courts of law, and so they "took the law into their own hands" and directly punished those who committed acts of violence or theft. This vigilante justice, a form of crime control in the West, was intended to serve as a supplement to the legal system, and those administering this justice took aim at individuals transgressing the criminal code. By the late 1870s, however, vigilantism gave way to mob violence that was aimed not at crime control, but at social control, and the primary targets of this violence were racial and ethnic minorities. After Reconstruction, vigilantism moved to the South, and mob lynchings of African Americans sharply increased.

Throughout the late 1800s and until the mid-1900s, state and local law enforcement officials allowed mob violence to run rampant as African-Americans were systematically targeted, often falsely accused of crimes, and then executed. The threat or actual use of lynching served as an effective social control and reinforced the Jim Crow laws that segregated the South and denied African-Americans equal footing with whites in virtually all areas of life. Whereas vigilantism in the West had been aimed at individuals transgressing an understood criminal code, mob violence in the South was aimed at a particular group and its goal was the systematic intimidation and control of this group.

In the late twentieth century, vigilantism became associated with urban crime and was sometimes seen as a reasonable response to ineffective crime control by the police. Bernard Goetz, the so-called "subway vigilante," gained wide notoriety when he shot four men who he said tried to rob him on a New York City subway train in 1984. He argued that he was avenging two muggings of which he had been the victim and that the four men were threatening his life. Goetz's actions and words resonated with some of the public, who were growing increasingly fearful of urban violence in the late 1970s and early 1980s. When one of the men, who had been paralyzed by the shooting, sued Goetz, Goetz asserted, "If you're injured, paralyzed or whatever while committing a violent crime against me, that's not my fault." He and his lawyers argued that he had a right to protect himself against a perceived threat to his life and that the shooting was a reasonable response to this threat. Many sympathized with Goetz, believing that he was acting in self-defense; many others vilified him for his actions.

More recently, some "militias" in the Northwest, most significantly, the Montana Freemen, have been using their own courts, which they call "citizen grand juries," to file complaints, usually against state and federal

THE LAW IN POPULAR CULTURE

Strange Fruit

Strange Fruit
Abel Meeropol
(1939)

> *Southern trees bear a strange fruit,*
> *Blood on the leaves and blood at the root,*
> *Black body swinging in the Southern breeze,*
> *Strange fruit hanging from the poplar trees.*
> *Pastoral scene of the gallant South,*
> *The bulging eyes and the twisted mouth,*
> *Scent of magnolia sweet and fresh,*
> *And the sudden smell of burning flesh!*
>
> *Here is a fruit for the crows to pluck,*
> *For the rain to gather, for the wind to suck,*
> *For the sun to rot, for a tree to drop,*
> *Here is a strange and bitter crop.*

This poem was written by teacher and union activist Abel Meeropol after seeing a photograph of the 1935 lynching of Robin Stacy in Fort Lauderdale. The music and lyrics were added later, and eventually performed by jazz legend Billie Holiday in 1937. "Strange Fruit" was very controversial—Holiday's recording label, Columbia Records, refused to record it, and *Time* magazine sharply criticized it as a piece of "musical propaganda."

officials. When these officials fail to appear, they are usually found guilty in absentia and sentenced to monetary liens, arrest, jail, or even death. Many analysts believe that after the Oklahoma City bombings in 1995, many militias have gone underground, but it appears that these common law courts are continuing to operate and that they serve as an alternative to civil courts in a number of states. While vigilantism is much more common in other countries, in particular, some South American nations like Colombia, there is a strong feeling in the United States that individuals have the right to take action to protect themselves, their loved ones, and their property, and that violence against persons who are perceived to be threats is justifiable.

LAWS CAN CHANGE NORMS

Usually, we think of law as reflecting social norms. As has been said, the primary function of law in the United States, as in other countries, is social control, that is, to ensure order and a predictability of behavior. This code of behavior is powerfully affected by the underlying norms that operate in a community. In some cases, law can not only reflect norms, it can change them as well. For example, it is widely accepted that Congress's passage of the 1965 Voting Rights Act profoundly increased the number of African American voters in the Deep South, particularly in Mississippi, Alabama, and Louisiana. In these states, registration of nonwhites jumped from as little as 5 percent of the eligible population to 71 percent between 1960 and 1970. This law created strict requirements for states to ensure the registration of minority voters and imposed serious sanctions on states that failed to meet these requirements. Most significantly, the law allowed for the voter registration system to be transferred from the state to the U.S. Attorney General to ensure compliance. The coercive power of this statute ensured that it would have an impact on the behavior of state and local officials charged with registering voters.

www ▶ ▶ ▶

Brown v. Board of Education

the landmark 1954 U.S. Supreme Court decision that struck down state laws that mandated separate schools for whites and nonwhites; many criticize this decision for failing to go far enough in mandating desegregation

www ▶ ▶ ▶

In theory, law can alter social norms, but in reality, it rarely does. For law to change norms, it must provide a very clear message about what is expected of individuals and it must establish that serious consequences will result from noncompliance with the new norms. Laws that conflict with existing norms often fail to meet these two requirements. First, they are often crafted in language that is ambiguous; and second, they must be implemented by law enforcement personnel and administrative and regulatory agents who may be acutely aware of how the law is out of step with public sentiment and who are unwilling to incur the public's wrath.

Many scholars believe that the U.S. Supreme Court's decision in *Brown v. Board of Education*, which mandates the desegregation of educational institutions, was not ultimately successful. There continued to be strong support for segregation, especially in the South, and these decisions did not offer a clear enough blueprint for how or when to achieve desegregation. By failing to set firm guidelines or clear sanctions for noncompliance, the Court lost the opportunity to help create a new social norm of racial integration. Moreover, the reluctance of law enforcement and administrative agents to move vigorously to desegregate the schools effectively undercut the Court's decisions. Similarly, the Court's unwillingness to base the right to abortion on firm constitutional footing, preferring to ground it on the amorphous privacy right, likely contributed to the chipping away of this right in the 1980s and 1990s, and ultimately, may be faulted for contributing to the reversal of the 1973 *Roe v. Wade* holding, which established the right to abortion. Moreover, some believe that the Court's ruling in *Roe* polarized opposition to abortion rights and encouraged opponents to aggressively lobby state and federal legislatures to roll it back. These cases didn't settle the ongoing debates about segregation and abortion; they established norms that conflicted with strongly held beliefs.

Roe v. Wade

the landmark 1973 U.S. Supreme Court case that struck down state abortion bans but polarized public opinion about abortion in the United States

SUMMARY

Law is only one of a set of social controls that operate to constrain behavior in a community, and usually law reflects the mores and norms of the community. Like all social controls, law outlines acceptable rules of behavior and establishes sanctions for noncompliance. What sets law apart from other controls, however, is that the role of the state is central in both creating the rules and imposing the sanctions. Moreover, these sanctions are almost always negative and exclusive: the state alone can impose the penalties, and in the criminal realm, these penalties can range from fines to imprisonment or death. In the United States, we require that punishment be proportional to the act, that is, that the punishment not be excessive, cruel, or unusual. In both the criminal justice and civil systems, the goal of compensation and retribution is central, and in the criminal system, this goal has gradually taken on a more punitive cast. Where law is controversial, that is, based on norms that are not widely held or are in a state of flux, the likelihood of noncompliance is greater than it would be if the law were based on widely accepted norms. We also need to recognize that there have been times in our nation's history when extralegal actors have enforced their own codes of behavior by effectively sidestepping the legal system through the use of vigilantism or mob violence. Finally, while law is based on social norms, it is limited in its ability to change these norms. The only times law has been able to alter norms have been when the law has articulated clear guidelines, established serious penalties for noncompliance with these new guidelines, and had enforcement agents willing to impose these sanctions.

SUGGESTED READING

John D'Emilio and Estelle B. Freedman, *Intimate Matters: A History of Sexuality in America* (Perennial Library/Harper & Row, 1988). This is an excellent book detailing both the practice and regulation of sex in the colonial era and early years of our nation's founding.

Alan M. Dershowitz, *The Genesis of Justice: Ten Stories of Biblical Injustice That Led to the Ten Commandments and Modern Law* (Warner Books, 2000). This book discusses the roots of the Judeo-Christian heritage, detailing the lessons taught in the Book of Genesis and the laws that derived from these stories.

Tara Heivel and Paul Wrangler, eds., *Prison Nation: The Warehousing of America's Poor* (Routledge, 2003). The essays in this book argue that our criminal justice system is biased against the poor and working class. It examines the conditions of prisons in the United States and explores the long-term effects of our ongoing war on drugs, which has resulted in a huge increase in the prison population.

Gale Williams O'Brien, *The Color of the Law: Race, Violence and Justice in the Post–World War II South* (University of North Carolina Press, 1999). This important book examines how race relations had begun to change in the period following World War II and explores the role of community groups in helping to challenge the long-established use of terror by groups like the Ku Klux Klan.

Patrick Minges, *Black Indian Slave Narratives* (John F. Blair Publishers, 2004). This book compiles many interviews of African Americans and Native Americans that were conducted by the Federal Writers' Project, a governmental program funded during the Great Depression. These interviews provide wonderful insight into the interactions and interrelationship of Native Americans and African Americans in the 1800s.

ACTIVE LEARNING

1. Examine the informal and formal norms that constrain your behavior each day. How regulated is your daily life? Which norms do you feel have a greater impact on your daily life—informal or formal norms? What are the origins of those laws that do affect your daily life? What social norms do these laws reflect?

2. Remember, some norms are static and others change over time. Can you identify some norm that *is* changing? You may want to use the Web for this—it is a great resource for research on norms.

CHAPTER 2

American Law and Legal Theory

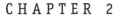

Theories of jurisprudence

theories that define what law is and how it functions

normative theories of jurisprudence

theories of law that focus on how law *should* function

empirical theories of jurisprudence

theories of law that examine how law *actually does* function

What is law? In the last chapter, we learned that laws are those rules of behavior that are written down by some governmental body and are backed by the threat of government-imposed sanctions for noncompliance. These sanctions are almost always negative and range from fine to imprisonment or death. But why are some norms made into law and not others? And perhaps more importantly, once a law is made, how does it actually function? **Theories of jurisprudence** *help us to answer both of these questions by giving us a framework within which to study the law. By using these frameworks, we can better understand why certain laws exist and what impact they have on our society. Generally, theories of jurisprudence are either normative or empirical.* **Normative theories of jurisprudence** *focus on how law should function, that is, the ideal role that law plays in our polity and wider society. In contrast,* **empirical theories of jurisprudence** *examine how law actually does function, by trying to determine what impact our laws have on our social and political structures. Beginning with the writings of the great Greek philosopher Aristotle in 350 BCE, and continuing until today, people have debated how to assess their laws and the relationship between law and justice. The focus of these writers has shifted over time—in some eras, they were focused on making sure that laws were just; in others, that law served divine purposes; in still other eras, that laws were created through known and established procedures. What ties these theories together, however, is an understanding that law plays a pivotal role in society, and that law must be evaluated and assessed in some way. Theories of jurisprudence do not simply take law as it is given—they hold it up against some yardstick or standard to determine whether it is legitimate.*

NORMATIVE THEORY: HOW LAW *SHOULD* FUNCTION

natural law

normative legal theory that argues that law should be based on religious or philosophical principles

Normative theorists focus on determining how law *should* function in an ideal society and concern themselves less with how law actually *does* function. They attempt to lay out a framework for assessing all law by emphasizing certain principles or goals. There are two main groups of normative theorists: **natural law** theorists, who focus on theoretical or philosophical principles and argue that law must be guided by these principles; and **positive law** theorists, who are concerned about the law as it is written down and who focus on the process by which law is made.

Natural Law: An Emphasis on Higher Principles

positive law

a form of normative legal theory that focuses on the law as it is written and the process by which law is made

All natural law theorists believe that higher principles govern our interactions, although they recognize that law does not always establish the norms of human behavior. In the ancient and medieval worlds, theorists were concerned about laying down principles for evaluating whether laws were just or consistent with divine law. In the modern era, theorists continue to focus on the relationship between the law as it is and the law as it should be, but they are looking at *specific* laws and attempting to determine whether these laws are legitimate. Natural law theorists believe that laws may be just or unjust, and they contend that we are obligated to obey only just laws.

■ **Ancient and Medieval Philosophers—Laying Down Principles** Aristotle was the first normative theorist. He used the principle of justice to understand the role that law should play in a society. For Aristotle, laws could be classified as either just or unjust. He argued that just laws were supreme and enabled men to perfect their condition and to become "the best of animals." But he warned that unjust laws could be used for the worst ends and could enable men to act more savagely than animals. Aristotle recognized that "what are good laws has not yet been clearly explained," but he remained convinced that "true" or good forms of government would have just laws, while perverted forms would have unjust laws. For Aristotle, justice probably had a different meaning than it does for us, since his notion of this term easily encompassed slavery and the complete subjugation of women!

divine law

infallible law that is God-given (according to those who subscribe to this belief) and has only to be discovered by human beings

Writing seven hundred years later, St. Augustine also attempted to evaluate the law according to higher principles. While Aristotle used his ideal of justice to evaluate laws, Augustine focused on whether the law was consistent with God's law, or **divine law,** which was infallible and all-encompassing. Augustine contended that human beings had known divine or "natural law" before the fall of Adam and Eve, and that while it was now hidden from human beings, it was superior to all of the man-made law that had followed.

Both divine and natural law existed independently of human law and were superior to it. Keep in mind that at the time that Augustine was writing, Roman Emperor Justinian was distributing his legal code, which covered a wide range of subjects. For Augustine, however, the Code of Justinian, like all others, had to be evaluated on the basis of whether it was consistent with God's law.

This focus on natural or divine law reemerged in the late medieval period, when St. Thomas Aquinas wrote his *Summa Theologica* (1266–1273), arguing that natural law should be the source of all human law and that those laws in conflict with this higher law were illegitimate. Even more clearly than either Aristotle or Augustine had done, Aquinas stated that law was either evil or divine and that only just laws had to be obeyed. He contended that evil in the world resulted from human beings deviating from the divine law, which was discoverable through human reason. Aquinas's view of law as evil or divine, and his belief that only just laws have to be obeyed, link him directly to both Aristotle and Augustine. Moreover, his writings reveal the central tension that continues into the present between natural law and positive law. But while philosophers in the ancient and medieval periods aimed at laying down the principles for evaluating positive laws, those in the modern era focused on evaluating the laws themselves. In the course of assessing these laws, they found that the laws were sometimes in conflict with natural law principles, and these theorists were left trying to reconcile the two sets of laws.

■ **Natural Law Theorists in the Modern Era—Focusing on the Law As It Is Written** Aquinas's view that there is a higher, natural law independent of the laws passed by human beings continued to resonate into the eighteenth century and beyond, as legal philosophers sought to understand the relationship between written, or positive, law and some higher law. Often this higher, natural law became the standard by which positive law could be evaluated. Even when more law began to be written down, both as court decisions and as legislation, the notion of natural law remained unchallenged. Moreover, the absence of positive law in the international domain encouraged many thinkers to believe that natural law governed the relationships between nation-states and constrained the actions of each individual state. They continued to see natural law as arising from the exercise of human reason.

During the Enlightenment this belief in human reason was part of a larger movement based on the understanding that all individuals have inherent worth and that they have rights that are guaranteed to them, regardless of what the laws decree. Many philosophers—among them Montesquieu, Hobbes, and Locke—believed that inalienable rights derived from natural law exist and that those rights protect individuals against the unjust laws passed by governments. Natural law was used to justify revolutionary movements in Europe and America in the 1700s. By the early 1800s many who sought to abolish slavery in the United States relied on natural law and the existence of an inalienable right to liberty to justify their position. Ancient and medieval philosophers also believed that law should be based on higher principles—for Aristotle, the ideal of justice; for Augustine and Aquinas, divine law that could be glimpsed through the exercise of human reason. Natural law theorists of the modern era focused on using natural law principles to evaluate existing laws. For them, natural law was a tool to ensure that individual rights and liberties were protected from governmental encroachment.

By the late 1800s and early 1900s, however, many philosophers and jurists began to challenge how natural law was being used to evaluate the government's laws. One of the most influential jurists of this time, Oliver Wendell Holmes, Jr., rejected the way that judges were using natural law principles to decide cases. He argued that this reliance on natural law hindered the progress of law. Instead of using these philosophical principles, judges should be pragmatic about which laws best advanced the society's goals. Specifically, he urged judges to work together with legislators in formulating laws that were socially useful. The focus on positive law, that is, law that is passed by governmental actors, began in the early 1900s and continued until the mid-1940s. During this period, natural law jurisprudence languished in the United States, as jurists, legislators, philosophers, and legal scholars increasingly relied on positive law to resolve existing and emerging problems, rejecting natural law as outdated and irrelevant.

World War II brought a renewed interest in natural law as the Nazis used positive law to justify and legitimate their genocidal regime. You might want to look at some of these laws, included on the website for this text. In the wake of the Nazi Holocaust, many scholars began to consider how natural law principles could be used to evaluate and possibly to temper positive law. Responding to Nazism, some philosophers began to argue once again that only just laws were binding. A number of writers, including American philosopher Lon Fuller, argued that Nazism exemplified the dangers inherent in relying exclusively on positive law. He and others argued that Nazi laws were not guided by higher values, truths, or reason; they were instead the result of a gross exercise of power. Fuller and others contended that by separating morals from law, the Nazis had been able to use the law as a weapon of terror and tyranny. He argued that the Nazis had accomplished this by creating a legal system that was not really a legal system at all. Fuller attempted to blend natural law principles with a reliance on positive law, developing his theory of **procedural naturalism**. According to this theory, the only legitimate legal systems are those that achieve social order by respecting the inherent autonomy of the individual and his or her ability to make choices. When the Reichstag passed its laws, which ultimately

www ▶ ▶ ▶

procedural naturalism

Fuller's theory that legal systems are legitimate only when they respect individual autonomy

served as the foundation of the Nazi campaign to exterminate all Jews and undesirables, they coerced or compelled individual actions; they did not guide behavior and enable individuals to make choices about what actions to take.

The Holocaust, a campaign waged by the National Socialist or Nazi government in Germany in the late 1930s and early 1940s, and made possible by laws passed by the German legislature, resulted in the death of more than 6 million people.

At the heart of Fuller's theory is an inherent belief that individuals are autonomous actors and that the law must respect and advance this autonomy. Fuller was essentially arguing what Enlightenment thinkers had argued two centuries earlier. The "rights revolution" ushered in by the civil rights movement of the mid-1960s revitalized much of the natural law theory that had been discarded in the early 1900s. Employing this theory, philosophers, legal scholars, and lawmakers began to ground their attempts to broaden civil rights protections to people of color and women by relying on arguments about inherent and/or inalienable rights. Ronald Dworkin was one of the first philosophers to use natural law principles to advocate this approach, and he continues to argue that law must be evaluated according to these principles. He envisioned an important role for judges in his system, contending that judges reach decisions by relying on a conception of "law as integrity." The common law's reliance on past decisions ensures that law has an internal consistency and coherence; however,

Dworkin notes that there are cases in which there is no precedent to guide a judge in her or his actions. It is here that the judge invokes her or his own moral principles.

For Dworkin, as for all natural law theorists, there is a complete overlap between law and morals, and it is in the "hard cases" for which there is no precedent that this overlap becomes most apparent. Like his natural law predecessors, Dworkin argues that there is a "right" and knowable answer to questions raised in courts of law and that it is the responsibility of judges to find this answer. He contends that judges would be able to know what to do, even in very difficult cases, by focusing on rights arguments rather than policy arguments. Dworkin assumes that there is a societal consensus about the existence of moral rights and that they have the force of law, even if existing laws do not recognize them. According to his **Rights Thesis,** judges have an obligation to discover the rights of the parties and to respect these rights when considering laws. He contends that the most profound obligation of the judge is to enforce preexisting rights. When legislatures pass laws that interfere with these rights, it is the obligation of the judge or judges to strike down these laws. For example, Dworkin argues that every person has the right to bodily integrity and that this right is grounded in our moral principles. Laws passed by legislatures that interfere with the exercise of this right have no moral foundation. Thus, in his book *Life's Dominion,* he contends that the debates about abortion and euthanasia are inherently spiritual debates about the intrinsic value of life. He argues that the state must remain neutral in this debate and that only laws that protect the individual's right to make these difficult decisions may be justified.

> **Rights Thesis**
>
> Dworkin's argument that judges have the obligation to respect individual rights when deciding cases

Legal Positivism: Focusing on the Written Law

In addition to natural law, which may or may not be written down, there is positive law, which is, by its very definition, written law. Since the Code of Justinian was penned in 550 CE, written laws have covered a broad array of activities. As we have already discussed, natural law theorists looked at these laws and attempted to determine whether they were consistent with higher principles. Where these man-made laws were inconsistent with divine or natural laws, these theorists had no qualms about concluding that the written laws were illegitimate. Many other philosophers were far less critical of the written law, however, and were eager to find that the laws themselves were an expression of either reason or progress. These theorists became known as **legal positivists,** and they enthusiastically promoted the codification or writing down of laws, believing that society was best served by having laws that were explicit and clear.

> **legal positivists**
>
> theorists who promote the codification of laws and argue that society is best served by having written laws that are explicit and clear

■ **Coke and Blackstone: The Earliest Proponents of Written Law** One of the first theorists to argue in favor of written law was **Sir Edward Coke,** writing in England in the late 1500s and early 1600s. Coke argued that royal prerogative, which was based on the divine right of kings, one of the principles of natural law at the time, was in fact illegitimate, and that written law was supreme. Where prerogative clashed with the laws of Parliament, it was to be opposed. Coke contended that all written law was based on ancient principles that were simply waiting to be discovered by judges and legislators. Code laws didn't just emerge spontaneously; instead, they were the expression of widely held principles that could not be challenged. Coke's work had a profound impact on the writings of many theorists, judges, and legislators who followed, including **Sir William Blackstone,** who picked up Coke's torch and penned his two-thousand-page treatise *Commentaries on the Laws of England,* compiling judges' decisions on a vast array of subjects, including contract, tort, property, and criminal law and criminal procedure.

Like Coke, Blackstone believed that all written laws were rooted in the customs and traditions of the community and reflected ancient law. At the time that Blackstone was writing, judges were the chief lawmakers and there were few laws passed by Parliament or other lawmakers. Then, as now, judges made law by deciding cases and writing opinions to justify their decisions. Blackstone was a zealous supporter of this judge-made law. He contended that the judge was the spokesman of communitarian principles that he discovered through the exercise of reason and then articulated in case holdings.

Blackstone argued that the primary function of government was to ensure the fundamental rights to security, liberty, and property ownership. According to Blackstone, there could be no unjust laws: if judges used their reason, the inevitable result would be the articulation of just laws. According to Blackstone, common law reflected the protection of individual liberty that was at the heart of ancient law, and the maxims or principles derived in case law had to be adhered to closely. Blackstone's *Commentaries* demonstrated how this unwritten customary law had been employed by judges, and it provided a virtual catalog of legal decisions. He justified the writing down of these decisions in annual "year books," public records, and law reports by contending that reporting allowed for law to be put into systematic form and encouraged uniformity. It bears noting that Blackstone's work was widely read, both in Great Britain and the American colonies, and constituted the authoritative guide to Anglo-American law for many years. Apprentices training to become lawyers became well-versed in Blackstone's *Commentaries,* and lawyers, including Abraham Lincoln, relied heavily on them.

In the late 1800s and early 1900s, legislatures began to engage more heavily in lawmaking. Some even argued that the laws made by legislators, known

code law

law made by legislators

historical jurisprudence

views law and legal institutions as evolving into the highest stage—that of written code law

sociological jurisprudence

theory that law is the product of social, political, and economic realities and can be used to bring about a better society

as **code law,** was superior to judge-made law. For example, in his 1861 book *Ancient World,* Sir Henry Maine zealously promoted his theory of **historical jurisprudence,** contending that there had been an evolution in legal ideas and institutions from the ancient to the modern worlds. The key to any evolution in cultural and legal development was the development of written law, particularly code law. American jurist Roscoe Pound, writing in the late 1800s and early 1900s, rejected the view of Blackstone and others who relied on case law and argued for a more proactive role for judges and legislators, believing that written law could be used to alleviate social problems. Pound was one of the founders of **sociological jurisprudence,** a theory that viewed law as a product of social, political, and economic realities.

■ The Development of Legal Positivism: Bentham, Austin, and Hart

Coke and Blackstone strongly believed that all written law was based on morals that were simply waiting to be discovered—and that judges were the most important interpreters of this moral code. In the late 1800s, many theorists had begun to challenge this view that all laws in a sense were inevitable and argued instead for laws that were rational and responded to societal needs and goals. Jeremy Bentham and John Austin, who founded the positivist school of jurisprudence, rejected the Anglo-American system's reliance on judge-made law, instead arguing that legislators should be the primary lawmakers. Bentham argued that the common law was insufficiently proactive and didn't provide notice to people about the rules of conduct they should follow. He contended that trying to follow this law was like "waiting for one's dog to do something wrong and then beating it." Bentham also claimed that the common law was not really accessible to most people—that one needed to be a judge or a lawyer to really understand its nuances.

In place of this common law, which was supposed to be based on some higher code of morality, Bentham advocated a code of law based on the principle of utility, which he called the **greatest happiness principle.** He claimed that most people act to maximize their pleasure and minimize their pain and that laws must reflect this principle. His theory, which became known as **utilitarianism,** was premised on the understanding that laws should be deliberately crafted by legislators and should follow the principle of social utility; that is, they should benefit the greatest number of people.

Bentham rejected the argument of natural law theorists that there were inalienable or natural rights. Instead, he contended that the only rights that individuals possess are those given to them by the sovereign, that is, the legitimate government. This heavy reliance on lawmaking by the government was embraced by Bentham's successor, John Austin, who also

greatest happiness principle

basis of the theory of utilitarianism; argues that law should benefit the greatest number of people

utilitarianism

philosophy based on the greatest happiness principle

contended that laws had to crafted by the sovereign in order to be legitimate. Austin developed the theory of **analytical jurisprudence,** arguing that there are no inherent or inalienable rights and that governments confer these rights because they advance the common good. Austin's legal theory relied heavily on the coercive nature of law. He argued that the only real laws are those that enable the sovereign to impose punitive sanctions on those who failed to conform their behavior.

This theory had two principles: first, that government, not community standards, traditions, or customs, is the source of all law; and second, that law is to be evaluated, not on the basis of goodness or justice, but in terms of whether the law is created pursuant to established lawmaking procedures. As long as the government has followed all procedures or standards for lawmaking, then it is assumed that the result is a legitimate law. Austin argued that law is morally neutral and can be studied scientifically by employing simple and knowable standards. While his predecessor Jeremy Bentham had rejected all judge-made law, Austin believed that this law could be used in a transitional context. But he concluded, much to the anger of both the British and Americans, that ancient Roman code law was actually more advanced than English common law, since it was based almost entirely on legislative enactments.

While this theory of utilitarianism relied heavily on the coercive nature of law, Austin's successor, H. L. A. Hart, saw law in a more nuanced way. Like both Bentham and Austin, Hart argued that law and moral principles had to be discussed separately. Discussions about the law should distinguish between what law is and what it should be. As long as the law is the product of a legal system that satisfies three conditions, or rules, it is law. First, the legal system that creates the law must have a rule of recognition, that is, an authoritative text that specifies how primary rules or laws are made. These rules not only inform citizens of what behaviors are prohibited but structure rights and obligations, as well. For example, criminal law defines those activities that are prohibited, and contract law creates a code of behavior for persons seeking to enter into contracts. Laws created pursuant to these rules have validity; those not crafted according to these rules do not. The second condition is that the legal system has a rule of change; in other words, it specifies how the rules that guide behavior will be altered. Last, the legal system must have a set of secondary rules that enables individuals to determine whether a primary rule has been violated. In the simplest legal systems, this is a system of adjudication, and judges interpret the rules. Altogether, these three rules structure the lawmaking process. If the public recognizes these three conditions as laying down the foundation for lawmaking, then they confer legitimacy on the legal system. Like Bentham and Austin, Hart contended that morality could not be used to test the legitimacy of a law. Even if a law was inconsistent with standards of morality, that inconsistency didn't void that law. Similarly, the mere fact that some action was morally desirable did not render that action law.

Sociological Jurisprudence

Natural law and positive law are both normative theories of jurisprudence—they describe what the law *should* be and aim at assessing the legitimacy of law based on general principles. Under natural law, laws that do not comport with divine will or human reason are illegitimate. Similarly, under the positive law theory of utilitarianism, laws that do not maximize the public good are not law; under the theory of analytical positivism, those laws that are not created pursuant to accepted procedures or by recognized lawmakers are not law. In a sense, both schools focus on the negative aspects of law: their primary inquiry is whether a law is legitimate, not whether law can be used in a proactive and positive way to achieve certain goals.

■ **The Progressive Movement** A new theory of jurisprudence that emerged in the early 1900s viewed law as a more positive force and urged that law be used to promote social welfare and the public good. By this time, the industrial revolution had begun to result in serious workplace injuries and harm, and the public was becoming aware of the difficult working conditions of men, women, and children in urban factories. It was not unusual for workers to toil for twelve to sixteen hours a day and to be forced to work seven days a week. There was little regulation of child labor, and children often worked in dangerous conditions, again, for many hours each day. Activists in what became known as the **Progressive Movement** began to lobby both Congress and state legislatures to enact laws that would protect workers and the general public from health hazards associated with industrialization. By the turn of the twentieth century, Progressives successfully lobbied many states to pass laws that regulated hours and working conditions for industrial laborers. This success was short-lived, however, as courts began to strike down most of these laws, concluding that they violated the individual's right to contract. Consider the case of *Lochner v. New York* (1905).

In a few rare cases from the Progressive Era, courts allowed state regulations to stand. For example, the Court upheld a state law limiting the hours worked by miners, holding that mining had such great health risks that

---

www ▶ ▶ ▶

Progressive Movement

a political and social movement that focused on how law could be used to protect workers and the public from health hazards that resulted from industrialization

---

Lochner v. New York

Progressive Era legislation setting maximum hours struck down because it violated the right to contract

1.1 Progressive Era Legislation Struck Down

LOCHNER V. *NEW YORK,* U.S. Supreme Court, 1905

The 1905 U.S. Supreme Court case *Lochner* v. *New York* (198 U.S. 45) is an excellent example of how contract principles were used to strike down a state law that intended to limit the hours and working conditions of bakers to sixty hours a week, with a maximum of ten hours a day. The state law had been passed because of the significant health hazards associated with job, and in particular, the chronic inflammation of the lungs and bronchial tubes caused by prolonged exposure to flour dust. In legislative hearings and at trial, testimony strongly suggested that bakers tended to be sicker than other workers and to die much sooner. Despite the fact that the hours limitations were intended to minimize these health hazards, the Court struck down the state law.

Writing for a majority of Justices, JUSTICE PECKHAM held that:

The statute necessarily interferes with the right of contract between the employer and employees concerning the number of hours in which the latter may labor in the bakery of the employer. The general right to make a contract in relation to his business is part of the liberty of the individual protected by the Fourteenth Amendment of the Federal Constitution. . . . Under that provision, no State can deprive any person of life, liberty or property without due process of law. The right to purchase or to sell labor is part of the liberty protected by this amendment unless there are circumstances which exclude the right . . . (p. 45)

There is no reasonable ground for interfering with the liberty of person or the right of free contract by determining the hours of labor in the occupation of a baker. There is no contention that bakers as a class are not equal in intelligence and capacity to men in other trades or manual occupations, or that they are not able to assert their rights and care for themselves without the protecting arm of the State, interfering with their independence of judgment and of action. They are in no sense wards of the State . . . It is a question of which of two powers or rights shall prevail—the power of the State to legislate or the right of the individual to liberty of person and freedom of contract. The mere assertion that the subject relates though but in a remote degree to the public health does not necessarily render the enactment valid. The act must have a more direct relation, as a means to an end, and the end itself must be appropriate and legitimate, before an act can be held to be valid which interferes with the general right of an individual to be free in his person and in his power to contract in relation to his own labor. (pp. 57–58)

QUESTIONS:

1) What law is challenged in this case?
2) How does the U.S. Supreme Court decide the case?
3) What is the Court's reasoning?
4) What goal or goals are advanced by the Court's decision?

Muller v. Oregon

Progressive Era
legislation upheld for
women workers
because it protected
maternal function

the regulation was justified. In ***Muller v. Oregon*** (1908), the U.S. Supreme
Court also upheld an Oregon law that limited the hours that women could
work in certain establishments—in this case, laundries—to ten hours a day.
In justifying its decision, which allowed women's work to be regulated even
though it had struck down a similar regulation for men only three years
earlier in *Lochner,* the Court held that "woman's physical structure and the
performance of maternal functions place her at a disadvantage which justifies a difference in legislation" (208 U.S. 412). And even though the law
directly interfered with women's right to contract, the Court argued that
society's need for "healthy mothers" justified the infringement. With these
rare exceptions, the judiciary, and in particular the U.S. Supreme Court,
struck down most of the labor legislation of this period.

The Court's strong belief in the principle of freedom of contract, coupled
with the view that businesses had virtually no liability for harm caused to
their workers and the general public, created an atmosphere that was very
conducive to maximizing profits, but which caused significant harm to large
sectors of the population. A number of writers began to sharply criticize
the Court's heavy reliance on contract principles and argued strongly in
favor of a more proactive and protective role for law. Their legal philosophy became known as sociological jurisprudence, and this theory envisioned a positive role for law in effecting social change. Those advocating
this theory argued that courts and legislatures should use law to achieve
social policy goals: law should be a means to these goals, rather than an end
in itself.

■ The Impact of Sociological Jurisprudence on Legal Study and Practice

Two of the strongest advocates of sociological jurisprudence were Roscoe
Pound, dean of Harvard Law School from 1916 to 1936, and Benjamin
Cardozo, judge on the New York State high court from 1914 to 1932 and
a U.S. Supreme Court justice from 1932 to 1938. Pound was totally dissatisfied with the classical common law tradition. He argued that judges'
strict reliance on precedent meant that case law was out of touch with
social reality and thus made no real contribution to the most pressing
issues of the day. He argued for the study of "**law in action**," which examined not only the formal rules of law but also the actual application and
interpretation of them. Pound envisioned a central role for judges in this
system, arguing that they should function as legislators and be given more
flexibility in interpreting statutes and resolving disputes. He argued that
the judge was more like a social engineer than the technician envisioned in
the classical common law tradition. While Blackstone had seen the judge
as simply discovering settled principles of law, Pound rejected what he
saw as the "mechanical operation of legal rules" and envisioned a much
more independent and innovative role. For Pound, law had to meet the

"law in action"

theory of jurisprudence
that focuses on the
actual enforcement and
interpretation of laws
and argues for a more
active role for judges

challenges posed by evolving political and social realities. He argued that laws that failed to satisfy society's need for both stability and change would not be effective.

Cardozo also saw the judge's role in much more dynamic terms. He claimed that "judge-made law is one of the existing realities of life" and that the process of judging is very much like legislating. He contended that judges make decisions by following a number of steps. First, the judge compares the present case with existing legal precedent and asks whether the factual basis of the cases is the same. If the facts are identical or closely related, the judge applies these existing principles. Where the facts differ, however, the judge has to make a choice about how to proceed. According to Cardozo, the judge could rely on history, tradition, or intuition, but he urged that the judge keep societal welfare and the public good in mind when making a decision. In one of his most famous cases, *MacPherson v. Buick Motor Company* (New York Court of Appeals, 1916), he struck down the doctrine of privity that limited product liability suits and protected manufacturers of defective products from having to pay damages for harm from these products. In this case, MacPherson bought a Buick with a defective wheel that broke apart, injuring him. Again, envisioning that law should promote the public good, Cardozo established that MacPherson could sue not only the dealership that had sold him the car but also the company that had manufactured the car.

Sociological jurisprudence was pragmatic; it looked at how law functioned and at its relationship with the wider society. For example, by focusing on how courts' strict reliance on contract theory actually hurt workers and the public by barring legislatures from passing laws that could ameliorate the harms associated with industrialization, advocates of sociological jurisprudence argued that law was having a negative societal effect. For these advocates, lawmakers had to be concerned with human needs and values. It was not enough for law to rely on logic. Lawmakers—that is, both judges and legislators—had to consider the practical effects of the law. The successor to sociological jurisprudence, legal realism, wholly rejected the view that judges make decisions based on legal doctrine. For proponents of sociological jurisprudence, however, law and legal doctrine were capable of evolution and could ultimately be the basis for a more just social order. Legal realists and those who followed looked at how the law actually did function; they had a much more negative view of its place in the larger society.

EMPIRICAL THEORY: HOW LAW *DOES* FUNCTION

While normative theories of jurisprudence, such as natural law, positivism, and sociological jurisprudence, consider how law *should* function, empirical theories examine how law actually *does* function. Empirical theories emerged in the mid- to late 1800s and reflected a growing concern about

`www ▶ ▶ ▶`

the shortcomings of natural law and positive law theories. The first of these, legal realism, sharply criticized the classical common law tradition; the remaining theories were critical of not only common law, but all positive law, and were concerned, to varying degrees, about the biases that they saw as inherent in the natural law tradition.

Legal Realism

legal realism

theory that all legal decisions are based on moral and political choices

www ▶ ▶ ▶

In the mid- to late 1800s, theorists were increasingly skeptical of the classical common law tradition espoused by Blackstone and others. Some of these theorists, who came to be known as legal realists, advocated a pragmatic and scientific approach to law, arguing that the common law's reliance on abstract principles like contract and property did not serve societal needs. Legal realists claimed that reliance on these principles skewed the law in favor of certain classes of people, principally, those with money and property. Central to **legal realism**, which some have termed legal pragmatism, was the belief that there is no such thing as an objective legal methodology and that all decisions are based in moral and political choices. This overlap between law and morals is reminiscent of natural law, but while natural law theorists saw morality as a positive force in shaping the law, legal realists viewed it much more skeptically.

The best-known and most influential legal realist was Oliver Wendell Holmes, who served on the Massachusetts Supreme Court from 1883 to 1902 and on the U.S. Supreme Court from 1902 to 1932. Holmes argued that judges did not really use logic and reasoning, the linchpins of the common law system, to settle cases. He argued instead that "the life of the law is not logic, but experience." He also raised serious questions about relying on past decisions to decide cases, contending that reliance on these cases could hinder a judge in developing a pragmatic approach to problems presented to him. His pragmatism also led Holmes to be sharply critical of the natural law tradition, contending that morals and law should be separated in order to facilitate the use of law as an instrument of social control. Moreover, Holmes argued that the roles of judge and legislator sometimes blurred, with judges engaged in "interstitial legislating," meaning that they filled in the blanks left open by legislators who crafted the laws.

In his books, articles, and judicial opinions, Justice Holmes argued that law should be analyzed not in terms of moral principles, like "right" and "duty," but in terms of its consequences. Holmes established the "bad man" theory of the law, which assumed that people are interested more in what will happen to them if they disobey the law than they are in abstract principles of right and wrong. Perhaps more than any other school of jurisprudence, legal realism focuses on actual behavior and on establishing remedies under the law. At its core, the legal realism that developed from the writings of Holmes and others was deeply skeptical of the classical common law

tradition and, in particular, its strict reliance on precedent. For legal realists, the law was simply a reaction to the social and political environment;
it was driven, not by neutral principles, but by issues of class and power
relationships. Over time, legal realism has spun off many other schools of
jurisprudence, which have examined the relationship between law and race,
gender, class, and the economic system.

Law and Economics

law and economics

well-accepted theory
that law functions
or should function
to maximize societal
wealth by promoting
market efficiency

The **law and economics** school of jurisprudence emerged in the United
States in the late 1960s. It is now the best-accepted theory of private law,
and in particular, property rights, among law school faculty members. Some
have argued, in fact, that this theory of jurisprudence has had a greater
effect on American law than any other theory in the last fifty years. The central assumption of the law and economics movement is that law functions,
or should be allowed to function, to maximize wealth in the society by promoting market efficiency. Legal economists assume that individuals are
rational actors who structure their activities in ways that enable them to
maximize their happiness.

In many ways, the law and economics movement is similar to the theory
of utilitarianism. Both theories seek to understand law by assessing the
extent to which it achieves the goal of utility or rationality, as opposed to
more amorphous ideals like justice and fairness. The central difference lies
in the fact that for legal economists, the only goal is the maximization of
wealth, while utilitarians have a more vague notion of what is socially desirable. The individual is the most important unit in the law and economics
movement, whereas utilitarians envision an important role for both the individual and the collective. For legal economists, the collective is important
only as it relates to the individual actor. For example, many legal economists
use **game theory** to explain and predict individual actions. In so doing, they
attempt to predict and explain how the strategies of other actors ultimately
affect the individual's decisions about how best to proceed.

game theory

theory used to predict
and explain how
individual decisions
are affected by the
strategies of other
actors

Law and economics actually envisions a less extensive role for the law,
since it assumes that rationality and bargaining will result in the efficient
distribution of property rights and that law will simply reinforce these market decisions. Where law interferes with market efficiency, that is, it would
not, and should not be permitted to, exist. This argument, that individuals
act to maximize their wealth or resources and that they act strategically
after considering what other players might do, has been applied to a number
of fields. For example, a recent study of regulatory law by Harrell Chesson
and others revealed that an increase in taxes on alcohol had a significant
effect on sexually transmitted disease rates, explaining that this increase
in the cost of alcohol had decreased alcohol consumption, which in turn
decreased risky sexual activity. This study concluded that individual actors

had acted strategically to maximize (or protect) their wealth: they had responded to the higher taxes by decreasing their alcohol intake, and in turn, had also lowered their risk of sexually transmitted diseases by reducing risky sexual behavior. There is significant controversy about whether law and economics is a useful tool for understanding and predicting criminal activity, as the following debate suggests.

DEBATE

Can law and economics be used to describe and predict how criminal law functions?

Yes:
For a number of years, law and economics has been used to describe and predict how law functions in a number of areas, including criminal law, tort law, contract law, and family law. For example, several studies employ the economics model to explain why people choose to engage in illegal activities. These scholars explain that when people think about committing criminal acts, they consider the possible punishments that will be inflicted if they are caught and then, based on their desire to optimize their wealth, make a decision about whether to commit these crimes. Similarly, law enforcement personnel can be seen as optimizing actors—they decide which offenders to punish based on their desire to maximize their resources. By using the law and economics model, we can better understand how people make decisions about whether to commit crimes and how the criminal justice system deals with these crimes.

No:
Some scholars argue that the law and economics model is far less useful in criminal law than it is in other fields. The problem with criminal law is that it is unclear what is being maximized—that is, the measure of wealth or resources that law seeks to optimize. Some of the difficulty here lies in the disagreement among policymakers about the goals of criminal law— if the goal is deterrence, that will be measured very differently than it would be if the goal were retribution, incapacitation, or rehabilitation. Without a clear sense of the ultimate goal, it is very difficult to either measure or influence behavior. Many also argue that criminal law is inherently political—that is, it targets certain behavior that those in power view as undesirable, and for this reason, it is less amenable to economic analysis. For example, the decision to bar certain activities often turns on a policy decision and not on a reasoned calculation of how this prohibition might maximize societal wealth. And similarly, those considering engaging in criminal activities do not always undertake careful analysis of the costs and benefits of such activities.

▮ Critical Legal Studies

critical legal studies (CLS)

belief that law is used to reinforce existing power structures

Critical legal studies (CLS) emerged as a school of legal thought in the mid-1970s, when a group of law professors began to challenge the goals and methods of legal education. While the CLS movement has largely dissipated, its key assumptions continue to have an impact on theories of jurisprudence. CLS writers reject much of natural and positive law theories, as well as law and economics jurisprudence. They argue that all three theories are misguided in their arguments that law is based on neutral principles: for natural and positive law theories, a belief in individual autonomy and rights; for law and economics, a belief in the neutral principle of market efficiency.

CLS shares many principles of the earlier legal realist school, perhaps most significantly, the belief that law is neither neutral nor based on principles that can be, or are, applied across cases. Like legal realism, CLS argues that law is an expression of political, economic, and social reality—legal rules are an outgrowth of this reality rather than a result of reasoning and logic. For this reason, both schools also reject the view that law is stable over time. They see judges' role as making law, as opposed to simply interpreting it or discovering existing legal principles. While some legal realists, like Justice Oliver Wendell Holmes, view the judges' role in a positive light, CLS scholars see it quite negatively. They think that judges are largely motivated by a desire to advance the interests of the elite.

CLS builds on legal realism's view of the interrelationship between law, politics, and society, but it goes further. Many CLS theorists contend that law is used to reinforce existing power structures in society; that is, not only is law not neutral, but it is used to advance those who are already advantaged in terms of race, gender, and class. In many ways, it incorporates much of **Marxist legal theory**, arguing that law is a tool used to reinforce the privileged status of the elite. Moreover, perhaps because these writers are disillusioned with the shortcomings of the civil rights movement, they contend that liberal legal theory, which relied on individual rights, ultimately distracted activists from taking steps that would result in legal change. Many of these writers contended that even landmark court cases would not adequately address racism in the larger society because ultimately the law would be used to reinforce this racism. They criticized the work of Ronald Dworkin and others, saying that rights language was itself so capable of being manipulated that it would ultimately harm those who most needed its protection.

Marxist legal theory

belief that law is a tool to reinforce the privileged position of the elite

According to CLS, law schools perpetuate the myths of the classical common law tradition by training future lawyers that logic alone can be used to understand how cases are decided. CLS criticizes this reliance on case law, contending that it is not based on principles of logic or reasoning. It is instead the result of power relations; the law could be used to support virtually any decision in a case. According to CLS, by shrouding these decisions in the aura of case law and larger principles, the legal method makes it virtually impossible to challenge the underlying social structures. CLS challenges the legal community to consider that law is not insulated from the larger society but is very much a part of it, and is a tool for advancing certain groups and for oppressing others. CLS scholars contend that law is not blind and rejects the view that law is, or should be, disinterested and neutral.

CLS scholars were perhaps most concerned with what they saw as the legitimizing function of law. They argued that the public viewed law as neutral and unbiased and that it legitimated what were, at heart, political and social decisions. CLS called for the deconstruction of central concepts like justice and neutrality and urged theorists to consider how these concepts actually functioned. The core of the CLS movement has largely dissipated and given way to "outsider jurisprudence," a collection of theories that are driven by the belief that the law is structured and functions to advantage white men at the expense of women and people of color. The most well-known of these theories are feminist legal theory and critical race theory; emerging schools of thought include Latino critical studies, Asian critical studies, queer critical studies, and white critical studies.

Feminist Legal Theory

Under the broad rubric of feminist jurisprudence, there are a number of very different theories about the role of gender in the law. All schools agree, however, that the law is dominated by patriarchal assumptions about gender roles and that legal institutions are biased in favor of men. This view of law as inherently biased is shared by legal realism and critical legal studies, and like CLS, feminist jurisprudence sees law as functioning primarily to reinforce existing inequalities. **Feminist jurisprudence** finds gender bias and inequity readily apparent in most fields of American law, including property, contract, criminal, and constitutional law. All feminist jurisprudential theories agree that civil rights protections cannot function to equalize power inequities between women and men because these laws are inherently biased in favor of men and traditional gender roles. Most of these theories proceed from the assumption that law enshrines, not only reproductive differences between men and women, but also larger societal and cultural norms about gender roles in the workplace and at home.

feminist jurisprudence
set of theories that describe how law and legal institutions are biased in favor of men

While various feminist theories agree about the gendered nature of American law and society, they disagree about what needs to be done to achieve political, social, and economic equality between the sexes. As a school of jurisprudence, feminist legal theory, which emerged in the 1960s, aimed at eliminating explicit gender discrimination in the law. Most theorists now agree that this initial goal has been achieved. For example, feminist jurisprudence has helped to make many policymakers and members of the public aware of sexism in the law, and lawmakers have begun to address such issues as domestic and sexual violence and sexual harassment in the workplace and educational settings.

There are at least four major schools of feminist jurisprudence: liberal feminism, relational feminism, radical feminism, and critical race feminism. Advocates of these theories profoundly disagree about whether changes in the law have brought about true equality between men and women, and about whether such equality is even possible in our society. While liberal feminism would argue that changes in law have had a monumental impact on gender roles, relational, radical, and critical race feminism would have a much more skeptical view of their overall significance.

liberal feminist jurisprudence

view that law must aim at gender-neutrality

■ Formal Equality or Liberal Feminism Formal equality or **liberal feminist jurisprudence** begins from the starting point that men and women are equal and that the law must aim at gender-neutrality. According to those who espouse this view, law should make few if any distinctions between the sexes and should seek to enable women to compete as men do, especially in the workplace. Often this school of feminism is said to seek formal equality: that is, it aims to place men and women on a level playing field by eliminating explicit gender bias in the law.

Many of our laws reflect this focus on formal equality. For example, the Fourteenth Amendment, ratified in 1868, mandates "equal protection of the laws," and the Nineteenth Amendment, passed in 1920, extends suffrage to women. More recently, the federal Equal Pay Act and Title VII of the 1964 Civil Rights Act required that employers pay women the same as they pay men for the same job and that they eliminate gender bias in human resource decisions. Furthermore, the U.S. Congress is again considering an Equal Rights Amendment to the Constitution that would require that men and women have equal rights in all areas of public life. This amendment, which was defeated in the 1980s and reintroduced in 2001, states: "Equality of rights under the law shall not be denied or abridged by the United States or by any State on account of sex."

www ▶ ▶ ▶

Formal equality assumed that women would catch up to men if they were provided with equal opportunities, and for this reason, this school of jurisprudence was focused on the passage of laws barring gender discrimination in education and employment. While the 1964 Civil Rights Act and and 1965 Equal Pay Act bar explicit discrimination, men and women continue to be segregated in different jobs, and women continue to earn far less than men—at the writing of this text, less than 61 cents for every dollar men earn. Women also perceive themselves as having more limited job opportunities than men, and the burden of childrearing continues to fall more heavily on women than it does on men.

■ Relational Feminism Some feminists have attempted to respond to these continuing gender inequalities by focusing on the differences between men and women and, in particular, on women's choices. These feminists, who embrace what is known as **relational or cultural feminist jurisprudence**, focus on what they argue are women's concerns about caring and community, which stand in stark contrast with men's concerns about rights and logic. This branch of feminist jurisprudence moves away from focusing on formal equality between the sexes and instead seeks accommodation of gender differences. For example, while Title VII of the Civil Rights Act bars employers from discriminating against pregnant women, some proposals advocated by relational feminists would allow employers to provide additional protections and accommodations to pregnant women than they offer to nonpregnant women or men to allow these women to remain in the workplace both before and after childbirth.

> **relational or cultural feminist jurisprudence**
>
> the theory that law must accommodate gender differences, specifically, the role of relationships in women's lives

Moreover, relational feminists sharply criticize liberal feminism's focus on individual autonomy, that is, the right of the individual to make choices. They emphasize instead the role of relationships in women's lives. Relational feminists contend that it is only by focusing on women's relationships with others that real parity between the sexes can be achieved. For example, relational feminists argue that in divorce proceedings, division of marital property must recognize the contributions made by a stay-at-home parent or homemaker. They argue that such an approach compensates the non-wage-earning partner and ensures a more just and equitable distribution of property. Many relational feminists argue that only by fully valuing women's relationships and commitments to others can women begin to achieve parity with men. Relational feminism contends that the focus on rights, justice, and autonomy that is the basis of much of our law does not adequately protect or advance women's basic interests and needs because these terms do not really address women's relationships to others.

Relational feminism has been sharply criticized for what some view as its reinforcement of women's stereotyped role as nurturer and caregiver. Some, especially radical feminists like Catherine MacKinnon, have argued that the "ethic of care" and calls to protect women's ability to maintain their primary roles as mothers and caregivers will ultimately thwart any real advance toward equality. These theorists contend that viewing women primarily in terms of these traditional roles reinforces women's role as subordinate to men.

dominance or radical feminist jurisprudence

theory of feminist jurisprudence that focuses on the power imbalances between the sexes and sees law as a tool for the oppression of women

■ **Dominance or Radical Feminism** Dominance or radical feminist jurisprudence focuses on the power imbalances between the sexes and sees law as a tool that consciously oppresses women. Like relational feminism, radical feminism recognizes the differences between men's and women's experiences, but radical feminism focuses on the inequalities and subordination that it views as central to women's lives. Unlike the other feminist theories, dominance feminist jurisprudence argues that the principle of equality will never achieve true equality, since law is only facially neutral and masks men's oppression of women. For this school, the most important question to be answered in assessing a law is whether its implementation continues the subordination of women. This theory of law is radical: it envisions a much different legal system that is based not on neutrality and rights, both principles that dominance feminists see as serving patriarchy, but on the different characteristics of men and women.

Catherine MacKinnon contends that men maintain their control over women by sexualizing them. Much of her work is focused on the use of pornography to reinforce male dominance, and she contends that by sexualizing women, that is, by making them sexual objects, men maintain their control. MacKinnon argues that pornography encourages men to see women *primarily* as sexual objects and that this view colors how men see women in all facets of life. MacKinnon argues that the sexualization of women is based entirely on men's desires and needs and that it ensures that men and women will never be equals. For MacKinnon and others, a mere tinkering with the legal system will not achieve social change; instead, what is needed is a radical restructuring of the entire legal apparatus based, not on the principle of equality, but on that of nonsubordination. For example, dominance feminists point out that formal equality has not reduced the wage inequality between men and women. They argue that a much more radical solution is needed to equalize pay, and they embrace the controversial system of comparable worth as a means of achieving this goal. Comparable worth is a direct response to the fact that women and men tend to be segregated into different jobs, and women's jobs tend to pay less than men's. Advocates of comparable worth assume that women's jobs pay less simply *because* they are held by women. They believe that compensation should instead be based on the skill, education, and training needed to perform a job. So, a nurse's job, which requires a relatively high degree of skill, education, and training, should be compensated on par with "men's jobs" that have similar requirements. Again, radical feminists seek to level the playing field by restructuring the entire legal system.

critical race feminism

belief that law reflects not only gender but race and class bias, as well

■ **Critical Race Feminism** Rooted in critical race theory, **critical race feminism** is based on the understanding that law reflects not only gender but race and class bias, as well. According to adherents of critical race feminism, liberal, relational, and even radical feminism focus too heavily on the needs and issues of white upper- and middle-class women and ignore the very different experiences of women of color, working class and poor women, and lesbian and transgendered women. These theorists argue that the intersection of race, ethnicity, sex, sexual orientation, and class has a powerful effect on individuals in society and that each category alone does not explain their combined effect in placing the individual into a privileged, or nonprivileged, position. Critical race feminists contend that where discrimination is based, not on sex, race, or class alone, but on a combination of these characteristics, its effects can be even more profound. These theorists point to the devastating effects of gender, race, class, and ethnicity discrimination in a number of fields of law, including employment law, criminal law, family law, and legal education.

www ▶ ▶ ▶

THE LAW IN POPULAR CULTURE

Mi Vida Loca

In examining the difficult lives of several Latina friends living in a poor neighborhood of Los Angeles, this film shows how race, class, and gender powerfully interact in contemporary urban America.

critical race theory

part of outsider jurisprudence, it assumes that law is biased against persons of color; proponents are known as CRITS

■ **Critical Race Theory** Like feminist jurisprudence, **critical race theory** is considered to be part of outsider jurisprudence. It proceeds from the assumption that American law has been structured and has functioned to promote the interests of whites, particularly white males, over persons of color. Critical race theory contends that the experiences, concerns, values, and perspectives of persons of color are systematically excluded from most discussions of law and that often unexamined assumptions about race lie at the heart of many of our laws. Critical race theory, which emerged in the late 1970s, sought to clarify the problematic relationship between race and law that has existed throughout American history—and which persists today. CRITS, as proponents of critical race theory are known, contend that racism is a systemic problem in the United States, embedded in not only the culture but also the law. Critical race theory posits that race is central to American culture and that the lives of individuals and groups in the United States are powerfully affected by conceptions of race and by the experience of racism. CRITS reject the argument that antidiscrimination provisions in the U.S. Constitution and elsewhere have effectively eliminated racism. They argue that while federal, state, and local governments are barred from explicitly discriminating against someone because of his or her race, and while the same prohibition has been extended to private employment, public accommodations, and education, the effects of centuries of slavery and racism linger. Like critical legal studies and theories of feminist jurisprudence, critical race theory contends that even terms that are supposed to be neutral, like justice, fairness, and equality, are used so as to advantage certain groups over others.

CRITS acknowledge that laws passed during the 1950s and 1960s did advance the cause of racial equality by striking down Jim Crow laws that had segregated African Americans in the South and by calling for integration of public schools throughout the nation. They contend, however, that the civil rights movement has stalled. While de jure segregation—that is, segregation under the law—has been eliminated, de facto segregation continues. We remain a segregated society, largely because patterns of residential segregation persist, and as a result, many Americans continue to go through life having little interaction with people of other races. CRITS point out that de facto segregation is more difficult to overcome than was de jure segregation, and that it requires a much more active and creative approach. Such an approach is not forthcoming in our law, which over the last several decades has evaluated laws and practices on the basis of racial neutrality—requiring that laws not advantage one race over any other. CRITS claim that this stance of neutrality actually reinforces the historical advantages of whites over other races by preventing lawmakers and others from adopting policies that would attempt to overcome historical obstacles to the advancement of racial minorities. According to most CRITS, American law focuses on direct forms of discrimination, which require explicit evidence of discrimination, and ignores more damaging indirect forms of discrimination, which have the effect of excluding people of color.

At the core of the CRIT movement is the argument that racial distinctions are based, not on *real* differences between people, but on the social construction of these differences. This social construction has been used to justify the preferential treatment of Anglo-American males throughout American history. Many justified the enslavement of Africans and African Americans because they believed that this group was not fully human and did not possess the intelligence of those of European descent. It was the "white man's burden" to Christianize and civilize these peoples through enslavement. In the 1840s, a similar argument was made to justify westward expansion of the United States. Policymakers and others rationalized this expansion under the doctrine of manifest destiny, that is, the belief that the United States was ordained by God to dominate these territories, and by corollary, that the displacement and genocide of Native Americans was justified. The "white man's burden" and manifest destiny were both based on the view that European Americans were superior to other racial groups and that this superiority conferred clear advantages, most importantly, the right to conquest and the wholesale destruction of peoples. CRITS point to this construction of race and racial superiority to demonstrate how social conceptions of the differences between races have been used to justify differential treatment, and to underline the fact that physical differences have been relatively unimportant.

Recently, scholars have extended critical race theory to discuss how groups other than African Americans have been treated under the law. For example, advocates of **Latino critical theory** (LATCRITS) have begun to explore how Latinos and Latinas are viewed in society and have focused on the majority beliefs that this group is not capable of assimilation and that this inability to assimilate can be seen in the refusal to abandon Spanish as their primary language. In response to this assumption that Latinos will not assimilate into the majority culture, some states and localities have passed laws that impose English-only rules that bar the use of second languages in public settings, including governmental offices and schools.

Similarly, scholars have begun to study the role of religion in American society and have pointed to the explicit use of religion to target individuals or groups, especially Muslims and Muslim Americans, in the wake of the September 11 attacks. With regard to both Latinos and Muslim Americans, particular cultural characteristics are being emphasized. Latinos' language and Muslim Americans' religion are being viewed as somehow hostile or dangerous to the majority culture. These characteristics are used to justify the explicit targeting of these groups under the law. LATCRITS and others agree with CRITS that societal prejudice and racism can very easily seep into our laws.

www ▶ ▶ ▶

Latino critical theory
theory of jurisprudence that views the law as reinforcing the majority culture and English language

CRITS, LATCRITS, and other scholars concerned about the effects of American law on Asians and Asian Americans criticize policymakers' focus on individual racism. They argue that more subtle institutional racism is in many ways more problematic to the cause of racial equality. This institutional racism is difficult to detect, and many scholars believe that because our law is so steeped in racism, a radical restructuring must take place before the institutional structures for lawmaking and implementation can be reformed to foster racial equality. Many argue that if we are seeking to ensure racial equality, we must first become race conscious so that we may reconstruct our social and political institutions to promote and ensure true equality.

Law and Postmodernism

postmodernism

view that there is no objective, knowable, or final truth and that standards and behaviors are powerfully shaped by certain groups and individuals

Postmodernism, which initially was introduced as a literary theory, has recently been applied to the study of law. The central tenet of **postmodernism** is that there is no objective, knowable, and final truth and that our standards and behaviors are guided by subjective views of those individuals and groups who are dominant in a society. The earliest postmodern thinkers—among these, French philosopher Michel Foucault—were strongly influenced by the experience of World War II and the Nazi Holocaust. Foucault rejected the Enlightenment principles of reason and justice, and he argued that the true human condition, which motivated most activities, was unreason, or madness. Writing several decades later, in 1978, Jacques Derrida applied Foucault's views to literary theory and contended that all language is inherently subjective and that, for this reason, it is impossible to communicate objective truths.

As used by legal theorists, postmodernism is based on this understanding that concepts like fairness, justice, and truth are not objective and instead are based on the experience of the dominant members of the society. Postmodern legal theory rejects traditional legal theory's assumption that there are principles of fairness, justice, and equity that may be discoverable through the exercise of reason. Many postmodernists attempt to "deconstruct" these principles, that is, to assess how they are actually used and implemented in the legal system. Through this deconstruction, theorists are able to point out the ways in which law and legal discourse are used to advantage or oppress particular groups. Postmodernists contend that law is not based on objective truths; it is, instead, the articulation of the norms of the cultural elite in society. Since there is no universal set of truths that can be articulated in the law, postmodernists argue that all experiences and truths are valid. Some within this school argue that narrative and storytelling are key to understanding the law because it is through these mediums that we can better understand the social realities that inform the larger legal system. For example, postmodernists contend that the law constructs race in ways that continue to advantage whites and that this construction can be understood through a close examination of the narratives and stories told by people of color. Similarly, at trial, the jurors and judge are given a choice of which narrative or story is most convincing, and lawyers often rely on widely accepted, although not always conscious, images and stereotypes.

This focus on narrative and storytelling has produced another fertile area for research known as the **law and literature school**. This school posits two reasons that literature is useful for understanding how the law operates. First, literature provides alternative frameworks for understanding social realities than those that are produced by the dominant culture. For example, Tom Wolfe's *The Bonfire of the Vanities* describes what happens when a car owned by a wealthy, white, married Wall Street broker fatally strikes a young black man in the Bronx. The broker's girlfriend, who was driving the car at the time of the accident, convinces him that he should not report the accident to the police, telling him that he knows little about the "jungle" that is the Bronx.

In addition to providing an alternative social framework for understanding law and society, the law and literature movement offers a way of conveying moral lessons to lawmakers and the public. We are socialized to accept certain norms through a variety sources including literature. In *Fair Is Fair: World Folktales of Justice,* Sharon Creeden compiles an assortment of folktales told throughout the world. She argues that these widely disseminated tales teach moral lessons about good and evil and about how law should function in society. She and others contend that our culture has an unmistakable impact on our conception of justice and fairness. Socialization about acceptable norms begins in early childhood, with the learning of fairytales and folktales. These norms are so deeply ingrained in our conscience that we have a kind of knee-jerk response to stories that tap into these norms. Think about how easy it is to state the lessons that popular Disney films like *101 Dalmatians, The Little Mermaid,* and *Snow White* teach. All of these films make a very simple point about what is acceptable and unacceptable behavior: they all have villains and heroes, and they all convey lessons to young and not-so-young viewers.

Like the law and literature school, the even more recent **law and popular culture school** contends that there is a strong relationship between law and the larger society, and that we can better understand our law through interdisciplinary lenses. In other words, by using examples from popular culture, we can better appreciate how law functions. Again, like law and literature and postmodernism in general, the law and popular culture school assumes that there are no absolute rules or guidelines in law and that our law and legal system are based on the views of the dominant group. Most scholars

law and literature school

theory of jurisprudence that views literature as helpful to our understanding of how law operates

law and popular culture school

theory of jurisprudence that suggests we can use popular culture to better understand how law functions

working in the area of law and popular culture explore one of two themes: first, they look at how our culture reflects the functioning of law and our legal system; and second, they examine how culture changes the law and the operation of the legal system.

The first argument, that popular culture—that is, television, film, popular music, and other media—can instruct people about how the law works, seems obvious. As a society, we are fascinated by the law, and one need only turn on the television to understand how much of our culture is caught up in discussions of law and the legal system. Consider the popularity of such programs as *Law and Order* (and its spin-offs, *Law and Order: Criminal Intent* and *Law and Order: Special Victims Unit*), *Ally McBeal*, *The Practice*, *100 Centre Street*, *Judging Amy*, *Oz*, and a host of "cop shows," including *CSI: Crime Scene Investigation* (and its spin-off, *CSI: Miami*) and *Homicide*. All of these popular television series provide information, and some misinformation, to viewers about the content and application of American law.

Some law and popular culture scholars make a second argument that is more difficult to support. They contend that our popular culture not only reflects the law, it also changes the law. For example, some have argued that mass media, with its focus on sensationalism and immediate gratification, has seeped into our real-life legal system and has begun to shape the ways in which legal "stories" are told and legal arguments presented. Building on the postmodern view that law is not based on any ultimate truths, this strand of law and pop culture contends that myth and symbolism stand in for these truths. Some contend that law is becoming more and more like our pop culture depictions of it. In his excellent book *When Law Goes Pop*, Richard K. Sherwin provides a number of cases where law imitates our popular culture. For example, he reports on the 1996 murder trial of Ronnie Jack Beasley, in which prosecutors told the jury that the defendant had viewed the movie *Natural Born Killers* nineteen or twenty times and that he had modeled himself on the character Mickey, a killer.

Storytelling is a central feature of trials, and these stories often rely on symbols and a shared cultural interpretation of events. Often the most notorious and well-known cases are those that focus on some ongoing conflict or controversy in the society. So, the trial of Andrea Yates, the Texas woman accused of drowning her five small children, raised serious questions about mental illness and criminal responsibility, which are issues that we fiercely debate in our society. Some analysts have also noted that the case's notoriety was due in no small part to the fact that it was a mother who killed her children, and this act ran directly counter to our closely held beliefs about the unbreakable bond between mother and child. Ultimately, the jury that found Yates guilty of capital murder and rejected her insanity plea was asked to consider whether she knew that she was doing something wrong when she killed her children. The jury did not consider the much more difficult and subtle questions about how her well-documented mental illness may have affected her decision to murder her children. Much of the testimony in the Yates trial turns on the prosecutor's view of Yates as an evil woman who unflinchingly and heartlessly took the lives of her children. The defense did not effectively counter this view of the evil mother but instead attempted to employ a more subtle depiction of Yates as someone whose depression effectively rendered her unable to choose not to commit murder.

Like other postmodernist schools, the law and pop culture school assumes that law does not create a set of inexorable truths and that legal norms are constructed from a number of sources, including social and cultural norms. All of these schools proceed from an understanding that terms like justice, fairness, morality, and equality ultimately are interpreted through the lens of culture, and most postmodernist writers believe that this culture tends to be dominated by elites.

SUMMARY

This chapter has explored different ways of understanding what law is and how it functions in American society. Normative theories of jurisprudence focus on concerns about how law *should* function in the larger society, while empirical theories explore how law actually *does* function. Many normative theories have deep roots, and the earliest discussions of law are several thousand years old. For example, our views of natural law are rooted in the ancient Greek and Roman worlds, as is the theory of positivism. Similarly, classical common law theory is based on the Anglo-Saxon legal tradition of the thirteenth and fourteenth centuries. In contrast, empirical theories are much more recent and derive from advances in the social sciences.

There are deep divisions among varying theories of jurisprudence. Even among normative theories, there are serious disagreements about the basis and role of law in society. Empirical theory draws heavily on an interdisciplinary approach and uses advances in the social sciences and humanities to understand how the law functions in the American system. This interdisciplinary approach gives way to even more significant disagreements among scholars as to the nature and use of law in the United States. The splintering of these empirical theories has yielded to a variety of approaches, some of them focusing on the impact of economics on the legal system; others examining the role of race, gender, ethnicity, and class; and still others focusing on the role of literature and popular culture. We are hard-pressed to predict which theories of jurisprudence will become preeminent in the twenty-first century, as scholars and lawmakers are examining both normative and empirical approaches.

SUGGESTED READING

Randy E. Barnett, *The Structure of Liberty: Justice and the Rule of Law* (Oxford University Press, 2000). In this important book, Barnett argues that our legal culture embraces a number of important natural law rights, specifically, the fundamental right of individuals to be free. This focus on the right to liberty provides an interesting backdrop for further discussion about individual freedoms in the post-9/11 United States.

Harrell Chesson et al., "Sex Under the Influence: The Effect of Alcohol Policy on Sexually Transmitted Disease Rates in the United States," Issue 43, *Journal of Law and Economics* 215 (2000). This article is an excellent example of how law and economics is being used to understand and predict human behavior. This article discusses how taxes on alcohol have effectively reduced the incidence of sexually transmitted diseases in some communities.

Patricia Ewick and Susan S. Silbey, *The Common Place of Law* (University of Chicago Press, 1998). This fascinating compilation of interviews with people about their encounters with the law pro-vides an excellent opportunity to talk about law and postmodernism.

Helle Porsdam, *Legally Speaking: Contemporary American Culture and the Law* (University of Massachusetts Press, 1999). Porsdam examines the complex relationship between American culture and American law. In one insightful passage, the author discusses a passage from Tom Wolfe's *The Bonfire of the Vanities*, which starkly reveals the existence of two very different social and legal realities for whites and nonwhites in the United States.

Richard A. Posner, *The Essential Holmes: Selections from the Letters, Speeches, Judicial Opinions, and Other Writings of Oliver Wendell Holmes, Jr.* (Chicago: University of Chicago Press, 1992). This book is written by Judge Posner of the Seventh Circuit Court of Appeals, a preeminent scholar in the law and economics movement. Judge Posner presents Justice Holmes's original writings and provides commentary about this very important twentieth-century jurist.

ACTIVE LEARNING

1. Aquinas contended that the fact that there was no written law didn't mean that a higher legal principle didn't exist. What might Aquinas have thought about the dramatic differences in working conditions throughout the world today? In some nations, like the United States and Canada, there are fairly extensive laws in place that limit workers' exposure to harmful substances; while in others, like Mexico, there are far fewer protective regulations in place. What happens when free trade begins to erase the boundaries between these nations? Is there some higher law that mandates how workers and the environment should be treated?

   What would Aquinas or the other natural law theorists have made of the United States' war against Iraq? Was this a "just" war? How would they evaluate justice? Which wars are just?

2. Find some law that you consider to be controversial (you may want to use a website like findlaw.com and look at legal news). Evaluate this law from the viewpoint of each of the schools that we've discussed in this chapter. Consider the following questions: Is it law? Is it legitimate? What does it say about how law functions?

CHAPTER 3

The Foundations of American Law

common law tradition

a tradition focusing on judge-made law; derived from the British common law system

code or civil tradition

a tradition focusing on law made by legislatures, chief executives, and regulatory and enforcement offices; derived from the legal system of ancient Rome

case law

the law that derives from judges' decisions in cases

The American legal system is a blend of two very different traditions: the **common law** *tradition, which comes from the British system, and the* **code or civil** *tradition, which has its basis in ancient Rome. In this chapter, we will examine the foundations of the U.S. legal system, in particular, the historical basis of this system. The common law and code law traditions, which derive from very different assumptions, often have different ideas about how law should be made and the role that law should play in society. Over the last hundred years, however, scholars and practitioners have tried to reconcile these ideas. We will closely examine the common law tradition and focus on the role of judge-made law in the United States, as well as on the huge expansion of code law in the last century. In addition, we will briefly examine the kinds of laws that operate in the American legal system today. One of the goals of this chapter is to expose students to court holdings and to begin to help them feel comfortable with this* **case law**. *To meet this goal, the chapter introduces case briefings and demonstrates how cases and briefings help us clarify the central principles that underlie court holdings.*

THE HISTORICAL FOUNDATIONS OF U.S. LAW: THE ANGLO-AMERICAN COMMON LAW TRADITION

The experience of the British colonists profoundly shaped the development of law in the United States. Even while colonists rejected British rule, they wholly adopted the common law system in place in England. This system was first codified, or written down, in the late 1100s. The written code was ultimately used to limit the power of the monarchy and nobility.

■ The Early Development of American Law: From 1066 to 1765

The British common law system has its roots in the early medieval period, when the king's courts recognized common customs that stood in stark contrast to the laws of the manor or to local courts. Over time, British common law grew more uniform, as writers began to clearly articulate the inherent rights of individuals and to write down the decisions of judges in important cases

Norman Conquest of 1066

invasion of England that resulted in a national legal system

Ranulf de Glanvill

compiler of a highly influential treatise on British laws who furthered uniformity among British courts by laying out the common laws of royal courts

primogeniture

the common law rule that the firstborn son alone inherits the father's estate—the rule adopted by British courts

gravelkind

the rule that divided the father's estate equally among all his sons

borough-English

the rule that gave all of the father's property to the youngest son

■ The Norman Conquest and the Codification of Law The Norman Conquest of 1066, and subsequent rule by Henry II in the twelfth century, enabled the elite to impose a national legal system of far greater scope than had been previously employed in England. In fact, King Henry's rule was characterized by the emergence of a "common law," that is, court decisions that made uniform those laws or policies that were national in scope. The common law was intended to address only these national policies and to ensure that the king's rule extended throughout the realm. For less important issues, Henry's legal system left lawmaking to local or church authorities. Henry and his advisors were especially concerned with creating a more uniform system of procedure and are credited with greatly expanding the use of writs and juries. This common law was first written down by one of the King Henry's closest advisors, **Ranulf de Glanvill**, who compiled his *Treatise on the Laws* and *Customs of the Realm of England* at some point between 1187 and 1189. Glanvill's treatise laid out the common laws of the royal courts and provided forms for initiating legal proceedings in a variety of contexts.

As is the case today, common law judges played an important role in this early period because they had the chief responsibility of announcing legal principles that would govern particular issues or problems. The judges did not merely uncover these principles; instead, they chose among competing rules of the game. For example, **primogeniture**, that is, the rule that the firstborn son will inherit his father's estate, was only one way that locals had of deciding questions of inheritance. Other methods of distributing property were more equal and equitable—one of these, the **gravelkind**, ensured that all sons would share in the estate. Others, like the **borough-English**, gave all of the father's property to the youngest son. And still others, perhaps the most radical, ensured that even daughters would have some inheritance! Common law judges embraced the rule of primogeniture, however, which was also used among the elite Anglo-Normans who conquered Britain.

■ The Magna Carta and the Inherent Rights of Individuals The common law that swept England in the 1100s soon came to be closely entwined with the idea that royal power should be limited to protect the rights of individuals. The **Magna Carta of 1215** was adopted in response to perceived excesses of King John, whom the barons accused of wielding power in an arbitrary and unfair manner. The Magna Carta, or "Great Charter," was the first attempt to limit the power of the sovereign and to assert that individuals had rights that were separate from those given to them by the Crown. The Magna Carta is primarily a list of grievances that the barons lodged with the king, and each of the principles established rights that were then protected under law. Several of the principles embraced in the Magna Carta are very familiar to us. In this document, one can glimpse the requirements of proportionality, due process, the privilege against self-incrimination, and the right to a jury trial—requirements that are central to our criminal due process protections today.

Magna Carta of 1215

the "Great Charter" aimed at limiting the power of the sovereign; it asserted that individuals had rights separate from those given to them by the king

www ▶ ▶ ▶

■ Toward Greater Uniformity: Henry of Bracton's *On the Laws* Henry of Bracton, the next writer to describe the common law tradition, helped to compile the book *On the Laws and Customs of England*. This work, written by various authors between 1220 and 1260, detailed the opinions of a number of judges on differing issues and built on Glanvill's earlier work. Bracton's *On the Laws* was considered to be the most important work on the common law tradition until Sir William Blackstone wrote his four-volume treatise in the 1700s. In his work, Bracton argued that he was merging Roman civil or code law and English common law, but he spent the bulk of his time and energy on the common law tradition. In fact, he relied heavily on the annual Year Books, which were published compilations of judicial decisions throughout the land. Like Glanvill's work, *On the Laws* played an important role in promoting uniformity in judicial holdings throughout the nation. Bracton praised England's use of unwritten law and custom, asserting that it was approved by the public and the Crown and found expression in the decisions of judges throughout the country. He compiled the judicial decisions he considered to be excellent examples of how unwritten law should function, so that these decisions would serve to guide other judges in the future. At the heart of Bracton's urgings was a strong belief in the principle of **stare decisis**, that is, that judges should adopt the reasoning of judges who had reached decisions in similar cases in the past. Bracton wrote that the king was required to follow not only the written law but unwritten law and custom, as well. And ultimately, Bracton's law, with its focus on "just" laws, was used to justify English revolution of 1689.

Henry of Bracton

one of the most important commentators on the common law tradition whose work promoted uniformity

www ▶ ▶ ▶

stare decisis

the principle that judges should rely on the reasoning of judges in past cases

Glorious Revolution of 1689

uprising that ended the rule of King James II in England and ultimately made the king and queen subject to the laws of Parliament

Bill of Rights

document that created protections to safeguard individual rights, among these, the free election of representatives, the prohibition against cruel and unusual punishment, and the right to a jury trial

www ▶ ▶ ▶

■ **English Bill of Rights and the Rise of Written Law** The work of Glanvill and Bracton laid the foundation for the **Glorious Revolution of 1689**, which ended the rule of James II and installed King William II and Mary II and brought about the passage of the **Bill of Rights**. Throughout the reign of King James II, the courts had been used to maintain his control over the nation and to significantly curtail Parliament's actions. For example, in the 1686 case *Gooden* v. *Hales* a royal court held that the king should have the power to suspend the Parliament and was allowed to strictly limit its activities. King James II suspended Parliament in 1685 and dissolved it in 1687. When James was overthrown, William and Mary were offered the crown on the condition that they accept the Bill of Rights, which held that the king would be subject to the laws of Parliament and that he could no longer dissolve the body or impose taxes without its approval.

The Bill of Rights first laid out all of the abuses of James II, among these, that he had suspended the operation of Parliament, raised an army without the approval of Parliament, mandated the quartering of soldiers in private homes, and permitted the imposition of excessive bail and cruel and unusual punishment. The Bill of Rights affirmatively established a list of protections to safeguard individuals against abuse by the Crown. Many of these are familiar to us; they were incorporated into the Bill of Rights that was ratified by the fledgling United States in 1791. The British Bill of Rights established other important principles that would guide the development of common law in Great Britain, its colonies, and the United States. Among these principles were the free election of representatives, the requirement that punishment be neither cruel nor unusual, and the requirement of a jury trial.

■ **William Blackstone and His Impact on Case Law** William Blackstone, perhaps more than any other writer, may be credited with advancing the common law tradition, not only in England but in the American colonies and United States. His four-volume *Commentaries on the Laws of England* (1765–1769) compiled case law on individual rights, property rights, torts, civil procedure, and property and criminal law. In his treatise, Blackstone distinguished between written and unwritten law, and like Glanvill, he praised unwritten, or judge-made, law, arguing that it encompassed not only general but local customs. Blackstone contended that this unwritten law was based in antiquity and binding on the judges who followed by virtue of its long usage and universal acceptance. To clarify this unwritten law, Blackstone turned to case reports or Year Books that had been published since the mid-1500s and compiled case holdings in courts throughout England. He used these reports to establish legal principles and relied on the principle of stare decisis to admonish later courts to follow these cases. Like other writers who had come before him, Blackstone argued that the British common law safeguarded individual liberty and ensured protection against the arbitrary exercise of governmental power. Blackstone's *Commentaries* was perhaps the most influential law book in Britain, her colonies, and her former colonies for more than a century. For example, Blackstone argued that once married, a woman no longer had any legal personhood. Under the doctrine of **coverture** her legal identity merged with that of her husband, and she could not own property, enter into contract, sue or be sued, or assert her own legal rights. Blackstone's arguments were used to support the view that women shouldn't have the right to vote. Not until 1920 did the Nineteenth Amendment confer on women this right. In addition, Blackstone's view that men were the masters of their wives and had the legal right to physically punish them for their transgressions was at least at the philosophical core of the argument that spousal abuse and battery were not crimes under the law.

coverture

the merging of a woman's legal identity with that of her husband

Blackstone's *Commentaries* had a profound effect on the American colonies and the new nation. His belief that inalienable rights are created by nature and God and held by all individuals became the core of the Declaration of Independence, the Constitution, and the Bill of Rights. The founders knew their Blackstone, and there are numerous examples drawn from the notes of the Constitutional Convention of delegates using Blackstone's writings as support for their positions. While the United States increasingly relied on statutory lawmaking in the 1900s, the influence of Blackstone and the common law tradition continues to be felt. In the last several years, the *Commentaries* has been cited by courts grappling with issues like the treatment of enemy combatants, the scope of the habeas corpus provision, death penalty appeals, and the placement of a tablet depicting the Ten Commandments in an Alabama courtroom. Interestingly, one British judge recently cited Blackstone as support for barring the separation of Siamese twins. William Blackstone has also made an appearance in American popular culture, as mobsters are known to refer to their lawyers as "Blackstone"!

www ▶ ▶ ▶

Common Law in the Colonial and Early American Period

The common law tradition was embraced by British settlers to the New World, who relied heavily on the laws of England, at least in civil matters. Most colonies imported British common law tradition in a wholesale manner: they considered that the laws of England automatically applied to the colonies. Colonists followed church or ecclesiastical law in most matters, but where they were compelled to employ civil law, they used the common law of England. In the early colonial period, most laws derived from religious codes and purported to have a basis in divine law. They were based on morality and barred many actions that today would not be actionable. For example, it was against the law in many of the colonies to swear, not attend church services, engage in premarital sex, be drunk, or engage in "inappropriate" activities on the Sabbath. Interestingly, throughout much of the colonial era, punishment was imposed by church authorities and not by the state. Courts were relatively unimportant and tended to reinforce church law and decisions.

Sometimes the coalescing of religious principle and law had troubling effects. For example, the **Salem witchcraft trials of 1692** resulted in the hanging of nineteen New Englanders, the pressing to death of one other, and the death in prison of four others, relied heavily on evidence that the accused had consorted with the devil. The convictions were largely based on **spectral evidence**, which alleged that the afflicted person had been visited in her or his dreams by the spectral form or spirit of the accused. This evidence was virtually impossible to refute. Much of the judges' questioning hinged on discussions of the religious beliefs of the accused, as well as whether they attended church regularly and could recite portions of the Lord's Prayer and Bible. Many of the witches and wizards were accused of bedeviling their neighbors, and these accusations rested on supposed physical evidence. Those afflicted often called out or had fits that could only be controlled by forcing the accused witch to touch the victim. Victims also testified that they had had visions of the witches and wizards in the company of the devil or that the spirits of people killed by these witches and wizards were calling out to them for vengeance. Even when the accused denied the accusations, the judges assumed that person had committed witchcraft, as can be seen in the examination of Sarah Good which is provided on the website.

In the early to mid-1700s religious law relaxed its iron grip on the colonies, and the colonists began to rely more heavily on the common law tradition. They crafted colonial charters that explicitly recognized the laws of Great Britain. And even after declaring independence, most states reestablished the British common law. There were a few states, specifically, Kentucky, New Jersey, and Pennsylvania, that passed **noncitation statutes** in the early 1800s. These statutes were an attempt to limit the impact of the common law by barring judges from relying on past rulings to reach their decisions. By the early 1820s, however, this attempt was abandoned, and all states implicitly recognized the validity of the common law. The common law tradition is still very important in the American legal system, and judge-made law continues to profoundly affect the development of law. Since the late 1800s, however, the United States has increasingly relied on code law crafted by legislatures, chief executives, and regulatory agencies.

Salem witchcraft trials of 1692

trials that resulted in the deaths of twenty New Englanders who were alleged to have consorted with the devil

spectral evidence

evidence based on testimony that the accused had appeared in spectral or spirit form to someone who claimed to be afflicted by the accused; evidence that was basically impossible for the accused to refute

www ▶ ▶ ▶

www ▶ ▶ ▶

noncitation statutes

passed in several states in the period immediately following the Revolutionary War, these laws tended to limit the impact of British common law by barring judges from relying on past rulings in deciding cases

THE LAW IN POPULAR CULTURE

The Crucible

This film depicts the 1692 Salem witchcraft trials, in which twenty-four suspected "witches" were hanged or pressed to death, or died in prison. In these trials, courts relied largely on spectral evidence—typically, the victim testified that he or she had dreamed that the defendant appeared in the form of a witch. Since it was virtually impossible to defend against this evidence, the mere accusation that someone was a witch was enough to result in a conviction.

THE AMERICAN LEGAL SYSTEM IN FLUX: THE TURN TOWARD CODE LAW

The American legal system has its historical basis in common law, and through the nineteenth century judges were the principal lawmakers largely because federal and state legislatures did not assume the central lawmaking function. Until the late 1800s, the generally slow, incremental rule making by courts was usually sufficient to structure relationships and to resolve disputes. As the United States became more industrialized in the late 1800s, however, the need for detailed rules, especially about the conduct of business, increased the pressure on legislatures to adopt a more proactive role. With social relationships becoming more complex, legislatures needed to codify rules that would establish both public and private rights and obligations. In many ways, lawmaking in the United States is a shared enterprise: legislators create laws that are then interpreted by judges. There are some areas in which the legislator or judge acts more independently; however, in a general sense, they are collaborators in the lawmaking enterprise.

Historical Roots of the Code Law Tradition

While common law is the historical foundation of the British legal system, civil or code law is the tradition in the rest of Europe. Many ancient civilizations had codes that proscribed certain conduct. For example, Chapter 1 discussed at length the Code of Hammurabi, which governed relationships in ancient Mesopotamia. Our code law system has its roots in the *Corpus Juris Civilis,* the code adopted by Roman Emperor Justinian in the sixth century in an attempt to organize and systematize Roman law. The *Corpus Juris Civilis,* often referred to as the **Code of Justinian,** aimed at staving off the collapse of the Roman Empire, and failing that, it sought to preserve Roman law for posterity. By compiling, organizing and codifying this law, the Code preserved Roman law for later use by Europeans.

Code of Justinian

an extensive legal code compiled by Emperor Justinian in the sixth century in an attempt to maintain control over the Roman Empire

Like other codes, the Code of Justinian laid out, often in great detail, those activities and relationships that were barred. The *Corpus* is made up of three sets of books—one of these, the *Institutiones,* is an introductory text on Roman law. The second book of this set classified different kinds of property and distinguished between property that can be privately owned and that which is either publicly owned or owned by the community. As can be seen on the website, the Code provides a detailed description of the things that can be owned and clearly defines ownership rights. It notes that most things can be privately owned, but identifies some property that is held in common by all, among these, air, running water, the sea, rivers, the shores, public buildings, and religious shrines or houses of worship. Take note of the level of detail in this Code—it is this kind of detail that usually characterizes code law.

www ▶ ▶ ▶

After the Roman Empire finally collapsed in the seventh century, its law tradition was preserved by the Roman Catholic Church. In the eleventh century, Roman law was revived and had a profound impact on social relations in the medieval period. This code law established guidelines for how people should interact and also provided a rationale for the guidelines. For example, by the third century, the Roman Empire had begun to revoke the rights of Jews by issuing laws that barred interfaith marriage between Jews and Christians, banned slaveholding by Jews, prohibited the building of new temples, and excluded Jews from government service. Anti-semitism was a feature of the Middle Ages, as well, as people used the Justinian Code as a model for tightening restrictions on Jewish religious practices and customs and ensuring the segregation of Jews and Christians in both public and private realms. Even the relatively moderate code enacted by Alfonso X, the Wise, of Castile, Spain, in 1265, barred Jews from government service. From the excerpt on the webpage, one can readily see that this code provision not only bars Jews from public office, it also provides a rationale for this prohibition. This code was later employed by Spain and her possessions in the New World, among these, Puerto Rico, Florida, and Louisiana.

www ▶ ▶ ▶

The Roman tradition spread to much of Europe and had a tremendous influence on the legal systems that developed in the medieval period and beyond. Through conquest and colonization, this code law system also spread to the New World, as Spain and France transported their code law tradition to their colonies. The first modern code law was created under Napoleon Bonaparte, who sought to unify France in large part by reforming a fragmented and inconsistent legal system. For example, the north of France was strongly influenced by its proximity to England. The common law tradition was firmly in place there, while the south of France employed Roman law. In addition, in the wake of the Revolution in 1789, more than fourteen thousand new laws were passed by the French Legislative Assembly, but they were neither unified nor widely disseminated to the public. When Napoleon came to power in 1799, one of his first tasks was to create a commission whose principal function was to organize and systematize the law into one single code. In 1804, this **Civil Code**, also known as the **Napoleonic Code,** was distributed.

Civil Code or Napoleonic Code

civil code created largely by Napoleon Bonaparte in the early 1800s in an attempt to ensure uniformity, establish individual rights, and consolidate his power in France

Like the other codes that we have discussed, the Napoleonic Code aimed at creating one single set of written rules that would govern everyone in France and would be clear and well understood. This Civil Code accomplished these goals: it established as law the principles embraced by the Revolution—namely, religious tolerance, free speech, the right to a jury trial, and the elimination of feudalism. The Civil Code also established the absolute right of individuals to own property and recognized the right of husbands and fathers to rule the household. Under the Civil Code, the master of the house had nearly total control over the actions of his wife and children. The Civil Code was followed by the Code of Civil Procedure and the Commercial Code, adopted in 1806 and 1807; the Criminal Code and Code of Criminal Procedure, promulgated in 1808; and the Penal Code, adopted in 1810. Together, these codes revolutionized the legal system in France by ensuring that the law was uniform and clear.

The Civil Code had a tremendous impact not only on France but on many other countries. Most immediately, Holland and northern Italy, which were conquered by Napoleon, adopted the Code, and many other countries later adopted it. The Civil Code remains in place in France and most of Europe today. Napoleon considered his Code to be his greatest accomplishment. Writing after his defeat at Waterloo and exile to the island of Elba, he reflected on his life, stating that "[m]y real glory is not the 40 battles I won—for my defeat at Waterloo will destroy the memory of those victories. . . . What nothing will destroy, what will live forever, is my Civil Code." His assessment of his own contribution to history now seems accurate: this Code is probably the most influential code law of the modern era; it remains a model for other nations contemplating changes in their legal system.

While the United States has a long common law tradition, the Napoleonic Code had an important impact here, as well. The Code was the sole basis for the laws adopted in the newly acquired Louisiana territory in 1808, and it remains in place in Louisiana, which alone among the states does not employ the common law tradition. In Louisiana, therefore, the code is expected to govern all situations and the courts have a very limited role in lawmaking. While states like New Jersey tend to have shorter and much more vague code laws, Louisiana's law is long and very complex. Box 3.1 contrasts code law provisions adopted by the state legislatures in New Jersey and Louisiana. Both of these laws establish that property owners have a responsibility for keeping their buildings in good repair. But notice how different these code laws are. The Louisiana law is much more detailed and aims at anticipating a variety of circumstances that might make a property owner liable for breaching the duty of upkeep. In contrast, the New Jersey law is simpler and provides far less guidance. In fact, New Jersey doesn't even address the specific factual circumstances that might give rise to an injury claim. Instead, in its Permanent Statutes, New Jersey only establishes a legal standard that must be used by judges considering all cases that result because of an injury, not just specific cases involving property claims.

[www ▶ ▶ ▶]

BOX 3.1
Contrasting the Criminal Codes in New Jersey and Louisiana

In Louisiana, the Civil Code is the principal source of law. Judges and courts have only limited roles in this system and are permitted only to apply this law. When they must interpret the law in a case, this interpretation usually cannot be used in future cases, and in this regard, Louisiana stands completely alone—all other states rely on both code law and common law. For example, New Jersey's law, in stark contrast to Louisiana law, is not laid out in painstaking detail and the judge has a much more important role because she or he is charged with fleshing out what is really only a skeletal outline. For example, in the following case, the New Jersey state judges applied the precedent of past cases to determine whether a property owner (the defendants-appellees here) had a duty to protect people visiting their garage sale (the plaintiffs-appellants here) from tripping over his grass. While you are reading this case, consider how the court relies on other courts' decisions in similar cases to assess whether the homeowners here were liable for the damages. This is a case based on tort law and, in particular, on negligence theory. Tort law is largely made up of common law holdings. Over time, these holdings are applied to factual situations that are considered to be very similar. This case raises a novel issue that has not been considered by any court yet, that is, whether there is a duty of care owed under negligence law to those attending garage sales. The court has little difficulty finding that the owner owes such a duty to shoppers and that existing negligence law can be readily employed to dispose of this claim. Keep in mind that at the core of the common law tradition is the understanding that judge-made law has binding force in future cases and that the challenge for this court is in determining how this precedent should be applied to the facts here.

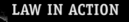

LAW IN ACTION

Common Law in New Jersey

FILIPOWICZ V. DILETTO, SUPERIOR COURT OF NEW JERSEY, APPELLATE DIVISION, 2002

`www ▶ ▶ ▶` (See *Law, Politics, and Society* website for a link to the complete decision.)

JUDGE NEWMAN delivered the decision of the court.

At issue here is the duty owed by a property owner to the public who are invited to the property where a garage or yard sale is conducted. In granting summary judgment and dismissing plaintiffs' complaint, the trial court found no duty owed to the injured party who fell where there was a three and one-half inch grade difference between the lawn and the sidewalk, which was covered over by grass. We reverse and hold that the property owner owed a reasonable duty of care to the public invited to attend the garage or yard sale to maintain the property in a reasonably safe condition.

The facts are straightforward. Plaintiff, Ruthann Filipowicz attended a garage sale at the home of defendants, Linda and Robert Diletto in Hamilton Township. The event was a multi-family sale organized by defendants and their neighbors. Defendants displayed their sales items on tables in the driveway. They also placed clothes on a corner of their front lawn where the driveway intersected with the sidewalk.

The sale began on a clear, dry day at 8:00 a.m. Plaintiff arrived at approximately 10:00 a.m. She parked near defendants' property. Plaintiff first visited the house across the street from defendants' house where she made a purchase. She then walked across the street, up the paved driveway of defendants' house and began browsing through the sales items. Nothing sparked her interest, so she proceeded to the items displayed on the lawn. At that time, someone approached the lawn to re-arrange the clothes on display. Plaintiff moved back, away from the clothes and toward the sidewalk to provide room for that person to work. Plaintiff turned to make sure no one was behind her, and so she would not step on anything. When plaintiff stepped backward she lost her footing and fell. She was wearing sneakers at the time.

Unknown to plaintiff, there was a three and one-half inch drop-off from the front lawn to the sidewalk. The drop-off was not visible to plaintiff from where she stood on the lawn or from where she approached the lawn. She noticed the drop-off only after she fell. According to plaintiff, the grass on defendants' lawn was tall, extended over the sidewalk and camouflaged the drop-off. Defendant Robert Diletto testified at a deposition that he and his wife lived in the house for about four years and were aware that the lawn was elevated above the sidewalk. During that time, he would mow and maintain the front lawn. As part of that maintenance, he would use an edge trimmer every third time he cut the grass.

Mary Grochala, a member of defendants' family, observed plaintiff's fall and went to assist plaintiff, but she declined help. Plaintiff later sought medical attention at a local hospital emergency room and, thereafter, received more extensive treatment, which included surgery.

LAW IN ACTION–(CONT'D)

On May 5, 1999, plaintiff filed suit against defendants alleging that they were negligent in failing to provide a safe walkway or adequate notice of the latent defects of their premises. Plaintiff contends that she has a permanent disability and still suffers from pain. Plaintiff's husband filed a loss of consortium claim.

On October 13, 2000, defendants moved for summary judgment contending that plaintiff could not make a *prima facie* case of negligence against defendants . . . The court determined that plaintiff failed to show that the elevation of the lawn constituted an unreasonably dangerous area or condition . . . On appeal, plaintiff contends that she was an invitee of defendants. Plaintiff maintains that the premises, during the garage or yard sale, became defendants' place of business. Plaintiff argues defendants owed plaintiff a duty to exercise reasonable care to ensure their place of business, here the property, was safe for plaintiff and defendants' other invitees.

To establish a *prima facie* case of negligence against defendants, plaintiff must establish all of the following elements: (1) duty of care, (2) breach of that duty, (3) proximate cause, and (4) damages suffered by the plaintiff. *Conklin* v. *Hannoch Weisman, 145 N.J. 395*, 417 (1996). The duty owed to a plaintiff is determined by the circumstance that brought him or her to the property. *Daggett* v. *Di Trani, 194 N.J. Super. 185*, 189 (App. Div. 1984). An invitee, in the legal sense, is "one who is on the premises to confer some benefits upon the invitor other than purely social." *Id.* at 189-90. (quoting *Berger* v. *Shapiro, 30 N.J. 89, 96* (1959)).

Defendants extended an open invitation to the general public to attend its garage or yard sale. Plaintiff accepted that invitation and entered defendants' premises to browse over their sales items. While she enjoyed attending garage and yard sales, that attraction did not deprive her of the status of an invitee. *Benedict* v. *Podwats, 109 N.J. Super. 402*, 408 (App. Div.), *aff'd, 57 N.J. 219* (1970). Plaintiff entered defendants' premises not to engage in a social gathering but to shop. Her presence alone, as a potential buyer, conferred a benefit upon defendants. *Hopkins* v. *Fox & Lazo Realtors, 132 N.J. 426*, 440-441 (1993); *Daggett, supra, 194 N.J. Super.* at 190. Plaintiff was an invitee on defendants' premises.

The standard of care due an invitee by a homeowner conducting a garage or yard sale is the same as the standard of care any property owner owes to any other invitee. As an invitee, defendants owed a duty to plaintiff to provide a "reasonably safe place to do that which is within the scope of the invitation." *Butler* v. *Acme Markets, Inc., 89 N.J. 270*, 275 (1982). The duty includes the obligation to "use reasonable care to make the premises safe, including the duty to conduct a reasonable inspection to discover defective conditions." *Handleman* v. *Cox, 39 N.J. 95*, 111 (1963); *Daggett, supra, 194 N.J. Super.* at 192 . . . To determine whether a person owes a reasonable duty of care toward another, the court must conduct a fact-specific and principled analysis to identify, weigh, and balance the relationship of the parties, the nature of the risk involved, the opportunity and availability to exercise care, and the public interests in the proposed solution. *Hopkins, supra, 132 N.J.* at 439. The solution must properly and fairly resolve the specific case and develop clear rules to govern future conduct. *Ibid.*

The imposition of a duty of reasonable care upon a homeowner conducting a garage or yard sale satisfies those concerns. Homeowners have a pre-existing and non-delegable duty toward

LAW IN ACTION—(CONT'D)

invitees to make reasonable inspections of the property and to remedy any reasonably discoverable defects. *Hopkins, supra,* 132 *N.J.* at 441. A homeowner is most familiar with his or her residence and is, therefore, in the best position to be aware of latent problems. *Id.* at 445. In preparation for a garage or yard sale, the homeowner advertises to the general public to attract shoppers to that sale. By responding to a homeowner's advertised garage or yard sale, the shopper gains permission, through invitation, to come on to the property and participate in that sale. The shopper may reasonably expect that implicit in the homeowner's invitation is some degree of responsibility for the safety of the shopper while he or she is visiting the premises . . . Here, plaintiff could reasonably believe the scope of the invitation extended to the lawn because defendants displayed sales items there. Consequently, she was within the scope of defendants' invitation at the time of the incident, and could have reasonably expected that the lawn would not be defective.

This duty is consistent with the traditional test of negligence. That test is what a reasonably prudent homeowner conducting a garage or yard sale would foresee and do to ensure the safety of shoppers entering the homeowner's premises to browse for sales items. *People Express Airlines, Inc.* v. *Consolidated Rail Corp., 100 N.J. 246,* 262 (1985). The duty is defined by knowledge of the risk of harm or the reasonable apprehension of that risk. *Ibid.* Defendants were aware of the drop-off between the lawn and sidewalk, but, nonetheless, they placed items there for sale. Defendants should have anticipated the presence of shoppers on their lawn. A reasonable homeowner conducting a garage sale under these circumstances

would have mowed the lawn and properly trimmed the edge so the elevation between the lawn and sidewalk was readily apparent to the shoppers, or would have warned the shoppers of the drop-off . . . The public interest will also be served by recognizing a duty of care on the part of a homeowner who holds a garage or yard sale. Generally, courts strive to ensure that the application of tort law will not only provide legal redress to an injured party but will also prevent accidents. *Hopkins, supra,* 132 *N.J.* at 448. To that end liability is imposed to deter tortious behavior. *Ibid.* Liability is imposed to discourage negligent practices by fostering reasonable conduct and creating incentives to minimize risks of harm. *Ibid.* Imposing responsibility here will further serve both goals of tort liability. It will ensure the safety of shoppers by encouraging homeowners who hold garage or yard sales to prepare their premises for the sale; and it will provide redress to those persons injured through the fault of those homeowners who fail to take such measures.

While this is the first time our courts have specifically addressed the duty of a homeowner who conducts a garage or yard sale, the duty applied is supported by well-established authority. The burden on homeowners is not onerous. It merely requires that in anticipation of a garage or yard sale, the homeowner exercise reasonable care to maintain the premises in a reasonably safe condition and to make a reasonable inspection to discover defective conditions.

Plaintiff next contends that the trial court erred in deciding the issue of whether defendants breached their duty of care to plaintiff. She maintains that the issue of whether the condition of the overgrown lawn and obstructed drop-off at the point of her fall was

LAW IN ACTION–(CONT'D)

defective and created an unreasonable risk of harm was an issue of material fact for the jury. We agree.

While it is within the province of the trial court to determine the legal status of a person coming on another's land, Benedict, supra, 109 N.J. Super. at 408, it is the function of the jury to determine the condition of the property and the reasonableness of defendants' care, Hopkins, supra, 132 N.J. at 451, and to determine the comparative fault of each party, Berger, supra, 30 N.J. at 102. The determination of what constitutes reasonable care under particular circumstances is to be resolved not by a judge but by a jury . . .

Reversed and remanded for trial.

QUESTIONS

1. What cases did the court rely on in reaching its decision? What was the court's decision?
2. What statutory or code law was used in this case? How did the court use this law?
3. What rule or rules come out of this case that could be used by other courts that were bound to follow this holding? How did the court justify its decision?
4. What are landowners in New Jersey now required to do as a result of the court's ruling here?

THE AMERICAN LEGAL SYSTEM: A BLEND OF COMMON LAW AND CODE LAW

Most states have legal systems that resemble the system in place in New Jersey: they have code laws, which may deal quite extensively with certain topics but barely mention others, and they have a common law, which is laid down by state judges and often fleshes out the code law. Sometimes the common law stands alone and there are no parallel code provisions; other times, common law exists to interpret the statutes or regulations that have been issued by other branches of the government. In the last century, state legislatures and the U.S. Congress have been actively engaged in lawmaking, and as a result, there has been a proliferation of code law. While these same bodies were unable or unwilling to make law throughout much of the 1700s and 1800s, they have now eagerly assumed this role. As a result, code law in the United States abounds. In Part II of this book, we will examine how courts, legislatures, chief executives, administrative agencies, and law enforcement agencies function and how they engage in lawmaking.

Growth in Code Law in the United States

National Conference of Commissioners on Uniform State Laws (NCCUSL) and American Law Institute (ALI)

organizations that seek to codify law and make it easier to use and more predictable

Uniform Commercial Code (UCC)

a code that governs contracts; intended to provide uniformity and consistency among states and to limit state variation in the making and enforcement of contracts

`www ▶ ▶ ▶`

Even in some areas of law where common law has historically existed with no code law counterpart, we have seen the creation of code law. Beginning in the late nineteenth century, a number of organizations, among these, the **National Conference of Commissioners on Uniform State Laws (NCCUSL)** and the **American Law Institute (ALI)** have drafted model laws that have attempted to codify law and make it simpler and more predictable. In many areas, these organizations have been successful. For example, all states have adopted, in whole or part, the **Uniform Commercial Code (UCC)**, which like other codes, ensures a consistency and uniformity of behavior for all parties engaged in private contractual arrangements. Until the UCC was adopted, nearly all of contract law was based on common law, but now all states rely on this code law. The NCCUSL and ALI continue to write model code laws, among these, the Uniform Probate Code and Uniform Child Custody Jurisdiction Act, which have been adopted in whole or part by the majority of states.

Most recently, the Conference has been engaged in writing a uniform law that would govern tort awards. This model law, the Uniform Apportionment of Tort Responsibility Act (2002), purports to ensure consistency among all the states in how blame and responsibility are to be determined in cases where there is more than one party at fault. This act attempts to address the wide variation among states in how negligence is apportioned and in how damages are assessed. Traditionally, tort law was a creature of the common law; however, courts have had very different ways of assigning blame. Many people believe that without code law, this inconsistency will likely continue. The model act is intended to help state legislatures take action to adopt laws that would then be consistent with the laws in other states. Groups like the NCCUSL and ALI have important roles to play in formulating model codes. These organizations, along with a number of states, like New York, are leaders in developing codes that historically have been adopted by many or most states.

Many areas of U.S. law that were once almost exclusively governed by common law are now also regulated by code law. One excellent example is sentencing in criminal cases. Until recently, judges were pretty much left to their own discretion to determine how much time a person convicted of a crime would actually do—while state and federal law generally stipulated a range of years, like three to five years for assault, it was the duty of the judge to determine the actual sentence. Increases in crime in the 1970s and early 1980s spurred state legislatures and Congress to "get tough on crime," and as part of this campaign, it was assumed that judges had employed much too lenient sentencing criteria. As a result, many states and the U.S. Congress created sentencing guidelines that aimed at starkly limiting judicial discretion. There is fierce debate about whether sentencing guidelines should be used. In 2004, the U.S. Supreme Court struck down federal and state guidelines, finding that they undermined the right to a jury trial because they allowed judges to mete out sentences based on "facts" that had not been introduced and thus had not been proven at trial. Many analysts question whether these recent Supreme Court decisions will change practice, and debate still rages on the question of whether mandatory sentencing guidelines should be imposed on courts.

♋

DEBATE

Do sentencing guidelines too tightly constrain judges?

Yes: For most of our nation's history, we left it to judges to use their expertise and judgment to decide sentencing in criminal cases. We assumed that judges were best able to make a determination about the proper sentence in these cases, and that judges would take into account a range of issues, like the age and marital status of the offender, his or her previous history and the circumstances of the crime. We viewed judicial discretion as a good thing—an essential element of the criminal justice system—and understood that judges needed to be able to consider the particulars of a crime and an offender in determining the proper sentence. If anything, we have an even greater need for judicial discretion now, when our courts and penal institutions are being flooded with cases. Moreover, it is ludicrous to argue that judges are unconstrained in their sentencing—the reality is that the guidelines replaced a system that was working very well. Judges were never deciding cases in an arbitrary way—they have always tried to square their decisions and sentences with those reached by judges in similar cases.

No: It was precisely the arbitrary nature of sentencing that helped to contribute to the huge increases in crime that we saw in the 1970s and 1980s. Why do I say this? Because offenders had no real notice of what their jail time would be and probably thought that judges would continue to treat them leniently. The sentencing guidelines not only make the criminals responsible for their act, they may actually deter crime by putting future offenders on notice about the harshness of sentencing. Moreover, these guidelines make sense—they are created by legislatures or commissions that are very much in touch with the public's sentiment and sensibilities about how particular crimes should be dealt with. Decision making by judges is simply not appropriate when we're talking about criminal law—this is an area of the law that the public is very interested in and wants to maintain substantial control over. It makes much more sense to allow democratically elected entities to set the parameters for sentencing.

Advantages and Disadvantages of Code and Common Law

There are benefits and drawbacks of both code and common law systems. Because common law systems rely on past court decisions and the principle of stare decisis, we assume that these systems are more stable over time. In theory, at least, stare decisis ensures that lawmaking is incremental, and that there are no big changes from one case holding to another. In addition, because common law is based on precedent and assumes that there is a rational, logical link between case holdings, we assume that this law is knowable and discoverable by those who understand the underlying case principles. The inherent conservatism of common law, however, may impair its ability to respond quickly and decisively to changed societal conditions. Moreover, because common law is made by courts, which are, by nature, reactive institutions, lawmaking is usually very slow and cannot be proactive. Courts and judges must wait for an issue to come before them in the form of a case in order to consider this issue. Furthermore, in making law, courts are limited to the two positions that are offered to them: generally speaking, courts cannot choose from options that are not presented to them by the formal parties in the litigation. As a result, lawmaking by courts is not only slow and incremental, it is piecemeal. An examination of case law in many areas reveals exceptions to these general principles: for example, courts do sometimes choose from options that are not presented by the formal parties, and they do at times ignore settled case law and make decisions that are in conflict with earlier case holdings. Generally speaking, however, the principle of stare decisis guides the operation of common law systems and guides decision making by judges.

In contrast, code law systems may be much more proactive, that is, better able to quickly deal with new issues or problems. Lawmaking by legislatures can be more systematic and better informed, and we assume that before code law is adopted, legislatures have closely examined the issues, options, and likely repercussions of the law. Legislatures can actively place an issue on their agenda and then carefully examine all sides of this issue. For example, in the wake of September 11, the U.S. Congress quickly considered and passed antiterrorist legislation. In contrast, courts concerned about terrorism or about a law being used to combat terrorism must wait until this issue is presented in the form of a case before they can engage in lawmaking. Code law systems are not only proactive, they can create law that is more uniform and can be applied to all conditions.

Code law is knowable—while changes in the common law might be predictable, one's ability to predict these changes assumes a legal education or ability to engage in logical reasoning, and still, the result may not be what was expected. In contrast, code law is written down and is generally more specific and more readily understood even by those without a legal education. Code law is also more adaptable to changes. On the other hand, this adaptability may also make code law very susceptible to changes in the larger political environment and may create law that is erratic and unstable. Moreover, by creating law that is intended to apply to all situations, code law may prove to be unworkable because it does not allow for sufficient flexibility. While judges can reason about whether precedent should be applied to a given factual situation, legislators assume that one law can cover a myriad of conditions.

In reality, the U.S. legal system is a blend of code and common law. The two legal systems coexist and interact in fascinating ways, and both judges and legislators are often making law that covers the same subjects or attempts to address the same problems. As has already been noted, there has been a huge increase in the amount of code law in the United States over the last century. This code covers a wide assortment of issues and behaviors. It is, however, often unclear and creates significant opportunities for courts to engage in lawmaking through the interpretation of ambiguous code provisions. For example, in the following case, the United States Supreme Court was charged with interpreting the establishment clause of the First Amendment to the United States Constitution. This clause states that "Congress shall make no law respecting an establishment of religion," and this prohibition has been extended to apply to the state legislatures as well.

The Constitution is a form of code law—it is our preeminent code law, meaning that it "trumps" all other code provisions, but it is nonetheless, a code law. Probably because there was so much disagreement among the framers of the Constitution about what the relationship between the church and the state should be, the establishment clause was written in ambiguous terms. It was this ambiguity that likely glossed over these differences and ensured that the Constitution and its amendments were ratified. But what does this clause actually mean? Are legislatures barred only from officially establishing a state religion, meaning that the state of Pennsylvania cannot establish Roman Catholicism as the state religion? Or should the establishment clause be read much more broadly as encompassing a strict separation of religious institutions and government? Over time, this vague clause has been interpreted quite differently by courts considering whether city, state, and federal laws are constitutional. In this case, *Zelman* v. *Simmons-Harris,* the U.S. Supreme Court examined the Pilot Project Scholarship Program of the Cleveland City School District and assessed whether this program, which allowed for parents of parochial school children to receive publicly funded vouchers, breached the separation of church and state.

LAW IN ACTION

The Interaction of Code and Common Law in the U.S.

ZELMAN V. SIMMONS-HARRIS U.S. SUPREME COURT, 2002

www ▶▶▶ (See *Law, Politics, and Society* website for a link to the complete decision.)

CHIEF JUSTICE REHNQUIST delivered the opinion of the Court.

The State of Ohio has established a pilot program designed to provide educational choices to families with children who reside in the Cleveland City School District. The question presented is whether this program offends the Establishment Clause of the United States Constitution. We hold that it does not.

There are more than 75,000 children enrolled in the Cleveland City School District. The majority of these children are from low-income and minority families. Few of these families enjoy the means to send their children to any school other than an inner-city public school. For more than a generation, however, Cleveland's public schools have been among the worst performing public schools in the Nation. In 1995, a Federal District Court declared a "crisis of magnitude" and placed the entire Cleveland school district under state control. See *Reed* v. *Rhodes*, No. 1:73 CV 1300 (ND Ohio, Mar. 3, 1995). Shortly thereafter, the state auditor found that Cleveland's public schools were in the midst of a "crisis that is perhaps unprecedented in the history of American education." Cleveland City School District Performance Audit 2-1 (Mar. 1996). The district had failed to meet any of the 18 state standards for minimal acceptable performance. Only 1 in 10 ninth graders could pass a basic proficiency examination, and students at all levels performed at a dismal rate compared with students in other Ohio public schools. More than two-thirds of high school students either dropped or failed out before graduation. Of those students who managed to reach their senior year, one of every four still failed to graduate. Of those students who did graduate, few could read, write, or compute at levels comparable to their counterparts in other cities.

It is against this backdrop that Ohio enacted, among other initiatives, its Pilot Project Scholarship Program, Ohio Rev. Code Ann. §§3313.974–3313.979 (Anderson 1999 and Supp. 2000) (program). The program provides financial assistance to families in any Ohio school district that is or has been "under federal court order requiring supervision and operational management of the district by the state superintendent." §3313.975(A). Cleveland is the only Ohio school district to fall within that category.

The program provides two basic kinds of assistance to parents of children in a covered district. First, the program provides tuition aid for students in kindergarten through third grade, expanding each year through eighth grade, to attend a participating public or private school of their parent's choosing. §§3313.975(B) and (C)(1). Second, the program provides tutorial aid for students who choose to remain enrolled in public school. §3313.975(A).

The tuition aid portion of the program is designed to provide educational choices to parents who reside in a covered district. Any

LAW IN ACTION-(CONT'D)

private school, whether religious or nonreligious, may participate in the program and accept program students so long as the school is located within the boundaries of a covered district and meets statewide educational standards. §313.976(A)(3) . . . Tuition aid is distributed to parents according to financial need. Families with incomes below 200% of the poverty line are given priority and are eligible to receive 90% of private school tuition up to $2,250. §§3313.978(A) and (C)(1). For these lowest-income families, participating private schools may not charge a parental co-payment greater than $250. §3313.976(A)(8).

The program has been in operation within the Cleveland City School District since the 1996-1997 school year. In the 1999-2000 school year, 56 private schools participated in the program, 46 (or 82%) of which had a religious affiliation. None of the public schools in districts adjacent to Cleveland have elected to participate. More than 3,700 students participated in the scholarship program, most of whom (96%) enrolled in religiously affiliated schools. Sixty percent of these students were from families at or below the poverty line. In the 1998-1999 school year, approximately 1,400 Cleveland public school students received tutorial aid. This number was expected to double during the 1999-2000 school year.

The program is part of a broader undertaking by the State to enhance the educational options of Cleveland's schoolchildren in response to the 1995 takeover . . .

In July 1999, respondents filed this action in United States District Court, seeking to enjoin the reenacted program on the ground that it violated the Establishment Clause of the United States Constitution . . . In December 2000, a divided panel of the Court of Appeals affirmed the judgment of the District Court, finding that the program had the "primary effect" of advancing religion in violation of the Establishment Clause. 234 F. 3d 945 (CA6). The Court of Appeals stayed its mandate pending disposition in this Court. App. to Pet. for Cert. in No. 01-1779, p. 151. We granted certiorari, 533 U.S. 976 (2001), and now reverse the Court of Appeals.

The Establishment Clause of the First Amendment, applied to the States through the Fourteenth Amendment, prevents a State from enacting laws that have the "purpose" or "effect" of advancing or inhibiting religion. *Agostini* v. *Felton,* 521 U.S. 203, 222–223 (1997) . . . There is no dispute that the program challenged here was enacted for the valid secular purpose of providing educational assistance to poor children in a demonstrably failing public school system. Thus, the question presented is whether the Ohio program nonetheless has the forbidden "effect" of advancing or inhibiting religion.

To answer that question, our decisions have drawn a consistent distinction between government programs that provide aid directly to religious schools, Mitchell v. Helms, 530 U.S. 793, 810–814 (2000) (plurality opinion); *id.,* at 841–844 (*O'Connor, J.,* concurring in judgment); *Agostini, supra,* at 225–227; *Rosenberger* v. *Rector and Visitors of Univ. of Va.,* 515 U.S. 819, 842 (1995) (collecting cases), and programs of true private choice, in which government aid reaches religious schools only as a result of the genuine and independent choices of private individuals, *Mueller* v. *Allen,* 463 U.S. 388 (1983); *Witters* v. *Washington Dept. of Servs. for Blind,* 474 U.S. 481 (1986); *Zobrest* v. *Catalina*

Foothills School Dist., 509 U.S. 1 (1993). While our jurisprudence with respect to the constitutionality of direct aid programs has "changed significantly" over the past two decades, *Agostini, supra,* at 236, our jurisprudence with respect to true private choice programs has remained consistent and unbroken. Three times we have confronted Establishment Clause challenges to neutral government programs that provide aid directly to a broad class of individuals, who, in turn, direct the aid to religious schools or institutions of their own choosing. Three times we have rejected such challenges.

In *Mueller*, we rejected an Establishment Clause challenge to a Minnesota program authorizing tax deductions for various educational expenses, including private school tuition costs, even though the great majority of the program's beneficiaries (96%) were parents of children in religious schools. We began by focusing on the class of beneficiaries, finding that because the class included *"all* parents," including parents with "children [who] attend nonsectarian private schools or sectarian private schools," 463 U.S., at 397 (emphasis in original), the program was "not readily subject to challenge under the Establishment Clause," *id.*, at 399 (citing *Widmar v. Vincent*, 454 U.S. 263, 274 (1981) . . . That the program was one of true private choice, with no evidence that the State deliberately skewed incentives toward religious schools, was sufficient for the program to survive scrutiny under the Establishment Clause.

In *Witters*, we used identical reasoning to reject an Establishment Clause challenge to a vocational scholarship program that provided tuition aid to a student studying at a religious institution to become a pastor. Looking at the program as a whole, we observed that "[a]ny aid . . . that ultimately flows to religious institutions does so only as a result of the genuinely independent and private choices of aid recipients." 474 U.S., at 487 . . . Our holding thus rested not on whether few or many recipients chose to expend government aid at a religious school but, rather, on whether recipients generally were empowered to direct the aid to schools or institutions of their own choosing.

Finally, in *Zobrest*, we applied *Mueller* and *Witters* to reject an Establishment Clause challenge to a federal program that permitted sign-language interpreters to assist deaf children enrolled in religious schools . . . Looking once again to the challenged program as a whole, we observed that the program "distributes benefits neutrally to any child qualifying as `disabled.'" *Id.*, at 10. Its "primary beneficiaries," we said, were "disabled children, not sectarian schools." *Id.*, at 12 . . .

Our focus again was on neutrality and the principle of private choice, not on the number of program beneficiaries attending religious schools. *Id.*, at 10–11 . . . Because the program ensured that parents were the ones to select a religious school as the best learning environment for their handicapped child, the circuit between government and religion was broken, and the Establishment Clause was not implicated.

Mueller, Witters, and *Zobrest* thus make clear that where a government aid program is neutral with respect to religion, and provides assistance directly to a broad class of citizens who, in turn, direct government aid to religious schools wholly as a result of their own genuine and independent private choice, the program is not readily subject to challenge under the Establishment Clause . . .

LAW IN ACTION—(CONT'D)

We believe that the program challenged here is a program of true private choice, consistent with *Mueller*, *Witters*, and *Zobrest*, and thus constitutional. As was true in those cases, the Ohio program is neutral in all respects toward religion. It is part of a general and multifaceted undertaking by the State of Ohio to provide educational opportunities to the children of a failed school district. It confers educational assistance directly to a broad class of individuals defined without reference to religion, *i.e.*, any parent of a school-age child who resides in the Cleveland City School District. The program permits the participation of *all* schools within the district, religious or nonreligious . . . Program benefits are available to participating families on neutral terms, with no reference to religion. The only preference stated anywhere in the program is a preference for low-income families, who receive greater assistance and are given priority for admission at participating schools.

There are no "financial incentive[s]" that "ske[w]" the program toward religious schools. *Witters*, *supra*, at 487–488. Such incentives "[are] not present . . . where the aid is allocated on the basis of neutral, secular criteria that neither favor nor disfavor religion, and is made available to both religious and secular beneficiaries on a nondiscriminatory basis." *Agostini*, *supra*, at 231 . . .

Respondents suggest that even without a financial incentive for parents to choose a religious school, the program creates a "public perception that the State is endorsing religious practices and beliefs." Brief for Respondents Simmons-Harris et al. 37–38. But we have repeatedly recognized that no reasonable observer would think a neutral program of private choice, where state aid reaches religious

schools solely as a result of the numerous independent decisions of private individuals, carries with it the *imprimatur* of government endorsement. *Mueller*, 463 U.S., at 399–399; *Witters*, 474 U.S., at 488–489; *Zobrest*, *supra*, at 10–11; *e.g.*, *Mitchell*, *supra*, at 842–843 (O'Connor, J., concurring in judgment) . . . Any objective observer familiar with the full history and context of the Ohio program would reasonably view it as one aspect of a broader undertaking to assist poor children in failed schools, not as an endorsement of religious schooling in general.

There also is no evidence that the program fails to provide genuine opportunities for Cleveland parents to select secular educational options for their school-age children. Cleveland schoolchildren enjoy a range of educational choices: They may remain in public school as before, remain in public school with publicly funded tutoring aid, obtain a scholarship and choose a religious school, obtain a scholarship and choose a nonreligious private school, enroll in a community school, or enroll in a magnet school. That 46 of the 56 private schools now participating in the program are religious schools does not condemn it as a violation of the Establishment Clause.

Justice Souter speculates that because more private religious schools currently participate in the program, the program itself must somehow discourage the participation of private nonreligious schools. *Post*, at 19–22 (dissenting opinion). But Cleveland's preponderance of religiously affiliated private schools certainly did not arise as a result of the program; it is a phenomenon common to many American cities . . .

Respondents and *Justice Souter* claim that even if we do not focus on the number of par-

LAW IN ACTION–(CONT'D)

ticipating schools that are religious schools, we should attach constitutional significance to the fact that 96% of scholarship recipients have enrolled in religious schools. They claim that this alone proves parents lack genuine choice, even if no parent has ever said so. We need not consider this argument in detail, since it was flatly rejected in *Mueller*, where we found it irrelevant that 96% of parents taking deductions for tuition expenses paid tuition at religious schools . . . The constitutionality of a neutral educational aid program simply does not turn on whether and why, in a particular area, at a particular time, most private schools are run by religious organizations, or most recipients choose to use the aid at a religious school. As we said in *Mueller*, "[s]uch an approach would scarcely provide the certainty that this field stands in need of, nor can we perceive principled standards by which such statistical evidence might be evaluated." 463 U.S., at 401 . . .

In sum, the Ohio program is entirely neutral with respect to religion. It provides benefits directly to a wide spectrum of individuals, defined only by financial need and residence in a particular school district. It permits such individuals to exercise genuine choice among options public and private, secular and religious. The program is therefore a program of true private choice. In keeping with an unbroken line of decisions rejecting challenges to similar programs, we hold that the program does not offend the Establishment Clause.

The judgment of the Court of Appeals is reversed.

[There was one concurrence in this case and three dissents. I have included the dissent of Justice Souter.]

JUSTICE SOUTER, with whom JUSTICE STEVENS, JUSTICE GINSBURG, and JUSTICE BREYER join, dissenting.

The Court's majority holds that the Establishment Clause is no bar to Ohio's payment of tuition at private religious elementary and middle schools under a scheme that systematically provides tax money to support the schools' religious missions. The occasion for the legislation thus upheld is the condition of public education in the city of Cleveland. The record indicates that the schools are failing to serve their objective, and the vouchers in issue here are said to be needed to provide adequate alternatives to them. If there were an excuse for giving short shrift to the Establishment Clause, it would probably apply here. But there is no excuse. Constitutional limitations are placed on government to preserve constitutional values in hard cases, like these . . . I therefore respectfully dissent.

The applicability of the Establishment Clause to public funding of benefits to religious schools was settled in *Everson* v. *Board of Ed. of Ewing*, 330 U.S. 1 (1947), which inaugurated the modern era of establishment doctrine. The Court stated the principle in words from which there was no dissent:

No tax in any amount, large or small, can be levied to support any religious activities or institutions, whatever they may be called, or whatever form they may adopt to teach or practice religion. *Id.*, at 16.

The Court has never in so many words repudiated this statement, let alone, in so many words, overruled *Everson* . . .

LAW IN ACTION—(CONT'D)

The [voucher] money [in Cleveland] will thus pay for eligible students' instruction not only in secular subjects but in religion as well, in schools that can fairly be characterized as founded to teach religious doctrine and to imbue teaching in all subjects with a religious dimension. Public tax money will pay at a systemic level for teaching the covenant with Israel and Mosaic law in Jewish schools, the primacy of the Apostle Peter and the Papacy in Catholic schools, the truth of reformed Christianity in Protestant schools, and the revelation to the Prophet in Muslim schools, to speak only of major religious groupings in the Republic.

How can a Court consistently leave *Everson* on the books and approve the Ohio vouchers? The answer is that it cannot. It is only by ignoring *Everson* that the majority can claim to rest on traditional law in its invocation of neutral aid provisions and private choice to sanction the Ohio law. It is, moreover, only by ignoring the meaning of neutrality and private choice themselves that the majority can even pretend to rest today's decision on those criteria . . .

The scale of the aid to religious schools approved today is unprecedented, both in the number of dollars and in the proportion of systemic school expenditure supported . . . The Cleveland voucher program has cost Ohio taxpayers $33 million since its implementation in 1996 ($28 million in voucher payments, $5 million in administrative costs), and its cost was expected to exceed $8 million in the 2001-2002 school year . . . These tax-raised funds are on top of the textbooks, reading and math tutors, laboratory equipment, and the like that Ohio provides to private schools, worth roughly $600 per child . . .

Everson's statement is still the touchstone of sound law, even though the reality is that in the matter of educational aid the Establishment Clause has largely been read away. True, the majority has not approved vouchers for religious schools alone, or aid earmarked for religious instruction. But no scheme so clumsy will ever get before us, and in the cases that we may see, like these, the Establishment Clause is largely silenced. I do not have the option to leave it silent, and I hope that a future Court will reconsider today's dramatic departure from basic Establishment Clause principle.

QUESTIONS

1. What is the law at issue? What was the reason that this law was passed? What importance do you think the justices give to these reasons?
2. How do the majority opinion and the Souter dissent justify their decisions? How do they treat existing precedent?
3. Many legal commentators have noted that *Zelman* is the first of many voucher programs that the Court will be faced with in the coming decade. The Court's decision in *Zelman* will likely serve as the precedent for evaluating future voucher cases. Can you identify the legal standard that will guide other cases involving school vouchers?

The majority opinion and the Souter dissent in *Zelman* illustrate the important role played by judges in interpreting code provisions. In this case, the Justices were charged with determining whether the Ohio state law was in accordance with the First Amendment of the U.S. Constitution. What is especially notable in these two opinions is the great extent to which the justices disagreed about how these laws should be interpreted and which cases should serve as precedent. For example, Chief Justice Rehnquist relied heavily on a number of cases in justifying his decision that the state law did not violate the establishment clause. In contrast, Justice Souter's dissent focused on a different case and provided a very different interpretation of the cases cited in the chief justice's opinion.

In many ways, this case illustrates the pitfalls of both the common and code law systems. Code law does not necessarily provide sufficient guidance to the justices in evaluating the constitutionality of this state law. For example, if the establishment clause were written more clearly and revealed the underlying goals of the framers, we would likely have a better sense of whether this law was permissible. Nor does the common law provide clear guideposts for understanding what the lessons of past case holdings have been. The fact that both opinions rely on legal precedent to arrive at starkly different results suggests the difficulty of assuming that stare decisis will lead inevitably to one conclusion. The Ohio law was passed in response to what were seen as failing schools; most significantly, it was passed to assist parents of children attending the Cleveland school district. Like other code laws, this law aimed at providing a comprehensive program for addressing a serious problem. In defending this law, its drafters had to address not only the law's underlying rationale and how it functioned, but they had to argue that this law was consistent with the Court's past holdings in similar establishment clause cases. *Zelman* is an excellent example of the difficulties of blending code and common law: this law had to be consistent with settled case law and it had to be based on good public policy. Ultimately, the majority and dissent disagreed on both counts: while the majority argued that it was consistent with code and common law principles, the dissent contended that it was based on neither policy nor common law holdings.

Criminal and Civil Law in the United States

In the United States, there are two main categories of law: civil law and criminal law. Criminal law encompasses breaches of the federal and state criminal codes that govern individuals and groups. In contrast, civil law outlines responsibilities and duties owed by one individual or group to another. Until recently, criminal law was the predominant form of law in the United States, but in the last several decades, there has been a dramatic expansion in the civil law field. Some of these areas of civil law have long existed. For example, contract and tort law, which govern relationships that arise out of either private contractual obligations or the common law principle of the duty of care, are well-established, as is the even older field of property law. Many new areas of law, however, have recently been developed, among these, corporation law, antitrust law, family law, environmental law, intellectual property law, labor and employment law, and administrative law. All have emerged and evolved in response to the restructuring and creation of new societal relationships. For example, the intellectual property field emerged in response to new intellectual discoveries and inventions. Existing law governing real property could not be used to structure relationships or resolve ownership disputes that arose in the area of intellectual property, and this field emerged to satisfy these demands. The theories of trademark, patent, and copyright continue to evolve as new technologies alter our conceptions of ownership and property.

Similarly, employment and labor law have continued to expand, as the common law principle of "at will" employment, which stated that an employee could be hired or fired for any reason at all, has given way to a heightened regulation of the employment relationship. For example, it is now against the law for employers or prospective employers to engage in certain discriminatory practices, among these, discrimination on the basis of race, sex, national origin, religion, disability, or age. In addition, employers have obligations to keep their employees safe from exposure to some occupational risks. Again, the expansion in employment and labor law corresponds to our understanding that the relationship between employer and employee has important public policy ramifications and that regulation of this relationship may foster important policy goals.

SUMMARY

What is the historical basis for American law? Our law comes from two different legal traditions—the common law and code law traditions—each with very different views of how law is made and how law functions in the wider society. The common law tradition derives from the British system, which focused on using law to limit the power of the monarchy. The common law comes directly from decisions made by judges in individual cases and passed on through adherence to the principle of stare decisis. This tradition focused on ensuring uniformity of case holdings and stability in the law over time. In contrast, the code law tradition focuses on lawmaking by legislatures and stresses the flexibility inherent in this tradition. While common law develops general principles of law to be applied in cases that come before judges, code law is made up of fairly detailed and complex statutes intended to be understood not just by the legislators who create them, but the general public, as well. As we will talk about in the next chapter, many nation-states blend two or more legal traditions, but the U.S. system, which blends common and code law, is fairly unusual. These are traditions that are in many ways less than compatible – while common law is reactive, code law is proactive; while common law lays out general principles, code law is much more detailed; and while common law focuses on stability over time, code law is capable of being altered immediately to respond to changes in the social or political environment. These two traditions interact in fascinating ways, and create a myriad of opportunities for lawmaking in the United States. In the second segment of the book, we will be talking about the shared lawmaking function, and about how courts, legislatures, chief executives, and enforcement agencies all compete to make law in the United States.

SUGGESTED READING

Paul O. Carrese, *The Cloaking of Power: Montesquieu, Blackstone, and the Rise of Judicial Activism* (University of Chicago Press, 2003). Carrese argues that judicial activism is not a novel practice and, in fact, was anticipated by Montesquieu and Blackstone. Montesquieu, who created the separation of powers construct, envisioned an important role for courts and probably saw them as equal to the other branches of government. Similarly, Blackstone viewed judicial power very favorably; he believed that through the exercise of logic, judges would discover an abiding and lasting truth.

Danny Danziger and John Gillingham, *1215: The Year of Magna Carta* (Touchstone Books, 2004). This short and engaging book provides a kind of snapshot of the year 1215, when the Magna Carta was created and the barons forced King James II to sign it. The authors stress that the historical context is key to understanding why this document emerged when it did and take the reader through the social, cultural, and political events of this important year.

Morton J. Horwitz, *The Transformation of American Law 1870–1960: The Crisis of Legal Orthodoxy* (Oxford University Press, 1994). This book explores the monumental shift in the American legal system that occurred from the post–Civil War period through to the civil rights movement. He argues that American law has changed dramatically during this period and that this change was necessary to accommodate the growing complexities and inequalities in our society.

Oliver Wendell Holmes, *The Common Law* (Dover Publishers, 1991). In this classic work on the common law tradition in the United States, Justice Holmes argues in favor of the common law, contending that judges *should* act as legislators, and in deciding cases, they should consider the political, social, and economic ramifications of their decisions.

Mary Beth Norton, *In the Devil's Snare: The Salem Witchcraft Crisis of 1692* (New York: Knopf Publishers, 2002). An excellent study of the Salem witchcraft trials, this book brings together the original source documents from this period and illuminates them with her insightful analysis. Norton contends that the witchcraft trials were the embodiment of the Puritans' fear of outsiders, particularly, American Indian tribes living close to Salem.

ACTIVE LEARNING

1. One of the chief functions of this chapter is to introduce students to the case brief. The website provides both a description of a legal brief and a sample brief from the *Filipowicz* case. Try your hand at briefing the *Filipowicz* v. *Diletto* case and then exchange your brief with others in your group. *Filipowicz* is a good case for a first brief because it involves tort law, which is a form of common law. There is no code law at stake in this case, and this simplifies students' task.

   To practice briefing, you should try your hand at *Zelman* v. *Simmons-Harris*. This much more complicated case involves both code law and common law—the code law is the U.S. Constitution and the state law at issue, the common law is the set of decisions reached by the Court in similar First Amendment cases.

2. Consider the federal and state sentencing guidelines in further depth. Both sets of guidelines were the subject of U.S. Supreme Court challenges heard in 2004 and 2005: *Blakely* v. *Washington*, *U.S.* v. *Freddie J. Booker*, and *U.S.* v. *Ducan Fanfan*. What do the guidelines do? Why have they been so controversial? What did the Court rule in these cases? What do these cases say about the relationship between code and common law in the United States?

CHAPTER 4

Comparative Context for American Law

What role does law play in a society? Does it come directly from the dominant culture, or is it imposed on the masses by a specialized law-making body? What goals does the law serve? Does it exist to reinforce philosophical ideals, like liberty and equality? Or economic principles, like capitalism or communism? Or religious creeds, like Islam, Judaism, or Roman Catholicism? In this chapter, we will discuss the legal traditions prevalent in the world today.

Nations have both legal traditions and legal systems. A legal system encompasses the rules and procedures that govern the making and enforcement of law—it's a kind of instructor's manual that tells people how the law and legal institutions can be used. A nation's legal tradition, in contrast, is much broader than its legal system. A society's choice of legal tradition tells us about its view of where law should come from and what goals it should serve. Nation-states usually have constitutions or other central documents that lay out the legal system, that is, the procedures to be followed for lawmaking. They also provide important information about the nation-state's legal tradition. In particular, these documents often clearly establish the goals that the law will serve or aspire to serve. For example, New Zealand's laws clearly state that the government will act to ensure liberty, democracy, nondiscrimination, and the protection of minority rights. In contrast, Saudi Arabia's constitution states clearly that it is based on Islamic law and that its goal is the protection and advancement of Islam.

There are four principal legal traditions in place in the world today: the **common law tradition,** *the* **code law tradition,** *the* **Islamic legal tradition,** *and the* **socialist legal tradition.** *Most nation-states have hybrid systems with characteristics of not only these four legal traditions, but others, as well. For example, many nations use a combination of code law and the Islamic legal tradition; others employ traditions drawn from Far Eastern culture or African tribal laws. Common and code law are*

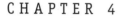

Islamic legal tradition

tradition that subordinates law to Islamic religious doctrine; only one nation is a pure Islamic state, where all law is based on religious code, but nearly forty others use Islamic law in combination with secular law

socialist legal tradition

tradition that focuses on the role of law in ensuring national security and in fostering the goals of socialism; used by only a few states

customary law

law that is not necessarily written down but is based on long-established patterns or rules of behavior

sometimes combined with **customary law,** *which derives from the daily experiences and customs of peoples. Even in traditions that have staunchly applied one system or another, there has been significant movement toward a mixed system. For example, the creation of the European Union has created significant incentives for both common law states like the United Kingdom and code law states like those of continental Europe to move in the direction of a hybrid tradition. This chapter examines the legal traditions operating in other nation states today and provides a comparative context for better understanding the unique features of the U.S. legal system. This chapter explores as well the development of legal systems and the relationship between law and economic development.*

THE COMMON LAW TRADITION

The common law tradition is the predominant tradition in Great Britain, Wales, and northern Ireland, Canada (except for Quebec), and a number of other nation-states that were colonies of the United Kingdom. As you may recall, the central feature of this tradition is case law, and judges are the lawmakers. In some nations that use this tradition, however, lawmaking is shared by more than one branch of government. In the United States all three branches of government participate in this activity. Even in the United Kingdom and its former colonies, the source and function of law is changing. For example, it has long been a tradition in the United Kingdom that law created by Parliament must be interpreted in light of existing case law. But when the UK joined the European Union in 1973, it agreed to abide by the mandate that member nations incorporate EU statutory law into their laws. By agreeing to be bound by EU law, the UK obligated itself to integrate principles that may be counter to existing case law into their law. This complex relationship between national and regional law has raised some difficult choices for decision-makers in the United Kingdom. In 1998, Parliament passed its Human Rights Act, which aimed at incorporating into British law the European Convention of Human Rights, to which the UK is a signatory. Under Section 2, British courts are charged with employing guidelines and decisions from the European Commission on Human Rights to interpret the act's provisions. Where British law is incompatible with Convention rights, the act establishes an extensive review procedure for judges to use to reconcile this incompatibility.

The case of *Regina* v. *Secretary of State for the Home Department* decided by the House of Lords in March 2003 and included on the website illustrates the challenge facing British courts charged with integrating international law into existing national law. In this case, the judges, who are members of the House of Lords, considered whether a man subjected to horrifying torture at the hands of the Sri Lankan government met the

www ▶ ▶ ▶

www ▶ ▶ ▶

British government's criteria for refugee status. Under British law and the law of the EU, the British government is obliged to employ the definition of "refugee" as it was given in the 1951 Geneva Convention on the Status of Refugees. In this case, the judges grappled with the definition of refugee, trying to understand whether the applicant fit within this definition. What is notable about this case is that the judges employed the Convention rules, rather than British law, in assessing whether this individual was eligible for asylum.

In reality, there is no "pure" common law system. Most countries with a historical common law basis are now mixed systems, employing both the common law tradition and some other tradition, usually civil law. Even Great Britain has created new code law, most notably in the area of tort law governing wrongful death. Up until recently, you could only bring suit against someone who harmed you if you were still alive—there was no common law covering wrongful death. Now your estate can sue for wrongful death under a statute that creates liability even where the person harmed has died. A number of countries have expressly adopted mixed systems, relying on code law to regulate some issues and common law to govern others. Still others have adopted systems that rely on both common law and customary law or Muslim law, and a few very small countries with homogenous populations employ a purely customary law tradition (Andorra, Guernsey Island (UK), and Island of Jersey (UK)). This customary law derives solely from tradition and custom, and it functions to protect and reinforce these traditions and customs. For example, on Guernsey Island, which is located in the Channel Islands between Great Britain and France, custom governs many important aspects of real estate transfers. Even though English is the official language in Guernsey and few speak French, real estate contracts are in French. Similarly, the requirement that all contracts be signed in open court on Friday is based on custom that dates from the medieval period.

www ▶ ▶ ▶

THE CODE LAW TRADITION

judicial review

the power of courts to review acts of the other branches, like statutes or agency regulations, and to strike them down as unconstitutional

In most code law systems, the court's role is much more limited than it is in nation-states with common law and does not encompass **judicial review**, which is the power to strike down laws passed by legislatures and chief executives. Although judicial review is a feature of many common law systems, the United Kingdom does not confer this power on its courts. U.S. courts have the broadest judicial review powers.

Most code law systems have their roots in the Napoleonic Code. When France colonized North America, Latin America, Africa, and the Far East in the 1700s and 1800s, it imposed its code law tradition on these peoples. Nation-states with a code law tradition rely heavily on the codification of

inquisitorial system

system used in nations with code law traditions; characterized by cooperation; in the criminal system, guilt is based on preponderance of evidence

www ▶ ▶ ▶

preponderance of the evidence

most of the evidence points to a finding of guilt or liability; greater likelihood than not that the person committed the act that he or she is alleged to have committed; in numeric terms, 51 percent or more of the evidence establishes guilt or liability

guilt beyond a reasonable doubt

so much of the evidence points toward guilt that no reasonable person would doubt that the person is responsible; in numeric terms, more than 99 percent of the evidence points toward guilt

advisory opinions

opinions rendered in response to a request for the highest constitutional court to weigh in on a law and issue an opinion that can guide lawmakers in dealing with this law; not binding on anyone, for advice alone; used in countries like France with a code law tradition

law. In addition, many code law nations like France have an **inquisitorial system**, unlike the adversarial system used in common law states like England and the United States. In such an inquisitorial system, there is an extensive pretrial period during which the judge and lawyers work together to gather and share information. During this period, the primary focus is on determining whether the person being investigated is guilty. While competition and confrontation characterize adversarial systems, cooperation is the rule in inquisitorial systems.

Roman law is the basis for many of the existing legal rules in Scotland and South Africa. In many areas of the law, Scotland looks to Roman code law as it was interpreted in what Scottish lawmakers term "institutional writings," which are core texts written more than two hundred years ago. English common law has had only a limited impact on "Scots' Law," as it is known, despite the fact Scotland is part of the United Kingdom. In some areas, Scots' Law is quite distinctive. For example, judges and juries in criminal cases may choose not only from guilty and not guilty judgments but from the judgment "not proven" as well. In cases where a jury reaches a verdict of not proven, this is understood to mean that the accused was guilty of the crime but that the prosecution did not offer a convincing enough case. In France's inquisitorial system, three-judge panels are directly engaged in gathering and evaluating evidence. There are typically no jury trials, and a determination of guilt is based on a **preponderance of the evidence**, as opposed to the British and American systems, which require a finding of **guilt beyond a reasonable doubt**. In the French system, preponderance of the evidence is established when the judges determine that it is more likely than not that the accused is responsible for committing an act. Consistent with the investigative function of French courts, there are fewer restrictions on the gathering of evidence or the interrogation of the accused. While the accused is not required to testify against himself or herself, the court may take this refusal into account and may hold it against the accused. Typically, there is no oral evidence at trial—instead, the lawyers present written dossiers to establish their cases.

There is no judicial review of code law; once passed, code law is supreme in the French system, as in all code or civil law systems. The French Constitutional Council, a body charged with evaluating statutes, can review these statutes before they are passed. The highest court in France, the French Supreme Court of Appeals, can issue nonbinding **advisory opinions** on novel civil issues. For example, the Law in Action feature that follows includes this court's advisory opinion about a proposal that would regulate abortion in France. Keep in mind that this decision is merely advisory, and the French legislature is free to disregard it. In stark contrast, consider the central role played by the U.S. Supreme Court in the abortion debate—our high court continues to sit in judgment of abortion laws passed by both Congress and the state legislatures.

LAW IN ACTION

4.1 Opinion of the Constitutional Council with Regard to the Voluntary Interruption of Pregnancy and Contraception Act (2001)

On 7 June 2001 the Constitutional Council received a referral from Mr Bernard SEILLIER [et al. . . . Senators] pursuant to the second paragraph of Article 61 of the Constitution, for constitutional review of the Voluntary Interruption of Pregnancy (Abortion) and Contraception Act.

THE CONSTITUTIONAL COUNCIL,

Having regard to the Constitution;
Having regard to Ordinance 58-1067 of 7 November 1958 enacting the Institutional Act governing the Constitutional Council, as amended, and in particular Chapter II of Title II thereof;
Having regard to Institutional Act 96-312 of 12 April 1996 on the statute of French Polynesia;
Having regard to the Civil Code;
Having regard to the Criminal Code;
Having regard to the Code of the Public Health;
Having regard to the observations of the Government, registered at the Secretariat-General on 15 June 2001;
Having heard the *rapporteur*;

On the following grounds:

1. The Senators making the referral submit to the Constitutional Council the Voluntary Interruption of Pregnancy (Abortion) and contraception Act, definitively passed on 30 May 2001, and challenge the constitutionality of sections 2, 4, 5, 8 and 19, in whole or in part;

Reprinted with the permission of Constitutional Council.

ON THE EXTENSION TO TWELVE WEEKS OF THE PERIOD DURING WHICH A PREGNANCY MAY BE TERMINATED WHERE THE PREGNANT WOMAN IS IN A SITUATION OF DISTRESS:

2. Section 2 of the Act referred, which amends section L2212-1 of the Code of Public Health, raises from ten to twelve weeks of pregnancy the period during [which] a pregnancy may be terminated where the pregnant woman is, because of her condition, in a situation of distress;

3. The applicants submit that this provision:

—Violates the principle of the safeguard of human dignity against any form of deterioration because, in particular, of the "unquestionable risk of eugenic practices tending to the selection of children that are to be born" since, they argue, it is possible at this stage of the growth of the foetus to detect "a larger number of anomalies" and "to distinguish the sex of the child to be born";

—Violates "the principle of the respect due to any human being from the commencement of its life" since the Act permits the interruption of the development "of a human being having reached the foetus stage", which "constitutes a potential human being" and is eligible for "strengthened legal protection";

—Violates, by disregarding the obligation of prudence which is incumbent on the legislature "in the absence of a

LAW IN ACTION–(CONT'D)

medical consensus" on these questions, the precautionary principle which constitutes a constitutional objective set by Article 4 of the Declaration of Human and Civic Rights of 1789;

—Violates the eleventh subparagraph of the Preamble to the Constitution of 1946 since the "change of nature and technique of the procedure" exposes women to increased risks;

4. It is not for the Constitutional Council, which does not have a general discretionary decision-making power comparable to that of Parliament, to call into question the provisions enacted by the legislature on the basis of the state of knowledge and techniques; it is always legitimate for Parliament, acting within its powers, to amend earlier legislation or to repeal it and substituting fresh provisions for it if necessary; the exercise of this power must not, however, have the effect of depriving constitutional requirements of their legal guarantees;

5. By raising from ten to twelve weeks the period during which a pregnancy may be voluntarily terminated where the pregnant woman is, because of her condition, in a situation of distress, the Act has not, in the current state of knowledge and techniques, destroyed the balance that the Constitution requires between safeguarding human dignity against any form of deterioration and the freedom of women under Article 2 of the Declaration of Human and Civic Rights; it follows from the second paragraph of section 16-4 of the Civil Code that the word

eugenics can only be used to qualify "any practice . . . tending to the organisation of human selection"; such is not the case here; by reserving the right to terminate pregnancy to "pregnant woman whose condition places them in a situation of distress", the legislature intended to exclude any fraud against the law and, more generally, any denaturing of the principles that it laid down, and these principles include "respect for the human being from the beginning of its life" under section L2211-1 of the Code of Public Health;

6. Contrary to what applicants state, the precautionary principle is not a principle of constitutional status;

7. Finally, if the termination of pregnancy is medically more delicate when practised between the tenth and twelfth weeks, it can, in the current state of knowledge and medical technique, be practised safely enough for women's health to be unthreatened; the Act referred comprises sufficient guarantees in this respect; it follows that the objection based on violation of the eleventh subparagraph of the Preamble to the Constitution of 1946 must be rejected;

ON THE PROCEDURE PRECEDING THE DECISION TO PRACTISE A VOLUNTARY INTERRUPTION OF PREGNANCY:

8. Section L2212-3 of the Code of Public Health, as amended by section 4 of the Act referred, relates to the first medical examination requested by a woman with a view to the interruption of her pregnancy and provides that a guidance file must be given to her, specifying its contents; the Act no longer requires this file to include

LAW IN ACTION—(CONT'D)

"the enumeration of the rights, aid and benefits given by the law to families, mothers, married or unmarried, and their children, and the possibilities offered by the adoption of a child to be born"; section L2212-4 of the same Code, as amended by section 5 of the Act referred, relates to the preliminary social consultation; under the first two paragraphs of this section as amended, this consultation remains obligatory only for non-emancipated women who are minors; it is merely "proposed" to major woman;

9. The applicants submit that the changes thus made to sections L2212-3 and L2212-4 of the Code of Public Health "call into question the level of the legal guarantees which were previously available to safeguard the mother's personal freedom" and no longer ensure that the pregnant woman will give her "free and enlightened assent, inherent in the exercise of freedom not to abort"; the Act accordingly violates the "constitutional principle of personal freedom";

10. Sections L2212-3 and L2212-4 of the Code of Public Health as amended respect the freedom of pregnant woman who wish to terminate their pregnancy; the information concerning aid and help available to mothers and their children is provided to women who are of age and have accepted the preliminary social consultation provided for by the first paragraph of section L2212-4 of that Code; this consultation "is systematically proposed before . . . the termination of pregnancy, to woman who are of age" and "comprises an individual interview in which she will be offered suitable assistance or advice on her situation"; under the second paragraph of the same section, the preliminary consultation is compulsory for non-emancipated woman who are minors; consequently, the disputed provisions do not violate the principle of freedom laid down by Article 2 of the Declaration of Human and Civic Rights; . . .

22. In this case it is not necessary for the Constitutional Council to raise other questions of constitutionality of its own motion;

Has decided as follows:

Article 1

Sections 2, 4, 5, 8 and 19(V) of the Voluntary Interruption of Pregnancy (Abortion) and Contraception Act are constitutional.

Article 2

This decision shall be published in the Journal officiel de la République française.

Deliberated by the Constitutional Council at its sitting of 27 June 2001, attended by Mr Yves GUÉNA, President, and Mr Michel AMELLER, Mr Jean-Claude COLLIARD, Mr Olivier DUTHEILLET de LAMOTHE, Mr Pierre JOXE, Mr Pierre MAZEAUD, Ms Monique PELLETIER, Ms Dominique SCHNAPPER and Ms Simone VEIL.

DISCUSSION QUESTIONS

1. How did this case come to the Constitutional Council?
2. What did the Council decide?
3. What laws was the Council relying on to decide this case?

In a code law system like France's, a court's decision is binding on the parties involved in a case, but the decision does not create precedent. While there are extensive individual rights and freedoms under French law, these are created almost totally under code law. This is very different from civil rights and liberties in the United States, which have been created and interpreted through the interplay of court decisions and legislative statutes. There are five principal French codes: the Civil Code, Code of Civil Procedure, Commercial Code, Criminal Code, and the Code of Criminal Procedure. In addition, there have been a number of French constitutions and amendments; the latest of these has been in effect since 1958. It bears noting that unlike the U.S. Constitution, the French Constitution provides little explicit guidance about the nature of individual rights. Article 66 of the constitution notes simply that

1. No one may be arbitrarily detained [and that]
2. The Judiciary, guardian of individual liberty, shall enforce this principle under the conditions stipulated by legislation.

The U.S. Constitution, in contrast, provides a virtual "laundry list" of civil rights and liberties. In fact, the first ten amendments, known as the Bill of Rights, details the freedoms that U.S. citizens and residents have come to rely on, including the right to free speech, religion, and assembly; the right to a fair and speedy trial; and due process of the law. In the U.S. system, lawmaking is shared by the three branches, but the **French Parliament** (*Parlement*) establishes rights and has the exclusive power to make law in the areas of civil rights and liberties, nationality, status, capacity, criminal law and procedure, currency, inheritance, labor law, education, and taxation. It also has the power to amend the Constitution. The French executive has the power to regulate all other areas, which are considered regulations and not within the purview of the legislature. One of the chief obligations of the Constitutional Court is to determine whether an issue would be subject to statutory or regulatory law, and thus whether if falls under the jurisdiction of the legislature or the executive. If the law is characterized as statutory law, it falls under the domain of the legislature; if it is regulatory law, it falls under the control of the executive. Like the United Kingdom, France is a member of the European Union and is obligated to reconcile domestic law with the law of the EU. French law in all areas is usually laid out in great detail. This process stands in stark contrast to the U.S. system, where rights are usually seen as rooted in constitutional guarantees and where courts play a central role in interpreting and protecting these rights.

It is important to note, however, that while most nations employ either code law or a mixed system in which code plays an important part, there are significant differences in the goals and functions of law in nations throughout the world. For example, the Islamic legal tradition, which subordinates law to the religious code, is very different from other code law

French Parliament

the key lawmaking body in France, it has a central role in the creation of French law

systems. Similarly, the socialist legal tradition, which uses law to foster the development of socialism and to redistribute resources so that the production and distribution of goods is centralized, has a structure and function that are distinct from other code systems.

ISLAMIC LEGAL TRADITION

Shari'ah

Islamic law that governs relationships between individuals and groups and is seen as the key Islamic legal text; it is interpreted by judges, who are said to be accountable to both Allah and the Muslim community

Only one nation-state employs the Qur'an exclusively in creating and implementing law today. The Republic of Maldives, a tiny nation made up of a group of islands in the Indian Ocean, is based solely on religious codes, as was the former Taliban regime in Afghanistan. Neither government had an independent secular government. In Maldives, the president is also the religious head of state, only those who adhere to Islam can be citizens, and all law is based on the religious code. While Maldives and the former Taliban regime are examples of pure Islamic regimes, nearly forty nation-states in northern Africa, the Middle East, and East Asia rely on the Islamic legal tradition to create and interpret the law. Islamic teachings are divided into two categories: the Hikmah, which provides guidance about faith and theology and is focused on the individual's relationship to God; and the **Shari'ah**, which is comprised of a number of sources, including the Qur'an; the Sunna, or teachings of the prophet Muhammad, which is also referred to as legal custom; and the Fiqh, or rulings of all the prophets, ijma or consensus among judges, and qiyas or legal analogy.

The Shari'ah also encompasses judicial consensus and analogical reasoning. It governs relationships between individuals and groups and is considered to be the key to Islamic law and the principal legal text. Shari'ah jurisprudence structures all economic, social, and political interactions; provides instruction on how war should be waged and on what punishments should be imposed on those who transgress the law; and mandates rules about oaths, etiquette, and the use of symbols. In fact, most of Islamic teaching is encompassed in the Shari'ah and not in the Hikmah—there is far less discussion of faith or theology in the Hikmah than there is of the rules governing individual conduct and relationships with others. The Shari'ah is interpreted by judges, and where this legal code does not impose a specific punishment for wrongdoing, it is the responsibility of the judge to determine what the punishment should be. In assessing punishment, judicial discretion is guided by a number of factors, and judges are said to be accountable to both Allah and the Muslim community. In 2000, one of the northern states in Nigeria, Zamfara, adopted Shari'ah law. Chapter VIII of its criminal code deals with a range of activities, including sex offenses, theft, defamation, use of alcohol, robbery, and other property offenses. Included in Box 4.1 are the provisions governing sex offenses and theft. When you read this code, you may want to consider the kinds of acts that have been criminalized, along with the nature of the punishments and the type of evidence that may be relied on for a conviction.

Under Shari'ah, a person who accuses another of rape has the burden of proving that she didn't consent to the act. If the rapist denies the allegation, the rape victim must find four witnesses, all of whom must be men, to testify that they witnessed the rape. Obviously, this is often quite difficult. The rape victim may face serious consequences—first, if she can't find witnesses willing to testify, she can be charged with defamation, which is punishable by lashing; and second, if she is married and cannot prove the allegation,

---

BOX 4.1
Zamfara State of Nigeria Shari'ah Penal Code Law, January 2000

CHAPTER VIII

HUDUD AND HUDUD RELATED OFFENCES

ZINA (ADULTERY OR FORNICATION)

126. Zina defined

Whoever, being a man or a woman fully responsible, has sexual intercourse through the genital of a person over whom he has no sexual rights and in circumstances in which no doubt exists as to the illegality of the act, is guilty of the offence of *zina*.

127. Punishment for Zina

Whoever commits the offence of zina shall be punished:-

(a) with caning of one hundred lashes if unmarried, and shall also be liable to imprisonment for a term of one year; or

(b) if married, with stoning to death *(rajm)*.

EXPLANATION: Mere penetration is sufficient to constitute the sexual intercourse necessary to the offence of zina.

RAPE

128. Rape defined

(1) A man is said to commit rape who, save in the case referred in subsection (b), has sexual intercourse with a woman in any of the following, circumstances:-

(i) against her will;

(ii) without her consent,

(iii) with her consent, when her consent has been obtained by putting her in fear of death or of hurt;

(iv) with her consent, when the man knows that he is not her husband and that her consent is given because she believes that he is another man to whom she is or believes herself to be lawfully married;

(v) with or without her consent, when she is under fifteen years of age or of unsound mind.

(2) Sexual intercourse by a man with his own wife is not rape.

EXPLANATION: Mere penetration is sufficient to constitute the sexual intercourse necessary to the offence of rape.

Brought to you by Zamfara Online Copyright © 2002

she can be found guilty of adultery and sentenced to death by stoning, or if she is unmarried, subject to one hundred lashes. The case of Amina Lawal—a divorced woman who gave birth to the child of a man who was not her husband, was convicted of adultery, and was sentenced to death by stoning—provides a window into how Shari'ah law functions. Ms. Lawal was divorced from her husband more than two years before she bore her child, and yet she was convicted of adultery. The man she identified as the father of her child denied any involvement with her, and charges were not brought against him. After Ms. Lawal's conviction by a Shari'ah court in Katsina State in northern Nigeria, she appealed with the assistance of several international human rights organizations, including Amnesty International. The Shari'ah Court of Appeals of Katsina State ultimately overturned the conviction, concluding that Ms. Lawal didn't fully understand the charges against her and wasn't able to effectively defend herself. At this point in time, there are a number of other adultery appeals pending. There have already been several amputation sentences carried out for people convicted of theft.

The Qur'an is considered to be the word of God: it cannot be challenged and is considered infallible and unchanging. But it bears noting that many of the provisions of the Qur'an are subject to differing interpretations and that Shari'ah courts often approach legal issues in very different ways. In early 1998, Osama bin Laden issued a **fatwa**, which is an interpretation of Islamic law, usually issued by learned scholars of the law, in which he called on all Muslims to kill every American in any area of the world. He stated that it was the "individual duty of every Muslim who can do it in any country in which it is possible to do it," and that all Americans, even civilians, were the enemy. When Islamic terrorists bombed the World Trade Center and the Pentagon, many saw the destruction as fulfilling this fatwa. In the wake of September 11, Muslim judges have issued conflicting legal rulings, or fatwas, about whether suicide bombers are martyrs or suicides. Some contend that these bombers are fulfilling their responsibilities to engage in jihad and will receive many blessings and honors in the afterlife; other judges conclude that these bombers are in reality suicides, and that the Qur'an condemns all who commit suicide to torment in hell.

Similarly, there continues to be fierce disagreement throughout the Muslim world about whether **honor killings** are justifiable under religious law. The criminal code in Jordan provides an exemption from murder charges for men who kill female relatives who commit adultery, and substantially reduces the term in prison for men who kill female relatives who commit acts that they view to be illicit. Most men eligible for this reduced term serve anywhere from three months to one year for their murder convictions. There has been a significant expansion in the use of Shari'ah law in recent years, even in those countries with secular legal systems. Currently, two countries are actively considering adding Shari'ah law to their code laws.

www ▶ ▶ ▶

fatwa
an interpretation of Islamic law usually issued by well-regarded scholars of the law

www ▶ ▶ ▶

honor killings
killing of female family members who have committed adultery; in Pakistan, Jordan, and some other Islamic states, men who commit these crimes are exempted from murder charges

www ▶ ▶ ▶

♋ **DEBATE**	**Should the international community take an active role in responding to the application of Shari'ah law in cases where this law violates international norms about human rights?**

Yes: The 1948 Universal Declaration of Human Rights, ratified by the General Assembly of the United Nations in the wake of World War II, guarantees that every human being will be treated with respect and dignity. Enshrined in this document is the principle of equality, which prohibits discrimination on a number of bases, including sex and religion. Shari'ah law explicitly mandates *unequal* treatment—women are barred from most employment, have little voice in the political or economic structures, and are completely subordinate to male family members. Women may be prosecuted and put to death for sexual crimes that are overlooked when committed by men, and adultery and rape laws expressly treat men and women unequally. In addition, under Shari'ah law, nations may engage in blatant discrimination against certain religious groups. For example, in Saudi Arabia, there is no religious freedom, and the practice of a religion other than Islam is illegal and punishable by imprisonment or physical abuse. In some nations, Muslims seeking to change their religion may be put to death.

No: When a nation has a large enough Muslim population, this population will eventually clamor for the institution of Shari'ah law. Shari'ah law governs all of life—including patterns of dress, speech, and social interaction—and it is logical for Muslims to expect that this code will become part of their secular law, too. Just because Western nations like the United States mandate the separation of church and state does not mean that the same norm should be imposed on states with Muslim majorities. These peoples should have the same right to self-determination that westerners have come to expect. The fact is that "humanitarian intervention" in the name of religious freedom will seriously undermine the right and ability of Muslim-dominated states to govern themselves. The Western media focuses on the most sensational applications of Shari'ah law, but these are fairly unusual cases. Before intervening in the domestic politics of these nations, human rights organization should look closely at the use of Shari'ah law and get a clearer picture of how this law actually functions.

Sunna

in addition to Shari'ah, this source of Islamic law establishes legal custom and tradition; there is significant disagreement about what the four schools of Sunna actually require

The second source of Islamic law, the **Sunna**, is believed to encompass the teachings of the prophet Muhammad. It is essentially a compendium of legal custom or tradition, and it has its basis in pre-Islamic Arab society, where tribal law or custom predominated. Again, there are differing interpretations about what the Sunna requires. For example, at the start of the Iraq War, Muslim clerics debated the role of the wider Muslim community in the war. Some clerics contended that the Qur'an and Sunna mandated that all Muslims take action to oppose the invasion of Iraq by the United States and UK, while others were more circumspect about the Muslim role. There are at least four different Sunna schools, the Hanifite, Shafi'i, Maliki, and Hanbali, and they sometimes employ very different approaches to legal issues or questions.

At this point in time, only the small Republic of Maldives relies exclusively on Shari'ah law; the vast majority of nation-states with Muslim majorities blend the Islamic tradition with some other system. Where these nation-states employ mixed systems, they may carve out particular areas in which Muslim law operates exclusively and other areas in which civil law governs. For example, in a mixed system, Muslim law may govern family matters, and Shari'ah courts may be the sole lawmakers in this area; in other areas, civil courts and law may function independently. Moreover, in some Muslim states, Islamic law will govern only Muslims; non-Muslims will be subject to the civil code. For example, Muslims may be required to follow Islamic teaching in the area of family law, but others may be governed only by the civil code, which may confer much different benefits and obligations on family members. In addition, in many of these nations, there are separate court systems set up to administer either religious or secular laws.

***Zaheer-ud-din* v. the State**

1993 Pakistan Supreme Court case that established that freedom of religion was *not* absolute and that in some conflicts between the Constitution and Islamic law, religious law would predominate

www ▶ ▶ ▶

There is some tension between religious and secular law in many Islamic states, and it is not always clear how these tensions are to be resolved. In some cases, secular law predominates; in other cases, religious law governs. For example, the Constitution of the Islamic Republic of Pakistan guarantees religious freedom; however, its penal code denies certain rights to specific Islamic sects and criminalizes all religious expression by these groups. In *Zaheer-ud-din* v. *the State*, a landmark case decided in 1993, Pakistan's Supreme Court upheld this discriminatory code, noting that freedom of religion is not absolute and may be limited by Islamic law. In other words, the Pakistani Supreme Court held that in a conflict between the constitution and Islamic law, religious law would be predominant. This may seem strange to many westerners, who assume that religious law and state law are or should be separate.

SOCIALIST LEGAL TRADITION

Most countries that rely on the socialist legal tradition also employ code law. Before the dissolution of the Soviet Union and Eastern European communist governments in the late 1990s, this tradition was prominent in a number of nation-states. Today, only a handful of countries utilize this tradition: Algeria, China, Cuba, Laos, North Korea, and Vietnam. In all of these countries, the socialist legal tradition or communist theory is combined with either French or Spanish code law or Muslim law. The judiciary is selected or appointed by either the legislature or executive committee in all of these countries. In Cuba, for example, the People's Supreme Court is elected by members of the legislature, and may include lay judges, who are expected to be representative of the population. This principle of representativeness is different from the U.S. tradition, in which judges are assumed to be neutral and independent of political pressures imposed by both the public and the other branches of government. In the socialist legal tradition, courts generally do not have judicial review and their decisions neither create precedent nor are binding on future cases.

The primary function of law in a socialist system is to advance the goals of socialism. There are three primary goals in this system: first, law is employed to foster the development of an economic system based on public ownership of the means of production; second, law is used to protect against internal or external threats to the socialist party and government; and third, law is used to raise citizens' "ideological consciousness" about the benefits of socialism and communism. Law does not operate independently of politics or economics in the socialist legal tradition; in fact, it is very consciously employed to ensure the development of the socialist economic system and to protect the existing party and governmental power structures. Joseph Stalin, who ruled the USSR for three decades between the 1920s and 1950s and was instrumental in defining how socialism would function, believed that law was merely a tool for advancing socialism and achieving the final goal of communism. He contended that the new law that emerged from socialism would be radically different from all existing legal systems, in that it would be used aggressively to advance the interests of the proletariat, or working people.

Under the socialist legal tradition, law is subordinate to the socialist party and to what this party perceives as the needs of the larger society. The United Kingdom's agreement to "return" Hong Kong to the People's Republic of China in 1997, after having leased the city for ninety-nine years, was viewed with a great deal of interest, since Hong Kong has a very vigorous and healthy free economy, in stark contrast to the far less industrialized and vibrant economy of China. In the years before and after the transfer of power, commentators were very concerned about how the merger with the PRC might affect Hong Kong's economy. The government of the PRC, also eager to sustain Hong Kong's economic growth, passed a series of laws that accomplished two, somewhat contradictory, goals. First, both Hong Kong and the tiny territory of Macao, which was also transferred in 1997, are separate jurisdictions from the PRC. Chinese law ensures the autonomy of Hong Kong, at least in terms of economic activities. In fact, a number of laws seem to freeze Hong Kong's status in structuring its economic affairs, allowing it substantial independence from mainland China.

At the same time, however, a series of laws have been passed that state specifically that Hong Kong and Macao are under the control of the PRC and that the Chinese government will be directing all foreign affairs and defense-related issues. Many remain concerned about how the merger will ultimately affect the political rights of individuals living in Hong Kong. Longtime residents of Hong Kong had become accustomed to living in a British commonwealth, where individual rights and liberties were protected under the law. It remains to be seen whether these citizens will continue to enjoy these protections, or whether residents of Hong Kong will have the much more limited set of rights that those living in the PRC have.

The constitutions of China, Cuba, and North Korea all explicitly state that the law should be used to protect the socialist party and its government and to advance its goals. In China, some of these goals have generated significant controversy, at least among international organizations. The Chinese Communist Party strongly advises its citizens that they should

www ▶ ▶ ▶

THE LAW IN POPULAR CULTURE

Red Corner

This film depicts a trial in the People's Republic of China. The socialist legal tradition uses law to promote the good of the community, and specifically, to advance socialist principles. This film demonstrates the stark differences in the Chinese and American criminal justice systems. While the American system focuses on individual due process protections, the Chinese system is much more focused on establishing guilt.

actively practice birth control, and this demand is enshrined in its family law. For example, Article 2 of China's matrimonial law states: "A marriage system based on freedom, monogamy and equality between man and woman shall be implemented [and that] [b]irth control shall be practiced." Similarly, this command to use birth control is present in Articles 6 and 16, which establish the age for marriage at 22 years old for men and 20 years old for women, in order to encourage "late child birth," and expressly state that both spouses are obligated to use birth control. In North Korea, the constitution explicitly establishes that the law is subordinate to party needs and interests. For example, Article 18 states that "[t]he law of the DPRK reflects the wishes and interests of the working people and is a basic instrument for State administration."

Similarly, under the socialist legal tradition, the law is used to help train citizens to be members of a socialist, or ultimately, communist society. For this reason, North Korea's constitution states that the role of law and the government is to "perfect the system of socialist law and promote the socialist law-abiding life" and to "train the working people to be builders of socialism and communism equipped with a profound knowledge of nature and society and a high level of culture and technology, thus making the whole of society intellectual (Articles 18, 40)." This use of law to promote a socialist culture is in keeping with the Soviet tradition, in which law was actively employed as a propaganda or "learning" tool. Like many other nations that have been colonized and occupied for long periods of time, the drive to preserve national and ethnic heritage in China and North Korea is very strong. The code law in these nations guards against the influence of Western culture. Interestingly, in some areas of the law, the Chinese government has largely adopted the laws of other nations. For example, Chinese laws governing contract and technology provide extensive procedures that transnational companies can follow when seeking entry into the Chinese economy. These laws guide the investment of foreign capital and the introduction of technology and are consciously employed to help entice companies and countries to invest in China.

While law is actively employed in the socialist legal tradition, the deeply entrenched role played by family and community continues to guide behavior in other domains. For example, under Chinese matrimonial law, many grievances between spouses are mediated by village or urban committees that are made up solely of members of the community. These committees have broad authority to grant monetary relief in cases of nonsupport or to call for law enforcement authorities in cases of child, spousal, or parental abuse. The primacy of the family unit is apparent under both Chinese and North Korean law, and family members have substantial obligations to provide for the support of children and parents. In the United States, only parents are obligated to provide support for their children—these children owe no reciprocal obligations to their parents. In contrast, in China, this support is owed by, not only parents, but grandparents as well, and adult children are held responsible for support of their parents. In sum, the socialist legal tradition employs a collective approach to rights and responsibilities. This approach is very different from the western tradition, which is based on the primacy of the individual. For example, Article 63 of North Korea's Constitution notes that "[i]n the DPRK the rights and duties of citizens are based on the collectivist principle, 'One for all and all for one,' " whereas the U.S. Constitution establishes that there are individual rights that the government may not abridge, even in the interest of the group.

LEGAL ANTHROPOLOGY AND THE EVOLUTION OF LEGAL SYSTEMS

We have been discussing the four main legal traditions in the world today. Many scholars assume that there is a connection between economic and political development and the kind of legal tradition employed in a community. Scholars of sociology and anthropology contend that in general, as a society becomes more industrialized, it moves from reliance on less formal mechanisms for resolving disputes to more structured and formalized systems. For example, a relatively small, homogeneous society may rely on custom and tradition to resolve disputes among its members, and there will likely be very little reliance on courts or a formal legal system. In contrast, a larger and more diverse society may find these informal mechanisms to be ineffective, since there are fewer shared norms among members of the community. For this reason, this kind of society will likely employ a more structured system of law to resolve disputes.

legal anthropology

a field of study that focuses on how different societies approach dispute resolution, and looks at how law functions as a social control and structures relationships; assumes a continuum, from less formal to more formal and complex legal systems

Emil Durkheim

sociologist writing in the late 1800s who argued that law is the expression of a nation-state's stage of development; as nations become more industrialized and specialized, the law also changes to become restitutive, and administrative and procedural law predominate

The study of **legal anthropology** began largely with the work of sociologist **Emil Durkheim**. Writing in the late 1800s, Durkheim argued that law is the expression, or the external index, of moral conditions in a society, and that as societies became more industrialized and occupations became more specialized, there was a profound change in the kinds of laws that were employed. In a less developed society, there was less division of labor, and people were tied together by what he called the collective conscience, which is the expression of the society's commonly held beliefs and sentiments. He classified the legal system in such a society as a repressive system and argued that individuals abided by the laws or customs because they feared the loss of something that they valued, like their life or property. Durkheim contended that this system was characterized by mechanical solidarity with the law and that collective punishment and responsibility were its benchmarks.

According to Durkheim, as a society became more industrialized, individuals began to assume specialized roles and there was a loosening of the collective conscience as the individual conscience began to emerge. Individuals began to be bound to the law not by mechanical solidarity but by what Durkheim called organic solidarity. In such a system, legal sanctions were

restitutive

aimed at making whole
the person who has
been injured

largely **restitutive**, as opposed to repressive, and the function of law was not to punish but to make whole or to return to a normal state of being. Durkheim claimed that this was a more advanced system. Perhaps not surprisingly, given his own cultural biases, he found these advanced systems in only a few areas of the world, specifically, parts of western Europe. He pointed out that in these advanced systems civil law predominated, and there was extensive use of administrative and procedural law. This system of law was focused on individual rights and responsibilities, and government's role increasingly was focused on the mediation or resolution of disputes between private parties. Drawing on much of the work of Charles Darwin and those who followed him, Durkheim constructed a theory of evolving legal systems, and he believed that legal systems inevitably evolved from primitive to advanced forms.

Durkheim focused on the nature of the punishments that were employed to determine a legal system's stage of development—primitive systems used repressive sanctions, while advanced systems employed restitutive punishments. In contrast, Max Weber, writing in the late 1800s, distinguished between stages of legal development by examining the relationship between law and political legitimacy. Weber argued that there are three ways in which people's actions can be controlled: through charismatic domination, traditional domination, or legal domination. Like Durkheim, Weber compared societies on a continuum of least to most developed, finding that those that employed legal domination were the most advanced in terms of their economic and social structures. Charismatic domination was based on the ability of a religious or political leader to command obedience through the operation of his or her personality or position; traditional domination was exerted through religious principles or traditions. Both charismatic and traditional domination were personal, in that individuals conformed their behaviors to the rules set down by some individual. In contrast, legal domination was based on obedience to rules or norms that are binding on all. This form of legal domination focused on the individual actor and assumed that he or she could choose whether to voluntarily submit to the authority of law. According to Weber, in a system of legal domination, the legal rules would be consistent and knowable: that is, the code would clearly and unambiguously establish those actions that were acceptable and unacceptable. He argued that legal systems relying on charisma and traditional domination were less developed than those relying on legal domination, and that for the modern state to emerge and capitalism to flourish, legal domination had to exist. In a system of legal domination, many different kinds of laws would emerge, among these, extensive code law governing domestic relations, contract, and commercial transactions. For Weber, the highest form that law would take would be administrative law, and he believed that the establishment of a bureaucratic structure was essential for the creation of a truly modern legal system.

The work of Durkheim and Weber laid the foundation for the more expansive examination of the evolution of legal systems by **H. L. A. Hart.** Hart explained that the transition from a primitive to a modern system of law was accomplished when three goals or rules were met: first, the rule of recognition, which allowed the society to identify which rules or laws had to be obeyed; second, the rule of change, which allowed the society to alter its rules; and third, the rule of adjudication, which allowed it to determine whether one of these rules has been violated. He drew on the work of legal anthropologists, who had examined the use of tribal law and custom in Melanesia, among Native American tribes like the Cheyenne, and in the Sudan. He concluded that primitive legal systems had rules that commanded automatic obedience and could not be readily changed. For Hart, the distinction between primitive and advanced societies lay in the existence of secondary rules. He argued that both primitive and advanced legal systems had primary "rules," that is, had rules that guided behavior and sanctioned noncompliance. Only advanced legal systems, however, had secondary rules, that is, rules *about* the rules, like the rules of recognition, change, and adjudication. To Hart, the existence of these metarules was key to determining the stage of legal development in a society.

Primitive legal systems have specific characteristics: legal rules are often synonymous with traditions, religion, or culture; there is heavy reliance on self-help, retaliation, and revenge; and criminal law is predominant. Throughout the early 1900s, the study of legal anthropology flourished, as scholars flocked to remote locations to study law in what they believed was a primitive stage of development. One of the most important legal anthropologists, **Bronislaw Malinowski,** focused his attention on the native peoples of the Trobriand Islands in New Guinea, which is located in the South Pacific. He argued that scholars had to study law in context and look at what was actually going on in a society. Malinowski rejected the simple conclusion by many that law did not exist in the absence of coercive institutions, and he used the Trobriand Islanders and their legal system as an example of how law might exist even though there was no formal system set up to enforce it. According to Malinowski, the native peoples of the Trobriand Islands had norms and the means of rectifying violations of these norms, even if they didn't have legal institutions. He contended that the principle of reciprocity guided the islanders and structured all of their rights and obligations. Malinowski directly challenged the view that "primitive" law was predominantly criminal: he contended that the Trobrianders' law was in essence a civil code and that it functioned as an effective means of social control for this tribe. For example, his widely known account of the "Coconut Palm Suicide," suggests the great degree to which individuals fully incorporated social norms about incest, and in so doing, undercut the need for any external institution, like police or courts, to step in. In effect, the person committing the crime took it on himself to exact the punishment.

Malinowski challenged the ethnocentric view that legal systems evolved to more advanced states and that "primitive" legal systems were implicitly inferior to more formal systems. Other scholars have also challenged this view and have argued that even primitive systems have complex, though often more subtle, legal arrangements. For example, all North American Indian tribes have legal systems that have been traditionally classified as primitive, since they rely on clan relationships and lack formal legal systems with courts and laws. A more nuanced and careful examination of these peoples now challenges this view. Many scholars contend that among the diverse tribes, laws have been central to structuring relationships and guiding behavior. These laws differ from our own and are likely to be unwritten and more informal. Similarly, even though the Kapauku Papuans of West New Guinea rely heavily on customary law, which is the hallmark of a primitive legal system, this law provides for extensive protection of private property, a feature that we usually associate with a very advanced legal system.

Traditionally, the work of legal anthropologists has been central to discussions about the development of law and legal systems. Much of this work has focused on studies of how law functions in particular societies or nation-states. More recently, some scholars have shifted their attention to the international community, which some commentators regard as the perfect example of a primitive legal system. There is no authoritative source of international law that is universally binding, and individual actors, here nation-states, can choose whether or not to abide by the standards of the larger community. Nation-states make this decision based on their own self-interest. Moreover, there is disagreement among nation-states about norms, and in some areas, this conflict is quite extreme. Simply pick up a newspaper or click on a news website for your daily dose of these conflicts. Ultimately, international organization is governed by custom and practice, as opposed to law, and even where law does exist, its binding authority may be questioned. Political leaders often mediate disputes, and international courts have only very limited authority to engage in dispute resolution. Many analysts would argue that international laws are not uniformly applied and that the law of might continues to predominate. The difficult transition to Iraqi self-rule that followed the U.S.-led invasion and occupation seems to exemplify the significance of military force in the international arena.

In sum, scholars are developing a more nuanced view of how legal systems change over time, and are beginning to think about the limitations of relying on formal laws in the international arena. Many scholars have also begun to question the view that legal systems inevitably evolve from primitive to modern forms. Up until recently, most theorists assumed that all modern legal systems were characterized by increasing reliance on code law. In the last several decades, however, some advanced legal systems have in fact *decodified* their laws. For example, even in highly industrialized nations like the United States, the creation of norms is sometimes left to community standards. The result of this is that these standards, which govern such subjects as obscenity and capital punishment, can lead to a variety of approaches. Similarly, resort to alternative dispute resolution devices, like negotiated settlements, mediation, and arbitration, has led to a **decodification of laws**. These devices are traditionally associated with less developed legal systems, and their emergence in a number of nation-states, including the United States and Japan, leads us to question whether we are inexorably moving toward exclusive reliance on the formal legal system for the resolution of disputes. Similarly, the reliance on judge-made law, even in nations that have historically employed the civil law tradition, results in a sort of decodification. And furthermore, the emergence of supranational law, like the laws of the European Union, has resulted in the decodification of law in member nations, who are compelled to adopt differing standards in those cases that concern EU matters. In the next few chapters, we will be discussing the international legal community and the trend in some industrialized nations, among these, the United States, to rely more heavily on alternative dispute resolution and community standards, both trademarks of what is theoretically a less developed legal system.

decodification of laws

the trend toward less formal means of resolving disputes in advanced legal systems

SUMMARY

This chapter explored the four major legal traditions operating in the world today: the common law tradition, the code law tradition, the Islamic legal tradition, and the socialist legal tradition. A legal tradition is different from a legal system in that a tradition is broader and encompasses information about where law comes from and what goals it serves, whereas a system is narrower and delineates the rules and procedures to be followed. The comparative approach offered by this chapter allows us to put the four traditions side by side and examine their sources and goals. For example, the four traditions clearly see law coming from different places—in the common law tradition, law comes from decisions reached by judges and handed down in subsequent cases through the principle of stare decisis; and in the code law tradition, law comes from legislatures. In the Islamic legal tradition and socialist legal tradition, law comes from outside of the political system—law in the Islamic tradition comes from religious texts and in the socialist tradition, law derives from socialist ideology. Similarly, this comparative approach allows us to contrast the goals of these systems—the common law tradition advances the goal of continuity and stability, while the civil law tradition allows for rapid innovation and responsiveness to changed societal conditions. The Islamic legal tradition overlaps with the religious code, and its primary purpose is to advance this code; similarly, the socialist tradition directly advances the goals of the socialist economic system. We noted that most legal traditions are a blend of at least two of these four predominant forms.

This chapter also explored the evolution of legal systems over time. Beginning with Emil Durkheim's work, legal sociologists and anthropologists have contended that legal systems evolve from primitive to more advanced forms, with primitive systems being more reliant on informal dispute resolution and the threat of punitive sanctions, while more advanced systems are marked by their greater reliance on courts and law for dispute resolution and by their increased use of administrative law. We discussed the work of Emil Durkheim, Max Weber, and H. L. A. Hart and noted that all assumed that legal systems progress from one stage to another in response to changes in economic and political development. Durkheim focused on the sanctions used in different systems and the overlap between law and external norms; Weber stressed the linkages between law and political legitimacy; and Hart concentrated on changes in the metarules, or rules about the rules or laws. Although most legal anthropologists and sociologists assume that legal systems progress over time, Bronislaw Malinowski and others argued that legal development is often more nuanced, and that even primitive systems have fairly complex and subtle legal arrangements. Finally, we talked about the emergence and development of supranational law, like the law of the European Union, and the decodification of law in some member nations.

SUGGESTED READING

Michael Byers, *Custom, Power and the Power of Rules: International Relations and Customary International Law* (Cambridge University Press, 1998). This book looks at the complex relationship between customary law and international law. Most advanced legal systems do not make much use of customary law, but where international relations are concerned, there is far less codified law and much greater reliance on the long-established patterns of behavior and custom that distinguishes customary law from other traditions.

Tom Ginsburg, *Judicial Review in New Democracies: Constitutional Courts in Asian Cases* (Cambridge University Press, 2003). In this study of how the adjudication of constitutional claims in Asia proceeds, Ginsburg argues that judicial review of statutes looks very different in these countries, largely because of their political and legal cultures.

Jean-Marie Henckaerts, Louise Doswald-Beck, *Customary International Humanitarian Law: Volume 1, Rules* (Cambridge University Press, 2004). This important study aims to establish grounds for humanitarian intervention in international relations. What the authors find is that customary law provides an excellent basis for such intervention.

Tim Koopmans, *Courts and Political Institutions: A Comparative View* (Cambridge University Press,

2003). This text compares the legal and political institutions of the United States, Great Britain, Germany, and France and concludes that on some issues the courts of one nation may behave more "politically" than do the courts of other nations.

Souad, *Burned Alive: A Victim of the Law of Men* (Warner Books, 2004). This book provides a horrifying first-hand account of the victim of an honor killing who survived burns to 90 percent of her body. The family of "Souad" tried to kill her because she had dishonored them by having a premarital affair and becoming pregnant. A good book to put a face on the ongoing debate about honor killings in some countries with an Islamic legal tradition.

ACTIVE LEARNING

1. While the U.S. Constitution doesn't explicitly give courts the power of judicial review, this power was established very early on in our history, in *Marbury* v. *Madison,* a case well-known to all law students, lawyers, and legal historians. In this 1803 case, Chief Justice John Marshall firmly established this power, stating: "It is emphatically the province and duty of the judicial department to say what the law is. Those who apply the rule to particular cases, must of necessity expound and interpret that rule. If two laws conflict with each other, the courts must decide on the operation of each."

   Now consider the fourth paragraph of the decision reached by the French Constitutional Council in its advisory opinion on the Voluntary Interruption of Pregnancy and Contraception Act, included in your textbook. This paragraph states:

   > It is not for the Constitutional Council, which does not have a general discretionary decision-making power comparable to that of Parliament, to call into question the provisions enacted by the legislature on the basis of the state of knowledge and techniques; it is always legitimate for Parliament, acting within its powers, to amend earlier legislation or to repeal it and substituting fresh provisions for it if necessary; the exercise of this power must not, however, have the effect of depriving constitutional requirements of their legal guarantees.

   Judicial review may in fact be antidemocratic, allowing courts to strike down acts passed by the democratically elected branches of government. But the lack of judicial review is a serious constraint on the operation and independence of courts. What goals do these two systems serve? Which system seems to be better suited to the modern democratic state?

2. There is substantial disagreement among Muslims about whether the 9/11 terror attacks were justified by religious law. The *Report of the 9/11 Commission* noted that beginning in February 1998, Osama bin Laden issued fatwa calling on all Muslims to murder any American in any area of the world and stating that it was the "individual duty of every Muslim

who can do it in any country in which it is possible to do it" (see find-law.com—Chapter 2 of the report). But consider the story at **http://www.islamfortoday.com/attacks.htm.** How do you distinguish bin Laden's call for jihad and justification of the terror attacks from the views of other Islamic clerics? Please discuss.

3. The case of *Regina* v. *Secretary of State for the Home Department* illustrates that for the United Kingdom, membership in the European Union requires that the courts in the United Kingdom employ statutory international law and convention rather than long-established common law. The assumption underlying this EU mandate is that the laws of this regional organization will trump those of each nation's legal system. Even though the United Kingdom has a common law tradition, this rule essentially requires that the civil law of the EU will govern, even if it is in conflict with common law rulings. The United States has no such mandate and staunchly defends its right to make its own laws, even where these laws conflict with those of the international community or regional organizations. On this point, the two legal systems, which are both based in the common law tradition, have sharply diverged. How do American courts determine refugee status? What laws or conventions do these courts rely on?

Consider the definition of refugee used by the U.S. Immigration and Naturalization Service. According to the INS, a refugee is entitled to political asylum if the attorney general determines that that person is unwilling to return to his or her country of origin "because of persecution or a well-founded fear of persecution on account of race, religion, nationality, membership in a particular social group, or political opinion." In a series of cases decided in the 1990s, the INS established that the refugee must establish that his or her fear of persecution is both "subjectively genuine and objectively reasonable" (*Arriaga-Barrientos* v. *INS*, 925 F.2d 1177, 1178 (9th Cir. 1991)). The refugee must provide "credible, direct and specific evidence" that establishes a reasonable fear of persecution (*Fisher* v. *INS*, 37 F.3d 1371, 1376 (9th Cir. 1994), and courts have required that this evidence demonstrate that there is a clear probability that persecution will result if the alien is deported. You may want to think about whether the definition of refugee used by the United States and the United Kingdom are consistent with each other. Which provides a broader umbrella for refugees seeking political asylum? Can you reconcile the different approaches of these two countries? Should there be a uniform standard? Why or why not?

CHAPTER 5

The United States and International Law

"Iraq Suicide Car Bomb Kills 68, Wounds 56"
"Ethnic Cleansing by Government and Militia Forces in Western Sudan"
"Haitian Rebels Still Armed and Active"

Click on your favorite news site, listen to the radio, or watch television, and you are probably bombarded by images and stories of violence in the world today. The United States continues to occupy Iraq, a nation-state that the U.S. government invaded or liberated—your choice of terms; civil war and genocide wrack the African nations of Rwanda and Ethiopia; and acts of extreme brutality continue to be perpetrated against individuals. What role does the law play in such a world? Every nation-state has some kind of legal tradition, but is there any code that governs the relationship between states or establishes even minimal protections for individuals? The fact is that there is a body of international law that requires that the international community establish and safeguard basic human rights protections. In this chapter, we'll discuss the sources of this law, its goals, and its effectiveness. We'll also explore the relationship between U.S. domestic and international law.

INTERNATIONAL LAW THROUGHOUT HISTORY

International law has existed in some form for thousands of years. For example, treaties and political alliances were common in the ancient world. There are historical accounts of such strategic arrangements from as early as 1400 BCE in the ancient civilizations of Mesopotamia, Syria, and Egypt. The ancient Greek city-states frequently engaged in such political alliances as they sought to protect themselves against common enemies and ensure the security of commercial transactions. Throughout history, political and strategic alliances were often reinforced by marriage as kinship bonds were

"just war"

war that is justified
by a principle higher
than the desire to
accumulate power

www ▶ ▶ ▶

sovereignty

the right of nation-
states to govern
themselves and to make
decisions based on their
self-interest

www ▶ ▶ ▶

Treaty of Westphalia

treaty marking the
beginning of the
modern era in
international relations;
established the nation-
state as the most
important actor

created among peoples. Such strategic alliances between governments or peoples were entered into because they provided some clear advantage or advantages that could not readily be ensured without such an agreement.

Beginning with St. Augustine in the fifth century, philosophers have debated whether international relations should be governed by some higher principle that serves the good, not only of the parties that participate, but also of the whole of the international community. For example, St. Augustine warned that force should be used only in the course of conducting a **"just war,"** that is, a war that was justified by some higher principle and not simply the desire to expand one's sphere of power. Hugo Grotius significantly expanded on this attempt to constrain war a thousand years later, in his 1625 work, *On the Law of War and Peace*. Grotius and others began to argue that the only just wars were those that were fought to ensure the protection of inalienable human rights. This concept of the just war eventually gave rise to international human rights law in the eighteenth and nineteenth centuries. Human rights law is an important area of international law, but many believe that there is an inherent conflict between this law and the supreme right of nation-states to govern themselves, which is known as **sovereignty**.

The nation-state has been the most important unit on the international scene since the 1648 **Treaty of Westphalia** ended the horrific Thirty Years' War that had destroyed much of Europe. The treaty recognized the preeminence of nations in Europe and clearly defined the territorial borders of these states. Moreover, the Treaty of Westphalia established that state sovereignty would be supreme; that is, each nation-state would have the right to govern itself and to control what happened within its borders. In this chapter, we will discuss how state sovereignty continues to powerfully shape international law. We will also assess the view of the United States toward international and regional law and its commitment to regional and international organizations. How does the U.S. desire to advance its own domestic goals continue to affect these relationships? The United States is embroiled in a number of international and regional conflicts, but in other areas, the United States is conspicuously absent. Should the United States be guided primarily by its own domestic needs, or does it have some larger responsibility for the needs of the global citizenry?

SOURCES OF INTERNATIONAL LAW

private law

law governing trans-
actions between
private entities, like
corporations

There are many different sources of international law—and many different lawmakers. Like nation-states, the international community has legislative bodies that make law, judges that engage in lawmaking through interpretation, and executive agencies that make law through the administering and enforcing of law. Many scholars divide international law into two main categories: **private law**, which governs transactions between purely

TABLE 5.1
Examples of Private and Public International Law

Private International Law	Public International Law
United Nations Convention on the Carriage of Goods by Sea	The Hague Convention on International Child Abduction
Convention on International Financial Leasing	Vienna Convention for the Protection of the Ozone Layer
Convention on International Interests in Mobile Equipment	Convention on Biological Diversity
United Nations Commission on International Trade Law (UNICTRAL) Model Law on International Commercial Conciliation	Convention on the Prohibition of the Use, Stockpiling, Production and Transfer of Anti-Personnel Mines and their Destruction

public law

law regulating relations between nation-states or nongovernmental agencies operating on behalf of a wider community

www ▶ ▶ ▶

International Court of Justice (ICJ)

the highest court in the international community

private entities, like corporations and commercial interests; and **public law,** which involves governmental units or nongovernmental organizations that operate on behalf of a wider community interest. International law binds not only nation-states and organizations but individual actors, as well.

The **International Court of Justice (ICJ),** the chief judicial arm of the United Nations, recognizes the following sources of law: international conventions or treaties; international custom; the generalized principles of law recognized by states; and judicial decisions of "the most highly qualified jurists" of nations (these court holdings provide "subsidiary" and not primary means for making determinations). Of these sources, most scholars agree that the ICJ gives primacy to treaty provisions and that conflicts between treaties and other forms of law are resolved in favor of the treaty provisions.

Treaties

treaty

a written agreement between two or more nation-states and governed by international law

North American Free Trade Agreement (NAFTA)

regional treaty between the United States, Canada, and Mexico intended to ease trade barriers and result in freer trade

Article 2 of the 1969 Vienna Convention on the Law of Treaties defines a **treaty** as "an international agreement concluded between States in written form and governed by international law, whether embodied in a single instrument or in two or more related instruments and whatever its particular designation," and a treaty may be called a convention, covenant, agreement, charter, or other term. Treaties can be made between two nations, called bilateral treaties, or more than two nations, called multilateral treaties. In addition, some treaties are regional in nature. For example, the **North American Free Trade Agreement (NAFTA)** went into effect in 1994. This agreement between Canada, Mexico, and the United States substantially eased trade barriers in an effort to strengthen the economies of all three nations.

A treaty that creates law must expound some new legal rule which is either ratified or tacitly adhered to by member nations. Treaties sometimes

Law of the Sea

customs and practices
governing use of the
seas, these have been
codified, most recently
in the 1982 UN
Convention on the Law
of the Sea

www ▶ ▶ ▶

hot pursuit

principle allowing a
nation-state to pursue a
vessel outside of its
own territorial waters
under international law

www ▶ ▶ ▶

**International
Convention for the
Suppression of the
Financing of
Terrorism**

treaty signed by more
than 130 states and
ratified by nearly 80
states, this treaty
targeted funding for
terrorist organizations

www ▶ ▶ ▶

ratification process

domestic law and
procedures that govern
the ratification of
international treaties

codify existing customs that govern relationships between nations. For example, the **Law of the Sea** is essentially a codification of customs and practices related to ocean use and navigation that have existed for hundreds of years. The first compendium of rules governing the sea was published in the seventh century and gradually gained acceptance among seafaring nations. Over time, these rules were accepted by individual nations and then by groups of nations. The 1982 United Nations Convention on the Law of the Sea codified much of what had been custom, practice, and domestic law. For example, the law of **hot pursuit**, which establishes that a nation-state may pursue a vessel into either international waters or the territorial waters of another nation-state if it believes that persons aboard the vessel have violated domestic law, derives from earlier wartime customs and practices that had been recognized by a number of nations, among these, England and Spain. "Hot pursuit" has recently been used to legitimize the actions of Southeastern Asian nations who have followed those suspected of a number of crimes, including piracy and illegal fishing, into international waters.

The decision about whether to enter into a treaty is almost always made voluntarily by the individual nation-state, and this decision is most often affected by a determination about whether the treaty advances the goals of the nation-state. In the last two hundred years, nation-states have increasingly relied on treaties to govern their relationships. There has been a proliferation of treaties in the last century as nations have employed these agreements, not only to end political conflict and violence, but to resolve other problems, as well. Some commentators see treaties as the major source of international law. Human rights, environmental protection, the atmosphere and space exploration, protection of marine and coastal areas, regulation of trade, and rules about diplomacy and war are heavily regulated by treaty law.

Treaties are often written and ratified in response to some crisis or serious problem in the international community. For example, the terror attacks against the United States on September 11, 2001, provided the impetus for a series of treaties proposed at the United Nations and elsewhere. One of these, the **International Convention for the Suppression of the Financing of Terrorism**, which entered into force on April 10, 2002, has been signed by 132 member states; of these, 79 nation-states have ratified the treaty, some with reservations, others without reservations. In the United States, as in many other member nations, the **ratification process** is governed by domestic law. Before a treaty can be ratified, it must be approved by some domestic agency. Under the U.S. Constitution, a treaty must be signed by the president, or his agent, usually the secretary of state, and then ratified by the Senate before it can enter into force. Treaties may also be tacitly agreed to; that is, even in the absence of formal ratification, a nation may agree to abide by the rules set forth in a treaty.

Kyoto Protocol to the United Nations Framework Convention on Climate Change

treaty that aims at controlling emission of carbon dioxide or greenhouse gases; President Clinton had signed and was set to send this treaty to the Senate, but upon assuming office President Bush withdrew support, arguing that the protocol undermined U.S. interests

www ▶ ▶ ▶

The United States has sometimes refused to sign or ratify treaties that have been accepted by virtually every other nation. For example, President Clinton signed the **Kyoto Protocol to the United Nations Framework Convention on Climate Change** (Kyoto Protocol) in 1998; however, in 2001, President Bush withdrew the United States from the protocol and refused to send the treaty to the Senate for ratification. The protocol obligated industrialized nations to cut their emission of carbon dioxide by 5–7 percent by 2012 in an effort to reduce the effects of this greenhouse gas on global warming. Some nations, like the United States, which produces 36 percent of the global emission of carbon dioxide, had to reduce emissions by 7 percent; other less developed nations were obligated to reduce emissions by lesser amounts or were exempted from the treaty. In explaining why the United States would not be bound by the Kyoto Protocol, the State Department contended that the protocol was fundamentally flawed, since it was based on political concerns rather than scientific fact and exempted two of the worst greenhouse gas emitters, China and India. President Bush contended that he also rejected it because it would have had a significant negative impact on the U.S. economy.

Customary Law

customary law

international law based on the customs or traditions of a community of nations

principle of reciprocity

ancient custom that ensured the safety of ambassadors and messengers by allowing retaliation against the ambassadors and messengers of those countries that harmed enemy envoys

www ▶ ▶ ▶

"comfort women"

the more than 200,000 Chinese and Korean women forced into sexual slavery during World War II; they sought damages in U.S. courts

The second source of international law is **customary law**, which is based on the customs or traditions of a community of nations. This is the oldest form of law, having existed in one form or another for thousands of years. Customary law is based on an implicit agreement among nations about how to deal with some issue or problem. These norms become accepted as custom only after they have been in use for a substantial period of time and are acceded to by a number of states. For example, the **principle of reciprocity** has governed the exchange of ambassadors or messengers between nations since ancient times. Under this principle, each state implicitly agreed that it would not harm envoys from other nations, and if a state did not abide by this custom, its own messengers could be harmed in retaliation.

Custom is often codified into treaties. For example, the customary right of a neutral ship to passage on the high seas was written into the Law of the High Seas. Even if a nation refuses to sign such a treaty, it remains bound by customary law. Moreover, customary law often has broader application than treaty-made law, and its principles are often defined more liberally. For example, there are estimates that more than two hundred thousand Chinese and Korean **"comfort women"** who were forced into sexual slavery by the Japanese government in the late 1930s and 1940s were tortured and raped by Japanese soldiers during this period. No existing international treaty laws enabled them to bring their case against the former

DEBATE

Should the Alien Torts Claims Act be used to combat international human rights violations?

Yes: This statute was passed in 1789, largely to ensure that pirates did not see our fledgling republic as a safe haven, but over time it has become an important weapon for punishing those who flagrantly disregard well-established human rights protections. In the last several decades, both Republican and Democratic administrations have encouraged the use of the ATCA to combat human rights violations. Victims often do not have any other effective route for achieving justice—at present, existing forums do not adequately punish wrongdoers, in part because there is no real enforcement mechanism. The ATCA uses the American court system, which is very well-regarded in the world today, to mete out punishment for those who would otherwise go unpunished. For example, using the ATCA and other laws, Holocaust victims were finally able to have their claims heard, and Swiss Banks agreed to pay out more than $1.25 billion for their role in the theft of victims' assets. The ATCA is not often used—in fact, it is usually reserved for the most egregious violations of human rights law—but it is an important mechanism for the enforcement of human rights law.

No: The courts have radically expanded the application of this law far beyond what Congress intended when it passed the law in 1789. The framers never intended that the law would be used the way it is being used at present—that is, by foreign nationals claiming they have been harmed by actions of other foreign nations on foreign soil. This reinterpretation of the act allows courts to replace American law with much more amorphous norms of international law, even where those norms are embodied solely in treaties that have not been ratified or in nonbinding resolutions or political statements. The activities that have been covered by the ATCA in the last decade are far beyond what is permitted under our system of democracy. If we want to provide a forum for victims of international human rights abuses, we should leave it to Congress or the president to do so. In fact, in 1991, Congress did provide a limited forum in its Torture Victims Act. Courts are ill-equipped to make policy decisions about how to best combat human rights violations, and allowing courts to assume this role may ultimately interfere with the ongoing war on terror by providing a tool to be used against our allies in their efforts to counter terrorist threats.

**Alien Tort Claims Act
(ATCA)**

U.S. statute that
empowers American
courts to hear cases
involving violations of
international treaty law
and customary law

`www` ▶ ▶ ▶

Japanese government, but customary law could be used to bring suit against
Japan. Unfortunately, they were unsuccessful in bringing suit in Japan, even
though international custom had long recognized that the kidnapping, rape,
and torture of women constituted a crime against humanity. Using a U.S.
law, the **Alien Tort Claims Act (ATCA)**, the women sued in federal district
court. The ACTA empowers American courts to hear cases involving both
breaches of international treaty law that the United States has signed and
the "law of nations," including customary law. The ACTA allows even
people who are not U.S. citizens to bring their human rights claims to
court—and in the case of the "comfort women" provided the only forum
for hearing their complaints.

Customary international law is broad and often encompasses codified, or
treaty-made, law. It also usually surpasses this law, because it creates a
broader cause of action and binds even those states that have not ratified a
treaty. The difficulty in applying customary law lies in being able to establish what this law says—without the clear guidelines set forth in treaty law,
decision makers are forced to infer those norms that have been recognized
under customary law. These interpretations may vary widely—with some
countries recognizing broader rights than others. Consider the ongoing controversy about the detainees in Guantánamo Bay. The U.S. Department of
Defense claims that detainees are not prisoners of war and that human
rights protections established under both customary law and human rights

*In the wake of the 9/11 attacks and subsequent laws passed by the President and
U.S. Congress, hundreds of non-citizens suspected of having ties to terrorist
organization were detained on Guantanamo Bay, a U.S. naval base in Cuba.*

statutes do not apply to these people. The administration claims that these individuals are enemy combatants and that the laws of war do not apply to them. According to the administration, it must treat these individuals humanely but its obligations extend no further. In contrast, human rights organizations like the International Committee of the Red Cross (ICRC) and Amnesty International claim that these detainees are prisoners of war and that they are entitled to certain protections under the customary laws of war and treaty law. Specifically, Amnesty International is arguing that individuals involved in armed conflicts are all entitled to customary and treaty protections and that the creation of an additional category of "enemy combatants" undermines long-established rules of war. The debate about Guantánamo Bay illustrates the ambiguity in customary law and the contradictory ways in which it may be interpreted.

Nonconsensual Sources

nonconsensual sources of law

those sources of law that are not written down but are inferred by domestic law—the two main sources are *jus cogens* and the decisions of some international and domestic courts; nation-states haven't explicitly agreed to be bound by these laws

jus cogens

set of norms based on unanimous or near unanimous agreement about acceptable behavior; derived from nations' laws

In addition to the two main consensual sources of law—treaties and custom, to which states consent to be bound either implicitly or explicitly, there are several **nonconsensual sources of law.** Under the statutes of the International Court of Justice discussed earlier in this chapter there are two such sources of law: those general principles of law that are recognized by all civilized nations, and judicial decisions and the teachings of certain influential jurists. These sources are nonconsensual in that they are not written down or explicit but are inferred, usually from the domestic laws in place in member nations. Moreover, all nations are bound to obey these laws—even if they want to, they may not exempt themselves. General principles of law comprise, not only those norms that bind together nations, but also those that are understood to be at the core of what it means to be a civilized nation. At the heart of these general principles is *jus cogens,* a set of norms that are based on a unanimous, or near unanimous, set of norms about behavior that is expressed in nations' domestic laws. Even though there are no international laws that bar piracy, slave trade, and torture, these activities are clearly prohibited under *jus cogens.*

Some have said that the notion of *jus cogens* comes closest to our understanding of natural law. Both concepts are based on the understanding that through reason or religion, human beings are imbued with an understanding of which actions are inherently wrong. Even in the absence of a law that bars murder or theft, we know that these actions are wrong. Similarly, *jus cogens* assumes that all civilized nations inherently recognize that they are barred from undertaking certain activities because these actions are wrong. Any domestic laws or international agreements that violate *jus cogens* are assumed to be null and void. At times, there is conflict between *jus cogens* and treaty law. For example, some analysts believe that the natural law principle of self-defense conflicts with the UN Charter. While both natural law and the charter establish that states have the right to take action when they have been attacked, the natural law theory moves beyond the charter provision by establishing the right to anticipate aggression from other nations and to take preventive action and the right to stage reprisals against nations that have caused harm.

Often these principles are established in the domestic laws of the individual states and then codified as international law. In 1989, the United Nations passed the **Convention on the Rights of the Child**, which barred capital punishment for juvenile offenders. This international law mirrored the domestic law of nearly all UN member nations. There are a few nation-states, among these, the United States, however, that allow the execution of juveniles. Some have argued that *jus cogens* reflects a near unanimous international norm and should prohibit all nation-states from allowing this practice. Until recently, U.S. lawmakers rejected this argument about *jus cogens*, relying instead on what they said was strong public opinion in favor of capital punishment. But in its 2002 decision in *Atkins* v. *Virginia*, the U.S. Supreme Court recognized *jus cogens* when it barred the execution of mentally retarded individuals. In this case, the Court recognized that within the international community, civilized nations do not put those with limited intelligence to death and that the American states had begun to bring their laws into alignment with this wider community. In its 2005 case, *Roper* v. *Simmons,* the Court extended this argument, and barred the imposition of the death penalty for individuals who were under the age of eighteen when they committed their crime. Arguing that a national and international consensus was evolving that the execution of juveniles constituted "cruel and unusual punishment," a majority of the Justices invalidated state laws that had allowed the practice. The Court relied upon a number of sources, including international laws barring the use of capital punishment in juvenile cases, and in so doing, used *jus cogens* to settle this case.

In addition to looking at domestic laws to establish *jus cogens,* the International Court of Justice and legal scholars sometimes examine the decisions of both international and domestic courts. The ICJ's decisions have no precedential value. They are not binding on anyone besides those states and individuals who are involved in the case, and relatively little case law comes out of the ICJ—the court hears only a handful of cases a year. This means that there really is no one authoritative source of case law in the international arena. For this reason, courts, and the ICJ in particular, must frequently rely on the decisions of other courts. Given this reliance, it is perhaps not surprising that the decisions of international courts often conflict. For example, the ICJ recently ruled that Congo's foreign minister, Abdoulaye Yerodia, could not be charged with human rights violations because of official immunity, but this ruling conflicted with the decision of the British high court that rejected the immunity claim and convicted Augustine Pinochet, the past president of Chile, of human rights abuses.

GOALS OF INTERNATIONAL LAW

law of conquest

the long-established custom that recognized the right of European nations to occupy and possess lands that they discovered in the New World

Universal Declaration of Human Rights

established that international law protects not only sovereign nations but individuals, as well

humanitarian intervention

decision by the United Nations or some other international or regional body to intervene in the domestic affairs of a nation to safeguard human rights

International Criminal Court

court created in 1998 to establish a permanent tribunal for hearing cases against government officials charged with human rights violations

There is more international law now, in terms of the number and scope of laws that impose obligations on nations, than there has ever been. Despite this fact, however, nations accept international law only when it is to their advantage, and for this reason, the impact of this law is relatively limited. For many years, international law has been based on the understanding that the right of the nation-state to act independently and in a self-interested way was preeminent. For example, during the 1600s and 1700s, European nations adopted a **law of conquest** that recognized their individual right to occupy and possess those lands that they "discovered," even though these lands were already occupied by aboriginal people. This discovery doctrine was based on their understanding that aboriginal peoples were uncivilized and had no exclusive right to possess territory. This doctrine fit in well with the prevailing view that nation-states had the right to act in their own best interest and that sovereignty was the most important principle in the international arena.

Until World War II, international law governed the relations between nation-states and focused much more on the rights of sovereign nations than on those of individuals. It was only after the global community became aware of the genocide perpetrated by the Nazis in Europe that attention began to shift to the protection of human rights. In 1948, the United Nations passed its **Universal Declaration of Human Rights**, which established that individuals had rights under international law and that the community of nations had an obligation to protect these individuals. This declaration, along with many other human rights laws, establishes that the protection of human rights is an important goal of the international community and that this goal will at times override the rights of nation-states to have exclusive control over what goes on within their borders.

Throughout the 1990s, the United Nations, the North Atlantic Treaty Organization (NATO), and other actors attempted to engage in **humanitarian intervention** in a number of countries, among these, Somalia, Bosnia-Herzegovina, Rwanda, Kosovo, and East Timor. In light of significant disagreement about whether international law and international organizations can be used to accomplish humanitarian goals, this aggressive attempt to use law to promote human rights was unprecedented. It has met significant resistance in the United States and elsewhere. At the same time, there has been a number of ad hoc criminal tribunals to try leaders of nations engaged in human rights abuses, among these, Serb leader Milosevic and leaders in Rwanda. In 1998, the **International Criminal Court** was created to establish a permanent tribunal for hearing cases against government officials charged with human rights violations. Even though the future of the ICC remains unclear, the creation of this permanent court to hear human rights claims strongly suggests that the protection of human rights has become an important goal in international law. Nevertheless, this goal sometimes conflicts with the long-established objective of international law, that is, the protection of the sovereign rights of nation-states. It remains to be seen how these goals will ultimately be reconciled.

THE EFFECTIVENESS OF INTERNATIONAL LAW

In the second half of the twentieth century, the sheer number of international laws exploded. There are now laws that seek to guide nation-states in many areas, among these, environmental protection, human rights, trade relations, and the waging of war. Many people, however, question

THE LAW IN POPULAR CULTURE

Deported to Torture

(2003—Denmark—part of Amnesty International Film Fest amnesty@andrew. cmu.edu) Until relatively recently, the overriding goal of international law has been the protection of nation-state sovereignty. The safeguarding of human rights has been far less important. This film highlights the limitations of the international legal system in ensuring human rights protections by depicting the real-life story of an eighteen-year-old Iranian citizen who was denied humanitarian asylum by the Danish government and was deported to Iran, where he was held captive and tortured for four years.

whether these laws are really effective. Unlike lawmaking within nation-states, international lawmaking does not have an authoritative legislature to enact laws, an executive branch to enforce these laws, or a judiciary to interpret the laws. Most significantly, there is no governing authority that can impose the will of the international community on those countries that choose not to abide by its laws. The primacy of the nation continues to be the central feature of our international laws. Even the United Nations, which was founded after World War II had devastated much of Europe, continues to defer to the nation-state. For example, while Article 2, section 4 of the charter establishes that member nations should not use force or the threat of force against any other nation, Article 51 recognizes the inherent right of nations to engage in self-defense, even when this means that they will undertake military action against other states.

www ▶ ▶ ▶

Most of the time, nation-states obey the law, perhaps because the norms themselves reflect a consensus about how best to handle some issue. This is true across many substantive areas. For example, there are general organizations, like the United Nations or the European Commission, which are umbrella organizations set up to achieve a variety of goals. There are also more specialized intergovernmental entities that exist outside the UN, like the Organization for the Prohibition of Chemical Weapons and the Asia and Pacific Coconut Community, both made up of nation-states and focused on some goal or problem. There are hundreds of such **intergovernmental organizations**, comprised only of nations, each organization having its own goals and policies. Some of these intergovernmental organizations have virtually universal membership—nearly every nation-state belongs to the organization; others are much smaller and have more specialized criteria for membership. In addition to these intergovernmental organizations, there are virtually thousands of **nongovernmental organizations** (NGOs), made up of private citizens who are concerned about some issue or problem. For example, Street Child Africa seeks to better the conditions of children and babies who live on the streets in countries in Africa, the International Committee of the Red Cross provides aid to those affected by war or armed conflict, and Amnesty International, puts pressure on nation-states that have violated international human rights law.

intergovernmental organizations

groups comprised of nations that address some specific issue or need, like the Asia and Pacific Coconut Community

nongovernmental organizations (NGOs)

groups comprising private citizens concerned about some issue or problem, like Street Child Africa or Amnesty International

www ▶ ▶ ▶

All of these organizations have goals and policies, and in most cases, nation-states respect these goals and comply with organizational norms. There are some situations, however, when nations violate the norms of the international community. It is in these cases that the weaknesses in international law become apparent. For many years, member nations of the United Nations saw the organization as essentially limited to providing economic and humanitarian assistance; it was not seen as a military entity. In the early 1990s, the function of the UN began to change, as the breakup of the Soviet Union radically altered global power politics. Beginning in this period, the

UN Security Council

one of the most important but controversial organs of the United Nations, its fifteen members address threats to international security and peace, and throughout the 1990s, embarked on several peacekeeping missions in Somalia, Kuwait, and Yugoslavia; it has five permanent members—China, France, the Russian Federation, the United Kingdom, and the United States—and ten rotating memberships

www ▶ ▶ ▶

UN Security Council, which has the power to embark on peacekeeping missions, took direct action to counter breaches or potential breaches of the peace. Under Article 39 of the UN Charter, the Security Council has the power to "determine the existence of any threat to the peace, breach of the peace, or act of aggression," and to decide on which actions should be taken to counter this threat. This peacekeeping role allowed the UN to intervene in Somalia, a central African nation torn apart by civil war in the early 1990s; in the Middle Eastern kingdom of Kuwait when it was invaded by Iraq in 1991; and in Yugoslavia, which was beset by ethnic conflict following the breakup of the Soviet-sponsored government in the early 1990s. Despite the apparent successes of the UN role in Kuwait and the former Yugoslav republics, many from both inside and outside of government continue to criticize the UN's peacekeeping attempts. Furthermore, the failure of the United Nations to provide sufficient aid to the Somali people is read as evidence of the organization's weakness.

People disagree about the peacekeeping role of the United Nations, and this disagreement has become even more vehement since the United States invaded Iraq in 2003 without the approval of the Security Council. Many see the UN, and the Security Council in particular, as manipulated by the member states and unable to take constructive action to deal with the problems that seem most difficult in our community, among these, the terrorist threat. Others argue that the only true path to global peace lies with international organizations and that relying on nation-states to counter threats will ultimately make the world less safe.

Some also question whether international law can be truly effective, given that it tends to place limits on only nation-states and not other actors. **Transnational organizations**, like corporations, play an important role in the international community and may profoundly affect the social and economic structure of nation-states, particularly those that are not highly industrialized. While corporations are bound to adhere to the law in place in the nation in which they operate, little transnational law governs their behavior. In fact, transnationals may intentionally "shop" for that nation-state with the most business-friendly environment. Usually, the most business-friendly countries are those with the fewest labor and environmental regulations. In fact, some international and regional agreements encourage companies to relocate to take advantage of more business-friendly laws. For example, the North American Free Trade Agreement (NAFTA), with its accompanying North American Agreement on Labor Cooperation (NAALC), dismantled barriers to free trade but did not create standards for minimum wages, child labor, employment discrimination, or occupational safety and health. As a result, some companies relocated to Mexico, which has the fewest laws governing occupational safety and health and less effective labor and employment laws.

Not only are the existing international laws capable of being manipulated by nation-states and transnationals, few effective mechanisms for enforcing

transnational organizations

groups or organizations that cross national borders and can have a profound impact on what's happening both inside a nation-state and among states. Among those groups with the most significant impact on international relations are corporations, which can have a profound effect on not only the laws of a nation but also its social and economic structures

World Court

entity made up of the Permanent Court of International Justice and the International Court of Justice; has jurisdiction to hear cases involving alleged violations of international law and to issue advisory opinions; cannot compel nation-states to participate in cases brought against them

www ▶ ▶ ▶

those laws are on the books. The **World Court**, made up of the Permanent Court of International Justice and the International Court of Justice and housed at the Hague in the Netherlands, has jurisdiction to hear cases arising out of violations of the international law and to issue advisory opinions on the law. Unlike domestic courts, which have the power to compel participation, this World Court cannot force those actors to submit to its jurisdiction. Moreover, this court only hears between two and four cases each year, and while its rulings in these cases are very important, the court has virtually no power to enforce its rulings. For example, in 1980, when the court ruled in favor of the United States in its complaint against Iran for the hostage taking of United States embassy workers, it was unable to compel Iran to comply with its ruling and release the hostages. Ultimately, the court's ruling was only one of a number of factors that led to their release. Other factors included the U.S. decision to freeze Iranian assets both in the United States and elsewhere and its intensive use of diplomacy.

The international community recently established a world criminal court. The Rome Statute of the International Criminal Court was ratified in 2002 to prosecute individuals accused of genocide, crimes against humanity, war crimes, or the crime of aggression. Up until this time, there had only been ad hoc tribunals for this purpose. They had been used to convict individuals of crimes against humanity in the former Yugoslavia (International Criminal Tribunal for the Former Yugoslavia) and Rwanda (International Criminal Tribunal for Rwanda). The ICC differs from the ICJ in that it was expressly created to prosecute and punish individuals, rather than states, for these crimes. No one has yet been prosecuted under this statute.

arbitration

a form of alternative dispute resolution that is widely used to resolve disputes among nations and transnational organizations, particularly commercial interests

www ▶ ▶ ▶

Rainbow Warrior

a vessel owned by Greenpeace that was sunk by France after protesting French nuclear testing; Greenpeace and the French government ultimately entered into binding arbitration that resulted in an award of several million dollars against French officials

Most disputes between nations and all disputes involving transnational organizations are resolved through **arbitration**. Similarly, intergovernmental or nongovernmental organizations are subjects for arbitration; they are not typically appropriate parties for adjudication in international courts. In arbitration, the two parties submit their dispute to a neutral third party, who examines all of the evidence and makes a determination. For example, in 1985, France bombed the ship *Rainbow Warrior,* which resulted in the sinking of the ship and the death of a sailor on board. *Rainbow Warrior* was owned and operated by environmental advocate Greenpeace and had been staging protests against France's nuclear testing in the South Pacific. *Rainbow Warrior* was registered under New Zealand law. Greenpeace and the governments of France and New Zealand chose to enter into binding arbitration of their claims, and ultimately, the cases were resolved by arbitrators who imposed damages against France in the millions of dollars. Arbitration has less formal procedures for gathering and evaluating evidence than does litigation, and the arbitrator's decision may or may not be binding on the parties. Like other forms of alternative dispute resolution, arbitration allows the parties to have a more central role in the resolution of their claims than they would have in litigation, and it allows them to have more control over how the claims are resolved.

THE RELATIONSHIP BETWEEN U.S. DOMESTIC LAW AND INTERNATIONAL LAW

United Nations Population Fund (UNPF)

a UN organization that provides contraceptive advice and contraception to nation-states, especially those that are less industrialized; the Bush administration withdrew American support for the UNPF because the administration believed that it advocated abortion as a form of birth control

Nation-states have substantial flexibility in either adopting or rejecting international laws, and the United States is very selective about the treaties it signs and the monetary contributions it makes to international organizations. The domestic agenda of the United States, and particularly, that of the president, may have a profound effect on the nation's stance on international policies and laws. For example, in early 2003, the Bush administration decided to withhold more than $35 million that it had pledged to the **United Nations Population Fund (UNPF)** because the administration contended that the fund advocated the use of abortion as a means of birth control.

Moreover, the relationship between domestic law and international law is somewhat unclear. Some nations, among these, many African nations, actually incorporate international laws into their domestic laws. For example, the judges in some African nations now consider whether punishment is "inhuman and degrading," a standard that is not present in the customary laws of these countries but is at the core of much of international law and the laws of other nations. Similarly, the European Union imposes the law of the community on each nation-state, and where community law conflicts with domestic law, EU law overrides the domestic law. In the United States, international and regional mandates have been viewed with some suspicion. While the U.S. Constitution mandates that international treaties are supreme and the law of the land, and that they override domestic laws when they are properly executed, the practice of the American government has been to refuse to ratify international treaties that it sees as conflicting with domestic law. For example, the United States has refused to sign most human rights treaties, arguing that these laws interfere with its sovereignty. Furthermore, the United States argues that while other nations might sign these laws, many will fail to implement them.

While the United States usually rejects the substitution of international norms for domestic ones, there have been a number of cases where American courts have employed international laws. These cases, however, have tended to involve issues that go beyond American borders. For example, in the following case, the U.S. Supreme Court used international custom governing salvage of property found on the high seas, a treaty between the United States and Spain, and the laws of Spain governing slavery to decide whether a group of Africans were free or slaves. You may want to consider how the Court sidestepped the highly charged political issue of whether these people would have been considered free or slave under American law. In the 1840s, the issue of slavery had become very contentious as abolitionists in the North began to press for the elimination of slavery in the South.

LAW IN ACTION

International Law in U.S. Courts

U.S. v. *Libellants and Claimants of Schooner Amistad*

[www ▶ ▶ ▶] (See *Law, Politics, and Society* website for a link to the complete decision.)

Mr. Justice STORY delivered the opinion of the Court.

This is the case of an appeal from the decree of the Circuit Court of the District of Connecticut, sitting in admiralty. The leading facts, as they appear upon the transcript of the proceedings, are as follows: On the 27th of June, 1839, the schooner L'Amistad, being the property of Spanish subjects, cleared out from the port of Havana, in the island of Cuba, for Puerto Principe, in the same island. On board of the schooner were the captain, Ransom Ferrer, and Jose Ruiz, and Pedro Montez, all Spanish subjects. The former had with him a negro boy, named Antonio, claimed to be his slave. Jose Ruiz had with him forty-nine negroes, claimed by him as his slaves, and stated to be his property, in a certain pass or document, signed by the Governor General [p. 588] of Cuba. Pedro Montez had with him four other negroes, also claimed by him as his slaves, and stated to be his property, in a similar pass or document, also signed by the Governor General of Cuba. On the voyage, and before the arrival of the vessel at her port of destination, the negroes rose, killed the captain, and took possession of her. On the 26th of August, the vessel was discovered by Lieutenant Gedney, of the United States brig Washington, at anchor on the high seas, at the distance of half a mile from the shore of Long Island. A part of the negroes were then on shore at Culloden Point, Long Island; who were seized by Lieutenant Gedney, and brought on board. The vessel, with the negroes and other persons on board, was brought by Lieutenant Gedney into the district of Connecticut, and there libelled for salvage in the District Court of the United States. A libel for salvage was also filed by Henry Green and Pelatiah Fordham, of Sag Harbour, Long Island. On the 18th of September, Ruiz and Montez filed claims and libels, in which they asserted their ownership of the negroes as their slaves, and of certain parts of the cargo, and prayed that the same might be "delivered to them, or to the representatives of her Catholic majesty, as might be most proper." On the 19th of September, the Attorney of the United States, for the district of Connecticut, filed an information or libel, setting forth, that the Spanish minister had officially presented to the proper department of the government of the United States, a claim for the restoration of the vessel, cargo, and slaves, as the property of Spanish subjects, which had arrived within the jurisdictional limits of the United States, and were taken possession of by the said public armed brig of the United States; under such circumstances as made it the duty of the United States to cause the same to be restored to the true proprietors, pursuant to the treaty between the United States and Spain: and praying the Court, on its being made legally to appear that the claim of the Spanish minister was well founded, to make such order for the disposal of the vessel, cargo, and slaves, as would best enable the United States to comply with their treaty stipulations. But if it should appear, that

LAW IN ACTION–(CONT'D)

the negroes were persons transported from Africa, in violation of the laws of the United States, and brought within the United States contrary to the same laws; he then prayed the Court to make such order for their removal to the coast of Africa, pursuant to the laws of the United States, as it should deem fit . . .

On the 7th of January, 1840, the negroes, Cinque and others, with the exception of Antonio, by their counsel, filed an answer, denying that they were slaves, or the property of Ruiz and Montez, or that the Court could, under the Constitution or laws of the United States, or under any treaty, exercise any jurisdiction over their persons, by reason of the premises; and praying that they might be dismissed. They specially set forth and insist in this answer, that they were native born Africans; born free, and still of right ought to be free and not slaves; that they were, on or about the 15th of April, 1839, unlawfully kidnapped, and forcibly and wrongfully carried on board a certain vessel on the coast of Africa, which was unlawfully engaged in the slave trade, and were unlawfully transported in the same vessel to the island of Cuba, for the purpose of being there unlawfully sold as slaves; that Ruiz and Montez, well knowing the premises, made a pretended purchase of them: that afterwards, on or about the 28th of June, 1839, Ruiz and Montez, confederating with Ferrer, (captain of the Amistad,) caused them, without law or right, to be placed on board of the Amistad, to be transported to some place unknown to them, and there to be enslaved for life; that, on the voyage, they rose on the master, and took possession of the vessel, intending to return therewith to their native country, or to seek an asylum in some free state . . .

Before entering upon the discussion of the main points involved in this interesting and important controversy, it may be necessary to say a few words as to the actual posture of the case as it now stands before us. In the first place, then, the only parties now before the Court on one side, are the United States, intervening for the sole purpose of procuring restitution of the property as Spanish property, pursuant to the treaty, upon the grounds stated by the other parties claiming the property in their respective libels. The United States do not assert any property in themselves, or any violation of their own rights, or sovereignty, or laws, by the acts complained of. They do not insist that these negroes have been imported into the United States, in contravention of our own slave trade acts. They do not seek to have these negroes delivered up for the purpose of being transported to Cuba as pirates or robbers, or as fugitive criminals against the laws of Spain. They do not assert that the seizure, and bringing the vessel, and cargo, and negroes into port, by Lieutenant Gedney, for the purpose of adjudication, is a tortious act. They simply confine themselves to the right of the Spanish claimants to the restitution of their property, on the facts asserted in their respective allegations . . .

No question has been here made, as to the proprietary interests in the vessel and cargo. It is admitted that they belong to Spanish subjects, and that they ought to be restored . . . The main controversy is, whether these negroes are the property of Ruiz and Montez, and ought to be delivered up; and to this, accordingly, we shall first direct our attention.

It has been argued on behalf of the United States, that the Court are [sic] bound to deliver them up, according to the treaty of 1795,

LAW IN ACTION–(CONT'D)

with Spain, which has in this particular been continued in full force, by the treaty of 1819, ratified in 1821 . . . The ninth article provides, "that all ships and merchandise, of what nature soever, which shall be rescued out of the hands of any pirates or robbers, on the high seas, shall be brought into some port of either state, and shall be delivered to the custody of the officers of that port, in order to be taken care of and restored entire to the true proprietor, as soon as due and sufficient proof shall be made concerning the property thereof." This is the article on which the main reliance is placed on behalf of the United States, for the restitution of these negroes. To bring the case within the article, it is essential to establish, First, That these negroes, under all the circumstances, fall within the description of merchandise, in the sense of the treaty. Secondly, That there has been a rescue of them on the high seas, out of the hands of the pirates and robbers; which, in the present case, can only be, by showing that they themselves are pirates and robbers; and, Thirdly, That Ruiz and Montez, the asserted proprietors, are the true proprietors, and have established their title by competent proof.

If these negroes were, at the time, lawfully held as slaves under the laws of Spain, and recognised by those laws as property capable of being lawfully bought and sold; we see no reason why they may not justly be deemed within the intent of the treaty, to be included under the denomination of merchandise, and, as such, ought to be restored to the claimants: for, upon that point, the laws of Spain would seem to furnish the proper rule of interpretation. But, admitting this, it is clear . . . that these negroes never were the lawful slaves of Ruiz or Montez, or of any other Spanish subjects. They

are natives of Africa, and were kidnapped there, and were unlawfully transported to Cuba, in violation of the laws and treaties of Spain, and the most solemn edicts and declarations of that government. By those laws, and treaties, and edicts, the African slave trade is utterly abolished; the dealing in that trade is deemed a heinous crime; and the negroes thereby introduced into the dominions of Spain, are declared to be free. Ruiz and Montez are proved to have made the pretended purchase of these negroes, with a full knowledge of all the circumstances. And so cogent and irresistible is the evidence in this respect, that the District Attorney has admitted in open Court, upon the record, that these negroes were native Africans, and recently imported into Cuba, as alleged in their answers to the libels in the case. The supposed proprietary interest of Ruiz and Montez, is completely displaced, if we are at liberty to look at the evidence of the admissions of the District Attorney.

If, then, these negroes are not slaves, but are kidnapped Africans, who, by the laws of Spain itself, are entitled to their freedom, and were kidnapped and illegally carried to Cuba, and illegally detained and restrained on board of the Amistad; there is no pretence to say, that they are pirates or robbers. We may lament the dreadful acts, by which they asserted their liberty, and took possession of the Amistad, and endeavoured to regain their native country; but they cannot be deemed pirates or robbers in the sense of the law of nations, or the treaty with Spain, or the laws of Spain itself; at least so far as those laws have been brought to our knowledge. Nor do the libels of Ruiz or Montez assert them to be such.

This posture of the facts would seem, of itself, to put an end to the Whole inquiry upon

LAW IN ACTION–(CONT'D)

the merits. But it is argued, on behalf of the United States, that the ship, and cargo, and negroes were duly documented as belonging to Spanish subjects, and this Court have no right to look behind these documents; that full faith and credit is to be given to them; and that they are to be held conclusive evidence in this cause, even although it should be established by the most satisfactory proofs, that they have been obtained by the grossest frauds and impositions upon the constituted authorities of Spain.To this argument we can, in no wise, assent. There is nothing in the treaty which justifies or sustains the argument. We do not here meddle with the point, whether there has been any connivance in this illegal traffic, on the part of any of the colonial authorities or subordinate officers of Cuba; because, in our view, such an examination is unnecessary, and ought not to be pursued, unless it were indispensable to public justice, although it has been strongly pressed at the bar. What we proceed upon is this, that although public documents of the government, accompanying property found on board of the private ships of a foreign nation, certainly are to be deemed prima facie evidence of the facts which they purport to state, yet they are always open to be impugned for fraud; and whether that fraud be in the original obtaining of these documents, or in the subsequent fraudulent and illegal use of them, when once it is satisfactorily established, it overthrows all their sanctity, and destroys them as proof. Fraud will vitiate any, even the most solemn transactions; and an asserted title to property, founded upon it, is utterly void. The very language of the ninth article of the treaty of 1795, requires the proprietor to make due and sufficient proof of

his property. And how can that proof be deemed either due or sufficient, which is but a connected, and stained tissue of fraud? This is not a mere rule of municipal jurisprudence. Nothing is more clear in the law of nations, as an established rule to regulate their rights, and duties, and intercourse, than the doctrine, that the ship's papers are but prima facie evidence, and that, if they are shown to be fraudulent, they are not to be held proof of any valid title. This rule is familiarly applied, and, indeed, is of every-days occurrence in cases of prize, in the contests between belligerents and neutrals, as is apparent from numerous cases to be found in the Reports of this Court; and it is just as applicable to the transactions of civil intercourse between nations in times of peace . . .

It is also a most important consideration in the present case, which ought not to be lost sight of, that, supposing these African negroes not to be slaves, but kidnapped, and free negroes, the treaty with Spain cannot be obligatory upon them; and the United States are bound to respect their rights as much as those of Spanish subjects. The conflict of rights between the parties under such circumstances, becomes positive and inevitable, and must be decided upon the eternal principles of justice and international law. If the contest were about any goods on board of this ship, to which American citizens asserted a title, which was [p. 596] denied by the Spanish claimants, there could be no doubt of the right of such American citizens to litigate their claims before any competent American tribunal, notwithstanding the treaty with Spain . . . [p. 598]

It is therefore ordered adjudged, and decreed by this Court . . . that the said negroes be and

LAW IN ACTION—(CONT'D)

are hereby, declared to be free, and that they be dismissed from the custody of the Court, and be discharged from the suit and go thereof quit without day.

QUESTIONS:

1. What did the U.S. Supreme Court rule in this case?
2. How did the Court sidestep the issue of slavery?
3. How might the Court have handled this case had it not tried to avoid the issue of slavery?

As the *Amistad* case shows, American courts will sometimes use international treaties and customs to settle cases. In addition, American laws may be the basis for claims brought by one individual against another for some action that took place in another country. For example, the Alien Tort Claims Act (ATCA) allows federal district courts to hear cases involving a violation of either the law of nations or a treaty to which the United States is a signatory. This law has recently been used by people who claim they have been subjected to torture by governmental officials in other countries. These individuals might not otherwise have a forum to bring their cases, and the ATCA provides such a forum, along with the possibility that damages might be imposed on these officials for their acts.

Moreover, the actions taken by the United States in the wake of the September 11 attacks strongly suggest that the government will extend its use of American law to cover other actions taking place abroad. For example, the United States continues to detain members of the Taliban whom it captured, along with other suspected terrorists, in Afghanistan during the overthrow of the Afghan government in October 2001. Many of these individuals have been detained on Guantánamo Air Force Base in Cuba and in military brigs in South Carolina so that they can be interrogated about their possible terrorist activities. These individuals are not granted the due process protections afforded under U.S. law, and the government justifies its treatment of these prisoners by contending that their continued detention and interrogation is necessary to ensure national security. Unfortunately, the war on terror is unlike any other conflict—the government readily acknowledges that it is not likely to end in one decisive military victory, but may continue for a long time to come. For detainees, this may mean years, or perhaps even decades, of continued imprisonment. Many commentators have questioned whether the prisoners are being protected under either domestic or international laws governing the rights of combatants, but as yet, the government firmly rejects the application of these laws.

Some of these detainees are U.S. citizens held on American soil; others are noncitizens held in Guantánamo Bay. In three cases decided in 2004, *Hamdi et al. v. Rumsfeld, Secretary of Defense, et al., Rasul et al. v. Bush, President of the United States, et al.,* and *Rumsfeld, Secretary of Defense v. Padilla et al.,* the U.S. Supreme Court rejected the government's argument that it could detain all enemy combatants indefinitely and that these individuals had no right to access American courts for hearings. In *Hamdi* and *Rumsfeld,* the Court held that U.S. citizens held in U.S. prisons had to be given a meaningful opportunity to present evidence that they were not enemy combatants. In *Rasul,* the Court held that noncitizen enemy combatants detained in Guantánamo Bay could challenge their detentions in American courts, since the naval base, while located in Cuba, was under the actual control of the United States. The actual effect of these cases is that U.S. courts may become embroiled in much of the controversy surrounding the detention of suspected terrorists. It remains to be seen how these courts will handle the possible flood of information about these detainees, and ultimately how they will balance the government's need for security against the right of citizens and noncitizens to challenge this detention. Also unclear is how these courts will use international law, and specifically, the laws governing prisoners of war, to decide these cases. Ultimately, future cases dealing with persons detained in the war on terror may provide excellent insight into how U.S. courts will employ international law in determining individual rights; they will also help us to better understand the role of law in international conflicts in which the United States becomes involved.

SUMMARY

International law, or the law that governs relationships between nations, has been around for thousands of years. Yet the period since World War II has seen a wide expansion in the scope and kinds of laws crafted to regulate the interactions between these states. In this chapter, we talked about the sources of international law—two of these are consensual, and the other two are nonconsensual. The consensual sources are either explicitly or implicitly agreed to by nation-states—these are treaties and customary law. Nonconsensual laws are imposed on states whether or not they agree with them and chief among these sources are general principles of law, known as *jus cogens,* and the decisions of international courts, like the International Court of Justice, and certain domestic courts. This chapter also examined the goals of international law, noting that the genocide wrought during World War II had created significant pressure on lawmakers to impose greater human rights protections. In fact, the period since World War II has been marked by much greater emphasis on human rights law at the expense of the traditional goal of international law, which is the protection of nation-state sovereignty.

Much discussion of international law focuses on whether this law is effective in achieving its goals. Nation-states continue to be the primary units in the global community, and the fact remains that there is no authoritative source of international law today. While most nation-states do agree with international law most of the time, they probably do so because these laws reflect a consensus about how to approach a problem or issue. This consensus is threatened, however, by the emergence and growth of other organizations, such as intergovernmental groups, nongovernmental organizations, and transnational entities, which often have only weak ties to nation-states. Finally, in this chapter we examined the relationship between international law and American law, noting that the United States has always been very selective about the laws that it chooses to abide by and that it has always made this decision based on a calculation of its own self-interest. We also noted that the war on terror, which has been launched both in the United States and abroad, raises serious questions, not only about whether the United States will abide by these laws, but about how U.S. law will be imposed abroad.

SUGGESTED READING

Michael Byers, *Custom, Power and the Power of Rules: International Relations and Customary International Law* (Cambridge University Press, 1998). This interdisciplinary study examines the development and role of customary law in the international community and argues that the relative power of nation-states is very important in explaining the rules that are generated.

Antonio Cassese, *International Law* (Oxford University Press, 2001). The author provides a wealth of information about the sources, creation, and enforcement of international law and about some of the most difficult issues in international politics today. Professor Cassese is the former president of the International Criminal Tribunal for the Former Yugoslavia.

Micheline R. Ishay, *The History of Human Rights: From Ancient Times to the Globalization Era* (University of California Press, 2004). An excellent study of the history of international human rights law, beginning with the Code of Hammurabi and continuing to the current era of glob-

alization, this book is organized around six questions, or themes, that provide cross-cultural analysis. It makes extensive use of historical source materials.

Patrick O'Meara, Howard D. Hehlinger, and Matthew Krain, *Globalization and the Challenges of the New Century: A Reader* (Indiana University Press, 2000). This book of important essays examines the impact of globalization on nation-states, specifically, its effect on ethnic conflict, national security, the global economy, and the environment.

Kelly-Kate S. Paese, *International Organizations: Perspectives on Governance in the Twenty-First Century* (Prentice-Hall Publishers, 2002, 2[d] edition). This book examines the role of international organizations in the global community by using critical theory, like Marxism, feminism, liberalism, and realism. It uses these theories as a lens through which to understand issues like human rights, global warming, and international and regional security.

ACTIVE LEARNING

1. The 1789 Alien Tort Claims Act, which grants "the [U.S.] district courts . . . original jurisdiction of any civil action by an **alien** for a **tort** only, committed in violation of the law of nations or a treaty of the United States" has been invoked in a number of cases. Among these is the recent case against Saddam Hussein, brought by a former Iraqi citizen, who claims that he was detained and tortured by Hussein's forces between 1997 and 2000. Consider how the federal district court resolved this case. You may want to think about the impact of this case on the on-going controversy over prisoner torture at Abu Ghraib (http://news. findlaw.com/hdocs/docs/iraq/ rasheedhussein70103cmp.pdf).

2. The Bush administration has repeatedly asserted that the Geneva Convention does not apply to the detainees at Guantánamo Bay. This international treaty is based on customary law and establishes guidelines for the humane treatment of prisoners of war. The administration argues that the detainees are not prisoners of war and so are not entitled to these protections. What do you think? Do you think the Geneva Convention applies or do you think that the detainees are outside the protection of the treaty? Do you think you could argue persuasively in favor of your opinion? Be prepared to make your case—either in a short written essay or in a radio or television spot. For the most persuasive argument, you may want to consider the opposing view and address its main concerns or arguments. For more information, you may want to view the Bush Administration's guidelines (http://www.defenselink.mil/ transcripts/ 2004/tr20040213-0443.html) or a recent federal district court decision that found that the detainees were prisoners of war (*Hamdan* v. *Rumsfeld,* http://news.findlaw.com/hdocs/docs/tribunals/ hamdanrums110804opn.pdf).

PART TWO

The Institutions of the American Legal System

There are many actors in the American legal system who create law: legislators, who actively engage in the creation of statutes; administrators, who are responsible for implementing these statutes, and who often make and interpret regulations that apply these laws; and judges, who make law through the adjudication of cases and the interpretation of statutory and regulatory law. In sum, lawmaking in the United States is a shared function—legislators, administrators, law enforcement personnel and judges are all actively engaged in the creation of law. While lawmaking is shared, however, it takes a different form depending upon the context—that is, who is making the law. For example, lawmaking by judges is very different than that by legislators, and lawmaking by police and law enforcement personnel, who are called upon to exercise discretion in implementing laws, is very different than it is by judges, legislators, or even other administrative actors. In this section, we will be discussing how each of these sets of actors engages in lawmaking, and we will explore how the context for making law can dramatically affect the kind of laws that are created. Throughout these chapters, we will be considering how law affects and is affected by the larger society, and we will be thinking about the actual operation of the law in society—which is what many sociologists and legal scholars term "law in action."

CHAPTER 6

The Structure of and Participants in the American Court System

Chapters 6 and 7 examine how American courts engage in lawmaking: Chapter 6 explores the somewhat unique structure of the judicial system and the key participants in cases; Chapter 7 looks at the many functions fulfilled by American courts and examines the use of alternative dispute resolution—where forums other than courts attempt to resolve conflicts. Together, these chapters cast light on the important role played by courts in making law and also suggest some of the serious shortcomings of judicial lawmaking in the United States.

THE STRUCTURE OF THE AMERICAN COURT SYSTEM

In reality, there are two separate and independent court systems operating in the United States: the federal judiciary created by the U.S. Constitution and various congressional statutes, and the state court systems created by state constitutions and statutes. Each state court system operates independently of other systems, using laws that are crafted by its own state legislature. All of these courts are largely insulated from each other, and it is fairly rare to have the same case heard by courts in different systems. In a very real sense, there are fifty different state court systems, all distinct in terms of the kinds of laws that they craft. Strangely, the best-known cases are those that are least common—that is, those cases that move from a state court system to the U.S. Supreme Court. Relatively few cases "jump" from one system to another, and nearly all cases remain in the court system in which they begin.

Dual Court System: Federal and State Courts

While there are many different court systems, there is a surprising uniformity in their structure. As shown in Figure 6.1, every federal and state court system has a three-tiered structure, which can be thought of as a pyramid—the "bottom" layer is the widest and has the largest number of cases; the middle and top layers have a progressively smaller number of cases. At the bottom of every pyramid are the trial courts. In the state courts, this bottom layer is itself two-tiered: state trial courts are composed of courts of limited jurisdiction as well as those of general jurisdiction. **Courts of limited jurisdiction** have responsibility for hearing only certain kinds of cases, like traffic or family cases; **courts of general jurisdiction** have much wider authority and can hear cases involving a greater range of issues. Limited jurisdiction courts greatly outnumber courts of general jurisdiction: there are 13,515 state courts of limited jurisdiction and only 2,040 general jurisdiction courts. And maybe not surprisingly, there are many more cases heard in courts of limited jurisdiction than there are in general jurisdiction trial courts. In fact, limited jurisdiction courts handle 66 percent of the state cases; only 34 percent of the cases are heard by general jurisdiction courts. Limited jurisdiction courts include small claims courts, domestic relations or family courts, juvenile courts, and traffic courts. In addition, limited jurisdiction courts usually handle much of the preliminary work in cases involving felony criminal charges.

State cases can move from limited to general jurisdiction trial courts, but to make this move, the parties must meet certain jurisdictional requirements. Typically, the case must involve a certain amount of money, a statutory or constitutional right, or a felony criminal charge. While state courts have both limited and general jurisdiction courts, federal district courts—the trial courts of the federal system—are only courts of limited jurisdiction. There are only two ways that you can have your case heard in these courts: either your case must involve some federal question (typically a federal statutory, regulatory, or constitutional claim), or there must be **diversity of citizenship**—that is, where citizens of two or more states are parties to lawsuits involving more than $75,000 in claims. If claimants fail to meet these requirements, the federal court will refuse to hear their case, and they will be forced to go to the state courts instead. Why should it matter if your case is heard in a state or federal court? As we'll be talking about in this chapter, federal and state laws often differ on the same subject, and sometimes these variations are quite significant, especially as the dispute moves from the trial to the appellate levels.

At the middle layer of both the federal and state systems are the **intermediate courts of appeals**, which provide a forum for those who are unhappy with the trial court's decision. The federal government and most state governments

courts of limited jurisdiction

courts that have responsibility for hearing only certain kinds of cases; exist in federal and state court systems

courts of general jurisdiction

courts with wide authority that can hear cases involving a range of issues; exist only in the state court system

diversity of citizenship

one of the two ways that cases come to the federal district court—to have diversity jurisdiction, the parties must be from different states and the case must involve at least $75,000

intermediate courts of appeals

courts that provide answers to questions of law that have arisen in trial courts; exist in both the federal and state systems; the federal and most state systems guarantee at least one appellate hearing

FIGURE 6.1
The State Court
System

SUPREME COURT

The state's court of last resort for appeals in civil and criminal cases: A state may have a single supreme court (48 states) or separate courts for civil and for criminal appeals (Oklahoma and Texas).

Name of court: Supreme Court (46 states), Court of Appeals (Maryland, New York), Supreme Judicial Court (Maine, Massachusetts), Court of Criminal Appeals (Oklahoma, Texas).

Number of justices: Varies from state to state; 3 justices (Oklahoma's Court of Criminal Appeals), 5 justices (16 states), 7 justices (26 states), and 9 justices (6 states).

▲

INTERMEDIATE COURT OF APPEALS

The state's main appellate court, handling routine appeals and subject to review in some cases by the state supreme court (39 states).

Name of court: Varies from state to state; most frequent is Court of Appeals (28 states).

Number of justices: Ranges from 3 (Alabama, Alaska, Hawaii, Idaho) to 88 (California); 27 states have 10 or more judges.

▲

TRIAL COURTS OF GENERAL JURISDICTION

Found in all states, the trial courts for more serious criminal and civil cases: may hear appeals from trial courts of limited jurisdiction.

Name of court: Varies from state to state; most frequent names are Circuit Court (15 states), District Court (16 states), and Superior Court (14 states).

Number of judges: More than 7,500 judges.

Jurisdiction: On the basis of geography (judicial districts) and subject matter (cases not delegated to trial courts of limited jurisdiction).

▲

TRIAL COURTS OF LIMITED JURISDICTION

Found in all but six states, the trial courts for less serious criminal and civil cases: may also handle preliminary matters, such as arraignments and preliminary examinations in more serious cases.

Number of judges: More than 13,000 judges.

Jurisdiction: Usually on the basis of geography (for example, municipal courts), although may also be specialized on the basis of subject matter (for example, traffic court) or the amount involved (for example, small claims court).

allow for a mandatory appeal at this level—meaning that most Americans have the right to at least this one appeal, provided that they allege the lower court has made an error in its interpretation of the law, and that they can pay for it or have counsel appointed to them in criminal suits. The federal appellate courts, known as the courts of appeals or the circuit courts, are divided into regions or circuits, numbered from one to eleven. They include the circuit for the federal circuit and the District of Columbia (see Figure 6.2 for geographic distribution). The exception to the rule that the dissatisfied party has the right to one appeal is the **double jeopardy** provision, which applies to both the federal and state governments and which bars the prosecutor from retrying a case against a criminal defendant who has been acquitted of charges. Double jeopardy protects only against a second trial *identical* to the first—it does not protect a defendant from being charged with the violation of other laws or the commission of other crimes not brought up in the initial trial. This is why some criminal defendants who are

double jeopardy

protection guaranteed by the Fifth Amendment and most state constitutions that assures that a defendant in a criminal case cannot be tried more than once for a single crime

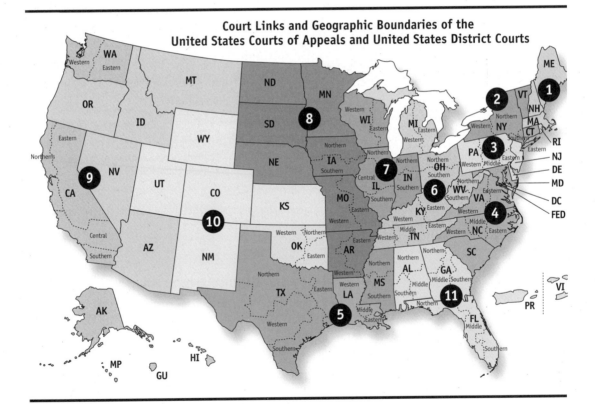

FIGURE 6.2
The Geographic Distribution of the Federal Courts of Appeals

acquitted of charges in a criminal trial may be sued and found liable of civil charges and why some defendants may be acquitted in one state but convicted in another. For example, Terry Nichols, who was found guilty of violating federal law for his role in the bombing of the Oklahoma City federal building in 1995, was also charged under Oklahoma law for committing murder. While his coconspirator, Timothy McVeigh, was put to death in 2001 for his part in the bombing, Nichols had been spared the death penalty by a federal jury. The goal of prosecutors in the state case was to convince the jury that capital punishment was the appropriate punishment for him. Like its federal counterpart, the jury in the state case deadlocked, and Nichols was not subjected to capital punishment.

court of last resort

exists in both the federal and state systems; court that hears appeals almost exclusively, and almost all of these are at the discretion of the judges or justices

Finally, at the top tier of both the federal and state systems is the **court of last resort**. In the federal system, this is the U.S. Supreme Court; in the state systems, this court goes by a variety of names, including the state supreme court, court of appeals, and superior court. Almost all cases brought to this top level are appellate cases, and nearly all of these are discretionary, meaning that the judges on this court have the right to choose whether or not to hear this case. It is popular, in the American vernacular, to speak of "taking one's case all the way to the Supreme Court." In reality, however, very few cases make it to the high court, since the justices exercise almost complete control over which cases they want to hear.

jurisdiction

the power to hear and resolve a case; created by federal or state constitutions or statute

The authority of a court to hear a case and resolve it is called **jurisdiction**, and jurisdiction is created by either the federal or state constitutions or by statute. For example, the jurisdiction of the U.S. Supreme Court is laid out in Article III, Section 2, of the U.S. Constitution, which establishes that "[t]he judicial Power shall extend to all Cases, in Law and Equity, arising under this Constitution, the Laws of the United States, and Treaties made, or which shall be made, under their Authority . . ." This means that the Supreme Court, or federal courts in general, can only hear cases that implicate issues involving the federal Constitution, laws, or treaties, or cases involving diversity of citizenship. The Constitution created only one specific court, that is, the Supreme Court, and left it to Congress to establish additional federal courts. Congress responded by creating both federal trial courts and appellate courts. And as the workload of these federal courts has grown, the number of courts has also increased. The jurisdiction of federal courts is strictly limited, and these courts are not able to hear other kinds of cases. All other issues or controversies are to be resolved by state law and by state courts. Like the federal court system, the state courts are creatures of both state constitutional law and legislative enactments. They create state courts and confer jurisdiction on these courts to apply and interpret state laws. For example, Article VIII, Section 1, of West Virginia's Constitution states that "[t]he judicial power of the state shall be vested solely in a supreme court of appeals and in the circuit courts, and in such intermediate appellate courts and magistrate courts as shall be hereafter established by the Legislature, and in the justices, judges and magistrates of such courts."

In both the federal and state systems, jurisdiction can change, as legislatures sometimes decide to reduce or expand the number of cases heard by their courts. The U.S. Congress has absolute power over the jurisdiction of the U.S. Supreme Court as it relates to appellate cases. Congress can decide to limit, or even eliminate, certain kinds of appeals from the Court's docket. In reality, Congress has only rarely taken this dramatic step; however, whenever there is anger or dissatisfaction with a Supreme Court holding, there are some legislators who argue that the Court should not be allowed to hear cases involving the underlying issue in the case. For example, for many years after *Roe* v. *Wade* struck down restrictive state abortion laws, some legislators in Congress argued that abortion cases should be eliminated from the Court's appellate jurisdiction. Had these legislators been successful, they probably could have removed abortion cases from the Court's docket.

Most of the action, in terms of sheer numbers, is in the separate state judiciaries, largely because the vast majority of laws that affect people within the United States are passed by state legislatures and implemented by state administrators and courts. In 2001, there were nearly 93 million filings in the state courts and fewer than 3 million filings in the federal courts. For that year, more than half the federal workload consisted of bankruptcy filings, which can only be heard by federal courts. Relatively few criminal and civil cases were heard by the federal courts, especially compared with the state courts. In 2001, federal courts disposed of about 300,000 filings, as contrasted with state courts, which heard nearly 30 million civil and criminal cases.

State law governs most relationships and day-to-day activities. For example, criminal laws are largely state laws, and every state has a detailed code that lays out prohibited activities and establishes penalties for engaging in those activities. State penal codes vary, and some states criminalize

Roe v. Wade

1973 U.S. Supreme Court case that struck down restrictive abortion laws and established that the right to privacy encompassed the right to choose abortion

TABLE 6.1
Examining the Work of State Courts

Cases Filed in State Trial Courts by Jurisdiction, 2002 (in millions)			
		Jurisdiction	
Case Type	Total	Unified/General	Limited
Traffic	57.6	14.1	43.5
Civil	16.3	7.7	8.6
Criminal	15.4	5.5	9.9
Domestic	4.6	3.3	1.3
Juvenile	2.0	1.3	0.7
Total	95.9	31.9	64.0

Note: Totals may not sum due to rounding.

activities that others do not. This variation among state laws is apparent in areas other than criminal law, as well. For example, marriage is governed by state law—if you want to get married, you have to meet requirements established by the law of the state in which you choose marry. You must apply for a marriage license, and you must have the marriage officiated by someone recognized by the state. Most professionals—for example, physicians, lawyers, and accountants, along with barbers and plumbers—are licensed under state law, which establishes the criteria that must be met for licensure. Many cities and counties also have their own municipal laws. For example, many municipalities passed laws prohibiting the use of hand-held cell phones while driving and smoking in public places long before state legislatures responded with their own laws.

The responsibility of state courts is to adjudicate claims arising under state law. Just as there is significant variation in the statutory laws in place among states, there are also considerable differences in the kinds of laws crafted by judges who are adjudicating cases in the state courts. Like state legislatures, state judges are under no obligation to ensure that their decisions are consistent with the decisions of judges in other states. For this reason, state common law can be very distinct, and judges may have very different approaches to the cases that they hear. Consider how differently judges in two different states disposed of the question of whether gun makers are liable for the injuries caused by their products. **Products liability law** governs the manufacture, sale, and distribution of goods that may pose a risk of harm to users or to other parties. This area of the law is created largely through the decisions of state courts, and in these two cases, the courts disagree on the issue of gun makers' liability. In the first case, *Ganim v. Smith & Wesson,* the Connecticut Supreme Court dismissed the case, finding that the City of Bridgeport and its officials lacked standing to bring the suit, since they had not alleged any specific legal right that had been infringed; in the second case, *City of Chicago v. Beretta USA Corp.,* an Illinois appellate court allowed the city's lawsuit to be brought, finding that the public nuisance law provided a legal foundation for its claims.

The two products liability cases suggest that courts in different states may have very different ideas about how the law should be interpreted. In these cases, both courts considered whether public nuisance law could be used to find that gun manufacturers were liable for injuries caused by their product. The variability across states is apparent, not only in products liability law, but in other areas, as well. For example, states have different requirements for imposition of the death penalty. When the so-called "D.C. Snipers," Lee Boyd Malvo, age 17, and John Allen Muhammad, age 42, were apprehended in the fall of 2002 after engaging in a killing spree that left thirteen dead in Virginia, Maryland, Alabama, Georgia, Louisiana, and Washington, D.C., there was significant wrangling over which entity would be able to try the suspects first. Ultimately, the contest was between the two states with

products liability law

law—mostly state law—governing the manufacture, sale, and distribution of goods that may pose a risk of harm to users or third parties

Ganim v. Smith & Wesson

the Connecticut Supreme Court dismissed this case, finding that city officials had no standing to bring a suit against gun manufacturers to recover damages for gun-related harm

City of Chicago v. Beretta USA Corp.

the Illinois appellate court allowed this case against gun manufacturers to proceed, based on public nuisance law

www ▶ ▶ ▶

the largest number of victims, Virginia and Maryland. Virginia, which allows capital punishment for minors, won this contest, after Maryland, which prohibits the imposition of death for juveniles, allowed its neighbor to take the lead. Bear in mind that any of the other states could also bring charges against the two suspects, and if convicted, these men would have to serve time for these state crimes.

Dual Court System: Trial and Appellate Courts

The American court system is actually dual in two ways: not only are there both state and federal courts, but these courts are also divided into trial and appellate levels. These federal and state trial and appellate courts have a different structure and a profoundly different function. In a **trial court**, the two opposing sides present to the judge or jury their version of the dispute or injury that is at issue. Often, there is significant disagreement about how a controversy arose or about the injuries that have been sustained. The sole function of the **fact-finder**, that is, the judge or jury, is to decide on the facts and to accept one party's version of what has happened. Because the trial court's sole function is to settle the facts in a case, this court is structured to facilitate fact-finding. Both parties are encouraged to present evidence and witnesses to support their version of what happened, and there are complex rules that govern the introduction of this evidence and these statements. Once the fact-finder determines the facts in the case, they are then obligated to apply the law as it has been interpreted by other courts. The trial process itself is strictly regulated by both federal and state constitutional law and statutory law. For example, **warrantless searches** by law enforcement personnel in criminal investigations are generally prohibited by both state and federal constitutional law, and prosecutors are usually prohibited from using this evidence at trial. Consider what was at issue in the case below. Specifically, focus on what the court ruled in this case, and how it applied the law.

While the principal function of trial courts is to determine the facts in a case and to apply the existing law to resolve the dispute or enforce the parties' rights, the function of an appeals court is much more complicated. An **appellate court** is not responsible for figuring out what happened in a case—that is left to the trial court. Instead, appellate courts concentrate on interpreting the laws that are at issue. Trial courts apply existing law; appellate courts interpret or resolve conflicts between laws. The focus in a trial is effectuating the rights of the parties, but in an appeals court, the focus is on the law—in fact, the parties become less important as cases "move up" through the appellate courts. There are at least two tiers of appeals courts—an intermediate tier of courts and a court of last resort. In some rare cases, courts may move from the state to the federal level, and where this happens,

---

trial court

court that resolves factual questions; engages in fact-finding and applies law

fact-finder

either a judge or jury in a trial court

warrantless searches

searches that take place without a warrant; if there is no valid exception to the warrant requirement, a judge can refuse to admit evidence from warrantless searches

appellate court

court with responsibility for deciding whether the law was applied correctly in the trial case

LAW IN ACTION

Fact-Finding in Trial Courts

ANTRON WASHINGTON, AS PARENT AND NEXT FRIEND OF TIFFANY WASHINGTON, PLAINTIFF, V. JEFF DEYOUNG, PAUL BOHNEY, AND WALGREEN CO., DEFENDANTS. U.S. DISTRICT COURT, N.D. ILLINOIS, EASTERN DIVISION, 2004 NO. 03 C 3161. JULY 29, 2004. MEMORANDUM OPINION AND ORDER

`www ▶ ▶ ▶` (See *Law, Politics, and Society* website for a link to the complete decision.)

DARRAH, J.

Plaintiff, Antron Washington ("Washington"), as parent and next friend of Tiffany Washington ("Plaintiff"), filed suit against Defendants, alleging racial discrimination in violation of 42 U.S.C. §§ 1981 and 1982. Presently before the Court is Defendants' Motion for Summary Judgment.

BACKGROUND

Paul Bohney is a Caucasian male who was the manager of the Walgreen's Park Forest, Illinois store. Bohney has been employed as a manager at Walgreen for fifteen years and has been assigned to several stores, including the Park Forest store. Jeff DeYoung is a Caucasian male who was an assistant manager at Walgreen's Park Forest store. DeYoung has been an assistant manager for Walgreen for seventeen years. Tiffany Gray is an African-American female teenager who attended eighth grade at Forest Trail Middle School during the 2001–2002 school year. Jameca Lipscomb and Alicia Shivers are also two African-American female teenagers who attended eighth grade at Forest Trail Middle School during the 2001–2002 school year.

Walgreen prohibits discrimination against employees, customers, vendors, and all other persons with respect to employment decisions, the making and enforcing of contracts, its sales practices, and its loss prevention and security practices. Walgreen's orientation guide states that all customers are to be served fully and fairly. It is Walgreen's pledge to treat all people "without regard to race, national origin, religion, sex, age . . ." Walgreen trains its employees, supervisors, and managers that the company prohibits discrimination as described above . . .

The Park Forest Walgreen store is located in a racially mixed community. At least half of the store's customers are African-American. During the 2001–2002 school year, the Park Forest store employed both African-American and Caucasian employees . . .

During the 2001–2002 school year, African-American and Caucasian customers, including middle school students, were often in the Walgreen store after school and purchased merchandise from the store. Virtually every weekday afternoon during the 2001–2002 school year, large groups of African-American and Caucasian middle school students went into the Park Forest Walgreen after school. Walgreen's employees increased their monitoring of the store when the groups of middle school students came into the store because of problems the store was having with these students. The students were often disruptive, rowdy, profane,

LAW IN ACTION—(CONT'D)

and rude to staff and other customers. The students often blocked the entrance and exits to the store, blocked aisle traffic, and engaged in fighting and play-fighting in the store and outside the store. Some middle school students were caught or suspected of stealing and damaging the store's products. The police were called on several occasions to handle problems with middle school students inside and outside the store . . .

Virtually every weekday between September 2001 and May 9, 2002, Plaintiff and two of her middle school friends went into and purchased items from the Park Forest Walgreen store after being dismissed from school . . . While in the store, Plaintiff believed that DeYoung followed her or watched her too closely. Plaintiff also alleges that when she and her friends went into the store, she heard a "code" called out over the store's announcement system. DeYoung's conduct nor the announcement of the code did not stop Plaintiff from going into or purchasing items at the store. Plaintiff never observed Caucasian customers being watched or followed by Walgreen's management. However, Plaintiff did observe other African-American customers being watched and followed by management.

Prior to May 10, 2002, DeYoung saw Plaintiff in the Walgreen store and believed that she and her friends were being disruptive and using foul language. DeYoung had also previously asked Plaintiff and her friends not to stand in the magazine aisle and read the magazines without purchasing the magazines. On one occasion when DeYoung asked Plaintiff and her friends not to read the magazines, Plaintiff believed that DeYoung had an "attitude . . ."

On one occasion, prior to May 10, 2002, DeYoung "locked" the automatic door to the Walgreen store, stood in the door, and told Plaintiff that she would have to show him her money if she wanted to enter the store. Plaintiff did not ask why DeYoung requested to see her money and did not show him any money. Prior to this date, DeYoung had not asked Plaintiff to leave the store nor had DeYoung made any comments to Plaintiff or her friends about her race.

Plaintiff and her friends went to the Walgreen store on May 10, 2002. Plaintiff went to the aisle that stocks potato chips. Plaintiff did not know what her friends were doing while she was in the aisle that stocks potato chips. As Plaintiff returned to her friends, DeYoung asked Plaintiff and her friends to leave the store because he believed that they had been in the store for a significant period of time without making a purchase and that one or more of them were being disruptive and profane. Plaintiff believes that DeYoung had an "attitude" when he told them to leave the store, telling them to "get out." Plaintiff did not ask DeYoung why he was asking her and her friends to leave the store. Plaintiff did not purchase the bag of potato chips that were in her hand and left the store . . .

After leaving the store on May 10, 2002, Plaintiff went home and told her mother and stepfather that Walgreen's assistant manager had asked her and her friends to leave the store. Less than thirty minutes after she had been asked to leave the store, Plaintiff returned to the store with her family and two friends. Plaintiff's stepfather, Washington, approached DeYoung and asked him why Plaintiff had been asked to leave

LAW IN ACTION–(CONT'D)

the store. DeYoung did not give Washington a specific answer but informed him about the problems the store was having with middle school students. Washington also asked Bohney why Plaintiff was asked to leave the store. Bohney told Washington that he did not know why Plaintiff had been asked to leave the store . . .

A few days after May 10, 2002, Washington sent a letter to one of Walgreen's then-district managers, Cheryl Gidcumb, complaining about DeYoung's treatment of Plaintiff. Shortly after he sent the letter, Gidcumb telephoned Washington and advised him that she would investigate his complaint. Gidcumb did not again contact Washington, and Washington did not contact her . . .

When Plaintiff was in the Walgreen store, she did not pay much attention to who else was in the store and/or whether those other persons were buying anything. Plaintiff believes that a Caucasian boy who was in the store on May 10, 2002, was treated better than she was treated. Plaintiff does not know the Caucasian boy's name nor how often he came into the store, how he conducted himself in the store, and whether he typically came into the store alone or with other students. Plaintiff observed the boy in the store both when she first entered the store and later, when she returned with her parents.

DeYoung and Bohney testified that they have asked non-African-American persons to leave the Walgreen store . . .

ANALYSIS

Summary judgment is proper if "the pleadings, depositions, answers to interrogatories, and admissions on file, together with affidavits, if any, show that there is no genuine issue as to any material fact." Fed.R.Civ.P. 56(c); *see also Celotex Corp.* v. *Catrett,* 477 U.S. 317, 322–23, (1986) (*Celotex*) . . . Summary judgment may be granted when no "reasonable jury could return a verdict for the nonmoving party." *Anderson* v. *Liberty Lobby, Inc.,* 477 U.S. 242, 248 1986) (*Anderson*).

Section 1981 prohibits discrimination in the making and enforcement of contracts. 42 U.S.C. § 1981(a). Under Section 1981, "making or enforcing" a contract includes the "making, performance, modification, and termination of contracts, and the enjoyment of all benefits, privileges, terms, and conditions of the contractual relationship." 42 U.S.C. § 1981(b). Similarly, Section 1982 prohibits discrimination in the purchase of personal property. 42 U.S.C. § 1982 . . .

To establish a claim under Section 1981, a plaintiff must show that: (1) she is a member of a racial minority; (2) the defendant had an intent to discriminate on the basis of race; and (3) the discrimination deprived the plaintiff of one or more of the rights enumerated in Section 1981, *i.e.,* the making and enforcement of a contract . . . Likewise, to establish a cause of action under Section 1982, a plaintiff must show that: (1) she is a member of a racial minority; (2) the defendant had an intent to discriminate on the basis of race; and (3) the discrimination deprived the plaintiff of one or more of the rights enumerated in Section 1982, *i.e.,* the purchase of personal property . . .

A *prima facie* case under Sections 1981 and 1982 include evidence that (1) the plaintiff is a member of a racial minority, (2) the defen-

LAW IN ACTION-(CONT'D)

dant had an intent to discriminate on the basis of race, and (3) the discrimination concerned one or more of the activities enumerated in the statute . . .

The parties do not dispute that the Plaintiff is a member of a racial minority. Defendants argue that the Plaintiff has failed to present evidence that the Defendants intended to discriminate against her because of her race. Defendants identify several undisputed facts which demonstrate that Plaintiff was allowed to purchase items at the store and that other African-Americans were also allowed into the store and allowed to purchase items prior to and after May 10, 2002. However, Plaintiff also testified in her deposition that only African-Americans were followed and watched while in the store and that when she entered the store, a "code" was broadcast over the intercom system; this same code was not broadcast when Caucasians entered the store. DeYoung and Plaintiff also have differing renditions of what occurred prior to DeYoung's asking the Plaintiff and her friends to leave the store as to whether Plaintiff and/or her friends were engaged in any conduct calling for DeYoung's ordering Plaintiff and her friends from the store. Furthermore, on May 10, 2002, a Caucasian juvenile was in the store for an extended period of time but was not asked to leave the store. Based on the above, genuine issues of material fact exist as to whether DeYoung's actions were racially motivated. Defendants also argue that the Plaintiff has failed to present evidence that she was denied the right to make a contract—to purchase the potato chips—because she never expressed her desire to purchase the chips before she left the store. However, when DeYoung told the Plaintiff and her friends to exit the store, Plaintiff had a bag of potato chips in her possession. After DeYoung ordered Plaintiff and her friends to leave the store, Plaintiff did not purchase the potato chips. These facts demonstrate a genuine issue of material fact exists as to whether DeYoung's conduct prevented Plaintiff from purchasing the potato chips. While DeYoung did not explicitly state that Plaintiff could not purchase the chips, he did order her to exit the store before she had the opportunity to purchase the chips that were in her possession.

Furthermore, Plaintiff has produced sufficient evidence from which a rational factfinder could infer that DeYoung's proffered reason for asking Plaintiff and her friends to exit the store was a pretext to discrimination. This evidence includes the disputed conduct of the Plaintiff and her friends prior to being ordered to leave the store and the disputed evidence of DeYoung's conduct toward Plaintiff prior to May 10, 2002 . . .

CONCLUSION

For the foregoing reasons, Defendants' Motion for Summary Judgment is granted in part and denied in part. The Motion for Summary Judgment is granted as to Plaintiff's claims against Bohney as an individual defendant and as to Walgreen for Plaintiff's claim for punitive damages. The Motion for Summary Judgment is denied as to all other claims.

N.D.Ill., 2004.

LAW IN ACTION—(CONT'D)

QUESTIONS

1. What did the federal district court rule in this case? Specifically, what factual question did this court resolve?
2. On which law did this court rely? Remember, trial courts take the law *as given;* they do not engage in legal interpretation.
3. What is summary judgment? What will happen with this case next?

they are almost always heard by the U.S. Supreme Court, which is the court of last resort for the entire nation.

Because appeals courts resolve questions of law, their structure is very different from that of trial courts. While trial courts typically have more participants, that is, they have the parties, their witnesses, including expert witnesses, and the fact-finders, appeals courts almost always include only the parties and the judges. There are no juries in an appeals court, because the sole function of a jury is to decide fact in a case. Since there are no facts at issue in an appeals case, there is no need for a jury. On appeal, there are no new factual questions introduced, and the appeals court will accept whatever determination of the facts has been reached by the judge or jury below. There are no jurors and no witnesses; instead, there is usually a panel of judges, ranging in number from three to twelve, depending on the court. Usually, intermediate level courts of appeals are composed of three judges; however, this is not always the case. For example, the courts of appeals in the federal system are made up of either three judges or all of the judges on the court. Typically, each court of appeals has up to twelve judges, and in some cases, the court will agree to hear a case *en banc,* meaning that it will hear the case with all judges present. Courts of last resort in the state and federal system are usually made up of a number of judges. For example, the U.S. Supreme Court is made up of nine justices. Where there is more than one judge, decision making is governed by majority rule—that is, a majority of the judges needs to reach agreement for the case to be decided.

collegial court

a court over which more than one judge or justice presides; members must work together to achieve agreement

This kind of court, where the judges need to work together to reach agreement, is called a **collegial court.** The judges or justices do not always agree about how a law should be interpreted, and sometimes a judge or justice will dissent from the decision reached by a majority of his or her brethren. In some cases, the judge or justice will write his or her own dissenting opinion, and in this opinion, he or she will lay out the reasons for

(See *Law, Politics, and Society* website for a link to the complete decision.)

majority opinion

court opinion that reflects the decision of the majority of judges or justices

concurring opinions

on a collegial court, the decisions reached by those judges or justices who do not agree with the reasoning of the majority

dissenting opinions

on a collegial court, the decisions reached by those judges or justices who do not agree with the decision reached by the majority

disagreeing with the majority. Judges or justices may also agree with the ultimate decision reached by the majority but write separately to explain how they think the decision should have been written. These separate opinions are called concurrences. In some cases, there may be a number of opinions written: there may be the **majority opinion**, that is, the opinion that reflects the decision of a majority of the judges or justices; and one or more **concurring opinions** and **dissenting opinions**, which lay out different approaches to the question at issue. In the following case, consider the central issue at play: here the U.S. Supreme Court was considering how to interpret two laws passed by Congress to deal with extortion—the Hobbs Act and the Racketeer Influenced and Corrupt Organizations Act (RICO). Note that Chief Justice William Rehnquist, who wrote the majority opinion, argued that laws should be interpreted to limit their application to antiabortion protestors, but Justice John Paul Stevens argued in his dissenting opinion that the laws could be used to limit protest activity that interfered with women's access to abortion. Again, note that there are no factual disagreements in this case—the Court takes as a given that Scheidler has attempted to block access to abortion clinics.

LAW IN ACTION

Legal Analysis and Interpretation in Appellate Courts

SCHEIDLER ET AL. V. NATIONAL ORGANIZATION FOR WOMEN, INC., ET AL., U.S. SUPREME COURT, 2003

`www ▶ ▶ ▶` (See *Law, Politics, and Society* website for a link to the complete decision.)

Rehnquist, C. J., delivered the opinion of the Court, in which *O'Connor, Scalia, Kennedy, Souter, Thomas, Ginsburg,* and *Breyer, J.,* joined. *Ginsburg, J.,* filed a concurring opinion, in which *Breyer, J.,* joined. *Stevens, J.,* filed a dissenting opinion.

Chief Justice REHNQUIST delivered the opinion of the Court.

We granted certiorari in these cases to answer two questions. First, whether petitioners committed extortion within the meaning of the Hobbs Act, 18 U.S.C. §1951. Second, whether respondents, as private litigants, may obtain injunctive relief in a civil action pursuant to 18 U.S.C. §1964 of the Racketeer Influenced and Corrupt Organizations Act (RICO). We hold that petitioners did not commit extortion because they did not "obtain" property from respondents as required by the Hobbs Act. We further hold that our determination with respect to

LAW IN ACTION—(CONT'D)

extortion under the Hobbs Act renders insufficient the other bases or predicate acts of racketeering supporting the jury's conclusion that petitioners violated RICO. Therefore, we reverse without reaching the question of the availability of private injunctive relief under §1964(c) of RICO.

We once again address questions arising from litigation between petitioners, a coalition of antiabortion groups called the Pro-Life Action Network (PLAN), Joseph Scheidler and other individuals and organizations that oppose legal abortion, and respondents, the National Organization for Women, Inc. (NOW), a national nonprofit organization that supports the legal availability of abortion, and two health care centers that perform abortions. Our earlier decision provides a substantial description of the factual and procedural history of this litigation, see *National Organization for Women, Inc.* v. *Scheidler,* 510 U.S. 249 (1994), and so we recount only those details necessary to address the questions here presented.

In 1986, respondents sued in the United States District Court for the Northern District of Illinois alleging, *inter alia*, that petitioners violated RICO's §§1962(a), (c), and (d). They claimed that petitioners, all of whom were associated with PLAN, the alleged racketeering enterprise, were members of a nationwide conspiracy to "shut down" abortion clinics through a pattern of racketeering activity that included acts of extortion in violation of the Hobbs Act.

The District Court dismissed respondents' RICO claims for failure to allege that the predicate acts of racketeering or the racketeering enterprise were economically motivated. See *National Organization for Women, Inc.* v.

Scheidler, 765 F. Supp. 937 (ND Ill. 1991). The Court of Appeals for the Seventh Circuit affirmed that dismissal. See *National Organization for Women, Inc.* v. *Scheidler,* 968 F. 2d 612 (1992). We granted certiorari and reversed, concluding that RICO does not require proof that either the racketeering enterprise or the predicate acts of racketeering were motivated by an economic purpose. See *Scheidler,* 510 U.S., at 256-262. The case was remanded to the District Court for further proceedings.

After a 7-week trial, a six-member jury concluded that petitioners violated the civil provisions of RICO. By answering a series of special interrogatory questions, the jury found, *inter alia,* that petitioners' alleged "pattern of racketeering activity" included 21 violations of the Hobbs Act, 18 U.S.C. §1951; 25 violations of state extortion law; 25 instances of attempting or conspiring to commit either federal or state extortion; 23 violations of the Travel Act, 18 U.S.C. §1952; and 23 instances of attempting to violate the Travel Act. The jury awarded $31,455.64 to respondent, the National Women's Health Organization of Delaware, Inc., and $54,471.28 to the National Women's Health Organization of Summit, Inc. These damages were trebled pursuant to §1964(c). Additionally, the District Court entered a permanent nationwide injunction prohibiting petitioners from obstructing access to the clinics, trespassing on clinic property, damaging clinic property, or using violence or threats of violence against the clinics, their employees, or their patients.

The Court of Appeals for the Seventh Circuit affirmed in relevant part . . .

We first address the question whether petitioners' actions constituted extortion in viola-

LAW IN ACTION—(CONT'D)

tion of the Hobbs Act. That Act defines extortion as "the obtaining of property from another, with his consent, induced by wrongful use of actual or threatened force, violence, or fear, or under color of official right." 18 U.S.C. §1951(b)(2). Petitioners allege that the jury's verdict and the Court of Appeals' decision upholding the verdict represent a vast and unwarranted expansion of extortion under the Hobbs Act . . .

Respondents, throughout the course of this litigation, have asserted, as the jury instructions at the trial reflected, that petitioners committed extortion under the Hobbs Act by using or threatening to use force, violence, or fear to cause respondents "to give up" property rights, namely, "a woman's right to seek medical services from a clinic, the right of the doctors, nurses or other clinic staff to perform their jobs, and the right of the clinics to provide medical services free from wrongful threats, violence, coercion and fear." Jury Instruction No. 24, App. 136. Perhaps recognizing the apparent difficulty in reconciling either its position that "giv[ing] up" these alleged property rights or the Court of Appeals' holding that "interfer[ing] with such rights" with the requirement that petitioners "obtain[ed] . . . property from" them, respondents have shifted the thrust of their theory. 267 F. 3d, at 267. Respondents now assert that petitioners violated the Hobbs Act by "seeking to get control of the use and disposition of respondents' property." Brief for Respondents *24*. They argue that because the right to control the use and disposition of an asset is property, petitioners, who interfered with, and in some instances completely disrupted, the ability of the clinics to function,

obtained or attempted to obtain respondents' property.

The United States offers a view similar to that of respondents, asserting that "where the property at issue is a business's *intangible* right to exercise exclusive control over the use of its assets, [a] defendant obtains that property by obtaining control over the use of those assets." Brief for United States as *Amicus Curiae 22*. Although the Government acknowledges that the jury's finding of extortion may have been improperly based on the conclusion that petitioners deprived respondents of a liberty interest, it maintains that under its theory of liability, petitioners committed extortion.

We need not now trace what are the outer boundaries of extortion liability under the Hobbs Act, so that liability might be based on obtaining something as intangible as another's right to exercise exclusive control over the use of a party's business assets . . . Whatever the outer boundaries may be, the effort to characterize petitioners' actions here as an "obtaining of property from" respondents is well beyond them. Such a result would be an unwarranted expansion of the meaning of that phrase.

Absent contrary direction from Congress, we begin our interpretation of statutory language with the general presumption that a statutory term has its common-law meaning . . . At common law, extortion was a property offense committed by a public official who took "any money or thing of value" that was not due to him under the pretense that he was entitled to such property by virtue of his office . . . In 1946, Congress enacted the Hobbs Act, which explicitly "expanded the common-law definition of extortion to include acts by private individuals . . ." While the Hobbs Act expanded

LAW IN ACTION—(CONT'D)

the scope of common-law extortion to include private individuals, the statutory language retained the requirement that property must be "obtained." See 18 U.S.C. §1951(b)(2).

Congress used two sources of law as models in formulating the Hobbs Act: the Penal Code of New York and the Field Code, a 19th-century model penal code. See *Evans, supra,* at 262. Both the New York statute and the Field Code defined extortion as "the obtaining of property from another with his consent, induced by a wrongful use of force or fear or under color of official right . . ." The Field Code explained that extortion was one of four property crimes, along with robbery, larceny, and embezzlement that included "the criminal acquisition of . . . property." §584 note, p. 210. New York case law before the enactment of the Hobbs Act demonstrates that this "obtaining of property" requirement included both a deprivation and acquisition of property . . .

We too have recognized that the "obtaining" requirement of extortion under New York law entailed both a deprivation and acquisition of property . . . Most importantly, we have construed the extortion provision of the Hobbs Act at issue in this case to require not only the deprivation but also the acquisition of property. See, *e.g., Enmons, supra,* at 400 . . . With this understanding of the Hobbs Act's requirement that a person must "obtain" property from another party to commit extortion, we turn to the facts of these cases.

There is no dispute in these cases that petitioners interfered with, disrupted, and in some instances completely deprived respondents of their ability to exercise their property rights. Likewise, petitioners' counsel readily acknowl-edged at oral argument that aspects of his clients' conduct were criminal. But even when their acts of interference and disruption achieved their ultimate goal of "shutting down" a clinic that performed abortions, such acts did not constitute extortion because petitioners did not "obtain" respondents' property. Petitioners may have deprived or sought to deprive respondents of their alleged property right of exclusive control of their business assets, but they did not acquire any such property. Petitioners neither pursued nor received "something of value from" respondents that they could exercise, transfer, or sell. *United States v. Nardello,* 393 U.S. 286, 290 (1969). To conclude that such actions constituted extortion would effectively discard the statutory requirement that property must be obtained from another, replacing it instead with the notion that merely interfering with or depriving someone of property is sufficient to constitute extortion.

Eliminating the requirement that property must be obtained to constitute extortion would not only conflict with the express requirement of the Hobbs Act, it would also eliminate the recognized distinction between extortion and the separate crime of coercion—a distinction that is implicated in these cases. The crime of coercion, which more accurately describes the nature of petitioners' actions, involves the use of force or threat of force to restrict another's freedom of action. Coercion's origin is statutory, and it was clearly defined in the New York Penal Code as a separate, and lesser offense than extortion when Congress turned to New York law in drafting the Hobbs Act. New York case law applying the coercion statute before the passage of the Hobbs Act

LAW IN ACTION–(CONT'D)

involved the prosecution of individuals who, like petitioners, employed threats and acts of force and violence to dictate and restrict the actions and decisions of businesses . . .

With this distinction between extortion and coercion clearly drawn in New York law prior to 1946, Congress' decision to include extortion as a violation of the Hobbs Act and omit coercion is significant assistance to our interpretation of the breadth of the extortion provision. This assistance is amplified by other evidence of Congress' awareness of the difference between these two distinct crimes . . .

Because we find that petitioners did not obtain or attempt to obtain property from

respondents, we conclude that there was no basis on which to find that they committed extortion under the Hobbs Act . . .

Because all of the predicate acts supporting the jury's finding of a RICO violation must be reversed, the judgment that petitioners violated RICO must also be reversed. Without an underlying RICO violation, the injunction issued by the District Court must necessarily be vacated. We therefore need not address the second question presented—whether a private plaintiff in a civil RICO action is entitled to injunctive relief under 18 U.S.C. §1964.

The judgment of the Court of Appeals is accordingly Reversed.

Justice STEVENS, dissenting.

The term "extortion" as defined in the Hobbs Act refers to "the obtaining of property from another." 18 U.S.C. §1951(b)(2). The Court's murky opinion seems to hold that this phrase covers nothing more than the acquisition of tangible property. No other federal court has ever construed this statute so narrowly.

For decades federal judges have uniformly given the term "property" an expansive construction that encompasses the intangible right to exercise exclusive control over the lawful use of business assets. The right to serve customers or to solicit new business is thus a protected property right. The use of violence or threats of violence to persuade the owner of a business to surrender control of such an intangible right is an appropriation of control embraced by the term "obtaining." That is the commonsense reading of the statute that other federal judges have consistently and wisely embraced in

numerous cases that the Court does not discuss or even cite. Recognizing this settled definition of property, as I believe one must, the conclusion that petitioners obtained this property from respondents is amply supported by the evidence in the record.

Because this construction of the Hobbs Act has been so uniform, I only discuss a few of the more significant cases. For example, in *United States* v. *Tropiano*, 418 F. 2d 1069 (1969), the Second Circuit held that threats of physical violence to persuade the owners of a competing trash removal company to refrain from soliciting customers in certain areas violated the Hobbs Act. The court's reasoning is directly applicable to these cases:

. . . The concept of property under the Hobbs Act, as devolved from its legislative history and numerous decisions, is not

LAW IN ACTION-(CONT'D)

limited to physical or tangible property or things (*United States* v. *Provenzano,* 334 F. 2d 678 (3d Cir. 1964); *United States* v. *Nedley,* 255 F. 2d 350 (3d Cir. 1958)), but includes, in a broad sense, any valuable right considered as a source or element of wealth (*Bianchi* v. *United States,* 219 F. 2d 182 (8th Cir. 1955)), and does not depend on a direct benefit being conferred on the person who obtains the property (*United States* v. *Green,* 350 U. S. 415 (1956)) . . .

The *Tropiano* case's discussion of obtaining property has been cited with approval by federal courts in virtually every circuit in the country . . . Its interpretation of the term "property" is consistent with pre-Hobbs Act decisions of this Court, see *Buchanan* v. *Warley,* 245 U.S. 60, 74 (1917) (property "consists of the free use, enjoyment, and disposal of a person's acquisitions without control or diminution"), the New York Court of Appeals, see *People* v. *Barondess,* 133 N.Y. 649, 31 N. E. 240 (1892), the California Supreme Court, *People* v. *Cadman,* 57 Cal. 562 (1881), and with our recent decision in *Carpenter* v. *United States,* 484 U.S. 19 (1987).

The courts that have considered the applicability of the Hobbs Act to attempts to disrupt the operations of abortion clinics have uniformly adhered to the holdings of cases like *Tropiano* . . . Judge Kearse's endorsement of the Government's position in *United States* v. *Arena,* 180 F. 3d 380 (CA2 1999), followed

this consistent line of cases. The jury had found that the defendants had engaged in "an overall strategy to cause abortion providers, particularly Planned Parenthood and Yoffa, to give up their property rights to engage in the business of providing abortion services for fear of future attacks." *Id.,* at 393 . . .

In my opinion Judge Kearse's analysis of the issue is manifestly correct. Even if the issue were close, however, three additional considerations provide strong support for her conclusion. First, the uniform construction of the statute that has prevailed throughout the country for decades should remain the law unless and until Congress decides to amend the statute. See *Reves* v. *Ernst & Young,* 494 U.S. 56, 74 (1990) . . . Second, both this Court and all other federal courts have consistently identified the Hobbs Act as a statute that Congress intended to be given a broad construction . . . Third, given the fact that Congress has enacted specific legislation responsive to the concerns that gave rise to these cases, the principal beneficiaries of the Court's dramatic retreat from the position that federal prosecutors and federal courts have maintained throughout the history of this important statute will certainly be the class of professional criminals whose conduct persuaded Congress that the public needed federal protection from extortion.

I respectfully dissent.

LAW IN ACTION-(CONT'D)

QUESTIONS

1. What was the history of this case?
2. What was the central holding of Chief Justice Rehnquist's decision? On what key question did Justice Stevens' dissenting opinion differ?
3. What is the impact of this case?
4. Imagine that you are NOW's legal counsel and it is the day after the Court has handed down this decision. How would you advise NOW to alter its legal strategy in the future? Do you think that RICO could be used to restrict the activities of pro-life/antiabortion protestors? If so, how would you advise using this law? In which factual scenarios could RICO be used? In which scenarios could the law *not* be used after *Scheidler?*

The opinions in this case suggest the extent to which appellate judges may disagree very strongly on how a law should be interpreted. Since judicial opinions create common law which binds all courts considering similar issues in the future, disagreement may be of critical importance. Dissenting opinions reflect a different view of how the law should be written, and in the past, dissents have later been used to craft majority holdings. For example, much of the reasoning in Justice Marshall Harlan's dissenting opinion in the 1896 case *Plessy* v. *Ferguson,* which allowed states to implement laws that segregated blacks from whites, was later employed by the Court in its 1954 case *Brown* v. *Board of Education,* which struck down segregationist laws. Again, the function of appellate courts is to interpret the law. It is important to note that judges or justices are not always in agreement about how a case should be handled, or about how the laws should be interpreted. Over time, these disagreements can become even more significant as various actors call for changes in the law.

PARTICIPANTS IN THE AMERICAN JUDICIAL SYSTEM

There are five key groups of participants in the American court system: juries, judges, litigants, lawyers, experts, and outside parties seeking to be heard. These participants play different roles in the litigation process, and over time these roles have changed, in part in response to changes in the functioning of courts. Perhaps most importantly, the evolution of law and the growing complexity in the kinds of cases heard by courts have placed substantial demands on all of these participants and have subtly altered the ways they can influence the lawmaking process.

Fact-Finders: Judges and Juries

At the trial court level, cases are presided over by judges, who have responsibility for fact-finding, either alone or with the assistance of a jury. The **right to a jury trial** is conferred by both the federal and state constitutions. Historically, the jury was intended to guard against abuses of power by the king or sovereign, and the right to a trial by jury was enshrined as early as 1215 in the Magna Carta. Initially, jury trials were intended to provide an alternative to the prevailing means of establishing fact in criminal cases. Throughout the Middle Ages, the facts of the case were determined by how the accused fared in any of a number of "ordeals," or trials, among these, the ordeals of water, glowing iron, or fire. According to the trial by iron or fire, a person accused of committing an act was compelled to walk on or carry a lump of burning coal or iron. The burn would be bandaged and examined in three days. If the burn was infected, the person was proven to be guilty; if the burn was healing or absent altogether, the person was adjudged to be innocent. Similarly, a person subject to the ordeal of water was thrown into cold water: if the accused floated, guilt was proven; if he or she sank, this proved innocence.

Clearly, there were some problems with these methods. First, many of the clerics who administered these ordeals were corrupt and willing to take bribes to ensure that the coals were not hot or that a wound would be found to be healing. Second, given the lack of antibiotics and the likelihood of death from either a burn or being thrown into cold water, the ordeals often meant death, regardless of whether one was actually guilty. Fact-finding through ordeals was enshrined in King William's Laws of Conquest, decreed after he conquered England in 1066. In these laws, William required that the accused defend himself through the ordeal of iron or wager of battle. Similarly, the ordeals of fire, iron, and water were portrayed in art, literature, and religion. Even now, we speak of a "trial by fire" as a test that must be overcome.

Jury trials were used more and more frequently in England throughout the 1500s and 1600s, and this right was firmly established in the British Bill of Rights, the Declaration of Independence, the constitutions of the former colonies, and the Sixth Amendment of the U.S. Constitution. This is one of those rights that many Americans view as absolute—but there are actually some serious limitations and constraints on the operation of the right. For example, there is no right to a jury trial in petty criminal cases, where a conviction would result in a prison term of less than six months. In addition, there is no right to a jury trial in certain kinds of cases—typically, those cases involving divorce and juvenile proceedings cannot be decided by a jury. In criminal cases, the jury is composed of twelve persons; in some state civil cases, the number may be less than twelve. In a series of cases heard since the 1980s, the U.S. Supreme Court has determined that the Sixth Amendment, along with the equal protection clause of the Fourteenth Amendment, bars the disqualification of jurors based on their race or sex. These cases ensure that the jury will be composed of the accused's peers and seek to eliminate the practice in some states of creating all-white or all-male juries.

bench or judge trial

trial in which the judge, rather than the jury, is the fact-finder

While one has a right to a jury trial in many criminal and civil cases, one also has the right to waive this jury trial in favor of a **bench or judge trial**. In criminal cases, the choice of whether to have a jury trial is in the hands of the person who has been charged; in civil cases, the two parties together choose whether to waive this right. The decision about whether to have a jury trial is based on an assessment of whether jurors will be more or less sympathetic to one's case than a judge might be. Most lawyers agree that jury trials are preferable in those cases in which the jurors would be sympathetic to their party's situation, but that bench trials are better in cases that are highly complicated or technical.

The role of the jury is to decide the facts of a case and to apply the law to these facts. In reality, however, there is nothing that strictly limits this role or prohibits a jury from interpreting or even disregarding the law. In fact, both John Adams and Thomas Jefferson noted that the jury trial served as a check on the lawmaking power of legislatures. This practice is called **jury nullification**. While judges almost always provide detailed instructions on the law to the jury, in theory, jurors have the right to disregard these instructions and make a decision based on their own assessment of the law. When juries engage in nullification, they may agree that a person has committed a crime but refuse to convict that person because they do not agree with the law, or they may act out of racial or gender prejudice or bias.

jury nullification

when a jury reaches a decision based, not on the facts, but on its interpretation or disregard of the law

While jury nullification is quite rare, it has a long historical record. The hit Broadway play and movie *Chicago* had its basis in the use of jury nullification in a series of cases heard by Chicago juries in the early 1900s. In these cases, women had killed their husbands or boyfriends after suffering repeated beatings at their hands. In these cases, there was no question that the women had murdered their husbands—in fact, in a number of cases, the women confessed to the police. And yet, juries disregarded this evidence and found them not guilty. More recently, juries in three separate cases engaged in nullification when they acquitted Dr. Jack Kevorkian of committing murder or manslaughter when he assisted with the suicide of three chronically ill people. A fourth trial ended in a mistrial, and it was only after Dr. Kevorkian videotaped the assisted suicide of a man suffering from Lou Gehrig's disease, sent the video tape to *60 Minutes,* and taunted the prosecutor's office that he would never be found guilty, that a Michigan jury convicted him of second degree murder. Jury nullification is very controversial—some echo the claims of Adams and Jefferson and see it as a check on the powers of courts and legislatures. Others warn that it can and has led to disparities in convictions and sentencing. They claim that jury nullification has allowed juries to look the other way when whites are charged with crimes against African Americans and to convict African Americans of more serious crimes than whites who have engaged in the same activities.

The number of jury trials in the United States appears to be on the decline, and in recent years, there have been serious questions raised about whether juries are representative of the population and about whether jury selection is itself tainted. Historically, **juror selection** has been guided by lawyers' folklore about what the best juror "looks like." Characteristics like race, age, sex, occupation, and religion, along with personal appearance and marital status, were assumed to provide hints of how a juror might decide in a given case. For example, the best jurors were assumed to be middle-aged men with sole responsibility for supporting their families engaged in white collar professions. Women were assumed to be "softer" on crime and criminals and more likely to vote with the injured party in civil suits. Similarly, the folklore said that African Americans were likely to vote with defendants in criminal cases and with injured plaintiffs in civil cases. Lawyers warned against having obese people on juries in civil suits, since they had less self-control and would more likely provide a windfall for the plaintiff; and against Catholics who would likely do the same. Cabinetmakers were to be avoided, since they were consumed with details and had difficulty seeing the big picture; nurses and teachers were members of "helping professions" and biased in favor of the disadvantaged in society. This folklore had little basis in fact and produced outcomes that were often unpredictable. Moreover, attorney folklore had an inherent race and sex bias; it encouraged lawyers to simply exclude racial minorities and women. Reliance on this folklore appears to have had lingering effects: when asked whether they have confidence in the ability of a jury to get to the truth in a case, African Americans are far more likely than are other races to respond by saying that they are not confident.

Today this race bias is exaggerated by class bias as well. Jury selection is now much more sophisticated, and many companies provide a full range of support services to lawyers who are trying to determine what the ideal juror or jury in their case would look like. These companies provide such services as mock trials to help lawyers craft their strategies, opening statements, and jury instructions and focus groups to assist lawyers in deciding on the most effective way of presenting information to jurors. In addition, many of these companies assist lawyers in creating jury questionnaires, which are used to select jurors, and other assessment devices to help lawyers use both verbal and nonverbal cues to choose jurors. The availability of these devices probably drives up the cost of bringing a suit or defending against a suit, and it is likely that these services are most accessible to those litigants who have the resources to pay for them. In

juror selection

the practice by which juries are chosen— once guided by lawyers' folklore about the ideal juror in a case; now dictated by much more scientific methods

environmental litigation brought by individuals or classes against corporations, it is now common practice for many companies to employ these sophisticated methods to limit their liability. Lawyers and litigants increasingly use social science and statistics to choose juries and test legal strategies, but these methods are costly and likely exaggerate class differences between the litigants.

Many companies provide a range of services—they determine what the ideal jury looks like, based on the facts of the case; they help construct jury selection questions to help lawyers ferret out the least sympathetic jurors; they assist lawyers in "theme preparation"—that is, they help them to try out different narratives for telling their client's story, including helping lawyers to have the most effective opening and closing statements; and they conduct mock trials to help lawyers predict how the trial might play out. Jury selection consulting is a booming business, but many question whether it interferes with the fact-finding function of juries. Ideally, juries should be made up of people from diverse backgrounds because this maximizes the chances that the truth will be discovered. When one side has the incentive

www ▶ ▶ ▶

THE LAW IN POPULAR CULTURE

Runaway Jury

Based on the John Grisham novel of the same name, this film underscores the importance of jury selection, especially in a highly controversial product liability case. Here, both sides in a class-action suit brought against a gun manufacturer attempt to use the jury to stack the deck in their favor.

and the resources to utilize jury selection devices, this fact-finding function may well be undermined, as jurors are selected, not on the basis of neutrality or even-handedness, but instead because of their sympathy with one party or the other.

Regardless of whether there is a jury in a trial, the judge plays a central role. It is the judge who structures the proceedings, rules on the evidence presented, and ultimately presents the jury with its instructions on the law. In a nonjury bench trial, the judge not only rules on the law, she or he is the fact-finder, as well. Judges are selected in different ways, depending on the court on which they sit. Federal judges are nominated by the president and confirmed by the U.S. Senate. These judges serve for life: there is no mandatory retirement age. Unless they are impeached or convicted of a serious crime, they stay on the bench until they retire or die. In contrast, state law governs the selection of state judges, and judges are selected through either popular election or nomination by the governor or a panel. Most state judges are elected and serve for a term of years, and most states allow judges to be reelected. Some analysts contend that **popular election** undermines the ability of state judges to make decisions based solely on the law and that elected judges are much more concerned about public opinion than about the law. In fact, the selection of judges in the federal system was expressly intended by the framers of the Constitution to limit the effect of public opinion on judicial decision making. The fact remains, however, that only one state, Rhode Island, grants life tenure to judges, and only two others, Massachusetts and New Hampshire, allow judges to serve until they reach the age of seventy. Every other state compels its judges to either be reappointed by the governor or legislative body or reelected in a general election.

Judges in both the state and federal systems tend to be very active in party politics. In many states, judges must identify their party affiliation, and this affiliation is of great significance in determining who the judges will be. In the federal system, the president typically nominates judges or justices with the same party affiliation as his own, and it is rare for a president to nominate someone who does not share this affiliation. In general, judges in the federal system come from an upper- or upper-middle-class background. Most federal judges have been educated at Ivy League schools, and the vast majority of federal judges were trained as lawyers. While state judges often share the class background of the federal bench, there is a bit more variability in terms of their class and education. State judges tend to be lawyers, but some state judges have other backgrounds, most often business experience.

The American judiciary is a highly unrepresentative institution. It is much more wealthy, white, and Protestant than the general population. Many analysts believe that this is a problem and argue that a more diverse judiciary would be more responsive to the needs of all Americans. In the federal

popular election
the most common method of choosing state court judges; raises concerns about the impact of public opinion on the judge's decisions

judiciary, presidents have often argued for some diversity in judgeships, and for many years, it has been assumed that there are specific "seats" on the most visible court, the U.S. Supreme Court, for African Americans, Jews, and women. President George W. Bush has signaled that when another vacancy opens on the high court, he will fill it with a Hispanic. It is unclear whether the occupants of these seats actually do decide cases in such a way that they "represent" the concerns or needs of their "constituency." But it's fascinating that many assume that the Court and courts in general should be representative of the population as a whole, and that demographic characteristics, like race, ethnicity, religion, and sex, affect how judges make their decisions.

Participants: Litigants, Expert Witnesses, and Outsiders

Cases come to court because someone seeks an authoritative settlement of a dispute that they are having or have had with another party. Without the litigants there are no cases and there can be no lawmaking by courts. A lawsuit must be initiated by someone whose rights have been violated, and this person must be able to identify the party who has harmed him or her and ask for a remedy that can be provided by a court of law. In different courts, these parties have different names: in trial courts involving civil matters, the plaintiff brings the suit against a defendant; in criminal trials, the prosecutor, a governmental actor, charges the defendant. At the appellate level, the parties go by the names of appellant and appellee, or in the U.S. Supreme Court and some state supreme courts, petitioner and respondent.

litigants

the two parties involved in a case: prosecutor and defendant in a criminal trial case; plaintiff and defendant in a civil trial case; appellant and appellee, or petitioner and respondent, in an appellate case

Because the American legal system is adversarial, **litigants** are the central players in the adjudication process. These are the formal parties—they present all of the factual issues and legal questions in the litigation, and judges are expected to choose from only those alternatives presented to them by the parties. The heavy burden placed on the litigants in an adversarial system can reinforce existing inequalities in society. For example, it is well known that those groups or individuals who are novices in the legal system, that is, who have never participated in litigation, are disadvantaged when their opponent is experienced in the litigation process. **Repeat players**—parties who come to court regularly—have a certain advantage, especially relative to these novices, known as **one-shotters**. Most often, repeaters are corporations, governments, or interest groups who go to court as part of larger strategy aimed at influencing public policy. These entities are typically advantaged in terms of resources like expertise, high-status connections, time, and money. One-shotters tend to be individuals who have far fewer advantages in terms of socioeconomic status or political connectedness. Repeat players' familiarity with how courts work and with the arguments

repeat players

those parties who are experienced in the litigation process; they have an advantage over one-shotters

one-shotters

novices in the litigation process; they have a disadvantage relative to repeaters

that may be most compelling to judges and juries give them a keen advantage, especially relative to one-shotters.

The second group of players who are important in litigation, especially at the trial court level, are **expert witnesses**. Expert witnesses are hired by either the plaintiff/prosecutor or the defendant in a trial, and these individuals try to get the judge or jury to view information presented to them in the light that is most favorable to their client. Expert witnesses are especially important when a case involves highly technical or complicated scientific or social scientific principles that are beyond the knowledge of the average judge or juror. For example, in the 1990s, criminal defense lawyers began to present a defense that is now known as the **battered woman syndrome**, and to establish this defense, they relied heavily on the testimony of expert psychologists and psychiatrists.

The earliest cases involved some act of violence by a woman against her mate or spouse. In these cases, the women had been beaten by their mate and had struck out at him by killing him, usually when he was asleep or incapacitated. These women argued that they acted in self-defense to stop their batterer from harming them or their children; however, traditional self-defense law requires that the person take action when faced with the risk of imminent harm. The fact that the batterer was not at the moment they struck out at him threatening them rendered this defense inapplicable. The defense presented evidence by psychologists and psychiatrists who were expert in the field of diminished capacity. These experts presented evidence that the women were not able to discern that the threat from their batterers was not imminent, because the sustained beatings had left them in a permanent state of terror. This defense of diminished or partial capacity has since been used by other defendants, including children and men who argue that their acts of violence can be explained by their mental illness or experience of being battered.

Expert witnesses have become even more important in the last decade, as jurors and judges are faced with the task of deciphering information that has become ever more complicated and technical. The importance of expert witnesses was apparent in the 1995 trial of O. J. Simpson for the murder of his wife and her friend. DNA experts offered differing conclusions about how the blood found at the murder scene could be used. The DNA in the blood matched Simpson's, but experts raised questions about how the samples might have been altered or tampered with by the Los Angeles Police Department and by their DNA labs. Their contradictory evidence may well have confused the jurors who likely based their acquittal of Simpson on their assumption that the LAPD was corrupt and racist, rather than that Simpson was clearly innocent.

The use of expert witnesses is apparent, not only in criminal trials, but in civil trials as well. For example, experts on addiction, cancer, and tobacco use have been central to the findings of a number of juries in tobacco cases

expert witnesses

specialists hired by either side to present information to the fact-finder about a factual issue

battered woman syndrome

increasingly used in the 1990s, a defense based on the diminished capacity of women who have been beaten repeatedly by their mate

that have resulted in astronomical awards to smokers or their estates for injuries sustained from cigarette smoking. Similarly, environmental litigation often hinges on the testimony of biologists, chemists, and others, who can introduce and interpret research findings in support of their clients. While it is usually true that both sides in any case can find some "expert" to back up their position, there are significant differences in the quality of expert testimony. Moreover, those litigants who have higher socioeconomic status typically can recruit better experts, as can those repeat players who are involved in a sustained course of litigation.

Expert witnesses are not as important in appellate cases, because these cases turn on interpretations of the law and not the facts, but there is another group of "experts" who do appear to play an important role at this stage. *Amici curiae,* or "friends of the court," are invited to file briefs in most cases at both the federal and state level, and very few constraints are actually placed on the filing of these briefs. These individuals and groups are not formal parties to a case. They are outsiders who are very interested in the outcome of the decision and in the law that is created as a result of the case holding. Typically, amici are organizations, like corporations, interest groups, governmental agencies, or professional organizations, who are also involved in lawmaking at the administrative and legislative levels. These groups are actively engaged in lobbying in these other forums, and they probably view amici participation as part of a larger strategy of influence.

amici curiae

briefs filed, usually before the U.S. Supreme Court or other high courts, by individuals or groups that are interested in the outcome of litigation but are not the actual litigants

Amici may file at any level; however, it appears that most amici activity is focused on the U.S. Supreme Court and on some state high courts. This preference for the court of last resort in both systems makes a lot of sense: these are the courts that are seen as making law for the larger system. In some important cases, there is also amici activity at the federal courts of appeals, probably because these are effectively the "last stop" for most cases, given that the U.S. Supreme Court grants review to only a handful of the cases presented to it. Amici are supposed to be friends of the court and to present unbiased information to the justices or judges to help them decide the case. The reality, however, is that they are much better friends to the parties: the vast majority of amici briefs are filed in support of one party or the other. Moreover, the arguments presented by some "friends" are likely heard more loudly by the judges and justices than others, and repeat amici have higher success rates, much like repeat litigants.

Lawyers

Lawyers have a complicated role in the American adversarial system: they are sworn to uphold the laws of this nation, but the public's perception of lawyers is largely negative. Historically, lawyers were viewed with some suspicion in England and the American colonies, and this distrust persists today. In 2002, the Litigation Section of the American Bar Association compiled its report on "Public Perceptions of Lawyers: Consumer Research Findings," and a summary of its findings is included on the website. As this summary strongly suggests, Americans are deeply ambivalent about lawyers: 60 percent agreed with the statement, "[m]ost lawyers are knowledgeable about the law and are interested in serving their clients," but another 34 percent believed that "lawyers deserve the bad reputation that they have."

Some of the public's mistrust of lawyers probably stems from the fact that the lawyer's role in an **adversarial system** is murky. The paramount responsibility of lawyers is to zealously protect the legal rights and interests of their clients. Every state has its own code of professional ethics for lawyers, and lawyers admitted to the bar in each state have an obligation to comply with this code of ethics. In each state's code, there is some provision that specifically states that a lawyer must promote and protect his client's interests. For example, Canon 7 of the New York State Bar Association's Code of Professional Responsibility informs that "A Lawyer Should Represent a Client Zealously Within the Bounds of the Law," and provides guidance to lawyers about how to accomplish this goal. Sometimes, lawyers have to make judgment calls about how to promote their client's interests without running afoul of the law, and often this judgment is a difficult one. There may be no applicable law to govern the activity; nonetheless, there may be a sense, among both the bar and the general public, that the lawyer has acted in an inappropriate or possibly dishonest manner.

Over the last century, lawyering has become more professionalized, and the criteria for becoming a lawyer have become more standardized and rigorous. Until the late 1800s, most lawyers did not attend a formal law school. Instead, they were trained by other lawyers as apprentices and then admitted into the bar association of their state after meeting certain requirements or passing an exam. Today, lawyers must attend an accredited law school to be eligible to sit for their state's **bar exam**. Most states also require that lawyers meet rigorous ethical and professional criteria before they may be admitted. Law schools themselves have a fairly standardized curriculum. Students are admitted only after completing their bachelor's degree. Most students have strong undergraduate records and have placed well on the **Law School Admissions Test (LSAT)**. The average age of a first-year law student is twenty-seven, and many law students have had significant work or extracurricular experience before beginning law school.

All first-year law students have pretty much the same complement of courses: all are required to take courses in contracts, torts, civil procedure, research and writing, criminal law, and constitutional law. In the second and third years of law school, students have relatively few required courses. Most students begin to take courses in their areas of interest by late in the second year or early in the third year. While students are not required to

---

[www] ▶ ▶ ▶

adversarial system

court system based on the principle that the truth will emerge in a trial from the clash between the two parties, or rather their lawyers; in this system, the lawyers have the responsibility to zealously protect the legal rights of their clients

[www] ▶ ▶ ▶

bar exam

a written test administered by the state bar association that all lawyers must pass before they can be admitted to practice law in that state

Law School Admissions Test (LSAT)

a standardized exam required by most law schools as part of the admissions process; scores range from 120 to 180

specialize in any area of the law, some students do choose to take elective courses in specific areas. The ranking of law students begins relatively early in their law school careers, and by the end of the first year, high rankings begin to confer certain privileges, such as lucrative and promising summer employment and possible membership on the board of editors for the law school's law review journal.

Law schools themselves are ranked, and these rankings are well-known by prospective law students, employers, and others. Generally speaking, a student's choice of law school will enhance or limit his or her prospects for employment later on. For example, one of the most prestigious appointments for new law school graduates is as a clerk for a federal court judge. Judicial clerks work closely with judges, helping them to read and analyze case law and the briefs presented by the parties. Clerkships with judges on the federal district courts or courts of appeals or with U.S. Supreme Court justices provide excellent opportunities for advancement in private practice, academia, or government service. Many of these clerks are chosen from a handful of schools, and in fact, in the last ten years, nearly all of the clerks at the U.S. Supreme Court have come from only a few schools—specifically, Harvard, Yale, and the University of Chicago. In admissions, there are very clear advantages conferred by socioeconomic class. For example, having had a grandparent, parent, or sibling attend a law school creates an advantage for a prospective student seeking admission. Similarly, having attended a prestigious college or university with similarly rigorous admissions criteria also carries with it a built-in advantage in the admissions game.

Many believe that the legal profession should be representative of all classes, races, and ethnicities in the United States. Unfortunately, however, there has been a dramatic decline in the number of applications and in the admissions of persons of color. This is troubling for at least two reasons. First, a legal education provides an avenue to middle- and upper-middle-class professional status; a decrease in the number of minority students probably means that at least one path to middle-class status is starkly limited. Second, diversity in the legal profession is an effective antidote to the bias and discrimination that continues to be apparent in the American legal system. The American Bar Association (ABA) and the American Association of Law Schools (AALS) are actively attempting to recruit persons of color to attend law schools. In association with specific law schools, organizations, and employers, the ABA and AALS have undertaken a number of programs aimed at enhancing diversity in the legal profession.

The U.S. Supreme Court has, in many ways, facilitated this push. In its 2003 decision in *Grutter* v. *Bollinger et al.,* the Court let stand the admissions policy at the University of Michigan Law School, which allowed the admissions committee to consider an applicant's race, among other factors, in evaluating applications. Ms. Grutter, a white woman denied admission to this elite law school, argued that the policy in place at this state school violated the equal protection clause of the Fourteenth Amendment, which bars state entities from treating people differently because of their race. The Supreme Court disagreed, finding that this policy, which enabled the committee to consider how an applicant could contribute to the life of the law school and enhance diversity, didn't violate the equal protection guarantee. Specifically, the law school was able to demonstrate that it had a "compelling interest" in fostering diversity and that diversity conferred benefits on all members of the law school community.

There is substantial variability in the kinds of jobs that law graduates do, and salary differentials reflect this variation. For 2002, the National Association of Law Placement (NALP) reported that the national median starting salary for law grads was $60,000—but those in private practice business earned a median of $90,000, while those in public interest advocacy earned a median salary of roughly $37,000. The best-paid lawyers have "made partner" in private practice and earn substantially more. Perhaps not surprisingly, many of the lawyers in these elite firms are white men. In 2003, attorneys of color made up 4 percent of the partners, and women constituted less than 17 percent. These numbers have seen a modest increase in the last decade, but it remains to be seen how recent efforts to promote diversity in elite law schools will affect the hiring and retention of attorneys of color in more prestigious and higher-paying jobs.

DEBATE

Is the lack of diversity among lawyers an issue that should be aggressively addressed?

Yes:

There is a striking lack of representation among people of color and women in both law schools and in the most prestigious positions in government and private practice. For example, while women are admitted to law schools in roughly the same number as men, people of color continue to be grossly underrepresented. And there are relatively few attorneys of color or women attorneys who are partners in our nation's major law firms or in leadership positions in government practice. Without better representation at the bar, women and people of color cannot fully exercise their influence. This is significant, because they are not fully able to represent their interests or to represent the interests of women or people of color in the judicial or legislative processes. In *Gruter*, a majority of the U.S. Supreme Court justices recognized the importance of all kinds of diversity, including ethnic and racial diversity, in law school classes and on the bar. They noted that law

DEBATE

Is the lack of diversity among lawyers an issue that should be aggressively addressed?–(Cont'd)

students and lawyers who are exposed to the viewpoints of those who look different have an advantage in litigation, especially given the fact that the U.S. population, and thus its judges and juries, are becoming increasingly diverse. In sum, diversity is good for both lawyers and the larger community.

No: The American bar is becoming more diverse. Women enter law school at the same rate, or in some places, at higher rates, than their male counterparts. And since 1993, women attorneys and attorneys of color have increased their numbers in large law firms and in partnership positions. The gains are modest but unmistakable. While diversity is an important goal, it makes little sense to pursue this goal at the expense of other, equally important values, among these, being judged on the basis of merit rather than on the color of one's skin or one's gender. Our culture prizes hard work and motivation, and people have a right to be evaluated on the basis of their achievements. In at least some law schools, there is an assumption that all people of color have been admitted through an affirmative action program and that none of these individuals are qualified. Ultimately, this assumption generates a sense of inferiority and continuing questions about the qualifications of women and people of color pervades both the law school community and the larger community of law firms and legal employers. In this way, affirmative action runs counter to the high value our culture places on individual merit and harms both the individual and the larger society.

SUMMARY

This chapter provided an overview of the structure of, function of, and participants in the U.S. court system. For each of the chapters that discusses a lawmaking institution, we will be examining these three aspects and asking the following questions: "What is the structure of this lawmaking institution?" "What is function of this institution?" and finally, "Who participates in lawmaking in this institution?"

The structure of the American court system is dual in two ways. First, there are both federal and state courts, and these courts operate largely independently of each other and may create significant variability and opportunity for innovation in the American system. This chapter introduced the concept of jurisdiction, explaining that jurisdiction is the power to hear and decide a case, and that jurisdiction is established by either federal or state constitution or statutory law. Second, the structure of the American court system is dual because in each federal and state system, there are both trial and appellate courts, and the structure and function of each of these is quite different. The trial court is set up to resolve questions of facts or disputes. It has fact-finders, like judges and juries, and evidence to accomplish this goal. In contrast, the appellate court exists to resolve questions about how a law is to be interpreted. There is no fact-finder and judges alone sit to determine whether the law has been correctly applied by the lower court.

This chapter also highlighted the three main groups of participants in the American court system—the fact-finders, either judge or jury, who sit to resolve questions of law or fact; the participants, which include the litigants, experts, and interested parties; and the lawyers. Each group has a distinct role to play in the American court system, and this role has changed over time. Specifically, we talked about changes in jury selection and trends in judicial selection. We also discussed the advantages that repeat litigants appear to have in the judicial process and the increasingly intense battle between experts and among interested parties filing *amici curiae* briefs. And finally, we talked about changes in the legal profession and about efforts to make the American bar more diverse and representative of the population. This chapter laid the foundation for a more extensive discussion of the functions of American courts, which follows in Chapter 7.

SUGGESTED READING

Clay S. Conrad, *Jury Nullification: The Evolution of a Doctrine* (Carolina Academic Press, 1998). This book explores the practice of jury nullification throughout U.S. history and asks critical questions about the positive and negative impact of this doctrine on American society.

Jonathan Harr, *A Civil Action* (Vintage Books, 1996). This is the book that the film was based on, and this book provides lots of detail about how this real-life environmental case emerged and ultimately was disposed of.

Forrest Maltzman, James F. Spriggs II, and Paul J. Wahlbeck, *Crafting Law on the Supreme Court: The Collegial Game* (Cambridge University Press, 2000). This impressive study looks at how interaction between the three institutions of government affect how the Supreme Court decides cases. It also examines how the Court's institutional features, like reliance on tradition and seniority, affect decision making.

Sandra Day O'Connor, *The Majesty of the Law* (Random House, 2003). Justice O'Connor has served on the U.S. Supreme Court for more than two decades and is widely viewed as the swing vote on most controversial cases heard by the Court. This book provides insight into the judicial philosophy of this very powerful jurist.

Suzanne U. Samuels, *First Among Friends: Amici Curiae, the Right to Privacy, and the U.S. Supreme Court* (Praeger Publishers, 2004). Drawing on the personal papers of retired Supreme Court Justices and the briefs filed in more than ten privacy cases heard since 1965, this study examines the impact of interest groups on Supreme Court decision making.

ACTIVE LEARNING

1. Note that in the federal court system, the intermediate courts, known as either the courts of appeals or circuit courts, are grouped into geographic zones. For example, the court that covers the region included in group 1 is known as either the Courts of Appeals for the First Circuit, or simply, the First Circuit, and it includes the states of Maine, New Hampshire, Massachusetts and Rhode Island, and Puerto Rico. These circuits were created by Congress in a series of laws beginning with the 1789 Judiciary Act, which established twelve geographic circuits. Why do you think Congress thought it wise to keep neighboring states together in the circuit system? How do you think these groupings affect the kinds of law that is made in these circuits? [Students may want to do some guided research to look into what's been written about the political dispositions of these circuits—e.g., the reputation of Seventh Circuit versus the Ninth Circuit on civil liberties, civil rights, and business cases.]

2. What goes on in trial courts? The only exposure most Americans have had to trials is in the media—either through fictional accounts or media reporting. To fully appreciate what goes on in the courthouse, observe a trial in your county or city. Write an account of your experience, focusing on the following questions: (1) What was this trial about—specifically, what law was at play? (2) Who were the litigants? (3) Who were the lawyers? (4) What was the quality of the legal representation—at the end of your observation, did you have strong feelings about how each team of lawyers was doing? (5) At the end of your observation, did you have some sense about who was right and who was wrong? Who do you think ultimately prevailed in your case?

CHAPTER 7

The Function of American Courts

*The primary function of courts is to resolve disputes between parties.
While courts and the law also function effectively as agents of social
control by establishing norms and ensuring a predictability of behavior,
it is their dispute-resolution function for which courts are best known.
When parties submit their disputes to a court of law for resolution, they
are seeking an authoritative settlement of their disagreement. They go to
court because this is the forum that they rely on to definitively adjudicate
or settle their claims. In this chapter, we will discuss the dispute-resolution
function, focusing on three aspects of adjudication: first, how disputes
get to court, that is, the stages of disputing and the resolution of disputes;
second, alternative dispute resolution, or the use of forums other than
courts to resolve conflicts; and finally, lawmaking by courts in the context
of the social and political system.*

COURTS AS FORUMS FOR DISPUTE RESOLUTION

Courts are set up primarily to resolve disputes between parties and to
enforce legal rights and responsibilities. The adjudication of cases is only
one function of courts. In addition, courts engage in lawmaking, operate
as agents of social control by interpreting and enforcing laws, promote or
discourage social change, and engage in dispute resolution. In some ways,
the dispute-resolution function is the most important of these roles. Unlike
the other institutions that we will discuss in Chapters 8, 9, and 10, courts
have no powers to engage in lawmaking proactively; that is, they cannot
initiate the lawmaking process. While legislatures, administrative agencies,
and law enforcement officials can proactively engage in lawmaking, courts
are reactive institutions. Courts and judges make laws in direct response to
disputes that are brought before them. Because court-made laws are tied so
closely to the adjudication process, the kinds of laws that courts make are

quite different from laws made by other institutions. Courts must wait to respond to a dispute before they can engage in lawmaking, and then, when the dispute arrives, courts are confined by the facts that are raised in that dispute. Disputes themselves impose certain constraints on courts: most significantly, they force judges to consider only those injuries and options that are presented by the litigants.

Stages of Dispute Resolution

three stages of dispute resolution

the predictable stages through which virtually all conflicts pass

pre-conflict or "naming" stage

stage at which the injured parties become aware that they have been harmed by the actions or words of another

conflict or "blaming" stage

stage at which the injured parties confront the person they believe has caused them harm and demand resolution

www ▶ ▶ ▶

dispute or "claiming" stage

the accused party refuses to compensate the injured party for the injuries and the injured party seeks resolution of the conflict by appealing to third party

"opt out"

decision not to pursue resolution of a dispute

"lumping it"

when the injured party decides to live with the injury and not to pursue resolution

avoidance

when the injured party removes him or herself completely from the offending relationship

Disputes are ubiquitous in society—there is potential for conflict in every human interaction. Very few disputes, however, are resolved and even fewer are resolved by courts. There are **three stages of dispute resolution**: a **pre-conflict or "naming" stage**, in which someone becomes aware that he or she has been injured by the actions or words of someone else; a **conflict or "blaming" stage**, in which the injured party confronts the party who has injured him or her; and a **dispute or "claiming" stage**, in which the injury is redressed.[1] Very few disputes are actually resolved: most do not proceed to the resolution stage because one or both of the parties have decided that they do not want to pursue resolution. In many cases, it is the person who is injured who decides to **"opt out"**—either by **"lumping it"** or by **avoidance**. When someone "lumps it," they decide to live with the injury or the damage and not to pursue a resolution; when someone avoids a dispute, they remove themselves entirely from the situation that has caused them harm. Moreover, people tend to move through the stages at unpredictable rates, and sometimes move backwards rather than forwards.

Let's look at a hypothetical case. If you have a landlord who doesn't periodically treat the premises for roaches and your apartment becomes infested, you have a number of options. First, assume that you have a right, under state or municipal law, to rent an apartment that is free from vermin. When you discover that you have an infestation and that you have legal right to have a vermin-free apartment, you enter into the pre-conflict stage. If you decide to confront your landlord with this problem, you will enter into the conflict or blaming stage. At this point, you and your landlord may resolve the problem, but if you do not, you may decide to enter the claiming or dispute stage. It may take a long time to move from stage to stage, and in fact, you may *not* move from one stage to the next. For example, you may decide that the rent is really, really low and that you don't want to involve your landlord in this, and you may even decide to hire your own pest control company. If you do this, you are probably "lumping" the dispute; that is, you are deciding to live with the problem or to resolve it

---

1 See William Felstiner, Richard Abel, and Austin Sarat, "The Emergence and Transformation of Disputes: Naming, Blaming and Claiming," 15 *Law and Society Review* 631–54.

yourself. Alternatively, you may decide to move out of this apartment and you may even forgo your security deposit. If you choose this course, you are really engaging in avoidance—meaning that you are removing yourself entirely from the situation that has caused injury.

Many disputes are never resolved. A person's willingness to pursue a real resolution of his or her claim is usually a function of a number of factors, among these, resources like time, money, and knowledge. A person who is not well-informed about his or her rights is not likely to move beyond the naming stage. Similarly, someone who is not aware that she or he has been injured at all or is not able to identify *who* has injured her or him will not move beyond this first stage. Consider the string of childhood cancers depicted in the book and film *A Civil Action*. For many years, no one made the link between the cluster of cancers found in the children residing around Woburn, Massachusetts, and the activities of several chemical companies. It was only after a few of the parents began to wonder why there were so many cases in their town that the dispute began to move into the second stage. Ultimately, some of the parents decided to sue the company and the case, *Anderson* v. *Cryovac,* was brought in federal district court. Many analysts have argued that this case demonstrates many of the pitfalls of relying on courts to resolve disputes. This case was ultimately settled out of court for a small fraction of what the parents had sought—and without any admission of wrongdoing by the companies.

The Language of Disputing

In many ways, the language of disputing and dispute resolution impose the most significant constraints on courts. Linguists contend that there is a language of disputing and that there are predictable patterns in how people talk about conflicts with others. According to linguists, disputes are transformed by the very act of talking about them. In their excellent work about the relationship between language and disputes, *Just Words: Law, Language and Power,* Conley and O'Barr present a language-based model of disputing, which focuses on the actual words used to describe conflicts. Conley, O'Barr, and others contend that disputes often emerge only after the person who has been harmed talks about his or her injuries with others; that is, blame only begins to emerge after the injured party has a chance to talk about how he or she has been harmed. Often, the person who is hearing about the injury will respond by asking ever more specific questions or by offering his or her own "story" to encourage the teller to provide more detail. The effect of this interaction between narrator and listener is to identify who is to blame for the injury. Again, think about how the very discourse about disputing shapes the actual dispute.

Once the injured party assigns blame or responsibility to one specific actor, she or he has the choice about whether to confront this person.

Again, the decision about whether to move to the next stage, the "blaming" stage, is highly dependent on the injured party's resources, relationship to the injurer, and sense of efficacy. Someone with few resources, in terms of time, money, or knowledge, in an ongoing and intimate relationship with the responsible party, or with a poor view of himself as someone who cannot make a difference or bring about change, is unlikely to move to this next stage. Conversely, someone in a position of relative superiority to her opponent, or with lots of resources, will likely make the decision to confront the person she views as responsible. If she does decide to confront the other party, chances are that that person will deny or limit his responsibility for the injuries. Usually, the denial sparks a new or slightly altered allegation by the grievant, which is also usually rejected. Rarely does the person accused of causing the harm admit responsibility—in fact, the linguistic "rule" about disputes is that they will be almost always rejected by the injurer.

Consider that before a dispute reaches the court, the parties have been involved in at least some discussion about it. It is almost always the fact that this discussion leads to subtle, or perhaps even dramatic, changes in the dispute itself. This is important to consider, since it is the legal claim itself and the injuries that flow from this complaint that are at the core of the case. When this case is litigated, the court will make a decision about whether the grievant's rights have been violated and whether the accused party is liable for this injury. The fact that the two parties have gone around at least once on this claim—that is, that the injured party has been rebuffed by the injurer, who has likely denied responsibility for the injury—may make this case more difficult to settle.

Judicial Resolution Changes the Dispute

When a dispute reaches the court it is because the parties seek some authoritative settlement of the dispute. They want a judge to make a determination about the controversy and about fault, and they want the judge to establish a remedy to compensate for damages. It is important to note, however, that framing a problem or dispute in such a way that it is appropriate for judicial resolution may dramatically affect what the dispute looks like. For a court to engage in dispute resolution, the problem or conflict must take the form of a case, and the dispute must be "translated" into the language of law, which is a language of rights and remedies. A case must be based on a legal right for which there is a remedy sanctioned by law. Thus, the dispute between the parties must be transformed into one that is much more formal and seeks specific tangible damages.

Moreover, by using a court to resolve the dispute, the parties are creating a zero-sum game, where one party must lose for the other party to win. By creating a win-lose game, adjudication inevitably alters the relationship between the parties. Moreover, even a win in court does not necessarily resolve the dispute or remove the underlying controversy between the parties. This is especially true when courts are called on to adjudicate claims between people who are in ongoing relationships. Consider how litigation transforms the following family law dispute, and consider the impact of this case on the relationships of all the involved parties. In this case, a father brought suit to have a court recognize his rights as the father of a child born to a woman who was married to another man. Note that the dispute in this case centered on the legal rights and responsibilities of parenthood, and consider how this case affected the relationships between the spouses and between the parents and the child.

LAW IN ACTION

How Adjudication Transforms a Dispute

C.C. V. A.B. SUPREME COURT OF MASSACHUSETTS, 1990

www ▶ ▶ ▶ (See *Law, Politics, and Society* website for a link to the complete decision.)

OPINION BY: Justice NOLAN

This case involves the question whether a man, who alleges that he is the father of a child, may bring an action to establish his paternity when the mother of the child is, and was at the time of the child's conception and birth, married to another man.

The plaintiff, C.C., filed a complaint in which he alleged that he is the father of a certain child. The plaintiff sought an adjudication of his paternity and a right of visitation with the child. The defendant, A.B., is admittedly the mother of the child.

The mother moved to dismiss the plaintiff's complaint. She alleged that she was married to a man other than the plaintiff when the child was born and argued that G. L. c. 209C, § 5 (*a*),

precluded the plaintiff's action . . . The mother, the plaintiff, and the Attorney General entered into a statement of agreed facts. The parties stipulate that the defendant is the mother of the child and that the child was born on May 19, 1986. At the time of the child's conception and birth the mother lived with the plaintiff and had sexual relations with the plaintiff. During the entire time that the mother lived with the plaintiff, including the time during which the child was born, the mother was married to another man. The mother and her husband have since reconciled, and they now live together.

When the child was born, she was given the plaintiff's last name. Moreover, the child's middle name derives from the plaintiff's first name. On the child's birth certificate, the plaintiff is listed as the father of the child. The child was

LAW IN ACTION–(CONT'D)

baptized in the plaintiff's religion on October 27, 1986. The plaintiff's name is recorded as the child's father on the baptismal record. In his affidavit, the plaintiff averred that, up until the time that he and the mother ended their liaison, he "cared for" the child. The plaintiff also affirmed his interest in maintaining a relationship with the child.

The mother acknowledges that the plaintiff may be the father of the child. After she took the child and left the plaintiff, the mother instituted an action against the plaintiff seeking custody of the child and support payments for the child . . . According to the mother, [General Laws c. 209C] § 5 (*a*) bars the plaintiff from bringing suit to establish the paternity of her child . . . The critical question in this case is whether the plaintiff may bring an action to establish paternity. It is not enough to conclude, as we do, that the enactment of G. L. c. 209C places no limit on the Probate Court's general equity jurisdiction. We must address the nature of an action to establish paternity.

The law has always drawn a distinction between legitimate and illegitimate children. See 1 W. Blackstone, Commentaries. A child who was not legitimate was, at common law, "filius nullius" (the son of no one) . . . The status of illegitimacy brought with it a host of social and legal disabilities . . . The English common law placed no obligation on the parents of an illegitimate child to support that child . . . The American courts adopted that view as well . . . An illegitimate child, being filius nullius, could inherit from neither parent under the common law . . . Until 1987, use of the word "issue," in the absence of anything indicating a contrary intent, was presumed to mean only legitimate children . . .

The common law severely burdened the illegitimate child, imposing harsh results on the child as punishment of the parents' actions. In recognition of the sad lot of illegitimate children, the common law generated a presumption of legitimacy . . . "The legal presumption always is, that a child born in lawful wedlock is legitimate . . ." While the law has always recognized that a child born to a married woman could nonetheless be an illegitimate child, it created a strong presumption to avoid that result. In England, the presumption could only be overcome by proof that the husband was "*extra quatuor maria* (beyond the four seas), for above nine months," or if "there is an apparent impossibility of procreation on the part of the husband, as if he be only eight years old, or the like." 1 W. Blackstone. The application of the presumption has changed somewhat, and it has become rebuttable. But the presumption may only be rebutted by "facts which prove, beyond all reasonable doubt, that the husband could not have been the father . . . " Accordingly, "it must be shown, 'beyond all reasonable doubt,' either that: (1) the husband had no access to the wife during the time of possible conception; (2) the husband was impotent; or (3) a properly conducted blood grouping test, administered by a qualified expert, definitively excludes the husband as a father . . . " In *P.B.C.* v. *D.H.*, 396 Mass. 68, 71 (1985), cert. denied, 475 U.S. 1058 (1986), we extended the scope of the presumption to include not only a child born to a married woman, but also a child conceived by a married woman.

Society has come to recognize that discrimination against illegitimate children is not justified. As noted, statutes were enacted at an early date to alleviate some of the hardships

LAW IN ACTION–(CONT'D)

thrust on illegitimate children by the common law. The United States Supreme Court has invoked the equal protection clause of the Fourteenth Amendment to the United States Constitution to strike down statutes discriminating against illegitimate children . . . It was the avoidance of those disadvantages which gave rise to the strict application of the presumption of legitimacy.

At the same time, the law has come to recognize an interest with which it had not historically dealt. The fathers of illegitimate children have certain rights, under the due process clause of the United States Constitution, to maintain a relationship with those children . . . In the constitutional sense, the father's interest is not one of a biological nature alone. Rather, the protected interest arises when there is a substantial relationship between a putative father and an illegitimate child . . . In a case with facts similar to the instant case, four Justices of the United States Supreme Court felt that a "natural father" had a protected liberty interest in the relationship with his child. *Michael H. v. Gerald D.*, 109 S. Ct. 2333, 2349-2363 (1989) (dissenting opinions of Brennan and White, JJ) . . .

The case sub judice involves a clash of the interests of the plaintiff, an unwed putative father, and the interest in preserving the legitimacy of the child that the plaintiff claims to have sired. We continue to adhere to the common law principle that motivated the presumption of legitimacy—that there is a strong interest in not bastardizing children. We are no longer convinced, however, that that interest can be protected only by requiring the rebuttal of a presumption by proof beyond a reasonable doubt. In view of the gradual betterment of the

illegitimate child's legal position, which weakens the purpose behind the presumption, coupled with the corresponding recognition of the interests of unwed putative fathers, we think that there is no longer any need for a presumption of legitimacy. The interests involved can be adequately protected by requiring that a putative father in the plaintiff's position be required to prove paternity by clear and convincing evidence . . .

The advances of modern science make determinations and exclusions of paternity much more accurate than was ever historically possible. In this context we think it preferable that a putative father in the plaintiff's position be able to produce the evidence he has on the issue of paternity . . .

We now proceed to the dispositive issue—whether a man in the plaintiff's position is entitled to bring an action to establish paternity pursuant to G. L. c. 215, § 6 . . . In the circumstances of this case, we think that the putative father has such a right. The parties' statement of agreed facts indicates, as already noted, that the mother, although married to another man, lived with the plaintiff at the time that the minor child was conceived and when the child was born. The plaintiff's name is listed as "father" on the child's birth certificate and on the child's baptismal record. The child bears the plaintiff's name. The mother has admitted that the plaintiff may be the father of the child. After the child's birth, the plaintiff, the mother, and the child lived together. The plaintiff has indicated, both by his actions and his words that he has an interest in continuing his relationship with the child. On this record, there is sufficient evidence of a substantial parent-child relationship between the plaintiff

LAW IN ACTION–(CONT'D)

and the child to allow the plaintiff to proceed with his paternity action.

The existence of a substantial parent-child relationship is, in our view, the controlling factor in determining whether this plaintiff may pursue his claim . . . It is the developed parent-child relationship of which both the plaintiff and the child were suddenly deprived, that the plaintiff seeks to renew. Accordingly, in cases such as this, the Probate Court must hold a preliminary hearing to determine the extent of the relationship between the putative father and the child. This is, in its nature, a fact-based question. The court must look at the relationship as a whole and consider emotional bonds, economic support, custody of the child, the extent of personal association, the commitment of the putative father to attending to the child's needs, the consistency of the putative father's expressed interest, the child's name, the names listed on the birth certificate, and any other factors which bear on the nature of the alleged parent-child relationship.

The requirement of showing a substantial parent-child relationship serves another important interest as well. In cases where the mother of a child is married and living with her husband, there is admittedly an extant marital relationship on which the plaintiff's action will intrude. The traditional family unit is at the core of our society. Despite a vast array of recent challenges to the traditional concept of the family, our civilization still places inestimable value on the importance of family life. Without regard to the outcome of a paternity case, even the very trial of such a case might place great strain on a unitary family. Where, however, the plaintiff has exhibited that he has had a substantial parent-child relationship with the child, it will certainly come as no surprise to the marital family that there is a question as to paternity. If the plaintiff cannot come forward with clear and convincing evidence of such a relationship, he will not be able to proceed beyond the preliminary stages of the action. The family will be protected against significant intrusion. If, on the other hand, the putative father can demonstrate that he has enjoyed a substantial relationship with the child, then his interest warrants protection and the interest in protecting a family which, by necessary implication, has already suffered substantial interference (by the acts of one of the marital partners) is greatly decreased. In these circumstances, the putative father should be allowed to proceed with his action . . .

QUESTIONS

1. What was happening in this case?
2. How did the court resolve the *legal* issue?
3. What bearing do you think the court's decision will have on the relationships in this case? For example, how do you think it will affect the relationship between the biological father and child? The biological mother and child? The biological mother and her husband? And maybe most significantly, the husband and child?
4. Could you have come up with a better solution? If you could have come up with an alternative, what would the basis of your decision have been? How would "the law" have factored into your decision?

Cases like this one starkly demonstrate how litigation pits the rights of one set of actors, here the mother and her husband, against another actor, here, the father. Consider how a judicial determination that the plaintiff is in fact the father will likely affect the relationships between the parties, and in particular, between the husband, the wife, and the child. One of the most serious drawbacks of relying on courts for the resolution of disputes is that they do not take full consideration of the context in which a case is heard. Because cases must focus on some specific act or period of time, they do not allow the decision-maker to take the situation as a whole and to consider how a case might affect persons outside of the litigation. Moreover, because cases are based on some injury in the past, they are by necessity, backward looking. In adjudication, decision-makers are limited in their ability to look into the future and to consider the likely impact of the decision on the parties. The transformation of this dispute meant that it became more formalized and confrontational, and it focused on the rights of the parties rather than the effect of the decision on the family unit as a whole.

THE LAW IN POPULAR CULTURE

I Am Sam

I Am Sam explores the pitfalls of relying on litigation to resolve highly sensitive issues. In this movie, child protective services attempts to remove custody of a young child from her mentally disabled father. This film asks important questions about how litigation alters disputes and forces a zero-sum solution, where the needs and interests of one party are swept aside to protect the legal rights of the other.

Limitations of Judicial Resolution of Disputes

Bringing a dispute to court does not necessarily mean that the dispute is resolved, or that the injured party is adequately compensated for damages suffered. Again, courts can only grant certain kinds of tangible relief. In *C.C. v. A.B.*, the appeals court ordered that the paternity suit could continue, and a lower court then concluded that the plaintiff was in fact the father and fashioned a shared child-custody arrangement. Ultimately, the parties are left to effectuate this agreement, and as anyone familiar with child support and custody cases can attest, even after a court order sets out support and custody arrangements, the parties themselves often engage in substantial "modification" of the order by disregarding it or altering its terms. Cases like this one, in which the parties have an ongoing relationship with each other, are probably the most difficult ones for courts to definitively decide. Again, remember that the function of courts is to *resolve* the dispute. Parties usually go to court because they don't want to simply manage the dispute—they want it to go away. But because this kind of case involves a relationship between people who are probably angry, sad, and/or disillusioned, it is unlikely that the court's holding can do anything more than to simply manage the underlying controversy or dispute.

Many people have argued that while the function of courts is to definitively resolve disputes, they are poorly suited to fulfill this function, at least in certain kinds of cases. In those cases that are highly contentious, either because the parties are in an ongoing relationship or have suffered grievous harm, or because the underlying issue is one that does not create any middle ground for agreement, courts may be unable to effectively promote dispute resolution. Moreover, the transformation of the dispute so that it is appropriate for a court to hear may itself make resolution impossible. Take the societal controversy over abortion, which provides a stark example of the limited capacity of courts to resolve certain kinds of disputes.

When queried about whether they believe that women should be able to have abortions, most Americans respond in the affirmative, but they voice significant reservations about the scope of this right. Most Americans reject the view that women should have an unlimited right to choose abortion and strongly condemn the use of abortion as a method of birth control. When courts have considered abortion cases, however, the controversy has been framed much more starkly as a contest between women's right to have abortion *at all* and either the state's right to protect the fetus *or* the fetus's right to life. In fact, the judicial controversy over abortion seems to be much different than the societal controversy. In court, there are two sides—the pro-choice and pro-life side—but neither really captures the sentiment of a majority of the population. Instead, the abortion debate is polarized, so that the two "camps" face off against each other. By using the language of rights, the controversy squarely pits women against either the state or their fetuses. It is not at all clear how these rights should be squared and whose rights should be given primacy. Again, the very discourse about rights and the zero-sum nature of litigation makes real resolution of the abortion controversy in courts difficult, if not impossible.

Many people wonder whether Americans are too litigious, that is, whether we rely too heavily on litigation to resolve our disputes. Clearly, law and courts are an important part of our popular culture: channel "surfing" on television quickly reveals that crime, punishment, and the law are common themes for TV series and movies. In the United States, there are many lawyers and the relative cost of legal representation is low. In addition, judges only very rarely impose penalties on those who pursue lawsuits that might seem frivolous. Moreover, over the last several decades, lawmakers, that is, judges, legislators, and administrators, have expanded the number and type of legal rights that may be protected by law. The "rights explosion" of the 1960s created rights and remedies for those who alleged they have been discriminated against on the basis of race, ethnicity, national origin, and sex. More recently, antidiscrimination prohibitions have been extended to those with disabilities and to those who allege they are victims of ageism. Similarly, environmental and products liability laws confer expanded protections on individuals and groups alleging a right to be free from certain harms. Law plays a prominent role in our society because of these factors—in terms of our popular culture, we have an abundance of lawyers to pursue cases, and we have an expansive view of the law as a tool to advance certain rights or ideals. Other factors also appear to be important, among these, the use of law to promote social change.

Requirements for Using Courts for Dispute Resolution

In order to use the courts to resolve disputes or to effect change, however, certain prerequisites much be met, and not every disagreement or controversy can be addressed by a court. The most important requirements before a court can hear a case and attempt to resolve a dispute are jurisdiction, justiciability, and standing.

Jurisdiction is the only real power that a court has, and it is conferred on a court either by the constitution or by a law. Without jurisdiction over a case, a court is powerless to adjudicate it. Unlike justiciability and standing, which are constraints that are self-imposed by courts, jurisdiction is imposed on courts by outside actors—either the framers of the constitution or the legislators. Usually, jurisdiction may be altered by laws that are passed after the initial constitutional or legislative provision. For example, in the 1960s, 1970s, and 1980s, the U.S. Supreme Court struck down a number of state or municipal laws that authorized or required public school students to observe a moment of silence or to pray. In the wake of these decisions, Congress considered several constitutional amendments that would have limited the Court's power to hear cases involving school prayer. These amendments failed, but had they succeeded, they would have removed the Court's jurisdiction over all of these cases, and in so doing, would have rendered the Court powerless to deal with this issue.

While jurisdiction is a power that is conferred on a court by an external actor, justiciability and standing are limitations on a court's power that are imposed by the court itself. **Justiciability** requires that the lawsuit being heard by a court involve a case or controversy that is appropriate for judicial resolution, and both the federal and state constitutions mandate that courts hear only those case or controversies that they have the jurisdiction to resolve. This **case or controversy requirement** basically means that a dispute must be one for which a court can provide a remedy, and that this remedy is both manageable and practical. There are three elements of justiciability: there can be no collusive or advisory suits, no unripe or moot suits, and no suits involving political questions. The first corollary is that the case must involve a real issue—not a hypothetical issue, but a genuine dispute between the parties. In the American system, courts cannot issue advisory opinions, and they cannot hear cases in which the opposing parties have colluded to bring a suit. In the U.S. system, courts have a somewhat narrow function, and they can only hear cases that involve real disputes. **Collusive suits** are those in which there is no controversy between the parties, and the parties are staging a lawsuit for their mutual benefit. Similarly, parties seeking an advisory opinion do not have any real dispute with each other, but want to have the court make a determination about either the legitimacy of a law or its likely resolution of some hypothetical lawsuit that might be heard in the future.

The second principle of justiciability is that the dispute itself must be at the proper stage for a court to hear it: it must be ripe—that is, the disagreement must have come to a head—but it cannot be moot, which means that it must still be relevant to the actors. Cases that are not yet ripe have come to the court before the controversy has really exploded. For example, an unripe case is one in which a party challenges the application of a law before the law has actually been implemented. If you think that your state's cell phone law is silly, you cannot bring a lawsuit challenging this law based on its mere existence. Your right to bring a lawsuit challenging this law only kicks in once the law has been enforced. On the other end of the spectrum, you cannot bring a lawsuit that is no longer ripe because of the passage of time, which is at the core of the mootness principle.

When a case is moot, it involves some controversy that is no longer relevant or real to the actors. For example, one of the first affirmative action challenges presented to the U.S. Supreme Court, *DeFunis v. Odegaard* (1974) was dismissed by the justices as moot. In this case, DeFunis challenged the admissions policy of the University of Washington Law School, which

justiciability

the requirement that courts handle only those conflicts that are appropriate for judicial resolution—there are three features of this principle: the conflict must be based on a legitimate case or controversy; it must be ripe, but not moot; and it must not involve a political question

case or controversy requirement

at the core of the principle of justiciability is the requirement that the case involve a genuine controversy and that it be a dispute for which a court can fashion a remedy—in short, it must not be collusive or ask for an advisory opinion

collusive suits

suits that do not involve a legitimate conflict; suits in which the parties are colluding to bring about the lawsuit

DeFunis v. Odegaard

case that demonstrates the principle of mootness—here the Supreme Court refused to hear an affirmative action case because the controversy was no longer present

 www ▶ ▶ ▶

he alleged practiced racial discrimination when it rejected his application but admitted a black applicant who he argued was less qualified. By the time this case was heard by the Supreme Court, a lower court had ordered DeFunis admitted and he had almost completed his law school classes. Since no one needs (or wants!) to be admitted to the same law school more than once, or to complete law school more than once, the Court ruled that DeFunis's case was now moot. Both ripeness and mootness center on the issue of time—cases that are dismissed because they are not yet ripe have come to the court too early, while those that are dismissed for mootness have come to the court too late.

political-questions doctrine

doctrine that a case is not justiciable if it turns on a question that is better answered by either the legislative or executive branch

The third corollary of justiciability is the **political-questions doctrine**. Courts will decline to hear those cases that they believe raise questions that are better settled by the other branches of government, that is, by the legislature or executive. For many years, the U.S. Supreme Court and other courts declined to hear lawsuits involving how voting districts had been created or modified. Periodically, legislative districts are redrawn to account for changes in population. Following the ten-year census, congressional districts are reconfigured to account for population increases and decreases. Historically, redistricting had been used as a tool for the ruling political party to cement its electoral advantage, and as a result, district lines were often oddly drawn to ensure that a particular legislator or party retained its advantage. For many years, the U.S. Supreme Court and other courts refused to hear cases involving redistricting, even when lines were drawn to disenfranchise groups of voters, usually African Americans. The courts justified their dismissal of voting rights cases by asserting that these cases involved a political question and that courts were an inappropriate forum for hearing these challenges. In a series of cases beginning in 1946, the U.S. Supreme Court held that questions about how district lines had been drawn had to be answered by state legislatures and that courts had no role in attempting to resolve these disputes. It was not until the 1962 *Baker v. Carr* case that the Supreme Court changed its position on this issue and began to hear cases involving voting rights. The Court rejected the political-questions doctrine in this case, alleging that redistricting had effectively deprived African American voters of their right to vote and had undermined the central principle of political equality, which is that every vote should have equal weight. Courts do continue to dismiss cases, however, that they believe are based on political questions. For example, in 1993, the U.S. Supreme Court refused to review the impeachment procedures employed by the U.S. Senate and rejected an appeal by a federal district court judge who had been impeached by that body.

www ▶ ▶ ▶

Baker v. Carr

landmark U.S. Supreme Court case that established that cases involving redistricting could be justiciable

www ▶ ▶ ▶

standing

having a legal right that has been impaired

The third constraint that courts impose on themselves is the requirement of **standing**. For a court to hear a case, it must be brought by the right person, that is, by someone who has a legal right that has been impaired. While jurisdiction focuses on the court and justiciability on the case or controversy, standing focuses on the person bringing the suit. To have standing, the person bringing the suit must demonstrate to the court that they have a legal stake in the case or that they have suffered some real injury. Courts are sometimes more flexible about this requirement; other times, less flexible. For example, after the Supreme Court's 2000 decision in *Friends of the Earth, Inc.* v. *Laidlaw Environmental Services,* it became much more difficult for citizens to bring suits alleging that companies violated environmental protection laws, thus limiting the ability of citizens to serve as watchdogs for these laws.

www ▶ ▶ ▶

ALTERNATIVE DISPUTE RESOLUTION

The use of courts to resolve disputes is a relatively recent phenomenon. Traditionally, people involved in disputes settled their problems without resorting to a governmental entity like a court. Either the grievants relied on a third party, like a tribal leader or elder, or they employed more direct methods, like interpersonal violence, to settle their disputes. Parties also relied on supernatural entities, like God or the devil, to rectify wrongs done to them. History is replete with examples of these alternative dispute resolution "devices." Think about dueling, fist fights, the invocation of heaven or hell, or vigilante justice and you'll have an excellent example of an alternative method. While most people don't want to rely on these devices to resolve their disputes, there is a growing movement aimed at decreasing reliance on courts through use of other dispute resolution methods. In fact, while Americans are fascinated with courts, it bears noting that litigation rates have not spiraled upward in the 1990s: instead, in some courts, like the federal district courts, the number of cases filed has actually dropped, in large part because grievants are looking for alternative forums. In other courts, the rate of increase has not been as great as it might have been had some parties not begun to rely on alternative dispute resolution devices.

Reasons to Rely on ADR

The requirements of jurisdiction, justiciability, and standing sometimes foreclose use of the courts to resolve disputes. For example, for same-sex couples, there is no legal right to marry and so the law doesn't govern the distribution of assets or child-custody decisions in the event that the relationship is dissolved. In these cases, parties turn to **alternative dispute resolution (ADR)** because they have no other recourse. In many other cases, people rely on ADR because of the enormous cost of litigation—bringing a case to court usually involves a huge expenditure of money and time. Moreover, relying on courts introduces the element of uncertainty, since the

alternative dispute resolution (ADR)

the use of some forum other than a court to resolve one's dispute

decision-maker (judge or jury) exclusively determines the outcome, and the litigants have little say in how the case will be resolved. This uncertainty is even more problematic because of the **zero-sum nature of litigation**: that is, because one party is definitely going to win and the other is going to lose. While the focus of litigation is on winning or losing, the focus of ADR is on crafting a solution to the problem. In addition, methods of ADR are private, and settlements do not become a matter of public record, as court decisions do. Many parties need or want to ensure that the award remains confidential. Because of these advantages, the parties themselves may choose ADR and may forgo the use of litigation, at least at the initial stages. In other cases, the decision about ADR is made for the grievants, because federal or state law mandates the use of some ADR method, again, at least for the initial complaint.

Forms of ADR

There are three principal forms of ADR: negotiation, mediation, and arbitration. In addition to these three methods, there are now a number of hybrids, which adopt the characteristics of more than one of these methods. Negotiation, mediation, and arbitration differ in terms of their complexity and formality. **Negotiation**, the least formal of the three devices, has the fewest procedures. It is also probably the most prevalent form of ADR. Negotiation is conducted between the two parties: there is no outside party to aid in the process, and the two parties themselves attempt to arrive at settlement. **Plea bargaining** in criminal cases is probably the most well-known form of negotiation; however, negotiation may be present in virtually every lawsuit and at all stages of litigation. For a successful negotiation, the two parties have to see settlement as the best course of action, and the outcome must be in the best interests of both. Negotiation is not imposed on the parties—they themselves choose it. In this way, negotiation is clearly preferable to litigation, because the parties themselves have the ultimate choice about whether to accept the settlement. Because negotiation involves only the two parties, however, it tends to reinforce inequalities between the parties. If one party has many more resources than the other, in terms of knowledge, experience, time, or money, these advantages can have a profound effect on the kind of negotiated settlement that is reached. In addition, since negotiation involves only the two central actors, it is not the appropriate forum to use when the parties have reached a stalemate and are unable or unwilling to work together.

Mediation may be the answer when communications between the parties have completely broken down. Mediation is slightly more formalized than negotiation in that it involves a third-party who may be chosen by some outside actor or by the parties themselves. The chief function of a mediator is to help the two parties to reach an agreement. This mediator, who is sup-

Margin glossary

zero-sum nature of litigation

in courts, necessity for someone to lose for the other to win; one of the obstacles to real resolution of a dispute

www ▶ ▶ ▶

negotiation

the least formal form of ADR; only the two parties are involved and to succeed, they must see agreement as in their mutual self-interest

plea bargaining

probably the most common form of negotiation

mediation

form of ADR in which a neutral and disinterested third person works with the parties to craft a solution that both parties must accept; fastest growing form of ADR

posed to be disinterested and neutral, should aid the parties in crafting a solution that is in both of their interests. As in negotiation, mediation will only work if the parties agree to the solution and both must see the settlement as in their best interests. Again, the advantage of mediation over litigation is that it is less costly, in terms of time and money, and it provides the parties with the chance to craft a settlement that is certain and that benefits both of them. Furthermore, mediation is more forward-looking. It enables the parties to focus on how they will interact in the future.

The **pretrial settlement conference**, where judges preside over a conference between the parties and may assist in the formulation of a settlement, is the most frequently used form of mediation. Mediation is being used, however, in a number of forums. In some cases, mediation is mandated by law or by contract. The Department of the Navy, for example, mandates the mediation of disputes, as do many private employers and unions. In other cases, mediation is chosen. Many environmental disputes are now mediated, as are other community-based disputes, among these, compensation for crime victims. Mediation is also becoming prevalent in the area of family law, as spouses seek more amicable ways of dividing their property and settling child custody. Many public and private universities also use mediation for students involved in conflicts with other students or with faculty or administrators.

The most effective mediator is one who is able to get the parties to focus on the most important issues and to see the settlement as in their best interest. Sometimes, mediators are experienced trial attorneys who can provide information to both parties about what might happen if their dispute were to go to trial. The mediator's role is sometimes quite narrow, and is confined to the facts introduced by the parties, and at other times it is much broader. For example, an **ombudsman** not only mediates the claim, he or she may also engage in a more extensive investigation of the facts surrounding the dispute. Again, the primary function of a mediator is to facilitate a settlement between the parties. The decision of the mediator is only binding if the parties choose that it be binding.

In contrast, the decision of an arbitrator may be binding on the parties. **Arbitration** is the most formal of the three ADR forms, and it is governed by a code of rules promulgated by the American Arbitration Association. Many **collective bargaining agreements**, which govern the relationship between an employer and union, have arbitration clauses, as do many other private contracts. Arbitration is stipulated in many international commercial contracts, and the parties may opt in or out of such arrangements; however, many corporations choose to use arbitration because they find that it provides a more predictable outcome and is less expensive than litigation. The arbitrator or arbitrators, who are neutral third parties, hear the claim and issue a decision. This decision may or may not be binding—it depends on the law or contract that governs the arbitration. The 1925 the **Federal Arbitration Act** was created to govern maritime and admiralty

---

pretrial settlement conference

probably the most common form of mediation; a judge presides over a conference between the parties and may help formulate a settlement

ombudsman

person who has more responsibility than a mediator and can engage in independent investigation of the claim

arbitration

the most structured form of ADR; uses an arbitrator, whose decision may or may not be binding on the parties

collective bargaining agreements

employment contracts between employers and unions may contain arbitration clauses

Federal Arbitration Act

congressional statute initially created to govern maritime and admiralty disputes; now extended to cover many other kinds of disputes

disputes; over time, it has been expanded to cover many other disputes, as well. The 1998 **Alternative Dispute Resolution Act** requires that federal district court judges offer parties in civil cases at least one form of ADR before proceeding to trial. Moreover, in the 2001 *Circuit City Stores, Inc.* **v.** *Adams* case, the U.S. Supreme Court upheld a mandatory arbitration clause in a private employment contract and found that even when an employee presented a discrimination claim, the employee could be compelled to employ arbitration before proceeding to trial.

The Court in *Circuit City* held that in cases where there is a valid employment contract that mandates the arbitration of any claim, the parties are bound by this document to go to the arbitrator before they go to court. The implementation of arbitral awards and appeals from arbitrator decisions are governed by either the Federal Arbitration Act, which governs disputes arising from the operation of many federal statutes, or the **Uniform Arbitration Act**, which has been adopted by thirty-five states and provides detailed guidance about arbitration under state law. Courts vigorously encourage the use of ADR because it reduces their tremendous caseload and allows parties to achieve a settlement within a much shorter time frame. If one of the parties is dissatisfied with an arbitrator's award, that party still has the right to proceed to adjudication; however, the judge usually has a much more limited role and may only confirm or modify the award. Rarely will the judge overturn an award.

Negotiation, mediation, and arbitration are the three main types of ADR; however, there are a number of hybrid forms that blend one or more of these processes. One of the most controversial of these is use of the **special master**, who has the power to conduct investigations, review the claims of multiple parties, and craft a binding settlement on the parties. Special masters have played an important role in some of the most controversial settlements in the last two decades; among these, the resolution of claims brought by Vietnam veterans who argued that they had been injured by the U.S. government's use of Agent Orange during the war; claims brought against Microsoft for monopolistic and anticompetitive practices; and lawsuits brought against the tobacco industry in some states. Most recently, the work of Special Master Kenneth R. Feinberg, authorized to administer the **September 11 Victim Compensation Fund of 2001**, has come under fire. In the wake of the September 11 attacks, the U.S. Congress passed a law establishing the fund, which was intended to provide compensation to victims of the attacks and their families. It was estimated that roughly 3,300 people who had been injured or killed in the attacks on the World Trade Center and the Pentagon would be eligible for compensation under the fund.

Congress created the fund to serve several purposes. First, it was part of the so-called airline bailout—it provided compensation to those victims who chose to "opt in," but in opting in, the victims and their families had to agree not to sue the airlines for negligence. The federal government paid for

---

Alternative Dispute Resolution Act

congressional statute requiring federal district court judges to offer at least one form of ADR before moving to trial in civil cases

Circuit City Stores, Inc. v. Adams

case in which the Supreme Court upheld a mandatory arbitration clause in an employment contract; in so doing, required a party alleging employment discrimination to arbitrate before he could litigate

Uniform Arbitration Act

act adopted by thirty-five states that regulates arbitration under state law

www ▶ ▶ ▶

special master

hybrid form of ADR that gives an individual wide-ranging power to investigate claims and craft a binding settlement

September 11 Victim Compensation Fund of 2001

fund created by Congress to provide an alternative to litigation for families of victims of the 9/11 attacks; Special Master Feinberg administered this fund

damages out of its own coffers, and in so doing, significantly limited the liability of the airlines. Second, the fund was intended to compensate victims and their families quickly and to ensure that the awards would be fairly predictable. Because the awards were underwritten by the government, there was no question that they would be paid. While negligence suits against the airlines might actually result in higher awards for some litigants, many feared that the industry would quickly be driven into bankruptcy and that many victims and their families would receive no compensation at all.

The guidelines created by Congress and fleshed out by Special Master Feinberg mandated that victims be compensated for noneconomic and economic harm and laid out a series of formulas for determining awards. Families of victims killed in the attacks are eligible for a noneconomic award of $250,000, with an additional $100,000 for each of the victim's dependents. In addition, the family is eligible for an economic award that aims at compensating for lost wages and takes into account the victim's age and income. The award is offset by collateral compensation, like life insurance, pension, and social security payouts. The average award after collateral offsets is estimated to be $1.5 million, and analysts estimate that the fund will award more than $4 billion in damages.

Special Master Feinberg has the responsibility for determining how the rather vague guidelines passed by Congress will be implemented, and some victims' families and lawyers have loudly criticized his assessments. In particular, they have been very dissatisfied with how he has determined economic loss. In May 2003, a federal judge in Manhattan dismissed three lawsuits brought by families against Mr. Feinberg, finding that he had not misused his discretion and that his awards were consistent with Congress's guidelines. Like an arbitrator, a special master's awards can be binding; however, the role of a special master is much more extensive than that of an arbitrator or even a judge. A special master is actively engaged in fact-finding and analysis, and she or he is responsible, not only to the parties who are directly involved in a dispute, but to potential claimants, as well. Typically, special masters oversee complex disputes that involve many parties, and often these special masters have expertise, not only in arbitration and mediation, but in more technical areas, as well.

LAWMAKING AND SOCIAL CHANGE

Courts occupy a unique position in the American political system. While their primary function is the adjudication of disputes, they also engage in lawmaking, and in so doing, may hinder or advance social change. From the time our nation was founded, some have criticized this lawmaking function. In particular, they have been concerned about the role of the

DEBATE

Did the Victim Compensation Fund fairly compensate victims and families of the September 11 attacks?

Yes: This fund allowed families and victims to expedite the hearing of their claims and to know, up front, how much they were likely to be awarded. By eliminating the need for lengthy trial cases and introducing certainty into the award, this fund allowed for psychological closure to begin. This is not a minor point—many of the victims and families of those injured in the 1988 downing of Pan Am flight 103 are still in court, trying to reach settlement in their cases. The fund allowed victims and families to avoid litigation and to receive the settlement monies very quickly. This was no small accomplishment, considering that many of these people needed the money—they had lost their primary wage earner and could not easily have afforded to wait a decade or more for settlement. The settlement awards were based on well-established guidelines used in other kinds of tort lawsuits. Consider also that if these cases had gone forward, they would have likely bankrupted the airline industry. So even if these victims and families had prevailed in court, the airlines might not have had the money to compensate them. The successes of this fund are already apparent—98 percent of eligible parties have received their awards and less than 2 percent of the families or victims of 9/11 have chosen to go to court.

No: Let us be very honest about this fund—it was a bailout for the airline industry, plain and simple. These attacks happened because the airlines placed their passengers at risk by failing to stop the terrorists from boarding the planes. The fund allows the airlines to dodge responsibility for their failures and shifts the cost of this failure to us taxpayers. This sets a dangerous precedent because it encourages companies to assume that the government will pick up the tab even if they are responsible for creating a dangerous situation.

In addition, the fund was based on a callous calculation of each life lost—these settlements were based on the jobs that the victims held, their age, whether they were married, and whether they had dependents. This is simply unfair and assumes that the loss of some families was greater than that of others. How can you put a value on human life? The lives of the police officers and firefighters lost cannot possibly be worth less than the lives of high-paid executives working in the towers, and yet that is the assumption on which the fund's guidelines are based.

the power of courts to
strike down acts of the
legislature and chief
executive; used relatively
infrequently by the
U.S. Supreme Court

U.S. Supreme Court in this system. Courts exercise the power of **judicial review**, meaning that they can strike down laws passed by the other branches of government if they find the laws to be in conflict with the federal or state constitutions.

Lawmaking by the U.S. Supreme Court

The U.S. Supreme Court is the final court of appeals in this system, and when this Court strikes down a law, the legislature, executive, or administrative agency must revise this law so that it is in accordance with the Court's holding. The potential power of judicial review is huge, but you may want to consider that it was not bestowed on the Supreme Court by any specific provision in the U.S. Constitution! Instead, the Court established this power itself in a series of cases beginning with the landmark 1803 case *Marbury* v. *Madison*. Every first-year law student is charged with deciphering this case, and it is arguably the single most important case decided by the Court in its long history. In *Marbury,* the Court announced that it alone had the power to decide or interpret what the Constitution says, and that it had the power to strike down laws that it viewed as conflicting with this document. While the high court exercises the power of judicial review relatively infrequently, the fact that it has this power certainly has some impact on how legislators and administrators formulate laws. Throughout our nation's history, some have fiercely criticized the power of judicial review, arguing that it undermines democratic rule. They contend that federal court judges, and Supreme Court justices in particular, are not democratically elected and that the power of judicial review allows them to strike down laws passed by those representatives whom the people have selected in direct elections. Consider that the Court has repeatedly struck down congressional statutes that made it a crime to desecrate the American flag in any way. While the vast majority of Americans strongly supported these laws, the Court nevertheless found that they interfered with the First Amendment freedoms of speech and expression.

■ **Judicial Selection** Others have countered by arguing either that there is an electoral connection to the selection of federal judges, since the president who appoints these judges and the senators who confirm them are democratically elected, or that there needs to be some insulation between the people and judges in order for democracy to function properly. Those who argue that the selection procedure itself allows voters to influence which judges are chosen focus on two facts. First, the president usually chooses judges who share his own philosophy, and the president expects that his appointees will decide cases in accordance with this philosophy. For example, while President George W. Bush criticized the politicization of the confirmation process in his May 2001 speech announcing his appointment of a group of federal judges, he nevertheless made a point of stating that his appointees shared his judicial philosophy. Moreover, the judges that he chose were far more conservative, in terms of civil rights and civil liberties issues, than the judges selected by his predecessor, Bill Clinton.

The Senate's role in confirming judicial appointees can also be highly politicized. Senate confirmation hearings are often very public events, especially when U.S. Supreme Court nominees are being questioned. Interest groups and prominent individuals are invited to weigh in on the qualifications and appropriateness of nominees. Organized interest groups can have a powerful role in the confirmation process—consider that vigorous lobbying by professional organizations and liberal interest groups is credited with defeating the confirmation of Robert Bork for the Supreme Court in 1985. President Bush, frustrated with the difficulty he has encountered in having his nominees confirmed, has taken a number of steps to blunt the impact of these interest groups. In 2003, President Bush announced that he would no longer consider the American Bar Association's long-standing practice of "rating" judicial nominees on their backgrounds and suitability for the bench. The president also thumbed his nose at the Senate Judiciary Committee, which rejected the nomination of the very controversial judge Charles W. Pickering, Sr., by using emergency powers to give him a recess appointment that didn't need Senate approval and remains in place until the end of 2004.

There are many who believe that there should be a link between the judiciary and the public; they point to the Senate's important role in the confirmation process as a link that should be respected, and if possible, strengthened. There are many others who argue, however, that there should be no direct link between judges and the public. They point out that democracies do not always protect the rights of the numeric minority and that insulating judges from the influence of the majority serves to safeguard these rights. These analysts point to the role of the courts in protecting the rights of racial minorities by striking down racist and discriminatory laws passed by state legislatures throughout the late 1800s and early 1900s. Clearly, these laws which strictly segregated African-Americans and whites and effectively confined African Americans to inferior positions in society, were passed by representatives who had been selected by a majority of the voting population in these states. Moreover, many of these laws continued to be quite popular well into the 1950s and 1960s. By stepping into this fray and striking down these laws, the U.S. Supreme Court was assuming an antidemocratic position, and there was fierce criticism of the Court's rulings throughout this period. While most people now believe that these laws were wrong and that the Court was justified in striking down these laws, holdings that invalidate state and federal laws continue to generate strong and vocal criticism of the Court. The Supreme Court's decisions in the areas of abortion, capital punishment, free speech, school prayer, and affirmative action have generated substantial opposition, as critics denounce the Court for undermining democratic rule.

■ **Role of the Court in a Democracy** Much of this discussion about the role of the Court in a democratic system focuses on whether the Court *can* or *should* be allowed to take action that brings about a significant change in social or political structure. Some people seriously question whether courts should occupy this position: they claim that in a democratic society, the courts should not be able to counteract the decisions of legislators and administrators. The question of whether courts should be able to exercise judicial review is largely a normative or philosophical one, and your opinion about this is probably guided by your views about law, society, and politics. The second question—whether courts *can* in fact bring about social change—is much more empirical. This question focuses on whether judicial decisions have a real impact on bringing about change in the larger social and economic structures. In the wake of the civil rights movement and the debate about abortion rights, some scholars began to question whether even landmark Supreme Court decisions made a difference. There has been a lot of argument about the real impact of these decisions on social and political debate, and some scholars believe strongly that these decisions did not bring about social change.

By examining the Court's decisions in desegregation and abortion cases, scholars like Gerald Rosenberg, who wrote *The Hollow Hope,* concluded that instead of promoting civil rights or abortion rights, these cases had the opposite effect. While the landmark cases were important in terms of their symbolic value, the ultimate effect of these cases may have been quite negative. In particular, *Roe* v. *Wade,* the case that established that there is a constitutional right to abortion, sparked a tremendous wave of opposition to abortion rights and to the Court's role in this debate. This opposition was hugely successful in crafting new abortion laws in the state legislatures, which were largely upheld by the Court in the 1990s. Rosenberg and other have argued that landmark cases sometimes have unintended effects—they encourage those who support the decision to believe that the battle has been won and to stop lobbying the courts, legislatures, and agencies. At the same time, they spark opposition efforts to overturn these decisions and often mobilize the opposition to take action. Thus, it is difficult to determine whether courts can bring about social change.

The symbolic impact of landmark Supreme Court decisions, however, cannot be underestimated. The Court's decision in *Brown* v. *Board of Education* clearly articulated an important shift in our views about racial segregation. Clearly, *Brown* generated huge opposition among, not only individuals, but also many elected officials. Among these were Alabama Governor George Wallace, who announced in his 1963 inaugural speech that he was "draw[ing] the line in the dust and toss[ing] the gauntlet before the feet of tyranny" and pledging his support for "segregation today . . . segregation tomorrow . . . segregation forever." But *Brown* represented a watershed moment in American legal history because it clearly rejected a view that had up until then been accepted by nearly all courts that had considered segregation, and that was the belief that having separate public accommodations, including schools, did not violate the equal protection guarantee of the Fifth and Fourteenth Amendments to the Constitution. Ultimately, *Brown* ran up against serious barriers to full implementation. Most importantly, it did little to address patterns of residential segregation or to counter trends that reinforced the increasing separation of racial groups into different communities.

Many point to *Brown* and *Roe* as examples of the inability of courts to produce social change, and it is probably true that controversial court decisions do not definitively settle an issue. But these decisions may better be viewed as part of the policy response to a problem or controversy. In our system of law, courts, legislators, executives, and administrators work in concert to create, implement, and modify law. All the branches of government are actively involved in making and interpreting law, and this function is not neatly bestowed on any one branch. In the following chapters, we'll be discussing the shared lawmaking role of these three branches and how this complex and fascinating system produces an almost continuous cycle of lawmaking and modification.

SUMMARY

This chapter examined two primary functions that courts are assumed to have—first, courts are assumed to function to resolve disputes; and second, many believe that courts can and should function to bring about social change. This chapter examined the stages of dispute resolution and noted that a dispute comes to court because one or both parties seek an authoritative resolution of their disagreement. Unfortunately, there are real limitations to using courts to resolve disputes. Chief among these is the fact that cases tend to be framed in terms of legal rights, are backward looking and reactive, require that one party lose in order for the other to win, and offer only the options sought by the parties.

This chapter also discussed how going to court transforms any dispute and may ultimately undermine efforts to resolve it. In addition, there are certain real limitations to going to court—the court must have the power to resolve the dispute; the right parties must be bringing the case; and the case itself must be appropriate for judicial hearing. These requirements of jurisdiction, standing, and justiciability foreclose many parties from bringing their disputes to court. In part because access to court is sometimes limited by these requirements and because courts are sometimes unable to craft a real solution that resolves the underlying controversy, parties are increasingly turning to alternative dispute resolution mechanisms. These mechanisms, chiefly negotiation, mediation, and arbitration, are already very much a part of our American legal system and will likely remain so far into the future. And finally, this chapter examined the claim sometimes made that law functions to promote social change, and it discussed some of the obstacles that interfere with this function.

SUGGESTED READING

Thomas F. Burke, *Lawyers, Lawsuits, and Legal Rights: The Battle over Litigation in American Society* (California Series in Law, Politics, and Society, 2) (University of California Press, 2004). This book argues that certain kinds of legislation generate litigation. It examines three different laws—the Americans with Disabilities Act, California's no-fault car insurance, and the Vaccine Injury Compensation Fund—in an attempt to identify what it is about these laws that has generated litigation.

John M. Conley and William M. O'Barr, *Just Words: Law, Language and Power* (University of Chicago Press, 1998). According to these authors, the language of law is one of power, and this power is manifest in the very process of litigation.

Michael J. Klarman, *From Jim Crow to Civil Rights: The Supreme Court and the Struggle for Racial Equality* (Oxford University Press, 2004). This excellent book places the highly controversial *Brown* v. *Board of Education* decision in historical context. It argues that the Supreme Court's ruling was both a response to wider societal pressures and a catalyst for further changes in race relations.

Larry D. Kramer, *The People Themselves: Popular Constitutionalism and Judicial Review* (Oxford University Press, 2004). This book argues that "the people" have an ownership stake in the U.S. Constitution and uses the *Marbury* v. *Madison* case to further explore the principle of popular sovereignty, or rule by the people, that is at the core of this document.

Tinsley E. Yarbrough, *Race and Redistricting: The Shaw-Cromartie Cases* (Landmark Law Cases and American Society) (University of Kansas Press, 2002). This excellent study examines landmark redistricting cases heard by the Supreme Court in the 1990s. These cases squarely raised the question of whether districts could be configured to advantage racial minorities. The author looks at a wealth of information—not just cases, but interviews with litigants and their lawyers—to understand how these cases were decided.

ACTIVE LEARNING

1. Read or view *A Civil Action* (or any other book involving toxic torts) and consider how the dispute moved from stage to stage, or how it stalled in one stage or another. Do you think that adjudication effectively

resolved the underlying dispute? Do you think there might have been more effective methods of dispute resolution?

2. "Log" a casual conversation with a friend or family members and notice how often we speak in the language of disputes—remember, disputes are everywhere, though few of them are ever resolved! After you log the conversation, read it—do you notice any patterns? Probably what you will see is that most dialogue is a dispute-seeking—that is, most conversations we have are in the form of question/answer, and we tend to home in on the problems or concerns of others, often asking increasingly specific questions. Did this happen in your conversation? How often did you or your conversation partner demonstrate empathy toward each other by saying things like "really?" "that is terrible" or just "hmmm"? Empathy is actually a valuable conversational skill that provides the space for partners to exchange information.

CHAPTER 8

Legislatures and Lawmaking

When most people think about lawmaking in the United States, they think about legislatures. The principal function of legislatures to create law, specifically, code law. Under the federal and state constitutions, the power to make law is expressly given to the legislative bodies. There is a **dual legislative system** *in the United States, meaning that there are separate and largely independent legislatures operating at the federal and state levels. This dual organization is a result of our federal system of government, where power is shared between the national and state governments, and responsibility for specific areas or policies is given to one set of actors or the other.*

dual legislative system

the two separate and largely independent federal and state systems

DUAL LEGISLATIVE STRUCTURE

Until the early 1900s, most legislation came out of state legislatures. Congressional lawmaking was far more limited than it is today, and state legislatures had most of the power to create, implement, and change domestic law. The **police power**, that is, the power to protect and maintain public health, safety, and morality, was lodged with the states, and the federal government generally did not interfere with state law. Since the 1930s, the power of the U.S. Congress to create and implement domestic law has waxed and waned—at times, Congress has been able to take broad action in its area of domestic law; at other times, its power has been starkly limited. For example, one of the most important sources of congressional power is Article I, Section 8, of the U.S. Constitution. This clause is the source of Congress's **commerce power**, which allows Congress to pass laws regulating trade with foreign nations and commerce between the states. From roughly 1937 through 1995, the U.S. Supreme Court interpreted Congress's power to regulate interstate commerce very broadly. Throughout this period, the Court allowed Congress to pass law that regulated

police power

the power of a legislature to protect the health, safety, and morality of its citizens; this power was recognized in the Tenth Amendment, which leaves to the state legislatures all powers not granted to the Congress and which has been the chief source of lawmaking power for the states

194

commerce power

the power to regulate trade among the states, known as interstate commerce, was given to Congress in Article I, Section 8, of the Constitution; the Supreme Court's interpretation of this power has sometimes been broad and other times narrow

www ▶ ▶ ▶

www ▶ ▶ ▶

implied powers

Congress not only has the right to take action to accomplish the explicit goals laid out in Article 1, Section 8; this clause also gives Congress the power to make laws that are "necessary and proper" to achieve these goals—this clause, also known as the elastic clause, is the source of Congress's implied powers

www ▶ ▶ ▶

activities, even if those activities occurred solely within one state's borders. Before 1937 and since 1995, however, the Court has quite dramatically limited Congress's commerce power and has decided that states should have responsibility for lawmaking when an activity occurs solely within state borders. The issue of whether commerce is intrastate (starting and ending solely within a state's borders) or interstate (occurring across those borders) is a difficult one. For example, in *U.S. v. Lopez,* the landmark case that most read as limiting Congress's commerce power, the Court struck down the 1990 Gun-Free School Zones law, which made it a federal criminal offense to carry a gun into a school zone. The Court held that this activity was occurring solely within one state and had no real economic impact on interstate commerce. In its decision, the Court rejected the argument that having guns on school grounds might affect the educational experience of students and thus might have a profound long-term impact on the national economy. Since *Lopez,* the Court has struck down a number of other congressional statutes, finding that they too exceeded the commerce power—among these, a law that provided a federal remedy for gender-motivated crimes (*U.S. v. Morrison*) and one that required that local police to perform background checks that would be used in a national registry of handgun owners (*U.S. v. Printz*).

Since the 1990s, the U.S. Supreme Court has also limited Congress's **implied powers**—these are the powers given to Congress in the last clause of Article I, Section 8, also known as the "necessary and proper" clause. This clause gives Congress very specific powers, among these, the power to tax, borrow money, coin money, and declare war. Since very early in our nation's history, the necessary and proper clause has been read as significantly broadening this list by allowing Congress to take any additional action that helps it perform these duties. Since the narrowing of the commerce clause, the necessary and proper clause has also been read in a more constrained way. For example, the *Morrison* and *Printz* cases turned on the Court's reading of both clauses, and in these cases, the Court demonstrated that it was much more willing to allow Congress to engage in lawmaking when it was acting pursuant to some explicit power that it read broadly. In 2003, the Court provided an example of this in its decision in *Jinks* v. *Richland County, S.C.* (123 S.Ct. 1667). In this case, the Court let stand a congressional statute that allowed the widow of an inmate who died while in the custody of a state penitentiary to bring suit in federal court. The widow alleged that state officials had lied about how her husband had died, and that the federal law allowed her to bring a separate lawsuit, even after a significant period of time had passed. Here, the justices found that this law was "necessary and proper" to achieve the goal of ensuring that witnesses and parties be truthful in court proceedings.

Although cases that affect the scope of Congress's lawmaking power receive a great deal of public attention, the fact is that state legislatures have always played a central role in lawmaking, and most U.S. law comes from the states, not from the U.S. Congress. While Congress has passed a number of criminal laws in the last several decades, most people agree that the framers of the U.S. Constitution intended to leave much of the power to make and enforce criminal law to the states. As a result, most criminal law is state law, and an examination of state penal codes reveals significant variation among the states. Some people believe that this variability is a good thing because it reflects the sometimes differing views of people about what acts should be criminalized. Others see this variability as much more troubling since it indicates that there is no one authoritative source of law in the United States.

The article about cyberstalking on the website illustrates the difficulties that are sometimes apparent in a system like ours, where many different actors are engaged in lawmaking. **Cyberstalking** is generally defined as the systematic harassment by a group or an individual of some individual by means of electronic communication. By 2003, nearly all state legislatures had enacted some form of cyberstalking ban; however, there is wide variability in the laws that have been passed, and there is no way to ensure that someone who crosses state borders, a relatively easy thing to do with the Internet, can be effectively prosecuted. This crazy quilt of state laws is made even more confusing by the fact that there is no unifying federal law.

Some people view the variation in states' criminal law in a positive light. They see this system as one that encourages experimentation and innovation. Others criticize the fact that the same action may be punished very differently depending on the state in which it was taken. In an attempt to smooth over some of the differences between the states and to facilitate the movement of goods and people across state borders, the framers of the Constitution included the full faith and credit clause in Article IV. Under this provision, states must recognize the public laws, records, and judicial proceedings of each other and must respect the privileges and immunities granted to citizens in other states. This clause is the reason that you don't have to get a driver's license for every state that you happen to drive through, and that a marriage license from one state is respected in others.

Recently, there has been a great deal of debate about whether the full faith and credit clause protects same-sex marriages entered into in Massachusetts, the one state that now recognizes these unions. In 1996, Congress passed the **Defense of Marriage Act (DOMA)**, which established that the federal government would only recognize marriages between a man and a woman and would not pay federal benefits, like social security, to same-sex couples. Interestingly, the DOMA also limited the application of the full faith and credit clause, by allowing states to refuse to recognize the same-sex marriages performed in other states. In late 2004, many Republican legislators, eager to pass a constitutional amendment that would bar all same-sex marriage, began to argue that the very law that they had so staunchly supported—the DOMA—was in fact unconstitutional, because it modified a constitutional provision. While the proposed constitutional amendment

www ▶ ▶ ▶

cyberstalking

the systematic harassment of an individual by means of electronic communication

Defense of Marriage Act (DOMA)

1996 Congressional statute stipulating that the federal government will only recognize marriage between a man and a woman and will not pay federal benefits to same-sex couples

www ▶ ▶ ▶

banning all same-sex marriage appears to be dead or dying, it remains to be seen whether this argument about the constitutionality of the DOMA will prevail in the courts.

Although criminal law and laws regarding marriage and divorce have traditionally been the province of the states, Congress has adopted its own criminal laws whenever a national, uniform law seemed to be necessary. For example, in the late 1800s, Congress passed a criminal law banning the transportation of women and children across state lines for immoral purposes—that is, it prohibited the trafficking of women and children for prostitution or other illicit sexual activity. Congress justified this law by stating that these activities affected individuals in more than one state and that regulation of this interstate transportation was justified as an extension of the commerce power. The U.S. Congress has continued to create criminal laws in the post-9/11 era. We see representatives considering a broad range of criminal prohibitions to counter domestic and international terrorism. To some extent, these laws appear to slight the traditional deference paid to state legislation in the area of criminal law; however, continuing concern about terrorist activities that cross state boundaries may make it more difficult to argue that Congress should not be able to act in this area. Some of these laws, among these, the Patriot Acts I and II, may very well run afoul of certain constitutional protections, among them, the right to privacy and the protection against unreasonable searches and seizures. It remains to be seen how the U.S. Supreme Court will handle challenges to these acts in the future.

CHARACTERISTICS OF LEGISLATIVE LAWMAKING

The lawmaking role is one that is shared not only by state and federal legislatures, but by legislatures and courts. As we discussed in Chapters 6 and 7, courts effectively create law in the American system. While lawmaking is shared, however, the kind of law that a legislature creates is quite different from that which courts make. As we saw in earlier chapters, judge-made law tends to be reactive. Judge-made law applies only to situations that are similar to the cases before the court. Judge-made law tends to be limited and not comprehensive. Judges are expected to choose from the options presented by the parties and not to consider the universe of options. And finally, judge-made law tends to be conservative and to protect the status quo, largely because of how the principle of stare decisis works. While judge-made law is open to interpretation by later courts and may in fact be modified significantly by reinterpretation, courts rarely expressly overrule an earlier judgment. For this reason, judge-made law is often less than clear.

Agenda-Setting

In contrast, law made by legislatures is very different. When a state legislature or Congress engages in lawmaking, it engages in an extensive process, and the actual passage of the bill is only a very small part of this process. At the start of the lawmaking process, an issue is placed on the legislative agenda, often because of the activities of some interested group or because of some highly visible and public event. In theory, any issue or social problem can be placed on the legislative agenda; this is very different from the agenda-setting that takes place in most courts, where the parties who bring their case before the court set the agenda. The important exception to this rule is the U.S. Supreme Court, which largely chooses which appellate cases it will hear. Legislators, on the other hand, are free to choose any issue or problem as a subject for legislation. In reality, legislators choose from only a narrow subset of issues when they set their agendas. Consider the agenda of the U.S. Congress: most of the bills that Congress considers are of concern to upper- and middle-class interests—very few issues are those of the poor or the working poor. Issues of class or class divisions rarely emerge on legislative agendas. The underclass is poorly represented when it comes to the agenda of our legislative bodies.

www ▶ ▶ ▶

The Lawmaking Process

political salience

issues that are of significant interest to voters or interest groups and that are usually placed on the legislative agenda

Legislatures are responsive to those issues with high **political salience**— what this means is those issues that are of great importance to most voters or to powerful interest groups will likely get legislators' attention. Thus legislators often respond to some issue that has erupted and has commanded media and public attention by quickly placing this issue on their agendas. When an internal Justice Department document was sharply critical of the ongoing interrogation and detention of thousands of largely Arab and South Asian men, the House Judiciary Committee placed this issue on its agenda by holding oversight hearings. At these hearings, the committee invited comment by many interested individuals and groups. Once an issue is placed on the agenda, the legislature engages in extensive fact-finding and analysis. The U.S. Congress and state legislatures all hold hearings on specific issues and on laws that are being considered. These hearings are expected to provide a wealth of information about the underlying problem and about possible solutions to the problem.

www ▶ ▶ ▶

fact-finding

one of the chief functions of legislative hearings— allows legislators to gather information about an issue

■ **Fact-Finding** Fact-finding is one of the main functions of legislative hearings. Through fact-finding, legislators expect to gather information about what action should be taken to deal with some issue. Because legislators themselves are generalists and usually lack the expertise to gather information on all possible topics, they rely heavily on the work of specialists. This is especially true when they are assessing legislation that deals with complex or sophisticated issues. Most of the work of Congress and the state legislatures takes place in **specialized committees**. These specialized standing committees have expertise in particular areas; for example, there are House and Senate ways and means committees, interstate commerce committees, labor committees, and foreign affairs committees. Not surprisingly, there is often overlap in the work done by the committees and subcommittees, and "turf battles" are not uncommon. The decision about which committee is responsible for an issue and has the power to craft the legislation is a very important one, and representatives sometimes must negotiate "jurisdictional" conflicts that arise between committees.

specialized committees

groups in the federal and state legislatures that have expertise in particular areas and usually provide much-needed information about proposed bills to the larger legislative body

When legislators begin to consider a bill, they usually invite interested parties to give testimony on that bill to the specialized committee or to one of its subcommittees. In May 2003, Congress invited the director of the American Civil Liberties Union Technology and Liberty Program on Government Data Mining to give testimony before the House Government Reform Subcommittee on Technology, Information Policy, Intergovernmental Relations and the Census about the impact of the Patriot Act on reducing the risk of terrorism and also on its impact on personal privacy (see website for the text of these hearings and use web icon). The technology issues were highly sophisticated, and legislators relied on specialists like this ACLU director to help them to assess the impact of the Patriot Act.

www ▶ ▶ ▶

■ **Crafting a Law** After choosing their agenda and collecting information about the topics or issues that interest them, legislators must decide whether to create legislation. If legislators decide to create a law, they must choose from among the available options—that is, they must decide how they will deal with a problem and then craft a solution in the form of a law. This law is often modified, sometimes very dramatically, in the course of the lawmaking process. In most states and in the U.S. Congress, a bill must pass through both houses of the legislature, and the bills that are approved by each house must eventually be identical. The president or governor has responsibility for signing this bill into law, and his or her opposition may only be overcome by a two-thirds majority vote of both houses.

Relatively few bills become law, and even the creation of a law does not necessarily mean that it will be enforced or that it will remain in the form in which it was initially passed. In fact, there is often significant modification of law, with or without the approval of the lawmaking body. This modification may take a number of forms: changes in the law may be the result of a formal amendment process or the result of informal action or inaction of those people who are most affected by the law. For example, when the U.S. Congress passed Title VII of the 1964 Civil Rights Act, which barred employment discrimination based on gender, it did not clarify whether the law also prohibited pregnancy discrimination. After the U.S. Supreme Court held that the law didn't prohibit pregnancy discrimination, Congress responded by passing the 1978 Pregnancy Discrimination Act, which specifically defined the gender prohibition as encompassing pregnancy.

Often, legislators pass laws that are quite ambiguous and leave it to administrative agencies to "flesh out" the law through regulations. Many times, this lack of clarity is the result of political compromise—an issue may be so controversial that legislators are only be able to achieve agreement by passing a law that is ambiguous. The work of clarifying this law is usually the responsibility of an administrative or regulatory agency. When the U.S. Congress passed the Endangered Species Act (ESA) in 1973, it barred the "taking" of endangered or threatened species of animals or plants. The definition of "taking" has been subject to a great deal of controversy.

www ▶ ▶ ▶

In 1975 the secretary of commerce broadly defined "taking" to include, not only the direct killing of a protected species, but destruction or modification of its habitat, as well. In 1982 Congress passed an amendment to the ESA that empowered the secretary to grant a permit virtually excusing action that was incidental to the taking of life or habitat. That is, where the killing of a species or destruction of habitat was not the primary purpose, but instead was a consequence of some action, that action would be excused. These two provisions seemed to be in direct conflict: the secretary's regulation prohibited habitat destruction, but the amendment seemed to allow it, provided the responsible party was able to show that he or she was motivated by some factor other than a desire to harm a species or its habitat.

The responsibility for clarifying ambiguous legislation also sometimes falls on judges, who are charged with determining the statutory intent of the legislators in order to interpret and apply the law. Ultimately, it was the U.S. Supreme Court that definitively determined how "taking" should be defined. In the 1995 case *Babbitt v. Sweet Home Chapter of Communities for a Great Oregon*, the Court ruled that the taking clause also prohibited habitat modification or destruction. An excerpt of this case follows: while reading, consider how the justices deferred to congressional intent in passing this law and to the expertise of the secretary in interpreting it.

Babbitt v. Sweet Home Chapter of Communities for a Great Oregon

1995 case in which the Supreme Court ruled that the definition of "taking" in the Endangered Species Act included the destruction of habitat

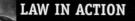

LAW IN ACTION

Clarifying Ambiguous Legislation

BRUCE BABBITT, SECRETARY OF INTERIOR, ET AL., PETITIONERS V. SWEET HOME CHAPTER OF COMMUNITIES FOR A GREAT OREGON ET AL. U.S. Supreme Court, 1995

www ▶ ▶ ▶ (See *Law, Politics, and Society* website for a link to the complete decision.)

JUSTICE STEVENS delivered the opinion of the Court.

The Endangered Species Act of 1973 . . . (ESA or Act), contains a variety of protections designed to save from extinction species that the Secretary of the Interior designates as endangered or threatened. Section 9 of the Act makes it unlawful for any person to "take" any endangered or threatened species. The Secretary has promulgated a regulation that defines the statute's prohibition on takings to include "significant habitat modification or degradation where it actually kills or injures wildlife." This case presents the question whether the Secretary exceeded his authority under the Act by promulgating that regulation.

Section 9(a)(1) of the Endangered Species Act provides the following protection for endangered species:

Except as provided in sections 1535(g)(2) and 1539 of this title, with respect to any endangered species of fish or wildlife listed pursuant to section 1533 of this title it is unlawful for any person subject to the jurisdiction of the United States to . . ."(B) take any such species within the United States or the territorial sea of the United States[.]" 16 U.S.C. 1538(a)(1).

Section 3(19) of the Act defines the statutory term "take":

The term "take" means to harass, harm, pursue, hunt, shoot, wound, kill, trap, capture, or collect, or to attempt to engage in any such conduct. 16 U.S.C. 1532(19).

The Act does not further define the terms it uses to define "take." The Interior Department regulations that implement the statute, however, define the statutory term "harm":

Harm in the definition of "take" in the Act means an act which actually kills or injures wildlife. Such act may include significant habitat modification or degradation where it actually kills or injures wildlife by significantly impairing essential behavioral patterns, including breeding, feeding, or sheltering. 50 CFR 17.3 (1994).

This regulation has been in place since 1975 . . .

A limitation on the 9 "take" prohibition appears in 10(a)(1)(B) of the Act, which Congress added by amendment in 1982. That section authorizes the Secretary to grant a permit for any taking otherwise prohibited by 9(a)(1)(B) "if such taking is incidental to, and not the purpose of, the carrying out of an otherwise lawful activity." 16 U.S.C. 1539(a)(1)(B) . . .

Respondents in this action are small landowners, logging companies, and families

LAW IN ACTION—(CONT'D)

dependent on the forest products industries in the Pacific Northwest and in the Southeast, and organizations that represent their interests. They brought this declaratory judgment action against petitioners, the Secretary of the Interior and the Director of the Fish and Wildlife Service, in the United States District Court for the District of Columbia to challenge the statutory validity of the Secretary's regulation defining "harm" particularly the inclusion of habitat modification and degradation in the definition . . . Respondents challenged the regulation on its face. Their complaint alleged that application of the "harm" regulation to the red-cockaded woodpecker, an endangered species, and the northern spotted owl, a threatened species, had injured them economically.

Respondents advanced three arguments to support their submission that Congress did not intend the word "take" in 9 to include habitat modification, as the Secretary's "harm" regulation provides. First, they correctly noted that language in the Senate's original version of the ESA would have defined "take" to include "destruction, modification, or curtailment of [the] habitat or range" of fish or wildlife, but the Senate deleted that language from the bill before enacting it. Second, respondents argued that Congress intended the Act's express authorization for the Federal Government to buy private land in order to prevent habitat degradation in 5 to be the exclusive check against habitat modification on private property. Third, because the Senate added the term "harm" to the definition of "take" in a floor amendment without debate, respondents argued that the court should not interpret the term so expansively as to include habitat modification . . .

II

Because this case was decided on motions for summary judgment, we may appropriately make certain factual assumptions in order to frame the legal issue. First, we assume respondents have no desire to harm either the red-cockaded woodpecker or the spotted owl; they merely wish to continue logging activities that would be entirely proper if not prohibited by the ESA. On the other hand, we must assume arguendo that those activities will have the effect, even though unintended, of detrimentally changing the natural habitat of both listed species and that, as a consequence, members of those species will be killed or injured. Under respondents' view of the law, the Secretary's only means of forestalling that grave result—even when the actor knows it is certain to occur—is to use his 5 authority to purchase the lands on which the survival of the species depends. The Secretary, on the other hand, submits that the 9 prohibition on takings, which Congress defined to include "harm" places on respondents a duty to avoid harm that habitat alteration will cause the birds unless respondents first obtain a permit pursuant to 10.

The text of the Act provides three reasons for concluding that the Secretary's interpretation is reasonable. First, an ordinary understanding of the word "harm" supports it. The dictionary definition of the verb form of "harm" is "to cause hurt or damage to: injure," Webster's Third New International Dictionary 1034 (1966). In the context of the ESA, that definition naturally encompasses habitat modification that results in actual injury or death to members of an endangered or threatened species.

Respondents argue that the Secretary should have limited the purview of "harm" to direct applications of force against protected species, but the dictionary definition does not include the word "directly" or suggest in any way that only direct or willful action that leads to injury constitutes "harm." Moreover, unless the statutory term "harm" encompasses indirect as well as direct injuries, the word has no meaning that does not duplicate the meaning of other words that 3 uses to define "take." A reluctance to treat statutory terms as surplusage supports the reasonableness of the Secretary's interpretation. See, e.g., Mackey v. Lanier Collection Agency & Service, Inc . . .

Second, the broad purpose of the ESA supports the Secretary's decision to extend protection against activities that cause the precise harms Congress enacted the statute to avoid. In TVA v. Hill (1978), we described the Act as "the most comprehensive legislation for the preservation of endangered species ever enacted by any nation." Id., at 180. Whereas predecessor statutes enacted in 1966 and 1969 had not contained any sweeping prohibition against the taking of endangered species except on federal lands, see id., at 175, the 1973 Act applied to all land in the United States and to the Nation's territorial seas. As stated in 2 of the Act, among its central purposes is "to provide a means whereby the ecosystems upon which endangered species and threatened species depend may be conserved . . ."

In Hill, we construed 7 as precluding the completion of the Tellico Dam because of its predicted impact on the survival of the snail darter . . . Both our holding and the language in our opinion stressed the importance of the statutory policy. "The plain intent of Congress in enacting this statute," we recognized, "was to halt and reverse the trend toward species extinction, whatever the cost. This is reflected not only in the stated policies of the Act, but in literally every section of the statute." Although the 9 "take" prohibition was not at issue in Hill, we took note of that prohibition, placing particular emphasis on the Secretary's inclusion of habitat modification in his definition of "harm." In light of that provision for habitat protection, we could "not understand how TVA intends to operate Tellico Dam without 'harming' the snail darter." Congress' intent to provide comprehensive protection for endangered and threatened species supports the permissibility of the Secretary's "harm" regulation.

Respondents advance strong arguments that activities that cause minimal or unforeseeable harm will not violate the Act as construed in the "harm" regulation. Respondents, however, present a facial challenge to the regulation . . . Thus, they ask us to invalidate the Secretary's understanding of "harm" in every circumstance, even when an actor knows that an activity, such as draining a pond, would actually result in the extinction of a listed species by destroying its habitat. Given Congress' clear expression of the ESA's broad purpose to protect endangered and threatened wildlife, the Secretary's definition of "harm" is reasonable . . .

Third, the fact that Congress in 1982 authorized the Secretary to issue permits for takings that 9(a)(1)(B) would otherwise prohibit, "if such taking is incidental to, and not the purpose of, the carrying out of an otherwise lawful activity," . . . strongly suggests that Congress understood 9(a)(1)(B) to prohibit indirect as well as deliberate takings . . . The permit process requires the applicant to prepare a "conservation plan" that specifies how he intends to "minimize and miti- gate" the "impact" of his activity on endangered and threatened species, 16 U.S.C. 1539(a)(2)(A), making clear that Congress had in mind foresee- able rather than merely accidental effects on listed species . . . No one could seriously request an "incidental" take permit to avert 9 liability for direct, deliberate action against a member of an endangered or threatened species, but respon- dents would read "harm" so narrowly that the per- mit procedure would have little more than that absurd purpose. "When Congress acts to amend a statute, we presume it intends its amendment to have real and substantial effect . . ." Congress' addition of the 10 permit provision supports the Secretary's conclusion that activities not intended to harm an endangered species, such as habitat modification, may constitute unlaw- ful takings under the ESA unless the Secretary permits them . . .

We need not decide whether the statutory definition of "take" compels the Secretary's interpretation of "harm," because our conclu- sions that Congress did not unambiguously man- ifest its intent to adopt respondents' view and that the Secretary's interpretation is reasonable suffice to decide this case . . . The latitude the ESA gives the Secretary in enforcing the statute, together with the degree of regulatory expertise necessary to its enforcement, establishes that we owe some degree of deference to the Sec- retary's reasonable interpretation . . .

III

Our conclusion that the Secretary's definition of "harm" rests on a permissible construction of the ESA gains further support from the legisla- tive history of the statute. The Committee Reports accompanying the bills that became the ESA do not specifically discuss the meaning of "harm," but they make clear that Congress intended "take" to apply broadly to cover indi- rect as well as purposeful actions. The Senate Report stressed that "'[t]ake' is defined . . . in the broadest possible manner to include every conceivable way in which a person can 'take' or attempt to 'take' any fish or wildlife . . ." The House Report stated that "the broadest possi- ble terms" were used to define restrictions on takings . . . The House Report underscored the breadth of the "take" definition by noting that it included "harassment, whether intentional or not." Id., at 11 (emphasis added). The Report explained that the definition "would allow, for example, the Secretary to regulate or prohibit the activities of birdwatchers where the effect of those activities might disturb the birds and make it difficult for them to hatch or raise their young." These comments, ignored in the dis- sent's welcome but selective foray into legisla- tive history, see post, at 14-16, support the Secretary's interpretation that the term "take" in 9 reached far more than the deliberate ac- tions of hunters and trappers . . .

The history of the 1982 amendment that gave the Secretary authority to grant permits for "incidental" takings provides further support for his reading of the Act. The House Report ex- pressly states that "[b]y use of the word 'inci- dental' the Committee intends to cover sit- uations in which it is known that a taking will occur if the other activity is engaged in but such taking is incidental to, and not the purpose of, the activity . . ." This reference to the foresee-

LAW IN ACTION—(CONT'D)

ability of incidental takings undermines respondents' argument that the 1982 amendment covered only accidental killings of endangered and threatened animals that might occur in the course of hunting or trapping other animals. Indeed, Congress had habitat modification directly in mind: both the Senate Report and the House Conference Report identified as the model for the permit process a cooperative state-federal response to a case in California where a development project threatened incidental harm to a species of endangered butterfly by modification of its habitat . . . Thus, Congress in 1982 focused squarely on the aspect of the "harm" regulation at issue in this litigation. Congress' implementation of a permit program is consistent with the Secretary's interpretation of the term "harm."

IV

When it enacted the ESA, Congress delegated broad administrative and interpretive power to the Secretary . . . The task of defining and listing endangered and threatened species requires an expertise and attention to detail that exceeds the normal province of Congress. Fashioning appropriate standards for issuing permits under 10 for takings that would otherwise violate 9 necessarily requires the exercise of broad discretion. The proper interpretation of a term such as "harm" involves a complex policy choice. When Congress has entrusted the Secretary with broad discretion, we are especially reluctant to substitute our views of wise policy for his . . . In this case, that reluctance accords with our conclusion, based on the text, structure, and legislative history of the ESA, that the Secretary reasonably construed the intent of Congress when he defined "harm" to include "significant habitat modification or degradation that actually kills or injures wildlife."

In the elaboration and enforcement of the ESA, the Secretary and all persons who must comply with the law will confront difficult questions of proximity and degree; for, as all recognize, the Act encompasses a vast range of economic and social enterprises and endeavors. These questions must be addressed in the usual course of the law, through case-by-case resolution and adjudication.

QUESTIONS

1. How did the two sides in this case differ in their definition of "taking"? What did each side argue?
2. How did the justices choose which definition they should adopt?
3. Why was this definition so important?
4. Why do you think a majority of the Court ruled in favor of Babbitt? What were these justices concerned about?

■ **Deference to Legislators** Courts tend to defer to the intent of the legislators who drafted a law when they are attempting to determine the proper interpretation of an ambiguous provision. Therefore, courts attempt to determine what legislators had in mind when they considered and passed legislation, and judges often look at hearings and amendments when they assess statutory intent. In Chapter 9, we will examine the role of administrative agencies in the lawmaking process. Because legislators often leave it to administrators to clarify or define provisions in code law, administrators often have a very important role to play in lawmaking. In fact, Congress and the state legislators often leave much of the actual interpretation of statutes to these administrative agents, and this is a huge source of lawmaking power for these officials. As in the *Sweet Home* case, a secretary of other administrator can play a central role in the interpretation of a law, even where this interpretation creates controversy among both officials and the public. Administrators exercise lawmaking power because legislatures delegate this power to them in the laws that create their agencies. While it might seem strange for legislatures to give away some of their lawmaking power, this delegation makes sense, because it allows legislatures to employ somewhat ambiguous language in controversial laws, while also enabling them to defer to the expertise and knowledge of specialized agencies.

PARTICIPANTS IN THE LEGISLATIVE PROCESS

There are three central players in the legislative process: the legislators, the chief executive, and lobbying groups. The roles of the legislators and the chief executive are fairly straightforward. Legislators place issues on the agenda, ask for and evaluate evidence provided in hearings and reports, formulate bills, analyze and modify bills, and decide whether to vote these bills into law. Similarly, the chief executive, that is, the president or governor, has an important and fairly straightforward role to play in this process. Most importantly, it is the function of the chief executive to help to get items onto the legislative agenda and to mobilize support among legislators for those bills that he or she favors. The role of the lobbyist, who is either an organized interest group or an individual consultant or group of consultants, is murkier. These groups or individuals attempt to influence the legislative agenda and the laws that are considered and passed. They provide legislators with a number of incentives to garner their support—among these, the votes of their constituencies; information, which may be sorely needed, especially when legislators are considering a law that is technical or beyond their level of expertise; or monetary contributions.

Legislators

qualifications for membership

the requirements for serving in Congress or the state legislatures; for members of the House and Senate, these are laid out in Article I, Sections 2 and 3, and impose age and residency requirements

The U.S. Constitution and state constitutions provide the principal guidelines for determining membership in the legislatures. Both sets of constitutions establish the **qualifications for membership**—that is, they require that legislators be a certain age and have residency in their district and in the United States for a certain length of time. Like the U.S. Congress, the vast majority of states are bicameral, meaning that they are made up of two houses, which have different qualifications, different terms of office, and different roles in the legislative process. Qualifications for House and Senate members differ. Representatives in the U.S. House must be twenty-five years old, have been a citizen for at least seven years, and be a resident of the state in which they run for office. In contrast, senators must be at least thirty years old, have been citizens for at least nine years, and be a resident of the state in which they run. In addition, the terms of office are quite different—House members are elected for two years, while Senators serve for six years.

Because House members are elected every two years, they are always concerned about the next election. As a result, they tend to be much more concerned about doing **casework** for their constituents than are senators. Casework is usually done at the request of the constituent—for example, if an individual is having difficulty getting her medical bills paid under Medicaid, the state medical assistance program, the representative may be able to facilitate this payment. The home office of the representative, located within the voting district, receives requests for casework and processes these requests. For this reason, the home office plays a central role in maintaining a positive connection between the legislator and his or her constituents. While representatives are, in a sense, always campaigning for the next election, the longer term in office affords senators much more freedom from casework and allows them to exercise more independence. Until 1913, senators had no direct connection with voters—they were chosen entirely by state legislatures. A constitutional amendment established the direct selection of senators. Each state has two senators, regardless of its size or population, and obviously, this is an advantage to smaller states, especially those with relatively small populations.

casework

the requests or problems of constituents that House members try to satisfy in order to assure reelection

Members of the House of Representatives and state houses serve in districts that may be reconfigured every ten years to take account of changes in population recorded in the U.S. census. There are 435 members of the House, and every state must have at least one representative—the total number of representatives is proportional to its population. In the 108th Congress, spanning 2002–2004, the states that increased the number of representatives were those that had enjoyed a population increase. They tended

THE LAW IN POPULAR CULTURE

Mr. Smith Goes to Washington

This classic 1939 film pits an idealistic outsider, Senator Jefferson Smith, a local hero and leader of the Boy Rangers, against forces of corruption and graft in the U.S. Senate and state political party. These forces engineer a smear campaign against Senator Smith in an attempt to force him from office, and in response, he stages a filibuster on the Senate floor in an attempt to clear his name. In this scene, Smith holds handfuls of telegrams from his constituents urging him to abandon his filibuster. He refuses, stating, "You think I'm licked. You all think I'm licked. Well, I'm not licked, and I'm gonna stay right here and fight for this lost cause even if this room gets filled with lies. . . . Somebody'll listen to me. . . ."

to be in the South and Far West. Those states that saw a decrease were those that suffered population losses, and they were almost all in the Northeast and Midwest. The big winners were Florida, Georgia, and Texas, which all gained two seats; the big losers were New York and Pennsylvania, which each lost two seats. Clearly, states with large populations, like California, Texas, New York, and Florida, have many representatives—California tops this list with 53, while those states with small populations have much smaller delegations—for example, Delaware, Montana, North Dakota, South Dakota, Vermont, and Wyoming have only 1 representative apiece.

A change in the number of representatives almost always means that legislative lines must be redrawn, a process known as **redistricting**. Perhaps not surprisingly—because redistricting can have profound effects on the fortunes of not only representatives, but members of the public, especially groups who tend to be numeric minorities in the population—fights often erupt over how the districts have been redrawn. A number of bitterly fought court cases stemmed from the redistricting that followed the 1990 census. In these cases, African Americans charged that they had far less effective representation as a result of the redrawn lines because they were split into a number of districts and their voting power was diminished. These individuals claimed that the state legislatures, which have responsibility for drawing all district lines, even those for the U.S. Congress, intended to minimize their political clout, in violation of the equal protection clause of the Fourteenth Amendment to the Constitution.

In a series of cases decided in the 1990s, the U.S. Supreme Court determined that state legislators could not draw district lines solely on the basis of race or ethnicity. District lines could be drawn, however, to give an advantage to one party over another, and in the 2000s, partisanship—that is, party affiliation—has been the focus of redistricting. The party that has a majority of members in the state house is permitted to draw lines so as to advantage its own party and to try to guarantee its continued predominance. In reality, drawing lines to advantage one party over another may have a significant impact on racial and ethnic groups, since many racial and ethnic groups tend to affiliate more strongly with one party or the other.

Representatives of the House, or its state counterpart, tend to be younger, and more diverse in terms of sex, race, ethnicity, and national origin than members of the Senate. As Table 8.1 shows, there is some representation of Hispanic Americans, African Americans, Asian/Native Hawaiian or Pacific Islanders, and Native Americans in the House in the 108th Congress (2002–2004); however, there are no Hispanic Americans or African Americans in the Senate, and there are only two Asian American/Native Hawaiian/Pacific Islander and one Native American senators. Relatively speaking, women are better represented—there are sixty-two women in the House and a record fourteen women in the Senate—but keep in mind that even these numbers fall far short of the actual proportion of women in the population, which now is in excess of 50 percent. You may want to note that representatives are younger than senators and that both groups have served for a considerable length of time.

Clearly, there is a racial, ethnic, and gender bias to representation in Congress. There is also a class bias in the House and Senate: the vast majority

---

redistricting

redrawing of lines for congressional districts to reflect changes in the population following the U.S. census, which is taken every ten years

www ▶ ▶ ▶

TABLE 8.1
Demographics for
the 108th Congress
(2002–2004)

House of Representatives (total number = 441 members and delegates)	Senate (total number = 100)
62 Women	14 Women
25 Hispanic Americans	0 Hispanic Americans
39 African Americans	0 African Americans
5 Asian Americans/Native Hawaiians/ Pacific Islanders	2 Asian Americans/Native Hawaiians/ Pacific Islanders
2 American Indians	0 American Indians
8 foreign born	0 foreign born
Average age = 53.9	Average age = 59.5
Average length of time in House = 9 years	Average length of time in Senate = 11 years

Source: Information drawn from the Congressional Research Service Report for Congress
(http://www.senate.gov/reference/resources/pdf/RS21379.pdf).

symbolic representation

representation based
on the assumption that
members of historically
disadvantaged groups
will support legislation
that serves the needs
and interests of these
groups

of members have college degrees, and most have graduate degrees as well. With the exception of some of the most visible celebrity representatives, like Sonny Bono, who represented a district in California before his death in 1998, most members have had careers in law or business, and nearly all are fairly affluent. In addition, Protestants continue to be the majority religion, although Roman Catholics are the most prevalent single religious sect. Many people are very concerned about the underrepresentation of racial, ethnic, and religious groups, and women, because this will affect the kind of laws that are passed. In fact, many believe that **symbolic representation**, that is, representation by members of historically disadvantaged groups, will ensure that the needs and interests of these groups are best protected. A number of studies strongly suggest that symbolic representation is important. Women tend to legislate differently than men do, and members of racial and ethnic minorities tend to sponsor and support bills that protect the interests of these groups. In addition, gay legislators tend to protect the interests of gays and lesbians in their communities.

This demographic bias is apparent in state legislatures, as well, as white Protestant men tend to be overrepresented while other groups are underrepresented. Among the more than six thousand senate and house districts in the fifty states, however, there is more diversity than in the U.S. Congress. Specifically, there is much more variation in the occupations and class of those elected to state office than there is in those elected to Congress. Furthermore, in some states, the number of women legislators hovers around one-third—for example, in Washington, 37 percent of legislators are women, and in California, Colorado, and Maryland, women occupy more than 30 percent of the positions. There is far more racial and ethnic diversity in the state senates and houses, as well.

Chief Executives

chief executive

governor or president, this person often plays a key role in the creation of legislation

Interestingly, the **chief executive**, that is, the governor or president, has an important role to play in the legislative process. Many people recognize this role in the executive's power to veto legislation. The chief executive also has an extremely important role to play in sponsoring laws. Article II, Section 3, of the U.S. Constitution establishes that the president "shall from time to time give to the Congress Information of the State of the Union, and recommend to their consideration such Measures as he shall judge necessary and expedient." Through this provision, the president can actively participate in lawmaking by Congress. Over time, this role has become increasingly important, and some commentators refer to the president as *legislator-in-chief* because of his central role in the law-making process.

State of the Union address

a speech the president and most governors make each year to let the public know what the chief executive's legislative priorities will be

The chief executives' agendas are usually laid out in their annual **State of the Union address** to Congress. An excerpt of President Bush's 2005 address is included on the website. Notice how the president specifically identifies his goals for the year and calls on Congress to work with him in passing these laws. The president typically provides Congress with a working draft of a bill, and legislators usually use this bill as a starting point. The only exception is where the president places a bill on the **fast track**, and presents it to Congress to be voted up or down, without any amendment. In addition to recommending legislation, the executive also engages in lawmaking through the vetoing of bills passed by the two houses. In the federal system, the president's veto is a qualified veto, meaning that it can be overridden by a two-thirds vote of each house. Veto overrides are relatively rare—in fact, since our nation was founded, there have been nearly 1,500 vetoes (600 of these by President Franklin D. Roosevelt, alone) and Congress has managed an override only 105 times.[1] Governors not only have the power to veto legislation, but many also have the power to use **line-item vetoes**. Using the line-item veto allows the governor to go through a law and strike down provisions with which he or she disagrees. In 1998, the U.S. Supreme Court overturned a congressional statute that would have conferred the line-item veto power on the president; however, for governors in forty states, this is a source of significant lawmaking power. The use or potential use of either the general veto power or the line-item veto underscores the great extent to which chief executives participate in lawmaking by legislatures.

fast track

when the president or governor places a bill on the legislature's agenda and requires that the body either accept it as written, with no modifications, or reject it

line-item vetoes

the power of the chief executive to veto particular sections of bills; some governors have this power, but the president does not

[1] Louis Fisher, *The Politics of Shared Power: Congress and the Executive*, (Washington, DC: 1998), Congressional Quarterly Press, 30.

The executive does not need to rely on the legislature to engage in law-making. As we'll discuss in the next chapter, the president and the state governors have their own sources of lawmaking power. Legislatures often delegate power to chief executives and their agencies to implement laws, and through delegation, executives and administrative agencies can exercise substantial discretion. In addition, the chief executive has the power to make proclamations and to issue executive orders, which are also very important sources of law.

www ▶ ▶ ▶

Lobbyists

Throughout our nation's history, we have viewed lobbyists quite skeptically. Our country's founders were very concerned about what they called "factions," that is, groups acting in their own self- (and selfish) interest, even when this disadvantaged other groups or individuals. James Madison, writing as *Publius* (roughly translated from Latin as "the people") in *Federalist* No.10 warned that it was human nature to organize into "factions," and that these factions could undermine the public good. He was hopeful, however, that a republican government could counter the effects of such factions by promoting the interests of the whole. Many people have written about interest-group lobbying and its influence on the lawmaking process. Some of them have argued that interest-group participation has a positive impact on legislation—that through the competition or clash of groups the best policy emerges. These writers, who espouse a **pluralist theory of democracy,** are optimistic about the effects of interest-group participation and claim that everyone has the opportunity to participate in group activity. This form of political participation, in their opinion, enables interested parties to have an impact on lawmaking. Others articulate an **elitist theory of democracy,** contending that the playing field is not level and that it favors those with more resources. This group argues that lobbying produces more opportunities for some groups to participate than it does for others, and that the elites reinforce their hold on policymaking through lobbying.

Those who adopt the pluralist view focus on the fact that everyone can participate in some form of lobbying. People can write letters to their representatives, contribute their time and money to support the efforts of groups that they believe in, sign petitions, participate in protest activity, and organize voting drives. Pluralists believe that it is the opportunity to participate in group activity that is central, and they focus on the competition between groups. Box 8.1 describes the activities of two such competing groups. As this box demonstrates, these groups have very different ideas about what tort reform should look like, and they have been competing with each other to influence Congress to adopt their own version of a law. Pluralists look at this competition and see a system that is functioning very well—they focus on the fact

www ▶ ▶ ▶

pluralist theory of democracy

theory based on the argument that through the clash of interest groups, the best policies will emerge

elitist theory of democracy

theory based on the argument that only some groups, the elite in the society, have access to the law-making process

BOX 8.1
Chamber's Last Stand
by Sheryl Fred (http://www.capitaleye.org/)

June 17, 2003 | The annual showdown over class-action reform between the U.S. Chamber of Commerce and the Association of Trial Lawyers of America usually ends in a draw. But this time around, with a Republican-controlled Congress and a massive pro-reform lobbying campaign, the stage may be set for a Chamber win.

In each of the last three sessions of Congress, class-action reform has passed the House only to die in the Senate. This year's legislation cleared the House June 12. The Senate's version, sponsored by Sen. Charles E. Grassley (R-Iowa), may reach a vote in the next two weeks.

"Class action legislation has been around for five years," Matthew Webb, director of legal reform policy at the Chamber, told the *National Law Journal* in May. "If it doesn't pass this year, it probably never will."

The Class Action Fairness Act would move certain lawsuits from state to federal courts. The Chamber and other supporters of the bill say the federal court system is better equipped to handle class actions—whose multiple plaintiffs often come from different states and whose settlements can be complex. They also argue that the reforms would prevent lawyers from venue shopping and prevent judges from hearing frivolous lawsuits.

Critics of the bill, led by ATLA, say moving more class actions to the federal courts, which are already backlogged with cases, would only delay compensation for injured parties. They also say federal courts are less likely to certify lawsuits as class actions, meaning many consumers' cases might never make it to the courtroom.

In an all-out push to get their side heard, the Chamber and its Institute for Legal Reform spent more than $28 million on lobbying in the last six months of 2002—more than double what it spent in the first half of the year and more than any other group. (It also gave more than $285,000 in individual, PAC and soft money contributions in the 2002 election cycle and has ponied up nearly $20,000 for 2004.)

Part of the Chamber's lobbying money has gone toward courting Democrats this session—a relatively new tactic for the Republican-leaning group. In April 2002, the group hired Griffin, Johnson, Dover & Stewart, a lobbying firm with strong Democratic ties, to reach out to the minority party.

So far, this appears to have been a good strategy. *The Hill* reported that the bill's supporters are "within striking distance" of the 60 votes needed to avert a Democratic filibuster in the Senate. Sens. Dianne Feinstein (D-Calif.), Mary Landrieu (D-La.) and Blanche Lincoln (D-Ark.) have backed an amended version of the bill. *Business Week* labeled the legislation "tort reform even a Democrat could love."

ATLA spokesman Carlton Carl admitted the Class Action Fairness Act has been "a bit of a moving target." But for the most part, trial lawyers are treating the bill as business as usual. Over the past five years, ATLA has spent about $2 million per year lobbying Congress and the White House. For each of the past seven election cycles, the association has ranked among the nation's top donors, giving more than $4 million (92 percent to Democrats) in the last cycle alone.

"Our strategy has worked," said Carl, who points to five years' worth of blocked class-action reform at the federal level.

But this year the Chamber has upped the ante. In addition to its massive lobbying cam-

Sheryl Fred, "Chamber's Last Stand" from *Capital Eye* (June 17, 2003), www.capitaleye.org/inside.asp?ID=88. Reprinted with the permission of the Center for Responsive Politics.

BOX 8.1
Chamber's Last Stand–(Cont'd)
by Sheryl Fred (http://www.capitaleye.org/)

paign, the group is spending millions of dollars on issue advertising. Ads portraying plaintiffs' lawyers as money-hungry wheeler-dealers give the impression that class-action reform is good for the economy—and good for consumers. In one print ad, the Chamber calls for a "Class Action Plaintiffs' Bill of Rights," mimicking the Patients' Bill of Rights, a health care reform measure long backed by ATLA.

Some of the country's top newspaper editorial boards seem convinced. "[N]o area of U.S. civil justice cries out more urgently for reform than the high-stakes extortion racket of class actions . . . ," the *Washington Post* editorialized June 14. "Passing this bill would be an important start to rationalizing a system that's out of control."

Carl, who said ATLA has no immediate plans to run its own issue ads on class-action reform, called the Chamber's message misleading. He said the legislation is just one more step in a longstanding effort to take away injured parties' ability to sue corporations.

"Corporate interests have spent billions of dollars to poison the minds of the American public," Carl said. "This bill is a gift to Enron. It's a gift to Halliburton. It's a gift to every wrongdoing corporation out there."

A spokesperson for the Chamber was unavailable for comment.

ATLA has had some success with its arguments in recent battles over other tort reform measures. A bill to limit medical liability is

stalled in the Senate, and asbestos litigation reform is still languishing in committee. But some say ATLA has done little to counter the massive campaign for class-action reform.

"They don't seem to have the fire in the belly on this one," said Victor Schwartz, general counsel of American Tort Reform Association (a proponent of the legislation) and a former trial lawyer himself. "They're used to fighting one bill at a time. This year, the plaintiffs' lawyers have had to fight three very different bills."

They've also had to fight a number of different adversaries, including the White House. In a speech to New Jersey small-business owners June 16, President Bush told the audience he "strongly supported" the House legislation and urged the Senate to act quickly.

More than 475 lobbyists are working full-time to get the measure passed, according to a recent report from Public Citizen, a consumer group opposed to class-action reform. Most of these lobbyists come from business associations, including the Chamber, the American Council of Life Insurers and the National Association of Manufacturers. Many others come from corporations facing big-ticket class-action lawsuits.

Despite their manpower, Schwartz said his colleagues should not assume victory just yet—not when ATLA, long a powerful force in Washington, is on the other side of the issue.

"ATLA has a way of making sure you don't get 60 votes," he said.

ATLA vs. the
Chamber:
A Political
Spending
Comparison

Campaign Contributions, 1989–2003^

Election Cycle	ATLA	U.S. Chamber of Commerce
1990	$ 1,719,942	$ 6,602
1992	$ 2,538,335	$ 2,169
1994	$ 2,509,538	$ 2,617
1996	$ 3,486,888	$ 758
1998	$ 3,117,776	$ 67,151
2000	$ 4,058,100	$ 548,249
2002	$ 4,242,638	$ 285,663
2004*	$ 2,000	$ 19,250
Total	**$21,675,217**	**$932,459**

*So far.
^Based on data released by the Federal Election Commission on May 26, 2003. Totals include PAC, soft money and individual contributions to federal candidates, party committees and leadership PACs, 1989–2003.

Lobbying Spending, 1998–2002 (millions)°

Year	ATLA	U.S. Chamber of Commerce
1998	$ 2.2	$ 17.0
1999	$ 2.4	$ 18.7
2000	$ 3.0	$ 18.7
2001	$ 2.2	$ 20.7
2002	$ 2.6	$ 41.5
Total	**$12.3**	**$116.6**

°According to federal lobbying reports filed with Congress.

Source: From www.capitaleye.org/ATLA.Chamber.chart.06.17.03.asp. Reprinted with the permission of the Center for Responsive Politics.

that these groups will compete with each other and that the group with the "better" law will ultimately win out. For pluralists, "better" is defined as the law that is in the best interest of the society.

While pluralists see the contest between the Chamber and the Trial Lawyers as an example of how competition between groups creates opportunities to participate in the lawmaking process, elitists view the situation much differently. These critics point to the fact that only certain groups have the resources to effectively participate in lobbying, and that wealth creates clear advantages in lobbying strength. Groups with wealth have much more impact on the lawmaking process. Wealth is defined as not only financial resources, but knowledge or expertise. Both the Chamber and the Trial Lawyers have both forms of wealth—they have money and they have expertise, and at least they believe that representatives are listening to what they have to say. The problem with privileging wealth is that it favors the upper classes while starkly disadvantaging middle- and lower-class individuals and groups. Those who focus on elitism look at the huge expenditures made by the Chamber and the Trial Lawyers and argue that groups with fewer resources have been effectively locked out of discussions about tort reform.

Most individuals and groups believe that lobbying has an effect on the kinds of laws that are passed by the Congress and state legislatures, and probably for this reason, there has been a huge increase in the resources that are devoted to lobbying. The Center for Responsive Politics estimates that more than $1.5 billion was spent lobbying the U.S. Congress in 2000, and they contend that most of this money was spent by organizations and businesses, not by private individuals. As you can see by looking at Table 8.2, lobbyist spending increased in nearly all industries in 2000. Even non-profit organizations have tried to get into the lobbying game, and a national nonprofit organization made information available on its website to public interest groups about "charity lobbying." Whether these nonprofits can compete effectively with for-profit entities is open to question, but they seem to think that they have to at least make the attempt.

Sector	2000	1999	1998	1997
Agribusiness	$ 78	$ 83	$119	$ 86
Communications/Electronics	$201	$193	$186	$154
Construction	$ 23	$ 24	$ 22	$ 17
Defense	$ 60	$ 53	$ 49	$ 49
Energy & Natural Resources	$159	$158	$149	$143
Finance, Insurance & Real Estate	$229	$214	$203	$177
Health	$209	$197	$165	$163
Lawyers & Lobbyists	$ 16	$ 18	$ 19	$ 13
Misc Business	$224	$193	$169	$150
Transportation	$138	$117	$115	$112
Ideological/Single-Issue	$ 85	$ 76	$ 76	$ 73
Labor	$ 27	$ 24	$ 24	$ 21
Other	$103	$ 87	$ 69	$ 66

TABLE 8.2
Total Lobbyist Spending (in millions)

WHERE ARE THE FIGURES FROM? Lobbyists have to file semiannual reports with the secretary of the senate and the clerk of the house identifying their clients, the lobbyists working for each client, and the amount of income they receive. Companies have to report their overall lobbying expenditures and the names of any lobbyists employed as part of an in-house lobbying effort. Data are periodically updated to reflect late filings and amendments.

Source: From www.opensecrets.org/lobbyists/index.asp?year=2000. Reprinted with the permission of the Center for Responsive Politics.

DEBATE

Do the lobbyists own Congress?

Yes: One writer asked the question, "Is Congress for Sale?" and to this I would loudly answer "Yes!" There is a bias from the very beginning in what Congress is doing, and this bias is in favor of those groups that make the biggest contributions to the representatives and senators. If you look at Congress's agenda, you will very quickly notice that its agenda is biased in favor of certain constituencies, and these are those groups that have sought to buy influence. Consider the fact that there are few bills on the agenda that protect the interests of the poor or even working class, but there are many that seek to protect the interests of those with financial resources.

Lobbyists meet many of the needs of legislators. First, they often provide much-needed information about how to vote on bills that may be outside the representative's field of expertise. Second, lobbyists can often deliver voters by informing the membership of the group they represent about how the legislator is promoting their interests. And third, lobbyists can provide much-needed resources to finance the ongoing campaigns of senators and representatives.

No: Lobbyists may *want* to own Congress, but the fact is that they cannot, because each group competes with other groups to provide information and other resources to legislators. In lobbying for influence, these groups help legislators to fully understand important societal debates and the likely repercussions of any laws before them. In this way, lobbyists help legislators to be better informed. The fact is that there is a lot of competition among interest groups, and the data from the Trial Lawyers Association and the Chamber of Commerce bear this out. No one group operates in isolation and the beauty of the American political system is that groups are constantly clashing, and that from this conflict, better and more responsive policies can be formulated. Not all lobbyists are high-powered representatives of business corporations; lobbying takes place every day, in a myriad of interactions between many groups of people in American society. Our right to petition our government representatives and to encourage them to be responsive to our interests is what makes our democracy great. By regulating the lobbying process, we risk interfering with the right to free speech and association, which are fundamental to our political culture.

Interrelationship Between the Branches in Lawmaking

Because the lawmaking role is shared by all three branches of government, there is a ranking of laws based on predominance. Generally speaking, constitutions "trump" statutes—that is, laws passed by legislatures—and statutes may override case law and administrative law. It bears noting, however, that there is a very complicated interplay between the branches, especially when one branch strikes down or attempts to override the actions of another. For example, in Chapter 6, we talked about how courts engage in lawmaking by deciding cases and writing opinions. In addition, U.S. courts have the power of judicial review; that is, they can strike down the laws passed by legislatures, the chief executive, and administrative agencies. Between 1995 and 2001, the U.S. Supreme Court took this power very seriously and struck down twenty-seven of the laws passed by Congress. This reliance on judicial review to strike down laws passed by Congress has been rather recent—while the Court has had this power since 1803, it has used it relatively infrequently. Nevertheless, the overturning of legislative statutes places the Court (or state high courts) squarely in the middle of legislative lawmaking.

Once the Court strikes down a statute, it is up to the legislature to decide whether to amend the law and pass it again or to simply accept the Court's decision and move on. Congress and the state legislatures do sometimes respond by passing new laws. For example, immediately after the U.S. Supreme Court invalidated a Texas state ban on flag-burning in its 1989 case ***Texas** v. **Johnson*** (491 U.S. 397), Congress passed the 1989 Flag Protection Act. The Court responded by striking down this law, too, in its 1990 decision in ***U.S.** v. **Eichman*** (496 U.S. 310). Neither Congress nor the state legislatures have passed any new antidesecration statutes, and the Court's holding in these cases appears to have established that unless a new constitutional amendment is passed, it will continue to strike down these laws.

When the court has not specifically barred the legislature from taking action but has instead provided a kind of road map to guide legislatures, the legislators will often respond by passing a new law. This was clearly the case when the Oregon state legislature passed its Death with Dignity Act in 1997, in response to the U.S. Supreme Court's 1997 decisions in a pair of cases, ***Washington State** v. **Glucksberg*** and ***Quill** v. **Vacco***. In these two cases, the Court upheld state bans on assisted suicide but seemed to leave it to state legislatures to craft laws to allow terminally ill, competent individuals to control some aspects of their deaths. Oregon voters almost immediately responded by passing their law, which enabled competent and terminally ill people to get access to medications that would hasten their deaths.

Texas v. Johnson

1989 Supreme Court case that struck down a Texas law that made it a crime to burn the American flag

U.S. v. Eichman

1990 Supreme Court case that struck down the 1989 Flag Protection Act, which was passed by Congress after *Texas* v. *Johnson*

www ▶ ▶ ▶

Washington State v. Glucksberg and Quill v. Vacco

a pair of 1997 Supreme Court cases that upheld state bans on physician-assisted suicide but left to state legislatures substantial discretion to decide whether terminally ill, competent persons have the right to aid in dying

It is through this kind of interaction between courts and legislatures that laws are often modified. Courts and legislatures also interact with administrative agencies to craft and change laws. As we discussed earlier, legislatures often delegate some of their lawmaking power to administrative agencies to implement their laws. These agencies use this power to create and implement regulations. While legislatures delegate some of this power, the ultimate responsibility for oversight of these agencies stays with the legislature. From time to time, legislatures hold **oversight hearings** where agency heads have to respond to questions or concerns raised about their activities and their regulations. For example, the **U.S. Equal Employment Opportunity Commission (EEOC)** has been called before the House and Senate Labor Committees to provide information about a number of its rules and regulations. In the late 1980s, the EEOC failed to respond to cases brought by women who were excluded from jobs by employers who were concerned about exposure to certain substances in their workplaces. These employer policies targeted all women, except those who could prove that they had undergone surgical sterilization; the policies effectively barred women from access to many jobs. The House committee held hearings to examine the EEOC's failure to investigate these claims, and ultimately ordered the agency to take action to bar employers from engaging in sex discrimination.

As we will discuss in Chapter 9, agencies have significant responsibility for making and enforcing laws in the American system. In fact, they sometimes take action that legislators don't like or find unacceptable. Where agency action sparks lawsuits, courts may also step in to strike down agency policies or regulations. In the American system, lawmaking is a shared enterprise—not only do the federal and state governments engage extensively in the making of laws; all of the branches of government participate in it. The next chapter examines the role of the chief executive and his or her agencies in the making and enforcement of laws.

oversight hearings

hearings held by legislatures to determine how administrative agencies are implementing statutes

U.S. Equal Employment Opportunity Commission (EEOC)

a federal administrative agency with responsibility for creating and enforcing regulations that implement employment discrimination laws

SUMMARY

In this chapter, we discussed the dual legislative system in place in the United States. The chief function of legislatures is to make laws, known as statutes or code law. Both the U.S. Congress and state legislatures have the power to engage in lawmaking—Congress's powers are laid out in Article I, Section 8, of the Constitution, and in particular, in the commerce power and implied powers clauses; the state legislatures have broad legislative powers under the police power. Over time, the relative powers of Congress and the state legislatures have waxed and waned. Sometimes Congress is the preeminent lawmaker; at other times the state legislatures hold greater sway. This dual structure creates significant variability in the kinds of laws that we have, and in some areas, this lack of uniformity may thwart the ability of the government to respond effectively to some issue or problem.

This chapter also discussed the characteristics of lawmaking by legislatures, distinguishing them from judicial lawmaking. In contrast to lawmaking by courts, legislative lawmaking is proactive. Legislatures have the power to set their own agendas and to respond quickly to issues or problems in the wider society. In addition, legislatures can engage in extensive fact-finding and can choose from a wide array of options. In this chapter, we also discussed how ambiguous legislation that is crafted to achieve political compromise may create significant opportunities for lawmaking by administrative agencies and courts.

In addition, this chapter examined the chief participants in legislative lawmaking, principally, the legislators themselves, the chief executive, and lobbying groups. We noted that state legislators and members of Congress are not representative of the population as a whole and discussed the powerful role that chief executives play in setting the legislature's agenda. We also highlighted competing theories about how interest groups participate in the lawmaking process, focusing on the pluralist and elitist theories of democracy. And finally, we explored the interrelationship between the lawmaking institutions, noting that the power of judicial review provides significant opportunities for shared lawmaking by courts, legislatures, and agencies.

SUGGESTED READING

Sarah A. Binder, *Stalemate: Causes and Consequences of Legislative Gridlock* (Brookings Institution, 2003). Binder argues that congressional gridlock has a long history and explores the constitutional provisions that likely contribute to this condition; she also examines how institutional features of Congress and modern elections exacerbate gridlock.

Brian Czech and Paul R. Krausman, *The Endangered Species Act: History, Conservation Biology, and Public Policy* (Johns Hopkins Press, 2001). This excellent book focuses on the historical background for the act and then examines the law itself from a policy dimension.

Richard F. Fenno, *Home Style: House Members in Their Districts* (Longman Classics Edition) (Longman, 2002). This is still the classic work on

the role of casework in assuring reelection to the House of Representatives.

David C. King, *Turf Wars: How Congressional Committees Claim Jurisdiction* (University of Chicago Press, 1997). King deftly examines how congressional committees function, focusing on how committees stake claims to particular issue areas, and the resulting fragmentation and overlap of committees with similar jurisdiction.

Alan Rosenthal, *The Third House: Lobbyists and Lobbying in the States* (Congressional Quarterly Press, 2001). This is one of a handful of books that focus on lobbying in the state legislatures and looks at how powerful interest groups can control lawmaking in this "third house" of government.

ACTIVE LEARNING

1. **Political Salience and the Legislative Agenda**—Do this on your own or with a group:

   First: brainstorm—what do you think is on Congress's agenda **today?**
   Second: check to see if you were right by looking at today's agenda (http://thomas.loc.gov/ and click on "Action Yesterday," under "Legislation").
   Third: think critically—were you right? What's missing from the agenda? What do you think accounts for these omissions?

2. **Critical analysis**—think about total lobbyist spending each year—who is well represented? Which groups are missing? Do you think it makes a difference?

3. **Guided research**—Assess what is happening in the debate about aid in dying. If you recall, the Supreme Court held that this was an area in which states had a great deal of discretion and were free to choose whether to allow competent persons with terminal illness and significant pain and suffering to access aid in dying. Oregon responded almost immediately by passing its aid in dying act. What have other states either considered or accomplished in this area? Start with any search engine (like Google or Dogpile), then enter "aid in dying" or "physician aid in dying" and state. Log state initiatives in this area and whether they have been successful.

CHAPTER 9

Chief Executives, Regulatory Agencies, Administrative Agencies, and Lawmaking

In August 2004, President George W. Bush floated the idea of replacing the federal income tax with a federal sales tax, which would tax goods at a flat rate. At a campaign forum in Niceville, Florida, President Bush stated: "It's an interesting idea," continuing, "you know, I'm not exactly sure how big the national sales tax is going to have to be, but it's the kind of interesting idea that we ought to explore seriously." Some lawmakers have argued strongly in favor of a simplified federal tax code—either a sales tax or a flat, single-rate tax—but others have passionately opposed such taxes, arguing that they are regressive and create a much heavier tax burden for the poor and middle classes while lightening the load for the wealthy.

As we discussed in Chapter 8, the president or governor can work with the legislature, helping it to formulate laws, or he or she can create law independently. The two chief sources of executive lawmaking power are **executive orders,** *which are laws issued by the chief executive, usually in response to some specific issue or problem, and* **administrative regulations,** *which are passed by executive branch agencies that have responsibility for implementing statutes. In addition, the president has the power to enter into treaties, which must then be ratified by the U.S. Senate, and executive agreements, which do not need the consent of the Senate. Both treaties and agreements establish or clarify relationships between the United States and other countries. The vast majority of international arrangements between the United States and another nation are the result of an agreement, not a treaty. These international agreements govern an array of subjects, among them, trade, arms control, and extradition. In addition, the executive has the power to grant pardons and reprieves to those convicted of most kinds of wrongdoing, another source of law-making, or rather, law dodging! And the executive has the power to veto*

executive orders

laws created solely by the chief executive, whose power to make law comes from federal or state constitutions

administrative regulations

laws passed by executive branch agencies that have responsibility for implementing statutes

legislation passed by the legislature, again, a negative source of lawmaking, but potentially a significant source of power.

This chapter explores the two chief sources of domestic lawmaking—executive orders and administrative regulations—and discusses how the executive's power to create and implement law has expanded dramatically over the last century. Until Franklin D. Roosevelt assumed the presidency in 1932, lawmaking by legislatures was predominant; during FDR's term in office, however, the chief executive assumed a much more prominent and independent role. Although the chief executive's power to act independently fluctuates, President George W. Bush and his advisers moved quickly in response to the terror attacks of September 11 to broaden the scope of presidential powers, especially in the areas of domestic intelligence and foreign affairs. President Bush effectively employed both executive orders and the powers of his executive branch agencies to expand the powers of the presidency.

EXECUTIVE ORDERS

Article II, Section 1, of the U.S. Constitution establishes that the "executive power shall be vested in a President of the United States," and state constitutions recognize similar powers for governors. Executive orders are used for a number of purposes.

Orders as Proclamations

proclamation

an executive order that recognizes some group or emerging issue and has largely symbolic value

`www ▶ ▶ ▶`

First, a president or governor can use an order to issue a **proclamation**. These proclamations are usually issued in recognition of some group or emerging issue, and this form of executive order has largely symbolic value. For example, in just one month (May 2003) President Bush issued fifteen proclamations—including proclamations establishing National Child's Day, Missing Children's Day, Maritime Day, Hurricane Awareness Week, Safe Boating Week, Jewish Heritage Week, Asian/Pacific American Heritage Month, and Older Americans Month.

Orders to Establish Task Forces

task forces

groups usually created pursuant to an executive order to study certain problems

In addition to using executive orders to issue mostly symbolic proclamations, the chief executive can employ orders to establish **task forces** to study certain problems. These task forces are usually composed of experts who are called on to evaluate an issue and to propose a plan of action. Governors and the president have created task forces to deal with a number of highly visible and not-so-visible problems. For example, Michigan Governor Jennifer M. Granholm established a task force in 2003 to study chronic wasting disease, a neurological disease affecting deer and elk in the state of Michigan and elsewhere. Governors in New York have created task forces to reform local government and modernize election procedures; and President George W. Bush has organized task forces to investigate corporate fraud, improve health care delivery for military veterans, carry out research on coral reefs, and protect children against certain environmental risks.

www ▶ ▶ ▶

Orders to Reorganize or Create New Agencies

Department of Homeland Security (DHS)

federal department created after 9/11 and given significant powers to investigate and prevent terror attacks in the United States

Executive orders are also used to create or reorganize executive branch departments or administrative agencies. This may not sound exciting, but it's a huge source of power! In October 2001, President Bush issued an order calling for the creation of the **Department of Homeland Security (DHS)** and a Homeland Security Council. This office was to be given significant powers to investigate and prevent terror attacks in the United States. Throughout 2002 and 2003, the president issued a number of orders transferring power from twenty-two existing agencies to the new Department of Homeland Security. Congress passed the Homeland Security Act in December 2002, establishing the agency as an executive department, and the Senate confirmed its first secretary, Tom Ridge, in January 2003.

The creation of this new department and the subsequent restructuring of other executive branch agencies and responsibilities is the most significant reorganization of the executive branch in more than fifty years. Among those agencies placed under the umbrella of the new DHS are the Coast Guard, Transportation Security Administration, Immigration and Naturalization Service, Customs Service, Animal and Plant Health Inspection Service, the Secret Service, the Federal Emergency Management Administration, and the Federal Protective Service. Why does this matter? The new Department of Homeland Security has wide-ranging powers and responsibilities, and centralization of these responsibilities is likely to have a considerable impact on how they are performed.

www ▶ ▶ ▶

Orders as Law

Fourth, the executive order can be used to craft new policies. One of the most famous executive orders was President Abraham Lincoln's Emancipation Proclamation, which effectively banned slavery in the confederate states. This proclamation was extremely controversial and cost Lincoln and his Republican Party many votes in the 1862 congressional elections. President Franklin D. Roosevelt also used an executive order to accomplish what is now recognized as a very controversial goal. His Executive Order No. 9066, issued in 1942, ordered the forced relocation of Japanese and Japanese Americans into camps on the West Coast. In the late 1990s, the federal government publicly admitted that it had violated the civil rights and liberties of these groups and paid reparations to the individuals and their families. President Roosevelt also made extensive use of these executive orders in his attempts to "jump start" the American economy during the Great Depression of the 1930s and 1940s, creating the Work Projects Administration, the Fair Employment Practices Commission, and the War Production Board.

military tribunals

committees, groups, or courts created after 9/11 to try noncitizens suspected of planning or participating in terror attacks against the United States; offer fewer criminal due process protections than civilian law; conducted largely by the Department of Defense

`www` ▶ ▶ ▶

While some executive orders are controversial, as in the case of the Emancipation Proclamation, the forced relocation of Americans of Japanese ancestry, and the economic policies of FDR's New Deal, others are not. For example, in 1916, President Wilson issued an executive order that established the Star Spangled Banner as the national anthem, and in so doing, recognized the armed forces' long-standing use of the anthem. Often, however, executive orders spark serious criticism both inside and outside of government. This was the case when President George W. Bush issued his executive order authorizing the use of **military tribunals**. This order was issued on November 16, 2001, in response to the September 11 attacks, and it authorized the detention and military trial of noncitizens suspected of planning or participating in terror attacks against the United States. This military order, issued by the president pursuant to his powers as commander in chief, justified the differential treatment of noncitizens as a matter of public safety and laid out procedures for using the military tribunals. The order identified those individuals who were subject to detention and military trial and delegated wide-ranging authority to the secretary of defense to amass evidence and conduct the trial. The defense secretary had the responsibility to provide for the safety of detainees and to establish procedures for trying them. The text of this order is provided in the Law in Action box that follows. Notably, under this order, the secretary could convene a commission that would decide guilt or innocence, possibly in secret, and could establish the rules of evidence and even order death without a unanimous decision.

Executive orders are law, with much the same legitimacy and power as statutes passed by legislatures and case opinions written by judges. In some states, like New Jersey, the governor's executive orders can actually override laws passed by the state legislature. The extent to which presidents and governors use these orders varies—some executives rely heavily on the orders to make policy, while others use them only infrequently. When executives use these orders frequently or when they create law that is unpopular or controversial, the other branches often raise concerns about the separation of powers. Under the separation-of-powers principle, no branch should have too much power and the three branches should be equals. Not surprisingly, there are times when one branch seems to be more powerful than

LAW IN ACTION

Controversial Executive Orders—President George W. Bush's Order Establishing the Use of Military Tribunals

"DETENTION, TREATMENT, AND TRIAL OF CERTAIN NON-CITIZENS IN THE WAR AGAINST TERRORISM," PUBLISHED IN THE FEDERAL REGISTER 11/16/01 (VOLUME 66, NUMBER 222), PAGES 57831–57836.

By the authority vested in me as President and as Commander in Chief of the Armed Forces of the United States by the Constitution and the laws of the United States of America, including the Authorization for Use of Military Force Joint Resolution (Public Law 107-40, 115 Stat. 224) and sections 821 and 836 of title 10, United States Code, it is hereby ordered as follows:

Section 1. Findings.

(a) International terrorists, including members of al Qaida, have carried out attacks on United States diplomatic and military personnel and facilities abroad and on citizens and property within the United States on a scale that has created a state of armed conflict that requires the use of the United States Armed Forces.

(b) In light of grave acts of terrorism and threats of terrorism, including the terrorist attacks on September 11, 2001, on the headquarters of the United States Department of Defense in the national capital region, on the World Trade Center in New York, and on civilian aircraft such as in Pennsylvania, I proclaimed a national emergency on September 14, 2001 (Proc. 7463, Declaration of National Emergency by Reason of Certain Terrorist Attacks).

(c) Individuals acting alone and in concert involved in international terrorism possess both the capability and the intention to undertake further terrorist attacks against the United States that, if not detected and prevented, will cause mass deaths, mass injuries, and massive destruction of property, and may place at risk the continuity of the operations of the United States Government . . .

(e) To protect the United States and its citizens, and for the effective conduct of military operations and prevention of terrorist attacks, it is necessary for individuals subject to this order pursuant to section 2 hereof to be detained, and, when tried, to be tried for violations of the laws of war and other applicable laws by military tribunals . . .

(g) Having fully considered the magnitude of the potential deaths, injuries, and property destruction that would result from potential acts of terrorism against the United States, and the probability that such acts will occur, I have determined that an extraordinary emergency exists for national defense purposes, that this emergency constitutes an urgent and compelling government interest, and that issuance of this order is necessary to meet the emergency.

Sec. 2. Definition and Policy.

(a) The term "individual subject to this order" shall mean any individual who is not a United States citizen with respect to whom I determine from time to time in writing that:

(1) there is reason to believe that such individual, at the relevant times,

    (i) is or was a member of the organization known as al Qaida;

    (ii) has engaged in, aided or abetted, or conspired to commit, acts of international terrorism, or acts in preparation therefor, that have caused, threaten to cause, or have as their aim to cause injury to or adverse effects on the United States, its citizens, national security, foreign policy, or economy; or

    (iii) has knowingly harbored one or more individuals described in subparagraphs (i) or (ii) of subsection 2(a)(1) of this order; and

(2) it is in the interest of the United States that such individual be subject to this order . . .

Sec. 3. Detention Authority of the Secretary of Defense. Any individual subject to this order shall be—

(a) detained at an appropriate location designated by the Secretary of Defense outside or within the United States;

(b) treated humanely, without any adverse distinction based on race, color, religion, gender, birth, wealth, or any similar criteria;

(c) afforded adequate food, drinking water, shelter, clothing, and medical treatment;

(d) allowed the free exercise of religion consistent with the requirements of such detention; and

(e) detained in accordance with such other conditions as the Secretary of Defense may prescribe.

Sec. 4. Authority of the Secretary of Defense Regarding Trials of Individuals Subject to this Order.

(a) Any individual subject to this order shall, when tried, be tried by military commission for any and all offenses triable by military commission that such individual is alleged to have committed, and may be punished in accordance with the penalties provided under applicable law, including life imprisonment or death . . .

(c) Orders and regulations . . . shall include, but not be limited to, rules for the conduct of the proceedings of military commissions, including pretrial, trial, and post-trial procedures, modes of proof, issuance of process, and qualifications of attorneys, which shall at a minimum provide for—

(1) military commissions to sit at any time and any place, consistent with such guidance regarding time and place as the Secretary of Defense may provide;

(2) a full and fair trial, with the military commission sitting as the triers of both fact and law;

(3) admission of such evidence as would . . . have probative value to a reasonable person . . .

(6) conviction only upon the concurrence of two-thirds of the members of the commission present at the time of the vote, a majority being present;

(7) sentencing only upon the concurrence of two-thirds of the members of the commission present at the time of the vote, a majority being present; and

(8) submission of the record of the trial, including any conviction or sentence,

LAW IN ACTION—(CONT'D)

for review and final decision by me or by the Secretary of Defense if so designated by me for that purpose.

[Other sections follow: they cover the obligation of other agencies to assist the Secretary of Defense, additional authority exercised by the Secretary, and the relationship between this order and other laws].

QUESTIONS

1. What exactly did this order do?
2. Who is affected by it?
3. According to this order, how are trials to be conducted? Normally, rules of evidence are much more stringent than these—while this order requires only that evidence "have probative value to a reasonable person," courts normally require that the evidence that is introduced not only be relevant, but that it be reliable and offered to prove some specific fact. Also, conviction for most felony crimes must be by the judge's vote or by a unanimous vote by the jury. Consider what's required here. How does it differ? Does this difference matter?
4. What is the role of the secretary of defense in establishing and reviewing the work of the tribunal?

the others. During times of national emergency or war, the powers of the chief executive tend to expand and those of Congress and the courts to contract. It remains to be seen how the separation of powers will ultimately play out in the war on terror. The Supreme Court's rebuff of the administration's open-ended detention of unlawful combatants may ultimately be read as halting the chief executive's expansion of power in the foreign policy realm. Similarly, the introduction of bills by some members of the House of Representatives, like the Terrorism Tribunal Act of 2001, may be read as an attempt to firmly establish separation of powers in foreign policymaking. This act, which didn't pass Congress, attempted to limit the use of military tribunals to those cases where national security was clearly at risk and also sought to develop specific procedures for employing these tribunals.

The legislature may take action to limit the executive's exercise of power, or it may not, again depending on what's happening both inside the institution and in the larger society. While these orders have the force of law, they may be overturned by congressional statute or court order, and both the legislature and the courts have invalidated executive orders that they have decided go beyond the powers of the executive branch. Generally

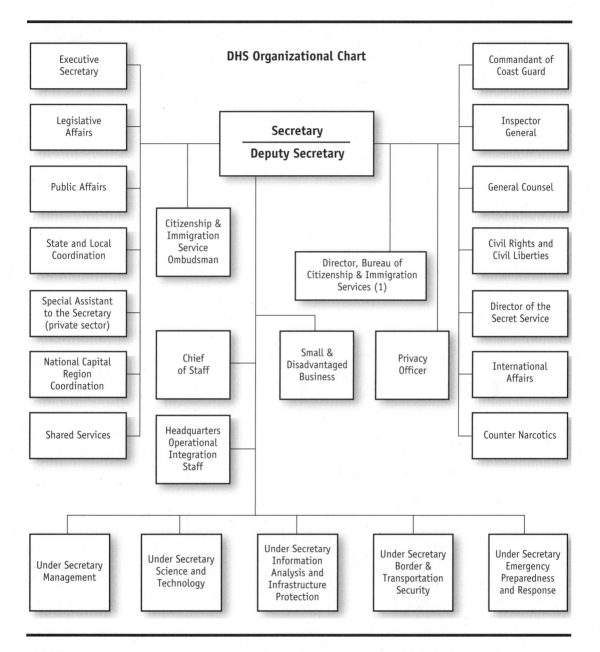

DHS Organizational Chart

Executive Secretary

Legislative Affairs

Public Affairs

State and Local Coordination

Special Assistant to the Secretary (private sector)

National Capital Region Coordination

Shared Services

Citizenship & Immigration Service Ombudsman

Chief of Staff

Headquarters Operational Integration Staff

Secretary

Deputy Secretary

Director, Bureau of Citizenship & Immigration Services (1)

Small & Disadvantaged Business

Privacy Officer

Commandant of Coast Guard

Inspector General

General Counsel

Civil Rights and Civil Liberties

Director of the Secret Service

International Affairs

Counter Narcotics

Under Secretary Management

Under Secretary Science and Technology

Under Secretary Information Analysis and Infrastructure Protection

Under Secretary Border & Transportation Security

Under Secretary Emergency Preparedness and Response

FIGURE 9.1
Organizational
Chart of
Department of
Homeland Security

The Department of Homeland Security was created in the wake of 9/11 and resulted in the most dramatic restructuring of the federal bureaucracy in more than 50 years, and consolidated control of 22 agencies and more than 180,000 federal employees.

speaking, the executive will seek the approval of the legislature, especially with regard to the creation of more controversial laws. For example, the Department of Homeland Security was first proposed by President Bush in his executive order in early 2002 and then endorsed by Congress in its Homeland Security Act and passed in late 2002. Figure 9.1 shows an organizational chart of the Department of Homeland Security.

Where chief executives do not expect approval, however, they may decide to go ahead and issue an order anyway. This is what happened when the Senate notified President Bill Clinton that it would not likely ratify the **Kyoto Accord**, a treaty that set deadlines for reducing greenhouse gases and imposed significant costs on the United States, which is by far the largest emitter of these gases. When President Clinton realized that his signature would not be ratified, he implemented part of the Kyoto Accord by issuing a series of executive orders and by employing the Kyoto standards in existing environmental laws, like the Clean Air Act, and in the administrative regulations issued by such agencies as the Environmental Protection Agency.

Kyoto Accord

an international treaty that set deadlines for reducing greenhouse gases at significant cost to the United States; parts of this treaty were implemented by President Clinton in a series of executive orders

THE LAW IN POPULAR CULTURE

The West Wing

Fictional President Josiah Bartlett must grapple with the challenges of the modern presidency. This award-winning program examines contemporary issues facing the president, among these, the role of the United States in the global community. Like the real president, Bartlett must face international crises, domestic turmoil, and party politics in the course of doing his job.

Even where the other branches do not oppose an executive order, members of the public may. While most legislators were silent about President Bush's controversial military tribunal order, there was strong opposition to this order by some civil liberties groups. From the very beginning, civil libertarians fiercely criticized this order and remain strongly opposed to any limitation on the due process rights of those suspected or accused of terrorist action. While this executive order was very visible and reported on by most news agencies, there are many other orders that attract little attention. For example, at about the same time President Bush issued his order authorizing the use of military tribunals, he also issued an order that blocked public access to presidential records indefinitely. Since the mid-1970s, there had been a movement toward greater disclosure of records, and President Bush's order marks a clear reversal of this trend. Some interested parties harshly criticized the president's decision to seal presidential records. The American Political Science Association and the American History Association, two groups of scholars who study the presidency, both complained about the order by writing letters to the House and Senate subcommittees on intergovernmental relations.

www ▶ ▶ ▶

EXECUTIVE DEPARTMENTS AND ADMINISTRATIVE AGENCIES

Chief executives oversee huge bureaucratic structures. Some agencies are independent of the executive branch. In the federal system, the Federal Reserve Board and the Federal Aviation Administration operate with little influence from the president or his cabinet. Alan Greenspan has served as chairman of the Federal Reserve Board under four presidents—Reagan, George Bush, Sr., Clinton, and George W. Bush, and has acted independently of all of them! When he makes decisions about interest rates, he does so without interference from the president or other executive branch personnel. Most agencies, however, are executive branch agencies, and the president or governor may have significant influence over their policies or day-to-day operations. Chief executives use this oversight to expand their lawmaking power.

Size of Bureaucratic Structures

The federal and state bureaucracies are mammoth—together they employ nearly 20 million people! There are more than 4 million federal employees and more than 15 million state and local government employees. The biggest employers are local governments, which have more than 11 million employees on the payroll. Most of these employees work in schools, hospitals, and police departments. They are the most visible governmental officials—

they are the public school teachers, firefighters, and police officers who perform much of the day-to-day governance in our communities. People are often surprised at just how many official government employees there are, but the real number may be even larger. Some labor analysts estimate that there are many more employed in the **"shadow government,"** and that this 20 million figure is far too low. Employees of this shadow government are not directly employed by the government, but are paid solely out of government coffers. Paul C. Light, founding director of the Center for Public Service at the Brookings Institute, estimates that there are more than 17 million additional federal "employees" in this shadow government, and that they are paid out of federal contracts with private companies, grants, and federal mandates. If he is right, then there are nearly 40 million people employed in the bureaucratic apparatus. Light and others claim that politicians' rhetoric about the benefits of smaller government has created the need for this shadow government, which is not included in estimates of total government employees.

"shadow government"

people who work indirectly for the federal government through federal contracts with private companies, grants, and federal mandates; possibly between 17 and 20 million people are employed in this shadow government

Scope of Administrative Law

In addition to sheer size, bureaucracies have wide-ranging powers and responsibilities in the United States. The most prevalent form of law in the United States is **administrative law**, which is created by federal and state administrative agencies. While the laws created by courts and legislatures get most media exposure, it is actually administrative law that is closest to us in terms of regulating our daily activities.

administrative law

law created by federal and state administrative agencies

Structure of Administrative Apparatus

Like both the legislative and judicial systems, the administrative apparatus in the United States is dual in structure. That is, there are parallel systems in the federal and state government, and in fact, there is significant duplication in the laws of these two levels of government. For example, there is a federal Department of Labor, created by a congressional statute. There are also state departments of labor, with some overlapping powers. These agencies establish workplace health and safety standards, set minimum wages and maximum hour limits, and regulate the relationship between unions and employers. The website provides an overview of the U.S. Department of Labor and its counterpart in California, the Department of Industrial Relations.

As the information on the website suggests, the U.S. Department of Labor and California Department of Labor share responsibility for many workplace issues and problems. Both agencies are responsible for enforcing laws that protect workers from exposure to certain harmful substances in the workplace. Often the permissible exposure level for these substances is determined by the federal or state agency. Generally, the agency in the federal Department of Labor responsible for workplace health and safety is the **Occupational Safety and Health Administration (OSHA)**, and OSHA's permissible level is really the "floor"—meaning that state agencies can usually establish more protective levels. This interaction between the federal and state agencies is sometimes problematic. This is especially true where there is variation both between and among federal and state policies, and where corporations operate in a number of different states, some with more protective laws, others with laws that parallel those adopted by the federal OSHA. Some people have argued that there should be uniformity in administrative regulations, and that inconsistency among states and between the federal and state governments creates uncertainty and a patchwork of different state laws. Given the dual nature of American government, however, this variation is probably unavoidable.

> **Occupational Safety and Health Administration (OSHA)**
>
> the federal agency charged with enforcing standards for occupational safety; its regulations usually establish a floor and state agencies can mandate additional protections

Creation of Administrative Agencies

Agencies are created in two ways—either through express or implied provisions in the constitution or through legislative statute. For example, under Article I of the U.S. Constitution, Congress has the power to regulate interstate trade. In 1887, Congress took the first major step toward creating a body of law to regulate this commerce, and established the **Interstate Commerce Commission (ICC)** to regulate the activities of transportation carriers. Similarly, the Department of Defense finds its authorization in Article II of the Constitution, which gives the president the role of commander in chief.

While some agencies and departments are creatures of the federal or state constitutions, most are established by legislative statute. Typically, a legislative body passes a statute that delegates power to an agency or agencies for implementation of the law. The power that is delegated is often very broad, and agencies are given the authority to create, interpret, and enforce rules that help them to implement the laws. For example, in 1969, the U.S. Congress passed the National Environmental Policy Act, which created the **Environmental Protection Agency (EPA)**. The agency was given expanded powers through Congress's later passage of the Clean Air Act (CAA) (1970), Clean Water Act (1972), Noise Control Act (1979), and Comprehensive Environmental Responsible Compensation and Liability Act (1980). See the website for the major laws that conferred broad

> **Interstate Commerce Commission (ICC)**
>
> one of the earliest regulatory agencies, established by Congress in 1887 pursuant to its constitutional power to regulate interstate commerce

> **Environmental Protection Agency (EPA)**
>
> agency created by Congress in 1969 under the National Environmental Policy Act and given expanded powers in a series of laws, including the Clean Air Act

enforcement power on the EPA. Many of the laws that empower the EPA are very vague. Consider the very statute that conferred power on to the EPA to formulate air quality standards. Under the Clean Air Act of 1970, it seemed the EPA was given broad powers. Specifically, the purpose of this statute was to develop a list of permissible exposure standards for all pollutants by 1975, but it left the EPA in charge of achieving this goal and this goal *remains* unmet. Why did the EPA fail in this task? The CAA was probably clearer than many other statutes about the purposes and goals to be achieved. It stated, quite clearly, that its goals were to "protect and enhance the quality of the Nation's air resources," and to promote "reasonable [governmental] actions . . . for pollution prevention." The EPA was unable to meet these goals, however, because over time, it became mired in conflicts with other agencies and with the president, and because it sparked significant resistance among business interests. Agencies like the EPA need the chief executive's support to pursue their goals effectively, but throughout much of the 1970s and 1980s, environmental protection grew more controversial and therefore less compelling to the president.

And even the CAA's purpose became less clear throughout this period. Specifically, agency heads and business leaders argued that only "*reasonable*" governmental actions could be taken, and that reasonableness should be determined in large part by how costly the regulation was to businesses and to consumers. In short, this statute, like many others, had enough ambiguity to allow agencies to be powerfully affected by politics. Ambiguities in statutes like this one allow agencies to interpret and implement those rules that agency heads think are appropriate. Because the chief executive usually has the power to appoint these officials, the chief executive exercises substantial clout in determining how the agency will function. Chief executives will often choose agency officials whose vision of a social issue or problem agrees with their own, even when this vision appears to be inconsistent with the statute that created the agency.

There is often fierce disagreement between presidential administrations about what environmental law requires. For example, in the mid-1990s, President Bill Clinton argued that emissions from aging coal-burning power plants should be reduced, and his EPA reflected this concern. In 1998, the EPA formulated strict rules that mandated alterations in the coal-burning power plants as part of the routine maintenance required under the CAA. Some companies complied, but many others did not, and those that failed to comply were fined. When President George W. Bush took office in 2001, his EPA head, Christine Todd Whitman, ordered that these rules be suspended. She worked closely with businesses to reach a negotiated settlement about upgrades. Thus, the Bush EPA has taken a much more conciliatory stance toward business, and has a much different interpretation of what is required under the CAA than did its predecessor.

Functions of Administrative Agencies

Executive branch agencies are responsible for implementing and enforcing the laws passed by the legislature and the chief executive. Their enforcement efforts center on three main functions: first, they must engage in rule making; second, they must investigate, and at times, prosecute, those who violate their rules; and third, they must adjudicate claims arising from their rules. In the course of performing these functions, agencies are heavily engaged in lawmaking.

■ **Rule Making** Lawmaking by legislatures tends to be somewhat incomplete, and legislatures often craft laws that are ambiguous or unclear. They engage in a **delegation of power** by giving agencies the authority to "flesh out" vague laws, to clarify inconsistencies in these laws, and to make law through the choices they make. Typically, the legislature will leave it to the agencies to fill in the blanks left by the lawmaking process, and in particular, legislators will allow agency heads to exercise substantial discretion in making the rules that implement the laws. Consider OSHA, the federal agency responsible for implementing the law. Over time, OSHA has had to make decisions about which workplace health and safety issues it wants to pursue, and about which rules would best serve workers' interests. In the 1990s, OSHA focused on workplace ergonomics and air quality in workplaces; these two issues were high on the agency's agenda. As a result, OSHA generated a number of rules to promote ergonomically safe workplaces and clean air. Other issues were given far less attention. The issue of reproductive hazards in the workplace, considered much more important in the 1980s and early 1990s, has effectively fallen off the agenda, despite the fact that reproductive and fetal toxins continue to exist in the workplace.

The rule-making process is highly regulated: new rules are considered by agency personnel and are published in the *Federal Register,* a government publication available to any interested person either in paper form or on the web. After publication, there is a notice and comment period, and parties interested in or affected by the rules are invited to provide information to the agencies about the probable impact of the new rules. This period may be extended at the agency's discretion. On the website, you can glimpse a notice published in the *Federal Register* in 2003 that informed the public that OSHA would allow the notice and comment period for its ergonomic rules to remain open.

After the notice and comment period, agency heads determine whether or not to implement the rule. Highly controversial rules will often spark lots of debate in the notice and comment period, and agencies sometimes abandon those rules that generate substantial opposition. When OSHA

delegation of power

the giving of law-making power to administrative agencies to create rules for the implementation of law by Congress and state legislatures; this power may be quite extensive, especially if the law is unclear or contradictory

Federal Register

a government publication that informs the public about any new rules being considered by an agency

 www ▶ ▶ ▶

www ▶ ▶ ▶

Indoor Air Quality Rules

proposed rules, withdrawn by OSHA in 2001 after more than six years of a highly critical notice and comment period

proposed its **Indoor Air Quality Rules** in 1994, these rules generated significant controversy, and ultimately, the agency withdrew them in 2001. One of the most difficult aspects of regulation is that there is insufficient data to guide regulators in some fields. For example, agencies like OSHA and the EPA are charged with limiting harmful exposure to environmental or occupational toxins; however, there is insufficient data to guide these agencies in determining the level of exposure at which substances become harmful.

Like lawmaking by legislatures, lawmaking by chief executives tends to be incomplete and ambiguous. For this reason, the rule-making function of executive branch departments and agencies charged with implementing executive orders is very important. For example, after President George W. Bush issued his directive establishing military tribunals, he gave the Department of Defense the authority to create rules to govern these proceedings. As a result, the Defense Department has proposed a series of rules on military tribunals. In March 2002 the department issued its rule on "Procedures for Trials by Military Commissions of Certain Non-United States Citizens in the War Against Terrorism." This rule implements the president's order by establishing the procedures that had to be followed in trying someone in a military commission. And in February 2003 the department issued its final rule on "Crimes and Elements of Trials by Military Commission," to guide it in bringing charges against individuals under the president's order.

www ▶ ▶ ▶

Sometimes, individuals and groups may challenge an agency rule in court and the agency will be called on to produce evidence in support of its rule. In a case discussed on the website, *American Trucking Association, Inc.* v. *Environmental Protection Agency,* the Circuit Court for the District of Columbia had to decide whether the EPA's rules were permissible under the Clean Air Act. When you read this case, note that the court is unsure about how to deal with scientific uncertainty; it seems more comfortable leaving judgment calls about the science to agency heads.

www ▶ ▶ ▶

■ **Investigation and Prosecution** After an agency creates rules to guide its enforcement efforts, it is also usually given the power to investigate and prosecute those who violate these rules. As we will discuss in Chapter 10, the decisions about whether to investigate or prosecute involve a substantial degree of discretion, and lawmakers must make the decision about whether they will in fact pursue enforcement efforts. Sometimes, agency heads will make a decision not to investigate or enforce existing rules. Throughout the 1980s, the U.S. Equal Employment Opportunity Commission was unsure about how to process claims of gender discrimination involving employer policies that barred women from certain workplaces because of employer concerns about exposure to reproductive toxins. Because the agency was unsure how antidiscrimination laws affected these policies, field offices, that is, offices outside of Washington, D.C., "warehoused" all claims that came to them and waited for the D.C. office to make a decision about how to proceed. Unfortunately, the main office was also unsure, and so there was no policy guidance until after the U.S. Supreme Court barred the use of these policies in 1991.

Even when an agency does take action to enforce its regulations, this may not result in uniform enforcement. For example, in early 2003, OSHA announced that it would be inspecting only those workplaces that it considered to be "high-hazard," that is, those in which there have been a higher than average number of injuries or illnesses. Employers must report the number of workplace-related injuries or illnesses suffered by their employees each year, and OSHA makes a decision to inspect those workplaces with the largest number of injuries. In 2003, the workplaces on this "primary list" had at least fourteen injuries or illnesses per one hundred workers, or had nine or more cases per one hundred workers of injuries resulting in days away from work. OSHA decided to pursue this targeted program because it did not have enough resources to inspect every workplace. This year, there will be only two hundred random inspections of workplaces not on the primary list.

■ **Adjudication** The third main function of administrative agencies is the adjudication of claims involving the laws they administer. Not every agency engages in adjudication—the law that creates the agency establishes whether this is a function that the agency may perform. Many state and federal agencies do perform this function; and principal among these are agencies charged with safeguarding employment discrimination, occupational safety and health, and environmental and consumer products safety. State and federal agencies often share this function and cooperate with each other to enforce state and federal laws. This cooperation is important, because in a number of areas, both the federal and state governments have passed laws that apply to the same activity.

The adjudication of claims is a complex activity, and it occurs on a number of different levels. First, the agency itself will make a determination about whether to pursue a case and will determine whether the evidence is sufficient to bring the case to an administrative hearing. Remember that because one activity may trigger both federal and state laws, the corresponding federal and state agencies need to know how they will approach the case, that is, which agency will have "first crack" at the case. In the area of employment discrimination, the federal EEOC has made a decision that it will allow states that have employment discrimination laws and agencies set up to enforce these laws to examine these cases first. Typically, the state

Yes: Federal bureaucrats with responsibility for enforcing administrative law tend to be highly skilled and have expertise in the area in which they are working. Agency personnel tend to be stable and remain from one administration to the next—these employees tend to be highly specialized and professionalized. For example, even after the transfer of power from President Clinton to President Bush in 2001, there was little turnover in employees in agencies like the Internal Revenue Service. What did change, of course, were the appointees to these agencies, but the new appointees also tend to have expertise, or at least experience, with the industry that they are charged with overseeing. For example, Secretary of Agriculture Mike Johanns, who was reared on a dairy farm in the heartland of America and served two terms as Nebraska governor, was known for being responsive to the needs of farmers and ranchers. In addition to having expertise, these appointees also tend to be fiercely loyal to the president who selects them and to the larger administration. And finally, high-ranking members of the federal bureaucracy tend to be very responsive to the issue networks of which their agencies are a part. Most analysts recognize that federal bureaucrats tend to work together with the regulated industry in crafting and enforcing new regulations. These issue networks enable administrators to get a clear picture of the impact of proposed rules on the affected industry and make for the crafting and implementation of more effective laws.

No: The federal bureaucracy is so enmeshed with the industries it regulates that it has been co-opted by these industries and can no longer operate independently. Agency heads are focused more on politics than they are on policy, and their ties to the regulated industry render them unable to consider the full range of policy alternatives when they deal with an issue or problem. The relationship between the agency, the regulated industry or constituency, and Congress is better characterized as an iron triangle than as an issue network. Each of these groups is highly dependent on each other—for example, legislators need the information and votes their constituencies offer, agencies look for the funding and grant of discretion that legislatures provide, and constituencies need the friendly laws and regulations that both the legislature and agencies may offer. This iron triangle is difficult, if not impossible, to penetrate, and this significantly reduces the opportunities that exist for alternative viewpoints or policies. In some areas of the law, the dependency is so complete that we speak of agency capture—that is, a situation in which the administrative agency is simply a pawn of the regulated industry or constituency.

Law Against Discrimination

New Jersey anti-discrimination law that provides more protection than its federal counterpart because it bars discrimination based, not only on race, color, religion, national origin, and sex, but on grounds like sexual orientation, as well

www ▶ ▶ ▶

agency will decide whether or not to pursue the case. The EEOC "steps out" for both strategic and policy-related reasons. First, it does so to preserve its own resources, choosing instead to have the state agency expend its time, money, and effort. This is a very compelling reason: in 2001, the D.C. office and its fifty field offices handled more than 80,000 claims, the largest number since the mid-1990s. Second, the EEOC defers to the state agency because state law may provide more protection to employees than is granted under the federal law. Where both the federal and state governments regulate an activity, the federal government almost always provides a floor, that is, some standard that provides minimal protection, but allows the states to impose a ceiling, or a more protective standard. In New Jersey, the Bureau of Enforcement (BOE) of the Division on Civil Rights has responsibility for enforcing the **Law Against Discrimination**, a state law that is actually more protective of employee rights than the federal law. New Jersey's LAD protects against discrimination on the basis of sexual orientation, while Title VII does not. When the BOE evaluates a case, it makes a decision about whether to sue the employer or to provide support to the employee. The time frame for the agencies to make their decisions is actually quite strict. If the state declines to pursue a case, it is moved to the federal EEOC, which must make a decision about whether there is "reasonable cause" to believe that discrimination occurred. If such a cause determination is made, the agency may either hold a hearing or attempt conciliation between the parties.

When the agency decides to attempt to resolve a grievance, its decision is not binding on the parties; the loser can always go to court after the agency issues its recommendations. It bears noting, however, that courts do seem to defer to the agency's decision in the case, probably because they recognize the agency's expertise. Employees who bring their cases to court despite an agency finding of no cause usually lose in court. While there is deference for agency decisions, this is not always the case, and some analysts have begun to suggest that courts are starting to question agency determinations.

Administrative Procedure Act

act that lays out guidelines that must be followed in administrative cases; usually more flexible than the procedures that must be used at trial

"Creppy Directive"

order issued by an INS judge immediately after 9/11 that allowed the agency to hold closed hearings in immigration cases; successfully challenged in the Sixth Circuit, which held that the INS had overstepped its powers

The **Administrative Procedure Act** lays out the guidelines that must be followed in administrative cases, and typically, there are fewer formalities in these cases than there are in court cases. Administrative hearings, however, must have certain minimal procedural guarantees. If these are lacking, a court will overturn the decision of the administrative judge or judges. For example, in 2002, the Sixth Circuit Court of Appeals barred the Department of Justice from conducting a secret bond hearing for Rabih Haddah, who was in the process of being deported for overstaying his visa. The DOJ wanted to bar all access to the hearing because it believed that Mr. Haddah was involved in channeling money to terrorist organizations abroad, and it wanted to limit his access to associates who might be able to take over his activities. To justify its closure of his hearing, the DOJ cited the **"Creppy Directive,"** a policy that had been put in place by Chief Immigration Judge

Creppy in the days immediately following September 11. Under this directive, the INS could simply classify a case as a special interest case and order that all hearings in connection to this case be closed to the press and the public, as well as to the defendant's family and friends. In this case, *Detroit Free Press* v. *Ashcroft* (303 F.3d 681), the Sixth Circuit struck down the INS's policy of blanket closure because the policy didn't require that the agency provide any specific information about why the case was so sensitive and because it undercut the defendant's due process rights. In this case, the circuit court weighed the government's need to protect the nation from terrorist attacks against the individual's interest in having a full and public hearing on the charges against him. It found that the INS had overstepped its powers.

`www  ▶ ▶ ▶`

SUMMARY

This chapter has explored lawmaking by the chief executive and administrative agencies in the federal and state governments. Chief executives, that is, the president and the governors, have broad discretion to make laws. They can make law unilaterally through the use of executive orders. These orders have a number of functions, many of them symbolic, but sometimes substantive, as well. We are living in an era when the president has moved quite dramatically in this area, using executive orders to accomplish a number of highly controversial goals, among these, the creation of military tribunals for the trial of noncitizens suspected of being involved in terror plots. Executive branch agencies also have significant lawmaking powers delegated to them by legislative bodies. This is a huge governmental apparatus, and as in the case of the chief executive, there is a separate and independent federal and state structure. The law that is made by these agencies, which is known as administrative law, is quite extensive. It governs much of our day-to-day lives. There has been significant debate about how to divide lawmaking responsibilities of the federal and state agencies, and also substantial disagreement about how effective these bureaucracies are in a number of policy domains.

SUGGESTED READING

Lief H. Carter and Christine B. Harrington, *Administrative Law and Politics: Cases and Comments* (Longman, 1999, 3rd edition). This is an excellent resource for learning about both the law and procedures governing administrative agencies. These authors explain in clear and engaging language what administrative law *is* and how it has functioned in the last one hundred years. They lay out key themes for examining administrative law and process, and they argue that law and politics are closely interwoven in this area.

Phillip J. Cooper, *By Order of the President: The Use and Abuse of Executive Direct Action* (University Press of Kansas, 2002). This book provides a solid overview of the use of executive orders throughout our nation's history, beginning with George Washington and continuing up through the presidency of George W. Bush.

Louis Fisher, *Nazi Saboteurs on Trial: A Military Tribunal and American Law* (University of Kansas, 2003). Fisher's book provides a detailed examination of the landmark 1942 case, *Ex parte Quirin*. At issue in this case was the decision of a military tribunal to execute six Germans who came ashore during World War II to commit acts of sabotage. Ultimately, the U.S. Supreme Court gave the executive branch wide discretion in this area and allowed the executions to go forward. This book helps to remind the reader that the ongoing debate about the use of military tribunals is not an entirely new one—we have long considered whether there are some circumstances that warrant expedited review and procedures, often at the expense of individual rights.

William G. Howell, *Power Without Persuasion: The Politics of Direct Presidential Action* (Princeton University Press, 2003). Howell encourages the reader to consider whether the separation-of-powers model is entirely useful in understanding the relationship between the branches of government. Howell argues that the president has a number of very important powers that he is able to exercise quite apart from the other branches, and that she or he is not as constrained in lawmaking as are the other institutions.

Cindy Skrzycki, *The Regulators: Anonymous Power Brokers in American Politics* (Rowman and Littlefield Press, 2003). Skrzycki, a columnist for the *Washington Post,* provides a much-needed view of who the regulators are in the administrative branch. She successfully unmasks these "anonymous" actors and helps us to understand how they actually do their jobs on a day-to-day basis. This book helps to humanize the vast bureaucracy and in so doing helps us to understand how these actors function.

ACTIVE LEARNING

1. Consider Section 1(f) of President Bush's Executive Order establishing military tribunals:

> Given the danger to the safety of the United States and the nature of international terrorism, and to the extent provided by and under this order, I find consistent with section 836 of title 10, United States Code, that it is not practicable to apply in military commissions under this order the principles of law and the rules of evidence generally recognized in the trial of criminal cases in the United States district courts . . .

What concerns do you think this article aims to address? What does it do to address them? Why would the president take this action? How does it change existing procedure governing the conduct of criminal trials?

You may also want to check out the final set of guidelines on military tribunals adopted by the Department of Defense (**DOD 2/03** final rule on "Crimes and Elements of Trials by Military Commission"). How does this help flesh out Section 1(f)?

2. Look at some regulation presently being considered by an administrative agency—you can start by tracking this regulation from the agency's initial publication of the rule in the *Federal Register* to publication of comments gathered during the notice and comment period. Consider how intensely the regulated industry participated in this notice and comment and think about how much input other parties might have. There is an excellent source for tracking all proposed rules, http://www.regulations.gov/, and from here you can see what has happened with rules proposed by many different agencies.

3. Take a good look at the White House website—it is full of information and very user friendly (http://www.whitehouse.gov/). What can you tell about how the president is making use of executive orders from this site? You can either search "executive order" or check out the executive order section of "In the News." Consider the many uses of these orders and how they function to make law unilaterally.

CHAPTER 10

Law Enforcement Personnel and Lawmaking

This final chapter on legal institutions focuses on the law enforcement system and its role in interpreting, enforcing, and making law in the United States. There really is no one law enforcement system in the United States—instead, policing is decentralized, with more than twenty thousand separate enforcement units, most of these at the municipal, county, or village level. This chapter examines the principal functions of law enforcement personnel and explores three central issues: first, how this decentralized structure affects law enforcement; second, how law enforcement officials function as agents of social control who are charged with balancing our need for security against our commitment to individual rights; and third, how law enforcement personnel use their greatest source of power, the exercise of discretion, to discharge their responsibilities.

Law enforcement officers have three principal functions:

1. *They must protect the public against acts of violence and disorder.*
2. *They must enforce the law by engaging in the investigation, apprehension, and punishment of wrong-doers.*
3. *They must serve on the "front lines," engaging in direct service to the communities they serve.*

These functions place law enforcement personnel in close contact with individuals and groups in society. To many people, the police are "the law"—the living personification of the American legal system. This direct contact with the public often places the police in highly controversial situations in which the exercise of discretion is critical.

As a culture, we are deeply ambivalent about the exercise of power by governmental organizations like the police. We want the police to protect us, but we aren't sure about how to limit the exercise of this power in order to guard against interference with individual rights. This distrust is apparent in our laws, political institutions, and popular culture. Our concern about public safety sometimes overrides our distrust of law enforcement agents, which leads many people think in we have to give these agencies more flexibility to conduct the war against terrorism the post-9/11 world.

DECENTRALIZED STRUCTURE AND ITS EFFECT ON LAW ENFORCEMENT

King's Court of the Star Chamber

chief law enforcement arm of the British monarchy during 1500s and 1600s; had unlimited power to search individuals and used this power to intimidate

www ▶ ▶ ▶

Our fear of a strong centralized police force goes back to our colonial roots. The British monarchy ruled with an iron fist throughout the 1500s and 1600s, and the early colonists were very aware of the kind of misuse of power that characterized the king's law enforcers. The **King's Court of the Star Chamber**, which was in place throughout this period, had broad and unlimited power to search any person, at any time, without any real suspicion. The Star Chamber used its powers to punish and intimidate the king's critics more than to fight crime. The Star Chamber was ultimately abolished in 1641, as Parliament sought to limit the monarchy's power. With this as a background, the colonists were wary of giving too much power to any policing unit, particularly one under the control of the federal government. Largely because of this fear, law enforcement has historically been decentralized in the United States, with municipal and county governments wielding most of the power.

In fact, for most of our history, law enforcement was strictly a local activity. Police departments as we know them emerged in the late 1800s as cities began to grapple with the perceived dangers of immigration and urbanization. From this period until the 1920s, law enforcement continued to be a function of cities and counties. Only two states, Massachusetts and Texas, had statewide police forces. In the 1920s, other states began to establish their own police forces, and in the 1920s and 1930s Congress began to expand the powers of federal law enforcement units like the Federal Bureau of Investigation. Up until this time, only the U.S. marshals, who were charged with safeguarding the public peace, especially on the frontier, had any real power. Over time, the authority of the marshals diminished, as those of federal agencies like the FBI, the Department of Alcohol, Tobacco and Firearms, and other agencies expanded.

Law enforcement continues to be primarily local. As Table 10.1 illustrates, of the nearly eight hundred thousand law enforcement officers employed in 2000, more than seven hundred thousand were employed at the state and local level—there are less than one hundred thousand employed as federal law enforcement agents. Moreover, of the seven hundred thousand state and local officers, the vast majority are employed by cities, counties, and municipalities, with only about one hundred thousand other state, special jurisdiction, or Texas constable officers. This decentralization means that both entry requirements and requirements for promotion are inconsistent. Moreover, this decentralized structure makes it difficult to develop or impose national or statewide standards or policies on officers.

TABLE 10.1
Law Enforcement
Personnel in the
United States

Type of Agency	Number of Agencies	Number of Full-time Sworn Officers
Total		796,518
All State and local	17,784	708,022
Local police	12,666	440,920
Sheriff	3,070	164,711
Primary State	49	56,348
Special jurisdiction	1,376	43,413
Texas constable	623	2,630
Federal*		88,496

Note: Special jurisdiction category includes both state-level and local-level agencies. Consolidated police-sheriffs are included under local police category. Agency counts exclude those operating on a part-time basis.
*Non-military federal officers authorized to carry firearms and make arrests.

Source: http://www.ojp.usdoj.gov/bjs/lawenf.htm

Before the 1940s, there were virtually no entrance requirements and no attempt to impose standards of police practice on officers in most police departments. During this period, departments became more professionalized and required officers to complete training programs. Again, these requirements were imposed almost entirely by municipalities: there was little state or federal oversight of the selection or training processes. There was also little oversight of police procedures or activities, and law enforcement officers exercised unlimited discretion in many parts of the country. In some cases, this discretion gave way to corruption and brutality, and the public began to clamor for the creation of standards for police departments. Consider the case of *Haley* v. *Ohio* (332 U.S. 596) decided by the U.S. Supreme Court in 1948—in this case, five justices signed the majority opinion while the remaining four dissented. The petitioner in this case, a fifteen-year-old African American boy, was held incommunicado for five days, during which time he was allegedly beaten by the police. He was questioned repeatedly by teams of police officers in a small room that was crowded with officers. The youth was denied access to his family and friends and to a lawyer who had been retained by his mother. Ultimately, he confessed to being the lookout in a robbery that resulted in homicide and was sentenced to life in prison. The Supreme Court threw out the confession and overturned the conviction.

In the 1960s, the Supreme Court handed down a number of decisions that limited police discretion and brutality by establishing standards for police behavior, particularly in the areas of interrogation, search, and seizure. Specifically, the Supreme Court's 1961 decision in **Mapp v. Ohio** mandated that police must have a valid warrant before conducting a search, and its 1966 decision in **Miranda v. Arizona** regulated the interrogation process by requiring that officers notify those in police custody of their due process rights. The standards that came out of these decisions were widely

www ▶ ▶ ▶

Mapp v. Ohio
Supreme Court's 1961 opinion mandating that police officers have a valid warrant before conducting a search

Miranda v. Arizona
Supreme Court's 1966 opinion requiring that officers give notice of criminal due process rights to anyone in their custody

recognized within a short period of time. Today's students can relate *Miranda*'s requirements in amazing detail, and nearly everyone can recall at least some portions of the warning. Many know the whole statement, which many police officers carry on a piece of paper inside their hats. I'll bet you know it, too—it starts, "You have the right to remain silent . . ."!

The U.S. Supreme Court's decisions in the generation of cases beginning with *Miranda* came out of the justices' serious concern about how police were performing their duties, and the decisions forced police departments to reconsider their interrogation and search tactics. These decisions have been widely criticized since the very beginning. Many people have argued that the Court's rules handcuff police officers and make them less effective at fighting crime. Some even argue that these rules resulted in an increase in criminal activity in the 1970s and 1980s. Ultimately, these decisions had only a limited impact on how police officers do their job, since decisions by later courts have allowed police officers to sidestep the rules. For example, from the beginning, police departments have argued that the requirement that police have a warrant to conduct a search should be subject to certain exceptions. The courts have now recognized many of these exceptions, among them the **plain view exception**, which allows police to access any evidence that is obvious to them even without a warrant, the **hot pursuit exception**, which allows officers to conduct a warrantless search of any vehicle or person of which they are in continuous pursuit, and finally the **vehicle exception**, which allows them to search any vehicle that they believe may be carrying illegal goods or substances. without having to first secure a warrant. Moreover, police officers can search any person they are arresting, again without needing a warrant. As a result of these exceptions, most searches are now warrantless.

Like the warrant rule, which has been chipped away over the last three decades, the *Miranda* **rule**, which requires that police inform suspects of their rights, has loosened whatever grip it may initially have had on police departments. In 2000, the U.S. Supreme Court reaffirmed *Miranda* in *Dickerson* v. *U.S.*, striking down a congressional law that had replaced the *Miranda* rule with a much more lenient test allowing police departments to show that the suspect had voluntarily given his or her incriminating statement. If the department could show voluntariness, the fact that the police officers had not read the *Miranda* rights would not matter, and the statement would be admissible. Despite this holding barring the use of the voluntariness standard, *Miranda* has actually become much less important over the last thirty years as courts increasingly have allowed into evidence incriminating statements made by people who were being questioned but were not yet in police custody. Many people have real doubts about the impact of *Miranda* on police procedure and have argued that police departments throughout the country have found ways to sidestep the rule.

---

plain view exception

an exception to the warrant requirement that allows police to access any evidence that is obvious to them

hot pursuit exception

an exception to the warrant requirement that allows police to search any vehicle or person of which they are in continuous pursuit

vehicle exception

an exception to the warrant requirement that allows officers to search any vehicle they believe may be carrying illegal goods or substances without having to first secure a warrant

Miranda rule

requirement that police inform suspects of their due process rights; has become less of a constraint on police departments over the last few decades

The decentralized structure of the law enforcement system has not only made it difficult to standardize and professionalize police practice but has also made coordination of agencies more problematic. Jurisdictions of many law enforcement agencies overlap, and this shared jurisdiction sometimes complicates enforcement efforts. This is especially true in the post–September 11 world. In the wake of the terror attacks, law enforcement agents were placed on heightened vigilance, and the Department of Homeland Security was created in part to coordinate the activities of, not only federal agencies, but state and local law enforcement units as well. In the event of another terrorist attack or fears of an imminent attack, the Department of Homeland Security can now bring most law enforcement departments within its control and could centralize much of our nation's policing activities. If the department were able to assume this role, it would be the first time in our nation's history that law enforcement agents would be directed from a distant, federal office. Given our political culture and historical distrust of a central policing authority, it is perhaps not surprising that some citizens have strongly criticized the expanded enforcement powers given to the Department of Homeland Security. In fact, some have begun to warn that this executive branch department could ultimately deploy military troops on domestic soil in pursuit of its war on terror—something that last happened in the Civil War.

POLICE AS LAW ENFORCERS AND AGENTS OF SOCIAL CONTROL

All law functions as a social control—that is, it seeks to protect the existing social and political order and to punish those who engage in aberrant behavior. In the American legal system, we expect that law enforcement personnel will work to ensure our safety, but at the same time, we are concerned about the impact their actions may have on individual rights. For this reason, we continue to try to balance our need for safety against our societal concern for individual rights and freedoms. Our concerns about individual rights are heightened by the substantial powers exercised by the federal and state governments. Unlike civil law, which is enforced principally by individuals filing civil suits, criminal law is enforced by public officials, and police officers are the first line of law enforcers. The state and federal governments have a monopoly on the criminal law—they create and implement criminal codes and they punish those who violate these codes.

Social Control

The goals of the criminal code are usually very clear, and often, there is wide societal consensus about these goals. Remember from Chapter 1 that a criminal code is often the first set of laws created in a community. Because

Do the Department of Homeland Security terror alert codes make us safe?

Yes:

The Color-Coded Threat Level System provides much-needed information to the public and to law enforcement and safety personnel about existing security threats. The Department of Homeland Security maintains this system, which grades the risk from low to severe, with corresponding color codes. Law enforcement and public safety officers all over the United States can use this code to gauge the terror threat and can know exactly when they should activate different plans to combat terrorism or respond to a specific threat. The goal of this system is to make security alerts uniform and to fully apprise public officials about ongoing terrorist activities. This color-coded system is intended to be used with the Homeland Security Threat Advisory, which provides specific warnings to officials who need this information to combat known threats to national security. In short, this system makes us safer by providing standardized information about terror threats to the people who need it most—law enforcement and safety officers on the front lines in the battle against terrorism.

No:

This system does not make us safer—it provides little in the way of information to either the public or to law enforcement and safety personnel. The five levels, ranging in color from green (low risk of terrorist activity) to red (severe risk of terrorist activity) are not specific enough to apprise the public of actual threats. For example, what is the real difference between a guarded risk of attack and a significant risk of attack? And how is the public to really understand these differences? We have been on and off the yellow/orange alerts (elevated risk of attack/high risk of attack), but no one has ever clarified why we moved between levels. In fact, we moved to the lower level directly *after* the presidential election in November 2004, prompting some to say that the higher alert might have been used for political reasons—that is, to keep the threat of terror high on the public's agenda and thus convince the public of the need to reelect the president. Perhaps even more troubling than this lack of clarity is the fact that these terror alerts may themselves make the public more afraid and thus more vulnerable to being terrorized. In the absence of clear evidence about why the alert has been raised, the American public may feel as if there is information that they simply are not getting that underscores some real and serious threat to them specifically. The accompanying fear actually serves the terrorists' goals very well—it makes us fear that we are not safe in our country and that the next attack is imminent. It is hard to go about your business when you are waiting for the next attack, and the alerts increase this sense of vulnerability without providing any real information about the actual threat.

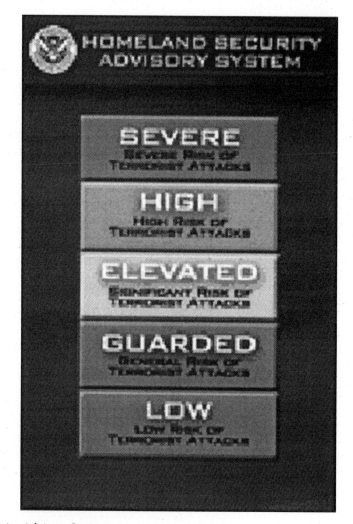

Homeland Security Advisory System
http://www.dhs.gov/dhspublic/display?theme=29SIDEBAR

the majority of people recognize that criminal laws exist to protect their lives and their property, they are very willing to cede control for law enforcement to the police. Many people now see law enforcement as the primary goal of police activity—and view social control as far less important. In reality, however, our law enforcement system was created, first and foremost, to reinforce existing social and political relationships, specifically, slaveholding.

slave patrol

the first American police force; charged with enforcing slave codes in the South in the pre–Civil War period

www ▶ ▶ ▶

The first American police force was the **slave patrol**, a group of men charged with enforcing the slave codes in the South. The slave codes, which were passed by southern states in the early 1700s, barred slaves from having weapons, from assembling, and from traveling beyond their plantations without passes. Slave patrols were also responsible for capturing and returning runaway slaves. Slave patrollers swore an oath to uphold the law—in one community, a patroller swore that he would "as searcher for guns, swords, and other weapons among the slaves in my district, faithfully, and as privately as I can, discharge the trust reposed in me as the law directs, to the best of my power." These patrollers saw themselves as agents of the law and believed that their communities depended on them to effectively execute slave codes. At first, slave patrols came together informally, but after some time had passed, the local community began to draw on militia lists or to rely on court-appointed patrols. Service on slave patrols was mandatory, and white men of all classes had an obligation to serve, although wealthy men might choose to pay a fine or find a substitute. Slave patrols had the primary responsibility for enforcing the state codes, and while newly established police departments helped, the patrols were the central players. As the testimony of some former slaves suggest, there was significant variation in how these patrols did their job, and this variation seems to have been a function of how the slave-holders wanted to have their slaves punished.

Like slave patrols, police officers in northern cities in the 1800s also functioned primarily as agents of social control. Until the 1840s, northern cities had resisted the call for public police forces, relying instead on private companies that provided part-time night watchmen and other workers. The increase in urban rioting and crime in the 1830s, however, changed all of this, and many cities created their own police forces in the 1840s and 1850s. By the mid- to late 1800s, the job of policing had expanded from simply riot and crime control to the enforcement of morality codes that barred gambling, prostitution, and public intoxication. Police were expected to control the "dangerous masses," that is, newly arrived immigrants and those arriving from rural areas, and they used these codes to do this. As Tyler Anbinder, author of *Five Points: The Nineteenth-Century New York City Neighborhood That Invented Tap Dance, Stole Elections and Became the World's Most Notorious Slum* has noted, during this period, police forces were more interested in maintaining the status quo, which placed Irish, Italian, and Eastern European Americans at the bottom rung, than they were in enforcing the criminal code. In fact, the residents of certain urban areas effectively performed this policing role when law enforcement agents refused to step in. Ultimately, the state government disbanded this ineffective and corrupt police force and, over the fierce opposition of the mayor and the officers, established a Metropolitan Police Force in 1857. The order disbanding the early police force is on the website.

www ▶ ▶ ▶

THE LAW IN POPULAR CULTURE

Gangs of New York

In 1846 there were no urban police forces—police and firefighters were privately paid and corruption was widespread. As depicted in this film, gangs roamed free in many cities, perhaps most notoriously, in New York, and native-born and immigrant groups often clashed, sometimes violently. This photo depicts such a clash in the poverty-stricken Five Points section of New York.

Policing Styles

Social control is still a very important function of law enforcement officials, who are called on to enforce the laws passed by other branches of government. Police departments have become more professionalized over the last century, and most require specialized training. There remains significant variation in the requirements for entry and promotion in departments across the country, but law enforcement officials are better educated and trained than they ever have been. Police departments have also become more diverse, in terms of gender, race, and ethnicity. Once an enclave of Irish-Americans, law enforcement agencies are much more ethnically balanced. In addition, a number of successful court challenges have permitted entry for women and African Americans, groups that had been excluded from law enforcement. In 1997, the Bureau of Justice Statistics reported that minorities comprised more than 21.5 percent of local law enforcement officers, up from 14.6 percent a decade earlier. It bears noting, however, that many police departments do not require college degrees and that they

legalistic style of policing

officers are expected to focus on strict compliance with laws on the books, and rank-and-file members are expected to closely follow guidelines

watchman style of policing

officers are allowed much more discretion in deciding which crimes to focus on, typically more serious violent crimes; police are expected to prevent crimes from being committed

service style of policing

departments using this style tend to see themselves as in a cooperative partnership with the local community; the public helps police to safeguard community; also known as community-oriented policing (COP)

www ▶ ▶ ▶

often give extra consideration to those applicants who have served in the military. As a result, there is a clear tendency to hire people who have more authoritarian personalities and who tend to adhere to the rules and procedures set down by those in positions of authority.

Law enforcement officials are on the front lines, serving as intermediaries between the public and the other governmental institutions. In the late 1960s, influential scholar James Q. Wilson distinguished between three different styles of policing. He said that policing style had a profound impact on how police performed their jobs and related to the community. According to Wilson, policing styles were either legalistic, watchman, or service-oriented. Police departments employing a **legalistic style of policing** were focused on strict compliance with the laws that were on the books, and typically, the rank and file were expected to closely follow police manuals and instructions. This style minimized discretion, and officers were expected to follow the orders of their superiors. In contrast, the **watchman style of policing** allowed officers much more discretion, and allowed them to pay less attention to crimes that they viewed as less serious, while focusing on more dangerous crimes. While legalistic departments expect their officers to react or respond to crimes that have already been committed, watchman departments assume that officers will be able to stop crime from being committed in the first place. Finally, departments employing a **service style of policing** were focused more on having a cooperative relationship with the community—and in fact, this style has become known as community-oriented policing, or COP. Police departments that use this style need to have strong ties to both the people and the organizations in a community, with police being just part of the law enforcement "equation"—the policing role is assumed, not only by officers, but by members of the community, as well. In cities or towns with COP, foot or bike patrols are common, as are citizen-watch or crime-watch activities, and police are much more active in providing information or support services to members of the community. COP relies much more on cooperation than do the more adversarial or confrontational approaches of the watchman and legalistic styles. Some writers argue that COP may result in less crime and better quality of life, in large part because the public helps the police to safeguard the community.

Wilson and others argue that policing style is determined by departmental culture, as opposed to being a choice that individual officers make, and this style is a function of a number of factors, some structural and some cultural. Among the institutional factors is whether the department has a strictly hierarchical structure—departments with such a structure tend to be more legalistic, while those that seek to provide officers with more leeway tend to have watchman or service styles. It is probably not a surprise that those departments that value officer creativity and initiative tend to adopt community policing styles, while those that value obedience and duty to superiors tend to use more legalistic styles. The political culture of the city, town, or county also seems to be very important in determining policing style. Obviously, if a community is very suspicious of the police and unwilling to partner with them to fight crime, community policing will probably be unsuccessful. High crime rates in the 1980s and early 1990s, along with allegations of police brutality in many cities, convinced a number of police departments to try to employ community policing tactics. One of the longest-lived community policing projects, in Portsmouth, Massachusetts, recently celebrated its fifteenth anniversary and won a regional award. Despite some success in many departments, serious obstacles remain, and some departments that had experimented with community policing are now abandoning this approach and focusing resources once again on more traditional police activities like investigations and arrests.

www ▶ ▶ ▶

Police Brutality

Police officers have the difficult job of reconciling two deeply held but conflicting values in American society—our desire to be safe and secure in our persons and homes versus our strong belief in the right of the individual to be free from governmental coercion and excessive control. The way law enforcement officers or departments mediate this conflict has a direct bearing on how the public sees them. As a culture, we expect that officers can balance these goals, and when they veer off too far in one direction or another, they are fiercely criticized. At the extreme, too heavy a focus on order and safety may border on police brutality.

According to Human Rights Watch, an international human rights organization, brutality is an issue in most urban police departments in the United States. A report issued by Human Rights Watch in 1998 reveals that these acts are committed by a small minority of officers. Human Rights Watch faults, not only these officers, but the departments that it claims protect these officers. While police officials abhor acts of brutality, police departments and officials must try to figure out how to fight crime without violating individual rights. Ultimately, courts must decide whether the police department has tipped the balance too far in the direction of public order and must balance safety against individual rights. Beginning in the 1960s, courts, and in particular, the U.S. Supreme Court, issued decisions that seem to oscillate between these two goals. In *Escobedo v. Illinois* (1964) the Supreme Court held that Mr. Escobedo's right to counsel, safeguarded by the Sixth Amendment to the Constitution, was violated when he was refused access to a lawyer, even though he had not been yet formally indicted. In stark contrast, in *Chavez v. Martinez* (2003), the pendulum had swung the other way, as the Court issued a decision that squarely favored order and public safety and gave the police much more discretion

www ▶ ▶ ▶

Escobedo v. Illinois

landmark 1964 Supreme Court decision that stated that criminal due process protections kicked in even before a formal indictment

www ▶ ▶ ▶

Chavez v. Martinez

landmark 2003 Supreme Court decision that allowed police to immediately question a person whom they had shot, even while emergency medical procedures were being performed on him

in fighting crime. In this case, Mr. Martinez was repeatedly questioned immediately after being shot by police officers. Mr. Martinez was blinded and paralyzed as a result of the shooting, and officers continued to question him even as he was being treated by emergency medical technicians and physicians. Here, the court concluded that the police's need for information about his encounter with the police outweighed any rights Martinez may have had.

By the mid- to late 1990s, police brutality was very much in the news, as the media reported on a number of very graphic and visible instances of brutality. The 1993 beating of Rodney King by Los Angeles Police Department officers, which was witnessed by fifteen to twenty officers and dozens of civilian by-standers and videotaped by one of these by-standers, squarely raised the issue of police brutality, particularly of the African American community. Similarly, the coercive tactics of the New York City Police Department were strongly criticized following the beating and sodomy of Abner Louima in 1997 and the shooting death of Amadou Diallo in 1999 by police officers. More recently, the death of a Harlem woman was ruled a homicide following the woman's fatal heart attack after police mistakenly raided her apartment, threw a concussion hand grenade, and handcuffed her. Media exposure and widespread criticism have convinced many police departments to review, and in some cases revise, their procedures for using deadly force. In 2001, former New York City Mayor Rudolph Giuliani and Police Commissioner Bernard B. Kerik gave the city's **Civilian Complaint Review Board** much broader powers to investigate and prosecute cases involving police brutality. Until 2001, the Review Board was not independent of the police department, and a 2001 report found that there were widespread delays in the investigation and prosecution of civilian complaints. Given sufficient resources to prosecute cases against police officers, the Review Board should function more effectively; but up until this point, deep budget cuts have made it difficult for the board to do its work.

Civilian Complaint Review Board

a panel that was given broad powers to investigate police brutality in New York City in the wake of a police shooting of an unarmed civilian in 1999

POLICE DISCRETION

Law enforcement agents stand on the "front lines," implementing the criminal codes created by the other branches. While this function might seem reactive because law enforcement personnel are charged with putting into place laws created by other governmental actors, they exercise a significant degree of discretion in the implementation of these laws. It is by the exercise of this discretion that law enforcement agents are engaged in making law. Like courts, legislatures, and executives, law enforcement agents are central actors in the American legal system. They may not be the ones who are creating law, but they are the ones who make the decisions about how the criminal code will be used, who will be investigated, and who will be charged with violations of this code.

The Need for Police Discretion

Law enforcement officers often argue that they need to be able to use their discretion in performing their duties. In many ways, this argument makes sense. Most police work focuses, not on investigation and arrest, but on maintaining order and preventing crime. And much of this work is situational: officers make decisions about how to react to some threat or breach of the peace based on the situation. An officer may respond differently to the same action depending on the context. The National Criminal Justice Research Service, an arm of the U.S. Department of Justice, describes such a scenario, noting that an officer may physically restrain an intoxicated person who is harassing a pregnant woman and her child on a busy street but take a less aggressive approach in dealing with the same drunk who is harassing a young man on a quiet street. Law enforcement officers argue that the exercise of discretion is essential to policing and that it is not always appropriate or effective to use the same approach in different situations. At times, police departments have attempted to limit the exercise of discretion by issuing manuals or rules and regulations and requiring that officers follow these in dealing with the public. Generally speaking, when departments have issued strict guidelines that significantly hamper the exercise of discretion and mandate a generic approach to policing regardless of the situation, they have found that law enforcement agents have been less effective. This is especially true when the officer must confront quality-of-life crimes, like drug or alcohol intoxication, drunk driving, gambling, prostitution, or minor traffic infractions or when dealing with the homeless or with persons suffering from mental illness. Officers are expected to use their good judgment in making determinations about whether to use force and about the degree of force to be used in their policing responsibilities. Most police departments have some guidelines for dealing with these situations, but officers retain a significant amount of discretion.

It appears that police discretion is expanding. In the 2001 case **Atwater v. Lago Vista,** the U.S. Supreme Court upheld the exercise of police discretion in making arrests based on minor infractions. In this case, the Court was asked to determine whether a Lago Vista police officer had exceeded his authority in arresting a driver who had not seat-belted her two children in her car. The Court held that the officer had the right to make the choice about whether to ticket the woman or to arrest her. The effect of this case has been to uphold the use of police discretion in situations involving arrest and in the use of warrantless searches—two situations where police discretion has become especially important. Americans do not have the right to be free from all searches—only those that are unreasonable or of places in which they have a reasonable expectation of privacy. When there is no such expectation, then there is no privacy right. For example, according to the U.S. Supreme Court, individuals do not have a reasonable expectation of privacy in their garbage, and so law enforcement agents may search peo-

www ▶ ▶ ▶

Atwater v. Lago Vista

2001 Supreme Court case that allowed police to exercise their discretion in deciding to arrest a woman who had not seat-belted her children into her car

www ▶ ▶ ▶

ple's garbage without a warrant and may use any incriminating evidence against them. Courts are increasingly limiting the protection against individual search and seizure, with the result that in many cases, there is no individual right or due process protection and the only guiding principle for law enforcement agents is their discretion.

Police discretion is likely to continue to expand. In fact, the war on terror has already considerably broadened the exercise of discretion by law enforcement agents. This expansion is apparent in a number of areas, among them, immigration and naturalization and search and surveillance. The Department of Justice, charged with enforcing both immigration and federal criminal law, has been actively involved in the creation and implementation of laws that expand the powers of federal law enforcement officials in these areas. Guidelines issued by the Immigration and Naturalization Service (INS), an agency within the Department of Justice, are included in the Law in Action box. In these guidelines, the INS justified its use of discretion, explaining that agents had to be allowed to exercise their best judgment in deciding which cases to prosecute. The agency also articulated some of the most important factors in deciding which cases to pursue.

The war on terror has also expanded the powers of law enforcement officers by allowing them to exercise more discretion in the areas of search and surveillance. Patriot Acts I and II passed by Congress in 2001 and 2003 broadened the powers of federal law enforcement agencies to conduct searches without warrants where terror activities were suspected. Specifically, the Federal Bureau of Investigation (FBI) and Central Intelligence Agency (CIA) were given the power to conduct searches without having to meet the more stringent probable cause requirement if they could demonstrate that they expected the search to yield information that would be relevant to a criminal investigation. These agencies were also allowed to use roving wiretaps and to monitor Internet communications without having to demonstrate that they had any concrete evidence linking suspects to specific criminal activities. This new search-and-surveillance standard broadened the discretionary powers of law enforcement agencies, enabling them to act largely independently of judicial oversight. Where once a judge would have to have ruled that there was probable cause to conduct a search or to engage in surveillance, these agencies are now permitted to make their own determinations about whether there is enough evidence to engage in these activities.

The Downside of Discretion

Discretion is the most important lawmaking power that law enforcement personnel are given, and it is the exercise of this discretion that may be most problematic. For many years, police departments declined to investigate or to make arrests in calls involving domestic violence. These cases were seen as involving private matters, and most police officers who were called to the

LAW IN ACTION

Prosecutorial Discretion Guidelines for the Immigration and Naturalization Service (2000)

Prosecutorial Discretion Guidelines

The use of prosecutorial discretion by the Immigration and Naturalization Service (INS) in deciding which cases to pursue has received increased attention since passage of the Illegal Immigration Reform and Immigrant Responsibility Act in 1996. Part of this legislation limited the authority of immigration judges to provide relief from removal in many cases, and persons facing removal have sought to avoid removal by other means, including prosecutorial discretion from INS.

Prosecutorial discretion is the authority that every law enforcement agency has to decide whether to exercise its enforcement powers against someone. INS, like other law enforcement agencies, has prosecutorial discretion and exercises it every day. In the immigration context, the term applies not only to the decision to issue, serve or file a Notice to Appear (NTA) when starting removal proceedings, but also to a broad range of other discretionary enforcement decisions. These include focusing investigative resources on particular offenses or conduct; deciding whom to stop, question and arrest; deciding whether to detain certain aliens in custody; settling or dismissing a removal proceeding; granting deferred action or staying a final removal order; agreeing to voluntary departure, permitting withdrawal of an application for admission, or taking other action in lieu of removing an alien; pursuing an appeal; or executing a removal order.

While INS can refrain from exercising its law enforcement authority against a particular person on a case-by-case basis, it cannot regular-ize someone's immigration status or grant a benefit that an alien is not legally entitled to receive. For example, INS has no discretion to admit into the United States an alien who is inadmissible and cannot adjust the status of a person who isn't qualified for adjustment. INS has prosecutorial discretion not to place a removable alien in removal proceedings, but it does not have prosecutorial discretion to approve a naturalization application by an alien who is ineligible for that benefit under the Immigration and Nationality Act.

Exercising prosecutorial discretion does not lessen INS' commitment to enforce the immigration laws to the best of the agency's ability. It is not an invitation to violate or ignore the law. Rather, it is a means to use the agency's resources in a way that best accomplishes INS' mission of administering and enforcing the immigration laws of the United States.

Factors Used in Determining Use of Prosecutorial Discretion

The factors that can be taken into account in deciding whether to exercise prosecutorial discretion favorably include the following:

- Immigration status
- Length of residence in the United States
- Criminal history
- Humanitarian concerns
- Immigration history
- Likelihood of ultimately removing the alien
- Likelihood of achieving enforcement goal by other means

LAW IN ACTION–(CONT'D)

- Whether the alien is eligible or is likely to become eligible for other relief
- Effect of action on future admissibility
- Current or past cooperation with law enforcement authorities
- Honorable U.S. military service
- Community attention
- Resources available to INS

Impact of Prosecutorial Discretion

Prosecutorial discretion is not a full or adequate substitute for the forms of relief previously available from an immigration judge prior to the changes in the law in 1996. In many cases, the exercise of prosecutorial discretion by INS leaves a person in limbo, at risk of future immigration enforcement action and unable to travel outside the United States without the fear of being denied readmission.

Although it is INS policy that a favorable exercise of discretion by an INS office should be respected by other INS offices unless the facts and circumstances have changed, the exercise of prosecutorial discretion does not grant a lawful status under the immigration laws, and there is no legally enforceable right to the exercise of prosecutorial discretion.

Ultimately, INS believes that a complete solution requires legislation to restore, to certain aliens affected by the 1996 changes, the possibility of a grant of relief by immigration judges during the removal process.

QUESTIONS

1. The trend toward prosecutorial discretion probably increases the powers of prosecutors, but at whose expense? Which individuals or groups are likely to see their powers reduced as a result of this new INS policy? Why? Is this a good thing?
2. Consider what the likely impact of mandatory sentencing rules will be on the balance of power between prosecutors and judges. If there is a mandatory sentence that accompanies the charges brought by a prosecutor, what will this mean in terms of the judge's discretion? Mandatory sentences were intended to limit the discretion of judges in criminal cases—why do you think that legislatures created these laws?

(http://www.immigration.gov/graphics/publicaffairs/factsheets/prosecut.htm)

November 28, 2000

scene were very slow to arrive. Once there, they did not engage in a full investigation of the incident. Batterers and their victims perceived that police would not vigorously address this issue, a perception that songwriter Tracey Chapman addressed in the lyrics of her song "Behind the Wall," which are on the website. It was only after women who had been injured or disabled by their batterers brought a series of lawsuits against the police departments in New York City; Oakland, California; and other cities that departments began to take these calls seriously and to train officers to deal with cases of domestic abuse. Perhaps the most famous of these cases involved a 1984 suit brought against the police department in Torrington, Connecticut, by a woman who was permanently disabled by her batterer.

Discretion may be essential to effective law enforcement, but this does not mean that officers are free to do what they please. They must make decisions about how to approach difficult circumstances, but their actions cannot be arbitrary, random, or at worst, discriminatory. In the best possible scenario, the exercise of discretion is guided by community values and professional standards. Police activities are also limited by civil rights and liberties protections granted under federal and state law. For example, the Fourth, Fifth, Sixth, Seventh, and Eighth Amendments to the U.S. Constitution impose significant limits on the exercise of discretion by law enforcement agencies. Specifically, the Fourth Amendment governs how police may conduct searches, surveillance, and seizure of evidence; the Fifth, Sixth, and Seventh Amendments regulate the trial process; and the Eighth Amendment creates limits on the punishment that can be imposed.

When law enforcement agents broaden their exercise of discretion to meet their own needs, or to engage in discriminatory activities, they are no longer acting in accordance with their authority. Sometimes, there is a very thin line between discretion and discrimination. For many years, law enforcement agents have employed profiles or proxies to apprehend criminals. In particular, in the area of drug trafficking, federal and state law enforcement personnel have used a list of characteristics that they identify with trafficking. When investigating trafficking on airplanes, police focus on passengers who have carry-on luggage only, pay for their tickets with cash, use the telephone immediately on exiting the airplane, and seem either too nervous or too calm. Law enforcement agents use profiles or proxies to target drug trafficking on interstate highways. Among the factors that raise suspicion are riding in a car with license plates from certain states (among these, Florida, California, and New York), riding alone, having many large plastic containers in the car, using a truck with a raised bed, and speeding. These profiles are created by a number of agencies, including the U.S. Drug Enforcement Agency and its counterparts at the state level. Moreover, law enforcement agencies have been permitted to use these proxies to justify "reasonable suspicion" to stop motorists. These stops, called **Terry stops** after the 1968 U.S. Supreme Court decision in *Terry* v. *Ohio,* typically allow officers to use their discretion in deciding to detain and search people who meet these profiles. The decision has been interpreted as requiring that officers show that there were a number of suspicious criteria and that the race of the suspect was not the only characteristic that triggered the stop.

The problem with these profiles or proxies is that they are not racially neutral and tend to target African Americans, even where members of this group have not engaged in any criminal activity. The use of **racial profiling** grew out of these proxies, and in the late 1990s, the practices of the New Jersey State Police, New York City Police Department, and Los Angeles Police Department came under fire as it was revealed these police depart-

www ▶ ▶ ▶

www ▶ ▶ ▶

Terry stops
stops that allow police officers to use their discretion in deciding to detain and search people who meet police profiles

www ▶ ▶ ▶

racial profiling
using race or ethnicity as a proxy for deciding whom to search and detain in a Terry stop; police are not permitted to use race as the sole criterion in deciding whom to stop; there must be other, suspicious characteristics that trigger the stop

www ▶ ▶ ▶

ments had been using race alone as a proxy for criminal activity. During this time, commentators began to identify a new "crime," that of "driving while black or brown," and revealed that racial profiling had been broadly used by police departments charged with investigating drug trafficking. It was revealed that many departments had specifically targeted racial minorities during routine traffic stops while bypassing whites.

The use of race to identify possible suspects was loudly criticized in the late 1990s and early 2000s, and many municipal and state law enforcement agencies vowed to change their practices. Many of these agencies agreed to keep records on routine traffic stops as a way of routing out racial profiling. The U.S. Justice Department's Civil Rights Division, responsible for safeguarding individual rights, vowed to be at the forefront of efforts to eradicate profiling; however, the war on terror has also affected this agency's activities, as it has struggled with the new law enforcement practice of targeting Arabs, Arab Americans, and Muslims. In fact, in June 2003, the Justice Department issued new guidelines on racial profiling that vowed to eliminate profiling but paradoxically allowed law enforcement officers to use the practice where it was necessary to safeguard national security. While law enforcement agents need to exercise discretion to do their jobs effectively, there remains significant disagreement about how much flexibility to provide these agents and about how to limit discretion to ensure that they do not abuse their powers. In the future, officers will almost certainly continue to walk a fine line between discretion and discrimination as they are called on to protect the public against domestic and international terrorism.

www ▶ ▶ ▶

SUMMARY

This chapter has explored the fourth institution for lawmaking in the United States—law enforcement agencies. Unlike the other three institutions, which are dual in structure, law enforcement in the U.S. is highly decentralized. There is no one (or even two) dominant law enforcers. Throughout American history, the public has been deeply ambivalent about the powers of law enforcement, and we have always believed that individual due process rights should be protected. U.S. law enforcement personnel perform a number of roles and perhaps the most important of these is protecting the existing social and political order. Of critical importance, the social control function has a long history dating back to the very beginning of law enforcement in this country. The first public law enforcement agents were members of slave patrols, charged with returning runaway slaves to their owners. In the mid- to late 1800s, police in urban centers had the responsibility for using moral codes to control immigrants, who were often viewed as dangerous and unpredictable. There are at least three different policing styles among police departments, and these vary according to their reliance on written guidelines and their relationship with the public. And finally, our deeply rooted concern about police power is often expressed in concerns about police discretion and frustration about police brutality.

SUGGESTED READING

Sally E. Hadden, *Slave Patrols: Law and Violence in Virginia and the Carolinas* (Harvard University Press, 2001). This excellent book examines the use of slave patrols and explores how these patrols functioned as effective agents of social control in the pre–Civil War South.

Tara Herivel and Paul Wright, *Prison Nation: The Warehousing of America's Poor* (Routledge Press, 2003). This important book examines how the nearly two million mostly poor people now in U.S. prisons live. The authors look at the huge increase in the number of inmates and examine their living conditions, focusing on issues like the privatization of prisons, forced work, medical care, rape, and prison litigation.

Jill Nelson, editor, *Police Brutality: An Anthology* (W.W. Norton, 2001). This edited volume explores brutality by focusing on the race, class, and gender biases in police practice. The writers also offer some solutions to this pervasive issue.

ACTIVE LEARNING

1. **Critical Thinking and Documentary Interviews:** Slave patrols and social control—At first, slave patrols came together informally, but after some time had passed, the local community began to draw on militia lists or to rely on court-appointed patrols. Service on slave patrols was mandatory, and white men of all classes had an obligation to serve, although wealthy men might choose to pay a fine or find a substitute. Read the story of Phoebe Lyons, who was a slave and gave testimony in the Ex-Slave Narratives that were compiled in the 1940s by the federal government. What did Ms. Lyons see the function of these patrols as being? Was there variation in how these patrols functioned? What accounted for this variation? Interview with Phoebe Lyons, Ex-Slave Narrative (The Ohio Historical Society: The African-American Experience in Ohio 18500) http://dbs.ohiohistory.org/africanam/det.cfm?ID=13924

2. **Critical Thinking and Guided Research: Human Rights Watch and police brutality**—Read the Human Rights Watch Report on Police Brutality in the United States (from http://www.hrw.org/reports98/police/uspo14.htm).

   Critical Thinking: Consider what the agency is arguing—what do they see as the primary contributor/s to police brutality in the United States. Do you agree? What factors do you think explain the use of brutality?

   Guided Research: Research one city examined in the report. What does the police code say about brutality or excessive force? Is it clearly defined? Interview someone on the force—what do they say about how existing police procedures can be used or even improved on to counter police brutality?

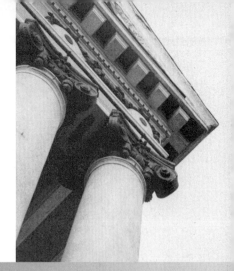

PART THREE

Controversial Issues in American Law

Part III explores the relationship between law and social policy in the United States by focusing on highly controversial issues in five areas: race and ethnicity, gender, class, medicine, and corporations. The laws relating to these areas have not been neutral; instead, they have tended to serve those in power—the elites—rather than the masses. Part III examines the nature of lawmaking in these domains and attempts to assess the extent to which our laws have been used to ensure equality, fairness, and justice.

By examining law and social policy, Part III integrates much of the material from Parts I and II. Here, we can explore the interplay between law, theories of jurisprudence, social norms, and the law-making process. Each chapter assesses the laws—that is, the statutes, regulations, and case holdings—that have been most significant in shaping legal norms over the last two hundred yers. Some of these norms have shifted dramatically over time. For example, the norms of owing slaves and barring women from voting have been rejected; in their place new norms have been adopted.

Part III demonstrates the extent to which law depends on the larger social conditions and shows how changes in political, social, and economic structures can ultimately produce changes in law. The theories of jurisprudence we discussed in Chapter 2 help us to understand America's approach to these issues. Both critical legal studies, with its focus on class struggle, and law and economics, with its assumptions about maximizing wealth, help us to explain the role of law in corporate America. Critical race theory and feminist jurisprudence help us to better comprehend the relationship between law, race, and gender. Sociologist Emil Durkheim's theory of social control and social facts give us a better appreciation of the central role that physicians play in the law governing medicne. And finally, the law and economics school provides an interesting vantage point for understanding the complex relationship between law and corporate America.

CHAPTER 11

Law, Race, and Ethnicity

Ideas about race and about racial superiority and inferiority are embedded in American political culture. Not surprisingly, our legal system reflects these ideas. Our most sacred legal text, the U.S. Constitution, was itself a compromise between those who embraced slavery and those who rejected it. Throughout our history Americans have been deeply ambivalent about the role of law in promoting and achieving racial equality. Maybe this ambivalence is inevitable, given the fact that our social and political culture promotes two ideals that are in many ways in conflict: freedom and equality. We have always been committed to the ideal of freedom—every schoolchild knows that the Plymouth Pilgrims fled Europe so that they would be free to practice their religion, and the concepts of liberty and freedom are the basis of our Declaration of Independence and our federal and state constitutions.

At the same time, Americans are committed to the ideal of equality. We may all understand what it means to be free: however, as a people, we have very different views of what equality requires. In its most narrow interpretation, equality is defined as **political equality**—*the requirement that all citizens have the right to vote and that all votes count equally. In its broader conceptions, equality may be defined as either* **social or economic equality,** *which mandates either that people have the same access to education and other resources that enable them to move ahead in the society, or alternatively, that everyone has a comparable standard of living. At this point in time, we accept the ideal of political equality—all citizens have the right to vote and attempts to systematically disenfranchise a group of voters are met with fierce resistance by law enforcement agents and the general public. We do not, however, all accept the ideals of either social or economic equality. In fact, we remain committed to the belief that individuals have a right to accumulate wealth and achieve socioeconomic status.*

political equality

all citizens have the right to vote and all votes count equally

social or economic equality

all people have the same access to education or other resources that enable them to move ahead, or all have a comparable living standard

www ▶ ▶ ▶

In this way, there is an inherent conflict between freedom and equality, particularly when one adopts a broader interpretation of equality. In the United States today, there is a yawning gap between the richest and poorest—in fact, more than 38 percent of the wealth is held by the richest 1 percent of the population and the bottom 40 percent of the population own less than 0.2 percent of the wealth. A broader interpretation of equality would require that there be some redistribution of assets at the very least, so as to ensure that all citizens have access to good quality education. This redistribution conflicts directly, however, with the ideal that everyone should have the right or freedom to accumulate as much wealth as he or she can and that government should not interfere with the exercise of this freedom by attempting to redistribute wealth through progressive taxes or other means. In Chapter 13, we will discuss American law and class and examine the role of law in protecting this individualist ideal.

In this chapter, we will talk about race and the law. We will focus on the historical treatment of Native Americans, Africans, and African Americans. We will also discuss the civil rights movement as well as institutional racism and affirmative action. Native Americans and African Americans are not the only groups that have suffered from discrimination in our nation. After arriving in this nation, those with many other heritages also found that the law did not provide a level playing field. This chapter focuses on Native Americans and African Americans, however, because of our nation's long legacy of unequal treatment under the law for these two groups.

critical race theory

theory of jurisprudence that assumes that racism is embedded in the law

Critical race theory *takes as its assumption the view that law is biased in favor of white northern Europeans and that racism is actually embedded in our law. CRITS argue that the experiences, concerns, values, and perspectives of people of color have been systematically excluded from discussions of law. As a result, our laws can only achieve a very limited form of equality. In this chapter, we will talk about how our recent laws bar direct or explicit discrimination based on race. CRITS argue that while our law now must be race neutral, this neutrality in effect undermines attempts to achieve real equality, since it preempts any real discussion about what must be done to eliminate the effects of racism in our institutions and larger society. For CRITS, even neutral terms like justice, fairness, and equality serve to advantage those in power. As CRITS see it, those in power are overwhelmingly white and Anglo. Similarly, LATCRITS, or advocates of Latino critical theory, contend that there is a hierarchy of culture and that our laws advance the dominant culture and language over others. Both CRITS and LATCRITS maintain that most perceived differences between groups of people are constructed in the majority culture and are not real. For example, our views of Latinos as people who are reluctant to assimilate into American culture, or of*

Muslims and Muslim Americans as potential threats to our security, are not based in reality but are socially constructed. Historically, such social constructions have been the basis of many of our laws and have undermined attempts to achieve real and lasting racial equality in the United States.

NATIVE AMERICANS AND THE LAW

Indian Removal Act (1830)

act mandating that all Native Americans east of the Mississippi give up their lands and move west

www ▶ ▶ ▶

General Allotment Act of 1887

act that allotted property to individual Native Americans and effectively gave the federal government title to more than 90 million acres of unclaimed tribal land

www ▶ ▶ ▶

www ▶ ▶ ▶

Throughout our nation's history, we have used the law to undermine the rights of Native American peoples, particularly with respect to their tribal lands. While the first treaty entered into with the Indians by the fledgling U.S. government in 1778 recognized the sovereign and independent Indian nations, later treaties served to disempower these nations and their peoples. While the young nation promised to cooperate with Native Americans, the westward expansion, begun in earnest with the 1803 Louisiana Purchase and Lewis and Clark's 1804 expedition to the Northwest, radically altered the relationship. By the early to mid-1800s, treaties starkly limited Native Americans' rights to occupy land by defining what was Indian territory while allowing the United States to occupy and own all remaining property. This treaty law enabled the federal government to claim huge tracts of land for westward expansion. In a series of treaties beginning in the early 1800s, Native Americans "sold" their lands to the federal government in exchange for an agreement to allow them to live on small parcels of land, known as reservations. The U.S. Supreme Court permitted this displacement, holding in one of its earliest cases, the 1823 case *Johnson* v. *M'Intosh* (21 U.S. (8 Wheat.) 543) that while the tribes held land by "Indian title," "discovery" by the European powers enabled these powers to make the ultimate decision about how these lands would be used. The **Indian Removal Act** (1830) mandated that Indians east of the Mississippi give up their lands and move west. As a result of horrific conditions, nearly one-third of all Native Americans perished in this forced relocation.

This relocation was accompanied by the government's attempts to "civilize" native peoples by imposing on them its view of property ownership by passing laws that aimed at encouraging individuals to give up hunting, fishing, and gathering in favor of "civilized agricultural pursuits." These laws called for the "allotment" of property to individuals, an ownership concept totally alien to Native Americans. Over time, these laws enabled the federal government to gain control of huge tracts of land. The **General Allotment Act of 1887** ultimately allowed the federal government to gain title to more than 90 million acres of tribal land that was not claimed by individuals.

Between 1778 and 1870, the United States entered into more than 370 treaties with the Indian nations. Of these, nearly two-thirds involved land concessions by Native Americans. Included here are examples of these treaties. The 1778 Treaty, entered into when the new nation was fighting its War of Independence against the British, is an agreement to provide mutual support between the United States and the Delaware Nation. The treaties between the United States and the Miami and the Nez Perce tribes are land-acquisition treaties. You may want to note that these two treaties ultimately resulted in the total removal of these tribes from their land. Many treaties were later disregarded by the U.S. government, which found it more expedient to remove reservation status and simply seize land that had been part of earlier treaties. The 1830 Indian Removal Act, which promised that those removed from their lands would occupy their new lands "forever," was disregarded within ten years, as Native Americans were again forced to relocate. The Delaware Nation, which occupied New Jersey and Pennsylvania, was relocated seven times over a 150-year period, ultimately landing in the Far West. In like manner, the U.S. government stripped the tribal lands of the Nez Perce Indians of their reservation status in 1855. This move ultimately led many members of the tribe to reject a new treaty and to engage in an armed uprising against the federal government in 1877. During this war, the tribe was almost anihilated, and in the end, the tribe was relocated.

These treaties not only enabled the federal government to acquire the Native Americans' tribal lands, they also cut off the tribes from any meaningful interactions with other nations or with the states. The federal government said that it was treating the Indian tribes as separate nations, and for this reason, argued that it alone could have relations with them. In reality, Native Americans were treated as subjects. While the federal government often backed out of its treaty obligations by requiring that the tribes renegotiate and relinquish reservation lands, the U.S. government insisted that the Native Americans were bound by treaty provisions. They were not allowed to move beyond the reservation boundaries, nor did they have any right to participate in the political process of the United States. The federal government sought to force their assimilation into the larger social and economic system. Christian missionaries were very active on the reservations during the mid- to late 1800s, and many Native Americans were encouraged to reject their own spiritual principles and to adopt Christianity. Native Americans were also drawn into the war over slavery. In part because the Seminole tribe in Florida had provided a safe haven for runaway slaves in the early 1800s, nearly every treaty included a provision that enabled fugitive slave hunters to have full access to reservation lands.

The unjust treatment of Native Americans that characterized nearly all of the laws passed during the 1800s was based on the view that Native Americans were uncivilized savages. Popular culture depicted American Indians as simple, superstitious people, who were inferior to Europeans and who could not be relied on to govern themselves. The illustrations provided

www ▶ ▶ ▶

on the website depict Indians as inhuman savages who prowled the frontiers seeking to kill or maim all settlers. In the first illustration, a white frontier woman is shown trying to protect herself and her child against the barbarous Indian; the second illustration depicts the Second Seminole War, part of the federal government's campaign to eradicate the Seminole tribe, and the Indians are shown killing women and children. While the federal government has taken steps to compensate some native peoples for their forced relocation and the loss of their tribal lands, it bears noting that we continue to view these people as "locked in history". Our popular culture continues to stereotype American Indians as somehow different—either more primitive or more in touch with nature. Native Americans living today are largely invisible in our popular culture, and we fail to consider the diversity in Native American cultures and language. Our laws also fail to appreciate or take account of differences in native cultures. There are more than 550 tribes recognized by the federal government, and there is tremendous diversity among these tribes in their languages and cultural practices. In fact, these tribes make up more than half of all languages and heritages recognized in the United States. Despite this, most Americans adopt a stereotypical view of Indians that is largely out of touch with the reality. Again, CRITS argue that these view are socially constructed, not based in reality, and that our laws have historically reinforced this perception of Native Americans as somehow less able to engage in real self-government.

Moreover, Native American tribes continue to have an ambiguous relationship with the rest of the United States. For example, even as late as 1994, President Bill Clinton issued an executive memorandum that restated what had been stated so many times before: that tribal governments are separate, sovereign nations, and that the federal government has a special relationship of trust with these tribes. This view of sovereign tribes existing within the territory of the United States has existed for nearly two hundred years. For much of this time, it was used as the justification for denying native peoples American citizenship and for withholding civil rights protections. While U.S. citizenship was conferred on Native American peoples in 1924, many other civil rights protections continue to be withheld. For example, the **Indian Civil Rights Act** (1968) conferred on native peoples the same rights that are established in the federal Bill of Rights, but this act did not provide an effective enforcement mechanism. As a result, even now there continue to be many cases in which American Indians are denied the right to vote for their tribal leaders, to decide where they will live, and to be given basic criminal due process rights, like the right to indigent defense. In addition, there is little enforcement of the **American Indian Religious Freedom Act** (1978), which aimed at ensuring that native peoples would be able to freely engage in the exercise of their religion, a right that had been denied to many peoples for hundreds of years.

Indian Civil Rights Act (1968)

conferred on native peoples the same rights that are in the Bill of Rights

American Indian Religious Freedom Act (1978)

act establishing the right to free exercise of religion for Native Americans

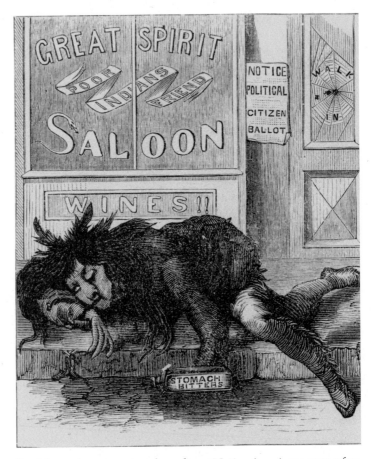

In eighteenth century popular culture, Native Americans were often depicted as sub-human and capable of acts of extreme violence against white women and children.

Many Native Americans have a much different existence than other Americans do. Residing on reservations that are governed by both tribal and federal law, they live largely ghettoized existences. The Native American poverty rate far outstrips that of the rest of the nation, medical care is woefully inadequate, and life expectancy is much lower than it is for other groups. In short, Native Americans are poorer, sicker, and die sooner than every other group in the United States. Furthermore, their ability to change their situation is constrained by the fact that they have only very limited control over governance or access to resources. Recently, the federal and state governments have agreed to allow casinos on tribal lands and to set aside state gambling bans in these casinos. Introduction of these casinos has provided much-needed employment and income, but native peoples continue to have shorter life expectancies, more poverty, greater levels of alcohol and drug addiction, and far less access to educational resources than most other Americans. Overt discrimination against Native Americans is prohibited by law, but the legacy of our government's treatment of these peoples continues. To eradicate traces of this discrimination, our law would need to be more than simply neutral—it would have to be used proactively to overcome the long-lasting effects of our policies on the lives of native peoples.

SLAVERY, JIM CROW, AND THE ANTIDISCRIMINATION LAW

Like Native Americans, African Americans have long been denied the protection of American law. The capture of Africans by European powers and the subsequent sale and enslavement of these people in the Americas began in the 1500s and slavery proved to be very profitable in the southern colonies and states throughout the 1700s and 1800s. The South's agricultural economy quickly grew dependent on slave labor as plantations expanded in size and number during this period. Until the Civil War, blacks sold or born into slavery were not viewed as people under the law—instead, the law saw them as property and protected their owners' property interest in them. The law of this period is very clear in denying basic human rights protections to Africans and African Americans. Like Native Americans, much of this history might be explained by critical race theory, which focuses on the ways in which law is used to benefit certain racial and ethnic groups at the expense of others. The Fourteenth Amendment to the U.S. Constitution mandates "equal treatment under the law," but interpretation of this amendment is quite limited and mandates simply that the law not use race as the justification for treating individuals or groups of people differently. The Fourteenth Amendment falls far short of requiring that individuals be guaranteed equality of outcome or result, or that there be a level playing field on which an individual's talents or merits can really be assessed. While our laws bar explicit race discrimination, they do little to counter the pervasive effects of race discrimination in the United States. Racism in the United States is now much more subtle and insidious, and many people believe that it has been institutionalized in our social structures and relationships. This institutionalized racism can only be countered by much more aggressive and proactive governmental policies and a broader interpretation of what equality requires.

Slavery and American Law

The U.S. Constitution itself allowed and in some ways probably encouraged the denial of basic rights for slaves: first, it was silent as to whether blacks

www ▶ ▶ ▶

**Missouri Compromise
(1820)**

a congressional statute
that paired the
admission of slave and
free states in an attempt
to ensure that neither
gained a political edge
as the result of
westward expansion

**Emancipation
Proclamation**

1863 executive order
issued by President
Lincoln decreeing that
all slaves were free

**Thirteenth
Amendment**

amendment to the U.S.
Constitution that pro-
hibited the practice of
slavery; ratified in 1870

**Fourteenth
Amendment**

amendment to the U.S.
Constitution that
guaranteed citizenship to
all people born or
naturalized in the United
States and barred states
from denying to them
the rights of citizenship
and depriving them of
due process or equal
protection of the laws;
ratified in 1870

Fifteenth Amendment

amendment to the U.S.
Constitution that
decreed that all men
could vote; ratified in
1870

Jim Crow

a series of far-reaching
laws passed in the
post–Civil War era that
segregated the races

and other minorities could be citizens, thus ensuring that this question
would be answered—in the negative—by the states; second, it explicitly
allowed the slave trade to continue until 1808; and third, it established
that each male slave would "count" as only three-fifths of a free man for
purposes of determining representation in the House of Representatives.
Furthermore, statutes enacted by Congress in the late 1700s and throughout the early to mid-1800s ensured that slave-holding states would maintain their political clout. For example, in a series of compromises including
the **Missouri Compromise** (1820), Congress agreed to pair the admission of
slave and free states to the union, thus ensuring that neither would have
more power as a result of westward expansion. Congress also passed a
number of fugitive slave laws that mandated the return of all escaped slaves
to their owners and allowed slave patrols and federal marshals to enter free
territory to capture runaways.

Lawmaking on the issue of slavery was characterized by political compromise and expedience until 1863, when President Abraham Lincoln
issued the **Emancipation Proclamation** decreeing that all slaves were free.
This proclamation was later followed by the **Thirteenth Amendment** to the
U.S. Constitution, which banned slavery. This amendment was coupled
with the Fourteenth and Fifteenth Amendments, which were both ratified in
1870. The **Fourteenth Amendment** guaranteed citizenship to all people
born or naturalized in the United States and barred states from denying the
privileges and immunities of citizenship; depriving individuals of their life,
liberty, or property without due process of law; and denying individuals
equal protection of the laws. The **Fifteenth Amendment** clearly stated that
men could not be denied the right to vote because of their race. Even in
these amendments, however, one can glimpse the political compromises that
were at the core of earlier laws—compromises that ultimately undermined
the enforcement of these amendments and allowed states to deny blacks the
right to vote well into the twentieth century. In fact, it was not until
Congress expressly stated that states and localities had the duty to ensure
that blacks were not denied the right to vote that African Americans were
guaranteed this right

Jim Crow Laws

After the Civil War; passage of the Thirteenth, Fourteenth, and Fifteenth
Amendments; and Reconstruction most southern states and many southern
cities began to enact laws that segregated blacks from whites and criminalized marriage or sexual relationships between blacks and whites. This code
of law became known as **Jim Crow**, named for the stereotypical African
American popularized in minstrel shows throughout the nation beginning
in the 1830s. In these shows, Jim Crow was a stupid and foolish character,
usually depicted as a dancing and singing simpleton. Jim Crow laws were
far-reaching, as can be seen in many of the examples provided on the web-

www ▶ ▶ ▶

site. The effect of these laws was to effectively block the enforcement of the Civil War amendments and to ensure that blacks would remain second-class citizens. Jim Crow segregated blacks from whites and barred blacks from accessing educational systems that were better funded and maintained, with the result that their opportunities for employment, housing, and public facilities were usually far inferior to the opportunities available to whites.

In those states and cities with extensive Jim Crow laws, there was significant support for these laws among whites, who sought to maintain their privileged status and who were very fearful of the impact that integration might have on their community's social hierarchy. Jim Crow functioned effectively as a tool of social control—it ensured that the existing social structures were not

BOX 11.1
Jim Crow Laws

From the 1880s into the 1960s, a majority of American states enforced segregation through Jim Crow laws (so called after an African American character in minstrel shows). From Delaware to California, and from North Dakota to Texas, many states (and cities, too) could impose legal punishments on people for consorting with members of another race. The most common types of laws forbade intermarriage and ordered business owners and public institutions to keep their clientele separated by race.
http://www.nps.gov/malu/documents/jim_crow_laws.htm

threatened and provided whites with the means for perpetuating their privileged position. Though slavery was abolished, Jim Crow effectively blocked efforts to ensure full citizenship for black men. It was not until the civil rights movement of the 1950s and 1960s that laws segregating blacks and whites were successfully challenged and Jim Crow began to be dismantled.

The Civil Rights Movement and the Voting Rights Act

Brown v. Board of Education

Supreme Court case that struck down state laws that mandated separate schools for white and nonwhite children

www ▶ ▶ ▶

Plessy v. Ferguson

Supreme Court case that had allowed "separate but equal" state-operated railway transportation for whites and nonwhites

www ▶ ▶ ▶

Civil Rights Act

an act tht barred discrimination in voting, public accommodations and facilities, education, federally assisted programs, and employment; passed in 1964

www ▶ ▶ ▶

In the period following World War II, black servicemen returning from war challenged their second-class status at home and the U.S. economy began to prosper. As a result, those opposed to segregation started to challenge these laws in the 1950s through acts of civil disobedience and by lobbying legislatures and courts. One of the earliest acts of disobedience was the refusal by Rosa Parks to give up her seat on a Birmingham bus to a white passenger. Her arrest and trial sparked a series of bus boycotts throughout the South and ultimately led the U.S. Supreme Court to rule that municipalities could not segregate transportation facilities on the basis of race. At the same time, legal challenges to segregated school districts led to the landmark Supreme Court holdings in the two *Brown v. Board of Education* cases in 1954 and 1955 that barred states and municipalities from segregating educational facilities on the basis of race. In this case, the Court explicitly overturned its earlier decision in the 1896 case *Plessy v. Ferguson*, in which it had allowed "separate but equal" state-operated railway cars. In contrast, the Court held in *Brown* that states that segregated on the basis of race were violating the constitutional guarantee of equal protection and that separate facilities were inherently unequal.

In the early 1960s, political pressure mounted for a statute barring discrimination in public accommodations, housing, and employment, and in 1964, the U.S. Congress passed its much awaited **Civil Rights Act**. Congress's power to pass this statute flowed directly from the Fourteenth Amendment to the Constitution, which charged Congress with implementing voting rights and civil rights protections established in the Thirteenth and Fourteenth Amendments. Perhaps not surprisingly, there was fierce opposition to this statute especially among southerners, who understood that the act would mean the end of Jim Crow. After much political compromise and bargaining, however, the law passed. The 1964 Civil Rights Act has eleven different sections, or titles, and these bar discrimination in voting, public accommodations and facilities, education, federally assisted programs, and employment. This statute charged different agencies with implementing each title—for example, the responsibility for enforcing the employment provision was placed on the Equal Employment Opportunity Commission. Over time, the administrative agencies responsible for enforcing the statute have been criticized for lax enforcement, but the impact of this law is undeniable. It is now illegal for state and local governments, private employers, and other organizations with significant ties to the public sector to engage in explicit discrimination based on race, ethnicity, national origin, religion, and sex.

hate crime statutes

laws adopted by municipalities, states, and Congress that make it a crime to engage in acts of violence motivated by racial, ethnic, or religious bias

[www ▶ ▶ ▶]

In recent years, many states and the federal government have enacted **hate crime statutes** that make it a crime to engage in acts of violence motivated by racial, ethnic, or religious bias. Many of these are sentence-enhancing laws—they increase jail time for those with a bias motivation. In 2004, a crowd of angry Long Island men ridiculed and beat a Sikh man who was wearing a turban, taunting him that his turban was "dirty curtains." One of these men was charged under the state hate crime law, which provides an additional penalty for bias crime, and he pled guilty to this charge. When municipal, state, and federal hate crime statutes were first adopted in the 1980s, many believed that they interfered with freedom of speech. The U.S. Supreme Court disagreed in its 1992 decision in *R.A.V. v. St. Paul,* finding that these laws were permissible, since they barred, not only speech, but action as well. Some of these laws have recently come under increased scrutiny, as courts have considered whether they are worded clearly enough to really provide notice about what activities are prohibited. But it seems clear that hate crimes statutes address a real need—there are more than twenty-five bias crimes committed each day, and this number is presumably on the increase, as evidence mounts of bias crimes against Muslims and Muslim Americans.

Institutional Racism

institutional racism

racism that is ingrained in the very fabric of society and cannot be eliminated without taking aggressive action

Most of our antidiscrimination law bars explicit or overt discrimination—that is, discrimination against a person or group specifically because of their race, ethnicity, national origin, religion, sex, or in some states, other characteristics as well. Since the 1960s, individuals and groups have been prohibited from treating people differently because of these characteristics; however, there remains a very wide disparity in the living conditions of Americans. This disparity may be glimpsed in a number of areas, including the criminal justice system, employment, and overall wealth. Many commentators believe that racism is now ingrained in the very fabric of our society—it has become a part of our social, economic, and political structures and cannot be eradicated without much more aggressive actions and laws. This **institutional racism** is starkly apparent in a number of areas, including the criminal justice system, employment relations, and distribution of household wealth.

■ **The Criminal Justice System** Many argue that the criminal justice system is one of the most visible and effective structures of institutional racism in the United States. They contend that U.S. criminal justice system is highly racialized because black and Hispanic men are grossly overrepresented in

this population. In 2002, 13 percent of black men and 43 percent of Hispanic men between the ages of twenty-five and twenty-nine were in prison, as compared with less than 2 percent of whites. In the 1990s, incarceration rates soared, as politicians elected on the promise to get tough on crime adopted laws that effectively lengthened prison terms, especially for drug offenses and quality-of-life crimes. In particular, drug convictions dramatically increased prison populations. People arrested for drug-related crimes make up nearly 60 percent of the federal prison population. In some cases, the new drug laws resulted in much harsher punishments for people of color than for whites. For example, the federal sentencing guidelines for the use and distribution of cocaine has a strong race dimension—the penalty for crack cocaine, which tends to be used and distributed by persons of color, is much more severe than that for powder cocaine, which is much more prevalent in wealthier white communities.

African American and Hispanic men are disproportionately represented at all stages of the criminal justice system—they are apprehended and convicted at much higher rates, and they serve significantly longer prison terms than white men involved in the same or similar crimes. In addition, African Americans and Hispanics are overrepresented on death row—they are much more likely to be sentenced to death than are whites, even when convicted of the same crime. Many politicians debate whether such a bias exists—for example, in 1996, President Bill Clinton placed a moratorium on use of the death penalty in federal cases, finding that nearly 80 percent of those sentenced to death were black. In 2003, Bush's attorney general, John Ashcroft, reinstated capital punishment in federal cases, brushing aside arguments that

DEBATE

Is the use of capital punishment inherently racist?

Yes: Look at the numbers: African Americans are grossly overrepresented on death row—they make up 12 percent of the U.S. population but 42 percent of federal and state defendants on death row. Since 1976, when the death penalty was reinstated, 40 percent of those executed have been either African American or Hispanic. Moreover, in death penalty cases where the defendant and victim were members of different races, courts have treated black defendants convicted of killing white individuals much more harshly—192 of these interracial cases involved black defendants and white victims, where only 12 cases involved white defendants and black victims. There are clear differences

Is the use of capital punishment inherently racist?–(Cont'd)

in the rate of prosecution and conviction of people of color and whites in the United States—in particular, African Americans are charged and convicted at much higher rates than their white counterparts. For some people, these different conviction rates are proof that people of color commit crimes at much higher rates and that the overrepresentation of African Americans on death row makes sense given these conviction rates. It is important to consider, however, that no one has ever proven that there is a relationship between the commission of crimes and race—instead, the relatively greater number of blacks on death row probably says more about the fact that police and courts are more likely to target this population and treat them less favorably than their white counterparts. The death penalty, like so many features of the criminal justice system, is mostly a tool to control black America—it keeps African Americans subordinate through the use of fear and intimidation.

No:
It is true that there are more African Americans on death row than one would expect to be there, based on the U.S. population, and this group is over-represented both on death row and in terms of those who have been put to death since the death penalty was reinstated in 1976. There is no proof, however, that this is unjust. There are more blacks on death row because they commit more death-eligible crimes. The criminal justice system is colorblind— it is penalizing the act of murder, not the color of someone's skin, and to argue that race is a substantial factor in sentencing decisions is simply wrong. It may be true that in the 1972 case *Furman* v. *Georgia* the U.S. Supreme Court struck down capital punishment, in large part because the justices concluded that the death penalty was being imposed in a racially discriminatory manner. In 1976, the Court allowed states to begin using capital punishment again, but only after they provided assurance that the sentencing decision was shielded from racial bias and prejudice. The system we have today is one where the defendant is punished because of the crime that he or she has committed, plain and simple. Overturning the death penalty because of unfounded concerns about race discrimination ultimately does much greater harm to racial minorities and the poor than use of this penalty ever could, because it is these groups that will ultimately be face-to-face with killers. If we're concerned about racial bias in the criminal justice system, then we must focus on the system as a whole and consciously take action to ferret out racism in all of its many facets.

THE LAW IN POPULAR CULTURE

Monster's Ball

Racism abounds in this moving film about the relationship between a death row inmate, his wife, and his executioner. This film poses probing questions about race and the criminal justice system, demanding that we consider how racism harms, not only the victim, but the racist as well.

the defendant's race figured heavily in the prosecutor's decision whether to recommend death.

■ **Employment** Many also believe that institutional racism is apparent in the work experiences of different racial and ethnic groups. Despite laws that mandate equal pay for equal work, African American men earn only 78 cents for every dollar earned by white men and Latinos earn only 67 cents for this same dollar. Presumably women of color earn even less than men, since on average, women earn less than 72 cents for every dollar earned by men. And education does not correct this inequality—white men with college degrees earned an average of $67,000 a year in 2001; in contrast, black and Hispanic college-educated men earned 30 percent less, and white women with college degrees earned 40 percent less—we can

www ▶ ▶ ▶

assume that for black and Hispanic college-educated women this number is even lower.

■ **Wealth** Maybe even more troubling than this wage disparity is the fact that there is a huge divide among Americans in terms of household wealth, and this divide starkly separates white Americans from everyone else. Wealth is a better indicator of economic well-being than salary, since it includes not only salary but also assets like homes; financial assets like cash, stocks, and bonds; and debt. As Box 11.2 demonstrates, there is a very wide gap between racial groups. In 2001, the net worth of families of color was roughly $17,000 and that of white families was nearly $121,000! Across the board, people of color fared far worse than whites—in not only income, but debt, stock holdings, and other financial assets, the already wide gap continued to broaden in 2001.

BOX 11.2
Racial Wealth Gap Has Widened
by *Betsy Leondar-Wright*

June 12, 2003 | The Federal Reserve does an economic survey every three years called the *Survey of Consumer Finances*. In 2001, they interviewed 4,449 families about their income, assets, and debts.

FROM 1995 TO 2001 . . .

• Typical families of color saw their net worth* fall 7% to $17,100 in those six years, while typical white families' net worth grew 37% to $120,900. (* Net worth equals assets minus debts.)

FROM 1998 TO 2001 . . .

• Overall the gap between the net worth of typical white families and families of color grew by 21%.

• Just in those three years, the net worth of typical families of color fell 4.5%, while white families' rose 17%.
• Comparing financial assets (money, stocks, bonds, etc.), asset-owners of color gained only $100 in those three years, compared with $5,800 gain for white asset-owners.
• Debtors of color added $3,100 of debt while white debtors added only $1,300.
• Stock ownership reached a few more people of color. But the typical shareholder of color owned $1,800 less stock at the end of the three years than the beginning; the typical white shareholder owned $200 more.

Source: "Recent Changes in U.S. Family Finances: Evidence from the 1998 and 2001 Survey of Consumer Finances," by Ana M. Aizcorbe, Arthur B. Kennickell, and Kevin B. Moore.

BOX 11.2
Racial Wealth Gap Has Widened–(cont'd)

THE STORY IN NUMBERS:

Median Net Worth (assets minus debts)

	1998	2001	% Change
People of color	$ 17,900	$ 17,100	– 4.5%
White people	$103,400	$120,900	+17%

Median Financial Assets (Money, stocks, bonds, etc. Excludes real estate, vehicles, businesses, art, jewelry, collectibles, etc.)

	1998	2001	% Change
People of color	$ 7,100	$ 7,200	+ 1%
White people	$32,700	$38,500	+ 18%

Median Non-financial Assets (Real estate, vehicles, businesses, art, jewelry, collectibles, etc. Excludes money, stocks, bonds, etc.)

	1998	2001	% Change
Families of color	$ 47,000	$ 56,800	+ 21%
White families	$157,900	$183,900	+ 16%

Median Debt (amount owed)

	1998	2001	% Change
Families of color	$16,900	$20,000	+ 18%
White families	$43,200	$44,500	+ 3%

Source: From United for a Fair Economy website (June 12, 2003), www.faireconomy.org/econ/RWG/SCF_Race_2003.html.

Institutional racism explains much of the racial disparity in our criminal justice system, employment relations, and overall household wealth. While our laws require colorblindness, the reality is often quite different. People's employment and educational opportunities, housing, and medical care are often strongly affected by race and ethnicity. Consider the possibility that institutional racism probably accounts for the fact that African Americans continue to be seriously underrepresented in upper management. Our laws clearly prohibit employers from making decisions based solely on race, and for this reason, blatant cases of discrimination are relatively easy for the employee or potential employee to win. For example, if an employer admits that he or she didn't hire an applicant because of the person's ethnicity, that employer will be found liable for violating antidiscrimination law. In this case, there is no question that the employer *intended* to engage in ethnic discrimination. It is much more difficult when an employer's policies or practices have the *effect* or *impact* of discriminating against a person or group of people because of their race or ethnicity. For example, if an employer only hires graduates from certain schools or applicants who perform extremely well on a certain exam, this may have a very negative impact on certain racial and ethnic groups. We know that educational advantages are closely tied to social class, and that class and race are closely related. In these kinds of cases, long-lasting patterns of institutional racism may have a profound effect on employment opportunities. But as a people, we loudly disagree about how the law should be used in these kinds of cases where an employer doesn't intend to discriminate, but the discriminatory effects of a policy are nonetheless clear.

Affirmative Action

equality of opportunity

equal access to resources that are needed to succeed

So what should be done about institutional racism? As a society, we seem to be committed to the ideal of **equality of opportunity**; that is, we agree that everyone should have the same chance to succeed. In the next chapter, we'll be talking about how people's class and wealth determine their position at the starting gate, but here we want to note that institutional racism probably makes it impossible for there to be a real equality of opportunity. CRITS argue that our debate about equality is very limited—we're looking only at explicit discrimination—and this narrow perspective ultimately distracts us from focusing on what needs to be done to achieve racial justice in the United States. These scholars contend that what is needed is not race-neutral language, or even equality of opportunity, but laws aimed at achieving equality of outcome. Many CRITS argue that at a minimum, we need a program that helps to achieve race parity in the United States.

Clearly, we are far from adopting such an approach. At this point in our history, our law mandates only racial neutrality and is openly hostile to more proactive attempts to achieve racial equality. Affirmative action, which has been very much in the news for the last several years, makes this position obvious. **Affirmative action** is based on an understanding that discrimination and racial and ethnic inequality have a long history and are embedded in our institutions and in society itself. While our law mandates that everyone be treated without regard for his or her race or ethnicity, real equality is impossible, given the disadvantages that continue to face ethnic and racial minorities in the United States. The fact is that there continues to be tremendous

affirmative action

programs that seek to address institutional racism by providing resources or opportunities to overcome inequities in education and employment

inequity in the areas of employment and education. For example, African American applicants continue to be poorly represented in our nation's institutions of higher education, and they are less likely to be hired and promoted than similarly qualified white applicants. Affirmative action programs exist largely in the areas of education and employment and are an attempt to ensure that everyone has the tools that they need to succeed.

Affirmative action first emerged in 1965, when President Lyndon B. Johnson created the **Office of Federal Contract Compliance** to ensure that individuals or corporations that had contracts with the federal government considered African American applicants when making hiring decisions. President Richard Nixon followed up on this in 1969, when he issued his **"Philadelphia Plan,"** which established timetables and goals for the employment of minorities in federal contracts. Many educational institutions and employers adopted affirmative action plans in the decades that followed, but many such plans were challenged in the courts.

Most courts have been unsure about how to proceed in response to affirmative action challenges. In a number of challenges, courts struck down affirmative action plans that set up different systems for evaluating minority and white applicants. Courts seem to be uncomfortable with allowing educational institutions and employers to assign a specific value to race when making decisions. Thus, many judges and justices have signaled that they are unwilling to let race be an overriding concern in the admissions or hiring process. For example, in 1978, the U.S. Supreme Court held that the University of California could consider a medical school applicant's race in making admissions decisions, but the state university system could not have separate admissions policies and requirements for minorities and whites. In the late 1990s, courts, state legislatures, and voters were much more openly hostile toward affirmative action. Voters in both California and Washington State approved initiatives that barred "preferential treatment" based on race, color, national origin, ethnicity, and sex in employment, education, and contracting; the Florida legislature prohibited the use of racial preferences in the state university system.

In 2003, the U.S. Supreme Court issued two landmark decisions on affirmative action in education. In *Grutter v. Bollinger* and *Gratz v. Bollinger,* the Court considered challenges to the admissions procedures in place at the University of Michigan. This top-tier public university has had a vigorous affirmative action plan for the last three decades. The undergraduate school awarded additional "points" to applicants from underrepresented minorities; the law school used a more flexible method of evaluating candidates and considered a number of variables that would enable them to enroll a diverse student body. Both the law and undergraduate schools stated that diversity was an important goal in admissions decisions. White individuals who had been denied admission to these schools alleged that they had been discriminated against because of their race and argued that the university

---

Office of Federal Contract Compliance

established by President Johnson to ensure that those with federal contracts considered African American applicants when hiring

---

"Philadelphia Plan"

President Nixon's plan to establish timetables and goals for the employment of minorities in federal contracts

---

www ▶ ▶ ▶

Grutter v. Bollinger and Gratz v. Bollinger

two Supreme Court cases challenging the use of affirmative action in a public university and law school—the law school program was upheld, that of the university was struck down as a quota system

had violated their constitutional rights. The University of Michigan responded by saying that their admissions decisions were guided by their commitment to having a diverse student body.

Ultimately, the Court upheld the law school's admissions process but struck down the one in place at the undergraduate school. The justices were sharply divided in these cases and disagreed about how a university could use race and ethnicity to assemble a diverse student body. These cases will probably establish the standards for affirmative action in higher education for generations to come. Included below is an excerpt of the majority opinion in the law school case, *Grutter* v. *Bollinger*. In reading this excerpt, you may want to think about the justices' rationale for permitting this program. Keep in mind that while these cases involved public universities, which must comply, not only with civil rights laws, but also with constitutional equal protection requirements, most people believe that they will set the pace for private universities and colleges, as well. Many of these private institutions also have affirmative action plans and have begun to fine-tune them so that they are in compliance with the Michigan decisions.

LAW IN ACTION

Affirmative Action in Education

BARBARA GRUTTER, PETITIONER V. *LEE BOLLINGER ET AL.* U.S. Supreme Court, 2003

www ▶ ▶ ▶ (See *Law, Politics, and Society* website for a link to the complete decision.)

JUSTICE O'CONNOR delivered the opinion of the Court.

This case requires us to decide whether the use of race as a factor in student admissions by the University of Michigan Law School (Law School) is unlawful.

The Law School ranks among the Nation's top law schools. It receives more than 3,500 applications each year for a class of around 350 students. Seeking to "admit a group of students who individually and collectively are among the most capable," the Law School looks for individuals with "substantial promise for success in law school" and "a strong likelihood of succeeding in the practice of law and contributing in diverse ways to the well-being of others." App. 110. More broadly, the Law School seeks "a mix of students with varying backgrounds and experiences who will respect and learn from each other." *Ibid.* In 1992, the dean of the Law School charged a faculty committee with crafting a written admissions policy to implement these goals . . .

LAW IN ACTION–(CONT'D)

The hallmark of that policy is its focus on academic ability coupled with a flexible assessment of applicants' talents, experiences, and potential "to contribute to the learning of those around them." App. 111. The policy requires admissions officials to evaluate each applicant based on all the information available in the file, including a personal statement, letters of recommendation, and an essay describing the ways in which the applicant will contribute to the life and diversity of the Law School . . .

The policy aspires to "achieve that diversity which has the potential to enrich everyone's education and thus make a law school class stronger than the sum of its parts." *Id.*, at 118. The policy does not restrict the types of diversity contributions eligible for "substantial weight" in the admissions process, but instead recognizes "many possible bases for diversity admissions." *Id.*, at 118, 120. The policy does, however, reaffirm the Law School's longstanding commitment to "one particular type of diversity," that is, "racial and ethnic diversity with special reference to the inclusion of students from groups which have been historically discriminated against, like African-Americans, Hispanics and Native Americans, who without this commitment might not be represented in our student body in meaningful numbers." *Id.*, at 120 . . .

Petitioner Barbara Grutter is a white Michigan resident who applied to the Law School in 1996 with a 3.8 grade point average and 161 LSAT score. The Law School initially placed petitioner on a waiting list, but subsequently rejected her application. In December 1997, petitioner filed suit in the United States District Court for the Eastern District of Michigan against the Law School, the Regents of the University of Michigan,

Lee Bollinger (Dean of the Law School from 1987 to 1994, and President of the University of Michigan from 1996 to 2002), Jeffrey Lehman (Dean of the Law School), and Dennis Shields (Director of Admissions at the Law School from 1991 until 1998). Petitioner alleged that respondents discriminated against her on the basis of race in violation of the Fourteenth Amendment; Title VI of the Civil Rights Act of 1964, 78 Stat. 252, 42 U. S. C. §2000d; and Rev. Stat. §1977, as amended, 42 U. S. C. §1981 . . .

The Equal Protection Clause provides that no State shall "deny to any person within its jurisdiction the equal protection of the laws." U. S. Const., Amdt. 14, §2 . . . We have held that all racial classifications imposed by government "must be analyzed by a reviewing court under strict scrutiny." *Ibid*. This means that such classifications are constitutional only if they are narrowly tailored to further compelling governmental interests . . . Although all governmental uses of race are subject to strict scrutiny, not all are invalidated by it . . . When race-based action is necessary to further a compelling governmental interest, such action does not violate the constitutional guarantee of equal protection so long as the narrow-tailoring requirement is also satisfied . . .

With these principles in mind, we turn to the question whether the Law School's use of race is justified by a compelling state interest. Before this Court, as they have throughout this litigation, respondents assert only one justification for their use of race in the admissions process: obtaining "the educational benefits that flow from a diverse student body . . ." In other words, the Law School asks us to recognize, in the

LAW IN ACTION–(CONT'D)

context of higher education, a compelling state interest in student body diversity . . .

[W]e have never held that the only governmental use of race that can survive strict scrutiny is remedying past discrimination . . . Today, we hold that the Law School has a compelling interest in attaining a diverse student body.

The Law School's educational judgment that such diversity is essential to its educational mission is one to which we defer. The Law School's assessment that diversity will, in fact, yield educational benefits is substantiated by respondents and their *amici* . . . We have long recognized that, given the important purpose of public education and the expansive freedoms of speech and thought associated with the university environment, universities occupy a special niche in our constitutional tradition . . . Our conclusion that the Law School has a compelling interest in a diverse student body is informed by our view that attaining a diverse student body is at the heart of the Law School's proper institutional mission . . .

As part of its goal of "assembling a class that is both exceptionally academically qualified and broadly diverse," the Law School seeks to "enroll a 'critical mass' of minority students . . ." [T]he Law School's concept of critical mass is defined by reference to the educational benefits that diversity is designed to produce.

These benefits are substantial. As the District Court emphasized, the Law School's admissions policy promotes "cross-racial understanding," helps to break down racial stereotypes, and "enables [students] to better understand persons of different races . . ." These benefits are "important and laudable," because "classroom discussion is livelier, more spirited, and simply more enlightening and interesting" when the students have "the greatest possible variety of backgrounds."

The Law School's claim of a compelling interest is further bolstered by its *amici*, who point to the educational benefits that flow from student body diversity. In addition to the expert studies and reports entered into evidence at trial, numerous studies show that student body diversity promotes learning outcomes, and "better prepares students for an increasingly diverse workforce and society, and better prepares them as professionals . . ."

These benefits are not theoretical but real, as major American businesses have made clear that the skills needed in today's increasingly global marketplace can only be developed through exposure to widely diverse people, cultures, ideas, and viewpoints . . . What is more, high-ranking retired officers and civilian leaders of the United States military assert that, "[b]ased on [their] decades of experience," a "highly qualified, racially diverse officer corps . . . is essential to the military's ability to fulfill its principle mission to provide national security . . ."

We have repeatedly acknowledged the overriding importance of preparing students for work and citizenship, describing education as pivotal to "sustaining our political and cultural heritage" with a fundamental role in maintaining the fabric of society . . . This Court has long recognized that "education . . . is the very foundation of good citizenship." *Brown* v. *Board of Education*, 347 U. S. 483, 493 (1954). For this reason, the diffusion of knowledge and opportunity through public institutions of higher education must be accessible to all individuals regardless of race or ethnicity . . . Effective participation by members

LAW IN ACTION–(CONT'D)

of all racial and ethnic groups in the civic life of our Nation is essential if the dream of one Nation, indivisible, is to be realized.

Moreover, universities, and in particular, law schools, represent the training ground for a large number of our Nation's leaders . . . Individuals with law degrees occupy roughly half the state governorships, more than half the seats in the United States Senate, and more than a third of the seats in the United States House of Representatives . . . The pattern is even more striking when it comes to highly selective law schools. A handful of these schools accounts for 25 of the 100 United States Senators, 74 United States Courts of Appeals judges, and nearly 200 of the more than 600 United States District Court judges. *Id.*, at 6.

In order to cultivate a set of leaders with legitimacy in the eyes of the citizenry, it is necessary that the path to leadership be visibly open to talented and qualified individuals of every race and ethnicity . . .

The Law School's goal of attaining a critical mass of underrepresented minority students does not transform its program into a quota . . . Here, the Law School engages in a highly individualized, holistic review of each applicant's file, giving serious consideration to all the ways an applicant might contribute to a diverse educational environment. The Law School affords this individualized consideration to applicants of all races. There is no policy, either *de jure* or *de facto*, of automatic acceptance or rejection based on any single "soft" variable. Unlike the program at issue in *Gratz* v. *Bollinger, ante*, the Law School awards no mechanical, predetermined diversity "bonuses" based on race or ethnicity . . . Like the Harvard plan, the Law School's admissions policy "is flexible enough to consider all pertinent elements of diversity in light of the particular qualifications of each applicant, and to place them on the same footing for consideration, although not necessarily according them the same weight." *Bakke, supra*, at 317 (opinion of Powell, J.) . . .

By virtue of our Nation's struggle with racial inequality, such students are both likely to have experiences of particular importance to the Law School's mission, and less likely to be admitted in meaningful numbers on criteria that ignore those experiences. See App. 120 . . . What is more, the Law School actually gives substantial weight to diversity factors besides race . . . By this flexible approach, the Law School sufficiently takes into account, in practice as well as in theory, a wide variety of characteristics besides race and ethnicity that contribute to a diverse student body . . .

In summary, the Equal Protection Clause does not prohibit the Law School's narrowly tailored use of race in admissions decisions to further a compelling interest in obtaining the educational benefits that flow from a diverse student body . . .

It is so ordered.

QUESTIONS

1. Why did the majority of the Court allow this policy but strike down the one in place at the undergraduate school?
2. How did the court justify this decision—specifically, how did it reconcile this decision to holdings in other, related cases? What was the rationale here?

LAW IN ACTION–(CONT'D)

3. What about historical disadvantage—did the justices accept this as a rationale in the majority opinion?
4. How do you think CRITS might assess this holding?

SUMMARY

In this chapter, we have been talking about how our law responds to issues of race and ethnicity. Through much of our nation's history, American law enshrined a belief in the racial superiority of whites and the inferiority of African Americans, Hispanics, and Native Americans, among others. The law assumed that a person's rights were powerfully affected by race and ethnicity, and until recently, law has been explicitly used to reinforce the advantages of whites. While the law no longer expressly privileges whites over others, it still does not effectively promote or ensure a truly race-neutral and equal society. Although constitutional amendments and civil rights laws now bar certain forms of racial and ethnic discrimination, the fact remains that many racial and ethnic minorities in the United States are living very different lives, in terms of social class, than their white counterparts. Our laws embrace a vision of equality that is, in many ways, limited. It mandates colorblindness and does not address the ways that racism and ethnic discrimination have become enshrined in our institutions, policies, practices, and social relationships. In large part this is because our ideal of equality does not encompass equality of opportunity or result, both of which are facets of social and economic equality. Instead, our laws focus on political equality, that is, the principle that every person has the right to participate in the political process and that every vote counts the same. In the next chapter, we will explore U.S. law as it relates to social class. Again, we will be talking about how a person's understanding of equality colors his or her ideas about how American law functions. In that chapter we will also discuss how the underlying tension between freedom and equality has been resolved in favor of freedom.

SUGGESTED READING

Derrick Bell et al., *Race, Racism, and American Law (Casebook Series)* (Aspen Books, 2004). This useful sourcebook for race and law provides a terrific overview of the theoretical issues surrounding this topic. The authors provide a clear analysis of some of the most pressing issues in the area of law and race, among these, voting rights, affirmative action, and institutional racism.

Peter H. Schuck, *Diversity in America: Keeping Government at a Safe Distance* (Harvard University Press, 2003). In this book, Schuck discusses the issue of diversity in terms of race, national origin, and religious belief, and he contends that diversity can be achieved, not only by government action, but also by inaction—that is, by allowing private actors to construct policies and programs to advance the cause of diversity. He also argues that our commitment to this ideal waxes and wanes in response to changes in the dominant culture, and that diversity often engenders opposition because it is a zero-sum game; that is, it takes from some to give to others.

Peter Wallenstein, *Tell the Court I Love My Wife: Race, Marriage, and Law—An American History* (Palgrave MacMillan, 2004). Here is an excellent and engaging book that describes intermarriage between black men and white women, beginning in the colonial era and continuing through *Loving* v. *Virginia*, the 1965 Supreme Court case that finally struck down laws criminalizing intermarriage.

David E. Wilkins, *American Indian Sovereignty and the U.S. Supreme Court: The Masking of Justice* (University of Oklahoma Press, 1997). This book examines fifteen Supreme Court cases involving Native Americans that had a profound impact on the land claims and citizenship rights of these people in the 1700s, 1800s, and 1900s.

D. Vann Woodward and William S. McFeely, *The Strange Career of Jim Crow* (Oxford University Press, 2001). This engaging book provides an excellent overview of Jim Crow laws adopted in the 1890s South. It argues that the laws that mandated racial segregation were the result not only of bias and bigotry but of political compromise as well. It contends that these laws came about because the South wanted them and the North was unable and in some cases unwilling to challenge them.

ACTIVE LEARNING

1. In October 2004, environmental activists and some leaders of the Goshutes tribe in Skull Valley, Utah, protested against a contract that the tribe signed with Private Fuel Storage (PFS), a private waste disposal company. This contract permits the company to come onto reservation land and to store 40,000 tons of nuclear waste in above-ground canisters. Protestors argued that PFS had exploited the economic vulnerability of the tribe; supporters in the tribe argued that the contract allowed the tribe to become economically viable. What do you think? Conduct a debate on this issue and argue in favor of or against the proposal—to strengthen your argument you may want to anticipate the opposing argument. (http://www.shundahai.org/Skull_Oct10_04.htm)

2. Consider that the 1954 *Brown* v. *Board of Education* struck down laws that had segregated the races into two different school districts. The impact of *Brown* was very slow in coming, and it seems also to have

been short-lived. By the1980s, it became clear that many school districts had in fact resegregated and that most children were not attending school with children of different races. How could this have happened? Results from the 2000 census suggest that patterns of residential and school segregation continue to exist and that segregation in both areas is highest for African Americans. Consider this analysis of the census findings. (http://lewis.sppsr.ucla.edu/special/metroamerica/factsheets/ LCMetroAm_DiscussPaper_3.pdf) Do you think that segregation is a problem? Why or why not? Consider also that there are serious questions about whether many public schools, especially in poorer districts, are providing an adequate educational experience to their students. Imagine that you are a legislative assistant—how would you advise the legislator you work for on actions to address segregation in the United States?

CHAPTER 12

Law and Gender

feminist jurisprudence

theories of law that are based on the view that law is patriarchal and reflects the dominant position of males in society

In Chapter 2, we discussed the different theories that explain how law functions in society. One of these empirical theories was feminist jurisprudence, which encompasses at least three distinct schools. All theories of **feminist jurisprudence** *maintain that our law is patriarchal and that it both reflects and reinforces the dominant position of men in our society. We talked about three of these schools—formal equality or liberal feminism, relational feminism, and dominance/radical feminism— and noted that they all agree that our law functions to advantage men. These three theories disagree strongly, however, about what must be done to eradicate sexism in the law and to promote real equality between men and women.*

In this chapter, we discuss the laws governing gender relations in three distinct areas—gender roles, reproductive rights, and gender identity and orientation. As you probably already know, the law in these areas is in a state of flux, as our ideas about gender, reproductive rights, and family roles continue to change. As a society, we are deeply ambivalent about the role of gender; that is, we are very unsure about how people's gender should affect their place in the society and about how equality can be achieved. Our laws reflect this deep ambivalence. Most Americans expect that both men and women should have equal opportunities, and that people's gender should not have an impact on their life choices. Despite this belief in equality, our laws often fall far short of ensuring equality of either opportunity or result.

IMMUTABLE CHARACTERISTICS AND EQUALITY

Under American law, equality mandates that similarly situated people be treated the same and that factors like race, color, national origin, religion, and sex have no impact on people's rights or position in society. The

LAW IN ACTION–(Cont'd)

The same opportunity does not result from the event of birth, as a matter of biological inevitability, in the case of the unwed father. Given the 9-month interval between conception and birth, it is not always certain that a father will know that a child was conceived, nor is it always clear that even the mother will be sure of the father's identity. This fact takes on particular significance in the case of a child born overseas and out of wedlock. One concern in this context has always been with young people, men for the most part, who are on duty with the Armed Forces in foreign countries . . .

When we turn to the conditions which prevail today, we find that the passage of time has produced additional and even more substantial grounds to justify the statutory distinction. The ease of travel and the willingness of Americans to visit foreign countries have resulted in numbers of trips abroad that must be of real concern when we contemplate the prospect of accepting petitioners' argument, which would mandate, contrary to Congress' wishes, citizenship by male parentage subject to no condition save the father's previous length of residence in this country. In 1999 alone, Americans made almost 25 million trips abroad, excluding trips to Canada and Mexico . . .

Principles of equal protection do not require Congress to ignore this reality. To the contrary, these facts demonstrate the critical importance of the Government's interest in ensuring some opportunity for a tie between citizen father and foreign born child which is a reasonable substitute for the opportunity manifest between mother and child at the time of birth. Indeed, especially in light of the number of Americans who take short sojourns abroad, the prospect that a father might not even know of the conception is a realistic possibility . . . Even if a father knows of the fact of conception, moreover, it does not follow that he will be present at the birth of the child. Thus, unlike the case of the mother, there is no assurance that the father and his biological child will ever meet. Without an initial point of contact with the child by a father who knows the child is his own, there is no opportunity for father and child to begin a relationship. Section 1409 takes the unremarkable step of ensuring that such an opportunity, inherent in the event of birth as to the mother-child relationship, exists between father and child before citizenship is conferred upon the latter.

The importance of the governmental interest at issue here is too profound to be satisfied merely by conducting a DNA test . . . [S]cientific proof of biological paternity does nothing, by itself, to ensure contact between father and child during the child's minority . . .

Having concluded that facilitation of a relationship between parent and child is an important governmental interest, the question remains whether the means Congress chose to further its objective—the imposition of certain additional requirements upon an unwed father—substantially relate to that end. Under this test, the means Congress adopted must be sustained . . .

In analyzing §1409(a)(4), we are mindful that the obligation it imposes with respect to the acquisition of citizenship by the child of a citizen father is minimal. This circumstance shows that Congress has not erected inordinate and unnecessary hurdles to the conferral of citizenship on the children of citizen fathers in furthering its

LAW IN ACTION–(Cont'd)

important objectives . . . Section 1409(a), moreover, is not the sole means by which the child of a citizen father can attain citizenship. An individual who fails to comply with §1409(a), but who has substantial ties to the United States, can seek citizenship in his or her own right, rather than via reliance on ties to a citizen parent . . . This option now may be foreclosed to Nguyen, but any bar is due to the serious nature of his criminal offenses not to an equal protection denial or to any supposed rigidity or harshness in the citizenship laws . . .

To fail to acknowledge even our most basic biological differences—such as the fact that a mother must be present at birth but the father need not be—risks making the guarantee of equal protection superficial, and so disserving it. Mechanistic classification of all our differences as stereotypes would operate to obscure those misconceptions and prejudices that are real. The distinction embodied in the statutory scheme here at issue is not marked by misconception and prejudice, nor does it show disrespect for either class. The difference between men and women in relation to the birth process is a real one, and the principle of equal protection does not forbid Congress to address the problem at hand in a manner specific to each gender.

The judgment of the Court of Appeals is Affirmed.

QUESTIONS

1. Why is the INS's distinction important to the petitioner in this case?
2. How does the Court validate this distinction?
3. To what extent is this decision based on gender stereotype?

As the decision in *Nguyen* suggests, the Supreme Court permits sex-based distinctions in the law as long as these distinctions are substantially related to important governmental interests. As the Court in *Nguyen* clearly stated, men and women have different reproductive functions—specifically, women alone are capable of becoming pregnant and bearing children. Because men and women are not situated similarly with regard to reproduction, laws may distinguish between them, provided that these laws are justified by some important governmental interest. The fact that men and women have different roles in human reproduction underlies many U.S. laws that treat women differently than men. The different treatment of men and women is also apparent in the areas of reproductive rights and family roles, which we shall discuss in the next section, where we ask how laws should accommodate the often very different roles of women and men in the areas of family roles and reproduction? If you remember, this is the central question for feminists, and different schools of feminist jurisprudence answer this question very differently.

GENDER ROLES

Sex

the biological differences between men and women

Gender

much broader than sex, this encompasses learned behaviors as well as societal expectations and responses with regard to maleness and femaleness

When we refer to **sex**, we're talking about the biological differences between men and women. **Gender** is much broader and encompasses learned behaviors, as well as societal expectations and responses. If you remember, most feminist jurisprudence is based on the assumption that law is patriarchal and serves the interests of men, but each theory of feminist jurisprudence has a different view about how law and society should bring about equality between men and women. The three main schools have sought, and at times been successful in helping, to change the law governing sex discrimination.

Discrimination Based on Pregnancy

Title VII

section of the 1964 Civil Rights Act that barred employment discrimination on the basis of race, sex, color, national origin, and religion

[www ▶ ▶ ▶]

[www ▶ ▶ ▶]

Equal Pay Act

act requiring that men and women be paid the same amount for the same job

Until relatively recently, employers were free to deal with their employees or applicants in any way they pleased—they could hire or fire for any reason or for no reason at all. No laws barred discrimination based on any characteristic, including sex or gender. This began to change in some states as early as the late 1940s, but in most places employment discrimination was permitted until 1964, when Congress passed the landmark Civil Rights Act and included in it **Title VII**, which barred discrimination in employment based on race, sex, color, national origin, and religion. Congress followed up Title VII with the 1965 **Equal Pay Act**, which aimed at ensuring that men and women occupying the same jobs were paid the same amount. At the core of these laws is the requirement that employers adopt a gender-neutral approach to employment relations—employers were required to treat men and women the same, regardless of their needs.

At the time, Title VII and the Equal Pay Act were groundbreaking, but their limitations soon became apparent. For example, when courts were called on to determine whether the Title VII sex prohibition also applied to pregnancy discrimination, they were unsure about how to proceed. Many courts, including the U.S. Supreme Court, strictly limited the law, saying that it didn't apply to pregnancy discrimination. The Court reasoned that employers were discriminating against one group of women, that is, pregnant women, and that it was treating this group differently from the other group of nonpregnant workers, which included both men and nonpregnant women. This very limited view of Title VII was quickly rejected by Congress, which amended the law to state that pregnancy discrimination was at its core discrimination based on sex. Faced with pregnancy discrimination claims, courts have had to be fairly creative. Where an employer admits that she or he fired a worker because the worker was pregnant, this is a very easy case—the employer has admitted to sex discrimination. But where the employer denies this claim, courts must engage in a more searching inquiry. They must determine whether an employer treated the pregnant woman differently from other workers who are similarly situated, that is, who have the same kind of disability. This requirement that employers treat similarly situated employees the same assumes that pregnancy is analogous, or can be made to be analogous, to other kinds of medical conditions.

Women's Work, Men's Work, and Pay Equity

This view of gender equality is strongly advocated by the formal equality school of feminist jurisprudence—it assumes that if the law is gender neutral, real equality between men and women will emerge. Unfortunately, however, workplace equality has not emerged. The Equal Pay Act has had only limited impact because jobs continue to be sex segregated—that is, most jobs are held largely by either men or women. And even more importantly, there is a **wage gap**—women's jobs continue to be paid far less than men's jobs. As a group, women earn 77 cents for every $1.00 earned by men, largely because of job segregation. Over a lifetime, this earning differential results in a gap of more than $523,000. More than one-half of all women are in low-paying sales, clerical, and service-industry jobs, and the more female a job, the less it pays. The General Accounting Office (GAO), the research arm of the U.S. Congress, has found that more than 20 percent of the pay disparity is *not* the result of factors like occupation, industry, race, marital status, or time on the job.

wage gap

difference between women's and men's earnings; women earn 77 cents for every dollar earned by men

www ▶ ▶ ▶

Some argue that women should simply switch jobs—they should try to occupy traditionally male jobs and reap the benefits of the wage gap. But the GAO study strongly suggests that even women in male jobs earn less, and it appears that as a job becomes more female, pay for this job begins a steady downward spiral. For this reason, the formal equality model, which demands that men and women be treated similarly and that the same job be compensated at the same rate regardless of the sex of the person in it, has serious limitations. A few states and municipalities have adopted a different approach to achieving pay equity. They have attempted to assess jobs based on several characteristics like skill, effort, experience, and education and then to calculate wages so that comparable jobs are paid at roughly the same rate, regardless of whether men or women occupy these jobs. This approach, termed **comparable worth**, which is based on a much more nuanced view of equality, has sparked a great deal of controversy. At this point, only a handful of state and local laws mandate the comparable-worth approach, and neither Title VII nor the Equal Pay Act has adopted it. Minnesota makes the most extensive use of comparable worth, and information about pay equity in Minnesota is provided on the state's home page. The comparable-worth model is based on the understanding that men and women occupy different

comparable worth

the attempt by some states and municipalities to compare jobs according to the skill, effort, education, and experience needed by the occupant of the job in an attempt to eliminate gender-based disparities in pay

job categories, and that women's work tends to be more service-oriented. Relational feminists argue strongly in favor of this model, arguing that women prefer work that focuses on relationships with others and that this work should be valued as highly as men's work, which tends to be less centered on service.

Sexual Harassment

Until the 1980s, employment discrimination law did not bar sexual harassment unless this harassment rose to the level of a *quid pro quo*—that is, unless an employee was forced to perform a sexual act as a condition of employment. Courts also refused to apply sex discrimination law to situations where the harasser was another worker, as opposed to the employer. In the late 1980s and early 1990s, however, the law of sexual harassment began to change as courts and legislatures adopted a much more flexible standard for establishing workplace harassment. Much of this change was the result of the work of the dominance or radical school of feminist jurisprudence. In arguing in favor of a broader definition of harassment, these theorists contended that the law had to be radically reconfigured to ensure real equality between the sexes. They insisted that gender neutrality, which is the goal of formal equality, would never be enough to eliminate men's dominance—instead, the law had to be sensitive to the nuances of control and dominance in order to eradicate men's control over women. Many of these theorists argued that the norm in law is a male norm and that this norm permits—even encourages—male aggression and dominance over women.

The formal model did not recognize sexual harassment claims, and as a result, employers were not required to eliminate harassment or deal effectively with employees who engaged in harassing behavior. Dominance feminists argued that equality required that employers have a broader obligation to their employees; employers must be held liable for workplace harassment. Largely because of their work, Title VII is now interpreted broadly to protect employees from being subjected to a **hostile work environment**. There is an established test for determining whether a workplace is hostile: first, the harassment must be unwelcome by the affected employee; second, the harassment must be based on a protected classification—that is, race, sex, color, national origin, or religion; third, the harassment must be severe enough to actually affect the terms, conditions, or privileges of employment; and finally, it must be committed by the employer or someone under the employer's control. To determine whether an environment is abusive or hostile, courts will consider whether a "reasonable woman" would perceive it to be. The law usually relies on the "reasonable person" standard, but dominance feminists reject this term,

hostile work environment

situation arising when an employer or someone under his or her control engages in harassment of an individual that becomes severe or pervasive enough to affect the employment relationship, thus creating a hostile work environment in violation of employment discrimination law

arguing that it is based on a male norm and doesn't always encompass the different experience that women have had. Because men have used their power to sexualize and oppress women, dominance feminists argue, practices like sexual harassment must be viewed from the victim's eyes, not those of the perpetrator.

Women's Work—Parenting and Paid Employment

While both the formal equality and dominance models assume that law can and should be changed to ensure sex and gender equality, relational feminism assumes that there are real differences between men and women and that the law should reflect these differences. For relational feminists, also known as cultural feminists, biological or sex differences are only part of the equation. The more important component is the fact that women, more than men, tend to view themselves *in relation* to others and that they tend to place high value on these relationships. Where men tend to speak in a language of rights, women speak in one of relationships. Laws must reflect these different approaches—in particular, they must be sensitive to the high value that women place on their relationships with their children, their parents, and others for whom they may be providing care.

Relational feminists argue for divorce and child-support laws that reflect the fact that women tend to be the primary caregivers for their children and thus their job opportunities and incomes are often more limited than those of men. As a result, divorce has a tremendous negative impact on the financial well-being of women and their children. Relational feminists argue that gender-neutral laws that assume that men and women are similarly situated with regard to their job prospects and potential income have led to the impoverishment of many women and their children. Similarly, relational feminism argues that Social Security laws must be changed to reflect the fact that women tend to be in lower-paying jobs and that these jobs are often interrupted by family and childcare responsibilities. Because women are not paid for their "work" with family members, they are not protected by the Social Security safety net and do not accumulate wages or retirement benefits.

For working-class women, this bind is even more problematic. In the mid-1990s, a long-established social welfare program, Aid to Families with Dependent Children (AFDC) was radically reconfigured, with the result that government subsidies for the poor have been dramatically slashed. These changes have had a profound effect on poor and working-class women and their families. Where the law had historically ensured that women with small children could rely on a safety net, the changes required all women to work, even those with infants and small children. While the new workfare rules required that women work or attend school as a condition for receiving medical benefits and subsidies, the law offered little in the way of quality childcare services. These changes have placed working-class and poor women in a difficult position as they scramble to secure childcare and a place in the paid workforce.

Glass Ceilings and Glass Elevators

glass ceiling

perceived barrier used to explain why women, people of color, and persons with disabilities can only rise to a certain level in management and are subtly kept out of the most elite corporate jobs

While poor and working-class women continue to struggle to keep their heads above water, many middle-class and professional women find themselves limited in career advancement by a **glass ceiling**. These women, along with people of color and persons with disabilities, claim that they can only rise to a certain level in management and are subtly kept out of the most desirable, and most elite, corporate jobs. The Federal Glass Ceiling Commission, which operated from 1991 through 1996, found that a variety of factors, many of them quite subtle, operated to disadvantage women, minorities, and persons with disabilities. Among these factors are continuing job segregation, the existence of what is termed an old-boy network, and sexual harassment in the workplace. The commission found that even when women worked the same number of hours, were willing to relocate, and had the same level of expertise and skills, they still found it difficult to gain entry into the most elite core of jobs.

glass elevator

perceived advantage used to explain why men in jobs occupied predominantly by women are presented with many more opportunities than their female counterparts

In contrast, men who enter female-dominated sectors often rise very quickly to the most lucrative and desirable jobs, a phenomenon referred to as the **glass elevator**. For example, even though most elementary school teachers are women, the few men who enter this sector seem to have a better chance of being promoted to the assistant vice principal and principal positions. Similarly, male nurses seem to advance quickly to head nurse and also appear to earn more than their comparably educated and skilled female counterparts.

REPRODUCTIVE RIGHTS

At this point in time, only women are capable of becoming pregnant and giving birth, and for this reason, laws that regulate reproduction have a much greater impact on women than they do on men. Laws governing access to birth control, abortion, and reproductive technology all raise difficult issues about the nature of equality in the American legal system and challenge us to consider how this essential difference should be accommodated or dealt with under the law.

Laws Governing Contraception

Comstock Law

a law passed by Congress in 1873 that sharply limited access to contraception

Griswold v. Connecticut

Supreme Court case that established that married couples have a right to privacy that protects access to contraception

www ▶ ▶ ▶
www ▶ ▶ ▶

Eisenstadt v. Baird

1972 Supreme Court case that extended the right to contraception to unmarried individuals

RU-486

a pill that can prevent conception if used within 72 hours of having sex

contraceptive equity laws

laws mandating that employers pay for contraceptives if they pay for other prescription drugs

www ▶ ▶ ▶

In 1873, the U.S. Congress passed what became known as the **Comstock Law**, which sharply limited access to contraception. This law, named after social crusader Anthony Comstock, prohibited the mailing of information about or advertisements for contraception and abortion. It had the wide support of religious crusaders and nineteenth-century feminists, like Susan B. Anthony and Elizabeth Cady Stanton, who believed that contraception would enforce male privilege and sexual dominance by eliminating the cost of sexual encounters, which had been pregnancy. The Comstock Law classified a wide range of material as obscene, including, not only risqué materials like postcards and photographs of scantily clad women, but medical texts as well. Most states responded to the Comstock Law by passing laws that regulated the distribution of contraception, with many requiring that licensed pharmacists dispense contraceptive devices. Largely because of the strong influence of the Roman Catholic Church, two states, Connecticut and Massachusetts, barred all access to contraception for both married and unmarried persons. In the 1965 case *Griswold v. Connecticut* the U.S. Supreme Court struck down the laws in these two states, finding that married people have a right to privacy that encompasses the right to access contraception. This right was extended to unmarried individuals in the 1972 case *Eisenstadt v. Baird*. Under *Griswold* and *Eisenstadt,* there is a presumption that laws limiting access to contraception are unconstitutional. In the last few years, however, controversy has erupted in this area, as governments have crafted laws that regulate contraceptives like **RU-486**, the "morning-after pill," which prevents conception if it is taken within 72 hours of sexual intercourse. This emergency contraceptive initially was given to rape victims, but it seems that its use has widened. Some state legislatures have considered banning the use of these contraceptives or requiring parental consent for the drug to be dispensed to girls under the age of eighteen. Other legislatures have considered and passed laws that would mandate that information about the morning-after pill be provided in sex education classes or that pharmacies post a sign noting the availability of the pills.

In response to the decision by many employers to offer prescription drug benefits to men using Viagra in the late 1990s, more than twenty states passed **contraceptive equity laws**, which mandated that employers who pay for other prescription drugs pay for their employees' contraceptives, which had been excluded from many plans for four decades. These contraceptive equity law were challenged by the Roman Catholic Church, which views contraceptive use as a sin and argues that forcing them to offer a prescription drug benefit violates the constitutional mandate that government should not undermine religious principles. Some states now have an exception for religious organizations like the Catholic Church and some Christian fundamentalist churches. But some state courts have not allowed such an exception. For example, in March 2004, the California Supreme Court threw out the Roman Catholic Church's challenge, arguing that the contraceptive equity law in that state was an antidiscrimination measure and that this purpose outweighed any marginal interference in the free exercise of Roman Catholicism. Courts must still decide cases involving specific exemptions in state contraceptive equity laws that would allow religious institutions like the Catholic Church to opt out of providing contraceptive benefits.

Most contraceptive devices are intended to be used by women. There are relatively few male contraceptive options. While this may change in the future, as drug companies experiment with hormonal implants for men, the fact is that laws that regulate contraception continue to fall more heavily on women. Even more significantly, to the extent that contraception is linked to abortion, access to it is likely to become more uncertain in the future. The Roman Catholic Church and many Evangelical and fundamentalist Christian churches explicitly link contraception and abortion, viewing both as unacceptable. Other groups have adopted a similar view. Some religious groups claim that both contraception and abortion are sinful because they reject the sacredness of human life; others contend that many forms of contraception are in fact abortifacients; that is, they interfere with the implantation of the fertilized egg or embryo.

Laws Governing Abortion

At roughly the same time that states were limiting access to contraception, they were passing laws that prohibited the use of abortion. In the mid-1800s, a number of groups, including the American Medical Association and many religious institutions, spearheaded what were successful attempts to criminalize abortion. By the time the Civil War was over, most states had laws that restricted abortion, and many of these criminalized the act at all stages of pregnancy. While it is true that most states treated abortion more leniently in the earliest stages, that is, before quickening (when the woman could feel the fetus moving), most states did bar abortion from even these early stages. The majority of these laws were aimed at health care providers, who were usually midwives, and imposed criminal penalties of these women. The AMA actively supported abortion regulation, in part as a way of controlling the provision of obstetrical services and of muscling out the midwives. These laws remained in place until the U.S. Supreme Court struck them down in the landmark 1973 decision *Roe* v. *Wade*.

In this decision, the Court held that the constitutional right to privacy that was recognized in the contraception cases as encompassing access to birth control also included the right to abortion. The Court did recognize, however, that some abortion regulations might be acceptable. The justices ruled that states could regulate access to abortion in the second trimester (roughly the fourth to sixth month of pregnancy) or if the regulations protected maternal health and that states could bar access to abortion altogether in the third trimester (the seventh through ninth month of pregnancy), since at that point fetuses became viable and able to survive outside the mother's womb. By balancing concerns about privacy rights, maternal health, and fetal life, the Court attempted to construct a framework for assessing state and federal laws that regulated abortion.

In the years following *Roe,* the Supreme Court had ample opportunity to employ their framework, as many state legislatures passed laws that limited access to abortion. Over time, the *Roe* framework was reinterpreted—some would say recreated—to assess these new state regulations. In 1992, on the cusp of overturning *Roe* v. *Wade,* the Supreme Court issued its decision in **Planned Parenthood of Southeastern Pennsylvania v. Casey,** which largely replaced the trimester approach with a new framework. In this case, the Court ruled that abortion regulations would be evaluated on the basis of whether they imposed an undue burden on women who sought access to abortion services. In the period before fetal viability, a state could regulate abortion as long as the regulations did not place a "substantial obstacle" in the path of the woman seeking an abortion. For example, state laws that required that a woman be informed about the procedure and then wait 24 hours before she could have an abortion were constitutional, since these laws didn't constitute substantial obstacles. But laws that barred access before viability or imposed onerous requirements, like requiring that the spouse or the father of the fetus be informed or consent to the procedure, were found unconstitutional. After viability, the state could impose more serious requirements and could even ban the procedure, as long as it provided an exception that would protect the life or health of the woman. In short, *Casey* significantly altered abortion law in that it allowed for much more state regulation in the first trimester and before viability than had been permitted under *Roe.* While the *Casey* decision did recognize that women have a constitutionally protected liberty interest in having access to abortion, it permitted much more leeway to states that sought to restrict access to this procedure.

In the years since *Casey,* the abortion debate has continued to play out in Congress, the state legislatures, and the courts. Abortion rights advocates, who continued to appeal to courts to limit the protest activities of pro-life groups, have used a variety of laws to combat these groups. Most recently, abortion rights advocates have sought to use federal extortion and racketeering laws, which had been intended to fight organized crime, to rein in protesters' activities. Abortion opponents have continued to press their case in the state legislatures, in many cases convincing these bodies to extend legal protection to fetuses and even embryos. In 2003, Congress passed the

---

Planned Parenthood of Southeastern Pennsylvania v. Casey

1992 Supreme Court case that replaced the trimester framework with the undue-burden test

www ▶ ▶ ▶

Stenberg v. Carhart

2000 Supreme Court case that stuck down a state ban on partial-birth abortions, finding that the law was too vague, didn't provide a maternal-health exception, and barred abortions before fetal viability

Norma McCorvey

the "Jane Roe" in *Roe v. Wade*—she now actively lobbies against the very case that she won more than three decades ago

first federal abortion law since *Roe*. The Partial Birth Abortion Act aimed at barring the use of what opponents called "partial-birth abortions" and what physicians term abortion through "intact dilation and extraction." This ban applies to previability fetuses and at this point has no exception to protect the health or life of the mother. A similar state ban was struck down by the U.S. Supreme Court in the 2000 case **Stenberg v. Carhart.** Three federal courts have now struck down the federal Partial Birth Abortion Act because it did not provide an exception for maternal health or life, and it is expected that the U.S. Supreme Court will ultimately rule on this issue. The intensity with which abortion rights advocates and their foes view this debate is suggested by their very disagreement about what the procedure itself should be called! Advocates seek to medicalize the procedure, probably because this is part of a larger strategy that would leave the decision in the hands of doctors and their patients. In contrast, abortion foes or pro-life advocates have been successful in using the term *partial-birth abortion*—and this obviously has very clear symbolic value.

Whether the right to abortion will survive this newest round of legislative activity is open to some debate. The right itself hinges on the Supreme Court's support of it, and a sizable number of justices have signaled that they do not view the right to abortion as raising fundamental liberty interests. As new justices join the Court, it is very possible that the right could again be placed in question. In early 2004, **Norma McCorvey**, the original Jane Roe in *Roe* v. *Wade* brought suit in the federal courts arguing that *Roe* should be overturned. She has made no secret of the fact that she now opposes the holding that recognized the right to abortion. She claims that in the years since *Roe* was decided, a great deal of evidence has been amassed about the psychological harm suffered by women who choose abortion. McCorvey asserts that states should be able to strictly limit and even prohibit access to abortion based on the harm the procedure does to the woman.

In many ways, the abortion debate is more contentious now than it has ever been. Advances in science and medicine have fueled the debate about when life begins and about the rights of embryos and fetuses. Advances in reproductive technology have raised questions about whether pre-embryos or embryos have rights independent of their parents, and about whether there is any duty owed to these beings. The debates about embryonic stem cell research, which uses cells from embryos to help treat certain genetic defects, and about the duty of parents to not "abandon" pre-embryos that are not used in *in vitro fertilization* treatment underscore this issue.

Similarly, ongoing debates about the rights of fetuses to sue for harm they have suffered in utero raise compelling questions about fetuses' rights to life and health. In some criminal cases where fetuses are injured or killed in the commission of a crime against their mothers, the district attorney has raised separate claims for these fetuses. The conviction of Scott Peterson was based on two separate homicide charges—one for the death of his unborn child and one for the death of his pregnant wife. Similarly, charges of child endangerment brought against pregnant women who test positive for illegal drugs squarely raise the question of whether fetuses have rights separate from those of their mothers and of whether fetuses can sue their mothers for neglect or endangerment. The argument made by some doctors in support of forced caesarian sections—that is, using a court-order to force an unwilling woman to submit to a C-section—is that they have two patients—the woman and her child—and that the needs of the child can sometimes outweigh those of the woman. At the heart of all of these debates are serious questions about a woman's right to bodily integrity and autonomy and the fetus's right to life. Abortion law and the regulation of motherhood have considerable repercussions on women's rights in the United States, and this is sure to continue.

GENDER IDENTITY AND ORIENTATION

Sex and gender are two distinct entities—sex is an assignment made at birth (you are either a boy or a girl), while gender is a learned identity. You are born male or female, but the traits, characteristics, and preferences that you learn to associate with this classification are part of what defines your gender. Unfortunately, this nuance is often lost in public debate and the sex/gender distinction is erased. The effect of this is that sex and gender are treated the same, and the assumption is that the sex that you are born with inevitably determines your gender role in society. Male and female are treated as either/or categories—you are born either male or female and this identity is fixed and clearly defined. In reality, gender is a much more subtle and less clearly defined category than sex. Being a boy or a girl, a man or a woman, does not mean that you are automatically assigned a clear gender role—gender is learned and may change over time. Our laws do not always reflect this understanding of gender roles, and we can see this lack of focus in laws that deal with sexual orientation and gender identity.

Sexual Orientation

Sexual orientation

the sexual preferences of individuals for their sex partners; usually described in terms of an individual's being gay or lesbian, heterosexual, or bisexual

Until very recently, our law enshrined heterosexuality as the prevailing norm. For people outside this norm, the law offered no protection, and in fact, in many states, homosexual contact was prohibited under the criminal code. **Sexual orientation** refers to the preferences of individuals for their sexual partners. Individuals are usually described as being gay or lesbian, heterosexual, or bisexual. Discrimination based on sexual orientation has a long history in the United States. Up until the Supreme Court's decision in *Lawrence et al.* v. *Texas*, states were permitted to ban sodomy as it applied to gays and lesbians. In this case, the Court held that a state criminal law that prohibited "deviate sexual intercourse with another individual of the same sex" violated constitutionally protected liberty and privacy rights. In the wake of *Lawrence,* there have been many other attempts in the courts and legislatures to establish legal protection for gays, lesbians, and bisexuals. Some of these have been successful—for example, in 2004, the Massachusetts Supreme Judicial Court held that the state ban on same-sex marriage violated the state constitutional guarantee of equal protection. A number of municipalities and the state of Vermont have already established that same-sex couples can enter into civil unions and thereby reap many of the financial benefits of marriage, including tax benefits, health insurance coverage, and inheritance rights. In addition, several states and a number of cities and counties have expanded their definition of sex discrimination to include discrimination on the basis of perceived or actual homosexuality or bisexuality. But there has also been a backlash against this movement.

In the 2004 elections, initiatives to create a state constitutional amendment banning gay marriage were successful in all eleven states where they were on the ballot. Some state courts have invalidated these amendments—for example, in Louisiana, a state court found that the initiative did not

The issue of whether same-sex couples had the right to marry emerged as an important public policy issue in the late 1990s and early 2000s, as some states and municipalities recognized that these couples had a legal right to marry or to create civil unions recognized under law.

www ▶ ▶ ▶

comply with ballot requirements. Nevertheless, the movement in favor of barring same-sex marriage is expected to continue well into 2006, when activists anticipate that there will be ballot measures in twelve to fifteen additional states. In addition, Congress remains resistant to extending antidiscrimination protections to those who claim that they have been discriminated against in employment, housing, or public services on the basis of their sexual orientation. Instead antidiscrimination bans are a literal patchwork—some states, cities, and counties ban discrimination based on sexual orientation while most do not. In part because of this, opponents of same-sex marriage are vigorously lobbying Congress and the state legislatures to propose and ratify an amendment to the U.S. Constitution that would limit marriage to heterosexual couples.

♋ DEBATE

Should same-sex couples be allowed to marry, and should states that don't want to allow same-sex marriage be compelled to recognize those marriages?

Yes:

There is a fundamental right to marry—our U.S. Constitution protects the right to liberty, and the right to choose whom to marry is intrinsic to this right. The U.S. Supreme Court has long recognized that marriage is a basic human right, and even though legislatures and executives may want to limit this right, they are not allowed to. Denying this right is a means of social control: consider that African Americans were denied the right to marry until slavery was abolished, and that until 1967, states continued to bar intermarriage between whites and people of color. And denying this right has serious repercussions for same-sex couples. State laws confer more than four hundred rights and privileges on married couples, and federal laws provide for an additional one thousand rights—these are rights and privileges that are denied to anyone but heterosexual couples. States may argue that same-sex marriage is deviant or that it violates the core of our religious principles, but the fact is that any marriage between two committed and loving people benefits the state and the larger community. There is no legitimate reason for denying this right based on sexual orientation, and this denial is in blatant violation of our right to liberty, protected in the federal and state constitutions. Many municipalities already recognize the benefits of conferring legitimacy on same-sex unions; and the Supreme Judicial Court of the Commonwealth of Massachusetts has recognized that the right to marry encompasses the right to be able to choose whom one will marry. Several other nations now recognize either same sex marriage or civil unions between same sex couples, among

DEBATE

Should same-sex couples be allowed to marry, and should states that don't want to allow same-sex marriage be compelled to recognize those marriages?–(Cont'd)

these, the Netherlands and Belgium, and several other nations are poised to pass laws recognizing these unions, among these, Canada and Spain. We need to move to the next level and agree that love and equality should be the basis for marriage laws, not outdated views of sex and sex roles.

No:

The right of homosexual couples to marry has never been recognized in the laws of the United States and this makes sense given that homosexual acts are prohibited by religious teachings. Marriage can only be between a man and a woman—by definition, this is a relationship that must be between heterosexual couples, and this we know from not only our religious principles and historical experience, but from common sense as well. The 1996 Defense of Marriage Act and countless state resolutions and laws explicitly state that marriage is only between a man and a woman. In the 2004 elections, the people of eleven states loudly condemned the homosexual lifestyle and roundly rejected the notion of gay marriage. Those who say that we need to extend the protections of marriage to those living a deviant lifestyle do not really understand that if we expand marriage to include homosexual couples we will ultimately destroy this holy institution. Those with strong values must stand up and be counted now. As Dr. James Dobson, founder of Focus on the Family, eloquently stated, if we interpret marriage to mean everything, it will ultimately mean nothing. We need to protect marriage from activist judges, like those on the Massachusetts Supreme Judicial Court, who are totally out of touch with the people, and we can only do this by passing a constitutional amendment expressly barring homosexual marriage.

Gender Identity and the Law

For some people, there is a clear conflict between the sex they were born with and the gender with which they identify. Many of these people define themselves as transgender. Some seek to have sex-reassignment surgery to reconcile this conflict—these are transsexuals—but many do not. A number of states and municipalities have attempted to address this disconnect by amending their sex discrimination law further to include, not only a ban on discrimination based on sexual orientation, but also a prohibition against gender-identity discrimination. For example, the City of Chicago recently amended its antidiscrimination laws to include gender-identity discrimination and defined this discrimination as "the actual or perceived appearance, expression, identity or behavior, of a person as being male or female, whether or not that appearance, expression, identity or behavior is different from that traditionally associated with the person's designated sex at birth." A similar law in place in New York City expands the definition of gender-based discrimination to include, not just discrimination based on people's actual or perceived sex, but also discrimination on the basis of their "gender identity, self-image, appearance, behavior or expression."

www ▶ ▶ ▶

The law in the area of sexual orientation and gender identity is continuing to change but is clearly meeting resistance at the national, state, and even local level. Gains brought about by the U.S. Supreme Court's decision in *Lawrence et al.* v. *Texas* have been minimized, and in some cases erased, by the vigorous lobbying of conservative, far right, and religious groups.

THE LAW IN POPULAR CULTURE

Boys Don't Cry

This film is based on the life and death of Teena Brandon, who was murdered because of her transgender sexual identity in 1993. Brandon's life and death underscore the failure of law and law enforcement agencies to adequately protect those whose gender does not fit neatly into the fixed and closed categories of male and female.

In many places, sex and gender continue to be conflated, and the result of this is that policymakers assume that one's sex is the sole determinant of one's gender and gender identity. Federal law defines sex very narrowly, and its discrimination bans apply to a narrow range of cases, usually involving stereotypical ideas about men's and women's capabilities, and pregnancy discrimination. Relatively few states have broadened this definition to include sexual orientation, and even fewer have expanded it to include sexual identity.

SUMMARY

Are men and women equal under the law? To a very great extent, your answer to this question depends on how you define equality. Like the debate about race equality in the United States, your perspective on gender equality is likely the result of what you think the government and law are obliged to do to ensure equality. If you believe in gender neutrality, that is, if you think that the law must treat men and women as equals and assume that they are similarly situated with regard to their positions in society, then you probably have relatively few complaints about the relationship between law and gender. If, however, you think that law must take into account the real differences between women and men, then you probably will give a less enthusiastic answer to this question. Men and women are different—they have different reproductive functions and distinct roles in the family. And in fact, our law does not act as if it is gender neutral; sex is treated differently than other immutable characteristics—like race, color, and national origin—that one is born with. The intermediate standard used to evaluate equal protection claims assumes that there are valid differences between the sexes. Instead of assuming that all gender-based distinctions are invalid, as we assume that all race-based ones are, our law allows for some differential treatment. Instead of requiring a compelling state interest for the law to stand, we require only that there be an important interest served.

Moreover, our laws do not move us in the direction of a more equal society. Despite the fact that we have laws that bar discrimination in employment, women continue to be paid less than men and perceive that they have fewer opportunities, especially in corporate America. In addition, the workplace is generally not set up to accommodate the needs of working parents or caregivers, and this burden falls more heavily on women since they tend to assume more of the responsibility for caregiving. Similarly, the debate about reproductive rights is far from over—abortion politics continue to be polarized, and this stark divide affects much of the debate about fetal rights in the areas of stem cell research and reproductive technology. In addition, laws governing sexual orientation and identity continue to be in a state of flux, and the issue of civil rights for gays and lesbians may ultimately divide the U.S. public in much the same way as the abortion debate.

This chapter has highlighted some of the most compelling controversies about law and gender in the United States today. We are a nation divided, not just by racial or class divisions, areas that we are also discuss in Part III of this text, but by gender as well. Perhaps it is not surprising that given these deep divisions, our laws are ambiguous and in many ways inconsistent. In the next chapter, we will continue our discussion of how law is affected by controversial issues and how it ultimately contributes to the debate about these issues in our society.

SUGGESTED READING

Evan Gerstmann, *Same-Sex Marriage and the Constitution* (Cambridge University Press, 2003). In this provocative book, the author explores whether there is a right to same-sex marriage protected by the Constitution. He examines how our theories of equality square with this proposed right. In addition, he asks important questions about whether this issue should be decided by the courts or by the people through either direct voting or representative democracy.

James Gruber and Phoebe Morgan, *In the Company of Men: Male Dominance and Sexual Harassment (The Northeastern Series on Gender, Crime, and Law)* (Northeastern University Press, 2004). Gruber and Morgan's book provides a different perspective on sexual harassment—it examines this problem as part of the larger workplace culture of male dominance. It offers a cross-cultural perspective by looking at sexual harassment and law in other countries.

Arlie Russell Hochschild and Anne Machung, *The Second Shift* (Penguin Books, 2003). An excellent book that uses interviews to explore the lives of two-career couples and the effect of working two "shifts," one at work and the second at home, on their careers, marriages, and children. Most women with small children now work outside the home. This book discusses how individuals and couples reconcile the inherent conflicts between paid and unpaid work.

William Saletan, *Bearing Right: How Conservatives Won the Abortion War* (University of California Press, 2004). This book explores how the politics of abortion have changed over the last thirty years, and how members of the moderate and far right have effectively co-opted this issue. This book is an excellent study of how interest-group activism shaped the agenda and discussion of this issue.

Dorothy M. Stetson, *Women's Rights in the U.S.A: Policy Debates and Gender Roles* (Routledge Press, 2004). This book looks at the role of gender in the creation of policy and law. It examines not only women in politics but also the politics of gender in the United States and provides an excellent overview of the issues of reproductive rights, education, family roles, employment, and sexuality.

ACTIVE LEARNING

1. Find the sexual harassment guidelines in place at either your college or your workplace. Bring them to class for discussion. Are the guidelines

clear? Do you know what is prohibited? Permitted? How comfortable are you with these guidelines? Why do you think your college or employer has put these guidelines in place?

2. Do you have any idea how much workers in particular fields make? Play a guessing game—you don't necessarily have to know the exact amount, just a sense of how much workers make relative to each other. Make a list of all the occupations you come in contact with daily and then analyze them. You may want to use the data accumulated by Washington State in its pay equity study—this study provides information not only about wages but also about the comparable-worth criteria (skill, effort, responsibility, education, and experience) that are used to compare jobs.

3. Debate: States have very different approaches to the issue of same-sex marriage. Look at http://www.gay-civil-unions.com/HTML/State_By_State/State_by_State.htm for a state-by-state analysis of marriage and civil union laws throughout the country. Also, consider the arguments for and against same-sex marriage and civil unions. A good starting point may be the list of pro arguments compiled on the webpage of Parents, Families and Friends of Lesbians and Gays http://www.pflag.org/education/marriage.html.

CHAPTER 13

Law and Class

There is a stark divide in American society. It is based largely on social and economic class. Throughout most of our nation's history, there has been a yawning gap between those who have resources and those who do not, and this gap has grown wider in the last forty years. **Social class** *is determined, not only by family name, but by educational attainment and job success, and this focus on achievement makes class a relatively fluid category. In the United States, social class is closely intertwined with economic class. While social class is based on one's family background or profession,* **economic class** *is determined by one's financial assets and resources. Both social and economic class are strong predictors of personal efficacy, self-esteem, and* **"life chances,"** *that is, the ability to get ahead, to wield influence in the wider society, and to pass one's social class along to one's offspring.* **Social stratification** *is said to characterize our society because there is grossly unequal access to opportunities and to the rewards that come from these opportunities. Despite the fact that class is viewed as fluid, it is actually fairly static; that is, there is little movement between classes. Social stratification and inequality have become institutionalized in the United States, and our law has operated to limit social mobility. In this chapter, we will discuss the role that American law has played in contributing to and reinforcing social stratification.*

As you may remember from Chapter 2, several schools of jurisprudence focus on the relationship between law, class, and the economic system. People who write from the point of view of either Marxist legal theory or critical legal studies contend that law is a tool of the ruling elite and that this elite uses law to reinforce its control over the political institutions and social and economic structures. This was at the core of what Karl Marx argued. He fiercely contended that those in power got there because of class advantage, specifically, their control over the means of production, and remained in power because of their control over governmental institutions, including the law and the courts. Preeminent sociologist Donald

Black also argued that law is not just a set of rules; even more importantly, it is a social control, instituted by the government to ensure conformity of behavior. In contrast to these schools of thought, the law and economics school, one of the most prominent theories of jurisprudence in law schools today, adopts a more positive perspective. This school argues that law is and should be used to maximize market efficiency—that is, to produce and distribute goods at the lowest cost—because in so doing it will make the larger society wealthier. These two sets of theories view the relationship between law and class very differently. For Marxist legal theory and CLS, the law reinforces existing privilege and is simply used as one of many tools for advancing the economic interests of the wealthiest. In contrast, law and economics theorists see that law can be used as a positive force to improve market efficiency, thus improving the living and working conditions of everyone in the society. In this chapter, we will examine the relationship between law and social and economic class in the United States.

IDEOLOGY, CULTURE, AND CLASS

Americans have long prized those with ingenuity, ambition, and intelligence, and most Americans believe that everyone has the responsibility to take care of themselves and to "pull themselves up by their bootstraps." Those who are rich *deserve* to be rich, and those who are poor are simply not working hard enough—they *deserve* to be poor. Our notions of class are mixed with our notions of morality—we question whether there really are deserving poor or undeserving rich. American culture very strongly reveres those who succeed despite their humble beginnings. Think about the personal stories and the mythologies of some of our most cherished heroes— Abraham Lincoln, born in a log cabin, who, through ambition, hard work, and a strong intellect, became one of our most respected presidents; Horatio Alger, who lived in the 1800s and preached the message of "Strive and Succeed" to poor young boys living on the streets in cities like New York; and Bill Clinton, born to a single working woman in the little town of Hope, Arkansas. In the United States, we assume that people can improve their positions by working hard and following the rules. We believe that class is determined by achievement and merit, not necessarily by birth or luck. As the polling data from the General Social Survey posted on our website suggests, most Americans believe that individuals are responsible for their own successes or failures. It is interesting to note, however, that many respondents also think that some of the blame for social and economic class should go, not just to the individual, but also to circumstances beyond the individual's control.

`www ▶ ▶ ▶`

Given this belief in individual ingenuity, it is perhaps not surprising that many Americans doubt that government should have a role in helping to redistribute wealth. Remember that we said in the introduction to Part III that there is an inherent tension between equality and freedom. One can see this tension very clearly when one considers class in the United States. For there to be a more equal society, that is, for there to be less social stratification, government would probably have to take some action to redistribute resources. For example, government might adopt a different tax structure that would limit the ability of wealthy individuals to pass their wealth down to their offspring. If government wanted to take this approach, they might do so by taxing estates at a higher level than they are currently taxed. Such an action would undoubtedly meet with vigorous opposition, as lawmakers and individuals objected to the government's attempt to limit their ability to dispose of their resources as they see fit. In this scenario, the goal of equality would clearly conflict with the goal of individual freedom. To many Americans, such a tradeoff would simply be unacceptable. Most Americans, even those at the lower rungs of the income and wealth ladder, still maintain some belief in their ability to get ahead and continue to think that they or their children will have a better life.

For most, this confidence about the future has little foundation in reality. In the last forty years, the rich have gotten much richer and the poor have gotten poorer; the middle class, according to many commentators, has virtually disappeared. As the chart from United for a Fair Economy that is posted on our website shows, in the last two decades, the bottom 40 percent of the population has suffered a *decline* of more than 75 percent in their net worth, while the top 1 percent have increased their net worth by more than 42 percent. The pie chart graphically depicts the tiny net worth of the bottom 40 percent of our population (not even 1 percent of the net worth is held by these people) and the staggering wealth of the top 1 percent, who own more than 38 percent of the net worth in our country. The remainder of the wealth is held largely by the next 9 percent of the population, who hold another 33 percent of all financial resources. Thus, the top 10 percent of the population has more than 70 percent of all wealth.

Differences in wealth translate directly into differences in health, educational resources, and housing. Class status directly correlates with morbidity—sickness—rates and mortality rates. Those from lower-class backgrounds tend to suffer from more health problems, such as low birth weight, heart and lung disease, high blood pressure, obesity, asthma, diabetes, and mental illness, and to engage in risk-taking behaviors, such as smoking and recreational drug and alcohol use and abuse, than do their upper-class counterparts. In the United States, childhood health is directly related to social class, and children in wealthy families tend to have a much better start, in terms of their health, than do those in less affluent families. Access to high-quality health care is skewed in favor of those who have financial resources and are well educated, and this sharpens the disparity in morbidity and mortality between the classes. At present, more than 37 million Americans are without health insurance and lack access to important preventive resources that would probably improve health and life expectancy. The prevalence of hunger and homelessness among the poor and working poor, particularly among children, also widens the health gap.

In a similar way, educational resources are also a function of social class in the United States. At the primary and secondary level, there is a wide disparity in the quality of education because elementary and secondary schools are funded by a combination of state and local moneys, and nearly all local funds come from property taxes. In some states, local funding is the biggest component of school funding, and this reliance on property taxes means that school funding is grossly unequal. Affluent school districts raise taxes from properties that are worth more and so generate more taxes. Consider the law in action example—*San Antonio Independent School District* v. *Rodriguez*—a case decided by the U.S. Supreme Court in 1973. Parents of students in poor school districts brought this challenge against the public school district, claiming that inequalities in funding violated the equal protection clause of the Fourteenth Amendment. When you read this case, consider how the Court handled the equal protection challenge

Some state courts have found that school financing that is largely dependent upon local taxes and local revenues creates huge inequalities among schools and thus violates state equal protection law. Those who have successfully challenged these funding schemes have argued that this kind of funding does not ensure that poor children have access to adequate educational facilities—note that the emphasis is on equity, not simple equality. Despite these findings, however, there are vast differences in the resources provided to students at the elementary and secondary levels, and this inequality probably has a significant impact on the quality of education.

We know that there is a substantial gap in the standardized test scores of children in different districts—children in affluent districts do far better than those in middle-class districts, and those in middle-class districts far outscore those in working-class or poor districts. Moreover, there is some evidence that the curriculum of these districts not only provides a competitive advantage or disadvantage in terms of the standardized tests, but may be subtly directing students into certain occupations. In one recent study, the researchers found that in school districts with the most affluent families, students are encouraged to engage in critical thinking and analysis, and there is far less focus on repeating tasks and following the teacher's instructions. In contrast, in working-class and poor districts, teachers focused their attention on helping students to complete simple tasks, to repeat these tasks, and to engage in simple fact recall; they spent less on the development of analytical thinking skills.

San Antonio Independent School District v. Rodriguez

1973 Supreme Court case that declined to subject class- and wealth-based distinctions that resulted in inequalities in school funding to strict scrutiny

www ▶ ▶ ▶

LAW IN ACTION

Class Distinctions in the Law and Equal Protection Analysis

SAN ANTONIO INDEPENDENT SCHOOL DISTRICT V. *RODRIGUEZ* U.S. Supreme Court, 1973

www ▶ ▶ ▶ (See *Law, Politics, and Society* website for a link to the complete decision.)

MR. JUSTICE POWELL delivered the opinion of the Court.

This suit attacking the Texas system of financing public education was initiated by Mexican-American parents whose children attend the elementary and secondary schools in the Edgewood Independent School District, an urban school district in San Antonio, Texas . . . In December, 1971, the [three-member federal district court] panel rendered its judgment in a per curiam opinion holding the Texas school finance system unconstitutional under the Equal Protection Clause of the Fourteenth Amendment . . . For the reasons stated in this opinion, we reverse the decision of the District Court.

The first Texas State Constitution, promulgated upon Texas' entry into the Union in 1845, provided for the establishment of a system of free schools. Early in its history, Texas adopted a dual approach to the financing of its schools, relying on mutual participation by the local school districts and the State . . .

Until recent times, Texas was a predominantly rural State, and its population and property wealth were spread relatively evenly across the State. Sizable differences in the value of assessable property between local school districts became increasingly evident as the State became more industrialized and as rural-to-urban population shifts became more pronounced . . . These growing disparities in population and taxable property between districts were responsible in part for increasingly notable differences in levels of local expenditure for education.

Recognizing the need for increased state funding to help offset disparities in local spending and to meet Texas' changing educational requirements, the state legislature, in the late 1940's, undertook a thorough evaluation of public education with an eye toward major reform. In 1947, an 18-member committee, composed of educators and legislators, was appointed to explore alternative systems in other States and to propose a funding scheme that would guarantee a minimum or basic educational offering to each child and that would help overcome inter-district disparities in taxable resources. The Committee's efforts led to the passage of the Gilmer-Aikin bills . . . Today, this Program accounts for approximately half of the total educational expenditures in Texas . . .

The State, supplying funds from its general revenues, finances approximately 80% of the Program, and the school districts are responsible—as a unit—for providing the remaining 20%. The districts' share, known as the Local Fund Assignment, is apportioned among the school districts under a formula designed to reflect each district's relative taxpaying ability . . .

The school district in which appellees reside, the Edgewood Independent School District, has been compared throughout this litigation with the Alamo Heights Independent School District. This comparison between the least and most affluent districts in the San Antonio area serves to illustrate the manner in which the dual system of finance operates, and to indicate the extent to which substantial disparities exist despite the State's impressive progress in recent years . . .

For the 1970-1971 school year, the Foundation School Program allotment for Edgewood was $356 per pupil, a 62% increase over the 1967-1968 school year . . . Alamo Heights enjoyed a similar increase under the Foundation Program, netting $491 per pupil in 1970-1971 . . .

Despite these recent increases, substantial inter-district disparities in school expenditures found by the District Court to prevail in San Antonio and in varying degrees throughout the State still exist. And it was these disparities, largely attributable to differences in the amounts of money collected through local property taxation, that led the District Court to conclude that Texas' dual system of public school financing violated the Equal Protection Clause. The District Court held that the Texas system discriminates on the basis of wealth in the manner in which education is provided for its people. Finding that wealth is a "suspect" classification, and that education is a "fundamental" interest, the District Court held that the Texas system could be sustained only if the State could show that it was premised upon some compelling state interest. *Id*. at 282–284. On this issue the court concluded that

[n]ot only are defendants unable to demonstrate compelling state interests . . . they fail even to establish a reasonable basis for these classifications (Id. at 284) . . .

We must decide, first, whether the Texas system of financing public education operates to the disadvantage of some suspect class or impinges upon a fundamental right explicitly or implicitly protected by the Constitution, thereby requiring strict judicial scrutiny. If so, the judgment of the District Court should be affirmed. If not, the Texas scheme must still be examined to determine whether it rationally furthers some legitimate, articulated state purpose, and therefore does not constitute an invidious discrimination in violation of the Equal Protection Clause of the Fourteenth Amendment.

. . . In concluding that strict judicial scrutiny was required, [the district] court relied on decisions dealing with the rights of indigents to equal treatment in the criminal trial and appellate processes, and on cases disapproving wealth restrictions on the right to vote. Those cases, the District Court concluded, established wealth as a suspect classification . . . [However] [t]he wealth discrimination discovered by the District Court in this case, and by several other courts that have recently struck down school financing laws in other States, is quite unlike any of the forms of wealth discrimination heretofore reviewed by this Court . . .

Only appellees' first possible basis for describing the class disadvantaged by the Texas school financing system—discrimination against a class of definably "poor" persons—might arguably meet the criteria established in these prior cases. Even a cursory examination, however, demonstrates that neither of the two distinguishing characteristics of wealth classifications can be found here. First, in support of their charge that the system discriminates against the "poor," appellees have made no effort to demonstrate that it operates to the peculiar disadvantage of any

LAW IN ACTION—(CONT'D)

class fairly definable as indigent, or as composed of persons whose incomes are beneath any designated poverty level. Indeed, there is reason to believe that the poorest families are not necessarily clustered in the poorest property districts . . . there is no basis on the record in this case for assuming that the poorest people—defined by reference to any level of absolute impecunity—are concentrated in the poorest districts.

Second, neither appellees nor the District Court addressed the fact that, unlike each of the foregoing cases, lack of personal resources has not occasioned an absolute deprivation of the desired benefit. The argument here is not that the children in districts having relatively low assessable property values are receiving no public education; rather, it is that they are receiving a poorer quality education than that available to children in districts having more assessable wealth. Apart from the unsettled and disputed question whether the quality of education may be determined by the amount of money expended for it, a sufficient answer to appellees' argument is that, at least where wealth is involved, the Equal Protection Clause does not require absolute equality or precisely equal advantages . . . Texas asserts that the Minimum Foundation Program provides an "adequate" education for all children in the State. By providing 12 years of free public school education, and by assuring teachers, books, transportation, and operating funds, the Texas Legislature has endeavored to guarantee, for the welfare of the state as a whole, that all people shall have at least an adequate program of education . . .

The State repeatedly asserted in its briefs in this Court that it has fulfilled this desire, and that it now assures "every child in every school district an adequate education." No proof was offered at trial persuasively discrediting or refuting the State's assertion.

For these two reasons—the absence of any evidence that the financing system discriminates against any definable category of "poor" people or that it results in the absolute deprivation of education—the disadvantaged class is not susceptible of identification in traditional terms.

As suggested above, appellees and the District Court may have embraced a second or third approach, the second of which might be characterized as a theory of relative or comparative discrimination based on family income. Appellees sought to prove that a direct correlation exists between the wealth of families within each district and the expenditures therein for education. That is, along a continuum, the poorer the family, the lower the dollar amount of education received by the family's children . . .

If, in fact, these correlations could be sustained, then it might be argued that expenditures on education—equated by appellees to the quality of education—are dependent on personal wealth . . . It is evident that, even if the conceptual questions were answered favorably to appellees, no factual basis exists upon which to found a claim of comparative wealth discrimination.

This brings us, then, to the third way in which the classification scheme might be defined—*district* wealth discrimination . . . the disadvantaged class might be viewed as encompassing every child in every district except the district that has the most assessable wealth and spends the most on education . . . The system of alleged discrimination and the class it defines have none of the traditional indicia of suspectness: the class is not saddled with such disabilities, or subjected to such a history of purposeful unequal treatment, or relegated to such a position of political powerlessness as to command extraordinary protection from the majoritarian political process.

We thus conclude that the Texas system does not operate to the peculiar disadvantage of any suspect class. But in recognition of the fact that this Court has never heretofore held that wealth discrimination alone provides an adequate basis for invoking strict scrutiny, appellees have not relied solely on this contention. They also assert that the State's system impermissibly interferes with the exercise of a "fundamental" right, and that, accordingly, the prior decisions of this Court require the application of the strict standard of judicial review . . . It is this question—whether education is a fundamental right, in the sense that it is among the rights and liberties protected by the Constitution—which has so consumed the attention of courts and commentators in recent years.

In *Brown* v. *Board of Education* (1954), a unanimous Court recognized that "education is perhaps the most important function of state and local governments." What was said there in the context of racial discrimination has lost none of its vitality with the passage of time . . .

Compulsory school attendance laws and the great expenditures for education both demonstrate our recognition of the importance of education to our democratic society. It is required in the performance of our most basic public responsibilities, even service in the armed forces. It is the very foundation of good citizenship. Today it is a principal instrument in awakening the child to cultural values, in preparing him for later professional training,

and in helping him to adjust normally to his environment. In these days, it is doubtful that any child may reasonably be expected to succeed in life if he is denied the opportunity of an education. Such an opportunity, where the state has undertaken to provide it, is a right which must be made available to all on equal terms . . .

Nothing this Court holds today in any way detracts from our historic dedication to public education. . . .

It is not the province of this Court to create substantive constitutional rights in the name of guaranteeing equal protection of the laws. Thus, the key to discovering whether education is "fundamental" . . . lies in assessing whether there is a right to education explicitly or implicitly guaranteed by the Constitution . . . Education, of course, is not among the rights afforded explicit protection under our Federal Constitution. Nor do we find any basis for saying it is implicitly so protected. As we have said, the undisputed importance of education will not, alone, cause this Court to depart from the usual standard for reviewing a State's social and economic legislation . . .

Even if it were conceded that some identifiable quantum of education is a constitutionally protected prerequisite to the meaningful exercise of either [freedom of speech or the vote] . . . we have no indication that the present levels of educational expenditures in Texas provide an education that falls short . . .

We have carefully considered each of the arguments supportive of the District Court's finding that education is a fundamental right or liberty, and have found those arguments unpersuasive. In one further respect, we find this a particularly inappropriate case in which to subject state action to strict judicial scrutiny. The present

LAW IN ACTION—(CONT'D)

case, in another basic sense, is significantly different from any of the cases in which the Court has applied strict scrutiny to state or federal legislation touching upon constitutionally protected rights. Each of our prior cases involved legislation which "deprived," "infringed," or "interfered" with the free exercise of some such fundamental personal right or liberty . . . A critical distinction between those cases and the one now before us lies in what Texas is endeavoring to do with respect to education . . . Every step leading to the establishment of the system Texas utilizes today—including the decisions permitting localities to tax and expend locally, and creating and continuously expanding state aid—was implemented in an effort to extend public education and to improve its quality.

It should be clear, for the reasons stated above and in accord with the prior decisions of this Court, that this is not a case in which the challenged state action must be subjected to the searching judicial scrutiny reserved for laws that create suspect classifications or impinge upon constitutionally protected rights.

We need not rest our decision, however, solely on the inappropriateness of the strict scrutiny test. A century of Supreme Court adjudication under the Equal Protection Clause affirmatively supports the application of the traditional standard of review, which requires only that the State's system be shown to bear some rational relationship to legitimate state purposes. This case represents far more than a challenge to the manner in which Texas provides for the education of its children. We have here nothing less than a direct attack on the way in which Texas has chosen to raise and disburse state and local tax revenues . . .

Thus, we stand on familiar ground when we continue to acknowledge that the Justices of this Court lack both the expertise and the familiarity with local problems so necessary to the making of wise decisions with respect to the raising and disposition of public revenues . . . the Court does well not to impose too rigorous a standard of scrutiny lest all local fiscal schemes become subjects of criticism under the Equal Protection Clause.

In addition to matters of fiscal policy, this case also involves the most persistent and difficult questions of educational policy, another area in which this Court's lack of specialized knowledge and experience counsels against premature interference with the informed judgments made at the state and local levels . . . Indeed, one of the major sources of controversy concerns the extent to which there is a demonstrable correlation between educational expenditures and the quality of education—an assumed correlation underlying virtually every legal conclusion drawn by the District Court in this case. Related to the questioned relationship between cost and quality is the equally unsettled controversy as to the proper goals of a system of public education.

. . . it would be difficult to imagine a case having a greater potential impact on our federal system than the one now before us, in which we are urged to abrogate systems of financing public education presently in existence in virtually every State . . .

. . . [I]f local taxation for local expenditures were an unconstitutional method of providing for education, then it might be an equally impermissible means of providing other necessary services customarily financed largely from local property taxes, including local police and fire protection, public health and hospitals, and public utility facilities of various kinds . . . It has simply never been within the constitu-

LAW IN ACTION—(CONT'D)

tional prerogative of this Court to nullify state-wide measures for financing public services merely because the burdens or benefits thereof fall unevenly depending upon the relative wealth of the political subdivisions in which citizens live.

In sum, to the extent that the Texas system of school financing results in unequal expenditures between children who happen to reside in different districts, we cannot say that such disparities are the product of a system that is so irrational as to be invidiously discriminatory. Texas has acknowledged its shortcomings, and has persistently endeavored—not without some success—to ameliorate the differences in levels of expenditures without sacrificing the benefits of local participation . . .

Reversed.

MR. JUSTICE BRENNAN, dissenting.

Although I agree with my Brother WHITE that the Texas statutory scheme is devoid of any rational basis, and, for that reason, is violative of the Equal Protection Clause, I also record my disagreement with the Court's rather distressing assertion that a right may be deemed "fundamental" for the purposes of equal protection analysis only if it is "explicitly or implicitly guaranteed by the Constitution." As my Brother MARSHALL convincingly demonstrates, our prior cases stand for the proposition that "fundamentality" is, in large measure, a function of the right's importance in terms of the effectuation of those rights which are in fact, constitutionally guaranteed . . .

Here, there can be no doubt that education is inextricably linked to the right to participate in the electoral process and to the rights of free speech and association guaranteed by the First Amendment. This being so, any classification affecting education must be subjected to strict judicial scrutiny, and since even the State concedes that the statutory scheme now before us cannot pass constitutional muster under this stricter standard of review, I can only conclude that the Texas school-financing scheme is constitutionally invalid.

QUESTIONS

1. What were the parents arguing in this case?
2. How does the Court resolve the equal protection challenge?
3. You have one of the four dissents in this case—the one penned by Justice Brennan. What was the central argument in this dissent?
4. Which decision—the majority opinion or the Brennan dissent—do you think was more compelling?
5. Why do you think the majority reached its decision? What do you think would have happened had the dissenters been in the majority?

This gap extends to education after high school. The wealthiest Americans tend to attend prestigious private colleges and universities, and to continue to develop ties that will allow them to enter the most highly paid professions. In contrast, the working class and poor are less likely to attend or to complete college. They may attend vocational schools that will provide skills and training that easily translate to the workforce, but they are far less likely to complete a four-year college degree. This gap has worsened in the last two decades, as college tuition rates have soared and as the amount of federal and state aid (as opposed to loans) has dramatically dropped. A college degree is a very significant variable in the American economy—it often determines whether an individual will enter into the middle class, and it is almost always necessary for class mobility, that is, for movement up the social-class ladder.

In addition to inequality in educational resources, there is a tremendous class gap in housing in the United States. This gap has widened considerably in the last few years as housing costs have skyrocketed in many states and metropolitan areas. By 2003, the average person had to earn $16.00 an hour to rent a two-bedroom apartment. In the most expensive housing markets, San Diego and San Francisco, renters needed to earn roughly $35.00 for the same apartment. The continuing economic downturn combined with steadily increasing housing costs forced many low-income individuals and families out of safe and affordable housing. It is estimated that 3.5 million people are homeless at some point during each year. Families are the fastest growing group in the homeless population, and 39 percent of the homeless are children. Another 5.4 million people either live in substandard housing or spend more than half of their incomes on housing. Those most at risk for homelessness are single mothers, children, the mentally ill, veterans, and the disabled. At the upper end of the housing market, single family residences in the most affluent areas sell in the tens of millions of dollars.

THE LAW AND SOCIAL CLASS IN THE UNITED STATES

Our laws reinforce these inequalities in wealth, employment, health care, education, and housing. The law is not neutral—it has the effect of highlighting and perhaps even heightening the disparity between rich and poor. Our culture is based on individualism, and our laws reflect this in a number of ways: first, our definition of equality requires only facial neutrality—that is, it requires only that the law not explicitly privilege one group of people over another. In addition, Americans generally do not think government should have an active role in distributing resources. And finally, Americans value individual economic action over collective activity like unionism. We tend not to see class in the United States—in fact, it is largely invisible. And most Americans do not view our society as stratified, despite the fact that is deeply divided along class lines. Because we perceive this to be an open society, where hard work is rewarded and everyone can get ahead if only they work hard enough, we tend to be skeptical about the permanence of social class.

www ▶ ▶ ▶

Equality Defined

Remember that we have been talking about the tension between equality and freedom, and one of the ways that we have dealt with this conflict is to define equality very narrowly. If equality were believed to require equality of opportunity or equality of result, the individual's right to be free, or in the economic sense, to accumulate resources without having the government's "hand" in his or her pocket, would be much more limited. Equality of result would mandate that everyone end up in pretty much the same place and that differences between people be equalized. In many industrialized nations, equality is defined in such a way that there is a redistribution of resources. As a result, there is not a large gap between the wealthiest and the poorest. Government has a much more prominent role in these nations and takes an active role in equalizing resources. Equality of opportunity is different from result—it doesn't require that everyone end up in the same place. It requires instead that there be a level playing field and that no one have an advantage or disadvantage that is not based on individual merit. For example, if equality of opportunity were the rule of thumb, there would be no advantage given to "legacies" in college or graduate school admissions—in other words, sons or daughters of graduates would not be given a preference, as they usually are, in the admissions process at elite institutions.

Our laws do not define equality as requiring either equal results or opportunities. Instead, we define equality in a very limited way—we require that there be formal equality, also known as political equality, but not social or economic equality. Formal or political equality requires simply that every person's vote count equally and that the law treat everyone the same *on its face*, that is, that it not explicitly discriminate or privilege certain groups. Writing in 1894, famous author Anatole France stated: "[t]he law, in its majestic impartiality, forbids the rich, as well as the poor, to sleep under bridges, to beg in the streets, and to steal bread" (*The Red Lily*, 1894), and this encapsulates our approach to equality. Our political culture, with its focus on individualism, precludes a broader interpretation. Instead, our law requires simple facial neutrality—that is, the law cannot expressly help or hinder any particular group. We believe in individualism and expect that hard work and intelligence ultimately will be rewarded. Despite the fact that our society is deeply stratified, we believe that the individual can rise above his or her background and move up in terms of social class.

THE LAW IN POPULAR CULTURE

Glengarry Glen Ross

While Americans tend to view one's class status as fluid, there is nevertheless significant class hostility. This film explores class dynamics and hostilities, showing how they are magnified during times of economic hardship. Here, real estate brokers are desperately trying to make a living after the market has soured. There is plenty of hostility in this film—the management and workers/brokers are in a highly confrontational relationship, and the workers/brokers are simply out to fleece the public.

Remember, there are three levels of scrutiny for equal protection analysis. The most stringent, strict scrutiny is reserved for classifications like race, color, and national origin. These are distinctions that the individual is born with and that have historically created significant disadvantages. It is very difficult for a law that distinguishes on the basis of one of these characteristics to pass muster, and in fact, such a law would be presumed to be invalid. To justify such a distinction, the government would have to show that it served a compelling state interest and was narrowly tailored to achieve this interest. The intermediate standard of review, reserved for sex-based distinctions in the law, requires that government show that the classification be based on an important interest and that it be substantially related to achieving that interest. All other distinctions, including those based solely on wealth or class, may be readily justified under the third tier of scrutiny, known as rational relationship. There is a presumption that laws based on these distinctions are valid; to successfully challenge them, the individual has the difficult job of showing that they do *not* further some legitimate state interest or that they are *not* rationally related to this interest. As you may recall, in *San Antonio Independent School District* v. *Rodriguez,* the Supreme Court easily disposed of the equal protection challenge, declining to subject class- or wealth-based distinctions in the law to more stringent analysis.

Government's Role in Redistributing Resources

Transfer programs

government programs that *transfer* funds from one group of people to another; provide resources to particular groups who are deemed worthy of funding

www ▶ ▶ ▶

Government has a very important role to play in the economy. Through its transfer and taxation policies, it can redistribute wealth and reduce the disparity between the wealthiest and the poorest. **Transfer programs** provide resources to particular groups in the society that are deemed worthy of funding. In the United States, we use programs like Social Security and unemployment insurance to provide monies to the disabled and their dependents, to the elderly, and to the unemployed. These programs essentially *transfer* money between two sets of "workers"—those who are employed and those who are not employed. In the United States, we do not rely heavily on transfer programs. Other industrialized nations, like Sweden, Finland, Canada, and the United Kingdom, employ a much greater range of programs, including those that fund child-care subsidies, universal health care, worker retraining programs, and housing funds. We are deeply ambivalent about social welfare programs in the United States—as a society, we are not sure that government should have an expansive role in ensuring a certain standard of living, and we are very cautious about large-scale governmental involvement in the economy. Probably because of our ambivalence, we accept only those transfer programs that seem to benefit those who are "worthy." Most Americans believe that Social Security should be available to those who are truly disabled and to their dependents, and we view Social Security retirement funds as almost sacred. In fact, most Americans don't even realize that Social Security is a transfer program—they tend to believe that they are paying into their own Social Security accounts, not that they are paying for someone else's retirement *right now.*

In the United States, health care costs are covered only for specific groups—disabled children covered by Social Security may be eligible for Medicaid or Medicare, depending on their state's laws. Medicaid provides coverage for the poor and indigent, and in most states, also for disabled children; Medicare funds the medical care of the elderly, and in some states, additional funds are available to children with certain diseases. Every state now provides some funding for the medical care of children from working-class families that earn too much money to be considered poor, but too little to pay for private insurance. These federal and state programs, however, do not provide universal health care access. For example, a large number of adults—some estimate upwards of 44 million people, about 20 percent of these children—are uninsured. In addition, the quality of health care varies, sometimes very dramatically, with social class.

Again, we rely relatively little on transfer programs in the United States. Some nations, like Finland and Sweden, make much greater use of these programs and the effect is that income is much more equalized. These countries provide much more extensive family benefits, like paid maternity and paternity leave, child-care subsidies, paid medical leave, and retirement benefits, along with greater funding for educational opportunities than what the United States government provides. Our government doesn't mandate any of these benefits—while workers may have a right to family or medical leave, this is not *paid* leave, and relatively little funding devoted to higher education is not loan-based. Again, our vision of equality is that everyone should have an equal right to these benefits, but making use of these policies or services requires that you be able to pay for them.

In addition to using transfer programs, governments may also use taxes to redistribute wealth. In the United States, not only do we rely heavily on taxes to fund government programs, we rely on highly **regressive taxes**, meaning that they place a relatively greater burden on those in the lower economic classes than they do on those who are wealthier. **Progressive taxes** have the potential to equalize wealth in a society by taxing the wealthier at a higher rate than the less affluent. Generally speaking, taxes on personal income and corporate income have a better shot at being progressive, since the rates can be structured so that more affluent people pay a higher percentage of their income in taxes. In reality, neither personal nor corporate taxes are progressive. As the data on the website show, those in the top income bracket pay taxes at a much lower rate today than they have at any time since 1933. In the 1940s, those in this bracket had a huge tax burden—they were taxed at a rate of more than 90 percent of their income. In contrast, the top tax bracket today is taxed at a 35 percent rate. Many commentators believe that the changes in the tax code implemented by George W. Bush in 2001–2003 will continue to shift the tax burden to the working and middle classes. Specifically, the decrease in the tax on capital gains and dividends and the increase in the amount of money that can be deducted for certain corporate expenses may enable those in the upper income brackets to keep a greater percentage of their income.

Income taxes generate a significant amount of dollars for the federal and state governments. The other forms of taxes that our government relies on are inherently regressive. State and local taxes on real estate, sales, and gasoline tend to consume a much larger share of the household income of poor, working- and middle-class Americans than they do for the wealthy. The same is true for payroll taxes, that is, taxes collected for the Social Security fund. Taxes on Social Security apply only to the first $88,000 of

regressive taxes

taxes that impose a proportionately heavier burden on people in the lower socioeconomic classes than they do on the wealthy

 www ▶ ▶ ▶

progressive taxes

taxes that impose a proportionately heavier burden on wealthier people and have the potential to equalize wealth in the society

earned income—no additional Social Security taxes are collected above this amount. Perhaps even more significantly, payroll taxes are paid by every working person—you may not owe any income taxes if your wages are low enough, but you will still be responsible for your Social Security taxes. As a result of these policies, not only are our tax laws not progressive—they are highly regressive! Some analysts say that these policies encourage efficiency and corporate investment, and this seems to be true. Before 1913, when the states ratified the Sixteenth Amendment, which permitted Congress to levy an income tax, we relied much more heavily on excise and customs taxes collected on imports. By shifting to an income tax, we were able to engage more freely in international trade and to fund government programs that helped us to industrialize and build a modern technological society. But the cost is clearly very high and has contributed to the growing wealth and income inequalities that we now see in the United States.

DEBATE

Should our taxation policies be more progressive?

Yes:

As a matter of fairness, the rich should pay more to support government programs—they simply have more and should contribute more. In the past, the rich *have* paid more. For example, in 1963, the top income bracket paid 91 percent in taxes. But now, the rich pay relatively little of their huge incomes in taxes. Since 2001, tax cuts have resulted in a reduction of tax rates on the richest taxpayers from 33 percent of their incomes to less than 26.7 percent. There were reductions in taxes placed on individual wages, earnings from investments, and corporate earnings, all of this resulting in more than $197 billion in tax cuts for the richest Americans. In addition, there was a repeal of the estate tax, which Congress is now considering making permanent, and which allows the rich to simply transfer their wealth to their children. What all of this means is that the richest are getting richer, even as poor and middle-income people become worse off, and federal, state, and local deficits are reducing governmental services. The richest Americans like to talk about how they accumulated their wealth through hard work, but as Mike Lapham of the organization Responsible Wealth put it, "It takes a village to raise a billionaire." Much of this wealth comes directly from the public's investment in research and development—we allow these people to use public money like tax deductions and government grants to finance their empire-building. Ultimately, the huge gaps between the richest and everyone else will destabilize our republic and undermine democratic rule. In the interests of fairness and the survival of our democracy, we should use tax policy to redistribute wealth more equitably.

Should our taxation policies be more progressive?–(Cont'd)

No:

We already have a progressive tax system, where those with more resources do contribute much more than those with less wealth. Consider that the top 5 percent of income earners pay more than 50 percent of the taxes, while the bottom 50 percent of income earners pay less than 5 percent of the taxes. Put another way, those who earn $200,000 or more each year, this is roughly 1 percent of all taxpayers, contribute 31 percent of the revenue, while those who earn less than $25,000, this is about 55 percent of the population, shoulder only 6 percent of the tax burden. We have never embraced the regressive tax policies adopted by other industrialized nations, but instead have always had tax laws that redistributed wealth from those with more resources to those with fewer resources. For example, more than fifty industrialized nations use the value-added tax (VAT) to generate revenue. The VAT taxes a product at each stage of production, and like sales taxes, is highly regressive, because it places a larger proportionate burden on the poor, who tend to spend much more of their income on goods. Instead, we use a more progressive tax system that imposes a much greater burden on the wealthy. This is acceptable, but we need to consider that imposing too great a burden on those with more resources is ultimately bad for the economy. A steeply progressive system harms the economy for two reasons: first, it diminishes the overall tax base, and sharply reduces the number of people paying taxes; and second, it eliminates many of the resources needed for new investment and economic growth. This kind of system interferes not only with economic freedom, by undermining the right of those with resources to make decisions about how to dispose of these resources, but also hurts the whole population, by stymieing innovation and expansion of the economy.

Economic Rights and Freedoms—Freedom of Contract and the American Worker

Our law reinforces class inequalities in a number of ways. As we've already discussed, equality is defined in such a way that all people must be treated the same—the law is neutral and wealth or class-based distinctions are presumed to be valid. In addition, our government has been less than enthusiastic about redistributing wealth through either transfers or taxes. Class inequality is also a function of our society's view of freedom and of the economic rights of individuals. The transformation of our economy from

www ▶ ▶ ▶

Lochner v. New York
1905 Supreme Court case that struck down New York State law limiting the number of hours a baker could work; the Court argued that the law violated the freedom of bakers to freely contract for the sale of their labor

primarily agricultural to industrial in the late 1800s created serious dislocations for workers. Throughout this period, there was little regulation of the workplace. Workers were expected to toil for long hours, often working eighteen hours a day for seven days a week. Children were employed in factories under working conditions that were harmful to their development, and workplace accidents were commonplace. In the late 1800s and early 1900s, some states attempted to pass laws that either limited the hours that a worker could work or established work hygiene rules to reduce the number of accidents. One of these states was New York, which passed a number of laws that limited workers' hours and attempted to regulate workplace conditions. These laws were challenged in several cases heard by the U.S. Supreme Court in the early 1900s. One of the most important of these cases was the 1905 case *Lochner v. New York.* In this case, the Court struck down a state law that limited the number of hours that a baker could work, finding that this law violated the right of workers to freely sell their labor.

In *Lochner,* the justices treated workers and employers as equals. They assumed that bakers had the choice about what their employment agreement

Industrialization created a demand for factory labor that was met in a number of ways, among these, through exploitation of child labor.

would look like and that they were able to choose or not choose the conditions of their employment—an interesting view of the employment relationship. The Court ultimately held that the state regulation could not stand because it interfered with the freedom of contract that was enshrined in the due process clause. When they made this decision, the justices gave this freedom of contract constitutional protection. In doing so, the Court essentially said that government didn't have a role to play in the employment relationship and that government couldn't craft laws that sought to protect the employee against employer excesses. While many labor laws establishing maximum hours and minimum wages were ultimately upheld by the Court, beginning with a series of cases decided in the late 1930s, the Court's view of workers as the equals of their employers continues to be a part of our law.

In fact, American law approaches the employment relationship in a fairly simplistic way. It assumes that the employee and employer are independent and can choose the conditions of employment. We assume that if we eliminate what we consider to be the most blatantly unfair practices, like race or ethnic discrimination in employment, that the employment relationship will need little more tinkering. Many American workers and the society as a whole are suspicious of unions. Even more importantly, our trade practices and regional and international trade agreements have undercut union support and membership, which has fluctuated, often quite dramatically. At its high point in the 1950s nearly 40 percent of the workforce was unionized. By 2002, however, only about 13 percent of the workforce, or 16 million workers, belonged to unions. The decline in union membership has been the result of a number of factors, among these, a sharp decrease in the number of people employed in manufacturing, which has been the traditional field for unionization, along with steep increases in employment in the service sector and white-collar jobs, which are typically not unionized. These economic shifts in the economy have occurred worldwide, but the declines in union membership have been steepest in the United States. In fact, the United States has one of the very lowest rates of union membership in the world today.

Some analysts argue that the decline in the strength of the union movement is the result, not only of larger changes in the economy, but of a deep-seated mistrust of unions. Whenever workers have attempted to engage in collective action, their actions were blocked by employers and courts until relatively recently. Until well into the 1930s, employees who attempted to create unions or to join unions were often charged with conspiracy. An 1827 jury in Philadelphia convicted tailors who had attempted to form a union of conspiracy and concluded that their actions had resulted in an injury to trade. Collective activity like strikes or slowdowns were harshly but effectively countered by employers and law enforcement officers. Not until the U.S. Supreme Court let stand the 1935 **National Labor Relations Act (NLRA)**, also known as the Wagner Act, were workers given the right to engage in collective action and to form unions. Ultimately, unionization

National Labor Relations Act (NLRA)

law passed by Congress in 1935 that established workers' right to engage in collective action and to form unions

www ▶ ▶ ▶

was permitted because lawmakers saw that it contributed to economic progress. When unions were first tied to organized crime and criminal activities, which began as early as the 1940s and continued well into the 1980s, suspicions among politicians and the public reemerged. Many Americans today question whether unions can really contribute to economic efficiency or better the working conditions of employees. For example, when the Major League Baseball Players Association considered striking in 2002 to protest changes in work rules, including attempts by owners to limit the ability of players to become free agents and to impose mandatory drug testing, there was little public support.

The public's lukewarm support was in many ways understandable. Our culture values individual initiative and expects that merit will enable individuals to move up in terms of social class. We continue to be very suspicious of collective activity, and this skepticism is reflected in the fact that more than one-third of the states have adopted **"right-to-work" laws** that enable workers to choose whether they want to join a union that is already in place in an employer's workplace. Before these laws were passed, workers usually didn't have a choice about whether to join the union when they were hired. Many workplaces were **"closed shops,"** meaning that union membership was a condition of employment. In right-to-work states where workplaces are "open shops," union strength is much diminished. Those who argue in favor of open shops make much the same argument that was made in the 1905 *Lochner* v. *New York*—that is, that individuals should have the opportunity to choose their working conditions, and this includes eliminating the "middle man," here, the labor union.

www ▶ ▶ ▶

"right-to-work" laws

state laws that allow workers to decide whether they want to join the union that operates in their workplace

www ▶ ▶ ▶

"closed shops"

workplaces where all employees must join the union

SUMMARY

This chapter has explored the relationship between social class and the law. Scholars in the law and economics school contend that law is and should be used to maximize wealth in the society; CLS and Marxist scholars, argue that law is a tool used by the economic elite to reinforce their power and control. In this chapter, we noted the increasing stratification and widening gap between the wealthiest and poorest in the United States. This stratification has resulted in huge disparities in wealth, as well as in educational, housing, and health care resources. We also talked about how our popular culture and belief in individual merit is manifest in our laws, and how our laws reinforce class stratification. We looked at three areas of the law and talked about how the law actually buttresses class distinctions. Specifically, we discussed how equality is defined in civil rights law, the role of government in redistributing wealth through tax law and laws governing wealth transfer, and the laws protecting our economic rights and liberties. Our law operates according to certain assumptions about the role of the individual in the economic system and assumes that economic efficiency should be the paramount value in this system. It could be argued that elements of both law and economics and CLS and Marxist legal theory are apparent in our legal system. On the one hand, our laws do make our market stronger and more efficient, at least by some measures. But on the other hand, these same laws do little to bridge the ever-expanding gap between the richest and poorest in our society.

SUGGESTED READING

Barbara Ehrenreich, *Nickel and Dimed: On (Not) Getting By in America* (Owl Press, 2002). In this important book, the author goes undercover, working as an unskilled laborer for poverty wages. Ehrenreich explores what happened when women were shoved off welfare after passage of welfare reform laws in the early 1990s and provides an in-depth look at how welfare law actually affects the lowest-wage workers in the United States.

Steve Fraser and Gary Gerstle, editors, *Ruling America: A History of Wealth and Power in a Democracy* (Harvard University Press, 2005). This is a survey of American history from the vantage point of class. It looks at how class and class conflict have played out in the United States from the colonial era until the present, and it examines the seemingly contradictory relationship between democratic rule and class stratification.

John Steele Gordon, *An Empire of Wealth: The Epic History of American Economic Power* (Harper Collins, 2004). This study examines how the American economy functions, examining key fig-ures and eras in economic development. The author argues that the American economy has both good and bad qualities—it is innovative and dynamic on the one hand, and the catalyst for tremendous inequalities, on the other.

Marc J. Hetherington, *Why Trust Matters: Declining Political Trust and the Demise of American Liberalism* (Princeton University Press, 2004). This book tries to explain the turn toward conservatism in American politics since the 1960s. The author claims that a decline in the public's trust of public officials explains this shift. He focuses on this shift's negative impact on redistributive taxation and transfer policies.

Mark Robert Rank, *One Nation, Underprivileged: Why American Poverty Affects Us All* (Oxford University Press, 2004). This book explores the impact of class stratification and poverty on American society and argues that the ideology of individualism does not fit well into the modern economy. He challenges the notion that the poor deserve to be poor, arguing in favor of a structural explanation for poverty.

ACTIVE LEARNING

1. To determine what your social class is, you may want to go to either http://www.socialclass.org/ or http://www.pbs.org/peoplelikeus/games/chintz.html. Are you surprised at what these games or surveys suggest about your social class? Did you think that this *was* your social class?

2. Read one or two of the school financing cases decided by the state courts. While *San Antonio Independent School District* v. *Rodriguez* foreclosed use of the federal equal protection clause for school finance cases, some challenges based on state equal protection clauses have been successful. Why have they been successful? What was different about these cases? For starters, see *Abbott* v. *Burke* (New Jersey), *Serrano* v. *Priest* (California), and *Tomblin* v. *Gainer* (West Virginia). For a complete list of these cases from 1970–1999, go to http://nces.ed.gov/edfin/pdf/2003020tab3_3.pdf.

CHAPTER 14

Law and Medicine

Biotechnology and medicine are critical sectors in the U.S. economy. In this chapter, we examine the impact of lawmaking on medicine and biotechnology. Specifically, we look at the role of physicians in the implementation of laws, the regulation of research and development, and the drug-approval process. The law in all three areas has changed dramatically as it attempted to respond to important developments in law and medicine. In Chapter 4, we talked about social norms and the evolution of legal systems. In particular, that chapter discussed Emil Durkheim's concepts of social norms as they were understood in the late 1800s and early 1900s. Durkheim believed that law is the expression of the norms of a society and that in a modern legal system, the goal of law is to compensate the individual for harm suffered and damages inflicted. According to Durkheim, laws are based on **social facts,** *that is, those ways of thinking, acting and feeling that are shared by the collective and have coercive power over the individual. Social facts and norms are helpful concepts for understanding the relationship between law and medicine.*

Although lawmaking in this area has undergone an important shift over the last several decades, clear norms continue to underlie our approach to this field. Perhaps most importantly, physicians are viewed as professionals who pursue or should pursue the interest of their patients. The doctor-patient relationship has protection in both law and medical practice, and the physician's primary duty under both law and medical ethics is to act in the best interest of his or her patient. This belief in the sanctity of the doctor-patient relationship is a social fact, and it animates much of our law in this area. This is not to say that there have been no changes in how our law treats physicians or on the obligations imposed upon them. Until the 1950s, research and development were not well regulated, and physicians practiced medicine with little governmental regulation. It was assumed that doctors would police themselves as a profession. There was also far less regulation of the development process for drugs and treatments. In the last several decades, however, issues relating to medical practice and to biotechnology have moved to the forefront of public debate, and the physician's obligation, both to his or her patient and to the larger society, has moved front and center.

DOCTORS, PATIENTS, AND THE LAW

American Medical Association

national organization of physicians that has played an important role in many medical-legal debates, among these, the debate about how to regulate abortion. The AMA's role in the regulation of abortion began with its campaign in the mid- to late 1800s to institute state abortion bans

The **American Medical Association** has had a prominent role in American society for more than one hundred years. Throughout this time, lawmakers who were contemplating regulations that pertained to medicine, science, and biotechnology have turned to physicians for their expertise and have often relied heavily on groups like the AMA. In at least three currently controversial areas, physicians have played a central role in the legal debate. In the controversies over abortion, aid in dying, and the use of medicinal marijuana, the law has conferred certain responsibilities, and a certain authority, on physicians. In these areas and others, American law has made the physician the central gatekeeper; that is, it has bestowed on physicians the responsibility for determining patient access to medical treatment.

Abortion

As we discussed in Chapter 12, the AMA and other physician groups played a pivotal role in the creation of abortion bans in the mid- to late 1800s. In fact, many of the abortion laws in place until the 1973 *Roe v. Wade* decision allowed a medical exception. Under this exception, women whose continued pregnancy endangered their lives or health could obtain an abortion. Physicians had the responsibility for determining whether the medical exception applied and thus served as gatekeepers. Even the *Roe* decision envisioned that physicians would continue to play an important gatekeeping role.

Under *Roe*, physicians were expected to provide information to women about the abortion procedure, and they ultimately had to determine how pregnancy and abortion would affect women's health. Many abortion laws passed since *Roe* effectively limit the physician's discretion. For example, many laws require that physicians provide their patients with specific descriptions of fetal development and of the abortion procedure and that they obtain parental consent before performing an abortion on a minor. Laws also now regulate some aspects of the abortion procedure—for example, federal law now bans what is termed the "partial-birth abortion," and many state laws regulate the disposal of fetal remains. Even with these

www ▶ ▶ ▶

limitations, however, physicians continue to play an important role in providing access to abortion. Perhaps most importantly, physicians can decide to opt out completely and refuse to provide any abortion services at all. This has happened in many areas of the country, as doctors have decided against providing abortion services. As a result, some states and counties face a severe shortage of physicians who will perform abortions.

Physicians also continue to be responsible for determining whether second- and third-trimester abortions are necessary to protect the life or health of the mother. Many state legislatures who opted to regulate abortion in the wake of *Roe* have severely limited access to abortion in these two trimesters. Courts have required that these states provide an exception to their abortion bans where the women's life and health is in serious jeopardy. This exception provides physicians with significant discretion in determining whether these abortions should go forward. For physicians, the downside has been that they are liable if a court determines that their medical judgment is incorrect. In other words, if a physician permits a second-trimester abortion to proceed and a court determines that the assessment that the procedure is necessary to save the life of the woman or protect her from serious and irreversible harm is incorrect, it can find the doctor legally liable. Moreover, in many states, the physician has a responsibility to protect the life, not only of the woman, but of the viable fetus, as well. If a fetus reaches viability, which happens at about the twenty-eighth week of pregnancy, many states mandate that the physician take steps to save his or her life. The abortion law in place in Ohio is typical of these regulations, and if you want to review this law, you can view it on our webpage. In an important sense, the physician serves, not only the patient seeking the abortion, but the fetus, as well.

Physician Aid in Dying

physician aid in dying
the practice by physicians of providing death-hastening medications, usually to terminally ill patients who have significant pain and suffering; barred in most states by laws that make it a crime to assist another in committing suicide, but permitted in some states in certain narrowly defined circumstances

Physicians also play a central role in the debate about **physician aid in dying**, and in fact, the debate about euthanasia has shifted in recent years to focus on the right of terminally ill individuals to receive physician aid in dying. In two cases decided in 1997, *Vacco v. Quill* and *Washington v. Glucksberg,* the U.S. Supreme Court ruled that state laws that banned physician aid in dying did not violate the constitutional rights of those who seek this assistance. Doctors and terminally ill patients in Washington and New York had sued their states, arguing that bans against assisted suicide violated two provisions of the U.S. Constitution. First, they claimed that when terminally ill persons enduring significant pain and suffering chose to hasten their death, this choice was constitutionally protected, and states couldn't impose an "undue burden" on this choice by making it difficult or impossible to

Vacco v. Quill and Washington v. Glucksberg

two cases in which the Supreme Court ruled that state laws that banned physician aid in dying did not violate the constitutional rights of those who seek this assistance

Death with Dignity Act

1997 Oregon law passed by voter initiative that allows individuals in Oregon who are terminally ill to access physician aid in dying

Ashcroft v. Oregon

case decided by a federal appeals court that upheld the Oregon Death with Dignity Act and struck down a policy directive issued by U.S. Attorney General John Ashcroft that would have barred doctors from using prescriptions to assist individuals in hastening their deaths under the federal Controlled Substances Act

exercise the choice. Second, the doctors and patients claimed that since states allowed individuals to refuse treatment, they had to also permit aid in dying for that group of individuals who are facing imminent death. Since Washington and New York didn't permit this choice, the parties argued that they violated the constitutional equal protection guarantee. The U.S. Supreme Court rejected both challenges, arguing that the U.S. Constitution didn't forbid states from enacting assisted-suicide bans, and that states had significant leeway in regulating aid in dying.

Voters in Oregon responded to the Court's decision quickly and decisively by using a voter initiative to pass the 1997 **Death with Dignity Act**. A physician may help individuals in Oregon who are suffering from a terminal illness by prescribing medication to hasten death. To access aid in dying, the individual must initiate a written request for the medication and two physicians must attest that the individual has been informed about his or her illness and that he or she is mentally competent to make this decision. This request must be witnessed by at least two additional people. The actual form that individuals in Oregon use to trigger the request for physician aid in dying is shown in Box 14.1. Under the Oregon law, the doctor's responsibility is extensive: she or he must ensure that the person who seeks aid in dying has given informed consent after having been informed about a wide range of issues, including his or her diagnosis, prognosis, and alternatives like hospice and palliative care. The physician must also meet extensive record-keeping and reporting requirements and may be liable for any failure to do so. Between 1998 and 2004, 171 people were reported to have used medication to hasten their deaths. Physicians have a central role in the implementation of the Oregon law—they not only serve as gatekeepers, limiting access to only those terminally patients whom they consider competent, but they are also the primary source of information about how the law is being implemented. While individual patients must swallow the medicine on their own, the physicians are on the frontlines providing access to it.

Perhaps recognizing the centrality of physicians to the Death with Dignity Act, U.S. Attorney General John Ashcroft issued a policy directive that interpreted the federal Controlled Substances Act (CSA) as banning use of prescription medicines to hasten death. The CSA requires that medicines be used for a "legitimate medical purpose," and Attorney General Ashcroft claimed that hastening death did not meet this requirement. He threatened that physicians who continued to use medicines to hasten death would not be allowed to prescribe any controlled substances. He also warned that physicians would be held criminally liable for providing aid in dying. An Oregon federal district court blocked the enforcement of this order, and the lawsuit is now pending in the Court of Appeals for the Ninth Circuit. In the 2004 case *Ashcroft v. Oregon,* the Ninth Circuit Court of Appeals upheld

LAW IN ACTION

Box 14.1 **Oregon Death with Dignity Act**

Under the Oregon Death with Dignity Act, a request for a medication as authorized by ORS 127.800 to 127.897 shall be in substantially the following form as follows:

REQUEST FOR MEDICATION
TO END MY LIFE IN A HUMANE
AND DIGNIFIED MANNER

I, _____, am an adult of sound mind.

I am suffering from _____, which my attending physician has determined is a terminal disease and which has been medically confirmed by a consulting physician.

I have been fully informed of my diagnosis, prognosis, the nature of medication to be prescribed and potential associated risks, the expected result, and the feasible alternatives, including comfort care, hospice care and pain control.

I request that my attending physician prescribe medication that will end my life in a humane and dignified manner.

INITIAL ONE:

_____ I have informed my family of my decision and taken their opinions into consideration.

_____ I have decided not to inform my family of my decision.

_____ I have no family to inform of my decision.

I understand that I have the right to rescind this request at any time.

I understand the full import of this request and I expect to die when I take the medication to be prescribed. I further understand that although most deaths occur within three hours, my death may take longer and my physician has counseled me about this possibility.

I make this request voluntarily and without reservation, and I accept full moral responsibility for my actions.

Signed: _____

Dated: _____

DECLARATION OF WITNESSES

We declare that the person signing this request:
(a) Is personally known to us or has provided proof of identity;
(b) Signed this request in our presence;
(c) Appears to be of sound mind and not under duress, fraud or undue influence;
(d) Is not a patient for whom either of us is attending physician.

_____ Witness 1/Date

_____ Witness 2/Date

NOTE: One witness shall not be a relative (by blood, marriage or adoption) of the person signing this request, shall not be entitled to any portion of the person's estate on death and shall not own, operate or be employed at a health care facility where the person is a patient or resident. If the patient is an inpatient at a health care facility, one of the witnesses shall be an individual designated by the facility.

[1995 c.3 s.6.01; 1999 c.423 s.11]

www ▶ ▶ ▶

the law, finding that Attorney General Ashcroft had overstepped his authority in trying to block physician aid in dying in Oregon. The court held that states, not the federal government, have the principal authority to regulate medicine and that if Congress wanted to regulate aid in dying, it would need to pass legislation.

Medical Marijuana

www ▶ ▶ ▶

war on drugs

program initiated in the early 1970s that targets all aspects of the production, distribution, and use of illegal drugs

Controlled Substances Act

federal law that prohibits the sale and distribution of marijuana across state lines

www ▶ ▶ ▶

Compassionate Use Act

initiative approved by California voters in 1996 that allowed patients and their primary caregivers to possess or cultivate marijuana without being penalized under state drug laws

www ▶ ▶ ▶

For nearly five thousand years, cannabis, the plant from which marijuana is derived, has been used to ease suffering and to facilitate recovery in cultures worldwide. There is evidence of medical use dating back to 2737 BCE, when Chinese emperor Shen Neng began prescribing the drug to treat a variety of ailments, including gout, rheumatism, and malaria. It was also widely used to treat pain and protect against and treat infections. As other drugs were developed, cannabis was used less, and in 1937, Congress joined a number of states in banning the use of marijuana. The **war on drugs**, which began in earnest in the early 1970s, targeted all drugs but focused especially on marijuana because many drug warriors claimed that use of this drug inevitably spiraled into use of more serious and addictive drugs. One of the laws that initiated this war was the 1970 **Controlled Substances Act**, which prohibits the sale and distribution of marijuana across state lines. This law and its state counterparts have lately been under intense fire, as advocates have fought to be able to use marijuana for medical purposes. These advocates, many of them physicians and individuals with medical illnesses, argue that marijuana is an effective drug for treating many illnesses, including multiple sclerosis. They also argue that marijuana alleviates pain and nausea, which are often associated with cancer and cancer treatments. Despite these arguments, the federal Drug Enforcement Agency continues to classify marijuana as a Schedule I drug, meaning that it has no medical use.

Advocates of medical marijuana have recently brought their case to the states, and in particular, to voters, and in 1996, California voters approved the **Compassionate Use Act**, which established that state drug laws would not "apply to a patient, or to a patient's primary caregiver, who possesses or cultivates marijuana . . . upon the written or oral recommendation or approval of a physician." Eleven other states and many municipalities have joined California in allowing physicians to prescribe marijuana for certain medical conditions or treatments. In many other states, researchers are permitted to study the therapeutic effects of the drug. Perhaps ironically, the drug Marinol, a cannabis-derived medicine that is administered in tablet form, rather than being smoked, is widely available to physicians, who use it to treat nausea and stimulate appetite, especially for patients with chronic illness. Like the debates about abortion and aid in dying, physicians and medical personnel play an important role in the medicinal marijuana

www ▶ ▶ ▶

Raich et al. v. Ashcroft
case currently before
the U.S. Supreme Court
that raises the question
of whether the federal
Controlled Substances
Act prohibits the
cultivation of medical
marijuana in California

www ▶ ▶ ▶

controversy. In all states and municipalities, there must be some assessment by a member of the medical community that use of the drug is therapeutic and aimed at treatment of a specific illness.

A case currently before the U.S. Supreme Court, *Raich et al. v. Ashcroft,* tests the limits of existing drug laws. At issue in this case is the conviction of a California woman under the federal Controlled Substance Act for cultivation of medical marijuana. She claims that the Controlled Substances Act only applies to drugs that enter interstate commerce and that her home-grown farm only cultivates the drug for local distribution. The Ninth Circuit Court of Appeals agreed with her, finding that the cultivation, use, and distribution of marijuana for medical purposes was a state activity and governed by state law alone.

Physicians are granted a prominent role and wide latitude in making treatment decisions in all three of the areas we have discussed: abortion, physician aid in dying, and medicinal marijuana. The norm that permits this latitude has animated lawmaking. While many pro-life advocates argue that abortion involves a woman's self-interested choice about whether to continue her pregnancy, laws are framed less in terms of women's liberty rights and much more in terms of medical practice. *Roe v. Wade* is still good law, and because of this, states and the federal government must recognize that there is some liberty or privacy interest in the abortion right. Perhaps because of this, lawmakers have turned their attention to the medical procedure itself. These laws regulate the abortion procedure but continue to recognize the rights and obligations of the physician. In fact, the only federal law that has regulated the abortion procedure itself, the so-called partial-birth-abortion ban, has been struck down by federal courts because it does not sufficiently protect women when their lives are endangered by continuing a pregnancy, a judgment that has historically been left to her physician. In 2004, federal district courts in New York, San Francisco, and Nebraska struck down the 2003 federal Partial Birth Abortion Ban. Similarly, the issue of euthanasia or aid in dying, which burst on the public scene in the early 1980s and has remained there since, has morphed into a debate about whether physicians can aid in hastening the death of their patients. While lawmakers are very reluctant to say that terminally ill persons have a constitutional right to die, they have been more willing to consider the rights and obligations that a physician may have to aid a patient who is suffering and in great pain. And finally, the larger debate about legalizing marijuana, on the fringe of American politics since the Controlled Substances Act of 1970 utilized its ban against marijuana use and distribution to kick off its war on drugs, has become a much narrower debate about the compassionate use of the drug to treat suffering. We believe that physicians have an important role in our society and that they act primarily out of concern about their patients. This social fact, as Durkheim would have noted, is very much a part of our social order and at the core of our laws.

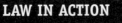

LAW IN ACTION

The Regulation of Medical Marijuana

RAICH ET AL. V. ASHCROFT U.S. SUPREME COURT, 2005

Alberto R. Gonzales, Attorney General, *et al.*, Petitioners *v.* Angel McClary Raich *et al.* June 6, 2005

Justice Stevens delivered the opinion of the Court.

California is one of at least nine States that authorize the use of marijuana for medicinal purposes. The question presented in this case is whether the power vested in Congress by Article I, §8, of the Constitution "[t]o make all Laws which shall be necessary and proper for carrying into Execution" its authority to "regulate Commerce with foreign Nations, and among the several States" includes the power to prohibit the local cultivation and use of marijuana in compliance with California law.

California has been a pioneer in the regulation of marijuana. In 1913, California was one of the first States to prohibit the sale and possession of marijuana, and at the end of the century, California became the first State to authorize limited use of the drug for medicinal purposes. In 1996, California voters passed Proposition 215, now codified as the Compassionate Use Act of 1996. The proposition was designed to ensure that "seriously ill" residents of the State have access to marijuana for medical purposes, and to encourage Federal and State Governments to take steps towards ensuring the safe and affordable distribution of the drug to patients in need. The Act creates an exemption from criminal prosecution for physicians, as well as for patients and primary caregivers who possess or cultivate marijuana for medicinal purposes with the recommendation or approval of a physician. A "pri-

mary caregiver" is a person who has consistently assumed responsibility for the housing, health, or safety of the patient.

Respondents Angel Raich and Diane Monson are California residents who suffer from a variety of serious medical conditions and have sought to avail themselves of medical marijuana pursuant to the terms of the Compassionate Use Act. They are being treated by licensed, board-certified family practitioners, who have concluded, after prescribing a host of conventional medicines to treat respondents' conditions and to alleviate their associated symptoms, that marijuana is the only drug available that provides effective treatment. Both women have been using marijuana as a medication for several years pursuant to their doctors' recommendation, and both rely heavily on cannabis to function on a daily basis. Indeed, Raich's physician believes that forgoing cannabis treatments would certainly cause Raich excruciating pain and could very well prove fatal.

Respondent Monson cultivates her own marijuana, and ingests the drug in a variety of ways including smoking and using a vaporizer. Respondent Raich, by contrast, is unable to cultivate her own, and thus relies on two caregivers, litigating as "John Does," to provide her with locally grown marijuana at no charge. . . .

On August 15, 2002, county deputy sheriffs and agents from the federal Drug Enforcement

LAW IN ACTION–(CONT'D)

Administration (DEA) came to Monson's home. After a thorough investigation, the county officials concluded that her use of marijuana was entirely lawful as a matter of California law. Nevertheless, after a 3-hour standoff, the federal agents seized and destroyed all six of her cannabis plants.

Respondents thereafter brought this action against the Attorney General of the United States and the head of the DEA seeking injunctive and declaratory relief prohibiting the enforcement of the federal Controlled Substances Act (CSA) to the extent it prevents them from possessing, obtaining, or manufacturing cannabis for their personal medical use. . . . Respondents claimed that enforcing the CSA against them would violate the Commerce Clause, the Due Process Clause of the Fifth Amendment, the Ninth and Tenth Amendments of the Constitution, and the doctrine of medical necessity. . . .

The question before us . . . is not whether it is wise to enforce the statute in these circumstances; rather, it is whether Congress' power to regulate interstate markets for medicinal substances encompasses the portions of those markets that are supplied with drugs produced and consumed locally. Well-settled law controls our answer. The CSA is a valid exercise of federal power, even as applied to the troubling facts of this case. . . .

Marijuana itself was not significantly regulated by the Federal Government until 1937 when accounts of marijuana's addictive qualities and physiological effects, paired with dissatisfaction with enforcement efforts at state and local levels, prompted Congress to pass the Marihuana Tax Act. . . . Then in 1970, after declaration of the national "war on drugs," federal drug policy

underwent a significant transformation . . . [P]rompted by a perceived need to consolidate the growing number of piecemeal drug laws and to enhance federal drug enforcement powers, Congress enacted the Comprehensive Drug Abuse Prevention and Control Act.

Title II of that Act, the CSA repealed most of the earlier antidrug laws in favor of a comprehensive regime to combat the international and interstate traffic in illicit drugs. The main objectives of the CSA were to conquer drug abuse and to control the legitimate and illegitimate traffic in controlled substances. . . . In enacting the CSA, Congress classified marijuana as a Schedule I drug. . . . Schedule I drugs are categorized as such because of their high potential for abuse, lack of any accepted medical use, and absence of any accepted safety for use in medically supervised treatment. By classifying marijuana as a Schedule I drug, as opposed to listing it on a lesser schedule, the manufacture, distribution, or possession of marijuana became a criminal offense. . . . Despite considerable efforts to reschedule marijuana, it remains a Schedule I drug.

. . . [R]espondents' challenge is actually quite limited; they argue that the CSA's categorical prohibition of the manufacture and possession of marijuana as applied to the intrastate manufacture and possession of marijuana for medical purposes pursuant to California law exceeds Congress' authority under the Commerce Clause.

In assessing the validity of congressional regulation, none of our Commerce Clause cases can be viewed in isolation. [There are] . . . three general categories of regulation in which Congress is authorized to engage under its commerce power. First, Congress can regulate the channels of

LAW IN ACTION–(CONT'D)

interstate commerce. Second, Congress has authority to regulate and protect the instrumentalities of interstate commerce, and persons or things in interstate commerce. Third, Congress has the power to regulate activities that substantially affect interstate commerce. Only the third category is implicated in the case at hand.

Our case law firmly establishes Congress' power to regulate purely local activities that are part of an economic "class of activities" that have a substantial effect on interstate commerce . . . (*Wickard* v. *Filburn*, 317 U. S. 111, 128-129 [1942]). As we stated in *Wickard*, "even if appellee's activity be local and though it may not be regarded as commerce, it may still, whatever its nature, be reached by Congress if it exerts a substantial economic effect on interstate commerce." *Id.*, at 125. . . . *Wickard* thus establishes that Congress can regulate purely intrastate activity that is not itself "commercial," in that it is not produced for sale, if it concludes that failure to regulate that class of activity would undercut the regulation of the interstate market in that commodity.

The similarities between this case and *Wickard* are striking. Like the farmer in *Wickard*, respondents are cultivating, for home consumption, a fungible commodity for which there is an established, albeit illegal, interstate market. . . . In *Wickard*, we had no difficulty concluding that Congress had a rational basis for believing that, when viewed in the aggregate, leaving home-consumed wheat outside the regulatory scheme would have a substantial influence on price and market conditions. Here too, Congress had a rational basis for concluding that leaving home-consumed marijuana outside federal control would similarly affect price and market conditions. . . . In both cases, the regulation is squarely within Congress' commerce power because production of the commodity meant for home consumption, be it wheat or marijuana, has a substantial effect on supply and demand in the national market for that commodity . . . That the regulation ensnares some purely intrastate activity is of no moment . . .

The exemption for cultivation by patients and caregivers can only increase the supply of marijuana in the California market. The likelihood that all such production will promptly terminate when patients recover or will precisely match the patients' medical needs during their convalescence seems remote; whereas the danger that excesses will satisfy some of the admittedly enormous demand for recreational use seems obvious. Moreover, that the national and international narcotics trade has thrived in the face of vigorous criminal enforcement efforts suggests that no small number of unscrupulous people will make use of the California exemptions to serve their commercial ends whenever it is feasible to do so. Taking into account the fact that California is only one of at least nine States to have authorized the medical use of marijuana . . . Congress could have rationally concluded that the aggregate impact on the national market of all the transactions exempted from federal supervision is unquestionably substantial. . . .

Under the present state of the law . . . the judgment of the Court of Appeals must be vacated. The case is remanded for further proceedings consistent with this opinion.

It is so ordered.

MEDICAL RESEARCH AND DEVELOPMENT AND THE LAW

Abortion, aid in dying, and medicinal marijuana are all good examples of policy areas where laws privilege the practice of medicine and where physicians are assumed to be acting primarily out of concern for their patients' best interests. In the areas of medical research and informed consent, however, laws reflect our concerns or fears that physicians and researchers are motivated by more self-interested motives. Perhaps because of this, medical research and development is an area that has been subject to much greater scrutiny by governmental bodies, especially since the 1970s. Extensive regulations govern the development of new research protocols and the investigation and approval of new drugs, and governmental control over these sectors is fairly intense. The public, or at least certain interest groups, have played an increasingly important role in the development of new drugs, and it is likely that this will continue well into the future. If law is an index of the moral conditions in a society, as Durkheim claimed, then our increasing regulation of this field reflects real concern about the conduct of research and development in the field of medicine.

Medical Research and Informed Consent

Tuskegee Syphilis Study

a study of untreated syphilis, conducted between 1932 and 1972, in which poor black men were not informed that they were test subjects and were not receiving treatment of their disease; public outcry against this study resulted in more protective regulations governing research on human subjects

National Research Act

federal statute passed in the wake of the outcry over the Tuskegee Syphilis Study that required all federally funded research projects involving human subjects to be approved by an institutional review board

Many regulations affecting medical research were adopted in the last fifty to sixty years, as regulators and the public learned of egregious practices involving research subjects. The Nuremberg Trials conducted after World War II brought to light horrific abuses by Nazi doctors who conducted medical research on human subjects. Much closer to home, a federally funded program studied the effects of syphilis on black men but withheld treatment. During the course of this study, which was known as the **Tuskegee Syphilis Study** and lasted from 1932 to 1972, poor black men believed that they were receiving effective treatment for their disease. In reality, however, treatment was deliberately withheld, so that researchers could study the disease's progression in those who were untreated. These men were never informed that they were actually research subjects and not patients, and many of these men suffered and died from the disease, despite the fact that penicillin was a widely available and effective treatment for syphilis.

In the wake of the Nuremberg Trials and the Tuskegee Syphilis Study, the U.S. Congress passed the **National Research Act**, which mandates that all federally funded trials involving human subjects be approved by an institutional review board or IRB. The National Commission for the Protection of Human Subjects of Biomedical and Behavioral Research issued the Belmont Report, which stated that all human research should be guided by the principles of justice, beneficence, and respect for all persons. Before someone

THE LAW IN POPULAR CULTURE

Miss Evers' Boys

This film depicts the relationship between black men who are subjects of the Tuskegee Syphilis Study and their nurse. The men, who are mostly poor and illiterate, are told that they are being treated for the disease, but they are receiving only placebos so that the medical establishment can study the effects of untreated syphilis on this group. Their nurse, Eunice Evers, shown with a patient above, knows that the men are not being treated and must provide comfort without revealing that they are being denied an effective cure.

---

informed consent

a central tenet of medical research; requires that a person consent to participate in clinical research, meaning that they be fully informed of the risks and benefits of clinical research

`www` ▶ ▶ ▶

can participate in clinical research, they must give **informed consent**; that is, they must be informed of the risks and possible benefits of treatment; in addition, the benefits of not receiving treatment must be described. Researchers must assess whether study participants understand these risks and benefits and whether they are capable of giving consent. The Food and Drug Administration's website lists the requirements for informed consent in experiments involving human subjects. The U.S. Department of Health and Human Services recognizes that some groups of people may be less able to consent to a research protocol and more susceptible to coercion or undue influence. Among these groups are children, prisoners, pregnant women, the mentally disabled, or those who are "economically or educationally disadvantaged." For some of these groups, there are specific rules that researchers must follow before enrolling participants. For prisoners, the federal rules require that the research involve questions that relate to the effects of incarceration; for children, the research must either involve only minimal risk or provide some direct benefit or benefit to other children with the same or similar illnesses. It is notable, however, that there are no additional rules for informed consent of those who are poor or uneducated.

Drug-Approval Process

Informed consent is of central importance in medical research, in large part because the development of new drugs and medical devices depends on human testing. The Food and Drug Administration was created to administer the 1938 Food, Drug and Cosmetic Act. Early on, the FDA focused on ensuring that misbranded, dangerous, or adulterated goods were not sold in interstate commerce. Over time, much of the FDA's work has become focused on the approval of new drugs and medical devices.

The process for approval of new prescription drugs and medical devices is cumbersome, time-consuming, and extremely costly. It is estimated that it takes between ten and fifteen years and costs upwards of $800 million to have a new drug approved, and more than 80 percent of the costs of this process are shouldered by pharmaceutical companies. To garner FDA approval, a new drug must survive three rounds of study—Phase I, which tests a relatively small group of volunteers in an attempt to determine whether a drug or device is safe; Phase II, which employs a larger group of patients to study not only safety but how effective the drug or device is; and Phase III, which uses a much larger group of patients, usually in multisite trials. The FDA may, and often does, reject a drug or medical device at any stage of the approval process.

In addition, even after the FDA has given approval, it may still exercise control over the medication, as the FDA did with the antipsychotic drug Zyprexa. In March 2004, the FDA asked Eli Lilly and Company, which manufactures the drug, to send a letter to physicians notifying them that labeling information for the drug would be changed to inform patients using this drug of the increased risk of hyperglycemia and diabetes. The FDA sometimes recalls drugs that it has approved. This often happens in cases where the label for a lifesaving drug is either misleading or wrong or where a drug is not being prescribed at a strength adequate to treat a medical condition. Recently, two very popular anti-arthritis drugs, Vioxx and Bextra, were linked to an increased risk of heart attack, and Vioxx was recalled. Drug companies almost always comply with the rules for drug approval and recalls, but when they fail to comply, they can be subject to both civil and criminal penalties. Where a controlled substance is involved, the Drug Enforcement Agency also has enforcement powers, and the DEA has targeted physicians for not complying with its regulations.

Experimental Drugs and the Drug-Approval Process

For a drug to be approved by the FDA, the researchers must prove that it provides a clear therapeutic benefit without exposing the patient to undue risk. Critics claim that the FDA has stifled innovation by imposing a lengthy and very costly drug-approval process. Especially fierce criticisms have been aimed at development of treatments or vaccines for diseases that are fatal. For example, by the mid-1980s, Acquired Immune Deficiency Syndrome, or AIDS, had killed tens of thousands of people and there was no effective treatment for the disease. AIDS activists condemned the FDA for its

Throughout the late 1980s and 1990s, ACT UP was very effective in using protest and civil disobedience to lobby aggressively for increased funding and support for AIDS research.

business-as-usual approach, and urged the agency to relax its approval process and allow for an expedited review of medications.

AIDS activists like the AIDS Coalition to Unleash Power, or **ACT UP**, staged protests, which they called acts of civil disobedience, to bring pressure to bear on governmental officials and to expedite the drug review process. ACT UP used tactics that were outside the mainstream, engaging in protest activities that were intended to maximize media exposure. For example, members staged "die ins," shut down the offices of the FDA by blocking access to the building, and delivered empty coffins to federal, state, and local officials. ACT UP politicized the drug-approval process and argued that those with life-threatening or serious illnesses had a right to access to drugs, even if these drugs were experimental. See the website for more information about ACT UP's activities in the early years of the AIDS epidemic.

In large part because of the protest activities of groups like ACT UP, the FDA created a **fast track** for AIDS drugs, allowing a number of medications to be distributed to patients before they had actually been approved. In 1994, the National Task Force on AIDS Drug Development was created to expedite the development of drugs. This expanded access is credited with stemming the tide of AIDS-related disease and death. Interestingly, a number of other activists have looked to the work of AIDS advocates to try to convince the FDA to expedite the approval process for other drugs. Breast cancer activists used some of the same kinds of tactics to try to convince the FDA to expedite cancer-fighting drugs. The **Food and Drug Administration Modernization Act of 1997** institutionalized the fast-track procedure for serious or life-threatening diseases. Under this law, researchers who are working on the development of drugs that address "unmet medical needs" may be eligible for a number of important benefits, among these, regular and frequent meetings with FDA officials and expedited clinical trials.

The FDA will probably be receptive to the use of fast-track approval in the future. In fact, in 2004, FDA commissioner Mark McClellan announced that the agency would try to encourage drug innovation by shortening Phase III and that it would decrease the number of review cycles for generic drugs. In addition, both the public and government officials are placing significant pressure on the FDA to encourage them to expedite research into treatments for bioterrorism. The mapping of the human genome has also intensified efforts to reform the FDA's drug-approval process. In particular, researchers and pharmaceutical companies are rushing to develop therapies to "fix" defective genes and to treat genetically influenced illness. Any such medical products, devices, or treatments would have to be FDA-approved. In addition, the field of **pharmacogenomics** is booming as researchers try to figure out how to use an individual's genetic blueprint to ensure that medical treatments—in particular, drug therapies—will deliver the maximum therapeutic impact. For the lucky researchers who unlock these fields, the financial reward will be tremendous, which only increases the huge incentive to try to accelerate the FDA approval process.

ACT UP

an activist group that staged protests to bring pressure on governmental officials to increase funding for AIDS research and to expedite the FDA's drug-review process; often outside the mainstream

 www ▶ ▶ ▶

fast track

streamlined procedures created by the FDA in the wake of the AIDS epidemic to expedite delivery of some experimental drugs to patients with Human Immunodeficiency Virus (HIV)

www ▶ ▶ ▶

Food and Drug Administration Modernization Act of 1997

act that institutionalized the fast-track procedure for experimental drugs being studied for possible treatment of serious or life-threatening illness

DEBATE

Should the FDA have a central role in regulating pharmacogenomics?

Yes: The FDA must have a central role in the debate about pharmacogenomics. The Human Genome Project makes it possible for us to specifically tailor drugs for treatment or prevention of disease according to an individual's genetic structure. Genetic engineering could revolutionize medicine by allowing for the replacement or repair of genetic material, as opposed to treating the manifestations of disease. In the absence of legal or regulatory safeguards, the use of genetic material could be commercialized and exploited for profit. If this happened, access to these new treatments could be limited to those who could pay, and those without the means would be denied access to cutting-edge technology. The U.S. health care system would truly become a two-tiered system, where those with money might have vastly different treatment outcomes than those with fewer resources. In addition, genetic medicine is in its earliest stages and continues to be fairly dangerous—in fact, in several trials, subjects have died after gene therapy compromised their immune systems. Without regulation, genetic engineering may spawn designer babies or designer medicine, where people seek treatment to achieve the "perfect" child or sculpt the "perfect" body. This area of medicine is at a very vulnerable and dangerous stage and FDA involvement is clearly needed to safeguard against abuse.

No: Unfortunately, in a number of areas, including AIDS research, the FDA has shown itself to be unable to respond effectively to the need for testing of experimental and cutting-edge therapies. This agency is incredibly risk-averse and is unwilling to take the chances necessary to develop innovative genetic testing and treatment plans. Ultimately, the agency fast-tracked AIDS drugs only in response to immense public pressure. We are hoping that the agency has learned its lesson and that it will look to develop cooperative relationships with pharmaceutical companies instead of trying to order them to take certain actions. We are not hopeful, however, about the prospects for a new agency approach. There is some evidence that gene therapy could be successful in treating a number of diseases, but there has been little movement by the FDA toward testing genetic therapies, and the agency continues to be immobilized by its concerns about the risks attendant on these therapies. At this point, testing on mice has already provided great insight into the testing and treatment of sickle cell anemia. Research in other areas, including diabetes and breast cancer research, is just as promising. The FDA needs to allow pharmaceutical companies to continue to develop these therapies. It needs to adopt a cooperative rather than a combative stance. The agency should not have a central role; instead, it should share its place with those who are already engaged in research and development in this important area.

In addition, recent controversies involving several drugs, including hormone replacement therapies and the diet drug Fen Phen, which were recalled after concerns about safety began to mount, will likely increase pressure on drug companies to ensure further testing both before and after the approval process.

The activities of large, transnational pharmaceutical companies also raise questions about drug testing and approval. Recently, the drug manufacturer Pfizer, Inc. was sued by thirty Nigerian families who claimed that the company conducted drug experiments on their children without their approval and that six children died as a result of these experiments. These families claim that Pfizer was testing an experimental drug, Trovan, to be used against meningitis. Pfizer researchers chose to use Trovan despite the availability of alternative medicines that had been tested and approved for the treatment of this fatal disease. Major pharmaceutical companies have also been accused of paying doctors in other countries to recruit patients and failing to provide any real guidance about informed consent requirements. As a result, many third-world citizens have been induced to participate in drug trials without giving informed consent. In some cases, the information given to them was misleading and inaccurate or participation was coerced. Some commentators have starkly criticized what they term the globalization of drug testing, claiming that pharmaceutical companies are avoiding the cumbersome drug-approval process in place in countries like the United States by shifting their attention to the third world, where there are few requirements for drug testing and little governmental oversight of pharmaceutical companies.

Controversies in Medical Research

Human Genome Project

an international collaboration of scientists who created a blueprint or map of all human genes, the entities that establish the basic structure and function of the human body that may ultimately be used to identify an individual's predisposition to certain medical diseases

In the last two decades, the drug-approval process has become more sensitized to politics and public opinion in the United States. Other areas of medical research have also become more controversial and susceptible to political decisions, as opposed to policy choices. Among these are the areas of stem cell research, fetal cell research, and cloning. All of these research avenues raise serious questions about the rights of embryos and fetuses. Researchers believe that fetal and embryonic tissue and cells may be very helpful in developing treatments for Parkinson's disease, Alzheimer's, strokes, spinal cord injuries, and other diseases or conditions. We now know much more about how the human body functions than we have ever known, and very recently, scientific research has yielded important insight about the very structure and composition of our genetic makeup. The **Human Genome Project**, which was completed in 2003, provides a complete blueprint of the basic building blocks of human life. The project, a work of international collaboration, has established the location and function of all of the genes in the human genome. If you recall from your basic biology courses, our genes are responsible for much of our physical makeup and perhaps even our behavioral predisposition, as well. Using this map, we may ultimately be able to identify each individual's predisposition to medical issues or diseases. **Genetic engineering**, which is only in its earliest stages, will use the map to expand its applications, and we may one day be able to alter the genetic structure of individuals or groups to lessen their risk of disease.

genetic engineering

using genetic information to treat disease or possibly to alter a person's predisposition to certain illnesses

While genetic testing and engineering have the potential to ease human suffering and ameliorate or eliminate certain diseases, many people worry about how it might be used to undermine individual rights. In the wake of 9/11, commentators have become increasingly concerned about the use of DNA profiling and testing—and about the impact of these practices on the right to privacy. There are serious concerns that genetic testing and screening might be used by employers, insurance companies, and even governmental institutions to identify individuals who might have a disposition toward certain diseases or even behavioral traits. While some analysts argue that our existing laws protect against such abuses, it remains to be seen how this information will ultimately be used. It is very likely that this striking advance in medical technology will place pressure on legislators and regulators to pass laws that protect individual rights, but serious questions remain about the shape that these laws will ultimately take.

SUMMARY

In this chapter, we have been discussing how law affects the practice of medicine and scientific research in the United States and the different social facts or norms that help us understand why these laws look the way they do. Throughout much of the last one hundred years, our laws reflected the assumption that the doctor-patient relationship was privileged and that physicians should be permitted to exercise significant autonomy in treating their patients. We discussed one area of the law, abortion, where the law continues to afford physicians considerable leeway and two other emerging areas, aid in dying and medicinal marijuana, where the law recognizes a special role for physicians. In all three areas, doctors argue that the needs of their patients should trump broad and amorphous arguments about public morality. Like doctors who fight to keep abortion safe and legal, doctors who administer aid in dying or prescribe medicinal marijuana are asserting that they should be permitted substantial latitude in making treatment decisions. Many of our laws reflect an acceptance of this argument. Somewhat paradoxically, while the law in many ways privileges the doctor-patient relationship, the increasingly complex regulations governing medical research seem to be based on the assumption that patients and research subjects should be protected from overzealous doctors and researchers. Our laws aim at ensuring that patients are autonomous and that they fully consent to taking part in research protocols.

This chapter also examined changes in the law governing the testing and approval process for new medications. We talked about how interest-group politics—especially the activities of AIDS activists—have had a powerful effect on the FDA's drug-approval process and have created a fast-track approval process for certain medicines. Finally, in this chapter, we examined developments in mapping the human genome and talked about how the use of genetic testing and profiling will inevitably create pressure for the passage of new laws in this area.

Where law regulates specific practices, like abortion, aid in dying, and medicinal marijuana, we are more likely to allow physicians leeway in providing care. This reflects the norm that the physician's primary responsibility is to the patient. Our experiences with medical research and development, however, lead us to question whether physicians or researchers act as selflessly in these areas. Specifically, the Tuskegee Syphilis Study and the slow federal response to the AIDS crisis lead many to believe that physicians and researchers may sometimes act in their own self-interest. Perhaps not surprisingly, this concern about professional ethics has opened the door to much greater regulation in these areas.

The public debate surrounding these public health issues has grown increasingly fierce, especially in the last decade. Even a cursory glance at the laws governing biomedicine reveals that law has lagged far behind scientific research. There are a number of serious challenges in the near future: among them crafting laws that readily adapt to the rapidly changing biomedical frontier and creating laws that respect the time-honored doctor-patient relationship. It remains to be seen how lawmakers will ultimately address these challenges, but it seems clear that medical and scientific technology will be the subject of an ever-expanding and varied array of federal, state, and municipal laws.

SUGGESTED READING

Michael C. Carroll, *Lab 257: The Disturbing Story of the Government's Secret Plum Island Germ Laboratory* (William Morrow, 2004). In this disturbing book, the author warns readers that biological research conducted on Plum Island, located off the shore of Long Island, New York, has the potential to unleash deadly diseases, either by accident or as a result of biological terrorism. The Plum Island research facility has been operation since World War II, and some commentators believe that a number of diseases, among these, West Nile virus and Lyme disease, were first developed in its labs. Serious concerns about safety prompt the author to strongly urge the closing down of this facility.

Kathleen Foley and Herbert Hendin, *The Case Against Assisted Suicide: For the Right to End-Of-Life Care* (Johns Hopkins Press, 2004). This volume serves as the counterpoint to the book written by Quill and Battin. Drs. Foley and Herbert argue strongly in opposition to aid in dying, presenting an opposing right, the right to end-of-life care.

Andrew Goliszek, *In the Name of Science: A History of Secret Programs, Medical Research, and Human Experimentation* (St. Martins Press, 2003). In this study of medical experimentation, the author chronicles the use of human subjects throughout the 1900s, beginning with the use of forced sterilization in the eugenics movement and continuing until today. The author argues that the Human Genome Project actually increases the potential for abuse in medical research.

Timothy E. Quill and M. Pabst Battin, *Physician-assisted Dying: The Case for Palliative Care and Patient Choice* (Johns Hopkins Press, 2004). Written by physician Timothy Quill as a counterpoint to the book by physician Kathleen Foley, this book examines the arguments in favor of physician aid in dying, focusing specifically on the experiences of Oregon and the Netherlands.

Leslie J. Reagan, *When Abortion Was a Crime: Women, Medicine, and Law in the United States, 1867–1973* (University of California Press, 1998). An excellent study of how physicians shaped abortion policy in the 1800s and how they justified much more restrictive abortion laws during this period.

ACTIVE LEARNING

1. Consider the model act on physician aid in dying that was recently created by lawyers, physicians, academics, and Hemlock Society members in Boston to help guide state legislatures that are considering adopting aid-in-dying laws. What are the responsibilities of physicians under this law? What do you think of this law—does it address the needs of those with terminal illnesses while still ensuring that states protect all human life? You can find the act at http://www.pbs.org/newshour/bb/health/die.html.

2. Consider the fast-track provision of the FDA Modernization Act of 1997. What goals do you think it advances? Why do you think this provision is included under the subheading "Improvements"? Note the inclusion of the "information program on clinical trials for serious or life-threatening diseases." Why do you think that Congress established this program? What's the relationship between these two aspects of the statute? You can find the statute on the *Law, Politics, and Society* website.

www ▶ ▶ ▶

CHAPTER 15

Law and Corporations

Fast-food giant McDonald's recently introduced healthier menu choices—like milk and juice instead of soda, and apple slices instead of french fries—in children's Happy Meals. McDonald's also began to provide nutritional information on menu choices and to suggest healthier choices for customers concerned about their fat, cholesterol, and caloric intake. Did this advertising and public relations campaign stem from new-found concern about its customers health, or is it at least in part a response to lawsuits filed by individuals and organizations concerned about the impact of fast food on children's and adults' health? In one lawsuit filed in 2003, a group of parents sued the fast-food giant for deceptive advertising, claiming that McDonald's violated consumer protections and products liability laws by offering meals that were "inherently dangerous" to children's health and not informing their parents of these dangers.

Corporations are subject to an array of federal, state, and local laws that regulate many of their activities. Laws regulate the relationship between employer and employee, product safety, the impact of the corporation's activities on the environment, and the company's business practices and investments. In turn, the activities of corporations affect the kinds of laws we adopt. Corporate regulations are largely the result of actions taken by state and federal administrative agencies, and they are enforced through agency practices and, occasionally, court orders. Business leaders and politicians are often highly critical of this regulatory environment. They call for less restrictive laws that encourage business efficiency, competition, and flexibility. In this chapter, we will discuss the relationship between law and corporate practices in the United States. In particular, we will explore three areas of the law: regulations that proscribe corporate investments and trading, environmental regulations, and products liability laws. In all three areas, the law has been shaped by political and social forces; it reflects our core values of individualism and wealth maximization.

law and economics

well-accepted theory that law functions or should function to maximize societal wealth by promoting market efficiency

*If you recall Chapter 2, we considered the **law and economics**, model of jurisprudence, which is one of the most influential theories used today to describe both how law should function in society and how law actually does function in society. This theory, which has been embraced by legal scholars and judges in the United States and abroad, posits that law should be evaluated on the basis of economic principles. These scholars claim that law and economics are closely interwoven and that the goal of both systems is or should be to maximize profit by allowing free choice. They believe that individuals make choices about how to act based on their calculation of the costs and benefits of different options. Ideally, law operates to provide information about these costs and benefits, and in so doing helps to structure human interactions. This school, which has roots going back to the late 1800s, gained ascendancy in the United States in the 1960s, but its core belief in market efficiency and its faith in the ability of individuals to choose that action that best maximizes profit and wealth can be glimpsed in many of our laws, especially those adopted in the industrial era. In this chapter, we will examine the relationship between law and corporate America and consider how our laws reflect core beliefs about how corporations function.*

right to contract

until 1937, the prevailing justification used by the U.S. Supreme Court in its decisions striking down state and federal employment laws

THE ROLE OF LAW IN THE ENTREPRENEURIAL SYSTEM

Sherman Antitrust Act

1890 law that banned the creation of monopolies because lawmakers and the courts were concerned about the negative effects of these structures on fair competition and economic growth

A key tenet of our political culture has always been a belief in individualism. So perhaps it is not surprising that until the late 1930s few laws regulated business practices in the United States. Even when our nation began to industrialize in the mid- to late 1800s and people began to appreciate the huge environmental and human costs of this industrialization, our governments were slow to craft and implement protective laws. When Congress and the state legislatures did pass laws, federal and state courts often struck them down, arguing that the workplace regulations interfered with the worker's **right to contract** for employment. For a long time, decision makers believed that individuals had a fundamental right to sell their labor and that their choices in that area should not be constrained by regulations. Only where courts were convinced that laws would protect free trade and open competition did they pass muster. The U.S. Supreme Court allowed the 1890 **Sherman Antitrust Act** to stand only because it was convinced that this act, which banned monopolies, would ensure fair competition and thus economic growth.

www ▶ ▶ ▶

laissez-faire

an economic model based on the assumption that markets operate best and are most efficient when they are free from governmental regulation

Many other laws, however, were struck down by the Court because the justices believed that they interfered with business practice. The Court's approach mirrored the economic model of **laissez-faire**, which was based on the belief that markets operated best and were most efficient and productive when the fewest restrictions were placed on them by governmental

Great Depression

economic collapse precipitated by the stock market crash of 1929 and marked by high unemployment, low wages, and widespread poverty; ultimately the catalyst for much greater government regulation of the economy

NLRB v. Jones & Laughlin Steel Corp.

1937 U.S. Supreme Court case upholding a federal law that protected unionization efforts; signaled the Court's willingness to allow more regulation of businesses; used to uphold federal and state regulation of the workplace relationship

Securities Act of 1933

law that imposed significant disclosure requirements on corporations offering stocks for sale to the public and barred the manipulation of securities prices through deceptive practices like insider trading; a result of concern about the 1929 stock market crash

1934 Securities Exchange Act

the law that created the Securities and Exchange Commission and empowered it to enforce reporting and disclosure laws

commerce power

the power of Congress to regulate aspects of the economy

bodies or other actors. Using this rationale, the Court struck down regulations that limited the number of hours or days that a worker could work or that tried to protect workers' health in highly hazardous workplaces, like mines and poultry processing plants. It was not until the 1929 stock market crash and the ensuing **Great Depression** had created serious dislocations in the economy, with high unemployment, staggeringly low wages, and widespread poverty, that the Court finally began to rethink its commitment to this model.

When the Court began to allow these regulations to stand in 1937, it did so because it believed that regulations were necessary for economic growth in the United States. In the 1937 case *NLRB v. Jones & Laughlin Steel Corp.,* the Court allowed the 1935 National Labor Relations Act to stand, and in so doing, permitted Congress to take action to protect workers who wanted to unionize. The Court justified its decision to protect unionization efforts by arguing that collective bargaining between workers and employers was "an essential condition of industrial peace," and allowed for more a more efficient and productive operation of the business.

The *Jones & Laughlin* decision signaled that the Court was willing to allow Congress and the state legislatures much greater latitude in regulating business practices. Not only were legislatures permitted to regulate the relationship between employer and employee, and to establish rules governing wages, hours, and working conditions, they were also allowed to craft laws that regulated corporate investment and trading. The federal **Securities Act of 1933** aimed at ensuring that there would not be another financial disaster like the 1929 stock market crash that precipitated the Great Depression. The Securities Act imposed significant disclosure requirements to ensure that investors were provided with better information on which to make investment decisions. Better-informed investors were more likely to be confident in the system; they would invest more enthusiastically; and these investments would ultimately pump more money into the economy. The **1934 Securities Exchange Act** created the federal Securities and Exchange Commission and empowered this commission to enforce these reporting and disclosure requirements.

It is interesting to note that both kinds of laws—those that regulated the employment relationship and those that regulated investment and trading— were based on the core belief that the laws should create an environment in which corporations could function more efficiently and generate more wealth. The Court ultimately accepted the view that Congress had the power to regulate the employment relationship and corporate investment and trading because it viewed these activities as being within Congress's **commerce power**—which is the explicit power to "regulate commerce with foreign nations, and among the several states, and with the Indian tribes," given to Congress in Article I, Section 8, of the U.S. Constitution. There has always been some disagreement about how much power this clause gives Congress to make laws that govern activities that occur within state boundaries:

those who want to limit Congress's power argue that most activities should be left to the states to regulate, while those who embrace Congress's role in the economy contend that this power is very broad. The Supreme Court itself has shifted back and forth between these two arguments. In a very early case, the 1819 case of *Gibbons* **v.** *Ogden,* the Court established that Congress had the power to regulate the operation of steamboats in the waters between New York and New Jersey, reading commerce very broadly as the power to regulate *traffic* between states. But it was not until *Jones & Laughlin* that Congress was allowed to regulate an activity—unionization—that was wholly intrastate and that was not directly related to the transport or trafficking of goods or services.

And while *Jones & Laughlin* was a springboard for the creation of federal laws governing a vast array of activities, including virtually all industrial and manufacturing activities, telecommunications, and most commercial dealings, the Supreme Court has dramatically narrowed Congress's commerce power in the last ten years. In a series of cases, the Court has argued that this clause allows Congress only to regulate activities with an economic basis; it has struck down laws that were really social policies, among them, gun control laws, laws related to violence against women, and several environmental laws (for example, see *U.S. v. Lopez, U.S. v. Morrison,* and *Solid Waste Agency of Northern Cook County* v. *U.S. Army Corps of Engineers).* The Court has been unwilling to accept the argument that these laws had a substantial impact on the national economy. It has insisted on a much narrower reading of the commerce power. In this shift, one can glimpse a return to the Court's earlier approach to regulation—and perhaps a return to a much more limited role for government in at least some kinds of regulations.

Gibbons v. Ogden

1819 U.S. Supreme Court case defining commerce broadly to include traffic between the states

DEBATE

Should the commerce power be defined narrowly?

Yes:

The framers of the Constitution intended that the federal government would have limited powers, and they enumerated the powers of Congress in Article I, Section 8, of the Constitution, among these, the power to regulate commerce among the several states. Over time, Congress has used this clause and others to substantially broaden its powers, often at the expense of the states. In part, Congress has done this by ignoring the "commerce" part of the clause—that is, it has used this clause without really demonstrating that what it was doing was closely related to any real commercial exercise. In 1995, the U.S. Supreme Court clarified these powers by striking down Congress's 1990

Should the commerce power be defined narrowly?–(Cont'd)

Gun-Free School Zones Act. This act had relied on the commerce power to create a federal criminal statute that punished those who came within one thousand feet of a school with a firearm. The Court struck down the law, finding that it was not related to any commercial or economic activity and that it intruded on the long-established powers of states to act independently in the area of criminal law. The commerce power was never intended to be a general grant of power to Congress to make whatever law it wanted—its focus on economic activity has always been clear. Violent crimes are not usually closely related to economic enterprise, and for this reason, Congress is barred from regulating these activities.

No:

Given our fast-paced interdependent economy, it is difficult and foolish to very narrowly define the commerce power, and there is no evidence that the framers intended to use this clause to cripple Congress and prevent it from taking effective action to regulate commerce between the states. The framers rejected a narrow interpretation of this congressional power. Even as early as 1816, the Supreme Court held that commerce was more than just traffic, that it was instead intercourse. It is ludicrous to argue, as the Supreme Court has in a series of decisions in the last decade beginning with *U.S. v. Lopez*, and continuing forward, that criminal activities like gun possession in school zones and violent sexual crimes against women have no bearing on interstate commerce. Clearly, both kinds of crimes have a significant impact on commerce because they interfere with the free flow of people, ideas, and education across state lines. Moreover, by using the power of judicial review to strike down congressional statutes like the Gun-Free Schools Law and the 1994 Violence Against Women Act, the Court is undermining the will of our democratically elected branches of government to make law on behalf of the public. This approach ultimately undermines our democratic principles and hamstrings Congress's ability to respond effectively to threats to our society.

While the Court seems to be limiting congressional power to broadly regulate economic activities, it has been less eager to limit the power of state legislatures to take action in this area. And in fact, in limiting federal activity, the Court may be opening the door for more state regulation of commerce. Even at the heyday of the commerce power, much of the action, in terms of economic policy and law, occurred at the state level. Even today, states regulate many aspects of the corporate activity—among these, the decision to incorporate, the entering into of contracts for goods and services, the use of

Uniform Commercial Code (UCC)

law created with substantial input by corporations; has been accepted by nearly all the states and governs many business transactions

www ▶ ▶ ▶

banking services and credit, and the dissolution of businesses. States claim the power to regulate business under their broad police powers, which allow states significant latitude in passing laws that protect the health, safety, well-being, and morality of residents. Nearly all state legislatures have adopted the **Uniform Commercial Code (UCC)**, which regulates many business practices, including the creation of leases, the transfer of stocks and other negotiable instruments, and the use of funds transfers and bank deposits. Many of these laws were drafted with significant corporate input and support, probably because the laws facilitate and encourage business interactions. Some commentators believe that such laws are excellent examples of the law and economics model in action. To take just one example, the UCC minimizes the costs of doing business by establishing the rules for making and enforcing contracts and encouraging individuals to contract with each other; in so doing, this law maximizes choices and profits.

It seems to be true, as most law and economics theorists claim, that the legal and economic systems operate in tandem, and our laws at least implicitly recognize the benefits of an entrepreneurial system. In many areas, the laws are crafted with subtle, or maybe not so subtle, input by corporations, and they reflect our basic belief in competition and individualism. In the remainder of this chapter we will explore the ways in which laws have shaped business dealings and focus on the expansion of law in this area by examining laws that regulate investments and stock trading, environmental impact, and products liability. Some analysts might say that laws are crafted in these areas because a free-market economy does not sufficiently protect individual rights, environmental protection, or consumer safety. Many law and economics scholars argue, however, that the laws provide basic information to individual actors, including corporations, about the costs and benefits of taking certain actions.

CORPORATE INVESTMENT AND STOCK TRADING

www ▶ ▶ ▶

It is hard to overstate the impact of the 1929 stock market crash and the subsequent Great Depression on our economy and the larger society—stocks lost more than 40 percent of their value in the first month following the crash, and annual national income declined from $87 billion in 1930 to $40 billion in 1933. At its worse, unemployment was 25 percent—which means that more than 15 million Americans were out of work. It is estimated that more than 250,000 people became homeless in the decade following the crash. In the cities, six out of every ten African Americans were unemployed. More than one-third of the population was below the poverty line, the high school dropout rate doubled in this period, and farm foreclosures dramatically increased. Thousands of businesses and financial institutions also failed in the years following the crash, and the crash produced horrific dislocations in family structure.

THE LAW IN POPULAR CULTURE

Grapes of Wrath

The title of this film and the book it was based on comes from the "Battle Hymn of the Republic":

> Mine eyes have seen the glory of the coming of the Lord,
> He is trampling out the vintage where the grapes of wrath are stored,
> He has loosed the fateful lightning of His terrible swift sword,
> His truth is marching on.

The film depicted the utter desperation of tenant farmers in Oklahoma who were thrown off their land in the wake of the Great Depression and forced to begin a long and difficult trek to find a new home.

Securities Act of 1933

law that regulated the registration and initial offering of stocks by corporations; precipitated by the 1929 stock market crash

Many believed that business leaders and stock brokers were to blame for the crash. They criticized these groups for not disclosing information about the real value of stocks and the overall health of the economy. In response to the stock market crash and in an effort to shore up investor confidence, Congress passed a number of laws aimed at ensuring full disclosure by companies offering stocks for sale. In 1933, Congress passed the **Securities Act of 1933**, which is also known as the "truth in securities law," because it requires that securities like stocks and bonds be registered with the government, and that companies offering these securities provide full and accurate information about their financial health. This information is usually provided in the prospectus for a stock offering, and this law bars the issuing of fraudulent or inaccurate prospectus statements. The 1933 law aimed at ensuring the proper operation of stock markets and exchanges by establishing requirements for the trading, purchase, and sale of securities, and Section 78 (j) barred the manipulation of securities prices through deceptive practices, including insider trading.

In 2004, home decorating maven Martha Stewart was convicted of lying to the Securities and Exchange Commission about why she sold shares of stock in the biopharmaceutical company *ImClone*. At trial, the SEC argued that she made the decision to sell after she acquired nonpublic information about the company from a broker friend. Stewart is perhaps one of the most visible targets of the SEC's stepped-up enforcement efforts. While the agency did little to enforce its laws against insider trading, false reporting, and securities fraud until the early 1960s, there was a surge of enforcement efforts in the 1980s and again in the early 2000s. The current upswing in enforcement was probably driven in large part by the bankruptcy of **Enron**, once the seventh wealthiest corporation in the Fortune 500, and one of the biggest company to collapse in American history. Enron's former chief executive officer, Jeffrey Skilling, and a number of other financial officers have either been charged with or convicted of engaging in securities fraud, insider trading, or the falsification of financial reports. Skilling faces 325 years in prison and $80 million dollars in fines for his role in the Enron scandal. Specifically, federal prosecutors believe that he violated the law against **insider trading**, which bars the trading of stocks based on information that is not available to the public. Prosecutors claim that he sold more than $60 million dollars in Enron stock one month after he left the company and with the knowledge that Enron was about to go bankrupt. The collapse of Enron had a tremendous negative effect on investors, including those who had invested in mutual funds that relied on its financial reports, and on company employees. Probably because of this high visibility of the Enron scandal, there have been a number of changes in securities law aimed at ensuring accurate financial accounting, among these, a requirement that CEOs personally verify corporate earnings reports.

Clearly, white-collar crime like securities and financial fraud, antitrust violations, and electronic fraud—the kind of crimes that Skilling is charged with—are incredibly costly to our economy. The FBI estimates that **white-collar crime**, characterized by deviance from legitimate business activities, costs the U.S. economy more than $300 billion each year. Securities fraud and insider trading is notoriously difficult to prosecute, and the SEC recognizes that the further away the "tippee" is from the brokers and managers who provide the information, the more difficult the case is to prosecute. Skilling's case is an unusual one, because this former CEO quit his job, then

www ▶ ▶ ▶

www ▶ ▶ ▶

Enron
once the seventh wealthiest corporation listed in the Fortune 500, this company went bankrupt in 2001, the largest company ever to do so; the resultant scandal surrounding accounting practices and insider trading have spawned a number of high-profile cases, including the federal cases against former CEO Jeffrey Skilling

www ▶ ▶ ▶

insider trading
the use of information that is not available to the public in making decisions to buy, sell, or transfer stocks; barred by the Federal Securities Act of 1934

white-collar crime
deviance from legitimate business activities; largely invisible and underreported, they cost the U.S. economy more than $300 billion each year

www ▶ ▶ ▶

www ▶ ▶ ▶

sold off all of his stock in a short period of time. Prosecutors may have an easier time proving that Skilling acted with inside information about Enron's future prospects than they do in most cases, where proof of insider trading is much more difficult to establish. Despite their huge costs, these crimes remain largely invisible, and there is a need for much greater coordination of enforcement efforts by federal, state, and local police.

Polling data suggests strongly that most Americans have confidence in business and industry in the United States—according to one poll, nearly 80 percent of Americans had either some confidence or a great deal of confidence in these institutions. But many Americans also believe that insider trading—that is, the use of material, nonpublic information to make decisions about stock trades—is fairly widespread, and some analysts caution that this cynicism could undermine consumer confidence in stock investments. In part to bolster consumer confidence, many companies now require that employees attend educational sessions in which they are informed about the long-range negative effects of insider trading on corporate profits. And ultimately, it may be the companies themselves that are more effectively able to police the practice.

WORKPLACE AND ENVIRONMENTAL LAW

Triangle Shirtwaist Factory fire

fire that killed 111 immigrant women in 1911 and sparked the passage of state laws protecting worker health and safety, although many of these laws were struck down by the Supreme Court

The stock market crash of 1929 demonstrated the dangers of relying exclusively on the laissez-faire economic model. This model, which had been the predominant force driving economic policy from the late 1800s until 1929, assumed that the economy would function best and be most efficient and productive if it were allowed to operate with the fewest number of restrictions. Even though it quickly became apparent that industrialization and urbanization created profound social and economic dislocations legislatures were very slow in adopting laws to protect the health of workers or the public. It was only after a number of horrific events, like the 1911 **Triangle Shirtwaist Factory fire**, which killed 111 immigrant women, that some states adopted laws aimed at protecting worker health. And even after states began to adopt these laws, the U.S. Supreme Court was hostile to them, striking down many laws that established minimum-wage and maximum-hour protections as violations of the constitutional right to sell one's own labor. In the midst of the Great Depression, the Supreme Court finally changed course, permitting Congress and the state governments to adopt these laws.

Silent Spring

book that served as an important catalyst for the modern environmental movement

These laws sought to ensure that workers would be paid a living wage and that they wouldn't be forced to work long hours without additional compensation, but they did little to protect workers or the general public from environmental hazards created by industrialization. The 1964 book *Silent Spring* by Rachel Carson was one of the most important catalysts for

www ▶ ▶ ▶

the modern environmental movement. In this book, Carson warned of a coming global apocalypse caused by the overspraying of pesticides, describing one town where spraying had killed every living creature. *Silent Spring* had a profound effect on some policymakers, including President John F. Kennedy, who was so moved by reading the book that he charged his Science Advisory Committee to examine the effects of pesticides on human and animal health. Soon after, Congress banned the pesticide DDT. This book for the first time brought to public awareness the health effects of chemicals and other environmental and occupational toxins, and the environmental movement of the 1970s was born with the public's strong reaction to this book.

www ▶ ▶ ▶

In time, policymakers adopted a wide array of regulations that affected corporations, among these, the National Environmental Policy Act, the Clean Air Act, and the Clean Water Act. The Environmental Protection Agency (EPA) and the Occupational Safety and Health Administration (OSHA), charged with enforcing these and other acts, are sometimes at odds with corporations about proposed rules and investigations. Corporations often accuse regulatory agencies of not taking into sufficient consideration the huge costs that environmental regulations impose on their businesses. These corporations often participate very aggressively in the rule-making process, and they often are highly critical of regulations that they think will hamper corporate efficiency, profit margins, and growth. By law, agencies like the EPA, the Consumer Products Safety Commission (CPSU), and OSHA must consider the costs of their regulations to corporations. When these costs are very high, these agencies may reconsider or even abandon proposed rules. When these rules are passed, corporations may continue to challenge them, sometimes going to court to prevent implementation.

www ▶ ▶ ▶

www ▶ ▶ ▶

voluntary overcompliance

corporate choice to go beyond existing environmental, products safety, and occupational regulations in an effort to protect themselves against liability

It is interesting to note, however, that many corporations are now engaging in a practice called **voluntary overcompliance**, and are choosing to not only abide by existing regulations but go beyond them and meet even more stringent environmental, products safety, and occupational standards. Corporations choose to overcomply basically because they recognize that existing regulations may not be sufficiently protective of consumer and employee health; thus, merely complying with existing regulations might not protect them from being sued for harm from exposure to toxins or products. They voluntarily overcomply as part of a management plan that seeks to minimize the real costs of manufacturing and production. Many companies have found that overcompliance not only helps to shield them from liability but that it raises the value of their stock and helps in negotiations with environmental lobbyists, unions, employees, and governmental agencies. Again, law and economics would explain this practice by noting that companies may use law to make decisions about how best to maximize their profits and minimize their losses, and in particular, to minimize their liability for environmental hazards.

Superfund

1980 law, also known as CERCLA, that administers the cleanup effort of toxic waste sites and imposes strict liability on all owners, even those who did not pollute the sites themselves

www ▶ ▶ ▶

strict liability

making someone totally responsible for damages, even in the absence of proof that the party caused the harm

It certainly makes sense for businesses to be concerned about liability. In the United States in particular, corporations are anxious about the hidden costs of doing business, among these, liability for environmental toxins and occupational hazards. Perhaps of greatest concern to businesses are laws like the 1980 Comprehensive Environmental Response, Compensation and Liability Act (CERCLA), known as **Superfund**. Superfund was set up to fund the cleanup of toxic waste sites, many of which were polluted by companies that were no longer in business or that had gone bankrupt. To ensure sufficient funding for these cleanups, Superfund uses a number of tactics. First, at various points in Superfund history, Congress has directly taxed all businesses in certain sectors, particularly the chemical and oil industries. Second, and even more contentious, is that the law has also made *all* property owners liable for *any* toxic substances on their land, including those that had been dumped by a previous owner. In other words, landowners have **strict liability** and are responsible for hazards that were created even before they themselves took ownership of the property. For the owners of commercial property, especially properties that have long been occupied and used for commercial purposes, this is a potentially huge liability. The Environmental Protection Agency administers the Superfund legislation in cooperation with state environmental agencies. Most businesses are very concerned about Superfund liability, and while there are some cases in which businesses have been directly aided by Superfund monies, the fact is that many companies are extremely fearful about the possibility that environmental toxins might be found on their property.

There is significant disagreement among law and economics theorists about how to best view these workplace and environmental regulations. Some analysts argue that the regulations provide information to companies about the real costs of doing business that can be used effectively to assess business practices. To the extent that these rules make businesses more efficient, they should be embraced, but if they do not aim at efficiency, either by providing information or deterring others from similar misconduct, they should not be adopted. Other law and economics theorists argue against such regulations, contending that their one-size-fits-all approach results in less efficiency and ultimately interferes with the goal of maximizing profit.

PRODUCTS LIABILITY

In addition to being concerned about liability under securities, corporate fraud, and Superfund legislation, businesses are increasingly concerned about liability that may attach to the products that they manufacture. Law and economics principles also play out here—as analysts try to figure out whether regulations and case decisions provide information to companies

caveat emptor

the prevailing norm in business dealings through the 1950s and 1960s; literally defined as "buyer beware," it made the buyer responsible for all defects of a product, even those that were hidden or not readily discoverable

about how best to manufacture some goods or provide some service. Others argue that these laws result in inefficiency. Some law and economics theorists note that we have moved from a *caveat emptor* approach to business dealings—where the buyer of the product must beware of hidden defects—to a *caveat fabricator* approach—where the builder must actively eliminate design defects. We have already talked about products liability in the context of the fast-food industry. Many laws regulate goods that are manufactured and processed in the United States, and also the production process itself. If you remember way back in Chapter 1, we started this book with a discussion of how ubiquitous much of this law is—law regulates much of the food we eat, the quality of the air we breathe and the water we consume, the cars we drive, and so on and so on. . . . Regulatory law sets standards for products and services and holds responsible those who fall short of these requirements. The body of law that makes corporations responsible for harm caused by the products they make is known as **products liability law**. It is the potential source of tremendous liability for companies. Corporations can be liable for harm that results from defects in the design, manufacture, or marketing of their products. For example, the company Hoffman-LaRoche, which makes the acne drug Accutane, has been sued for birth defects suffered by babies whose mothers took the drug and by individuals and families who claim that use of the drug resulted in severe depression, and in some cases, suicide. Similarly, Firestone, for almost one hundred years the supplier of tires to the Ford Motor Company, has been the subject of many lawsuits alleging that the tires used on the Ford Explorer had defects that resulted in tread separation. The company is being sued not for only defective design but for defective manufacture of the product as well. And gun manufacturers, tobacco companies, and drug companies are all being sued for defective marketing or inadequate warnings to consumers about the inherent risks of using guns, cigarettes, or drugs. In other cases, people sue companies to recover the costs of indirect effects from faulty products.

caveat fabricator

a central tenet of products liability law; defined as "builder beware," it makes the manufacturer or distributor of goods responsible for both direct and indirect harm that befalls the buyer

www ▶ ▶ ▶

products liability law

law that makes corporations liable or legally responsible for harm that results from defects in design, manufacture, or marketing of their products

Deceptive Marketing and Fraud—Tobacco and Smoking-Related Illness and Death

Souders v. Philip Morris, Inc.

California appellate case that made tobacco companies responsible for marketing and advertising policies in force during a period of immunity

Throughout the 1990s and early 2000s, plaintiffs brought lawsuits against tobacco companies, claiming that the companies had intentionally withheld information about the harmful effects of cigarette smoking and that as a result, they had become addicted to cigarettes and developed serious and life-threatening diseases. A Florida jury handed down the largest ever punitive damages award in 2000, finding that a group of tobacco companies was liable for $145 billion in damages to a group of smokers and former smokers. In the following Law in Action case, *Souders v. Philip Morris, Inc.*

www ▶ ▶ ▶

(104 Cal. App.4th 15), a California state appeals court was being asked to review the decision of a trial court in a similar case, this time involving a claim brought by a husband and his deceased wife. In *Souders*, the tobacco companies claimed that they were not liable because the California state legislature had granted immunity from products liability cases for a ten-year period, even though legislators later revoked immunity for tobacco cases. Consider how the appeals court in this case responded to the plaintiffs' arguments that Philip Morris should be liable for certain advertising and marketing policies that it adopted during the immunity period, because these policies lied to smokers about the health hazards associated with cigarettes that it claimed were safer than existing brands. Just so you know, when a party files a demurrer under California law, they are admitting that what is alleged is factually true, but they are contending that these facts have no legal relevance.

LAW IN ACTION

Tobacco Litigation

SOUDERS V. *PHILIP MORRIS*, 104 CAL. APP. 4TH 15 (2002)
COURT OF APPEAL OF CALIFORNIA, SECOND APPELLATE DISTRICT, DIVISION THREE

www ▶ ▶ ▶ (See *Law, Politics, and Society* website for a link to the complete decision.)

OPINION: PERLUSS, J. *—Plaintiffs and appellants Donald Souders, individually and as guardian ad litem for Sandra Souders, Barbara Souders, Ben Souders, Elizabeth Souders and Jessica Souders; Donald Souders, Jr.; David Souders; Ann Souders; and the Estate of Mary Schuler (the Souderses) appeal from a judgment of dismissal [of] the personal injury and wrongful death causes of action in the complaint.

The sole question presented is whether the Souderses' claims for injuries and wrongful death allegedly caused by smoking, which accrued in 1999, but which are based on conduct that occurred prior to January 1, 1998, are barred by former Civil Code section 1714.45 (the Immunity Statute) . . .

In *Myers* v. *Philip Morris Companies, Inc.* (2002) (*Myers*) the Supreme Court answered

that question: "The Immunity Statute applies to certain statutorily described conduct of **tobacco** companies that occurred *during* the 10-year immunity period, which began on January 1, 1988, and ended on December 31, 1997. With respect to such conduct, therefore, the statutory immunity applies, and no product liability cause of action may be based on that conduct, regardless of when the users of the

LAW IN ACTION–(CONT'D)

tobacco products may have sustained or discovered injuries as a result of that conduct. That statutory immunity was rescinded, however, when the California Legislature enacted the Repeal Statute, which as of January 1, 1998, restored the general principles of tort law that had, until the 1988 enactment of the Immunity Statute, governed tort liability against **tobacco** companies. Therefore, with respect to conduct falling *outside* the 10-year immunity period, the **tobacco** companies are not shielded from product liability lawsuits." (*Id.* at p. 832.)

Because the Souderses' personal injury and wrongful death causes of action allege conduct by Philip Morris and B&W that occurred prior to January 1, 1988, we reverse the judgment of dismissal.

FACTUAL AND PROCEDURAL BACKGROUND

1. *The plaintiffs.*

Donald Souders and his wife Mary Schuler smoked cigarettes manufactured by Philip Morris and B&W for more than 30 years, beginning sometime prior to 1969, when they were both minors. On July 12, 1999, Donald Souders was diagnosed with emphysema and terminal heart disease attributable to his smoking. Mary Schuler died on July 20, 1999 as a result of damage to her heart caused by smoking. Sandra, Barbara, Ben, Elizabeth, Jessica, Donald, Jr., David and Ann Souders are the children of Donald Souders and Mary Schuler and the surviving heirs of Mary Schuler.

2. *Proceedings in the trial court.*

The Souderses filed this action against Philip Morris and B&W, as well as several other **tobacco** manufacturers and retailers, on November 18,

1999. The complaint contains causes of action for negligence, strict products liability and other torts, as well as claims for breach of express warranty and for violation of Business and Professions Code sections 17200 and 17500. The complaint alleges that Mary Schuler's death and Donald Souders's injuries were caused by smoking cigarettes manufactured by Philip Morris and B&W and that Philip Morris and B&W had engaged in wrongful conduct in connection with the manufacture and marketing of cigarettes dating from the 1950's.

Philip Morris and B&W demurred to the product liability causes of action on the ground that they were barred in their entirety by the provisions of former section 1714.45. The trial court sustained the demurrer, ruling that the 1997 amendment did not apply retroactively to conduct that occurred prior to its January 1, 1998 effective date . . .

The order of dismissal was entered on May 3, 2000. The Souderses filed a timely notice of appeal.

3. *Our initial decision on appeal and the Supreme Court's transfer order.*

In a decision filed on March 7, 2001, we reversed the judgment of dismissal, holding amended section 1714.45 applied to personal injury and other tort causes of action against **tobacco** manufacturers that accrued on or after January 1, 1998 . . . On May 16, 2001, the Supreme Court granted review and ordered briefing deferred pending its decision in *Myers*. On October 30, 2002, the Supreme Court transferred the case back to us "with directions to vacate [our] decision and to reconsider the cause in light of *Myers* v. *Philip Morris Companies, Inc.* (2002) 28 Cal.4th 828 [123

LAW IN ACTION–(CONT'D)

Cal. Rptr. 2d 40, 50 P.3d 751] and *Naegele v. R.J. Reynolds Tobacco Co*. (2002) 28 Cal.4th 856 [123 Cal. Rptr. 2d 61, 50 P.3d 769]." (*Souders v. Philip Morris Inc*. (Oct. 30, 2002, S096570).)

ISSUE

Does the Souderses' complaint state facts sufficient to constitute causes of action for personal injuries and other torts against Philip Morris and B&W under *Myers* and *Naegele v. R.J. Reynolds Tobacco Co, supra*, 28 Cal.4th 856 (*Naegele*)?

DISCUSSION

1. *Standard of review*.

(1) In reviewing an order sustaining a demurrer, we independently review the complaint to determine whether the facts alleged state a cause of action under any possible legal theory . . . We must give the complaint a reasonable interpretation, "treat[ing] the demurrer as admitting all material facts properly pleaded." (*Ibid*.)

2. *Section 1714.45*.

a. *The original version of section 1714.45: the Immunity Statute*.

(2) As originally enacted in 1987, effective January 1, 1988, section 1714.45 granted **tobacco** companies "complete immunity in certain product liability lawsuits . . ." (*Myers, supra,* 28 Cal.4th at pp. 831–832) . . .

b. *The 1997 amendment: the Repeal Statute*. Effective January 1, 1998, section 1714.45 was amended to delete "**tobacco**" from subdivision (a), enumerating those consumer items entitled to statutory immunity from product liability actions, and to state explicitly that this section does not exempt the manufacture or sale of

tobacco products by **tobacco** manufacturers from product liability actions. Additional changes were made to reflect the Legislature's intent in enacting this amendment . . .

3. *The Supreme Court decisions in Myers and Naegele*.

In *Myers* the [California] Supreme Court considered the following question . . . "Do the amendments to Cal. Civ. Code § 1714.45 that became effective on January 1, 1998, apply to a claim that accrued after January 1, 1998, but which is based on conduct that occurred prior to January 1, 1998?" . . . Because the Repeal Statute is not retroactive, the court concluded the plaintiff Betty Myers has no product liability claim against the defendant **tobacco** companies for their conduct in manufacturing and distributing cigarettes during the statutory immunity period . . .

Noting, however, that Myers began smoking cigarettes in 1956 and continued to do so until 1997 . . . , the Supreme Court also held the Repeal Statute "removed the protection that the Immunity Statute gave to **tobacco** companies for their conduct occurring *before* the Immunity Statute's effective date . . ." Thus, plaintiff Myers was entitled to pursue her tort claims against the **tobacco** company defendants for their conduct prior to January 1, 1988 (and after Dec. 31, 1997, as well) under general tort law principles.

Having decided in *Myers* that former section 1714.45 continues to provide immunity for **tobacco** companies in product liability actions for conduct during the 10-year period the Immunity Statute was in effect, in *Naegele*, the companion case to *Myers*, the Supreme Court considered what forms of conduct by **tobacco**

LAW IN ACTION–(CONT'D)

companies come within the Immunity Statute's protection . . . To the extent the plaintiff alleged the **tobacco** companies manipulated the addictive properties of their cigarettes through additives, however—for example, adding ammonia to the "nicotine delivery system"—the defendants are not protected from product liability lawsuits during the immunity period . . .

4. *The Souderses' complaint states causes of action for personal injuries and other torts under Myers and Naegele.*

(5) The Souderses' personal injury and wrongful death causes of action allege conduct by Philip Morris and B&W beginning some time prior to 1969 and continuing through the beginning of the 10-year statutory immunity period of former section 1714.45. Accordingly, the Souderses may pursue each of those causes of action under general tort principles . . .

Allegations that Philip Morris and B&W misrepresented the addictive nature of nicotine and developed and utilized high-nicotine **tobacco** in their product blends do not avoid the immunity bar for the period from January 1, 1988, through December 31, 1997. However, because the Souderses' claims assert misconduct by the **tobacco** companies prior to January 1, 1988, the demurrer to these causes of action should have been overruled. In addition, to the extent the Souderses have alleged defendants "add[ed] ammonia, or otherwise alter[ed] the PH of the **tobacco,** enhanced the delivery of nicotine, thereby increasing addiction and/or dependence" and thus have alleged Philip Morris and B&W exposed the Souderses to a risk other than those inherent in **tobacco** products, the Immunity Statute provides no protection for the defendants.

DISPOSITION

The judgment of dismissal is reversed . . .

QUESTIONS

1. What had happened in the trial court in this case?
2. What was the relevance of the California Supreme Court's decisions in *Meyers* and *Naegele?*
3. How did this appellate court respond to the Souderses' arguments? What was the court's rationale?
4. Consider that this was the first state case to allow lawsuits to go forward, even for conduct during the ten-year immunity period. What do you think will be the effect of this decision on cases that are pending? Do you think it will open the door to more litigation?
5. How do you square this decision with law and economics principles?

Tobacco companies continue to be under fire for their manufacture, distribution, and marketing of cigarettes, and there have now been many successful lawsuits both in the United States and abroad. Forty-four state attorneys general have filed lawsuits against tobacco companies, and

Master Settlement Agreement

California appellate case that made tobacco companies responsible for marketing and advertising policies in force during a period of immunity

www ▶ ▶ ▶

Racketeer Influenced and Corrupt Organizations Act (RICO)

the basis for a federal lawsuit against the tobacco industry, asserting that the companies acted as an "enterprise" and conspired to run their businesses through fraud and deception

www ▶ ▶ ▶

there have been four individual state settlements followed by a **Master Settlement Agreement** to cover the claims brought by the remaining forty states. Under the Master Settlement Agreement, seven tobacco companies agreed to pay the states $206 billion to reimburse them for the costs of smoking-related illness and medical treatment and to embark on a $1.5 billion antismoking campaign. Some analysts have criticized the agreement, claiming that it is a relative drop in the bucket for these companies, considering the huge profits they have derived over more than fifty years of selling cigarettes. Perhaps these claims will be answered by the ongoing suit brought by the U.S. Department of Justice and its attorney general, who are arguing that tobacco companies acted together to deceive the American public about the real health effects of smoking and to market cigarettes to young people, and that the companies violated the **Racketeer Influenced and Corrupt Organizations Act (RICO)**. Under RICO, the U.S. attorney general seeks to force tobacco companies to "disgorge" all the profits they earned over the last fifty years. In addition, the suit aims to prevent the companies from engaging in deceptive advertising in the future, force them to reveal all information they have about the health dangers of smoking, and make them pay all health care costs associated with smoking in the future.

Indirect Effects of Faulty Products—The Fast-Food Industry and Obesity

www ▶ ▶ ▶

Products liability law comes mostly from common law, specifically, the body of cases brought by individuals who have been harmed by faulty products. Liability extends far beyond the initial point of manufacture, and it includes, not only the direct effects of the faulty product, but more indirect effects, as well. For example, when a nightclub fire in Rhode Island killed almost one hundred people in 2003, victims' families sued not only the band, whose indoor pyrotechnics started the fire, and the owners of the nightclub, who failed to take down a foam door that fire inspectors had repeatedly identified as being a violation of the fire code. Families also sued the company that manufactured fire insulation material in the club, alleging that this material did not stop the spread of the fatal fire. Today plaintiffs are suing fast-food companies for the contribution their products have made to childhood and adult obesity, even though everyone recognizes that there are a number of other contributing factors, among them, a lack of exercise and too much television-watching. Many companies have begun to try to keep track of their buyers or users so that they can alert them when and if they become aware that their products pose a risk of harm. For example, many manufacturers of children's products now urge consumers to complete registration cards and submit them so that the company can more easily recall, repair, or replace defective products.

Damages

www ▶ ▶ ▶

compensatory damages

monetary award used to make victims whole and place them in the same position they were in before being harmed

www ▶ ▶ ▶

punitive damages

monetary award used to punish the wrong-doer, usually by assessing damages that are three times the compensatory damages

www ▶ ▶ ▶

Romo v. Ford Motor Company

here the U.S. Supreme Court drastically reduced the jury's punitive damage award in an SUV rollover crash

When judges and juries assess products liability cases, they attempt to determine the full extent of the injuries suffered by the person bringing the case. Courts decide on damages by trying to figure out how much the person has actually lost—that is, the loss of earnings, the medical expenses, and the extent of pain and suffering endured as a result of the injuries. These damages, calculated as a dollar amount, are known as **compensatory damages**, which are intended to get victims to the same place they would be in if they had not suffered the injury. Some courts also impose **punitive damages**, which are intended to punish the wrongdoer and to encourage other companies to be more careful in their design, manufacturing, and marketing. While compensatory damages are intended to compensate for actual losses, punitive damages are usually treble (or three times) the compensatory award. For example, in the 2003 case *Romo v. Ford Motor Company*, the U.S. Supreme Court reduced the punitive damage award from $290 million to $23.7 million, an amount that was roughly three times the compensatory damages, for Ford's liability in a rollover crash that killed three people and injured two. There is significant concern about the effects of large punitive damage awards on corporate solvency—in fact, a number of companies that manufactured asbestos went out of business after juries demanded that they pay large punitive awards to workers who succumbed to lung disease after exposure to the material. At this point in time, twenty-five states have passed tort reform laws intended to limit these awards to either treble damages or some specified amount.

How do we square the huge increase in products liability cases and laws with law and economics jurisprudence? What do damages represent? Many law and economics theorists argue strongly that damage awards should truly represent damage done by one party to another so that companies can assess the costs and benefits of taking action that may harm others or the environment. There is substantial concern in the American system about awards that go beyond simply compensation—for example, when a jury or judge decides to award punitive damages, which punish the transgressor rather than compensating the victim. This kind of award introduces an element of uncertainty into the model since it does not represent damages that can be readily determined and assessed. For law and economics it is key that companies understand the real costs of doing business so that they can use these costs to determine how to become more efficient. It is much more difficult for companies to do this when they must factor in the cost of punitive awards when determining the ultimate costs of manufacturing or distribution. For this reason, many law and economics scholars would argue for a transparent system of compensation, where damage awards reflect the actual harm done to a person or to the community.

SUMMARY

This chapter has examined the role of law in regulating the activities of corporations in the United States. As in so many other areas, our law has changed largely in response to the demands of the economic system. When the Industrial Revolution took hold, the law changed to accommodate the need to protect interstate commerce and competition. After the stock market crash of 1929 and resulting Great Depression, we again used law to deal with the social and economic dislocations suffered in some degree by nearly all American workers and business owners. The resulting laws regulating corporate investment and trading have been enforced more or less vigorously at different times in our history, but these laws remain on the books, setting the standard for corporate governance and investment. Similarly, when public consciousness of industrialization's threat to the environment grew, the law responded, creating new standards to guide corporations and the larger public.

Much of this law has been created by federal and state legislatures, but it bears noting that courts continue to play an important role in setting the parameters for debate. It was the courts that ultimately made the decision to allow Congress to play a more prominent role in the regulation of interstate commerce. And the courts played an important part in the expansion of economic policies and laws governing monopoly and anticompetitive tactics. The courts also weighed in on the important issues of environmental pollution and products liability. In all of these areas, courts have taken a central role in establishing the rules that guide corporate behavior, and in nearly all cases, this role has been controversial. In large part, this controversy grows out of our political culture, which values corporate initiative and independence and is suspicious of interference with market forces. This perceived tension between law, market efficiency, and competition is very much apparent in larger discussions about the real costs of administrative and regulatory law. We can expect that debates about the role of law in the economy will continue and that they are likely to shift to the international arena as the European Union and many nation-states seek to become more competitive while also adhering to international, regional, and national laws that protect the environment and worker health.

SUGGESTED READING

Robert Cooter and Thomas Ulen, *Law and Economics,* 4th ed. (Addison-Wesley Series in Economics, 2003). This casebook provides an excellent overview of law and economics, including an examination of how this theory of jurisprudence enhances our understanding of tort, contract, property, and criminal law.

Colin Gordon, *New Deals: Business, Labor, and Politics in America, 1920–1935* (Cambridge University Press, 1994). This book looks at the way in which government, organized labor, and corporations interacted to create policy in the period immediately before and after the Great Depression.

Richard A. Posner, *Antitrust Law,* 2nd ed. (University of Chicago, 2004). This classic text examines antitrust law from the standpoint of law and economics, arguing that these laws must be evaluated by determining whether they promote the economic welfare of the larger society.

Clifford Rechtschaffen and Eileen P. Gauna, *Environmental Justice: Law, Policy, and Regulation* (Carolina Academic Press, 2002). Offering an excellent overview of the field of environmental law and politics, this book evaluates both litigation and more collaborative approaches to achieving environmental justice.

ACTIVE LEARNING

1. Group Project: Go to http://www.corpwatch.org/ and choose an article (this site is always being updated). Read the article and devise solutions to the problems. How would you address these problems? Would you seek the cooperation of the corporation that is involved? Why or why not? What would an advocate of the law and economics school counsel?

2. Film and Essay: View or read *A Civil Action,* based on an actual case brought by people who claimed that they were harmed by by a group of companies that dumped toxic substances. What did the plaintiffs argue? Was their argument compelling? Do you think that the truth won out in this case? Why or why not? What role did the litigation process itself play in revealing or hiding the truth?

3. Debate: Consider the ongoing case brought by the Department of Labor against the tobacco industry (go to *http://www.usdoj.gov/civil/cases/tobacco2/*). Read some of the papers filed by both sides (there are a lot to choose from!). Read some of the testimony as well. Which side makes a more compelling argument? What elements of the opposing argument are convincing? Be prepared to debate the relative merits and shortcomings of each side's argument.

Glossary

ACT UP: an activist group that staged protests to bring pressure on governmental officials to increase funding for AIDS research and to expedite the FDA's drug-review process; often outside the mainstream

Administrative law: law created by federal and state administrative agencies

Administrative Procedure Act: act that lays out guidelines that must be followed in administrative cases; usually more flexible than the procedures that must be used at trial

Administrative regulations: laws passed by executive branch agencies that have responsibility for implementing statutes

Adversarial system: court system based on the principle that the truth will emerge in a trial from the clash between the two parties, or rather their lawyers; in this system, the lawyers have the responsibility to zealously protect the legal rights of their clients

Advisory opinions: opinions rendered in response to a request for the highest constitutional court to weigh in on a law and issue an opinion that can guide lawmakers in dealing with this law; not binding on anyone, for advice alone; used in countries like France with a code law tradition

Affirmative action: programs that seek to address institutional racism by providing resources or opportunities to overcome inequities in education and employment

Alien Tort Claims Act (ATCA): U.S. statute that empowers American courts to hear cases involving violations of international treaty law and customary law

Alternative Dispute Resolution Act (1998): congressional statute requiring federal district court judges to offer at least one form of ADR before moving to trial in civil cases

Alternative dispute resolution: the use of some forum other than a court to resolve one's dispute

American Indian Religious Freedom Act (1978): act establishing the right to free exercise of religion for Native Americans

American Medical Association: national organization of physicians that has played an important role in the regulation of abortion, beginning with its campaign in the mid- to late 1800s to institute state abortion bans

Amici curiae: briefs filed, usually before the U.S. Supreme Court or other high courts, by individuals or groups that are interested in the outcome of litigation but are not the actual litigants

Analytical jurisprudence: theory that rejects natural law and argues that the only rights we have are those that are given to us by the government

Appellate court: court with responsibility for deciding whether the law was applied correctly in the trial case

Arbitration: a form of alternative dispute resolution that is widely used to resolve disputes among nations and transnational organizations, particularly commercial interests

Arbitration: the most structured form of ADR; uses an arbitrator, whose decision may or may not be binding on the parties

Ashcroft v. Oregon: case decided by a federal appeals court that upheld the Oregon Death with Dignity Act and struck down a policy directive issued by U.S. Attorney General John Ashcroft that would have barred doctors from using prescriptions to assist individuals in hastening their deaths under the federal Controlled Substances Act

Atwater v. Lago Vista: 2001 Supreme Court case that allowed police to exercise their discretion in deciding to arrest a woman who had not seat-belted her children into her car

Avoidance: when the injured party removes him- or herself completely from the offending relationship

Baker* v. *Carr: landmark U.S. Supreme Court case that established that cases involving redistricting could be justiciable

Bar exam: a written test administered by the state bar association that all lawyers must pass before they can be admitted to practice law in that state

Battered woman syndrome: increasingly used in the 1990s, a defense based on the diminished capacity of women who have been beaten repeatedly by their mates

Bench, or judge, trial: trial in which the judge, rather than the jury, is the fact-finder

Bill of Rights: document that created protections to safeguard individual rights, among these, the free election of representatives, the prohibition against cruel and unusual punishment, and the right to a jury trial

Blackstone, Sir William: writer whose hugely influential *Commentaries on the Laws of England* compiled British judges' holdings and focused on making law uniform

Borough-English: the rule that gave all of the father's property to the youngest son

Brown* v. *Board of Education: the landmark 1954 U.S. Supreme Court decision that struck down state laws that mandated separate schools for whites and nonwhites; many criticize this decision for failing to go far enough in mandating desegregation

Bruce Babbitt, Secretary of Interior, et al., Petitioners* v. *Sweet Home Chapter of Communities for a Great Oregon et al., Respondents: 1995 case in which the Supreme Court ruled that the definition of "taking" in the Endangered Species Act included the destruction of habitat

Case law: the law that derives from judges' decisions in cases

Case or controversy requirement: at the core of the principle of justiciability is the requirement that the case involve a genuine controversy and that it be a dispute for which a court can fashion a remedy—in short, it must not be collusive or ask for an advisory opinion

Casework: the requests or problems of constituents that House members try to satisfy in order to assure reelection

Caveat emptor: the prevailing norm in business dealings through the 1950s and 1960s; literally defined as "buyer beware," it made the buyer responsible for all defects of a product, even those that were hidden or not readily discoverable

Caveat fabricator: a central tenet of products liability law; defined as "builder beware," it makes the manufacturer or distributor of goods responsible for both direct and indirect harm that befalls the buyer

Chavez* v. *Martinez: landmark 2003 Supreme Court decision that allowed police to immediately question a person whom they had shot, even while emergency medical procedures were being performed on him

Chief executive: governor or president, this person often plays a key role in the creation of legislation

***Circuit City Stores, Inc.* v. *Adams* (2001):** case in which the Supreme Court upheld a mandatory arbitration clause in an employment contract; in so doing, required a party alleging employment discrimination to arbitrate before he could litigate

City of Chicago* v. *Beretta USA Corp.: the Illinois appellate court allowed this case against gun manufacturers to proceed, based on public nuisance law

Civil disobedience: the view that individuals have no obligation to obey laws that they deem unfair or unjust

Civil law: law whose primary goal is the enforcement of rights and obligations usually between private entities

Civil Rights Act: and act that barred discrimination in voting, public accommodations and facilities, education, federally assisted programs, and employment; passed in 1964

Civilian Complaint Review Board: a panel that was given broad powers to investigate police brutality in New York City in the wake of a police shooting of an unarmed civilian in 1999

"Closed shops": workplaces where all employees must join the union

Code law tradition: legal tradition that emerged in Code of Justinian in sixth century; now the predominant tradition in the world; relies on non-judge-made sources of law

Code of Justinian: an extensive legal code compiled by Emperor Justinian in the sixth century in an attempt to maintain control over the Roman Empire

Code or civil law tradition: a tradition focusing on law made by legislatures, chief executives, and regulatory and enforcement offices; derived from the legal system of ancient Rome

Coke, Sir Edward: one of the first legal positivists, he argued against the divine right of kings and for written law

Collective bargaining agreements: employment contracts, often between employers and unions; may contain arbitration clauses

Collegial court: a court over which more than one judge or justice presides; members must work together to achieve agreement

Collusive suit: suit that does not involve a legitimate conflict; one in which the parties are colluding to bring about the lawsuit

Comfort women: the more than 200,000 Chinese and Korean women forced into sexual slavery during World War II; they sought damages in U.S. courts

Commerce power: the power to regulate trade among the states, known as interstate commerce, was given to Congress in Article I, Section 8, of the Constitution; the Supreme Court's interpretation of this power has sometimes been broad and other times narrow

Commerce power: the power of Congress to regulate aspects of the economy

Common law tradition: tradition that arose in Great Britain and was the foundation for the American legal system; relies on judge-made law and the principle of stare decisis

Comparable worth: the attempt by some states and municipalities to compare jobs according to the skill, effort, education, and experience needed by the occupant of the job in an attempt to eliminate gender-based disparities in pay

Compassionate Use Act: initiative approved by California voters in 1996 that allowed patients and their primary caregivers to possess or cultivate marijuana without being penalized under state drug laws

Compensatory damages: the monetary award used to make victims whole and place them in the same position they were in before being harmed

Comstock Law: laws passed by Congress in 1873 that sharply limited access to contraception

Concurring opinion: on a collegial court, the decisions reached by those judges or justices who do not agree with the reasoning of the majority but do agree with the decision

Conflict/"blaming" stage: stage at which the injured parties confront the person they believe has caused them harm and demand resolution

Contraceptive equity laws: laws mandating that employers pay for contraceptives if they pay for other prescription drugs

Controlled Substances Act (1970): federal law that prohibits the sale and distribution of marijuana across state lines

Convention on the Rights of the Child: UN treaty that barred capital punishment for juveniles; this is also *jus cogens,* since nearly all nation-states bar this practice

Court of last resort: exists in both the federal and state systems; court that hears appeals almost exclusively, and almost all of these are at the discretion of the judges or justices

Courts of general jurisdiction: courts with wide authority that can hear cases involving a range of issues; exist only in the state court system

Courts of limited jurisdiction: courts that have responsibility for hearing only certain kinds of cases; exist in federal and state court systems

Coverture: the merging of a woman's legal identity with that of her husband

Creppy Directive: order issued by an INS judge immediately after 9/11 that allowed the agency to hold closed hearings in immigration cases; successfully challenged in the Sixth Circuit, which held that the INS had overstepped its powers

Criminal due process rights: those rights that protect individuals against arbitrary and unreasonable actions taken by the government in enforcing the criminal code

Criminal law: law whose primary goal is the protection of persons and property and maintenance of public order; government is the central actor

Critical legal studies: belief that law is used to reinforce existing power structures

Critical race feminism: belief that law reflects not only gender but race and class bias, as well

Critical race theory: part of outsider jurisprudence, it assumes that law is biased against persons of color; proponents are known as CRITS

Customary law: law that is not necessarily written down but is based on long-established patterns or rules of behavior

Customary law: international law based on the customs or traditions of a community of nations

Cyberstalking: the systematic harassment of an individual by means of electronic communication

Death with Dignity Act: 1997 Oregon law passed by voter initiative that allows individuals in Oregon who are terminally ill to access physician aid in dying

Decodification of laws: the trend toward less formal means of resolving disputes in advanced legal systems

Defense of Marriage Act: 1996 statute stipulating that the federal government will only recognize marriage between a man and a woman and will not pay federal benefits to same-sex couples

DeFunis v. Odegaard: case that demonstrates the principle of mootness—here the Supreme Court refused to hear an affirmative action case because the controversy was no longer present

Delegation of power: the giving of lawmaking power to administrative agencies to create rules for the implementation of law by Congress and state legislatures; this power may be quite extensive, especially if the law is unclear or contradictory

Department of Homeland Security: federal department created after 9/11 and given significant powers to investigate and prevent terror attacks in the United States

Deterrence: the most controversial goal of criminal law; it focuses on using punishment to dissuade either the individual offender or the larger public from breaking the law in the future

Dispute/"claiming" stage: the accused party refuses to compensate the injured party for the injuries and the injured party seeks resolution of the conflict by appealing to a third party

Dissenting opinion: on a collegial court, the decisions reached by those judges or justices who do not agree with the decision reached by the majority

Diversity of citizenship: one of the two ways that cases come to the federal district court—to have diversity jurisdiction, the parties must be from different states and the case must involve at least $75,000

Divine law: law that was God-given (according to those who subscribe to this belief) and had only to be discovered by human beings

Dominance, or radical feminist, jurisprudence: theory of feminist jurisprudence that focuses on the power imbalances between the sexes and sees law as a tool for the oppression of women

Double jeopardy protection: protection guaranteed by the Fifth Amendment and most state constitutions that assures that a defendant in a criminal case cannot be tried more than once for a single crime

Dual legislative system: the two separate and largely independent federal and state systems

Durkheim, Emile: sociologist writing in the late 1800s who argued that law is the expression of a nation-state's stage of development; as nations become more industrialized and specialized, the law also changes to become restitutive, and administrative and procedural law predominate

Economic class: position in society based on financial assets and resources

Eisenstadt v. Baird: 1972 Supreme Court case that extended the right to contraception to unmarried individuals

Elitist theory of democracy: theory based on the argument that only some groups, the elite in the society, have access to the lawmaking process.

Emancipation Proclamation: 1863 executive order issued by President Lincoln decreeing that all slaves were free

Empirical theories of jurisprudence: theories of law that examine how law *actually* functions

Enron: once the seventh wealthiest corporation listed in the Fortune 500, this company went bankrupt in 2001, the largest company ever to do so; the resultant scandal surrounding accounting practices and insider trading have spawned a number of high-profile cases, including the federal cases against former CEO Jeffrey Skilling

Environmental Protection Agency (EPA): agency created by Congress in 1969 under the National Environmental Policy Act and given expanded powers in a series of laws, including the Clear Air Act

Equal Pay Act: act requiring that men and women be paid the same amount for the same job

Equality of opportunity: equal access to resources that are needed to succeed

Escobedo v. Illinois: landmark 1964 Supreme Court decision that stated that criminal due process protections kicked in even before a formal indictment

Executive orders: laws created solely by the chief executive, whose power to make law comes from federal or state constitutions

Expert witnesses: specialists hired by either side to get the fact-finder to present information about a factual issue

Fact-finder: either a judge or jury in a trial court

Fact-finding: one of the chief functions of legislative hearings—allows legislators to gather information about an issue

Fast track: streamlined procedures created by the FDA in the wake of the AIDS epidemic to expedite delivery of some experimental drugs to patients with Human Immunodeficiency Virus (HIV)

Fast track: when the president or governor places a bill on the legislature's agenda and requires that the body either accept it as written, with no modifications, or reject it

Fatwa: an interpretation of Islamic law usually issued by well-regarded scholars of the law

Federal Arbitration Act (1925): congressional statute initially created to govern maritime and admiralty disputes; now extended to cover many other kinds of disputes

Federal Register: a government publication that informs the public about any new rules being considered by an agency

Feminist jurisprudence: theories of law that are based on the view that law and legal institutions are patriarchal and reflect the dominant position of males in society

Fifteenth Amendment: amendment to the U.S. Constitution that decreed that all men could vote; ratified in 1870

Folkways: informal norms that are part of day-to-day living and guide dress, patterns of speech, and interactions with others

Food and Drug Administration Modernization Act of 1997: act that institutionalized the fast-track procedure for experimental drugs being studied for possible treatment of serious or life-threatening illness

Formal norms: social controls that are imposed on the individual by some outside actor—either a nongovernmental entity, or a governmental control, known as a law

Fourteenth Amendment: amendment to the U.S. Constitution that guaranteed citizenship to all people born or naturalized in the United States and barred states from denying to them the rights of citizenship and depriving them of due process or equal protection of the laws; ratified in 1870

French Parliament (*le Parlement*): the key lawmaking body in France, it has a central role in the creation of French law

Game theory: theory used to predict and explain how individual decisions are affected by the strategies of other actors

Ganim v. Smith & Wesson: the Connecticut Supreme Court dismissed this case, finding that city officials had no standing to bring a suit against gun manufacturers to recover damages for gun-related harm

Gender: much broader than sex, this encompasses learned behaviors as well as societal expectations and responses with regard to maleness and femaleness

General Allotment Act (1887): act that allotted property to individual Native Americans and effectively gave the federal government title to more than 90 million acres of unclaimed tribal land

Genetic engineering: using genetic information to treat disease or possibly to alter a person's predisposition to certain illnesses

Gibbons v. Ogden: 1819 U.S. Supreme Court case defining commerce broadly to include traffic between the states

Glass ceiling: perceived barrier used to explain why women, people of color, and persons with disabilities can only rise to a certain level in management and are subtly kept out of the most elite corporate jobs

Glass elevator: perceived advantage used to explain why men in jobs occupied predominantly by women are presented with many more opportunities than their female counterparts

Glorious Revolution of 1689: uprising that ended the rule of King James II in England and ultimately made the king and queen subject to the laws of Parliament

Goodridge v. Department of Public Health: 2004 Massachusetts Supreme Court case that held that the state ban on gay marriage violated the equal protection clause of the state constitution

Gravelkind: the rule that divided the father's estate equally among all his sons

Great Depression: economic collapse precipitated by the stock market crash of 1929 and marked by high unemployment, low wages, and widespread poverty; ultimately the catalyst for much greater government regulation of the economy

Greatest happiness principle: basis of the theory of utilitarianism; argues that law should benefit the greatest number of people

Griswold v. Connecticut: 1965 Supreme Court case that established that married couples have a right to privacy that protects access to contraception

Grutter v. Bollinger and Gratz v. Bollinger: two Supreme Court cases challenging the use of affirmative action in a public university and law school; the law school program was upheld, that of the university was struck down as a quota system

Guilt beyond a reasonable doubt: so much of the evidence points toward guilt that no reasonable person would doubt that the person is responsible; in numeric terms, more than 99 percent of the evidence points toward guilt

Hamdi et al. v. Rumsfeld, Secretary of Defense; Rasul et al. v. Bush, President of the United States, and Rumsfeld, Secretary of Defense v. Padilla et al. (2004): cases in which the Court rejected the U.S. argument that it could detain enemy combatants indefinitely; in the *Hamdi* and *Rumsfeld* cases, the U.S. Supreme Court argued that U.S. citizens had to be given meaningful opportunity to present evidence; in *Rasul* the Court held that even noncitizens could gain access to American courts

Hart, H. L. A: believed that as legal systems evolved, they moved through three discrete stages; when a society developed metarules, known as rules of recognition, change, and adjudication, it had moved to the most advanced stage

Hate crime statutes: laws adopted by municipalities, states, and Congress that make it a crime to engage in acts of violence motivated by racial, ethnic, or religious bias

Henry of Bracton: one of the most important commentators on the common law tradition whose work promoted uniformity

Historical jurisprudence: views law and legal institutions as evolving into the highest stage—that of written code law

Honor killings: killing of female family members who have committed adultery; in Jordon and some other Islamic states, men who commit these crimes are exempted from murder charges

Hostile work environment: situation arising when an employer or someone under his or her control engages in harassment of an individual that becomes severe or pervasive enough to affect the employment relationship, thus creating a hostile work environment in violation of employment discrimination law

Hot pursuit exception: an exception to the warrant requirement that allows police to search any vehicle or person of which they are in continuous pursuit

Hot pursuit principle: principle allowing a nation-state to pursue a vessel into another nation-state's domestic waters under international law

Human Genome Project: an international collaboration of scientists which created a blueprint or map of all human genes, the entities that establish the basic structure and function of the human body; the map may ultimately be used to identify an individual's predisposition to certain medical diseases

Humanitarian intervention: decision by the United Nations or some other international or regional body to intervene in the domestic affairs of a nation to safeguard human rights

Implied power: Congress not only has the right to take action to accomplish the explicit goals laid out in Article 1, Section 8; this section also gives Congress the power to make laws that are "necessary and proper" to achieve these goals—this clause, also known as the elastic clause, is the source of Congress's implied powers

Incapacitation: a goal of criminal law that aims at protecting society by incarcerating criminals or putting them to death

Indian Civil Rights Act (1968): conferred on native peoples the same rights that are in the Bill of Rights

Indian Removal Act (1830): act mandating that all Native Americans east of the Mississippi give up their lands and move west

Indoor Air Quality Rules: proposed rules, withdrawn by OSHA in 2001 after more than six years of a highly critical notice and comment period

Informal norms: social controls that are self-imposed by the individual

Informed consent: a central facet of medical research; requires that a person consent to participate in clinical research, meaning that they be fully informed of the risks and benefits of clinical research

Inquisitorial system: system used in nations with code law traditions; characterized by cooperation; in the criminal system, guilt is based on preponderance of evidence

Insider trading: the use of information that is not available to the public in making decisions to buy, sell, or transfer stocks; barred by the Federal Securities Act of 1934

Institutional racism: racism that is ingrained in the very fabric of society and cannot be eliminated without taking aggressive action

Intergovernmental organizations: groups comprised of nations that address some specific issue or need, like the Asia and Pacific Coconut Community

Intermediate courts of appeals: courts that provide answers to questions of law that have arisen in trial courts; exist in both the federal and state systems; the federal and most state systems guarantee at least one appellate hearing

Intermediate scrutiny standard: intermediate between the strict scrutiny and rational relationship tests, this standard is used to evaluate gender-based distinctions; requires that states justify their gender-based laws by showing that they are substantially related to an important governmental interest

International Convention for the Suppression of the Financing of Terrorism (2002): signed by more than 130 states and ratified by nearly 80 states, this treaty targeted funding for terrorist organizations

International Court of Justice (ICJ): the highest court in the international community

International Criminal Court: court created in 1998 to establish a permanent tribunal for hearing cases against government officials charged with human rights violations

Interstate Commerce Commission (ICC): one of the earliest regulatory agencies, established by Congress in 1887 pursuant to its constitutional power to regulate interstate commerce

Islamic legal tradition: tradition that subordinates law to Islamic religious doctrine; only one nation is a pure Islamic state, where all law is based on religious code, but nearly forty others use Islamic law in combination with secular law

Jim Crow laws: far-reaching laws passed in the post–Civil War era that segregated the races

Judicial review: the power of courts to review and strike down laws passed by the executive or legislative branches; used relatively infrequently by the U.S. Supreme Court

Jurisdiction: the power to hear and resolve a case; created by federal or state constitutions or statutes

Jurisprudence: theories that define what a law is and how it functions

Juror selection: the practice by which juries are chosen—once guided by lawyers' folklore about the ideal juror in a case; now dictated by much more scientific methods

Jury nullification: when a jury reaches a decision based, not on the facts, but on its interpretation or disregard of the law

Jus cogens: set of norms based on unanimous or near unanimous agreement about acceptable behavior; derived from nations' laws

Just war: war that is justified by a principle higher than the desire to accumulate power

Justiciability: the requirement that courts handle only those conflicts that are appropriate for judicial resolution—there are three features of this principle: the conflict must be based on a legitimate case or controversy; it must be ripe, but not moot; and it must not involve a political question

King's Court of Star Chamber: chief law enforcement arm of the British monarchy during 1500s and 1600s; had unlimited power to search individuals and used this power to intimidate

Kyoto Accord: an international treaty that set deadlines for reducing greenhouse gases at significant cost to the United States; parts of this treaty were implemented by President Clinton in a series of executive orders

Laissez faire: an economic model based on the assumption that markets operate best and are most efficient when they are free from governmental regulation

Latino critical theory: theory of jurisprudence that views the law as reinforcing the majority culture and English language

Law Against Discrimination: New Jersey antidiscrimination law that provides more protection than its federal counterpart because it bars discrimination based, not only on race, color, religion, national origin, and sex, but on grounds like sexual orientation, as well

Law and economics: well-accepted theory that law functions or should function to maximize societal wealth by promoting market efficiency

Law and literature school: theory of jurisprudence that views literature as helpful to our understanding of how law operates

Law and popular culture school: theory of jurisprudence that suggests we can use popular culture to better understand how law functions

"Law in action": theory of jurisprudence that focuses on the actual enforcement and interpretation of laws and argues for a more active role for judges

Law of conquest: the long-established custom that recognized the right of European nations to occupy and possess lands that they discovered in the New World

Law of the Sea: customs and practices governing use of the seas, these have been codified, most recently in the 1982 UN Convention on the Law of the Sea.

Law School Admissions Test (LSAT): a standardized exam required by most law schools as part of the admissions process; scores range from 120 to180

Legal anthropology: a field of study that focuses on how different societies approach dispute resolution, and looks at how law functions as a social control and structures relationships; assumes a continuum, from less formal to more formal and complex legal systems

Legal positivists: theorists who promote the codification of laws and argue that society is best served by having written laws that are explicit and clear

Legal realism: theory that all legal decisions are based on moral and political choices

Legalistic style of policing: officers are expected to focus on strict compliance with laws on the books, and rank-and-file members are expected to closely follow guidelines

Legislator-in-chief: the governor or president, who often uses his or her office to play an active role in the creation of legislation

Liberal feminist jurisprudence: view that law must aim at gender-neutrality

Life chances: ability to get ahead, wield influence, and pass one's social class along to one's offspring; closely related to social and economic class

Line-item veto: the power of the chief executive to veto particular sections of bills; some governors have this power, but the president does not

Litigants: the two parties involved in a case: prosecutor and defendant in a criminal trial case; plaintiff and defendant in a civil trial case; appellant and appellee, or petitioner and respondent, in an appellate case

Lochner v. _New York_: 1905 Supreme Court case that struck down Progressive Era New York State law limiting the number of hours a baker could work; the Court argued that the law violated the freedom of bakers to freely contract for the sale of their labor

"Lumping it": when the injured party decides to live with the injury and not to pursue resolution

MacPherson v. _Buick Motor Company_: struck down the principle of privity, and thus paved the way for product liability suits against manufacturers

Magna Carta of 1215: the "Great Charter" aimed at limiting the power of the sovereign; it asserted that individuals had rights separate from those given to them by the king

Majority opinion: court opinion that reflects the decision of majority of judges or justices

Mala in se: acts that are viewed as evil in themselves, like murder and rape

Mala prohibita: activities that are prohibited by law but about which there is substantial societal disagreement, including "victimless" crimes

Malinowski, Bronislaw: a legal anthropologist who argued that scholars had to look to see how a legal system was actually operating; his study of Trobriand Islanders blurred the lines between primitive, transitional, and modern legal systems

Mapp v. _Ohio_: Supreme Court's 1961 opinion mandating that police officers have a valid warrant before conducting a search

Marxist legal theory: belief that law is a tool to reinforce the privileged position of the elite

Master Settlement Agreement: California appellate case that made tobacco companies responsible for marketing and advertising policies in force during a period of immunity

Mediation: form of ADR in which a neutral and disinterested third person works with the parties to craft a solution that both parties must accept; fastest growing form of ADR

Military tribunals: committees, groups, or courts created after 9/11 to try noncitizens suspected of planning or participating in terror attacks against the United States; offer fewer criminal due process protections than civilian law; conducted largely by the Department of Defense

Miranda **rule:** requirement that police inform suspects of their due process rights; has become less of a constraint on police departments over the last few decades

Miranda v. Arizona: Supreme Court's 1966 opinion requiring that officers give notice of criminal due process rights to anyone in their custody

Missouri Compromise (1820): a congressional statute that paired the admission of slave and free states in an attempt to ensure that neither gained a political edge as the result of westward expansion

Mores: informal norms that are based on common values and establish rules for moral behavior; more intensely held than folkways

Muller v. Oregon: Progressive Era legislation upheld for women workers because it protected maternal function

Napoleonic Code: civil code created largely by Napoleon Bonaparte in the early 1800s in an attempt to ensure uniformity, establish individual rights, and consolidate his power in France

National Labor Relations Act (NLRA): law passed by Congress in 1935 that established workers' right to engage in collective action and to form unions

National Research Act: federal statute passed in the wake of the outcry over the Tuskegee Syphilis Study that required all federally funded research projects involving human subjects to be approved by an institutional review board

Natural law: normative legal theory that argues that law should be based on religious or philosophical principles

NCCUSL and ALI: organizations that seek to codify law and make it easier to use and more predictable

Negotiation: the least formal form of ADR; only the two parties are involved, and to succeed, they must see agreement as in their mutual self-interest

NLRB v. Jones & Laughlin: 1937 U.S. Supreme Court case upholding a federal law that protected unionization efforts; signaled the Court's willingness to allow more regulation of businesses; used to uphold federal and state regulation of the workplace relationship

Noncitation statutes: passed in several states in the period immediately following the Revolutionary War, these laws barred judges from relying on past rulings in deciding cases in an attempt to limit the impact of British common law

Nonconsensual sources of laws: those sources of law that are not written down but are inferred by domestic law—the two main sources are *jus cogens* and the decisions of some international and domestic courts; nation-states haven't explicitly agreed to be bound by these laws

Nongovernmental organizations (NGOs): groups comprising private citizens concerned about some issue or problem, like Street Child Africa or Amnesty International

Norma McCorvey: the "Jane Roe" in *Roe* v. *Wade*—she now actively lobbies against the very case that she won more than three decades ago

Norman Conquest of 1066: invasion of England that resulted in a national legal system

Normative theories of jurisprudence: theories of law that focus on how law *should* function

North American Free Trade Agreement (NAFTA) (1994): regional treaty between the United States, Canada, and Mexico intended to ease trade barriers and result in freer trade

Occupational Safety and Health Administration (OSHA): the federal agency charged with enforcing standards for occupational safety; its regulations usually establish a floor and state agencies can mandate additional protections

Office of Federal Contract Compliance: established by President Johnson to ensure that those with federal contracts considered African American applicants when hiring

Ombudsman: person who has more responsibility than a mediator and can engage in independent investigation of the claim

One-shotters: novices in the litigation process; they have a disadvantage relative to repeaters

Opt out: decision not to pursue resolution of a dispute

Oversight hearings: hearings held by legislatures to determine how administrative agencies are implementing statutes

Pharmocogenomics: the study of how genetics affects one's response to drug therapy

Philadelphia Plan: President Nixon's plan to establish timetables and goals for the employment of minorities in federal contracts

Physician aid in dying: the practice by physicians of providing death-hastening medications, usually to terminally ill patients who have significant pain and suffering; barred in most states by laws that make it a crime to assist another in committing suicide, but permitted in some states in certain narrowly defined circumstances

Plain view exception: an exception to the warrant requirement that allows police to access any evidence that is obvious to them

Planned Parenthood of Southeastern Pennsylvania v. Casey: 1992 Supreme Court case that replaced the trimester framework with the undue-burden test

Plea bargaining: probably the most common form of negotiation

Plessy v. Ferguson: 1986 Supreme Court case that allowed "separate but equal" state-operated railway transportation for whites and nonwhites

Pluralist theory of democracy: theory based on the argument that through the clash of interest groups, the best policies will emerge

Police power: the power of a legislature to protect the health, safety, and morality of its citizens; this power was recognized in the Tenth Amendment, which leaves to the state legislatures all powers not granted to the Congress and which has been the chief source of lawmaking power for the states

Political equality: all citizens have the right to vote and all votes count equally

Political salience: issues that are of significant interest to voters or interest groups and that are usually placed on the legislative agenda

Political-questions doctrine: doctrine that a case is not justiciable if it turns on a question that is better answered by either the legislative or executive branch

Polygamy: marriage between more than two people

Popular election: the most common method of choosing state court judges; raises concerns about the impact of public opinion on the judge's decisions

Positive law: a form of normative legal theory that focuses on the law as it is written and the process by which law is made

Postmodernism: view that there is no objective, knowable, or final truth and that standards and behaviors are dominated by powerful groups and individuals

Preconflict/"naming" stage: stage at which the injured parties become aware that they have been harmed by the actions or words of another

Preponderance of the evidence: most of the evidence points to a finding of guilt or liability; greater likelihood than not that the person committed the act that he or she is alleged to have committed; in numeric terms, 51 percent or more of the evidence establishes guilt or liability

Pretrial settlement conference: probably the most common form of mediation; a judge presides over a conference between the parties and may help formulate a settlement

Primitive legal systems: systems in which laws are synonomous with traditions, religion, or culture; retaliation and revenge are key; and criminal law is predominant

Primogeniture: the common law rule that the first-born son alone inherits the father's estate—the rule adopted by British courts

Principle of reciprocity: ancient custom that ensured the safety of ambassadors and messengers by allowing retaliation against the ambassadors and messengers of those countries that harmed enemy envoys

Private law: law governing transactions between private entities, like corporations

Private property rights: in the United States, the claim of individuals to make decisions about real property and personal property in which they have an ownership interest

Procedural naturalism: Fuller's theory that legal systems are legitimate only when they respect individual autonomy

Proclamation: an executive order that recognizes some group or emerging issue and has largely symbolic value

Products liability law: law that makes corporations liable or legally responsible for harm that results from defects in design, manufacture, or marketing of their products

Products liability law: law—mostly state law—governing the manufacture, sale, and distribution of goods that may pose a risk of harm to users or third parties

Progressive Movement: a political and social movement that focused on how law could be used to protect workers and the public from health hazards that resulted from industrialization

Progressive taxes: taxes that impose a proportionately heavier burden on wealthier people and have the potential to equalize wealth in the society

Proportionality: the requirement that the punishment fit the crime, that is, that it be neither too lenient nor excessive

Public law: law regulating relations between nation-states or nongovernmental agencies operating on behalf of a wider community

Punitive damages: monetary awards used to punish the wrongdoer, usually by assessing damages that are three times the compensatory damages

Punitive restitution: a goal of criminal law that focuses on both punishment and compensating the victim

Qualifications for membership: the requirements for serving in Congress or the state legislatures; for members of the House and Senate, these are laid out in the Constitution, Article I, Sections 2 and 3, and impose age and residency requirements

Racial profiling: using race or ethnicity as a proxy for deciding whom to search and detain in a Terry stop; police are not permitted to use race as the sole criterion in deciding whom to stop; there must be other, suspicious characteristics that trigger the stop

Racketeer Influenced and Corrupt Organizations Act (RICO): the basis for a federal lawsuit against the tobacco industry, asserting that the companies acted as an "enterprise" and conspired to run their businesses through fraud and deception

Raich v. Ashcroft: case currently before the U.S. Supreme Court that raises the question of whether the federal Controlled Substances Act prohibits the cultivation of medicinal marijuana in California

Rainbow Warrior: a vessel owned by Greenpeace that was sunk by France after protesting French nuclear testing; Greenpeace and the French government ultimately entered into binding arbitration that resulted in an award of several million dollars against French officials

Ranulf de Glanvill: compiler of a highly influential treatise on British laws who furthered uniformity among British courts by laying out the common laws of royal courts

Ratification process: domestic law and procedures that govern the ratification of international treaties

Rational relationship test: the easiest test for a state to prove; used to evaluate virtually all distinctions in the law *other than* those based on race, color, national origin, and sex; requires only that the distinction be rationally related to a legitimate state interest

Redistricting: redrawing of lines for congressional districts to reflect changes in the population following the U.S. census, which is taken every ten years

Regressive taxes: taxes that impose a proportionately heavier burden on people in the lower socioeconomic classes than they do on the wealthy

Rehabilitation: a controversial goal of the criminal justice system—over the last several decades, it has given way to retribution and incapacitation

Relational, or cultural feminist, jurisprudence: the belief that law must accommodate gender differences, specifically, the role of relationships in women's lives

Repeat players: those parties who are experienced in the litigation process; they have an advantage over one-shotters

Restitutive: aimed at making whole the person who has been injured

Retribution: the oldest goal of criminal law; encompasses both simple retribution ("an eye for an eye") and pecuniary compensation

Right to a jury trial: the right established in both the federal and state constitutions to have a jury as the fact-finder in a trial

Right to contract: until 1937, the prevailing justification used by the U.S. Supreme Court in its decisions striking down state and federal employment laws

"Right to work" laws: state laws that allow workers to decide whether they want to join the union that operates in their workplace

"Rights revolution": in the 1960s, courts and legislatures began to recognize many new legal rights, particularly for individuals

Rights Thesis: Dworkin's argument that judges have the obligation to respect individual rights when deciding cases

Roe v. Wade: the landmark 1973 U.S. Supreme Court case that struck down state abortion bans but polarized public opinion about abortion in the United States and allowed physicians to play an important role in the abortion decision by providing information to women and making assessments about how abortion, pregnancy, and childbirth might affect a woman's health

Romo v. Ford Motor Company: 2003 U.S. Supreme Court case that substantially reduced punitive damages from $290 million to $23.7 million, an amount that was three times the compensatory award against the car manufacturer in a case involving an SUV rollover crash

RU-486: a pill that can prevent conception if used within 72 hours of having sex

Salem witchcraft trials of 1692: trials that resulted in the deaths of twenty New Englanders who were alleged to have consorted with the devil

San Antonio Independent School District v. Rodriguez: 1973 Supreme Court case that declined to subject class- and wealth-based distinctions that resulted in inequalities in school funding to strict scrutiny

Securities Act of 1933: law that regulated the registration and initial offering of stocks by corporations; precipitated by the 1929 stock market crash

Securities Act of 1934: law that imposed significant disclosure requirements on corporations offering stocks for sale to the public and barred the manipulation of securities prices through deceptive practices like insider trading; a result of concern about the 1929 stock market crash

September 11 Victims Compensation Fund of 2001: fund created by Congress to provide an alternative to litigation for families or victims of the 9/11 attacks; Special Master Feinberg administered this fund

Service style of policing: also known as community-oriented policing (COP); departments using this style tend to see themselves as in a cooperative partnership with the local community; the public helps police to safeguard the community

Sex: the biological differences between men and women

Sexual orientation: the preferences of individuals for their sex partners; usually described in terms of an individual's being gay or lesbian, heterosexual, or bisexual

Shadow government: people who work indirectly for the federal government through federal contracts with private companies, grants, and federal mandates; possibly 40 million people are employed by this shadow government

Shari'ah: Islamic law that governs relationships between individuals and groups and is seen as the key Islamic legal text; it is interpreted by judges, who are said to be accountable to both Allah and the Muslim community

Sherman Antitrust Act: 1890 law that banned the creation of monopolies because lawmakers and the courts were concerned about the negative effects of these structures on fair competition and economic growth

Silent Spring: book that served as an important catalyst for the modern environmental movement

Slave patrol: the first American police force; charged with enforcing slave codes in the South in the pre–Civil War period

Social class: position in society based on family name, educational achievement, and job success

Social control: device that establishes norms to guide individual and group behavior

Social facts: ways of thinking, acting, and feeling that are shared by the collective and have coercive power over the individual

Social or economic equality: all people have the same access to education or other resources that enable them to move ahead, or all have a comparable living standard

Social stratification: grossly unequal access to opportunities and rewards in a society

Socialist legal tradition: tradition that focuses on the role of law in ensuring national security and in fostering the goals of socialism; used by only a few states

Sociological jurisprudence: theory that law is the product of social, political, and economic realities and can be used to bring about a better society

Souders v. *Philip Morris, Inc.:* California appellate case that made tobacco companies responsible for marketing and advertising policies in force during a period of immunity

Sovereignty: the right of nation-states to govern themselves and to make decisions based on their self-interest

Special master: hybrid form of ADR that gives an individual wide-ranging power to investigate claims and craft a binding settlement

Specialized committees: groups in the federal and state legislatures that have expertise in particular areas and usually provide much-needed information about proposed bills to the larger legislative body

Spectral evidence: evidence based on testimony that the accused had appeared in spectral or spirit form to someone who claimed to be afflicted by the accused; evidence that was basically impossible for the accused to refute

Standing: having a legal right that has been impaired

Stare decisis: the principle that judges should rely on the reasoning of judges in past cases

State of the Union address: a speech the president and most governors make each year to let the public know what the chief executive's legislative priorities will be

Stenberg v. *Carhart:* 2000 Supreme Court case that stuck down a state ban on partial-birth abortions, finding that the law was too vague, didn't provide a maternal-health exception, and barred abortions before fetal viability

Strict liability: making someone totally responsible for damages, even in the absence of proof that the party caused the harm

strict scrutiny standard: the most stringent equal protection test that can be applied to laws that distinguish among people, usually on the basis of race, ethnicity, and color—for the laws to stand, the government must show that the laws are narrowly tailored to serve a compelling interest

Sunna: in addition to Shari'ah, this source of Islamic law establishes legal custom and tradition; there is significant disagreement about what the four schools of Sunna actually require

Superfund: 1980 law, also known as CERCLA, that administers the cleanup effort of toxic waste sites and imposes strict liability on all owners, even those who did not pollute the sites themselves

Symbolic representation: representation based on the assumption that members of historically disadvantaged groups will support legislation that serves the needs and interests of these groups

Task forces: groups usually created pursuant to an executive order to study certain problems

Terry stops: stops that allow police officers to use their discretion in deciding to detain and search people who meet police profiles

Texas v. *Johnson:* 1989 Supreme Court case that struck down a Texas law that made it a crime to burn the American flag

Texas v. *Lawrence:* 2003 Supreme Court case that struck down a state sodomy ban that applied only to gays and lesbians

Thirteenth Amendment: amendment to the U.S. Constitution that prohibited the practice of slavery; ratified in 1870

Three stages of dispute resolution: the predictable stages through which virtually all conflicts pass

Title VII: section of the 1964 Civil Rights Act that barred employment discrimination on the basis of race, sex, color, national origin, and religion

Transfer programs: government programs that *transfer* funds from one group of people to another; provide resources to particular groups who are deemed worthy of funding

Transnational organizations: groups or organizations that cross national borders and can have a profound impact on what's happening both inside a nation-state and among states; among those groups with the most significant impact on international relations are corporations, which can have a profound effect on not only the laws of a nation but also its social and economic structures

Treaty: a written agreement between two or more nation-states and governed by international law

Treaty of Westphalia (1648): treaty marking the beginning of the modern era in international relations; established the nation-state as the most important actor

Trial court: court that resolves factual questions; engages in fact-finding and applies law

Triangle Shirtwaist Factory fire: fire that killed 111 immigrant women in 1911 and sparked the passage of state laws protecting worker health and safety, although many of these laws were struck down by the Supreme Court

Tuskegee Syphilis Study: a study of untreated syphilis, conducted between 1932 and 1972, in which poor black men were not informed that they were test subjects and were not receiving treatment of their disease; public outcry against this study resulted in more protective regulations governing research on human subjects

UN Population Fund (UNPF): a UN organization that provides contraceptive advice and contraception to nation-states, especially those that are less industrialized; the Bush administration withdrew American support for the UNPF because the administration believed that it advocated abortion as a form of birth control

UN Security Council: one of the most important but controversial organs of the United Nations, its fifteen members address threats to international security and peace, and throughout the 1990s, embarked on several peacekeeping missions in Somalia, Kuwait, and Yugoslavia; it has five permanent members—China, France, the Russian Federation, the United Kingdom, and the United States—and ten rotating memberships

U.S. Equal Employment Opportunity Commission (EEOC): a federal administrative agency with responsibility for creating and enforcing regulations that implement employment discrimination laws

U.S. v. Eichmann: 1990 Supreme Court case that struck down the 1989 Flag Protection Act, which was passed by Congress after *Texas* v. *Johnson*

Uniform Arbitration Act: act adopted by thirty-five states that regulates arbitration under state law

Uniform Commercial Code (UCC): a code that governs contracts; intended to provide uniformity and consistency among states and to limit state variation in the making and enforcement of contracts

Universal Declaration of Human Rights (1948): established that international law protects not only sovereign nations, but individuals, as well

Utilitarianism: philosophy based on the greatest happiness principle

Vacco v. Quill and Washington v. Glucksberg: two cases in which the Supreme Court ruled that state laws that banned physician aid in dying did not violate the constitutional rights of those who seek this assistance

Vehicle exception: an exception to the warrant requirement that allows officers to search any vehicle they believe may be carrying illegal goods or substances without having to first secure a warrant

Vigilante justice: actions by persons outside of government who step in to ensure order and the protection of life and property

Voluntary overcompliance: corporate choice to go beyond existing environmental, products safety, and occupational regulations in an effort to protect themselves against liability

Wage gap: difference between women's and men's earnings; women earn 77 cents for every dollar earned by men

War on drugs: program initiated in the early 1970s that targets all aspects of the production, distribution, and use of illegal drugs

Warrantless searches: searches that take place without a warrant; if there is no valid exception to the warrant requirement, a judge can refuse to admit evidence from warrantless searches

Washington State v. Glucksberg and Quill v. Vacco: a pair of 1997 Supreme Court cases that upheld state bans on physician-assisted suicide but left to state legislatures substantial discretion to decide whether terminally ill, competent persons have the right to aid in dying

Washington v. Glucksberg and Quill v. Vacco: 1997 Supreme Court cases that held there is no due process liberty right that bars states from banning physician aid in dying

Watchman style of policing: officers are allowed much more discretion in deciding which crimes to focus on, typically more serious violent crimes; police are expected to prevent crimes from being committed

Weber, Max: argued that the most advanced legal systems were those that employed legal domination, and in this system, the individual

White-collar crime: deviance from legitimate business activities; largely invisible and underreported, they cost the U.S. economy more than $300 billion each year

World Court: entity made up of the Permanent Court of International Justice and the International Court of Justice; has jurisdiction to hear cases involving alleged violations of international law and to issue advisory opinions; cannot compel nation-states to participate in cases brought against them

Zaheer-ud-din* v. *the State: 1993 Pakistan Supreme Court case that established that freedom of religion was *not* absolute and that in some conflicts between the constitution and Islamic law, religious law would predominate

Zero-sum nature of litigation: in courts, the necessity for someone to lose for the other to win; one of the obstacles to real resolution of a dispute

Bibliography and Suggested Readings

Chapter 1

S. Beth Atkin, *Voices from the Fields: Children of Migrant Farmworkers Tell Their Stories* (Little, Brown & Company, 1993)

Edward Ball, *Slaves in the Family* (Random House, 1998)

Yogesh Chadha, *Gandhi: A Life* (John Wiley & Sons, 1999)

John D'Emilio and Estelle B. Freedman, *Intimate Matters: A History of Sexuality in America* (Perennial Library/Harper & Row, 1988)

Alan M. Dershowitz, *The Genesis of Justice: Ten Stories of Biblical Injustice That Led to the Ten Commandments and Modern Law* (Warner Books, 2000)

Lawrence M. Friedman, American Law in the 20th Century (Yale University Press, 2002)

Richard Goodbeer, Sexual Revolution in Early America (Johns Hopkins University Press, 2002)

John Owen Haley, *Authority Without Power: Law and the Japanese Paradox* (Oxford University Press, 1994)

Barbara A. Hanawalt, *Of Good and Ill Repute: Gender and Social Control in Medieval England* (Oxford University Press, 1998)

Tara Heivel and Paul Wrangler, eds., *Prison Nation* (Routledge Press, 2003)

Jon Krakauer, *Under the Banner of Heaven : A Story of Violent Faith* (Doubleday; 1st edition, 2003)

Michael McGerr, *A Fierce Discontent: The Rise and Fall of the Progressive Movement in America, 1870–1920* (Free Press, 2003)

R. Robin Miller and Sandra Lee Browning, *For the Common Good: A Critical Examination of Law and Social Control* (Carolina Academic Press, 2004)

Patrick Minges, *Black Indian Slave Narratives* (John F. Blair Publishers, 2004)

Gale Williams O'Brien, *The Color of the Law: Race, Violence and Justice in the Post–World War II South* (University of North Carolina Press, 1999)

Jaroslav Pelikan, *Interpreting the Bible & the Constitution* (Yale University Press, 2004)

Mary Prince and Sara Salih, eds., *The History of Mary Prince: A West Indian Slave* (Penguin Books, 2001)

Jeffrey Reiman, *The Rich Get Richer and the Poor Get Prison: Ideology, Class and Criminal Justice* (Pearson Allyn & Bacon; 7th edition, 2003)

Gerald N. Rosenberg, *The Hollow Hope: Can Courts Bring About Social Change?* (University of Chicago Press, 1991)

Sally S. Simpson, *Corporate Crime, Law, and Social Control* (Cambridge University Press, 2002)

James Spradley and David W. McCurdy, *Conformity and Conflict: Readings in Cultural Anthropology* (Pearson Allyn & Bacon; 11th edition, 2002)

Laurence Steinberg and Elizabeth S. Scott, "Less Guilty by Reason of Adolescence Developmental Immaturity, Diminished Responsibility, and the Juvenile Death Penalty," 58 *American Psychologist*, No. 12, 1009–1018 (2003)

Linda Stone, *Kinship and Marriage* (Westview Press, 1997)

Gregory Howard Williams, *Life on the Color Line: The True Story of a White Boy Who Discovered He Was Black* (Plume, 1996)

Fareed Zakaria, *The Future of Freedom: Illiberal Democracy at Home and Abroad* (W. W. Norton, 2003)

W. W. Zellner and William M. Kephart, *Extraordinary Groups: An Examination of Unconventional Lifestyles* (Worth Publishing; 6th edition, 1998)

Chapter 2

Randy E. Barnett, *The Structure of Liberty: Justice and the Rule of Law* (Oxford University Press, 2000)

William Blackstone, *Commentaries on the Laws of England* (University of Chicago Press, 1979)

Benjamin Cardozo, *Nature of the Judicial Process* (Yale University Press, 1960)

Harell Chesson et al., "Sex Under the Influence: The Effect of Alcohol Policy on Sexually Transmitted Disease Rates in the United States," 43 *Journal of Law and Economics* 215 (2000)

Sharon Creeden, *Fair Is Fair: World Folktales of Justice* (August House Publishers, 1997)

Ronald Dworkin, *Life's Dominion: An Argument About Abortion, Euthanasia, and Individual Freedom* (Vintage Books, 1994)

Ronald Dworkin, *Sovereign Virtue: The Theory and Practice of Equality* (Harvard University Press, 2000)

Isaac Erhlich, "Crime, Punishment, and the Market for Offenses," 10 *Journal of Economic Perspectives*, No. 1, 43–67 (1996)

John Finnis, *Natural Law and Natural Rights* (Clarendon Press, 1980)

Lon Fuller, *The Morality of Law* (Yale University Press, 1977)

H. L. A. Hart and Raz Bulloch Hart, *The Concept of Law* (Clarendon Press, 1997)

Oliver W. Holmes, *The Common Law* (Dover Publishers, 1991)

Nina Jaffe and Steve Zeitlin, *The Cow of No Color : Riddle Stories and Justice Tales from Around the World* (Henry Holt & Company, 1998)

Richard A. Posner, *The Essential Holmes: Selections from the Letters, Speeches, Judicial Opinions, and Other Writings of Oliver Wendell Holmes, Jr.* (University of Chicago Press, 1992)

Richard A. Posner, *Economic Analysis of Law* (Aspen Publishers, 1998)

John Rawls, *Political Liberalism* (Columbia University Press, 1995)

John Rawls, *A Theory of Justice* (Belknap Publishers, 1999)

Austin Sarat and Thomas R. Kearns, editors, *Law in the Domains of Culture* (University of Michigan Press, 2000).

Richard K. Sherwin, *When Law Goes Pop: The Vanishing Line between Law and Popular Culture* (University of Chicago Press, 2000)

Roberto Unger, *The Critical Legal Studies Movement* (Harvard University Press, 1986)

Chapter 3

William J. Bernstein, *The Birth of Plenty : How the Prosperity of the Modern World Was Created* (McGraw-Hill, 2004)

William Blackstone, *Commentaries on the Laws of England* (University of Chicago Press, 1979)

Daniel J. Boorstin, *The Mysterious Science of the Law: An Essay on Blackstone's Commentaries* (University of Chicago, 1996)

Danny Danziger and John Gillingham, *1215: The Year of Magna Carta* (Touchstone Books, 2004)

Lawrence M. Friedman, *American Law in the 20th Century* (Yale University Press, 2002)

Hendrik Hartog, *Man and Wife in America: A History* (Harvard University Press, 2002)

Oliver Wendell Holmes, *The Common Law* (Dover Publishers, 1991)

Morton J. Horwitz, *The Transformation of American Law 1780-1860* (Harvard University Press, 1979)

Morton J. Horwitz, *The Transformation of American Law 1870–1960: The Crisis of Legal Orthodoxy* (Oxford University Press, 1994)

Alan B. Morrison, ed., *Fundamentals of American Law* (New York University Press, 1996)

Mary Beth Norton, *In the Devil's Snare: The Salem Witchcraft Crisis of 1692* (Knopf Publishers, 2002)

Robert D. Stacey, *Sir William Blackstone and the Common Law: Blackstone's Legacy to America* (ACW Press, 2003)

Chapter 4

Kevin Avruch, *Culture and Conflict Resolution* (United States Institute of Peace Press, 1998)

David J. Bederman, James Crawford, and John Bell eds., *International Law in Antiquity* (Cambridge

Studies in International and Comparative Law) (Cambridge University Press, 2001)

Harold J. Berman, *Law and Revolution,* Vol. 2, *The Impact of the Protestant Reformations on the Western Legal Tradition* (Belknap Publishers, 2004)

Thomas F. Burke, *Lawyers, Lawsuits, and Legal Rights: The Battle over Litigation in American Society* (University of California Press, 2004)

Michael Byers, *Custom, Power and the Power of Rules: International Relations and Customary International Law* (Cambridge University Press, 1998)

Antonio Cassese, *International Law* (Oxford University Press, 2001)

John M. Conley and William M. O'Barr, REVIEW ESSAY: Back to the Trobriands: The Enduring Influence of Malinowski's Crime and Custom in Savage Society: Bronislaw Malinowski. 1985 [1926]. Crime and Custom in Savage Society, 27 *Law & Social Inquiry* 847 (Fall 2002)

Tom Ginsburg, *Judicial Review in New Democracies: Constitutional Courts in Asian Cases* (Cambridge University Press, 2003)

H. Patrick Glenn, *Legal Traditions of the World: Sustainable Diversity in Law* (Oxford University Press, 2000)

H. L. A. Hart, *The Concept of Law* (Oxford University Press, 1997)

Jean-Marie Henckaerts and Louise Doswald-Beck, *Customary International Humanitarian Law,* Vol. 1, *Rules* (Cambridge University Press, 2004)

Herbert Jacob, Erhard Blankenberg, Herbert M. Kritzer, Doris Marie Provine, and Joseph Sanders, *Courts, Law, and Politics in Comparative Perspective* (Yale University Press, 1996)

Bruce E. Johansen, ed., *Enduring Legacies: Native American Treaties and Contemporary Controversies* (Praeger Publishers, 2004)

Robert Alan Jones, *Emile Durkheim: An Introduction to Four Major Works* (Sage Publications, 1986. Pp. 24–59)

Robert A. Kagan, *Adversarial Legalism: The American Way of Law* (Harvard University Press, 2003)

Tim Koopmans, *Courts and Political Institutions: A Comparative View* (Cambridge University Press, 2003)

James T. McHugh, *Comparative Constitutional Traditions (Teaching Texts in Law and Politics 27)* (Peter Lang Publishing, 2002)

Martha Mundy, Alain Pottage, Chris Arup, Martin Chanock, Pat O'Malley, Sally Engle Merry, and Susan Silbey, eds., *Law, Anthropology, and the Constitution of the Social: Making Persons and Things (Cambridge Studies in Law and Society)* (Cambridge University Press, 2004)

Laura Nader, *Law in Culture and Society* (University of California Press; Reprint edition, 1997)

Laura Nader, *The Life of the Law: Anthropological Projects* (University of California Press, 2002)

Richard A. Posner, *Law and Legal Theory in England and America (Clarendon Law Lecture)* (Oxford University Press, 1996)

Xin Ren, *Tradition of the Law and Law of the Tradition: Law, State, and Social Control in China (Contributions in Criminology and Penology)* (Greenwood Press, 1997)

Alison Dundes Renteln and Alan Dundes, *Folk Law: Essays in the Theory and Practice of Lex Non Scripta* (University of Wisconsin Press, 1995)

Thane Rosenbaum, *The Myth of Moral Justice: Why Our Legal System Fails to Do What's Right* (HarperCollins, 2004)

Austin Sarat and Thomas R. Kearns, eds., *Law in the Domains of Culture (Amherst Series in Law, Jurisprudence, and Social Thought)* (University of Michigan Press, 2000)

Souad, *Burned Alive: A Victim of the Law of Men* (Warner Books, 2004)

Rennard Strickland, SYMPOSIUM: INDIAN LAW INTO THE TWENTY-FIRST CENTURY: Wolf Warriors and Turtle Kings: Native American Law Before the Blue Coats, 72 *Washington Law Review* 1043 (October 1997)

Max Weber on Law in Economy and Society (Harvard University Press, 1954)

Chapter 5

Gary Jonathan Bass, *Stay the Hand of Vengeance: The Politics of War Crimes Tribunals* (Princeton University Press, 2001)

Michael Byers, *Custom, Power and the Power of Rules: International Relations and Customary International Law* (Cambridge University Press, 1998)

Antonio Cassese, *International Law* (Oxford University Press, 2001)

Richard A. Clarke, *Against All Enemies: Inside America's War on Terror* (Free Press, 2004)

Catherine Connolly and Julie Tennant-Burt, "The NAFTA Labor Agreement and U.S. Employment Discrimination law," 24 *Social Justice* (1997)

Robert Cooper, *The Breaking of Nations: Order and Chaos in the Twenty-First Century* (Atlantic Monthly Press, 2004)

Yves Dezalay and Bryant G. Garth, *Dealing in Virtue: International Commercial Arbitration and the Construction of a Transnational Legal Order (Chicago Series in Law and Society)* (University of Chicago Press, 1998)

Robyn Eckersley, *The Green State: Rethinking Democracy and Sovereignty* (MIT Press, 2004)

Francis Fukuyama, *State-Building: Governance and World Order in the 21st Century* (Cornell University Press, 2004)

Lawrence E. Harrison and Samuel P. Huntington, *Culture Matters: How Values Shape Human Progress* (HarperCollins, 2001)

K. J. Holsti et al., eds., *Taming the Sovereigns: Institutional Change in International Politics (Cambridge Studies in International Relations)* (Cambridge University Press, 2004)

Micheline R. Ishay, *The History of Human Rights: From Ancient Times to the Globalization Era* (University of California Press, 2004)

Mark W. Janis and John E. Noyes. *International Law: Cases and Commentary* (West Group; 2d edition, 2001)

Margaret E. Keck and Kathryn Sikkink, *Activists Beyond Borders: Advocacy Networks in International Politics* (Cornell University Press, 1998)

Michael T. Klare, *Resource Wars: The New Landscape of Global Conflict* (Owl Books, 2002)

Sean D. Magenis, "Natural Law as the Customary International Law of Self-Defense," 20 *Boston University International Law Journal* 413 (Fall 2002)

National Commission on Terrorist Attacks, *The 9/11 Commission Report: Final Report of the National Commission on Terrorist Attacks Upon the United States* (W. W. Norton, 2004)

Patrick O'Meara, Howard D. Hehlinger, and Matthew Krain, *Globalization and the Challenges of the New Century: A Reader* (Indiana University Press, 2000)

Kelly-Kate S. Paese, *International Organizations: Perspectives on Governance in the Twenty-First Century* (Prentice Hall Publishers; 2d edition, 2002)

Byoungwook Park, "Comfort Women During WWII: Are U.S. Courts a Final Resort for Justice?" 17 *American University International Law Review* 403 (2002)

Philippe Sands, ed., *From Nuremberg to The Hague: The Future of International Criminal Justice* (Cambridge University Press, 2003)

Chapter 6

Jeffrey Abramson, *We, the Jury: The Jury System and the Ideal of Democracy* (Harvard University Press, 2000)

Carl T. Bogus, *Why Lawsuits Are Good for America: Disciplined Democracy, Big Business, and the Common Law* (New York University Press, 2001)

D. Graham Burnett, *A Trial by Jury* (Vintage Press, 2002)

Clay S. Conrad, *Jury Nullification: The Evolution of a Doctrine* (Carolina Academic Press, 1998)

David L. Faigman, *Laboratory of Justice: The Supreme Court's 200-Year Struggle to Integrate Science and the Law* (Times Books, 2004)

Charles Fried, *Saying What the Law Is: The Constitution in the Supreme Court* (Harvard University Press, 2004)

Hiroshi Fukurai and Richard Krooth, *Race in the Jury Box: Affirmative Action in Jury Selection (SUNY Series in New Directions in Crime and Justice Studies)* (SUNY Press, 2003)

David J. Garrow, *Liberty and Sexuality: The Right to Privacy and the Making of Roe v. Wade* (University of California Press, 1998)

George S. Grossman and Rennard Strickland, *The Spirit of American Law* (Westview Press, 2000)

Jonathan Harr, *A Civil Action* (Vintage Books, 1996)

Randolph N. Jonakait, *The American Jury System (Contemporary Law Series)* (Yale University Press, 2003)

David E. Klein, *Making Law in the United States Courts of Appeals* (Cambridge University Press, 2002)

Thomas H. Koenig and Michael L. Rustad, *In Defense of Tort Law* (New York University Press, 2002)

Herbert M. Kritzer and Susan S. Silbey, *In Litigation: Do the "Haves" Still Come Out Ahead?* (Stanford University Press, 2003)

Laura Langer, *Judicial Review in State Supreme Courts: A Comparative Study (SUNY Series in American Constitutionalism)* (SUNY Press, 2002)

Anthony Lewis, *Gideon's Trumpet* (Vintage Books, 1989)

Forrest Maltzman, James F. Spriggs II, and Paul J. Wahlbeck, *Crafting Law on the Supreme Court : The Collegial Game* (Cambridge University Press, 2000)

Kevin T. McGuire, *Understanding the U.S. Supreme Court* (McGraw-Hill, 2001)

Sandra Day O'Connor, *The Majesty of the Law: Reflections of a Supreme Court Justice* (Random House, 2003)

Walter K. Olson, *The Rule of Lawyers: How the New Litigation Elite Threatens America's Rule of Law* (Truman Talley Books, 2003)

Richard A. Posner, *Law, Pragmatism, and Democracy* (Harvard University Press, 2003)

Suzanne U. Samuels, *First Among Friends: Amici Curiae, the Right to Privacy, and the U.S. Supreme Court* (Praeger Publishers, 2004)

Gerald M. Stern, *The Buffalo Creek Disaster: How the Survivors of One of the Worst Disasters in Coal-Mining History Brought Suit Against the Coal Company—and Won* (Vintage Books, 1977)

G. Alan Tarr, *Judicial Process and Judicial Policy-making* (Wadsworth Press, 2002)

Scott Turow, *One L: The Turbulent True Story of a First Year at Harvard Law School* (Warner Books, 1997)

Chapter 7

Kevin Avruch, *Culture and Conflict Resolution* (United States Institute of Peace Press, 1998)

Alexander M. Bickel, *The Least Dangerous Branch: The Supreme Court at the Bar of Politics* (Yale University Press, 1986)

Christopher M. Burke, *The Appearance of Equality : Racial Gerrymandering, Redistricting, and the Supreme Court (Contributions in Legal Studies)* (Greenwood Press, 1999)

Thomas F. Burke, *Lawyers, Lawsuits, and Legal Rights: The Battle over Litigation in American Society (California Series in Law, Politics, and Society 2)* (University of California Press, 2004)

John M. Conley and William M. O'Barr, *Just Words: Law, Language and Power* (University of Chicago Press, 1998)

Jane K. Cowan, Marie-Benedicte Dembour, and Richard A. Wilson, eds., *Culture and Rights: Anthropological Perspectives* (Cambridge University Press, 2001)

Yves Dezalay and Bryant G. Garth, *Dealing in Virtue: International Commercial Arbitration and the Construction of a Transnational Legal Order (Chicago Series in Law and Society)* (University of Chicago, 1998)

L. F. Felstiner, R. L. Abel, and A. Sarat, "The Emergence and Transformation of Disputes: Naming, Blaming, and Claiming," 15 *Law and Society Review* 631–54 (1980)

Roger Fisher, *Getting to Yes: Negotiating Agreement Without Giving In* (Houghton Mifflin, 1992)

Mary Ann Glendon, *A Nation Under Lawyers: How the Crisis in the Legal Profession Is Transforming American Society* (Harvard University Press, 1996)

Michael J. Klarman, *From Jim Crow to Civil Rights: The Supreme Court and the Struggle for Racial Equality* (Oxford University Press, 2004)

Larry D. Kramer, *The People Themselves: Popular Constitutionalism and Judicial Review* (Oxford University Press, 2004)

Peter Lovenheim and Lisa Guerin, *Mediate, Don't Litigate: Strategies for Successful Mediation* (Nolo Press, 2004)

Bernard Mayer, *Beyond Neutrality: Confronting the Crisis in Conflict Resolution* (Jossey-Bass, 2004)

Robert L. Nelson, William Bridges, and Mark Granovetter, eds., *Legalizing Gender Inequality: Courts, Markets and Unequal Pay for Women in America (Structural Analysis in the Social Sciences)* (Cambridge University Press, 1999)

William E. Nelson, *Marbury v. Madison: The Origins and Legacy of Judicial Review* (University Press of Kansas, 2000)

Michael Palmer, Simon Roberts, William Twining, and Christopher McCrudden, eds., *Dispute Process: ADR and the Primary Forms of Decision Making (Law in Context)* (Cambridge University Press, 1998)

James T. Patterson, *Brown v. Board of Education: A Civil Rights Milestone and its Troubled Legacy* (Oxford University Press, 2001)

Cass R. Sunstein, *One Case at a Time: Judicial Minimalism on the Supreme Court* (Harvard University Press, 2001)

Tinsley E. Yarbrough, *Race and Redistricting: The Shaw-Cromartie Cases* (Landmark Law Cases and American Society) (University Press of Kansas, 2002)

Chapter 8

Douglas J. Amy, *Real Choices/New Voices* (Columbia University Press, 2002)

Margaret P. Battin, Rosamond Rhodes, Anita Silvers, and M. Pabst Battin, *Physician Assisted Suicide: Expanding the Debate (Reflective Bioethics)* (Routledge Press, 1998)

Sarah A. Binder, *Stalemate: Causes and Consequences of Legislative Gridlock* (Brookings Institution, 2003)

Bonnie B. Burgess, *Fate of the Wild: The Endangered Species Act and the Future of Biodiversity* (University of Georgia Press, 2001)

Charles M. Cameron, Randall Calvert, and Thrainn Eggertsson, eds., *Veto Bargaining: Presidents and the Politics of Negative Power (Political Economy of Institutions and Decisions)* (Cambridge University Press, 2002)

Edward T. Chambers and Michael A. Cowan, *Roots for Radicals: Organizing for Power, Action, and Justice* (Continuum International Publishing Group, 2003)

Matthew A. Crenson and Benjamin Ginsberg, *Downsizing Democracy: How America Sidelined Its Citizens and Privatized Its Public* (Johns Hopkins Press, 2002)

Brian Czech and Paul R. Krausman, *The Endangered Species Act: History, Conservation Biology, and Public Policy* (John Hopkins Press, 2001)

Roger H. Davidson and Walter J. Oleszek, *Congress and Its Members* (Congressional Quarterly Press, 2002)

Michael X. Delli Carpini and Scott Keeter, *What Americans Know About Politics and Why It Matters* (Yale University Press, 1997)

Linda L. Emanuel, *Regulating How We Die: The Ethical, Medical, and Legal Issues Surrounding Physician-Assisted Suicide* (Harvard University Press, 1998)

Richard F. Fenno, *Home Style: House Members in Their Districts* (Longman Classics Edition) (Longman, 2002)

Louis Fisher, *The Politics of Shared Power: Congress and the Executive* (Congressional Quarterly Press, 1998)

Kenneth M. Goldstein, *Interest Groups, Lobbying, and Participation in America* (Cambridge University Press, 1999)

Robert Justin Goldstein, *Flag Burning and Free Speech: The Case of Texas v. Johnson* (University Press of Kansas, 2000)

William G. Howell. *Power Without Persuasion: The Politics of Direct Presidential Action* (Princeton University Press, 2003)

David C. King, *Turf Wars: How Congressional Committees Claim Jurisdiction* (University of Chicago Press, 1997)

John W. Kingdon, *Agendas, Alternatives, and Public Policies* (Longman Classics Edition) (Longman; 2d edition, 2002)

Vasan Kesavan and J. Gregory Sidak, "The Legislator-in-Chief," *William and Mary Law Review* 44 (2002)

Ken Kollman, *Outside Lobbying* (Princeton University Press, 1998)

Jamin B. Raskin, *Overruling Democracy: The Supreme Court vs. the American People* (Routledge Press, 2003)

Steven J. Rosenstone and John Mark Hansen, *Mobilization, Participation, and Democracy in America* (Longman Classics Edition) (Longman, 2002)

Alan Rosenthal, *The Third House: Lobbyists and Lobbying in the States* (Congressional Quarterly Press, 2001)

Andrew Rudalevige, *Managing the President's Program: Presidential Leadership and Legislative Policy Formulation (Princeton Studies in American Politics)* (Princeton University Press, 2002)

Eric Schickler, *Disjointed Pluralism: Institutional Innovation and the Development of the U.S. Congress* (Princeton University Press, 2002)

Barbara Sinclair, *Unorthodox Lawmaking: New Legislative Processes in the U.S. Congress* (Congressional Quarterly Press, 2000)

Sidney Verba, Kay Lehman Schlozman, and Henry E. Brady, *Voice and Equality: Civic Voluntarism in American Politics* (Harvard University Press, 1996)

John R. Wright, *Interest Groups and Congress: Lobbying, Contributions and Influence* (Longman, 1995)

Chapter 9

David Gray Adler and Michael A. Genovese, *The Presidency and the Law: The Clinton Legacy* (University Press of Kansas, 2002)

Stephen Breyer, *Breaking the Vicious Circle: Toward Effective Risk Regulation* (Harvard University Press, 1995)

Dan Briody, *The Iron Triangle: Inside the Secret World of the Carlyle Group* (John Wiley & Sons, 2003)

Lief Carter and Christine Harrington, *Administrative Law and Politics: Cases and Comments* (Addison-Wesley Publishers; 3d edition, 1999)

Craig E. Colten and Peter N. Skinner, *The Road to Love Canal: Managing Industrial Waste before EPA* (University of Texas Press, 1995)

Ken Conca and Geoffrey D. Dabelko, *Green Planet Blues: Environmental Politics from Stockholm to Kyoto* (Westview Press, 1998)

Phillip J. Cooper, *By Order of the President: The Use and Abuse of Executive Direct Action* (University Press of Kansas, 2002)

Robert M. Cox, Jr., *EPA and Superfund: A Small Business Story* (Washington House, 2001)

Catherine Crier, *The Case Against Lawyers* (Broadway Books, 2002)

Louis Fisher, *Constitutional Conflicts Between Congress and the President* (University Press of Kansas, 1997)

Louis Fisher, *Nazi Saboteurs on Trial: A Military Tribunal and American Law* (University Press of Kansas, 2003)

Philip B. Heymann, *Terrorism, Freedom, and Security: Winning Without War* (MIT Press, 2003)

Phillip K Howard, *Death of Common Sense: How Law is Suffocating America* (Warner Books, 1996)

William G. Howell, *Power Without Persuasion: The Politics of Direct Presidential Action* (Princeton University Press, 2003)

Kenneth Mayer, *With the Stroke of a Pen: Executive Orders and Presidential Power* (Princeton University Press, 2002)

Rosemary O'Leary, *Environmental Change: Federal Courts and the EPA* (Temple University Press, 1995)

Mark R. Powell, *Science at EPA: Information in the Regulatory Process* (Resources for the Future, 1999)

Andrew Rudalevige, *Managing the President's Program: Presidential Leadership and Legislative Policy Formulation (Princeton Studies in American Politics)* (Princeton University Press, 2002)

Cindy Skrzycki, *The Regulators: Anonymous Power Brokers in American Politics* (Rowman & Littlefield Press, 2003)

Richard D. Stone, *The Interstate Commerce Commission and the Railroad Industry: A History of Regulatory Policy* (Praeger Publishers, 1991)

Cass R. Sunstein, *After the Rights Revolution: Reconceiving the Regulatory State* (Harvard University Press, 1993)

Jacqueline Vaughn Switzer, *Environmental Politics : Domestic and Global Dimensions* (Wadsworth Press, 2003)

Mark Tushnet, *The New Constitutional Order* (Princeton University Press, 2004)

Norman J. Vig and Regina S. Axelrod, *The Global Environment: Institutions, Law, and Policy* (Congressional Quarterly Press, 1999)

Chapter 10

Geoffrey P. Alpert, Roger G. Dunham, and Alfred Blumstein, eds., *Understanding Police Use of Force: Officers, Suspects, and Reciprocity (Cambridge Studies in Criminology)* (Cambridge University Press, 2004)

Ronald Banaszak, *Fair Trial Rights of the Accused: A Documentary History* (Greenwood Press, 2001)

Gordon Bazemore and Scott Senjo, "Police Encounters with Juveniles Revisited," in 20 *Policing: An International Journal of Police Strategy and Management,"* No. 1, 60–82 (1997)

Richard A. Clarke, *Against All Enemies: Inside America's War on Terror* (Free Press, 2004)

Steve Coll, *Ghost Wars: The Secret History of the CIA, Afghanistan, and Bin Laden, from the Soviet*

Invasion to September 10, 2001 (Penguin Books, 2004)

Sally E. Hadden, *Slave Patrols: Law and Violence in Virginia and the Carolinas* (Harvard University Press, 2001)

David A. Harris, *Profiles in Injustice: Why Racial Profiling Cannot Work* (W. W. Norton, 2003)

Tara Herivel and Paul Wright, *Prison Nation: The Warehousing of America's Poor* (Routledge Press, 2003)

Milton Heumann and Lance Cassak, *Good Cop, Bad Cop: Racial Profiling and Competing Views of Justice in America (Studies in Crime and Punishment, 10)* (Peter Lang Publishing, 2003)

Jill Nelson, ed., *Police Brutality: An Anthology* (W. W. Norton, 2001)

Richard Gid Powers, *Broken: The Troubled Past and Uncertain Future of the FBI* (Free Press, 2004)

Howard Rahtz, *Understanding Police Use of Force* (Criminal Justice Press, 2003)

Wesley G. Skogan and Susan M. Hartnett, *Community Policing, Chicago Style (Studies in Crime and Public Policy)* (Oxford University Press, 1999)

Gary L. Stuart, *Miranda: The Story of America's Right to Remain Silent* (University of Arizona Press, 2004)

Ralph B. Taylor, *Breaking Away from Broken Windows: Baltimore Neighborhoods and the Nationwide Fight Against Crime, Grime, Fear, and Decline* (Westview Press, 2000)

Athan Theoharis, *The FBI & American Democracy: A Brief Critical History* (University Press of Kansas, 2004)

Dan Verton, *Black Ice: The Invisible Threat of Cyber-Terrorism* (McGraw-Hill Osbourne Media, 2003)

Samuel Walker, *Police Accountability: The Role of Citizen Oversight* (Wadsworth Press, 2000)

Chapter 11

Joshua G. Behr, *Race, Ethnicity, and the Politics of City Redistricting: Minority-Opportunity Districts and the Election of Hispanics and Blacks to City Councils (African American Studies)* (SUNY Press, 2004)

Derrick Bell, *Silent Covenants: Brown v. Board of Education and the Unfulfilled Hopes for Racial Reform* (Oxford University Press, 2004)

Derrick Bell et al., *Race, Racism, And American Law (Casebook Series)* (Aspen Books, 2004)

Sheryll Cashin, *The Failures of Integration: How Race and Class Are Undermining the American Dream* (Public Affairs, 2004)

Faye J. Crosby, *Affirmative Action is Dead; Long Live Affirmative Action* (Yale University Press, 2004)

Dog Mary Crow, *Lakota Woman* (Perennial, 1991)

Nicholas DeGenova et al., *Latino Crossings: Mexicans, Puerto Ricans, and the Politics of Race and Citizenship* (Routledge Press, 2003)

E. J. Dionne, Jr., et al., *One Electorate Under God: A Dialogue on Religion and American Politics (Pew Forum Dialogues on Religion & Public Life)* (Brookings Institution, 2004)

Leon Fink et al., *The Maya of Morganton: Work and Community in the Nuevo New South* (University of North Carolina Press, 2003)

Brett Duval Fromson, *Hitting the Jackpot: The Inside Story of the Richest Indian Tribe in History* (Atlantic Monthly Press, 2003)

Grace Elizabeth Hale, *Making Whiteness: The Culture of Segregation in the South, 1890–1940* (Vintage Books, 1999)

Ian F. Haney-Lopez, *White by Law: The Legal Construction of Race (Critical America Series)* (New York University Press, 1998)

Ian F. Haney-Lopez, *Racism on Trial: The Chicano Fight for Justice* (Belknap Publishers, 2003)

Matthew Frye Jacobsen, *Whiteness of a Different Color: European Immigrants and the Alchemy of Race* (Harvard University Press, 1999)

Mahmood Mamdani, *Good Muslim, Bad Muslim: America, the Cold War, and the Roots of Terror* (Pantheon Books, 2004)

W. Dale Mason, *Indian Gaming: Tribal Sovereignty and American Politics* (University of Oklahoma Press, 2000)

Barack Obama, *Dreams from My Father: A Story of Race and Inheritance* (Three Rivers Press, 2004)

Charles J. Ogletree, *All Deliberate Speed: Reflections on the First Half-Century of Brown v. Board of Education* (W. W. Norton, 2004)

Leonard Peltier, *Prison Writings: My Life Is My Sun Dance* (St. Martin's Griffin, 2000)

Samuel Walker, *The Color of Justice: Race, Ethnicity, and Crime in America* (Wadsworth Press, 2003)

Peter Wallenstein, *Tell the Court I Love My Wife: Race, Marriage, and Law—An American History* (Palgrave MacMillan, 2004)

David E. Wilkins, *American Indian Sovereignty and the U.S. Supreme Court: The Masking of Justice* (University of Texas Press, 1997)

D. Vann Woodward and William S. McFeely, *The Strange Career of Jim Crow* (Oxford University Press, 2001)

Chapter 12

Clara Bingham and Laura Leedy Gansle, *Class Action: The Story of Lois Jenson and the Landmark Case That Changed Sexual Harassment Law* (Anchor Press, 2003)

Gene Burns, *The Moral Veto: Framing Contraception, Abortion, and Cultural Pluralism in the United States* (Cambridge University Press, 2005)

Rebecca J. Cook, Bernard M. Dickens, and Mahmoud F. Fathalla, *Reproductive Health and Human Rights: Integrating Medicine, Ethics, and Law (Issues in Biomedical Ethics)* (Oxford University Press, 2003)

Martha Fineman and Terence Dougherty, *Feminism Confronts Homo Economicus: Gender, Law, And Society* (Cornell University Press, 2005)

Evan Gerstmann, *Same-Sex Marriage and the Constitution* (Cambridge University Press, 2003)

James Gruber and Phoebe Morgan, *In the Company of Men: Male Dominance and Sexual Harassment (The Northeastern Series on Gender, Crime, and Law)* (Northeastern University Press, 2004)

Arlie Russell Hochschild and Anne Machung, *The Second Shift* (Penguin Books, 2003)

N. E. H. Hull and Peter Charles Hoffer, *Roe v. Wade: The Abortion Rights Controversy in American History (Landmark Law Cases and American Society)* (University Press of Kansas, 2001)

Catherine MacKinnon, *Women's Lives, Men's Laws* (Belknap Publishers, 2005)

Dale T. Mortensen, *Wage Dispersion: Why Are Similar Workers Paid Differently?* (MIT Press, 2003)

Robert L. Nelson, William Bridges, and Mark Granovetter, eds., *Legalizing Gender Inequality: Courts, Markets and Unequal Pay for Women in America* (Cambridge University Press, 1999)

Martha C. Nussbaum, *Hiding from Humanity: Disgust, Shame, and the Law* (Princeton University Press, 2004)

Deborah L. Rhode, *Speaking of Sex: The Denial of Gender Inequality* (Harvard University Press, 1999)

Sue V. Rosser, *The Science Glass Ceiling: Academic Women Scientists and the Struggle to Succeed* (Routledge Press, 2004)

William Saletan, *Bearing Right: How Conservatives Won the Abortion War* (University of California Press, 2004)

Suzanne U. Samuels, *Women's Rights, Fetal Rights: Gender Equality in the Workplace* (University of Wisconsin Press, 1995)

Johanna Schoen, *Choice and Coercion: Birth Control, Sterilization, and Abortion In Public Health And Welfare* (University of North Carolina Press, 2005)

Dorothy M. Stetson, *Women's Rights in the U.S.A: Policy Debates and Gender Roles* (Routledge Press, 2004)

Leslie Woodcock Tentler, *Catholics and Contraception: An American History* (Cornell University Press, 2004)

Joan Williams, *Unbending Gender: Why Family and Work Conflict and What to Do About It* (Oxford University Press, 2001)

Chapter 13

David Brody, *Labor Embattled: History, Power, Rights* (University of Illinois Press, 2005)

David Brooks, *Bobos In Paradise: The New Upper Class and How They Got There* (Simon & Schuster, 2001)

David Cole, *No Equal Justice: Race and Class in the American Criminal Justice System* (New Press, 1999)

John De Graaf et al., *Affluenza: The All-Consuming Epidemic* (Berrett-Koehler Publishers, 2002)

Barbara Ehrenreich, *Nickel and Dimed: On (Not) Getting By in America* (Owl Press, 2002)

Steve Fraser and Gary Gerstle, eds., *Ruling America: A History of Wealth and Power in a Democracy* (Harvard University Press, 2005)

John Steele Gordon, *An Empire of Wealth: The Epic History of American Economic Power* (HarperCollins, 2004)

Lawrence Otis Graham, *Our Kind of People: Inside America's Black Upper Class* (Perennial Books, 2000)

Tara Herivel and Paul Wright, *Prison Nation: The Warehousing of America's Poor* (Routledge Press, 2003)

Marc J. Hetherington, *Why Trust Matters: Declining Political Trust and the Demise of American Liberalism* (Princeton University Press, 2004)

Annette Lareau, *Unequal Childhoods: Class, Race, and Family Life* (University of California Press, 2003)

Katherine S. Newman, *No Shame in My Game: The Working Poor in the Inner City* (Vintage Books, 2000)

Mark Robert Rank, *One Nation, Underprivileged: Why American Poverty Affects Us All* (Oxford University Press, 2004)

Jeffrey Reiman, *The Rich Get Richer and the Poor Get Prison: Ideology, Class, and Criminal Justice* (Allyn & Bacon, 2003)

Paula S. Rothenberg et al., *Race, Class, and Gender in the United States: An Integrated Study* (Worth Publishing, 2000)

David K. Shipler, *The Working Poor: Invisible in America* (Knopf Publishers, 2004)

Robert Smith Thompson, *The Eagle Triumphant: How America Took Over the British Empire* (John Wiley & Sons, 2004)

Michael Tigar, *Law and the Rise of Capitalism* (New York University Press, 2000)

Rhonda Y. Williams, *The Politics of Public Housing: Black Women's Struggles Against Urban Inequality* (Oxford University Press, 2004)

William Julius Wilson, *When Work Disappears: The World of the New Urban Poor* (Vintage Books, 1997)

Chapter 14

Marcia Angell, *The Truth About the Drug Companies: How They Deceive Us and What to Do About It* (Random House, 2004)

Howard Ball, *The Supreme Court in the Intimate Lives of Americans: Birth, Sex, Marriage, Childrearing, and Death* (New York University Press, 2002)

M. Pabst Battin, *Ending Life: Ethics and the Way We Die* (Oxford University Press, 2005)

Eric Blyth and Ruth Landau, *Third Party Assisted Conception Across Cultures: Social, Legal and Ethical Perspectives* (Jessica Kingsley Press, 2004)

Martin Booth, *Cannabis: A History* (Thomas Dunne Books, 2004)

Michael C. Carroll, *Lab 257: The Disturbing Story of the Government's Secret Plum Island Germ Laboratory* (William Morrow, 2004)

Mitchell Earleywine, *Understanding Marijuana: A New Look at the Scientific Evidence* (Oxford University Press, 2002)

Kathleen Foley and Herbert Hendin, *The Case Against Assisted Suicide: For the Right to End-Of-Life Care* (Johns Hopkins Press, 2004)

Andrew Goliszek, *In the Name of Science: A History of Secret Programs, Medical Research, and Human Experimentation* (St. Martins Press, 2003)

Merrill Goozner, *The $800 Million Pill: The Truth behind the Cost of New Drugs* (University of California Press, 2004)

Lester Grinspoon and James B. Bakalar, *Marijuana: The Forbidden Medicine* (Yale University Press, 1997)

N. E. H. Hull et al., *The Abortion Rights Controversy in America: A Legal Reader* (University of North Carolina Press, 2004)

James H. Jones, *Bad Blood: The Tuskegee Syphilis Experiment* (Free Press, 1993)

Terrance McConnell, *Inalienable Rights: The Limits of Consent in Medicine and the Law* (Oxford University Press, 2000)

Timothy E. Quill and M. Pabst Battin, *Physician-assisted Dying: The Case For Palliative Care and Patient Choice* (Johns Hopkins Press, 2004)

Leslie J. Reagan, *When Abortion Was a Crime: Women, Medicine, and Law in the United States, 1867–1973* (University of California Press, 1998)

James Shreeve, *The Genome War: How Craig Venter Tried to Capture the Code of Life and Save the World* (Knopf Publishers, 2004)

John Sulston and Georgina Ferry, *The Common Thread: A Story of Science, Politics, Ethics and the Human Genome* (National Academies Press, 2002)

Arthur G. Svenson and Susan M. Behuniak, *Physician-Assisted Suicide: The Anatomy of a Constitutional Law Issue* (Rowman & Littlefield, 2002)

Stuart J. Youngner et al., *Transplanting Human Tissue: Ethics, Policy, and Practice* (Oxford University Press, 2003)

Chapter 15

Elizabeth Cohen, *Making a New Deal: Industrial Workers in Chicago, 1919–1939* (Cambridge University Press, 1991)

Robert Cooter and Thomas Ulen, *Law and Economics* (Addison-Wesley Series in Economics; 4th Edition, 2003)

Martha A. Derthick, *Up in Smoke: From Legislation to Litigation in Tobacco Politics* (Congressional Quarterly Press, 2004)

Frank H. Easterbrook and Daniel R. Fischel, *The Economic Structure of Corporate Law* (Harvard University Press, 1996)

David D. Friedman, *Law's Order: What Economics Has to Do with Law and Why It Matters* (Princeton University Press, 2001)

Stanton A. Glantz and Edith D. Balbac, *The Tobacco War: Inside the California Battles* (University of California Press, 2000)

Colin Gordon, *New Deals: Business, Labor, and Politics in America, 1920–1935* (Cambridge University Press, 1994)

John R. Lott, Jr., *More Guns, Less Crime: Understanding Crime and Gun Control Laws* (University of Chicago Press, 1998)

Carrick Mollenkamp et al., *The People vs. Big Tobacco: How the States Took on the Cigarette Giants* (W. W. Norton, 1998)

Massimo Motta, *Competition Policy: Theory and Practice* (Cambridge University Press, 2004)

Robert T. Nakamura and Thomas W. Church, *Taming Regulation: Superfund and the Challenge of Regulatory Reform* (Brookings Institute, 2003)

Adam Penenberg, *Tragic Indifference: One Man's Battle with the Auto Industry over the Dangers of SUVs* (Harper Business, 2003)

A. Mitchell Polinsky, *An Introduction to Law and Economics* (Aspen Publishers, 2003)

Richard A. Posner, *Economic Analysis of Law* (Aspen Publishers, 2002)

Richard A. Posner, *Antitrust Law* (University of Chicago Press, 2004)

Clifford Rechtschaffen and Eileen P. Gauna, *Environmental Justice: Law, Policy, and Regulation* (Carolina Academic Press, 2002)

Kristin S. Shrader-Frechette, *Environmental Justice: Creating Equality, Reclaiming Democracy* (Oxford University Press, 2002)

Cass R. Sunstein et al., eds., *Behavioral Law and Economics* (Cambridge University Press, 2002)

Studs Terkel, *Hard Times: An Oral History of the Great Depression* (W. W. Norton, 2000)

Andrew Zimbalist, *May the Best Team Win: Baseball Economics and Public Policy* (Brookings Institution, 2003)

Index